MW01102606

PUZZLER'S GIANT BOOK OF CROSSWORDS
56

Penny Press is the publisher of a fine family of puzzle magazines and books renowned for their editorial excellence.

This delightful collection has been carefully selected by the editors of Penny Press for your special enjoyment and entertainment.

Puzzler's Giant Book of Crosswords, No. 56, November 2015. Published four times a year by Penny Press, Inc., 6 Prowitt Street, Norwalk, CT 06855-1220. On the web at PennyDellPuzzles.com. Copyright © 2015 by Penny Press, Inc. Penny Press is a trademark registered in the U.S. Patent Office. All rights reserved. No material from this publication may be reproduced or used without the written permission of the publisher.

ISBN-13: 978-1-59238-076-3
ISBN-10: 1-59238-076-X

Printed by Quad/Graphics, Taunton, MA U.S.A. 10/13/15

PENNY PRESS PUZZLE PUBLICATIONS

✦ PUZZLE MAGAZINES ✦

All-Star Word Seeks
Approved Variety Puzzles
Classic Variety Puzzles
   Plus Crosswords
Easy & Fun Variety Puzzles
Easy Crossword Express
Family Variety Puzzles & Games
Fast & Easy Crosswords
Favorite Easy Crosswords
Favorite Fill-In
Favorite Variety Puzzles
Fill-In Puzzles
Garfield's Word Seeks
Good Time Crosswords
Good Time Easy Crosswords
Good Time Variety Puzzles
Large-Print Word Seek Puzzles

Master's Variety Puzzles
Merit Variety Puzzles & Games
Original Logic Problems
Penny's Famous Fill-In Puzzles
Penny's Finest Favorite Word Seeks
Penny's Finest Good Time Word Seeks
Penny's Finest Super Word Seeks
Quick & Easy Crosswords
Spotlight Celebrity Word Seek
Spotlight Movie & TV Word Seek
Spotlight Remember When Word Seek
Tournament Variety Puzzles
Variety Puzzles and Games
Variety Puzzles and Games
   Special Issue
Word Seek Puzzles
World's Finest Variety Puzzles

✦ SPECIAL SELECTED COLLECTIONS ✦

Alphabet Soup
Anagram Magic Square
Brick by Brick
Codewords
Crostics
Crypto-Families
Cryptograms
Diagramless
Double Trouble
England's Best Logic
   Puzzles
Flower Power

Frameworks
Large-Print Crosswords
Large-Print Cryptograms
Large-Print
   Missing Vowels
Letterboxes
Match-Up
Missing List Word Seeks
Missing Vowels
Number Fill-In
Number Seek
Patchwords

Places, Please
Quotefalls
Share-A-Letter
Simon Says
Stretch Letters
Syllacrostics
The Shadow
Three's Company
What's Left?
Word Games
   Puzzles
Zigzag

✦ PUZZLER'S GIANT BOOKS ✦

Crosswords   Sudoku   Word Games   Word Seeks

PUZZLE 1

ACROSS
1. Used a cuspidor
5. Male party
9. Tropical ant
13. Hounds' prey
14. Subway fare
16. Pitcher
17. Single-file
19. Love too much
20. Green veggie
21. Abba ____
22. Bands
24. Fancy dance
25. Boot country
26. Turn down
29. Deprived
31. Do penance
32. Decline
34. "____ the ramparts..."
36. Secure
37. Heel
38. Fool
39. Golf norm
40. Fakes
42. Actress Sophia
43. Five cents
45. Expired
46. Bete ____
47. In the past
48. Fuel gas
50. Irish lake
51. Nozzle
54. Fibber
55. Sixty
58. Hostels
59. Tanker
60. Poker entry
61. Marquis de ____
62. Collections
63. Lager

DOWN
1. Boutique
2. Window glass
3. Sphere
4. Drink with scones
5. Mr. Ed's home
6. Sum
7. Similar
8. Muffin
9. Roman official
10. Timbers
11. Head: Fr.
12. War god
15. Snared
18. Pester
23. Unusual
24. Baseball play
25. Footnote abbrs.
26. Grate
27. "____ Frome"
28. Necktie
30. Indian home
32. Climb a peak
33. Take it on the ____
35. Tear
38. Nitwit
40. Peel
41. Toward this point
42. Bowling alleys
44. Rough
45. Nonconformists
47. Welcome
48. Yale students
49. Actress Louise
50. ____ Stanley Gardner
51. Dial sound
52. Commedia del'____
53. Co-worker
56. Towel word
57. Taxi

5

PUZZLE 2

ACROSS
1. Informers
5. Pintail duck
9. Enthusiasts
13. Small case
14. Inferior
16. Rocker Billy
17. 007 movie
19. Defense gp.
20. Reply: abbr.
21. Singer Burl
22. Rue
24. Handbill
26. Walking stick
27. Indisposed
28. Lathe spindles
32. Deserves
35. Cross a stream
36. Request
37. Male deer
38. Lays open
39. Tolled
40. Volume
41. Evict
42. Makes coins
43. Evaluate
45. Moral wrong
46. Rhythmic swing
47. Demolish
51. Scrape
54. Thailand, once
55. Marsh elder
56. Saturate
57. Wedding-band spot
60. Sound
61. Restrict
62. ____ Descartes
63. Lawyers: abbr.
64. Baboons
65. Comedian Johnson

DOWN
1. Stately
2. Make amends
3. Oklahoma city
4. Comic Caesar
5. Pivot
6. French painter
7. Work units
8. Opposite of WNW
9. Detective's clue
10. Hebrew month
11. Short letter
12. Lock opening
15. Chores
18. Stuffs
23. Finale
25. New York resort area
26. Mark of omission
28. Telegraph inventor
29. Verve
30. Fast time
31. Droops
32. This: Sp.
33. Over
34. Sloping walk
35. Gounod opera
38. Water heaters
42. Florida city
44. Help
45. Arrow stems
47. Actress Hasso
48. Jungle cat
49. Occurrence
50. Street show
51. Movie dog
52. High shoe
53. Talk wildly
54. Small cut
58. Bataan native
59. FDR gp.

PUZZLE 3

ACROSS

1. Rush or dust
5. Magna ____
10. Remotely
14. Diva's song
15. Good-by: Sp.
16. Arm bone
17. Colorado park
20. Compass pt.
21. Greek harp
22. Prize money
23. Jungle king
24. New Zealand native
26. French spa
28. Soft mineral
29. Last mo.
32. Icebox assaults
33. B'nai ____
34. "I ____ Rock" (Simon and Garfunkel hit)
35. Ripens
36. Spinet
37. Slaloms
38. Viral illness
39. British coins
40. Met offering
41. Cowboy Ritter
42. Frenzy
43. Scolds severely
44. Writer Alistair
46. Spanish custard
47. Head part
49. Fraternal gp.
50. Tibetan gazelle
53. New Mexico park
57. Taj Mahal site
58. Alaska native
59. ____ of tears
60. Ball holders
61. Water holder
62. Writer Seton

DOWN

1. Green plum
2. Algerian port
3. Italian money, formerly
4. Father
5. Grand ____
6. Enhance
7. Plentiful
8. Preteen
9. Fire residue
10. Soothsayer
11. Southern island
12. Ampersands
13. Demolish, in England
18. Inventor Howe
19. Historic time
23. Box tops
24. Pine Tree State
25. Palo ____
26. Two below par
27. New Orleans area
28. Smidgen
30. Arab princes
31. ____ Grande
32. Finn craft
33. Bender
36. Pikes ____
37. Bridge length
39. Actor's articles
40. King of Norway
43. Parade entries
45. Earthen pots
46. Adjust a lens
47. Shoo!
48. Zoo pen
49. Brainstorm
50. ____ Canaria
51. Just
52. Bewildered
54. Satchel
55. Everybody
56. ____ Marie Saint

PUZZLE 4

ACROSS
1. Engrossed
5. Rock-music magazine
9. Actress Ina
14. Wagnerian solo
15. Gait
16. Avoid
17. Conifers
19. Friend of Pythias
20. Not original
21. Quiver
23. Susa's land
25. Bacchanal's cry
26. Takes pleasure in
30. ____ spumante
32. Postal service inits.
35. Fills a van
36. Slowpoke
37. ____ alai
38. Squad or admiral
39. French dialect of the Acadians
40. Small mountain lake
41. Rile
42. Aesop ending
43. English essayist Francis ____
44. Galilee, for one
45. Imposing
46. Servile one
47. Shakespeare's was a melancholy one
49. Make a sweater
51. Alhambra site
54. Flavoring
59. Like Old Norse poems
60. Kind of dive
62. Confuse
63. Israeli port
64. ____'acte
65. Swiss/American psychiatrist
66. Cattail
67. Existence, to Cato

DOWN
1. Ranee's man
2. Landlocked sea
3. Ancient Briton
4. Appropriate
5. Sales pitches
6. Bearcat
7. Diamonds, to some
8. Aerie
9. Torment
10. Texas mission
11. Logger
12. Golden calf
13. Hawaii's state bird
18. Victims
22. Coat with solder again
24. Every ____ (all)
26. "The King"
27. Bete ____
28. Fop
29. "____ to Billy Joe"
31. First king of Israel
33. Torshaven's islands
34. Alley Oop's big pet
36. Hindu garment
39. Dealt
40. Tic-____-toe
42. Threatening one
43. Hand-dyed textile
46. Connected
48. Enfeebled
50. Mother-of-pearl
51. Metric weight
52. Uncivil
53. Not closed
55. Dirk
56. German numeral
57. Immature newts
58. Streeter's " ____ Mable"
61. Tennis point

8

PUZZLE 5

ACROSS
1. Float
5. Valley
9. Dutch commune
12. Jai ___
13. Like notebook paper
14. Roman poet
15. Richard Thomas film
18. By birth
19. First name in mystery
20. ___ Lauder
21. Tints
22. Make esteemed
24. "Gunsmoke" star
27. Begin
28. Bona fide
29. Pentateuch
30. Not high or low
33. "I have it here ___"
38. ___ Angeles
39. Ogle
40. "___ in Love"
41. Church words
42. In an indolent manner
44. Athwart
46. Randall or Martin
47. Once more
48. Do road repair
49. Pastry
52. Strauss composition
56. Supervisor
57. Estate house
58. Equal
59. Kwa language of Western Africa
60. Director Preminger
61. Scarlett's home

DOWN
1. Caution
2. Sheltered
3. Wash out
4. "My country, ___ of thee . . ."
5. Phones
6. Feed the kitty
7. Moon vehicle: abbr.
8. Godzilla's stomping ground, once
9. A Peron
10. Cafe
11. Rim
13. Old harps' kin
14. Assault
16. Low islands
17. Sketch over
21. "The Farmer in the ___"
22. Jacket or collar
23. Ointment
24. Seed coat
25. Nevada town
26. Captures
27. Nova and Vega
30. Actress Rogers
31. Print type: abbr.
32. Contradict
34. Nut
35. Average grades
36. Berry and Kercheval
37. Misty
41. The Ram
42. Sweetheart
43. Afresh
44. Ruddy
45. Reason
46. Forbidden
47. Ecclesiastic's title
48. Football kick
49. Supplication
50. Roman road
51. Poet Pound
53. ___, amas, amat
54. Singer "King" Cole
55. Suitable

9

PUZZLE 6

ACROSS
1. Patron saint of Norway
5. Old-fashioned oaths
10. Crosspatch
14. Shower
15. Military force: Fr.
16. Lounging garment
17. Snick's mate
18. Brown bread
19. Sioux
20. Broadway
23. Actress Arlene ___
24. Stripling
25. Previously
28. Stress
33. "What's in ___?"
34. Venerable
35. Catnip
36. ___ Porsena
37. Victories
38. Fabric nap
39. Command for DDE
40. Indians
41. Bandleader Shaw
42. Goes back in
44. Freezing rains
45. Cereal
46. Lampreys
47. Old East-West highway
53. Pungency
54. Composition for nine
55. "The Old Gray ___"
57. Type of code
58. Bolivia's 1st president
59. "___ for All Seasons"
60. Saucy
61. Gladden
62. Negative votes

DOWN
1. Goddess of plenty
2. Lengthy
3. Actor Mischa ___
4. Liberties
5. "Please Don't ___ Daisies"
6. Grumble
7. Hong Kong nanny
8. Actor Arnaz
9. Colonizers
10. Swarms of people
11. Roster
12. "It's ___!"
13. Honeymaker
21. Swiss river
22. A breeze
25. Hay packer
26. Maternally related
27. Danish island group
28. Warsaw inhabitants
29. Male sheep
30. Merge
31. Ignited again
32. Dueling weapons
34. Crowning glory
37. Sham
38. Newspaper employee
40. State: Fr.
41. Actress Sheedy
43. Confection
44. Divan
46. Use
47. Infrequent
48. Unique thing
49. Spirit
50. Indian of Peru
51. "___ Camera"
52. Medical picture
53. Faucet
56. Printers' measures

PUZZLE 7

ACROSS

1. Time indicator
5. Fragrant compound
10. Homer's son
14. Malevolent
15. Accra's land
16. Together, in music
17. So long
18. Kern tune of 1923
20. Fire-truck gear
22. Exotic
23. Roast: Fr.
24. Uses crayons
26. Last king of Troy
29. Author of "Giant"
31. Forest warden
33. Victory symbols
34. ___-de-lance
37. Rainbow
38. Fencing swords
40. Stratagem
41. Bath rug
42. Mountain pool
43. Card game for two
45. Sense of taste
47. Eyed amorously
48. Tempestuous
50. Tennyson poem
52. Small sandpiper
53. Heathrow or Dulles
56. Precarious place
59. Pilot's maneuver
61. Awry, to a Brit
62. Separate
63. Como or Garda
64. Parched
65. Garb for a ranee
66. Winter weather

DOWN

1. Understand
2. Egg-shaped
3. Actress Naldi
4. Duds for a big bash
5. White heron
6. Actor Omar ___
7. Follows
8. High-school subj.
9. "Norma ___"
10. Waco university
11. Robin of song
12. Poems, to a bard
13. Appalachian st.
19. Broad valleys
21. Capitol feature
24. Montana Indian
25. Vastly overweight
26. Sedate
27. ___ avis
28. What's ___ for me?
30. Happening
32. Domain
34. Roll up
35. Punta del ___
36. Bulrush
39. Implore
40. Toys
42. Dessert for Mimi
44. ___ d'etat
45. Tan silk fabric
46. Political refugee
48. Proscenium, once
49. Moth or lily
51. Mountain crest
52. Madrid Mmes.
53. 6th Jewish month
54. Horse color
55. Fast-food order
57. "___ Boot"
58. Ecology org.
60. Comic-book blow

PUZZLE 8

SLOGANS

ACROSS
1. Pigpen
4. Broadway's Rivera
9. Filmdom's Farrow
12. Jacob's first wife
14. Of a certain grain
15. Cacophonies
16. Virginia: "Thus ___"
19. Unleavened-dough product
20. Compass dir.
21. Pianist/singer John
22. African native
24. Ceylon or Elba: abbr.
25. Iowa: "Our Liberties We Prize and Our Rights ___"
33. '75 Wimbledon winner
34. Envelops
35. Untidy one
37. Depot: abbr.
38. "The Great ___"
39. Dander
40. Grasp
42. Lieu
44. "I can't believe ___ the whole thing"
45. Massachusetts: "By the sword we seek peace, but ___ liberty"
48. Tit for ___
49. 19th letter
50. France's Delon
53. Treasure or road
56. Large drake
60. West Virginia: "___ Always Free"
63. Chinese dynasty
64. Arcade or dreadful
65. Chicago paper, for short
66. Peterborough's prov.
67. Growing out
68. Brewed beverage

DOWN
1. TV's Maxwell
2. Honduran seaport
3. Deviates
4. Romaine
5. Abhor
6. Lay ___ the line
7. Head: Fr.
8. "___ Wednesday"
9. Coin plant
10. "___ the Woods"
11. Org.
13. "Panama ___"
15. J.R.'s town
17. Small sailboat
18. Take a nap
23. TV alien
24. Officeholders
25. Launder
26. Impede legally
27. Moby Dick, e.g.
28. Very, in music
29. Nature of 23 Down
30. Perfect
31. Homer epic
32. "El ___" (American Playhouse film)
36. Lager
41. "The ___ Game"
42. Tennis unit
43. Coloring
44. Press
46. Argot
47. Client
50. Munitions
51. Rib-to-hip area
52. "Charley's ___"
53. Demeanor
54. Dancer Pavlova
55. Confined
57. Pub missile
58. Toledo's lake
59. Singer McEntire
61. Mimic
62. Hurricane center

PUZZLE 9

ACROSS
1. Colleen
5. Fleur-de-____
8. Grizzly
12. Matty of baseball
13. Alabama town
15. Singer Fitzgerald
16. Actor Sean ____
17. One who propels a raft
18. Reclined
19. Tangled
21. Displayed conspicuously
23. Eldritch
24. Morose
25. Homeless cats
27. Concur
31. Border lake
34. Museum display
35. Changes
36. Goes fast
37. Taj ____
39. ____ even keel
40. Scatters about
42. Ohio Northern University location
43. Beauty spot
44. "Over ____"
45. Tempestuous
47. Twisted-horned African beasts
49. Out in front
53. Actor Jeff ____
56. Actor Brian ____
57. Turkish pound
58. Prophets
60. Indigo plant
61. Raring to go
62. Missouri's ____ Mountains
63. Ascend
64. Ancient Persian's kin
65. German spa
66. ____ off

DOWN
1. Run out
2. Coeur d'____, Idaho
3. Underwater detection device
4. Frankie Carle's theme song
5. Zodiac sign
6. Haley/Jeffreys recording
7. Odors
8. "You ____" ("The Three Caballeros" hit)
9. Dash
10. "It's a Sin to Tell ____"
11. Author Ayn ____
13. Secret watcher
14. Asian sea
20. Permit
22. Enthusiasm
24. Frances Burnett heroine
26. Batters
28. Splitsville
29. Of an epoch
30. Serf
31. Formerly
32. Dr. Westheimer
33. About
35. Winglike
38. Fusses
41. Actress Tuesday ____
45. Nothing to ____ at
46. ____-jongg
48. In addition
50. Tennessee ____ Ford
51. Flavoring herb
52. Expunged
53. Bivalve
54. Bees' home
55. Saharan
56. Inquire
59. Engine tracks: abbr.

13

PUZZLE 10

ACROSS
1. Boxers do it
5. Sermon subject
10. Actor Ladd
14. Folk myth
15. Positive terminal
16. Tramp
17. Skin ailment
18. Watches
20. Esther Rolle series
22. Bumstead dog
23. Historic age
24. ___ centum
25. Actress Signoret
29. Chewed out
33. Cut of pork
34. Terminal
35. Singer Davis
37. Anthony Newley song
41. Spanish aunt
42. Hereditary
43. "___ Three Lives"
44. ___ checkers
46. Malay sword
48. Food fish
49. Cry of surprise
50. Metric quart
53. The moment's fleeting
59. "Romeo and Juliet" song
61. Elliptical
62. Actress Miles
63. Peak
64. Aquatic worm
65. Hymn ending
66. Laws
67. ___ of Wight

DOWN
1. Metal refuse
2. Somewhat, in music
3. Italian river
4. Hollow stalk
5. Parody
6. Inner self
7. Large book
8. Fruit coolers
9. Cotton knot
10. Have ___!
11. Places
12. Burrows et al.
13. Intrusive
19. Think
21. KO count
24. Teacher's nickname
25. Key opening
26. Column style
27. Minor Prophet
28. United
29. Contradict
30. Heroic poem
31. Writer Zola
32. "___ at Sea"
34. Cupid et al.
36. Yield
38. Snub
39. Obligation
40. Even score
45. "The ___ Cometh"
46. Bureaus
47. British pilots: abbr.
49. Divert
50. Molten rock
51. Article
52. Grow weary
53. Pamplona bull
54. Angered
55. California city
56. Currier and ___
57. English count
58. Wild plum
60. Airwaves agcy.

ACROSS

1. Hoax
5. Scottish island
10. Town map
14. Sandwich filler
15. Rope loop
16. Right-hand man
17. North Carolina college
18. Yucca
20. Candide's tutor
22. Highways: abbr.
23. Put to flight
24. Identical
26. Bend
29. African trees
34. Whittler
36. Bounders
37. Bobble bait
38. Nichols hero
39. Marry in haste
41. Female horse
42. Criminal group
43. Hebrew measure
44. Puff, e.g.
46. Flowering tree
49. Emissary
50. Ins and ____
51. Futile
53. Pickle spice
55. ____ matter
59. Poplar
62. Venetian resort
63. Algonquin
64. Actress Linda
65. March date
66. Theology schools: abbr.
67. Italian poet
68. Eldest: Fr.

DOWN

1. Tramp
2. Hawaiian dance
3. Ever and ____
4. Rhizophora
5. Pear variety
6. Perches
7. Flag maker
8. Bat wood
9. New: Ger.
10. Rapid speech
11. Former Italian coins
12. Thirst quenchers
13. Ski-lift seat
19. Weapons: Sp.
21. Easy stride
24. Ginger cookie
25. Totaled
26. Rascal
27. Verboten
28. Small antelope
30. Oak nut
31. Old saw
32. Actress Leslie
33. Exhausted
35. Send money
40. Meadows
41. Tulip poplar
43. Eye: pref.
45. Invade
47. Actor Nick et al.
48. Airplanes: Fr.
52. "____ to bed"
53. Writer Schary
54. Bit of gossip
55. Extinct birds
56. "Veni, ____, vici"
57. "East of ____"
58. JFK's mother
59. Metric amounts: abbr.
60. Clear profit
61. Mountain State: abbr.

PUZZLE 11

15

PUZZLE 12

ACROSS
1. Coddle
5. Davenports
10. Cummerbund
14. Norse capital
15. Get up
16. Reverberation
17. Uniform ornaments
20. Make clothes
21. Dutch cheese
22. "Goodnight ____"
23. Unadorned
24. Irish nobleman
26. Flaunt
29. Unpredictable
32. Lake Albert tribesman
33. Used a lever
34. Extinct bird
36. Snubbing
40. Pedal digit
41. Barrel bands
42. Feminine suffix
43. Cargo
45. Ran after
47. G-man Eliot
48. Actor Everett
49. Coral island
52. Do pull-ups
53. Bikini top
56. Muscular
60. Judge's bench
61. Oyster gem
62. Climbing plant
63. Church recess
64. Shouts
65. Cookie man

DOWN
1. TV's "Who's the ____?"
2. Tennis great
3. Play a horn
4. Second person
5. Rider's seat
6. Mountain nymph
7. Solid
8. Viper
9. Caribbean ____
10. Private
11. Need liniment
12. Chinese god
13. Watering tube
18. Heavy metal
19. Harangue
23. Celtic poet
24. Seed coverings
25. Made angry
26. Treaty
27. Indifferent
28. Straightedge
29. Spew lava
30. Copies: abbr.
31. French tale
33. Exclamations of contempt
35. Ripened
37. Escutcheon
38. Gluttons
39. Peruse
44. Intertwine
45. Refrigerates
46. Workman
48. Boor
49. Israeli Eban
50. Snare
51. Ball and lag endings
52. Anthracite
53. Hat edge
54. Gambling city
55. Drinks that sound helpful
57. CIA agent
58. "____ Haw"
59. Miss Gabor

ACROSS

1. Coin openings
6. Glasgow native
10. Ring
14. Subject
15. Travel
16. Otherwise
17. Stadium
18. Days of ____
19. Information
20. Universal
22. Tranquilizes
24. Told a fib
26. Animated
27. Roof part
31. Arab chief
34. Cove
35. Zones
39. Pare
40. Glue
42. Bucket
44. Prosperity
46. Boat
47. Pitcher
48. Kind of scout
49. Indian's abode
53. Word before box or shed
55. Tells
58. Support
63. Historical times
64. Wind indicator
66. Vibrant
67. Locale
68. Selves
69. Defies
70. Understands
71. Charge
72. Exhausted

DOWN

1. Hart
2. Wisdom
3. Frank
4. Fork part
5. Red
6. Mode
7. Dove sound
8. Belonging to us
9. Birch or sycamore
10. Bicycle part
11. Gladden
12. Daisylike flower
13. Minimal
21. Ambiance
23. Pub missile
25. Meal course
27. Tear
28. Again
29. Escape
30. Inform
32. Convened
33. Sherbet
36. Milky gem
37. Unusual
38. Autograph
40. Fido's foot
41. "____ You Lonesome Tonight?"
43. Give permission
45. Yard parts
46. Sentimental songs
48. Also
49. Ringlet
50. Ghostly
51. Dish
52. Alleviates
54. Corpulent
56. Perpetually
57. Heroic narrative
59. Smack
60. Make weary
61. Balanced
62. Musical pause
65. "To Have and Have ____"

PUZZLE 13

17

PUZZLE 14

ACROSS
1. Manage
5. Cooking vessel
8. Crone
11. Kitchen hot box
12. Entity
14. Logger's tool
15. Tardy
16. Unclothed
17. Under the weather
18. Wide awake
20. Sirs, in Spain
22. Sticky stuff
24. Plant seeds
25. Gorges
29. Revolutionary
33. "___ to Billy Joe"
34. Musical sense
36. Respectful fear
37. Marked down
40. Enthusiast
43. Maiden name word
45. Rock's Steely ___
46. Military school
50. Daily darkness
54. Recreation
55. Weight loss plan
57. Butter substitute
58. Lincoln's nickname
59. Baseball's Musial
60. Not far
61. Unrefined
62. Fast plane
63. Dried up

DOWN
1. Soft-drink flavor
2. Egg-shaped
3. Singer Seeger
4. Vitality
5. Wordplay
6. Burden of responsibility
7. Ocean cycles
8. Head growth
9. Wheel shaft
10. Solidifies
13. Male voice
19. As well
21. Be in arrears
23. Washington bill
25. Pro's opposite
26. Commotion
27. Butterfly catcher
28. Glum
30. Vampire, e.g.
31. Ram's mate
32. Robert E. ___
35. Ruby-colored
38. Rearmost part
39. Feats
41. Moving truck
42. Pungent bulbs
44. Gives off
46. Remote
47. Castro's country
48. Again
49. Favorable votes
51. Open delight
52. Get word
53. Ripped
56. Explosive letters

PUZZLE 15

ACROSS
1. Coop
5. Swab
8. Drama
12. Greasy
13. Everyone
14. Get up
15. Gingko, e.g.
16. Poorest
18. Family car
20. Motive
21. Agreements
23. Expert
26. Cooking herb
29. Badgered
31. Extinct bird
32. Come to the rescue
33. Roof part
34. Eccentric one
36. Hostels
37. Vapor
38. Strange
40. "___ Alibi"
41. National bird
45. Grand
49. Highway
51. Actress Barbara ___
52. Baseball stat
53. Biblical preposition
54. Rents
55. Chat
56. Finest

DOWN
1. Folding bed
2. Melodies
3. Mirth
4. Stared
5. Heavenly dish
6. Cheer for a matador
7. Like some skirts
8. Proper
9. Prevaricate
10. Donkey
11. Thus far
17. Type of jockey
19. Orangutan
22. Texas fare
23. Blueprint
24. Guns an engine
25. "___ to Joy"
26. Soft drink
27. Sums up
28. Sailor
30. Entertainer Olin
31. Boxer or poodle
32. Keener
35. Astonishes
36. Crete mountain
39. Summarize
40. Domestic fowl
42. Chow
43. Solo
44. Nibbles
45. Singer Torme
46. Fruit cooler
47. New York athlete
48. Kind of nest egg: abbr.
50. Period

PUZZLE 16

ACROSS

1. Equal
5. Atlas parts
9. Convertible, e.g.
12. Soothing plant
13. Exam type
14. Corrida cry
15. Mandarin
17. Nothing
18. Confused
19. Offensive
21. White poplar
24. Rim
25. Blemish
26. Cherished
30. Author Levin
31. Step
32. Contend
33. Consecrate
35. Historical age
36. Rocker Billy ___
37. Burdened
39. Outspoken
41. Waterless
43. Roe
44. Controversial
49. Asian holiday
50. Always
51. Skin
52. Sooner than, poetically
53. Author Carnegie
54. Koppel and Turner

DOWN

1. Basketball coach Riley
2. High note
3. Time period
4. Stately
5. Additional
6. Opera highlight
7. "Peter ___"
8. Slim
9. Economized
10. Landed
11. Depend
16. Opposite of WNW
20. Turkish title
21. Among
22. Nude
23. Remove
24. Actress Sedgwick
26. And others: abbr.
27. Singer King Cole
28. Ireland
29. Actor James ___
31. Berated
34. Actress Kaminska
37. Ignited
38. Conform
39. Elect
40. "___ the Rainbow"
41. Cain's brother
42. Certain steak order
45. Actress Gabor
46. Hive denizen
47. Showed the way
48. Overhead railways

CODEWORD

Codeword is a special crossword puzzle in which conventional clues are omitted. Instead, answer words in the diagram are represented by numbers. Each number represents a different letter of the alphabet, and all of the letters of the alphabet are used. When you are sure of a letter, put it in the code key chart for easy reference and cross it off in the ALPHABET BOX below the diagram. Three letters have been given to start you off.

Code key chart:

1	2 O	3	4	5	6	7 R	8	9	10	11	12	13
14	15	16 D	17	18	19	20	21	22	23	24	25	26

Grid:

11	2	16	17	10	■	20	7	13	6	■	9	2	10	22
13	19	2	5	17	■	10	18	25	17	■	13	10	2	17
4	2	10	18	16	■	2	5	17	25	■	5	18	4	17
24	17	17	25	■	■	4	17	26	■	■	17	5	17	25
■	■	9	2	13	4	22	■	9	13	7	17	4	4	■
4	12	7	17	26	16	■	■	2	26	25	■	■	■	■
23	18	17	■	10	2	15	17	25	14	17	■	12	18	22
17	24	17	■	■	13	10	17	■	■	■	■	2	7	17
26	17	16	■	16	17	23	10	17	22	17	■	4	18	8
■	■	9	13	7	■	■	17	10	16	17	4	22	■	■
4	22	7	2	19	17	■	1	3	13	24	17	■	■	■
22	7	13	11	■	14	3	25	■	■	11	18	25	22	
13	18	16	17	■	20	2	2	16	■	21	3	7	2	7
11	13	18	16	■	13	25	22	17	■	17	7 R	2 O	16 D	17
23	10	2	6	■	16	17	13	7	■	22	17	25	4	17

ALPHABET BOX

A B C D̸ E F G H I J K L M N O̸ P Q R̸ S T U V W X Y Z

21

PUZZLE 18

ACROSS

1. Stop
4. "M*A*S*H" star
8. Raise
12. ___ Grande
13. Henhouse
14. "God's Little ___"
15. Skill
17. Viewed
18. Remodel
19. Object of value
20. Mixture of greens
23. Couple
24. Yoke of ___
25. Maundy ___
30. Tavern beverage
31. Fine dishes
32. Anger
33. Convince
35. Shoe part
36. Write
37. Complete
38. Rubs
41. Gulls' cries
43. Inactive
44. Thought
48. Bitter dispute
49. Writing fluids
50. Spanish shout
51. Simple
52. Sprinkle
53. Victory

DOWN

1. Age
2. Quick bite
3. Speck
4. Behaved
5. Noisy
6. Extinct bird
7. Gorilla, e.g.
8. Cowboys' ropes
9. Frosts
10. Unattached
11. Camp shelter
16. Persia, today
19. Atmosphere
20. Cleansing bar
21. Wheel rod
22. Sly look
23. Sand ridge
25. "More ___ You Know"
26. Concealed
27. Eat sparingly
28. Region
29. Shout
31. Hints
34. Quick
35. Gardening aid
37. Coil
38. Spouse
39. Theory
40. Additionally
41. Bill of fare
42. Lodge members
44. Offer
45. Promise solemnly
46. Actor Wallach
47. Lair

ACROSS

1. Listen
5. Shack
8. Site
12. Shangri-la
13. Fireplace residue
14. Big trucks
15. Went on horseback
16. High school souvenir
18. Composi-tions
20. ___ good to be true
21. Desert fruit
23. Pitfalls
27. Defeat
31. Barn's neighbor
32. Tennis expert
33. Nail's cousin
35. Beaver's project
36. Roe
38. Lantern fuel
40. Cozy abodes
42. Plunge
43. Fool
45. Maxims
49. ___ eel
53. Thespian's quest
54. Foul-smelling
55. "___ to Joy"
56. Loosen
57. Whirlpool
58. Pump purchase
59. Luge

DOWN

1. Present
2. Tumults
3. Cincinnati's nine
4. Works dough
5. Needle's hiding place?
6. Manipulate
7. "___ Girl"
8. Trellises
9. ___ Grande
10. Self
11. Solicit
17. Spoil
19. Thanks-giving side dish
22. Fouled-up
24. White House staffer
25. Scheme
26. A few
27. Frank
28. Whim
29. Apparel
30. Patios
34. Actress Natalie ___
37. Thickset
39. Certain tires
41. Rested
44. Kermit
46. Aim
47. Different
48. Sesame or poppy
49. Before, to a bard
50. Young fellow
51. Windup
52. Tarbell or Wells

23

PUZZLE 20

ACROSS

1. Craze
4. Rim
8. Catcher's glove
12. Before, poetically
13. Brad
14. Concept
15. Horse operas
17. Hit hard
18. Arrived
19. Web-footed birds
20. Apologetic
22. Evenhanded
24. Revise
25. Slope
29. High tennis shot
30. Suez ____
31. Mire
32. New students
34. Rushed
35. Soft throw
36. Spoils
37. Bird's noise
40. Combine
41. Air
42. Extra work period
46. Pleased
47. Sherry, e.g.
48. Plaything
49. Simple
50. Minus
51. Lamb's parent

DOWN

1. Not many
2. "Butterflies ____ Free"
3. Portray
4. Foe
5. Venture
6. Whitney's invention
7. Chicago trains
8. Skinflints
9. At rest
10. Afternoon gatherings
11. Domesticated
16. Vinegary
19. One quarter of a pint
20. Personality
21. Scent
22. Penalties
23. Actor Arkin
25. Radio buffs
26. Rude
27. Composition for two
28. Whirlpool
30. Mince
33. Consistent
34. Chimney substance
36. Wearies
37. Parrot's home
38. Hawaiian dance
39. Historical epochs
40. Authors
42. Nocturnal bird
43. Contend
44. Cut down
45. Potato bud

PUZZLE 21

ACROSS
1. Swat
4. Sore
8. Jambalaya
12. Anger
13. Achieves
14. Imitate
15. Well-dressed birds
17. Withered
18. High
19. Herons
21. Adjust to
23. Small fly
24. Fashion
25. Bends
26. Actor/director Reiner
29. Hubbub
30. Doze
31. Earlier than now
32. Prohibit
33. "Family ___"
34. Evergreens
35. Legal claim
36. Cobblers' concerns
37. Grotto
40. Libel
41. Space
42. Gazelle
46. Dock
47. Tailless amphibian
48. Clumsy boat
49. Merit
50. Flan necessity
51. Tint

DOWN
1. Verve
2. "Where the Boys ___"
3. Military building
4. Grownup
5. Wind
6. Layer
7. Perfumes
8. Stylish
9. Grow weary
10. Throw off
11. Joins
16. Gawk
20. Struggle for breath
21. Sheik
22. Early 20th-century art form
23. "Fried ___ Tomatoes"
25. Estrange
26. Train tracks
27. Monster
28. Foreman
30. Recipe direction
34. Rotten
35. Memorize
36. Winter toys
37. Shawl
38. Callas specialty
39. Swerve
40. Without a date
43. Festive drink
44. Jimmy
45. ___ out a living

25

PUZZLE 22

ACROSS
1. Split
5. Wipes gently
9. Day before Thur.
12. Marriage pledges
13. Eve's first home
14. Baled commodity
15. Tidings
16. Sideways
18. Necklace unit
20. Equipped
21. Perch
23. Counterfeit
25. Fin. fund
26. Elliptical
28. Short rests
32. Persian or Siamese
33. Award
35. Mom's partner
36. Additional
38. Nevada gambling city
39. Legume
40. Hordes
42. Foals
44. Incompetent
47. Southern vegetable
48. "___ Exposure"
51. Water bird
54. Pullover shirt
55. Actor Roberts
56. Korea's continent
57. Stale
58. Fad
59. Want

DOWN
1. Badge metal
2. "___ to Billy Joe"
3. Dories
4. Curvy letters
5. Feat
6. Sum up
7. Beseech
8. Skulk
9. Impulse
10. Assuage
11. Stained
17. Songbird
19. Small particle
21. Kind of pudding
22. Verbal
23. Loses color
24. King of comedy
27. Part of speech
29. Clapping
30. Pound or Frost
31. Health resorts
34. Wrestling hold
37. Radiate
41. Different
43. Heart or lung
44. Biblical preposition
45. Playwright Coward
46. Cartoon's Flintstone
47. "___ upon a time . . ."
49. Gay Nineties, e.g.
50. Surrey
52. Deceive
53. Tyke

PUZZLE 23

ACROSS
1. Colorado Indians
5. Polite address
8. Weary
12. Sad sound
13. Garden tool
14. Region
15. Huge
17. Lairs
18. Absent
19. Shoat's home
21. Record
24. Morse ____
25. Boisterous
26. "Are You ____ Tonight?"
30. Football's Marino
31. March King
32. Caspian or Caribbean
33. Gazelle
35. Level
36. Ready to eat
37. Actor Jeremy ____
38. Blade case
41. Point-winning serve
42. Labels
43. ____ rug
48. Encourage
49. Young man
50. Soda
51. Porgy's love
52. Optic organ
53. Sacred

DOWN
1. Exploit
2. Can
3. Id's companion
4. Camouflage
5. Inoculation
6. Debt note
7. Answer
8. Emblems
9. Metal sources
10. Tenant's concern
11. "The Big ____"
16. Silent
20. Inspiration
21. "M*A*S*H" star
22. Borrowed sum
23. Baseball ploy
24. Auto type
26. Means of evasion
27. Norway's capital
28. Cruel
29. Snacks
31. Slash
34. Eliminates
35. Horn or toast
37. Drink cooler
38. Cigar remnant
39. Rabbit
40. Breakfast fare
41. Assistant
44. Singer Charles
45. Also
46. Everything
47. Set down

PUZZLE 24

ACROSS
1. Spiked club
5. Officer
8. Weathercock
12. Stench
13. Tint
14. Century plant
15. Reflect
17. Emblem
18. Gear tooth
19. Fastener
21. Space
24. Lawn
26. Alfresco
28. Startle
33. Clinton's attorney general
34. Slave leader Turner
36. Yoked animals
37. Spare
39. Gabbed
41. Baseball's Staub
43. City trains
44. More wholesome
47. Pullover
49. Rabbit
50. Shimmers
55. Singer Murray
56. Eternity
57. Inkling
58. Student's need
59. Excavated
60. Suggestion

DOWN
1. "Mr. ____"
2. Fruit cooler
3. Cape ____, Massachusetts
4. Singer Clapton
5. Humiliation
6. Away
7. Molts
8. Immense
9. Actor Guinness
10. Ark builder
11. Conger
16. Roman garment
20. Burro
21. Writer Vidal
22. Acme
23. Confined
25. Bedouins
27. Neither's partner
29. Corn core
30. Wheel part
31. Rod's partner
32. Boundaries
35. Making lace
38. Exist
40. Farewells
42. Encouraged
44. Window part
45. Jars
46. Stink
48. Engrave
49. Owned
51. Baseball's Gehrig
52. Poet Siegel
53. Sister
54. Place

PUZZLE 25

ACROSS
1. Stain
5. ____ Morgana
9. Periods
14. Wine: pref.
15. Eliot's Bede
16. Get up
17. Speed
18. Town on Lago di Garda
19. Of the cheek
20. Hardwood
21. Goes the long haul
23. Organic compound
25. Chemical suffix
26. Minister
28. Boast
30. Body cavity
33. Actress Mary ____
34. So ____ (amen)
35. Mens ____ in corpore . . .
36. These may break bones
39. Bloodsucking arachnid
40. Family or shoe
41. Befuddle
42. Large boat
43. Chap
44. Cleans the blackboard
45. Southern constellation
46. "Sir, we are ____ of singing birds" (Johnson)
47. Construction workers
52. Be indebted
55. Biblical spy
56. Al or Lesley
57. Presently
58. Straighten
59. "Lovely ____, Meter Maid"
60. Infamous fiddler
61. Has an apartment
62. "When I was ____ . . ." ("H.M.S. Pinafore")
63. Interrogates

DOWN
1. Marsh bird
2. Legumes
3. With it
4. Dance or hold
5. More swiftly
6. Lady Caroline Keppel's "Robin ____"
7. Soft mineral
8. Out of control
9. Gentling
10. In high dudgeon
11. "____ and Otis"
12. Famous Biblical twin
13. Spanish painter
21. Delivery bird?
22. Puts firmly in its base
24. Blue-chip, e.g.
26. Starchy staple
27. Moving
28. Poet William Rose ____
29. Taken for a ____
30. Sedimentary rocks
31. Anoint
32. Judge's docket
34. Cow's home
35. Fountain treats
37. Get the wrinkles out of
38. Weeds
43. Diving birds
44. Group of nine
45. Concerning
46. Large artery
47. Wound remainder
48. Story
49. Actor Ken ____
50. City SSE of Delhi
51. Loam or marl
53. Toil
54. Slaughter of baseball
57. Literary collection

PUZZLE 26

ACROSS
1. Rooms in Spain
6. Night light
10. "Born Free" heroine
14. Disjoined
15. Long
16. Give temporarily
17. Barrier
18. Citizens: suff.
19. Archaic expletive
20. Annoy
22. Dessert
23. Aware of
24. Horn
26. Supple
30. Northern home
32. Publicizes
33. Birthright seller
35. Exchange
39. Vacation time
41. Stabbed
43. Clio and Thalia
44. Sound again
46. Floor piece
47. Left-hand page
49. Northern European kingdom
51. Stick
54. NBA's Archibald
56. Letter's first word
57. Judge
63. Chlorophyll-containing plant
64. Cheers
65. Claw
66. Mountain pass
67. Lake
68. African antelope
69. Republic of Ireland
70. Celtic
71. Descartes et al.

DOWN
1. Secure
2. High spot
3. Ms. Turner
4. Sparks
5. Take over
6. Former VP Agnew
7. Fairy queen
8. Dill
9. Close again
10. Voter base
11. Tender or reserve
12. Cad
13. Mathematician, sometimes
21. Submit a contest solution
25. Short letter
26. Open hand
27. Place
28. Eye part
29. Solemnly declare
31. Effusive language
34. Bishoprics
36. Sere
37. Take out
38. Heaven on earth
40. Employer
42. Mails
45. Eels
48. Type of control
50. Having more liquid
51. Saw
52. Indian city
53. Horrible one
55. French river
58. Winged
59. Sound of congestion
60. Actor Thicke
61. Sound
62. Terminals

PUZZLE 27

ACROSS

1. Narodnaya's range
5. Narrative
9. Wooden shoe
14. Han or Napoleon
15. Inspired reverence
16. Run off to marry
17. Verve
18. Pealed
19. Sir Arthur ___ Doyle
20. Dick Van Patten TV series
23. Cereal grain
24. Termination
25. Put through a sieve
29. Food fish
31. Louisville Slugger, e.g.
34. Rich soil
35. Convene
36. Lincoln's nickname
37. Highway rig
41. Guido's high note
42. Casks
43. Kind of beam
44. ___ Aviv
45. Jerk's offering
46. Scold
47. Diving seabird
48. Limb
49. Kaufman-Ferber play
56. "Last Tango in ___"
57. Immediately
58. ___ avis
60. Originated
61. Embellish
62. Astringent
63. Creed
64. Fitzgerald or Logan
65. Stair

DOWN

1. Consume
2. Function
3. Asian mountain range
4. "The ___, Hot Summer"
5. Scottish plaid
6. Expect
7. Camera eye
8. Rim
9. Fraction of a minute
10. Spoken
11. Sound of a large bell
12. Colorful fish
13. Decade
21. Raise
22. Under, to Keats
25. Ice pellets
26. Plain twill-weave fabric
27. Splendid
28. Ember
29. Actress Berger
30. Cuts down
31. Very light wood
32. Red as ___
33. ___ Haute
35. Anthropologist Margaret ___
38. Elicit
39. Varnish material
40. Auricle
45. Twilight
46. Starr of the comics
47. Herbaceous plant
48. Coral reef
49. Challenge
50. An Age
51. Wrath
52. Indigo plant
53. Mardi ___
54. Cease!
55. Factual
56. Touch lightly
59. Elect. unit

PUZZLE 28

ACROSS
1. Noisy impact
5. Andy or Al
9. Chocolate tree
14. Matador's victim
15. Exchange premium
16. Biblical land of riches
17. English watercress
18. Singer Jagger
19. Curbs
20. "Don't Shoot the ___"
23. Northern constellation
24. Like Willie Winkie
25. "The Secret ___"
27. Kettle metal
31. Spanish streets
33. Edgar ___ Poe
34. Skirt or van
35. Vaulted church part
38. Inlets
39. Juniper
40. Appeal
41. Trifles
42. Goddess of discord
43. Bargained
44. Frequent letter-writer
46. Gemstones
47. Smelting refuse
49. Pub quaff
50. "48 ___"
51. Stall
58. Greek fabulist
60. Duty list
61. Via Appia, for one
62. Surgeon's prefix
63. Hurry
64. Ponce de ___
65. Violinist Mischa ___
66. Keen desires
67. Enactments

DOWN
1. Dance move
2. Mischievous Norse god
3. Bailiwick
4. "September ___"
5. Home on wheels
6. Nimble
7. Desire to eat chalk, e.g.
8. Slow as molasses
9. Livestock enclosure
10. Be a copycat
11. Easy task
12. Eldest girl: Fr.
13. Actor/director Welles
21. "A Prayer for ___ Meany"
22. Florida air-force base
26. Harvester
27. Go or grocery
28. Potpourri
29. Feign sleep
30. Football player, at times
31. Polite
32. Tropical cuckoos
34. Naomi's later name
36. Hawk
37. Has a bite
39. Flower part
43. Bambi, e.g.
45. Japan, in Japan
46. Puffs up
47. Classic western
48. Angler's basket
49. River of song
52. Pretentious
53. Olden times
54. Plow the field
55. Virginia willow
56. Kitty's plaint
57. Gray sea eagles
59. ___ pro nobis

ACROSS
1. Receded
6. Scrub
10. Designer Cassini
14. Hag
15. Brainstorm
16. Slangy negative
17. Younger child's garb
19. Moran or Gray
20. "A Chorus Line" number
21. Diner sign
22. Heraldic emblem
24. Hodgepodge
25. Competent
26. Scholarly showoff
29. Brave
33. Auguries
34. Jauntily neat
35. Village People hit
36. Compassionate
37. Chews the fat
38. Salute
39. Ms. Lanchester
40. "Damn Yankees" vamp
41. ____ tov (good luck)
42. Enlists again
44. Vintner's workplace
45. Campus figure
46. Grease
47. Overwhelm with noise
50. Small rail
51. Ring victory
54. Medley
55. Preowned
58. VIP's transport
59. Historic times
60. Like a bireme
61. Endure
62. Coty or Descartes
63. Ceremonies

DOWN
1. Sound return
2. Muffin ingredient, sometimes
3. Off-white
4. Remnant
5. Humbles
6. Side-to-side measure
7. Commotions
8. Stitch
9. Purses
10. In all directions
11. Actress Singer
12. Homeric opus
13. Hackman or Autry
18. A Coast
23. Sprite
24. Slavishly
25. Bryant or Ekberg
26. Stud or draw
27. Author Zola
28. Stupid
29. Russian range
30. Astonish
31. More aloof
32. Loiter
34. Rose's protector
37. Scouring powder
41. Balcony
43. Golfer's gadget
44. Tip off
46. Slack
47. Ken or Barbie
48. Director Kazan
49. Draws a bead
50. Read
51. Sour
52. Trouser part
53. ____ and ends
56. Before, in poesy
57. "Bali ____"

PUZZLE 29

PUZZLE 30

ACROSS
1. Actor Kaplan
5. Faint
10. Roller coaster, for one
14. Milky-white stone
15. Keep an ___ the ground
16. Pernicious
17. National geyser site
20. Put two and two together
21. Shampoo stage
22. Raves
23. Breathe hard
24. Noisy bird
25. Owning
28. Playlet
30. Color
33. In debt
34. Indigo
35. Fortitude
36. Cheech and Chong song
39. Sound like a donkey
40. Steer
41. Un-conventional
42. Affirmative
43. Telephone inventor
44. Minister
45. "Annabel Lee" poet
46. Darn
47. Goes hang gliding
50. Atlantic or Indian
52. Stellar lion
55. Wassailing tunes
58. Is sick
59. Terra
60. President's office
61. Taylor/Burton film
62. Marshal
63. "Nautilus" commander

DOWN
1. Spanish artist Francisco de ___
2. Mimicked
3. Type of eagle
4. Extension
5. Using needle and thread
6. "Fuzzy Wuzzy ___ fuzzy ..."
7. Table scraps
8. Indian tribe
9. Persona ___ grata
10. Reimburse
11. Tennis's Lendl
12. Soil
13. Wapitis
18. Navel fruit
19. Part of QED
23. Little finger
24. Actress Ireland
25. Pastime
26. Conscious
27. Passports
28. Gastropod
29. Firing oven
30. Pursues
31. In ___ (in the womb)
32. City in the Ruhr River valley
34. Adam's son
35. Squash container
37. Sloth's home
38. Cassidy or Gleason
43. "Who's the ___?"
44. Swell
45. Telescope component
46. Hostess Perle
47. Picket-line buster
48. The Buckeye State
49. Singer Guthrie
50. General Bradley
51. Singer Vikki ___
52. Deep and abiding emotion
53. Western actor Jack ___
54. Scandinavian capital
56. Earl Grey, e.g.
57. Director Howard

34

PUZZLE 31

ACROSS
1. Showily aesthetic
5. Ethiopia's Selassie
10. Decreases
14. Handle with ___
15. Before
16. Shipshape
17. 4th Thursday of November
20. Cleopatra's reptile
21. Nice summers
22. Passage
23. Glen
24. Part of the lower back
26. Tractable
29. Ribbons
32. Befuddled
33. Florida cape
34. ___ Grande
36. 2nd governor of Plymouth Colony
40. Choice: abbr.
41. Cunning
42. To ___ (precisely)
43. Flower-shaped ornament
45. Eccentricities
47. Siouxan
48. Not this
49. Slanting
52. Astronomer Sagan
53. Append
56. 17 Across, e.g.
60. Chopped
61. Pungent vegetable
62. Hard-to-find
63. Comedian Conway et al.
64. Pakistani coin
65. Blinkers

DOWN
1. Proceedings
2. Stadium sounds
3. Plumbing element
4. Desire
5. Disco dance
6. Cherub
7. "How sweet ___"
8. Actress Ullmann
9. Hebrew priest
10. Locomotive
11. Hospital furniture
12. False god
13. Eye ailment
18. On an even ___
19. Hammered
23. TV tuner
24. Vers ___
25. Highly spiced stew
26. Crows' cousins
27. Willow with flexible twigs
28. Viola's big brother
29. Falsehood
30. Exercises
31. River to the Danube
33. Hit hard
35. Pindar products
37. "By the Time ___ Phoenix"
38. Detroit product
39. ___ accompli
44. Not liquids
45. Seat of authority
46. Flower or paper
48. Nevada lake
49. Med. school course
50. Kind of dancer
51. Piece of news
52. Cartridge or paper
53. Call it ___
54. Challenge
55. Stains
57. And not
58. Sky god
59. Furor

PUZZLE 32

ACROSS

1. Roman statesman
5. Pale purple
10. Cart
14. Norwegian king
15. Poetry Muse
16. Chest sound
17. Lawn tool
18. Female fox
19. Eight: pref.
20. Perforates
22. Kitchen apparatus
24. Remedied
26. Stare
27. ___ system
30. Isolate
34. With hand on hips
36. Innocent
37. Baseball stat
38. Tardy
39. "___ Theme"
41. Transmitted
42. Baboon
43. Actress Best
44. ___ de corps
46. Command
49. Inquisitive
50. ___ spumante
51. Ant
53. Underside
55. Straight course
59. Asian river
60. Sins
63. Slaughter of baseball
64. ___ avis
65. Escalates
66. Printing term
67. Low card
68. Hoofer Davis
69. Food fish

DOWN

1. Business abbr.
2. Jai ___
3. Seize
4. Conquered
5. Weight lifter
6. Eye parts
7. Remiss
8. Gobbled
9. Gathering
10. Slobbers
11. Mobsters
12. Der ___ (Adenauer)
13. Time period
21. Restrain
23. S-shaped molding
25. Corrupt morally
27. Mixed greens
28. African mammal
29. Printed material
31. Sine ___ non
32. Mr. Kovacs
33. Unkempt
35. Veterans
40. Blackbird
41. Sparkling clean
43. Outside: pref.
45. Old dagger
47. Wandering animal
48. Symbol
52. Untidy
53. Starr of football
54. The Tentmaker
56. Division word
57. Yule song
58. Punta del ___
61. By way of
62. Doctrine

ACROSS

1. Hyde or Central, e.g.
5. Impression
10. Precious
14. Toward shelter
15. Earn
16. Actor Lincoln
17. Sympathize with
18. Rules of conduct
20. A Gabor
21. Daring
22. Taunt
23. Liberate
25. Kind of dive
27. Org.
28. "___ of a Lesser God"
32. Mark or wind
34. Fame
35. Holiday time
36. Dobbin's dinner
37. Showy flower
38. Matures
39. Falsehood
40. "Inferno" author
41. Sparkle
42. Sanctions
44. Boston ___
45. Deck post
46. Assaulted verbally
49. Ledge
52. Means of travel
53. Actor Wallach
54. Navigation room
57. Irish islands
58. Actor Arkin
59. Born sooner
60. Measure
61. Secret group
62. Rinds
63. March date

DOWN

1. "___ Moon"
2. Functioning
3. Settled the score
4. West or Largo
5. Tax
6. Singer Haggard
7. Parched
8. ___ and tonic
9. Common abbr.
10. "You Can ___ on Me"
11. "___ Cinders"
12. Iowa college town
13. Pasadena bowl
19. Sicilians' country
21. Plinth
24. Terminates
25. Excelled
26. Lean and strong
28. Coagulates
29. Kind of nurse
30. Flush
31. Cozy retreat
32. Painted metalware
33. Downpour
34. Civet's cousin
37. Former
38. European mountains
40. Move with the tide
41. Object
43. Rectangular
44. Handyman's tool
46. Swiss city
47. Make happy
48. Has a meal
49. Quarrel
50. Hawaiian seaport
51. Ardor
52. Discourteous
55. Short flight
56. Comedian Olsen
57. Pierre's friend

PUZZLE 33

PUZZLE 34

ACROSS

1. Gentle as a ____
5. Dog-paddled
9. Witch town
14. Spoken
15. Neaten
16. Two times
17. Latvian port
18. Touched ground
19. Oahu greeting
20. British queen
23. "Believe It or ____"
24. Pipe elbows
25. "____ Miniver"
27. Meager
30. Fixed portions
35. Human trunk
36. Ballad
37. Tree stem
38. Bewilderment
39. Shovel
40. Storage box
41. Tenant's payment
43. Jaguar and puma
44. Snapshot
46. Mobile homes
48. Inferior race horse
49. Play on words
50. Propane
51. Dismiss
54. Restoration
60. Toward the rear
62. Angel's instrument
63. Border
64. Musical show
65. Formerly
66. Part
67. Equine
68. Unwanted plant
69. Snow coaster

DOWN

1. Body of tradition
2. Seed coat
3. Wise men
4. Sports jackets
5. Unvarying
6. Beguiling tricks
7. Mine passage
8. Legend
9. Way up
10. Piercing instrument
11. Social bigwig
12. Resound
13. Carnivore's diet
21. Too
22. Likeness
26. U-boat
27. Commence
28. Strength
29. Stadium
30. Protective trenches
31. Concludes
32. Automaton
33. Cream of the crop
34. Mister: Sp.
36. Shadowbox
39. Landscape
42. Gratuity
44. Appeal
45. Tethers
47. Prowled
48. Grilled
50. Mockery
51. Autos
52. Encourage
53. Wheel hub
55. Food, slangily
56. Bowling alley
57. False god
58. Eye amorously
59. Necessity
61. Hint

PUZZLE 35

ACROSS

1. Scrabble piece
5. Singer Billy
9. Swiss river
12. Expressed
13. Concerning
15. "Do ___ others . . ."
16. Religious recluse
17. Talkative
19. Gridiron player
20. Sorrows
21. Flowers
22. Circles
24. Tiny pest
25. Go quickly
27. ___ at (ogle)
31. Places for earrings
32. Lucille ___
33. Valley
34. Priestly vestment
35. Home on wheels
38. Comic Taylor
39. Fastened
41. Has title to
42. Miss Hopper
44. Shuffle
46. Tasty bit
47. Penpoints
48. Doctrine
49. Take for granted
52. Bad temper
53. Pronoun
56. Unwieldy
58. Field measure
59. "___ Grit"
60. Delhi garment
61. Derma
62. Position
63. Minus
64. Snakes

DOWN

1. Weighty volume
2. Steel base
3. Green sailor
4. Wapiti
5. Rattletrap
6. Orchestra members
7. Eternities
8. Carry with effort
9. Ampersands
10. Suit to ___
11. McKuen et al.
14. Glimmer
15. Joined
18. "Dies ___"
20. Poorest in quality
23. Neighbor of Wash.
24. Vexes
25. Louvers
26. Baby's woe
27. Potato state
28. Long rulers
29. Leave out
30. Flower part
32. Cries noisily
36. Muggers
37. French river
40. Vienna's river
43. Before, poetically
45. Wordless performer
46. Brawls
48. Multiplied by
49. Performs
50. Confident
51. Dirt
52. Drill
54. Stumble
55. Lawmakers: abbr.
57. Actor Mineo
58. Sound ___ bell

39

PUZZLE 36

ACROSS

1. Capture
4. Old silver coin
9. Wound mark
13. Land measure
15. "Plaza ____"
16. Nuts
17. "____ Head" (Frank Sinatra film)
19. Bovary or Lazarus
20. Stories
21. Woody Allen film
23. Religious belief
25. ____ good example
26. Elves' employer
29. Basker's reward
31. Russian revolutionary
34. Embraces
36. Turmeric
38. Have a feast
39. Islet
40. Suit makers
43. Palm leaf
44. Tragic king
46. Kind of cycle
47. Nutmeat
49. Join
51. Termite
53. Social class
54. Musical composition
56. Trot, pace, and canter
58. Roads
61. Continue
65. Scotto song
66. Demeanor
68. Gender: abbr.
69. Vandyke, e.g.
70. Spend it in Milan, once
71. Treasures
72. Feel
73. Seek payment from

DOWN

1. False god
2. Hurt
3. Alcoholic drink
4. Apart
5. Dusk
6. Cavity
7. Old English letters
8. Spins
9. Rained icy particles
10. Fellow travelers
11. Summit
12. Holler
14. Opts
18. Filled with delight
22. Conger
24. Pitcher Ron
26. Climb
27. Foreign
28. Swimming pool
30. Modern: pref.
32. Fiord
33. Fraser of tennis
35. Perched
37. Flood refuge
41. A Gershwin
42. Military area
45. Iterates
48. Scoundrel
50. Be sorry
52. Comes to a point
55. Uses a dagger
57. Sultan's decree
58. Warbled
59. Shoe or family
60. "Graf ____"
62. Arthurian lady
63. Beige
64. Actor Stockwell
67. Griddle

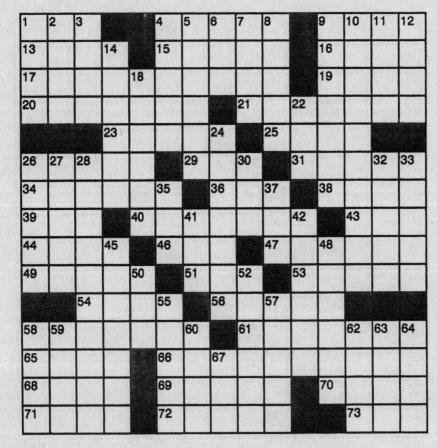

40

PUZZLE 37

ACROSS
1. Mr. Twain
5. Book of maps
10. Spelunker's spot
14. Soon
15. Free
16. Spoken
17. "Leave —— Beaver": 2 wds.
18. Bald bird
19. Loch of legend
20. Throw away
22. Teach
24. Equipment set
25. Olympian Owens
26. More mature
29. Track circuit
30. Daily routine
34. Parched
35. Fiver
36. Cat
37. Family room
38. More mannerly
40. Downcast
41. Deer horn
43. Pull
44. A —— farewell
45. Change the alarm clock
46. Tad
47. Ready cash
48. Narrow gradually
50. Respectful title
51. Kingly abodes
54. Movies
58. Religious ceremony
59. Pilfer
61. Bridal headwear
62. Fragrance
63. Thorax
64. Writer Bombeck
65. Church benches
66. Hits like Ruth
67. Relax

DOWN
1. Domestic worker
2. Against
3. Corrupts
4. Rapped
5. Vigilant
6. Frog's kin
7. Naval diary
8. Napping
9. Plants-to-be
10. Hide
11. Region
12. Enormous
13. Or ——!
21. Atmosphere
23. Theater employee
25. Custodian
26. Conning-tower device
27. Actress Dunne
28. Half quarts
29. "Diamond ——"
31. Buffalo
32. Ridiculous
33. Lingerie item
35. Because
36. "Chosen" quantity
38. Flower part
39. Plaything
42. Mail items
44. Always
46. Donate
47. Time measure: abbr.
49. Nuisances
50. Grain storage buildings
51. Farm product
52. Military assistant
53. Put away, aboard
54. Play personnel
55. A —— pittance
56. Points a weapon
57. Louver strip
60. Historical period

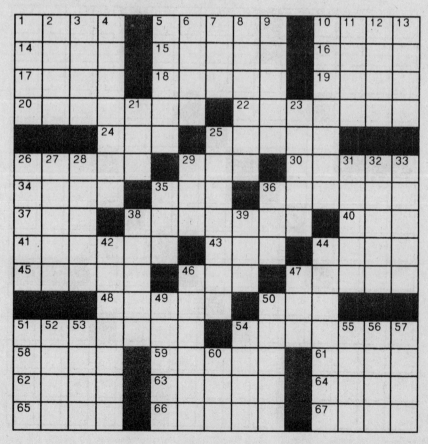

41

PUZZLE 38

ACROSS

1. Fast equines
6. Canvas cover, for short
10. Punta del ——
14. Italian explorer
15. Yesterday: Fr.
16. "Exodus" author, with 39 Down
17. Sitting Bull's right-hand man: 2 wds.
19. "Othello" villain
20. Make lace
21. Rifles
22. Pity
24. Appearing
26. Small role
27. Consume
28. Mata ——
29. Thorough-fare: abbr.
32. George M. ——
35. Trite
37. Stratford's river
38. Governs
40. River curve
41. Associates
43. Overbearing
44. Overhead trains
45. Leave out
46. Actress Farrow
47. Author Havelock
49. Sweeper's aid
53. Open wound
55. Sudden spurt
56. Gold: Sp.
57. Yearning
58. Long shots: 2 wds.
61. —— curtain
62. Singer Adams
63. Fake gems
64. Regrets
65. Criticizes
66. Spirited mount

DOWN

1. Bank depositors: abbr.
2. —— aves
3. Diminish
4. Dickens
5. Dark and gloomy
6. Strap
7. Tunes
8. Legal matter
9. Readies
10. Upper crust
11. Marine creatures: 2 wds.
12. African republic
13. Son of Seth
18. Search
23. Moslem prince
25. Intended
26. Spelunker's milieu
28. Composer Gustav
30. Sawbucks
31. Whirlpool
32. Headland
33. Track shape
34. Good-luck charm
36. Ger. craft: hyph.
38. Memoran-dum
39. See 16 Across
42. —— contendere
43. Chess pieces
46. Command to a dog team
48. Property attachments
49. "The —— of Hazzard"
50. Sheriff's group
51. Mountain ridge
52. Snooped
53. Den
54. Beige
55. Hold fast
59. Oklahoma city
60. Rodent

ACROSS

1. Cyprinid fish
4. Israeli port
9. Quite —— (lots): 2 wds.
13. Indigo
14. "To fetch —— of water": 2 wds.
15. Extinct bird
16. Tyson's milieu: 2 wds.
18. Hwys.
19. Win by ——: 2 wds.
20. Wrath
21. Sheep shelters
22. Practical
24. Penitentiary
25. Santa ——
26. Wiser
29. Buss
32. Irony
34. Pooch
36. Australian bird
37. Truck
38. Top kick: abbr.
39. Actress Merkel
40. Joke
41. Singer Caruso
43. Tiff
44. Wisconsin city
46. Mel of baseball
48. Carry on
49. Lee and Grant, e.g.
54. Leg bone
56. —— diem
57. Proportion
58. "His Eye —— the Sparrow": 2 wds.
59. 1982 Nolte film: 2 wds.
61. Salamander
62. Bear
63. Poetic nights
64. Slippery
65. Bucephalus, e.g.
66. Thing, in law

DOWN

1. —— ear . . .: 2 wds.
2. Mason-—— Line
3. Actress Landi et al.
4. Crying ——
5. Spring month
6. Most just
7. Penalty
8. Sch. subject
9. Nimble
10. Kept inside: 2 wds.
11. —— fixe
12. Throw
13. Desert garments
17. No, to a Frau
21. Omission mark
23. New Orleans rte.: 2 wds.
24. Zircon
27. Odds and ends: abbr.
28. Ms. Barrett
29. Barrel
30. Mosque priest
31. College football event: 2 wds.
33. Soil: prefix
35. Hood's gun
37. Queen: Sp.
42. Stage role
43. Wanderer
45. Petite
47. Area: abbr.
50. Mr. Ford
51. "—— Grows in Brooklyn": 2 wds.
52. Pride members
53. Miss Piggy et al.
54. Fork feature
55. Got it!: 2 wds.
56. Section
59. NBC rival
60. Finis

PUZZLE 39

PUZZLE 40

ACROSS
1. Cloth belt
5. Religious service
9. Pant
13. Three musicians
14. Broadway employee
16. Toward shelter
17. Fairy-tale monster
18. Waken
19. Hard to find
20. —— de la Paix
21. Ripped
22. Leather worker
24. Honorable ——
26. Walking stick
27. Stopover
28. They make a house beautiful
32. Brief
35. Comedienne Judy
36. Compete
37. Skin opening
38. Uncovers
39. Sherlock trademark
40. Chicken —— king: 2 wds.
41. Rescued
42. Mah-jongg pieces
43. Gave in
45. "The —— without a Country"
46. Ship deserters
47. Held a feather to one's nose
51. Injure
54. For fear that
55. Single
56. Lovely flower
57. Bellows like Leo
59. Secret language
60. Coal excavation site
61. Feel
62. Secondhand
63. Ceases fasting
64. Water grass
65. Crimson and scarlet

DOWN
1. TV's "The Secret ——"
2. Debate
3. Ambulance squealer
4. Weeding tool
5. Leave behind
6. Oak nut
7. Daze
8. Distress signal
9. January birthstone
10. Actor Ladd
11. Withered, to a poet
12. Gaze narrowly
15. Keeps
21. Hue
23. Actress Baxter
25. Run out of steam
26. Minded
28. Peeled
29. Cruel
30. Ready for plucking
31. Detects with the eyes
32. Sail support
33. Cavity
34. Verbal
35. Caverns
38. Rams repeatedly
39. Nursery color
41. Unexpected difficulty
42. Diplomacy
44. Wipes out pencil marks
45. Failed to hit
47. Concise
48. Not tight
49. Terminated
50. Boy Scouts' acts
51. Ten cents
52. Opera highlight
53. After-dinner candy
54. Highway division
58. "—— the land of the free"
59. Mongrel

PUZZLE 41

ACROSS
1. Talk back
5. Clique
8. Tears
12. Songstress Logan
13. Paving liquid
14. Penn. port
15. Lumber
16. Summer: Fr.
17. Scrabble piece
18. —— and thread
20. Pencil rubber
22. At any time, in poetry
23. Drink slowly
24. Began
28. Combine
32. Ventilate
33. Medic
35. Paddle
36. Chinese canines, for short
39. Male geese
42. Caribbean ——
44. Teachers' gp.
45. Caused to lean
48. Marred, as a fender
52. Fit to ——: 2 wds.
53. Wise bird
55. Make reference to
56. Actor Auberjonois
57. "Norma ——"
58. Writer Ferber
59. English streetcar
60. Curvy letter
61. Back end

DOWN
1. Stitched
2. African lily
3. Wild plum
4. More despondent
5. Drove a car
6. Consume
7. Kilmer poem
8. Record a second time
9. Blue flag
10. Heap
11. Prophet
19. Rent
21. Circular border
24. Easily fooled person
25. Make a knot
26. Noah's boat
27. Canine animal
29. Fish eggs
30. Long-nosed fish
31. Sounds of hesitation
34. Birthday cake lights
37. Think highly of
38. Use the eyes
40. Maiden name designation
41. Ballerina
43. Worship
45. Small pie
46. Roman road
47. Russian river
49. Neap, e.g.
50. Sicilian volcano
51. Precious
54. No longer is

PUZZLE 42

ACROSS
1. False face
5. Do sums: 2 wds.
10. Kitties
14. —— spumante
15. Genus of grasses
16. Italian city
17. Avoid
18. Whirlybird
20. Summon: 2 wds.
22. Old Italians
23. Factual
24. Assail
25. Tender
27. Veto
28. Clothing frames
32. Frigid
33. Pitcher spout
34. 5th President
35. Scream
36. Gondola float
38. Spanish cheer
39. Rocket stages
41. Suitable
42. Plummet nail
43. Tropical eel
44. Chessman: abbr.
45. Lathery
46. Wall recess
48. Japanese ship
49. English thicket
52. Satellite's descent
55. Blimps
57. Genus of ants
58. To shelter
59. Rent
60. Feline sound
61. Buss
62. Sp. maidens
63. Seabirds

DOWN
1. Bulk
2. Tennis star
3. Aviation daredevil: 2 wds.
4. Related
5. Western resort
6. Atop
7. Indian river
8. Genderless
9. Spotted cavies
10. Sousa march, "El ——"
11. Address notation: abbr.
12. Shoe form
13. Gentlemen
19. Fairy king
21. Animal hair
24. Wright craft
25. English philosopher
26. Do without
27. Nothing
29. Airborne exterminator: 2 wds.
30. Tropical nut trees
31. Shabby
33. —— Cruces
34. Witticism
36. Howling
37. Choose
40. Nursemaids
42. Family identity
44. Asian Pass
45. —— Vicente
47. Covers the upper part of a room
48. Lawgiver
49. Coyote State: abbr.
50. Philippine tree
51. Maddens
52. Flat-topped hill
53. Broad collar
54. Playing marbles
56. Isolated column

ACROSS
1. Wager
4. —— Cruces
7. Green gem
11. Summer quaff
12. Stack
13. Actor Thicke
14. "Private ——" (Hawn film)
16. Mail
17. Whole
18. Confusion
20. Guitarist Paul
21. Graf's game
25. Shopping center
28. —— Guidry
29. Poetic work
30. Miner's quest
31. Russian rulers
33. Author of "The Raven"
34. Caspian, e.g.
35. Mimic
36. Beatles song
37. Ms. Dee
39. Supped
41. Corn unit
42. Associate
46. Press
49. Call to mind
51. Singer Tennille
52. Kiln
53. Take it on the ——
54. Pipe part
55. Marry
56. Period

DOWN
1. Slugger Ruth
2. "East of ——"
3. Canvas shelter
4. Rickey ingredients
5. Cassius Clay
6. Upper House member
7. Actor Robards
8. Pub brew
9. —— Cupid
10. Finale
12. Trim
15. Hill-climber of rhyme
19. Lairs
22. Yep's opposite
23. Matinee ——
24. Ooze
25. Playwright Hart
26. Vicinity
27. No-no for Mrs. Sprat
28. "Norma ——"
31. "GWTW" plantation
32. Nickname for Piaf
36. Ship's wheel
38. Jeans fabric
39. Possessing weapons
40. Adolescent
43. Qualified
44. Rip
45. Columnist Bombeck
46. "—— Magic"
47. Decompose
48. Billfold item
50. Night before a holiday

PUZZLE 43

PUZZLE 44

ACROSS
1. Clog, e.g.
5. Speak
10. Tablet
13. Long times
14. Dishcloth
15. Low
16. "—— hath both spoken unto me ..." (Isa. 38:15): 5 wds.
19. Offspring
20. Hardy girl
21. Set of beliefs
22. Male deer
23. Lifework
25. Chompers
28. Van Gogh's town
29. Terrible tsar
30. Avow
31. Color
34. "And —— and fetched ..." (I Kings 7:13): 3 wds.
38. Dutch city
39. Moran et al.
40. N.Y. canal
41. Lion group
42. Takes forcefully
44. Actress Dahl
46. Golf instructors
47. Actor Delon
48. "—— Magic Moment"
49. Youth org.
52. "Lo, —— all this ..." (Job 13:1): 4 wds.
56. Inquires
57. Rub out
58. Dill
59. Avenues: abbr.
60. Irrigate
61. Grant

DOWN
1. Bastes
2. Santa's sounds: 2 wds.
3. Son of Judah
4. Id ——
5. " . . . for-saking all ——"
6. Sunday meat
7. Pointed tools
8. —— Aviv
9. Hebrew priest
10. Recipient
11. Son of Jacob
12. Act
15. Denudes
17. Twinkler
18. Partition
22. Dangle
23. Stuffs
24. Female voice
25. TV's Wallace
26. Roman poet
27. Country road
28. Make amends
30. Skid
31. That girl's
32. Single thing
33. Fr. summers
35. Calm
36. O'Neill character
37. Observes
41. Works
42. Novelist
43. —— Hashanah
44. Tilted, nautically
45. Grades
46. Stage
47. Wine vessels
48. The one there
49. Part of N.B.
50. Germ
51. Pay up
53. Fir tree
54. Historic time
55. Pouch

PUZZLE 45

ACROSS

1. Bird's beak
4. Chore
8. Tar
11. Tops: hyph.
12. Garret
14. Lose brightness
15. Dieter's weakness: 2 wds.
17. Source of a bitter drug
18. Mexican menu choice
19. Garden plant
21. Gold: Sp.
22. ____ Aviv
23. ____ -a-brac
24. Vehicle
25. Pitcher Paige
28. Start of an oak tree
31. Sometimes part of a full house: 2 wds.
33. Flatfish
34. Strain
35. Mustn't do: hyph.
36. Equinox to equinox: 2 wds.
38. Breakouts in adolescence
39. Some Polynesians
40. Wind dir.
41. Breathe rapidly
42. Cooking vessel
43. Bout finish: abbr.
46. With reason
48. Supplying with oxygen
50. Slave
51. Turkey type
53. Fifty percent
54. Belgian town
55. ____ of sunshine: 2 wds.
56. Tarzan Ron
57. Classify
58. Abyssinian title

DOWN

1. ____ never (ultimatum): 2 wds.
2. Before Febrero
3. Borscht ingredient
4. Steele periodical, with "The"
5. Coral island
6. Greek porch
7. Scout Carson
8. Strong wind
9. Aroma
10. Quilters' gathering
11. Regarding: 2 wds.
13. Mapped
14. No way!:
16. Silo missile
20. Indian groom
23. With less covering
24. Bakery delicacy: 2 wds.
25. Of the Mets' old stadium
26. Business science: abbr.
27. Unaspirated
28. Dolt
29. Dove sounds
30. Wide-mouthed jar
31. Italian city
32. Mayday initials
34. Before long: 3 wds.
37. Horse color
38. "____ Is Born": 2 wds.
40. Most painful
42. Falk or Fonda
43. Jeweled headband
44. Nut-bearing trees
45. Just
46. Aquatic animal
47. Paris airport
48. Bread: prefix
49. Ski-lift: hyph.
50. Haggard title
52. High points

PUZZLE 46

ACROSS
1. Debating side
4. Betting protection
9. Before, poetically
12. Toast topping
14. Type of willow
15. Blue-green
16. First garden
17. Asparagus unit
18. Desire
19. Drowsy
21. Car-club events
23. Wreath
24. P.O. purchases
25. Sliver
30. Some
31. Walk, slangily
32. Line of rotation
34. "Green ——"
38. "I cannot tell ——": 2 wds.
39. Furious
41. Busy place
42. Men
44. Head: Fr.
45. Notion
46. Switch positions
48. Fidgety
50. Bridge support
53. Dirt
54. CPA
55. "—— for Tomorrow"
58. Bulgarian
59. Canine name
61. Cupid
63. Tennis great
64. Expel
65. Alaskan city
66. Recent: prefix
67. Chairs
68. Damp

DOWN
1. Enemy
2. Auto pioneer
3. Spool
4. "General ——"
5. Catch sight of
6. Gambling cube
7. Cogwheels
8. Printing mistakes
9. Supply
10. Tricks
11. Devours
13. Soap opera: 4 wds.
15. Another soap opera: 3 wds.
20. Nightfall, to a poet
22. Actress Turner
25. Kind of rug
26. —— vault
27. Pork cut
28. Door sign
29. Broadway's "Big ——"
33. Location
35. Astronaut Sally
36. Holiday times
37. Bodies of water
40. Sundaes, e.g.
43. Agitated state
47. Sleep sounds
49. One —— customer: 2 wds.
50. Beat
51. Potato state
52. Small orchard
54. Clumsy —— ox: 2 wds.
55. Faction
56. Boast
57. Where the heart is
60. By way of
62. Matched group

ACROSS

1. Successful: 2 wds.
6. Gaelic language
10. Guam harbor
14. Unattached
15. Classified: hyph.
17. Mains
18. From the —— (publicly)
19. Bat wood
20. Get —— of: 2 wds.
22. Neckline shape
23. Nestling
25. Meal scrap
26. "—— Gay"
28. Has to
30. Chicago airport
33. Thorne Smith character
35. Moccasin
36. Greek porch
40. Excel
42. Most outstanding: 2 wds.
44. —— nostrum
45. Society girl
47. Weds secretly
48. Kenya native
50. Whitecaps
51. Fins
54. Mail center: abbr.
56. Blind strip
59. Peer Gynt's mother
60. Actor Charlton et al.
64. "—— Crazy": 2 wds.
65. Redhead:

hyph.
67. Edge: 2 wds.
69. Dining surfaces
70. Yearns
71. Wood sorrels
72. —— -daisy
73. Courageous

DOWN

1. Greek flasks
2. Loud
3. Upper excess weight
4. Simple sugar
5. Worrywart
6. Clear sky
7. Chimney locale
8. Pour forth
9. —— est percipi
10. Legislation
11. Utah city

12. Drive away
13. Lost: 2 wds.
16. Sniggler
21. Souped-up cars: 2 wds.
24. Paramount
27. Wise elders
29. Coterie
31. Chapeau
32. Statesman Dean
33. Cowboy Mix
34. Gametes
37. First-rate
38. Disclose, to bards
39. Donkey
41. Legume
43. Chosen: Fr.
46. Circus tents: 2 wds.
49. ". . . who lived in

——":
2 wds.
51. Ipso ——
52. Violinist Stern
53. Ipsissima ——
55. English sweetheart
57. Malarial fevers
58. Stowe character
61. Two of Caesar's last words
62. Organ valve
63. Dross
66. Literary monogram
68. Old Fr. coin

PUZZLE 47

51

PUZZLE 48

ACROSS
1. Surrealist
5. Hawaiian farewell
10. Bivouac
14. Astride
15. 1925 Peace Nobelist
16. Hautboy
17. Brat
18. Incense resin
19. Booty
20. Impromptu
23. Balderdash!
24. Acknowledge
25. Propounds
28. Israeli port
30. Federal publisher: abbr.
33. Apportion
34. Beige
35. Writer Ambler
36. Impromptu: 4 wds.
39. English river
40. Once more
41. Relative
42. Burro
43. Alack!
44. Rue
45. "—— Hopkins"
46. Cup handle
47. Impromptu
55. —— about: 2 wds.
56. Mortise and ——
57. Church area
58. Female singer
59. French historian
60. Coatrack
61. Corset bone
62. —— and wiser
63. Convinced

DOWN
1. Cat's-paw
2. Peak
3. Astray
4. Room decors
5. Experts
6. French composer
7. Debtor
8. Blood: prefix
9. Pons ——
10. Punctuation mark
11. —— Deia, Chad
12. Dairy sounds
13. Special favorite
21. Slogan
22. Ram's dam
25. Italian staple
26. Oil flasks
27. Pivots
28. Yearns
29. Personnel
30. Actress Garson
31. —— -nez
32. Double quartet
34. Lab heater
35. Resettlers
37. High voice
38. —— a time: 2 wds.
43. Publicize
44. Actor Rob
45. Atomize
47. Element
48. —— Scotia
49. Grist
50. Writer Bagnold
51. Completed
52. Poi source
53. Daredevil Knievel
54. Exploit
55. GI wear

ACROSS

1. Tempo
5. Jumble
9. Chinese food fryer
12. Milky gem
13. Buffalo's lake
14. Kimono tie
15. Andean nation
16. Pioneer's fuel
18. Information
20. Wide valleys
21. Alpine songs
24. ____-Hur
25. Entertain
26. Dirtier
30. Fled
31. Droop
32. Lyric poem
33. Aspired
36. Trace
38. Buck's mate
39. Felt the loss of
40. Thespian
43. Tastes
44. Emergency treatment
46. Flying saucers
50. Had a meal
51. Carney and Garfunkel
52. Singer Fitzgerald
53. Type of grass
54. Take it easy
55. Colored

DOWN

1. Mom's man
2. Primate
3. Horseless carriage
4. Dodges
5. Lifts
6. Opera song
7. Title of respect
8. Listened to
9. Angora or alpaca
10. Woodwind
11. Goats' young
17. Magic stick
19. Beer's cousin
21. Three feet
22. Poet Khayyam
23. Beach feature
24. Annoy
26. Insane
27. Charged particles
28. Brink
29. Bulrush
31. View
34. Fusses
35. Grinding bowl
36. Tilt
37. Put forth
39. Middle
40. A long way off
41. Metropolis
42. Maple, for one
43. Rests
45. Exist
47. Soar
48. Bullfight cheer
49. Melancholy

PUZZLE 49

PUZZLE 50

• HOW'S THE WEATHER? •

ACROSS
1. Wanes
5. In a ____ (dazed)
8. Special goodie
9. Debate
11. Silly
12. Startles
13. Road distance
16. Mild weather climate
19. Rotisserie part
23. Doctors' gp.
24. Linen vestment
25. Listens to
26. Kind of attack
29. Sinew
32. "Little Orphan ____"
33. Patricia ____ of films
34. Type of bran
35. Reel's companion
37. Sherbets
38. Hopeless souls
40. Pig's home
41. TV producer Charles
42. Yes, to Henri
43. Platt and Sullivan
45. 551, to Romans
47. Used a chair
48. Actor Kingsley
49. Female rabbit
51. Sigma's follower
53. "____ the season ..."
56. Playmate
59. Hideout
60. Canadian prov.
61. "You dirty ____"
62. Sir Geraint's wife
65. Soothes
66. Soldiers' groups
68. Hindu gowns
70. Refine ore
71. Response, briefly
72. Gym pad
73. Church section
74. Winter weather event
80. Actor Gordon
81. Parlors
83. Singer Frankie ____
85. Connecticut, e.g.
86. Muppet
87. Hurricane center
88. Transmitted

DOWN
1. Sea eagle
2. Tempo
3. Deadly poison
4. Goblet feature
5. College gp.
6. Fairy tale heavy
7. Bubble source
8. Even-steven
9. According to
10. Heart
12. Bowers
13. Road diagram
14. African-born model
15. Bowling alley
17. Slacks
18. Antiquity
20. Window components
21. Rainbow
22. Lao-____
25. Falling weather objects
27. "Othello" villain
28. Sudden wet weather
29. Foot end
30. Spike of maize
31. Touch-me-____
36. Colors
39. Egyptian river
44. Miami's county
46. "____ the Night"
50. Writer Ferber

54

51. Yarns
52. Without a purpose
54. Bank statement abbr.
55. Soda sippers
56. American poet
57. Knock sharply
58. Part of TGIF
59. Lantern
63. "____ La Douce"
64. Watch face
65. Civil War abbr.
67. Switch positions
69. Sault ____ Marie
74. Crack up
75. Musical symbol
76. ____ for the road
77. Bullfight cheers
78. Unusual
79. Wisc.'s neighbor
80. Horse command
82. Grazed
84. Insect egg

PUZZLE 50

PUZZLE 51

ACROSS
1. Keen humor
4. Pout
8. Choir singer
12. Lyric poem
13. Lineage chart
14. Chess piece
15. Guarantee
17. Office group
18. ___ to riches
19. Bold
21. Writer/director Edwards
23. Ember
24. Lasso
25. Soldier's clergyman
29. Kimono sash
30. Layers
31. Female deer
32. Speculated
34. Specks
35. Clothes stand
36. Jeweler's weight unit
37. Toward the top
40. Acquire
41. Comedian Danny
42. Deceptive
46. Shade trees
47. Christmas song
48. Novel
49. Mailed
50. Sticky stuff
51. ___ whiz!

DOWN
1. Exclamation of surprise
2. Mountain overlooking Troy
3. Turtle
4. Actor's platform
5. Large vases
6. Allow
7. Piano part
8. Horrify
9. Neighbor of Vietnam
10. Deuces
11. Solely
16. Libertine
20. Strikes
21. Forehead
22. Timber wolf
23. Impudence
25. Going around
26. Decorating
27. Tiny bit
28. ___ egg (savings)
30. Wild duck
33. Most arid
34. Raised platform
36. Crack filler
37. Hawaiian guitars
38. Faintly colored
39. Song of worship
40. Scottish valley
43. Bud's partner Costello
44. Victory sign
45. Lamb's ma

ACROSS

1. Huge
5. Deface
8. Planted
12. New York canal
13. Cheer for a toreador
14. Honolulu's island
15. Actress Moreno
16. Tear
17. Steel ingredient
18. Kareem's game
21. Grow
22. Total
25. More trite
29. "___ Through the Tulips"
31. Angel's headgear
32. Seep
33. Follows
36. Tree frog
38. In the past
39. Intense light beam
41. Triumphant
46. Medicinal plant
49. Rose fruit
50. Gumbo ingredient
51. Flaps
52. Building addition
53. Labels
54. Leave
55. Golf peg
56. Favorable votes

DOWN

1. Action word
2. Operatic melody
3. Perches
4. Tropical wood
5. Cement
6. Excuse
7. Meal
8. Loam
9. Rower's tool
10. What person
11. Religious sister
19. Before, in verse
20. Hawaiian wreath
22. On the summit of
23. Nap
24. Venison
25. ___ butter
26. Zest
27. As well
28. Singer Rawls
30. Edgar Allan ___
34. Yale nickname
35. Fragrant bag
36. Populate
37. Miscalculate
40. Subway gate
41. Waistcoat
42. Jot
43. Approve
44. Strong desire
45. Back talk
46. Dined
47. Careless
48. Kimono sash

PUZZLE 52

PUZZLE 53

ACROSS
1. Emotionless
5. Molecule
9. Deposit eggs
12. Formal song
13. Bossa ____
14. Ram's counterpart
15. Bombast
16. What get painted after fingertips
18. Gratify
20. Little ____ Riding Hood
21. Malt brew
23. Endive or Caesar
27. Church bench
30. Puppies
32. "The Dating ____"
33. Elliptical
35. Tennis instructor
36. Flat
37. Grow weary
38. Morays
40. Army insect
41. Snow coasters
43. Tongue part
44. Chewing ____
46. Discouraged
51. Thirst quencher
55. General's assistant
56. Historical period
57. Breeze makers
58. Pelt
59. Twice five
60. Dirt
61. Congeals

DOWN
1. Find fault
2. Spoken
3. Queue
4. Info
5. Gazelle
6. Also
7. Concluded
8. Mops of hair
9. Orchid necklace
10. Punching tool
11. Affirmative answer
17. Old saying
19. Down in the dumps
22. White heron
24. Volcano's output
25. Prayer response
26. Fender damage
27. Cauldrons
28. Malevolent
29. Merchandise
31. Most firm
34. Ridge
39. Health establishment
42. Catches waves
45. Form of address
47. Lip
48. Trek
49. Work on a manuscript
50. Animal lairs
51. Ante
52. Bard's before
53. Singer Morrison
54. Wildebeest

PUZZLE 54

ACROSS
1. Dust cloth
4. Mr. Lincoln
7. Moist
11. Cain's mother
12. Embankment
14. Ohio Indian
15. Precious
17. Fabric nap
18. Have a go at
19. Merchant
21. Sandwich part
24. Top banana
25. Apiece
26. Salad staple
30. Bat wood
31. Feather adhesive
32. Utter
33. Reflection
36. Present
37. Skin opening
38. Tortoise racers
39. Pure
42. Blood-brother
43. Wander
44. Aviator's vehicle
49. Pass over
50. Trickle
51. Dawn moisture
52. Unites
53. Singer Grant
54. Be indebted to

DOWN
1. Stir (up)
2. Actress Gardner
3. Solidify
4. Grant
5. "Rosemary's ___"
6. Building wing
7. Set out
8. Parched
9. 1,760 yards
10. Influential equal
13. Mailbox item
16. Mormon State
20. You dirty ___!
21. Whip
22. Hotheaded
23. Reverberate
24. Start with a clean ___
27. Manipulator
28. Handle with ___
29. Potato buds
31. Sewing fiber
34. Overthrows
35. Procured
36. Talk show host Arsenio ___
38. Content
39. Gloat
40. Catcher's place
41. Zealous
42. High school event
45. Lyricist Gershwin
46. Commotion
47. Unused
48. Sheep's mom

59

PUZZLE 55

ACROSS
1. Naughty
4. Telephone
8. Release money
12. Capitalize on
13. Continent
14. Farm unit
15. Stretch
17. Actress Donna ____
18. Majorette's prop
19. Close at hand
21. Smidgen
23. Swallowlike birds
27. Bawl
30. Porky of cartoons
32. Unearthly
33. Compensated
35. Congregated
37. Went on horseback
38. Aquatic animal
40. Wash the floor
42. Grown boys
43. Topics
45. Shake
47. Stench
49. Walks the floor
53. Opposite of west
56. "Are You ____ Tonight?"
58. Color of the sky
59. Eternally
60. Veto
61. Warp
62. Sinks below the horizon
63. Pigpen

DOWN
1. Electric light
2. On a voyage
3. Dimple
4. Short snooze
5. Fireplace residue
6. Charge against property
7. Bowling alleys
8. Obstruction
9. Expert flier
10. Fury
11. Directed
16. "I ____ Rhythm"
20. Dazzle
22. Not bright
24. "____ Here to Eternity"
25. Tendency
26. Observed
27. Identify
28. Promise
29. Rise to the bait
31. Emerald, e.g.
34. Downgraded
36. Haul
39. Primary color
41. "The Pickwick ____"
44. Shoe bottoms
46. Cooking fuel
48. Traipse
50. Pros and ____
51. Radiate
52. Alluring
53. Taper off
54. Brew
55. Bask
57. Mesh

PUZZLE 56

ACROSS
1. Informant
4. Baseballer Pee Wee___
9. Morose
12. Comedian Olsen
13. Held title to
14. Snivel
15. Hot Mexican dish
17. Dedicate
19. Pastry
20. Spanish mister
21. Worked the garden
23. ___ capita
24. Salty drop
27. Piece of corn
28. Openings
29. Sidestep
30. ___ this moment
31. Took as one's own
33. Not out
34. Edge
36. Scull
37. Model Carol ___
38. One of the Great Lakes
39. Shirt sleeve
40. Unrefined minerals
41. Inception
43. Prompt
44. Idle chatter
46. Fred Flintstone's pal
49. Era
50. Duck
52. Affirmative word
53. Pole
54. Showy flower
55. Use a needle

DOWN
1. Bosh
2. ___ carte
3. Attitude
4. Character
5. Feminine sheep
6. Printer's measure
7. Passover feast
8. Heaven on earth
9. Made points
10. Craft
11. Color fabric
16. Assistance
18. Signified one's will
20. Ship-welcoming city
21. ___-ho!
22. Western movie
23. Authority
25. Lithe
26. Charters
28. "___ to the West Wind"
29. That girl
31. Spy
32. Scottish cap
35. Raged
37. Sporting grounds
39. Penthouse
40. Your and my
42. Soak through
43. Actor Grant
44. Stock value
45. "Long ___ and Far Away"
46. Actor Kingsley
47. Organ of sight
48. Slow growing evergreen
51. Execute

PUZZLE 57

ACROSS
1. 24 hours
4. ___ Minor
8. On the summit of
12. Momma sheep
13. Lemon peel
14. Challenge
15. John Wayne movies, typically
17. Warning
18. Singles
19. Type of rehearsal
20. Highway divider
23. Professional charge
24. Egg-shaped
25. Conjectures
29. Library
30. Flavorless
32. Paleozoic, for example
33. Adversaries
35. Primary pipe
36. Dined
37. Seethed
39. Mantle
42. ___ on the dotted line
43. Ajar
44. Newsletter
48. "A ___ for Us"
49. Prod
50. Part of to be
51. Glasgow guy
52. Necessity
53. Teacher's ___

DOWN
1. Moisture
2. Wonder
3. Word of approval
4. Coliseum
5. Seductress
6. Country hotels
7. TV spots
8. Admires a great deal
9. Housebroken
10. Raw metals
11. Quill writers
16. Labor
19. Achievement
20. Method
21. Neck and neck
22. Copenhagen native
23. Amusement
25. Step on the ___
26. Official stamp
27. Buffalo's lake
28. Beach material
30. Nip
31. Actor Marvin
34. Iron attractor
35. Not yours
37. Foolish talk
38. Leered
39. Droves
40. Grand
41. Audition tape
42. Positive
44. Roll
45. Type of dance
46. Wrath
47. Butterfly catcher's tool

62

PUZZLE 58

ACROSS
1. Maul
4. "More ___ You Know"
8. Star of "Moonstruck"
12. Pollster's inquiry
13. Saint's headdress
14. Hawaiian party
15. Staggered
17. What ___ is new?
18. Interrogate
19. Very large ponds
20. Distribute
23. In the distance
25. Pious platitudes
26. Pickier
30. Historic age
31. Go getters
32. New York town
33. Ambassador
35. Playwright Coward
36. Was in arrears
37. Blustery
38. Straighten
41. Tennis shot
42. Tedious
43. Rustic rug
48. "Little Man ___" (Foster movie)
49. Possesses
50. Before, in verse
51. Aroma
52. Red vegetable
53. ___ King Cole

DOWN
1. Square of butter
2. Past
3. Saturated
4. Not those
5. Listen
6. Ginger ___
7. Agree
8. Becomes free of fog
9. "The Incredible ___"
10. Soothe
11. Regrets
16. Rigid
19. Neighbor of Vietnam
20. Chilled
21. Rani's garb
22. ___, crackle, pop!
23. Presently winning
24. Knox or Ticonderoga
26. Advance
27. Press clothes
28. Ogled
29. Depend
31. Duck feathers
34. Lumberjack
35. Pen points
37. Most unfavorable
38. Palo ___
39. Onus
40. Division word
41. Country path
43. Irish rocker Geldof
44. Ram's mate
45. Tenn. neighbor
46. Pension fund: abbr.
47. Fish catcher

63

PUZZLE 59

ACROSS

1. Kind of basketball shot
5. Be mistaken
8. Traveler Marco ____
12. Largest continent
13. Cattle sound
14. Desertlike
15. What Frosty the Snowman will do in spring
16. Church seat
17. Nevada town
18. Light wind
20. Chalkboard item
22. And not
23. Mom's mate
24. Bugs Bunny's milieu
28. Flower part
32. Spanish cheer
33. "The ____ Shoes"
35. Actress Lupino
36. Lone Star State
39. Packaged
42. Daisy ____
44. Night before Christmas
45. Narrate again
48. Slipper
52. Actress Barbara
53. Donkey
55. Heart
56. ____ on the vine
57. Twentieth letter
58. Notion
59. Puts to paper
60. Cup handle
61. Bread unit

DOWN

1. Part of a door
2. ____-friendly
3. "The Last ____" (film)
4. Inventor's protection
5. Monarch
6. Shad's output
7. Used oars
8. Colorful march
9. Minerals
10. "What's My ____?"
11. Bouquet
19. Place to see wild animals
21. Seance sound
24. Camp bed
25. Stout
26. Film critic Reed
27. Fresh
29. Bit of advice
30. Cool drink
31. Tyke
34. Bureau
37. Reparation
38. "My Gal ____"
40. Burt's TV wife in "Evening Shade"
41. Writing tool
43. Overjoy
45. You ____ what you sow
46. Advantage
47. Juvenile
49. Fuddy-duddy
50. Region
51. Table extension
54. Vast amount

PUZZLE 60

ACROSS
1. Museum display
4. Take it on the ____
7. Luxurious resort
10. Train track
12. "____ to Billy Joe" (Benson film)
13. Flunk
14. 5,280 feet
15. Peculiar
16. Vex
17. Bargains
19. Reside
21. Rival
22. Untruth
23. Glide
26. Shopkeepers
30. Samovar
31. Conifer
32. ____ is me!
33. Garden bloom
36. Napped kid leather
38. Vermilion
39. Daylight source
40. Locked up
42. Sill
45. Remove rind from
46. Pinky ____
48. "To the ____ of the Earth" (Powell film)
50. Eager
51. Before, in poems
52. Violent anger
53. Marry
54. Squeal
55. Boston ____ party

DOWN
1. Upper limb
2. Sudden police visit
3. Scrabble piece
4. Slack
5. Tack on
6. Busybody
7. Go with the wind
8. Tablet
9. Strong beer
11. Turns, as pages
13. Emancipated
18. "Salem's ____"
20. Be victorious
23. 8 fluid ounces
24. Native metal
25. Rock star Adam ____
26. By way of
27. Have debts
28. Curtain fixture
29. Look at
31. "____ on the Roof"
34. Encouraged
35. Society page word
36. Take to court
37. Beneath
39. Frozen rain
40. Bear's home
41. Dry
43. Small fly
44. Brink
45. Fido's foot
47. Epoch
49. Dead, White, or Black

PUZZLE 61

Diagramless crosswords are solved by using the clues and their numbers to fill in the answer words and the arrangement of black squares. Insert the number of each clue with the first letter of its answer, across and down. Fill in a black square at the end of each word. Every black square must have a corresponding black square on the opposite side of the diagram to form a symmetrical pattern.

ACROSS

1. Easy stride
5. Russian news agency
9. Land measure
10. Cream of the crop
12. British gun
13. Work hard
15. Tree fluid
16. Ike's command: abbr.
17. Favorite
18. Nautical hail
20. Batter's ploy
21. Navigating device
23. River mouth
24. Milky gem
25. Pop
26. Put into place
27. Perfect score
28. Jones or Thumb
31. Camera stand
33. Hollywood and ____
34. Large artery
35. Whit
36. "High ____"
37. Soon

DOWN

1. Highland girl
2. Eight: prefix
3. Mixture
4. Night, to poets
5. Crochety
6. Choir voice
7. Title of respect
8. Condition
11. Happening
14. Kett of the comics
16. Long time
19. Actor Holbrook
20. Cot
21. Failed to win
22. "Aida," for one
23. Spanish gentleman
25. Auto type
27. Dorothy's dog
29. Aware of
30. Intend
32. Paid athlete
33. By way of

PUZZLE 62

ACROSS

1. Uncooked
4. Snoop
7. Lasso
9. Fib
10. Spillane's sleuth
11. Winter footwear
12. Bivouac
13. Pose
14. Sass
15. Heavy weight
16. The sun
17. Ogre
21. Lamb's mom
22. Put down
23. Guido's note: 2 wds.
24. Tolerated
27. Chart
28. Joke
29. Likely
30. Aviate
31. Ceramic piece
32. Rage
34. Ridicule
37. Metal source
38. Make amends
39. Finish
40. Runty rug

DOWN

1. Male sheep
2. Devoured
3. Armed conflict
4. Scheme
5. ____ Grande
6. Still
7. Highway entrance
8. Little devil
10. Greeted
11. Storage places
12. Circus worker
13. Offspring
15. Plaything
16. Observe
17. Bonkers
18. Shirley of films
19. Gladden
20. Knock
22. Table support
25. Unattractive
26. Baseball's Knight
29. Assistant
30. Allen or Astaire
31. Soft metal
32. Enemy
33. Vase
34. Water barrier
35. Greek letter
36. Decay

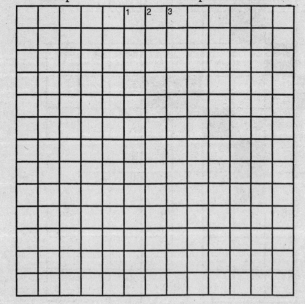

PUZZLE 63

ACROSS

1. Defect
5. Blueprint
9. Jot
10. Curved bone
13. Lasso
14. Midday
15. Song for one
16. Lyric poems
17. Grate harshly
18. Stop
19. Immediately following
20. Ginger drink
21. Marsh
22. Torrid
24. Army commander
27. Kingly
31. Rhythmic swing
32. Young boy
34. Mother sheep
35. Brief look
38. Passed by
40. Atmosphere
41. For each
42. Medley
43. Take by theft
45. Suspended
49. Plead
51. Noisy bird
52. By way of
53. Lichen
56. Distant
58. Farm worker
59. Poker pot
60. Null
61. Secret language
62. Sacred picture
63. Snakelike fish
64. Aid in crime
65. Salamander
66. Torso

DOWN

1. Closing act
2. Untie
3. Upon
4. Pale
5. Immediately
6. Ore vein
7. Pinnacle
8. Cozy home
10. Speckled horse
11. Unwell
12. The two
15. Refuge
17. Dust cloth
21. Untrue
23. Decree
25. New Haven tree
26. Undulate
28. Of course!
29. Reverent dread
30. Went in front
32. Panther
33. Back street
35. Cooking fuel
36. Ignited
37. Wrath
39. Seed container
44. Away
46. Dodged
47. Nonagenarian's age
48. Stripling
50. Donated
51. Hoosegow
53. Water pipe
54. Formerly
55. Pack away
57. Enemy
58. Vagabond
61. Taxi

Starting box on page 562

CHANGAWORD

PUZZLE 64

Can you change the top word into the bottom word (in each column) in the number of steps indicated in parentheses? Do not change the order of the letters, and change only one letter at a time. Proper names, slang, and obsolete words are not allowed.

1. **WORK** (3 steps)   2. **FIRE** (4 steps)   3. **BACK** (4 steps)   4. **LEAF** (4 steps)

LOAD   SALE   SEAT   MOLD

PUZZLE 65

ACROSS

1. Flop
4. Head covering
7. Female bovine
10. Article
12. Fast
14. Corn bread
15. Window glass
16. Enlist
17. Shoestring
18. Religious songs
20. Alternate
22. Wager
23. Cooking vessel
24. Gang
26. Mae or Key
29. Equitable
30. Exist
32. Tip
33. Place
34. Jane or John
35. Walk
36. Emerald Isle
39. Fashion
40. Tease
42. Baby
43. Inclines
46. Separately
49. Spoil
50. Postage square
53. Honk
55. They're for hugging
56. Cabs
57. Smell
58. Gosh!
59. Sportscaster Barber
60. Firmament

DOWN

1. Scoop
2. Beehive State
3. Refuse to admit
4. Metal cylinder
5. Quick to learn
6. Dock
7. Outer garment
8. A sole time
9. Very little
11. "The ___ of the Wedding"
12. Remainder
13. Decline
14. Blue ___ special
19. Unused
21. Drag
24. Small boat
25. Horseman
27. Caesar or Cobb
28. Track down
29. Nourished
31. Needle aperture
35. Spud
37. Actor Jeremy ___
38. Pinch
39. Cleaning implement
41. Most suitable
42. Timothy Hutton film
43. Certain
44. Citrus fruit
45. Headliner
47. Fishing poles
48. Captured
49. Tatter
51. Cutting tool
52. Halfway
54. Undertake

Starting box on page 562

PUZZLE 66   Quotagram

Fill in the answers to the clues. Then transfer the letters to the correspondingly numbered squares in the diagram. The completed diagram will contain a quotation.

1. Body's framework
$\overline{23}\ \overline{49}\ \overline{21}\ \overline{17}\ \overline{29}\ \overline{5}\ \overline{31}\ \overline{35}$

2. The day after today
$\overline{4}\ \overline{9}\ \overline{26}\ \overline{47}\ \overline{10}\ \overline{28}\ \overline{27}\ \overline{8}$

3. Macaroni or potato
$\overline{39}\ \overline{42}\ \overline{11}\ \overline{34}\ \overline{36}$

4. Hocked
$\overline{43}\ \overline{15}\ \overline{1}\ \overline{19}\ \overline{38}\ \overline{12}$

5. In any case
$\overline{46}\ \overline{2}\ \overline{20}\ \overline{45}\ \overline{33}\ \overline{32}\ \overline{7}\ \overline{48}$

6. Piercingly
$\overline{40}\ \overline{6}\ \overline{13}\ \overline{24}\ \overline{16}\ \overline{30}\ \overline{18}$

7. Delighted
$\overline{41}\ \overline{37}\ \overline{44}\ \overline{3}\ \overline{25}\ \overline{14}\ \overline{22}$

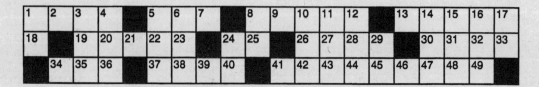

PUZZLE 67

ACROSS

1. Composer Khatchaturian
5. Shiny mineral
6. Mastered
7. Toast starter
11. Studio
15. Pancetta, e.g.
16. Enraged
18. Not any
19. Straighten
20. Batman portrayer West
24. Saltpeter
25. Styles
26. Falsehood
27. Strict
28. Bugs's snack
30. Turkish ruler
31. Edmond O'Brien film
35. Soft cheese
36. Morning fare
37. "The Highwayman" poet
38. Eat
39. Missouri feeder
44. Legitimate
45. Printer's direction
46. Commodities
47. Arabian gulf
48. Himalayan priests
49. Road sign
51. Unusual
52. Endeavor
55. Calla lily
56. Deride
57. Discerned

DOWN

1. Asian nurse
2. Basmati, e.g.
3. Sharp
4. ___ of it (celebrated)
8. Nova ___
9. Tinted
10. Oddball
11. Strike violently
12. Hawaiian city
13. "Metamorphoses" poet
14. Languish
17. Detected
20. Bell town
21. Mend
22. Very much
23. Practices
24. Evening person
27. Fervor
29. Some votes
31. Fits of weeping
32. Radiate
33. Bird on Maui
34. "___ a Song Go Out of My Heart"
35. Ravel work
37. Consumer advocate
40. European industrial region
41. Weapon, to Juan
42. Equipment
43. To be, to Pliny
44. Shoe part
50. Spooky
53. Solid shape
54. Govt. agts.

Starting box on page 562

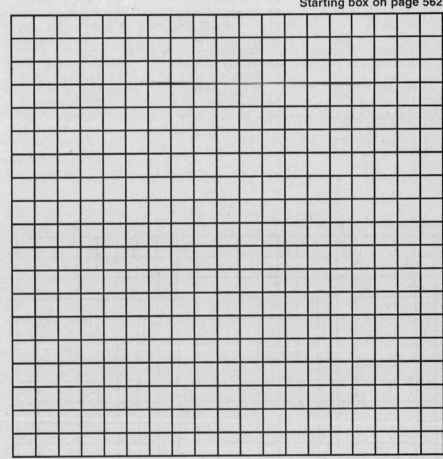

Deduction Problem   PUZZLE 68

One Saturday night, the Adlers went to a dance club with three other couples (the Rubins, the Tuckers, and the Turners). During one song, each of the four women (Angela, Janice, Judy, and Paula) danced with the husband of one of her friends. From the information provided, determine the full name of each woman and the last name of the man with whom she was dancing.

1. Mr. Adler was dancing with Mrs. Rubin.

2. Judy and Mr. Turner danced together.

3. Angela was dancing with Janice's husband.

4. Paula was dancing with Mr. Adler.

PUZZLE 69

ACROSS
1. Hindu stratum
6. Billy ____ Williams
9. Cut short, at Cape Canaveral
10. Writer Alexander
15. She, in Paris
17. "____ Hay" (Huxley)
18. "The ____ Purple"
19. Flamenco clickers
21. Excuse
22. Cooking staple
23. Author Phillip
25. Georgia or Cal
26. Baseball's Bucky
27. Highway incline
30. Large beer mug
34. TV E.T.
37. Indo-European
39. Great ____ Lake
40. Soft cheese
41. Heavenly bread
42. Property attachments
44. Units of volume
45. Cinch
46. Vegas opening
47. Prime and inflation
48. "____ Came Running"
49. Windy city: abbr.
52. Ruth's mother-in-law
54. Existed
55. Trace
57. Stops (the villain)
59. Mr. Kadiddlehopper
63. Facility
64. "The Man from ____"
65. Sidekicks
67. Mine excavation
69. Narcissus's other lover
70. Stogy, e.g.
72. Western bulrushes
73. Baseball's Durocher
74. Comic Buster
76. Trickle
77. Burden
81. Cave weapon
83. Rural structure
86. Actor Murphy
88. Airport for 49 Across
89. Economic slump
91. High-IQ group
92. One of Columbus's three
93. Big party: hyph.
94. Pilgrim John
95. Mink's kin
96. French possessive
97. Honks

DOWN
1. Actor James
2. Mr. Doubleday
3. ____ voce
4. Iseult's lover
5. And so on: abbr.
6. Art ____
7. African antelope
8. Famed cow
10. Shoo!
11. Disappearing places
12. "____ Restaurant"
13. San Francisco height: 2 wds.
14. Jackie's second
16. Collar or jacket
20. Coldest place on earth
24. Pester
28. Bait fish
29. Kind of hat
31. Speaker's platform
32. Mr. Knievel
33. Comic Jay
35. Feel warmly towards
36. Actor Parker
38. Neck parts
40. Smile from ear to ear
43. North Pole resident: 2 wds.
44. Poetry's cousin
49. Storage receptacle
50. Gap
51. Shoe part
53. Other: prefix
56. Amerind dwellings
57. Intensify
58. As soon as
60. Riff
61. Singer Adams
62. Million: prefix
66. Bag
68. ____ Santo, Brazil
71. Actor Gilbert
75. Angel of mercy
78. Evict
79. Sonora farewell
80. Electron tube
82. Orson or Andy
84. Slow tempo
85. Eightsome
87. Grandson of Adam
88. Grandma, in Berlin
90. I'm all ____
92. Kitty

Starting box on page 562

PUZZLE 70

ACROSS

1. Vegetable container
4. Article
8. Autumn
12. Egg-shaped
14. Praise highly
15. African lily
16. Shy
18. Frosts
19. Debatable
20. Hands-on lecture
23. Feather scarf
24. Sprite
25. Stubborn
28. Alternate
30. Equipment
31. Back of a boat
33. Crimson
36. Hawaiian garland
37. Allege
38. Lyric poem
39. House extension
40. Lament
41. Ache
42. Bird's flapper
43. Hovel
45. Light brown
46. Devour
47. Compassionate: hyph.
54. Magician's rod
55. Emotional state
56. Postpone
58. Otherwise
59. ____ of Capri
60. Charge per unit
61. Antlered animal
62. Adolescent
63. Modern

DOWN

1. Folding bed
2. Eager
3. Nominate
4. Blue flag
5. Diplomacy
6. Always
7. Tableland
8. Close kin
9. Standoffish
10. Crazy bird
11. Allow
13. Flexible
17. Portal
21. Negative vote
22. Aquatic bird
25. Eye amorously
26. Spool of film
27. Brad
28. Blood vessel
29. Upper limb
31. Fake coin
32. Sailor
33. Speckled horse
34. Revise copy
35. Contradict
37. Against
40. Obey
41. Rapid talk
42. Roam
43. Ocean
44. Difficult
45. Uptight
47. Yarn
48. Radiate
49. National flower
50. Golfing goal
51. First garden
52. Verve
53. Social appointment
54. Marry
57. Bow wood

Starting box on page 562

CATEGORIES

PUZZLE 71

For each of the categories listed, can you think of a word or phrase beginning with each letter on the left? Count 1 point for each correct answer. A score of 15 is good, and 21 is excellent.

	FLAVORINGS	ANIMALS	MUSICAL INSTRUMENTS	VEHICLES	FOOTWEAR
C					
L					
O					
P					
S					

PUZZLE 72

ACROSS

1. Calico or Manx
4. Stadium yell
5. No-no for Jack Sprat
8. ___ today, gone . . .
9. Harsh sound
13. Castle light
15. Worship
17. Sapor
18. Upper crust
19. Mitchell book: 4 wds.
23. Slovenly sort
26. Extent
27. Keats works
29. Reverence
30. Capture
32. Alkali
33. French city
36. Softened
38. Poetry Muse
40. Asian range
41. Handicraft
42. TV picture
43. M. Chagall
44. '70s Italian president
47. ___ guzzler
48. Hairdo
49. Night prior
51. Summer hue
52. Spanish rivers
54. Alas, in Aachen
56. Winchester, e.g.
58. Shades
62. Songs for two
65. Bed
66. Blades
67. Protection
68. Vermont resort
70. Yen
71. Cribbage piece
73. Gold: Sp.
74. Mr. Gehrig
75. Matched pairs
78. Pungent root
80. Of ___ (long ago)
82. Hemingway book: 4 wds.
89. Let up
91. Establish the truth of
92. Keen
93. Monster
94. Contribute to the poker pot
95. Kazakh sea
96. Compass point: abbr.
97. Bottom line
98. Grads-to-be

DOWN

1. Doctrine
2. Moses's brother
3. Stephen Crane book: 5 wds.
5. Weekday: abbr.
6. Bible book
7. Cooper book: 5 wds.
8. Witch
9. Prime or exchange
10. Bat wood
11. Sault ___ Marie
12. Church seat
13. Take care of
14. Ye ___ Shoppe
16. Ram's mate
17. Quaker's pronoun
20. Alaskan dwellings
21. Attempt
22. Kind of column
24. Have bills
25. Garden spot
28. Close tightly
30. Reno's state: abbr.
31. "Exodus" character
33. Machine part
34. Winglike part
35. Spike of corn
37. Length x width
39. Pekoe, e.g.
45. Blue Eagle inits.
46. Age upon age
49. Sin
50. Roman seven
53. Poky
54. Tempo word
55. Mongrel
57. St. Tropez summers
58. Residence
59. Nasser's inits.
60. Energy unit
61. Wind pt.
63. Craggy height
64. Sellout sign
68. Crafty
69. Also
71. Ashen
72. Newspaper execs
76. Feminine ending
77. Him and her
78. Boffo review
79. Malaga Mrs.
81. Black, to poets
83. Bath, e.g.
84. Footed vase
85. Un
86. More certain
87. Les ___-Unis
88. ___ et poivre
90. Lager's kin

Starting box on page 562

72

PUZZLE 73

ACROSS
1. Live outdoors
5. Communications medium
6. Pack down
10. Buries the hatchet: 2 wds.
12. ____ Antoinette
13. "La ____ aux Folles"
14. Deposition
16. Lose color
17. Astonish
18. Solution: abbr.
19. Have feelings
20. Finis
21. Spar
22. Leatherneck
26. Expertise
27. Deputy
28. Tread
30. ____ and carrots
31. Pay homage
33. Fear
36. After Mar.
39. Pianist Peter ____
40. Divest of rank
42. Podiatrists' concerns
44. "The Foggy, Foggy ____"
45. Lucky number
47. Records
49. Actress Moran
51. Piquant
52. Actor Vincent
53. Wrath
54. Deceived
55. Forehead
56. "My country, ____ of thee . . ."
57. Wharf
58. R.R. depot
61. Picnic pests
63. Joker
64. Calcium carbonate rock
67. Sousa group
68. Thoughts
69. Froths
71. Canvas shelter
72. Sorties
73. "Desire under the ____"

DOWN
1. Bar of soap
2. Summer cooler
3. Hit or ____
4. Scowls
5. Frenzy
6. Scottish cap
7. Length times width
8. Vikings' home: abbr.
9. Domesticated animals
10. Manufactured
11. Inventor's protection
12. Patch
13. Wheeled shopping basket
15. "Name That ____"
16. Hooked
19. Packing box
21. "Monster ____"
22. Atlas entry
23. Mellowed
24. Brings up children
25. Skirt panels
29. Stoma
32. Use oars
34. "You ____ My Sunshine"
35. Frogmen
36. Fore and ____
37. Bog fuel
38. Fixed
41. Danger
43. Extreme fear
46. French resort
48. Ragout
50. Composer Rorem
52. Six-shooter
54. ____ julep
55. Chickadee, e.g.
56. Soviet news agency
57. Gives a bad review
58. Narrow opening
59. Ocean movement
60. Prayer ending
62. Trap
63. Side and box followers
65. Have lunch
66. And others, to Ovid: abbr.
67. Four-posters
70. LBJ's beagle

Starting box on page 562

MIX 'EM MAXIM

PUZZLE 74

Rearrange the letters in the silly sentence below to spell out a familiar saying.

THREE MINKS ON TILE, PETE

Saying: __ __   __ __ __ __ __   __ __ __ __ __   __ __ __ __ __ __ __ __ __

PUZZLE 75

ACROSS

1. Bend
5. Press
6. Opera hero, often
8. Cook in a skillet
11. Dash
13. Adhesive
14. Is mendacious
16. Council city
17. Extol
19. "The ____ Gatsby"
20. Beer mug
22. Jimmies
23. Rend
25. Heavenly hunter
26. Meeting offering
28. "The ____ and Daniel Webster"
29. Abut
31. Hair-raising
33. Convince
36. Kind of wrap
37. Uncertainty
40. Void
41. "____ Love"
42. Proclaim loudly
43. Spot
45. Uncle's wife
46. Scurries
48. Mesh
49. ____ Lama
52. Bagel, e.g.
53. Songstress Carter

DOWN

1. Scout Carson
2. High dudgeon
3. Nary a one
4. Small hill
7. Soras
8. Fido's tormentors
9. Litter's littlest
10. Up to now
12. Straight
13. Unseasoned
15. Animal fat
16. Vocal group
18. Tool's buddy
19. Big smile
21. "A Boy ____ Sue"
22. Golf teacher
24. Wanders
25. Linseed ____
27. Fatigued
28. Arid
29. Pitcher's error
30. Galena or cinnabar
31. Commence
32. Dunce-hat shape
34. Fortune
35. Entice
36. Incline
38. Shrub
39. Not so hot
40. Azure
42. Outlaw
44. Pine
47. Kind of gin
50. "____ the President's Men"
51. Sickly

Starting box on page 562

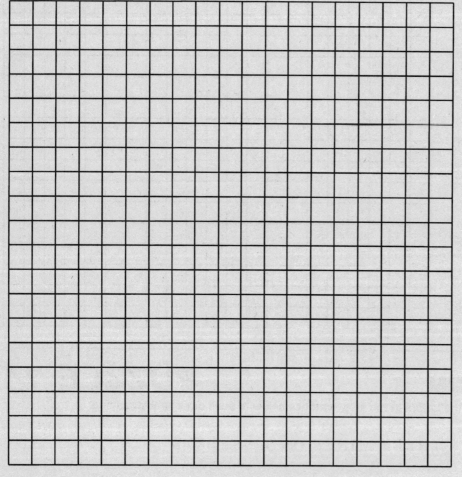

74

PUZZLE 76

ACROSS
1. Declines
5. Corrosive
9. County center
10. Actress Lee
11. Boss or poll
13. Help in crime
14. Conductor Caldwell
16. City on the Rio Grande
19. Pick up the bill
22. Go for a spin
25. Winglike
27. Cassini and others
29. Papal cape
30. Census data: 2 wds.
35. For any reason: 2 wds.
36. Stinks
37. Pianist Peter
38. Decay
40. Darns
43. "____ My God to Thee"
47. Consumed
50. Fashion
51. Frogman
53. Defendant's answer
54. Split
55. Transmit
56. Coaster

DOWN
1. Double curve
2. Plays the odds
3. Vamp Theda
4. Commence
5. Asian sea
6. Castro's country
7. Via Appia, for one
8. Old-fashioned
12. State of conflict
15. "Crimes of the ____"
17. Whimsical
18. Fatty liquids
20. Asian range
21. Powder ingredient
23. Turn down
24. Victorian oaths
26. Thing, at law
28. Prevent
29. Actor Davis
30. Mover's vehicle
31. Thing
32. Weed among grain
33. Solo
34. Golf club
39. End-table pieces
41. Pop
42. Mixes
44. Function
45. British prime minister
46. Interpret a text
48. Iniquitous
49. Glacial snow
52. Burgundy or cherry

Starting box on page 562

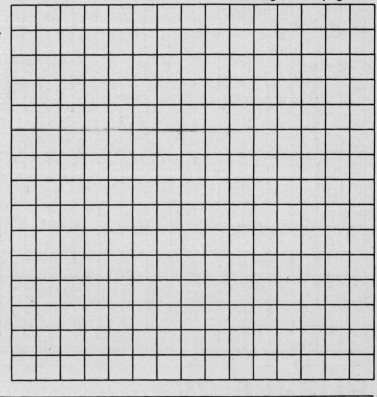

QUOTAGRAM   PUZZLE 77

Fill in the answers to the clues below. Then transfer the letters to the correspondingly numbered squares in the diagram. The completed diagram will contain a quotation.

1. Direction
   $\overline{1}\ \overline{40}\ \overline{20}\ \overline{27}\ \overline{38}\ \overline{13}$

2. German city
   $\overline{19}\ \overline{36}\ \overline{10}\ \overline{33}$

3. Sufficient
   $\overline{22}\ \overline{23}\ \overline{2}\ \overline{16}\ \overline{29}\ \overline{18}$

4. Respond
   $\overline{4}\ \overline{37}\ \overline{28}\ \overline{6}\ \overline{21}$

5. Steak order
   $\overline{31}\ \overline{42}\ \overline{11}\ \overline{8}\ \overline{26}\ \overline{15}$

6. Removed the center of
   $\overline{24}\ \overline{9}\ \overline{41}\ \overline{5}\ \overline{35}$

7. Price
   $\overline{17}\ \overline{25}\ \overline{14}\ \overline{7}$

8. Secluded
   $\overline{3}\ \overline{30}\ \overline{39}\ \overline{12}\ \overline{34}\ \overline{32}$

1	2	3	4	5	6	7	8	9	10	■	11	12	13	14	■
15	16	17	18	■	19	20	21	■	22	23	24	25	26	27	28
29	30	31	32	33	34	■	35	36	37	38	■	39	40	41	42

PUZZLE 78

ACROSS
1. Blunt end
5. Distress signal: abbr.

Starting box on page 562

8. Expect
9. She-sheep
10. Press, as clothes
11. Against
13. Uses cash
15. Ground grain
18. Center of a wheel
21. Opera highlight
22. Walking stick
23. Bacterium
24. Greedy
25. Loyal
28. Encourage
29. Twelve-inch lengths
30. Pagan god
33. Marine bird
34. Sand hill
35. Conclusion
36. Nasty look
37. Specimen
42. Hurl
46. Actor's part
47. Mimic
48. Notion
49. Moved swiftly
50. College VIP

DOWN
1. Boat
2. Ripped
3. On top of
4. Stoop
5. Ocean
6. Possess
7. Matched pieces
12. Likeness
13. Shut noisily
14. Tonsorial service
16. Before
17. Ventilate
19. Basic amount
20. Cot
22. Public vehicle
25. Gull-like bird
26. Bursts
27. American Indian
28. Wide-awake
29. Service charge
30. Out of a job
31. Immediately owed
32. First number
38. Like the Sahara
39. Fashion
40. Appeal
41. Slender
43. Boat paddle
44. Mineral spring
45. Japanese coin

PUZZLE 79

WORD MATH

In these long-division problems, letters are substituted for numbers. Determine the value of each letter. Then arrange the letters in order from 0 to 9, and they will spell a word or phrase.

1

0	1	2	3	4	5	6	7	8	9

```
               A N T
       _____
CAN   | M U S E U M
        M E A A
        _____
        N U I U
          C A N
          _____
          A E E M
          A N P T
          _____
            N N C
```

2

0	1	2	3	4	5	6	7	8	9

```
                  A R E
         _____
RODEO   | G R A Z I N G
          R O D E O
          _____
          Z A D R N
          O D D I E
          _____
          R A D N Z G
          A D D E Z R
          _____
            A D Z J A
```

3

0	1	2	3	4	5	6	7	8	9

```
                C O Y
        _____
ECHO   | S H A K E S
         N E H C
         _____
         F A O E
         E C H O
         _____
         C Y O K S
         C O H H Y
         _____
           E O K E
```

76

ACROSS

1. Amazes
5. Actress MacGraw
8. South Seas island
9. Hearts and clubs
11. Culture medium
12. Foreshadow
14. Tennis unit
15. Guido's high note
16. Household servant
18. Send back
21. Metric weight
23. Canine
24. Time period
25. Negative vote
27. Sparked electrically
29. Arachnid
30. Rodents
31. Pigeon dwellings
32. Id's companion
33. Stir
34. Fish-eating bird
36. Used to be
38. Goes by
41. Stitches
43. Offer
44. Colloid
46. Proclaimed
48. Rant's partner
49. Persons
50. Solar disk
51. Dampen
52. Saucy

DOWN

1. Arabian robes
2. Bet
3. On cloud nine
4. Knight's title
5. Atmosphere
6. Ignited
7. Component
9. Vended
10. Hitch
12. Writing tool
13. Movie makers
17. Ventures
19. Watched carefully
20. Playing marble
22. Incensed
26. Word of permission
27. Exist
28. Storms
29. Styles
31. Crow's call

35. Cancel
37. Lambs' dams
38. Pastry treats
39. Do sums
40. Cut off
42. Freight barge
43. Van Allen ____
45. Period before Easter
47. Regret
48. Knock

PUZZLE 80

Starting box on page 562

Word Math

PUZZLE 81

In these long-division problems letters are substituted for numbers. Determine the value of each letter. Then arrange the letters in order from 0 to 9, and they will spell a word or phrase.

1

0	1	2	3	4	5	6	7	8	9

```
              S T Y
YENS | S T A I N E D
       I Y L I S
       T Y W A E
       L Y S L E
       Y T Y W D
       E E E E D
       I W L W
```

2

0	1	2	3	4	5	6	7	8	9

```
              K I N
IOTA | E N G A G E
       V K T K
       A K N R G
       A T E T I
       A O R K E
       A N N T N
       K G K N
```

3

0	1	2	3	4	5	6	7	8	9

```
              P A L
OAKS | C A R E S S
       A L L A
       O W C R S
       S E K P
       E S L S
       E O S L
       C A P
```

77

PUZZLE 82

ACROSS
1. Musical ensemble
5. Camp beds
9. Butter substitute
10. Boxing site
12. Garden intruders
14. Pavarotti, e.g.
15. Precipice
16. Lock of hair
19. Harrow rival
22. New York island
24. Enthusiastic review
25. Mob action
27. Say one's piece
29. Division word
30. Sculptor, e.g.
33. Go apace
34. Mr. Linkletter
35. Observe
36. Pub brew
37. On one's toes
40. Paper fastener
42. Char
43. Garden intruders
45. Put by
46. Fool
47. Hound
51. Rile
52. Hackneyed
53. Elizabeth II to Edward VIII
57. More ashen
60. Lively dance
61. Barrel slat
62. Wash
63. "The ____ of Laura Mars"
64. Snick and ____

DOWN
1. Orange or Gator
2. Downwind
3. Require
4. Los Angeles team
5. Singer Stevens
6. Magnetite, e.g.
7. Circus sites
8. Express contempt
11. Locale
13. Isolate: 2 wds.
17. Old Glory element
18. Kind of net
20. Manifest
21. Undiluted
23. Musical tone
26. Wool weight
28. Buss
31. Clique
32. Athletic ensemble
33. In dreamland
34. Halt
36. Apportion
37. Mule parent
38. Look before you ____
39. Roof overhangs
41. Whale groups
44. "The Perils of Pauline" et al.
48. "Lights out" music
49. Thrill
50. Kind of race
54. Spirit
55. Sheltered inlet
56. Fencing sword
58. Poet Merriam
59. Legal matter

Starting box on page 562

PUZZLE 83 CHANGAWORD

Can you change the top word into the bottom word (in each column) in the number of steps indicated in parentheses? Do not change the order of the letters, and change only one letter at a time. Proper names, slang, and obsolete words are not allowed.

1. CAMP (4 steps)   2. WILD (3 steps)   3. CORK (3 steps)   4. MOLE (7 steps)

FIRE   BIRD   SOLE   SKIN

PUZZLE 84

ACROSS
1. Act in a pretentious way
5. Hero
9. Walk through water
13. At all times
14. Indian boat
16. Eastern continent
17. Grow
18. Proverb of luck: 5 wds.
22. European stag: 2 wds.
23. Depart
24. Seasoning for turkey stuffing
26. Alkaline solution
27. MacDonald's place
29. Aladdin's-lamp spirit
30. Egyptian deity
33. Ticket for a postponed game: 2 wds.
35. Killer cetacean
36. Comfortable
37. Singing voice
38. Place
41. Among
43. Shows grief
45. Made laws
50. Bet on a loser: 4 wds.
55. Pacify
56. Festival
57. Tenant's contract
58. Plunder
59. Style
60. Colored
61. Measure

DOWN
1. Discontinue
2. Greedy
3. Small plateau
4. Victim
5. Cake decorator
6. Mr. Garroway
7. United, of old
8. Master
9. Joker
10. Timber tree
11. Old phone part
12. Artist's frame
15. Spies
17. Split
19. Turn a ____ to: 2 wds.
20. Type of chemistry
21. Dried grass
25. Actress Moran
28. Holy city of Islam
29. 12 dozen: abbr.
30. Attendants of grooms: 2 wds.
31. Repeating
32. Firmament
34. Hawaiian dance
38. Compassion
39. Cry of disgust
40. Larceny
42. Actress Arlene
43. Ice runner
44. Influence
46. College girl
47. Salver
48. Existence
49. Exploit
50. Soothing substance
51. Plant of the lily family
52. Coagulate
53. Van Winkle
54. Mineral source

Starting box on page 562

SUM WORDS PUZZLE 85

This puzzle adds words instead of numbers, which makes it sumwhat different. Answer the top two clues in each problem with words containing the number of letters indicated in parentheses. Then rearrange these letters to find the Sum Words answer. If the math-od eludes you, try working backwards!

1.
	Ceremony	(4)
+	Scottie's family	(4)
=	Woodwind instrument	(8)

2.
	Brag	(5)
+	Prong	(4)
=	Stubborn	(9)

3.
	River in England	(4)
+	Nerve network	(4)
=	Remodel	(8)

4.
	Marathon	(4)
+	Food fish	(4)
=	Chicory	(8)

PUZZLE 86

CHALLENGER

ACROSS

1. Boot liners
5. Asian nursemaid
6. Superlative ending
9. Soccer great
10. Stanza: abbr.
11. Take ____ view of
15. Similar: abbr.
16. Actress Miles
17. Venetian resort
18. Math functions
21. Storms
24. Table scrap
25. Petrarch work
26. Geraint's wife
27. Carpets
28. Liberates
29. Reasons for action
33. Roll-call response
34. Author Macdonald
35. Get one's ducks ____
36. Butter portions
37. Aviation prefix
38. Wild
39. Ireland
40. Composer Khachaturian
41. FM
48. Stratagem
49. Hyde Park vehicle
50. Hoard
51. Kingly title
52. Pome
53. Uprising participant
54. Halt
55. Caution
56. Dance attire
57. Boca ____, Fla.
59. Lively ____
60. Equine hue
61. Kind of hat
62. Morse unit
63. Cloth junctions
64. Theme ____ (musical form)
67. Broadway's Billy
68. Wee devils
69. Costa ____
71. Seth's son
72. Break a fast
73. Neat as ____
74. Draft inits.
75. Pup or circus
76. Norse verse collection

DOWN

1. Hemingway nickname
2. Changed for the better
3. Pas de ____
4. Cabinet part
6. Turns inside out
7. Dried up
8. Great changes
11. Straightens
12. Actress Keaton
13. Runs in neutral
14. Largest portion
16. Brink
19. Plus ____
20. Trunk
21. Che et al.
22. From scratch
23. Amer. soldiers, for short
27. Tunes again
29. Irk
30. Unique sort
31. Bible weed
32. Baghdad's land
33. "____ Janos" (Kodaly)
34. Actual
36. Select
37. Calla lily, e.g.
39. Noun suffix
40. Jewish month
42. Wyatt of the West
43. Algerian port
44. Brisk gait
45. Atom
46. Radioman's word
47. Drip
51. Mouthlike opening
52. Singer Page
53. Twenty quires
54. Barrel slats
55. Legal documents
56. Mauna ____
57. Prattled
58. ____ to bed
59. Adjusts
60. Cancel
61. Peel
63. Took potshots
65. "____ corny as Kansas . . ."
66. Emulate Cicero
70. Architectural pier

Starting box on page 562

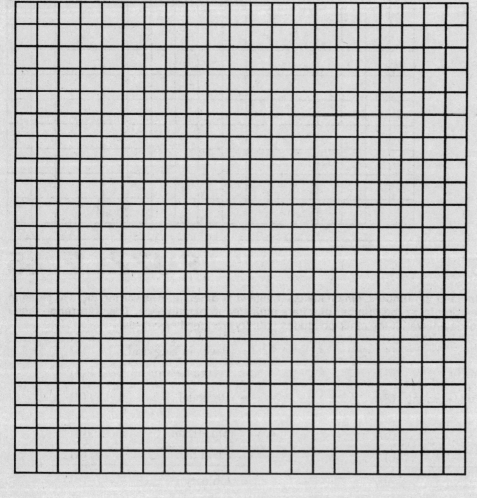

80

PUZZLE 87

ACROSS
1. Small crow
4. Inventor Whitney
5. Outlaw
6. Trash
9. Pub potable
12. Neglect
13. Newsman Rather
14. Hole
15. Fuss
16. Racetrack deal
17. Stamp adhesive
19. Fool
22. "My Gal ___"
24. Service or gloss
25. Pool circuit
27. Historical period
28. Rider's controls
30. Individual
31. Support
32. Ancient
33. Novel
34. Cozy room
36. ___ and haw
37. Doctor's charge
39. Crude metal
41. Tom Hanks movie
42. River inlet
43. Ladder part
44. Capable
45. Pebbles
47. Grizzly's child
48. Nickname for Lincoln
49. Legal matter

DOWN
1. First performance
2. Alack!
3. Asti product
6. Thick cord
7. Give off
8. Suitable
9. Cartwright son
10. Young man
11. Space chimp
16. Knife
17. Type of rummy
18. Increases
20. Solitary
21. Window section
22. Caribbean, e.g.
23. Extremely dry
24. Bottle cap
26. Sunday seat
28. Caviar
29. Shade tree
35. Nick's wife
36. Warmth
37. Delicate
38. Easter presents
40. Shred
41. Roll
43. Dressing gowns
45. Wound memento
46. Toothpaste holder

Starting box on page 562

TIE-IN

PUZZLE 88

Place a 3-letter word on the dashes to complete a word on the left and to begin another word on the right. For example, HEN between EART and NA would complete EARTHEN and begin HENNA.

PUMP __ __ __ DRED   PORT __ __ __ NT
GAR __ __ __ IZEN   ATT __ __ __ URE
SH __ __ PT   BIT __ __ __ OR
SCAR __ __ __ TUCE   CA __ __ __ OT
PAR __ __ __ NET   CON __ __ __ TAIN

81

PUZZLE 89

BRICK BY BRICK

Rearrange this stack of bricks to form a crossword puzzle. The clues will help you fit the bricks into their correct places. Row 1 has been filled in for you. Use the bricks to fill in the remaining spaces.

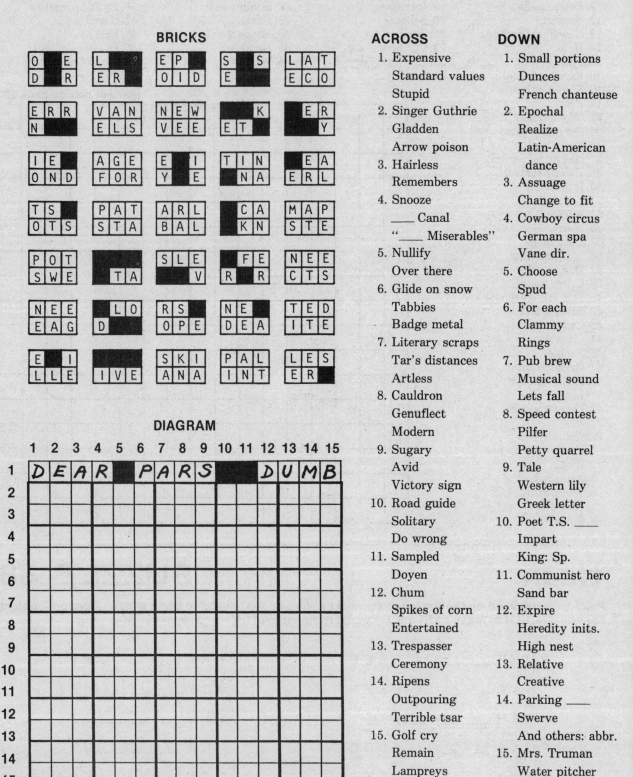

BRICKS

DIAGRAM

ACROSS

1. Expensive
   Standard values
   Stupid
2. Singer Guthrie
   Gladden
   Arrow poison
3. Hairless
   Remembers
4. Snooze
   ___ Canal
   "___ Miserables"
5. Nullify
   Over there
6. Glide on snow
   Tabbies
   Badge metal
7. Literary scraps
   Tar's distances
   Artless
8. Cauldron
   Genuflect
   Modern
9. Sugary
   Avid
   Victory sign
10. Road guide
    Solitary
    Do wrong
11. Sampled
    Doyen
12. Chum
    Spikes of corn
    Entertained
13. Trespasser
    Ceremony
14. Ripens
    Outpouring
    Terrible tsar
15. Golf cry
    Remain
    Lampreys

DOWN

1. Small portions
   Dunces
   French chanteuse
2. Epochal
   Realize
   Latin-American
   dance
3. Assuage
   Change to fit
4. Cowboy circus
   German spa
   Vane dir.
5. Choose
   Spud
6. For each
   Clammy
   Rings
7. Pub brew
   Musical sound
   Lets fall
8. Speed contest
   Pilfer
   Petty quarrel
9. Tale
   Western lily
   Greek letter
10. Poet T.S. ___
    Impart
    King: Sp.
11. Communist hero
    Sand bar
12. Expire
    Heredity inits.
    High nest
13. Relative
    Creative
14. Parking ___
    Swerve
    And others: abbr.
15. Mrs. Truman
    Water pitcher
    Cozy rooms

Clues to all the 6- and 7-letter entries in this crossword puzzle are listed first, and they are in scrambled order. Use the numbered clues as solving aids to help you determine where each one goes in the diagram.

6-LETTER ENTRIES

Highest point
Jacks
Actress Merle ____
Confusion
This or that
____ Corps
Lithe
Insist on
Most rational
Lustrous fabric
Orange and black bird
Lying face up
Stiffened
Polar feature

7-LETTER ENTRIES

Place of refuge
Extremist
Interest-rate term
President's men

ACROSS

7. Evergreens
11. Type of lettuce
15. "____ da Capo"
16. "Exodus" hero
18. "Uncle Sam" cartoonist
19. Mr. Chaney
20. Raided the refrigerator
21. Yearning
23. Learning
25. ____ bull
26. Caspian, for one
27. Annoy
28. Army doc
30. Shaving mishaps
34. Farrow of films
37. Actor Andrews
38. Keeshan a.k.a. Captain Kangaroo
39. Extremely
40. Sack
42. ____ overboard!
43. Scat queen
47. Poet Merriam
48. Baseball's Pee Wee
50. Belief
51. Thing: Lat.
52. Caboodle's companion
54. Clansman: abbr.
55. Orient
56. Put together
60. Pat
61. Hail: Lat.
62. Despise

66. Lassie's foot
67. Adam's address
69. Chicago trains
70. Take five

DOWN

1. "____ Squad"
2. Burrows or Vigoda
3. Outstanding
4. In a snit
5. "____ Shall Escape"
6. Culmination
8. Shah's country
9. Perils
11. Pacific island
12. Fe
13. Cherry type
22. Foray

25. ____ Bill
28. Boston school: abbr.
31. Photography addicts
36. Wall section
41. Understand
44. Queries
53. Barter
55. ____ de Valera
56. Ann or May
57. Ellipse
58. Tidings
59. American Indians
60. Fool
63. Do needlework
64. Pinky ____
65. Commentator Koppel

PUZZLE 91

ACROSS
1. Food thickener
5. Overfill
9. Turf
12. Boob ____
13. Pitcher Hubbell
14. "Ben ____"
15. Anchovy sauce
16. Government agent
18. Anger
20. Queen's address
21. Reverie
23. Ship-shaped clocks
26. Light beer
29. Necessary
31. Had a hamburger
32. Public
34. Western republic: abbr.
35. Kind of oil
37. Full of cavities
39. Top
40. Moluccas island
42. Avatar of Vishnu
44. Glossy paint
48. Impresario
51. Body: pref.
52. Chit
53. Actress Ralston
54. Monad
55. Hot air
56. Happy place
57. Ship's officer

DOWN
1. Luzon natives
2. Bolt
3. First victim
4. Flow out
5. Spectacle
6. Old Dutch wine measure
7. Hedge tool
8. Hostess Maxwell
9. Disgraceful
10. Radio's "____ Gal Sunday"
11. Thirsty
17. Trap material
19. Blooper
22. Anoint
24. Melt together
25. Do in
26. Lhasa priest
27. On one's toes
28. Openhanded
30. Patriot Allen
33. Quit
36. Oral
38. Cow's third stomach
41. Showed again
43. Propose
45. Noted Lisa
46. Issue
47. Departed
48. Sty dweller
49. Brown kiwi
50. Prior to, to a bard

PUZZLE 92

ACROSS
1. Money for the pot
5. "Harper Valley ____"
8. Hindu garment
12. Of ships: abbr.
13. Several eras
14. Actress Anna ____
15. Chart for painters
18. Unofficial title of respect: abbr.
19. Disintegrate
20. Inventor Whitney
21. Asian river
23. Neighbor of Windsor
25. Overcast
27. Region
30. Greet
31. Secrete
32. Trousers line
35. Fastened, at sea
37. Columnist Bombeck
38. Concerning: 2 wds.
39. Cry
41. African veld creature
43. Govt. agcy.
46. Lack of character
49. Brilliant hue, in Spain
50. Able was I ____ . . .
51. Villa d'____
52. Marsh growth
53. Clump of ivy
54. Burden for Pelion

DOWN
1. Noun suffix
2. Slangy negatives
3. Tropical sea hue: 2 wds.
4. DDE's command
5. Certain gates
6. Dorothy's dog
7. Positive electrodes
8. Compass pt.
9. Thoughtfulness
10. Stagger
11. Crucifix letters
16. Honey drink
17. Hand out
22. School-bag item
24. Yellow pigment
25. Ill. city
26. Computer system
28. Beautiful poem
29. Buttons, for one
33. Neighbor of Mex.
34. Wooden hammer
35. Washed lightly
36. Stops
39. Wound mark
40. Seep
42. Atmospheric prefix
44. Fast jets
45. At a loss
47. Tattered
48. Modernist: pref.

84

PUZZLE 93

ACROSS

1. "The World According to ____"
5. Actor Karloff
10. Voucher
14. Salmagundi
15. By oneself
16. Vehicle
17. Terra firma
18. Overseer
20. Adam's leaf
21. Pine fruit
22. Actress Gold
23. Pitcher's hill
25. Comedian Orson ____
27. Commences
29. Cheerleader's props
32. Kilns
33. "Throw ____ from the Train"
34. Police notice: abbr.
36. Convenes
37. "____ the Greek"
38. Continent
39. First cardinal number
40. Categorizes
41. Group of eight
42. Aftershocks
44. Compulsion
45. VIP car
46. Less diluted
47. Drag behind
50. ____ doute
51. Actress Novak
54. Expert: 2 wds.
57. Actor Mostel
58. Ms. Sommer
59. Oscar nominee in "The Great Dictator"
60. Black-____ Susan
61. "Untouchable" man
62. Cooling: 2 wds.
63. ____ est percipi

DOWN

1. Trevino's game
2. Jai ____
3. Circus emcee
4. Seedcase
5. Majorettes' sticks
6. Charlie Chan portrayer
7. "The Name of the ____"
8. Pen fluid
9. Punctuation mark: abbr.
10. Gambling place
11. Shacks
12. Natives: suff.
13. Whig's opponent
19. Territory of Brazil
21. Slices
24. Table leavings
25. Plays with bad reviews
26. Actress Samms
27. Mediocre: hyph.
28. Spoil
29. Certain wines
30. Lock openers: 2 wds.
31. Double agents
33. San Juan castle
35. Flying mammals
37. Camera lens type
38. Farmland measure
40. Facial expression
41. Yours and mine
43. Blue bloods
44. "Crocodile ____"
46. Frenzy
47. Government agents: hyph.
48. Rattle
49. Questions
50. Japanese wine
52. Infuriates
53. Style
55. Pooh's friend
56. "Star Wars" hero Solo
57. Zuider ____

QUOTAGRAM — PUZZLE 94

Fill in the answers to the clues below. Then transfer the letters to the correspondingly numbered squares in the diagram. The completed diagram will contain a quotation.

1. Fly like an eagle
   ‾12‾ ‾29‾ ‾18‾ ‾23‾

2. Groups of related people
   ‾4‾ ‾38‾ ‾16‾ ‾10‾ ‾8‾ ‾32‾ ‾15‾ ‾26‾

3. Flaw
   ‾1‾ ‾40‾ ‾3‾ ‾27‾ ‾34‾ ‾21‾

4. Pace
   ‾39‾ ‾13‾ ‾5‾ ‾20‾

5. Roundabout course
   ‾31‾ ‾11‾ ‾30‾ ‾22‾ ‾36‾ ‾14‾

6. Alumni gathering
   ‾37‾ ‾17‾ ‾25‾ ‾19‾ ‾2‾ ‾24‾ ‾28‾

7. Pathfinder
   ‾33‾ ‾6‾ ‾35‾ ‾7‾ ‾9‾

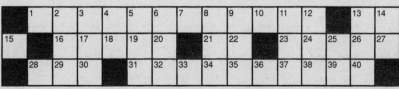

85

PUZZLE 95   CODEWORD

Codeword is a special crossword puzzle in which conventional clues are omitted. Instead, answer words in the diagram are represented by numbers. Each number represents a different letter of the alphabet, and all of the letters of the alphabet are used. When you are sure of a letter, put it in the code key chart and cross it off in the alphabet box. A group of letters has been inserted to start you off.

Code key chart:

1	14
2	15
3	16
4	17
5	18
6	19
7	20
8	21
9 B	22
10	23 L
11	24 A
12	25
13	26

Alphabet box:

A̶ N
B̶ O
C P
D Q
E R
F S
G T
H U
I V
J W
K X
L̶ Y
M Z

PUZZLE 96   Trade-Off

The answers to the two clues in each line below are 6-letter words that differ by only one letter, which we have given you. In the example, if you trade off the P from STRIPE with the letter K in the same position, you get STRIKE. The order of the letters will not change.

Example: Chevron   S T R I P E   S T R I K E   Hit

1. Full-grown   M _ _ _ _ _   N _ _ _ _ _   Essence

2. Metal fastener   _ _ _ P _ _   _ _ _ B _ _   Horse's home

3. Smokestack   F _ _ _ _ _   T _ _ _ _ _   Burrow

4. Uncomplicated   _ I _ _ _ _   _ A _ _ _ _   Taste

5. Jet of liquid   _ _ _ _ T _   _ _ _ _ _ E   Escort

6. Quantity   N _ _ _ _ _   L _ _ _ _ _   Wood

86

CIRCULAR CROSSWORD

PUZZLE 97

To complete this Circular puzzle, fill in the answers to the Around clues in a clockwise direction. For the Radial clues, move from the outside to the inside.

AROUND (Clockwise)

1. Ridge
6. Strawberry's stick
9. Spanish house
13. Trap
16. Type of examination
20. Parking device
21. U.N. statesman: 2 wds.
22. Hebrew letter
23. Building extension
24. Network
25. Guessing too high
28. Estrange
30. Deteriorated
32. Old French coin
33. Reverses to one's advantage:
   3 wds.
35. At a distance
36. Criterion: abbr.

37. ____ once: 2 wds.
38. Comrade
39. Man preparing for holy
   orders: abbr.
40. New Haven school
41. Onager
42. Octagonal sign
43. Comedian Louis and family
44. Author Rand

RADIAL (Out to in)

1. Without principles
2. Silversmith/patriot
3. French season
4. Singer Brewer
5. Builds
6. Except
7. Bryant and Loos
8. Uproar

9. Snooze
10. Tilted
11. Dispatched
12. Crocheted blanket
13. Ringo, for one
14. Eases
15. Silver-tongued
16. Cantankerous
17. Sense
18. Lawyer: abbr.
19. Elbowroom
26. Foam
27. Woody's son
29. Exile isle
31. Horse ____ different color:
   2 wds.
34. TV's Tarzan

PUZZLE 98

ACROSS

1. One ____ million: 2 wds.
4. Puncture
8. Fall short
12. Cut the grass
13. Contrition
15. Rainfall
17. Seed coating
18. Defeats
19. Collective
22. In favor of
23. Dwellings
24. Douglas pine
25. Have a good cry
28. Encourage
29. Careless
30. "____ Back, Little Sheba"
31. Actor Adams
32. 2000 pounds
33. Director Polanski
34. Gang
35. Regress
36. Defame
39. Contend
40. Involvement
45. Begins
46. Duo
47. Golf props
48. Annoyance
49. Stitch

DOWN

1. Mischievous child
2. Scandinavian country: abbr.
3. Overwhelm
4. Steeples
5. Lukewarm
6. Indigo source
7. Morsel
8. Parking timer
9. Amazonian dolphinlike animal
10. ____-free (not punished)
11. Washington VIPs: abbr.
14. Hand drum
16. Mark of omission
19. ____ roe
20. Vagrant
21. Last word in prayer
22. Predicament
24. Ventilator
25. Any
26. Actor Sharif
27. Angled
29. Tennis stroke
30. Envy
32. Japanese gateway
33. Meal
34. Helm and Dillon
35. Lassos
36. Roasting stake
37. Lion's pride
38. Pennsylvania port
39. Quote
41. Tam
42. "____ a Wonderful Life"
43. Have creditors
44. Immediately

PUZZLE 99

ACROSS

1. Small shark
5. Actress Dawber
8. Harbor
12. It's ____!: 2 wds.
13. Samuel's mentor
14. Great Lake
15. Texas: 3 wds.
18. Answer
19. Jeweler's weight
20. Take it on the ____
21. Diving duck
23. "____ Smart"
25. Commences
27. Blackboard adjunct
31. Shower
32. Actress Anna
33. Little hooters
36. Iron and tin
38. Take to court
39. Level
40. Health resort
43. Pester
45. Hoover, for one
48. Texas coastal city: 2 wds.
51. Singing voice
52. "We ____ Not Alone"
53. Membership fees
54. Rex or Oliver
55. Tie the knot
56. Copies

DOWN

1. Converse
2. Hautboy
3. Hairstyle
4. Hurricane's center
5. Flower parts
6. Winglike
7. Desert image
8. Favorite
9. Of the mouth
10. "Educating ____"
11. Pour
16. Shoo!
17. Ending for gang or mob
22. Ocean birds
24. Savor
25. Broadway hit sign
26. Playing marble
28. Arises: 2 wds.
29. Conger
30. Hospital workers: abbr.
34. Ballet skirt
35. Teeter-totter
36. Ensnared
37. Always
40. Wound mark
41. Raft propeller
42. Comedian Johnson
44. Land measure
46. Suit to ____: 2 wds.
47. Young girl
49. Seed container
50. Apple cider girl

BRICK BY BRICK

PUZZLE 100

Rearrange this stack of bricks to form a crossword puzzle. The clues will help you fit the bricks into their correct places. Row 1 has been filled in for you. Use the bricks to fill in the remaining spaces.

ACROSS

1. Orient
   Nobleman
   Nimbus
2. Woe is me!
   High society
   Roman poet
3. Arizona river
   Respect
   Hoarfrost
4. Knowledge
   Peddler
5. Finale
   Individual
   Pay dirt
6. Peculiar
   Relying on
7. Pitfalls
   Brag
   Scottish river
8. Pipsqueak
   Picnic pest
   Rich soil
9. Malt brew
   Sandwich stores
   Testaments
10. Sudden
    Piece
11. Actress
    Gardner
    Devotee
    Spy gp.
12. Stock units
    Florida city
13. Maize
    Overact
    Toward the
    mouth
14. To shelter
    Fido's pal
    English
    princess
15. Peruse
    Shabby
    Land title

DOWN

1. National bird
   English trolley
   Wound mark
2. Foreigner
   Regulation
   Cavity
3. Mixed greens
   Dill, of old
   Locale
4. Russian king
   Choose
   Worked for
5. Drowses
   Bird of peace
6. After
   Pencil rubbers
7. Unaccompanied
   Indonesian
    island
   Stooge
8. Peal
   Quinine water
   Great affection
9. Sioux
   Squealers
   Destined
10. Edgy
    Bread store
11. Once, of old
    Claret, e.g.
12. Paper wasp
    Kindled
    Burden
13. Eager
    False god
    Chili con ___
14. Exec's car
    Actress Patricia
    Senseless
15. Polish river
    Jewels
    Appended

BRICKS

Bricks (rows of paired letters):
VID | ALE | ▮TR | ANT | S▮E
IME | REA | BOA | LIS | A▮H

N GE | E▮R | ▮▮▮ | KEL | EOR
E▮▮ | D▮S | TRA | E▮O | AVA

AND | LEA | R▮A | OVE | UST
RAD | END | Y▮D | EED | ST▮

T▮▮ | NNE | ▮L▮ | RES | LIT
▮DE | EED | WI▮ | N▮E | ONO

VEN | IC▮ | RUN | SHA | DOR
ORE | ▮▮F | ALE | COR | ▮▮▮

▮▮▮ | ▮LA | E▮O | BIT | OAM
CIA | MOT | R▮R | AN▮ | LLS

ODD | MET | ALA | RNI | ING
PS▮ | ▮▮▮ | GIL | ▮ON | DEE

DIAGRAM

	1	2	3	4	5	6	7	8	9	10	11	12	13	14	15
1	E	A	S	T	▮	B	A	R	O	N	▮	H	A	L	O
2															
3															
4															
5															
6															
7															
8															
9															
10															
11															
12															
13															
14															
15															

89

PUZZLE 101

Place the answer to each clue into the diagram beginning at the corresponding number. Words will overlap with other words.

ACROSS

1. "Crossing the ___"
3. Unaccompanied
4. Come in last
5. Sargasso, for one
10. Utah's lily
11. Bridal dress
12. Title holder
13. Prefix meaning work
14. Acquired
18. "The Clan of the ___ Bear"
19. Gold lode
20. Clumsy
21. School organization: abbr.
22. Piquant
23. Russian co-op
24. Legendary archer
27. Carried on
30. Rewrite
32. Roman road
34. Discord goddess
35. Egyptian goddess
37. Michigan's ___ Royale
41. Asterisk
42. Place in order
43. Synthetic fabric
45. Solitary
47. Told a fib
48. Waxed cheese
49. Aswan and Hoover
50. Fish appendage

DOWN

1. Beneath
2. Hurry
3. Heroic tale
5. "___ Stoops to Conquer"
6. Rage
7. Once more
8. Baby nocturnal bird
9. Warming device
10. Keep
15. Pedal digits
16. Postal item
17. Love god
18. Bovine
19. Blue-white twinkler in Lyra
20. Ghandi's land
22. Towel cloth
25. Theme
26. Grant or Marvin
29. Natural fuel
31. Telephone feature
33. Succinct
36. Export
38. Utter
39. Bread grain
40. Odds and ___
42. Each and every
44. Long
46. Ego

PUZZLE 102

ACROSS
1. Instant kind of city
5. Beijing's land mass
9. Maxim
12. Away from the wind
13. Antimacassar
14. GI's address
15. Container's weight
16. Hautboy
17. Murmur
18. Deviation
20. Heavy suit fabric
22. Cousin: abbr.
23. Misfortunes
25. "___ Gynt"
26. Rouses feelings in
28. Residence
30. Wing
32. Flop
33. Synthetic rubber
35. Digest
39. Awful
40. Rabbit ___
43. "___ pro nobis"
44. Cry of defeat
46. Dwight Gooden, for one
48. Field
49. Glaze
51. Unaspirate
52. ___ Clemente
53. Large rodent
54. Monitor lizard
55. Anything high-flown: 2 wds.
56. Leftovers
57. Defeat

DOWN
1. Mongolians
2. Small kite
3. Orange-flower oil
4. Rain like crazy
5. Coral island
6. Prophetess
7. Wedding words: 2 wds.
8. Senate votes
9. Holy
10. Highest point
11. Suitor
19. Wedding path
21. Strophe-antistrophe's follower
24. In the dumps
27. Honey badger
29. Explode
31. Chopper
33. In direct succession
34. Secrets
36. Hold fast
37. Prize rings
38. Mom
39. Seaweed
41. To the side
42. Ceremonies
45. "Little Sir ___"
47. Billy
50. Paddle

PUZZLE 103

ACROSS
1. Bristle
5. "And ___ we go!"
9. Ouse tributary
12. Mangle
13. Coffee type
14. Vein output
15. Capital of Iceland
17. City of Serbia
18. Tempted
19. Memphis god
20. Gem surface
23. Evergreen
24. Leave
25. Goal
30. Have a session
31. Much-cooked bulb
32. By way of
33. To a certain extent
35. For fear that
36. Bronx attraction
37. Pelts
38. Help
40. Appointments
43. Sister
44. Provisions bag
48. Bobble
49. Smell
50. Woodwind
51. Distorted
52. Robe
53. Lots

DOWN
1. Dear ___
2. Before, poetically
3. Plaything
4. Sock
5. Somewhat open
6. Billow
7. Desirous
8. Gab
9. Artificial
10. Domingo highlight
11. Net
16. Stick out
19. Hole
20. Actor Parker
21. Leaf angle
22. The public
23. Fish feature
25. Insect
26. Wire measure
27. ___ George
28. River of France
29. Singer Cole and others
31. What have we here?
34. Received
35. Flexible
37. Pronoun
38. Once more
39. Die cutter
40. Pedestal part
41. Swear
42. Sea bird
44. Pig
45. Arab garment
46. Study
47. Locker

MAGIC WORD SQUARE

PUZZLE 104

Solve this puzzle as you would a regular crossword. Then arrange the answers to the 8 starred clues to form a word square in the middle of the diagram, so that 4 words read across and 4 read down. The circled letters in the Magic Word Square will reveal the answer to the riddle given at clues 20 and 81 Across.

ACROSS
*1. Quaker's pronoun
5. Peach seeds
9. Little, in Glasgow
12. London area
16. Feeling his ____
*17. Being: Lat.
18. Under the weather
19. Entreat
20. First half of the riddle: 4 wds.
24. Afloat
25. Container weight
26. Left-hand pages
27. "My country, ____ . . ."
28. Pack away
29. Baseball statistic: abbr.
30. Start
33. Poetic nights
34. Accuse
38. Cauldron
39. Grazing ground
40. Meetings
44. Woman's short coat
47. Author of "Annabel Lee"
48. Cooks in an oven
49. "The ____ Strikes Back"
52. Rocker Adam
53. Lamented
54. Minister
58. Greek letter
59. Before, to Shelley
60. Belt
63. Phi ____ Kappa Society
67. Rapidity
69. Land of ____
71. Functions
72. Babylonian god
73. "____ Bailey"
*76. Butts
77. Vaulted
81. Second half of the riddle: 4 wds.
84. Knot
85. Soft drink
86. Baseball's Speaker
87. Italian fortress near Padua
88. Grand move in bridge
89. Assenter's answer
90. Jeanne d'Arc et al.
91. Marsh plant

DOWN
1. Wilder's "Our ____"
2. Representation of laughter: hyph.
3. State: Fr.
4. Possessions
5. Nuisances
6. Mideast democracy: abbr.
7. African fly
8. Calm
9. Tendons
10. 1055, for Cicero
11. Vibrant
12. Winding
13. Globes
*14. Angelic headgear
15. "Hear ye!"
21. Part of a monogram: abbr.
22. Club for Palmer
23. Croat's neighbor
30. Select
31. And not
32. Porky's pad
*35. Swiss peaks
36. Swimming contest
37. Hearing essentials
41. Short car trip
42. Ripped
43. Pip
*44. Ensnare
45. Mrs. Chaplin
46. Hingle and O'Brien
*49. Rulers: abbr.
50. Largest amount
51. Two
55. Golf mound
56. Mesabi deposit
57. Scarlet
61. Patriotic hymn
62. Water game
63. Pouches
64. Birthright seller
65. Tries to induce
66. Affirm
67. Soothsayer
68. Performer
70. Procrastinate
72. Consecrate
73. Prohibitions
74. Hydrocarbon compound
75. Icelandic poem
*78. Certain posture
79. Being: Sp.
80. Land title
82. HST's successor
83. C'est la ____

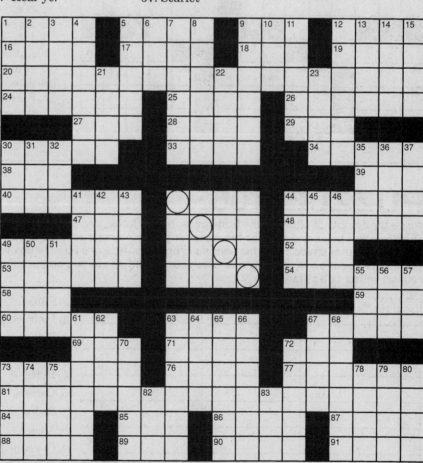

PUZZLE 105

ACROSS

1. Peruvian mammal
6. Ancient calculators
11. Bother
14. Auditory
15. Conestoga
16. Pool stick
17. Subway gate
18. Helps
19. Psychic ability: abbr.
20. Cure
21. Embarrassment color
22. Disturbed
24. Relieve
27. Completely
28. Lamp controller
31. Apprehends
36. Beach color
37. Despot
39. Encounter
40. Abundant
42. Baseball failure
43. Unadorned
44. Roads: abbr.
45. Homager
48. Faint
49. Sweat
51. Stops
53. Purpose
54. Charges
55. Tricks
58. Water runner
60. Fly alone
64. Precept
65. Take charge of
67. Fooled
68. Night before a holiday
69. Top-notch scout
70. Correct
71. Papa
72. Position
73. Repairs

DOWN

1. Bind
2. Ancient string instrument
3. Cantata air
4. Polo hammer
5. "Cakes and ____"
6. Knowing
7. Infant
8. Antiquated
9. Army bed
10. Affront
11. Frozen nondairy desserts
12. Sham
13. Retained
23. Vertical
25. Piece of legislation
26. Coy
27. Fitting
28. Gird
29. Forgo
30. Deduce
31. Reason
32. Social insects
33. Peruses
34. Weird
35. Plant parts
38. Lion's yell
41. Literary composition
45. Vitality
46. Expert
47. Brenda or Bruce
50. Fish sign
52. Presuppose
54. Dismissed
55. Begged
56. Volcanic outflow
57. Was obligated
58. Long tale
59. Pottery oven
61. Golf tournament
62. Opposite of borrow
63. ____-on favorite
66. Head covering
67. Beaver's handiwork

PUZZLE 106   ESCALATOR

Place the answer to clue 1 in the first space, drop a letter, and arrange the remaining letters to answer clue 2. Drop another letter and arrange the remaining letters to answer clue 3. The first dropped letter goes into the box to the left of space 1 and the second dropped letter goes into the box to the right of space 3. Follow this pattern for each row in the diagram. When completed, the letters on the left and right, reading down, will spell related words or a phrase.

1. Pure
2. Instruct
3. Pain
4. Sulker
5. Itinerary
6. Correct
7. Reply
8. Abates
9. Overwhelms
10. Interior
11. Eats
12. Remit
13. Stupor
14. Packing case
15. Rip
16. "The ____ of Wrath"
17. Extra
18. Harvest

94

PUZZLE 107

ACROSS
1. Cabbage salad
5. Rotate
9. Phi ____ Kappa Society
13. Desire
17. "Town Without ____"
18. Interval
19. Affirm
20. Expanse
21. Shakespeare's river
22. No taxation without ____
25. Opponent
27. Conceited
28. Don't spill the ____
29. Pinnacle
30. Pear variety
31. Posterior
33. Bills
36. Tight
37. Kind
38. Soda
41. ____ Stanley Gardner
42. Overseer
43. Allotment
44. Regret
45. Flightless bird
46. Stouts
47. Mimickers
48. Examination
49. Actress Post
51. Concur
52. Prices
53. "Three cheers for the ____": 4 wds.
57. Pigs
59. Satire
60. Merited
63. "Family ____"
64. Allow
65. Aimlessly
67. Road covering
68. Beast of burden
69. Commonplace
70. Revise
71. Plateau
72. Nevertheless
73. "Days of ____ and Roses"
74. Stocking mishap
75. Trainee
76. Feathered limb
77. Canines
78. Prohibit
79. Closed car
82. Fly aloft
83. Sate
87. Merry-go-round locales: 2 wds.
91. Egyptian river
92. Dryer debris
93. Healing plant
94. Eight, to Caesar
95. Enthusiasm
96. Clothes hanger
97. Teases
98. Ages and ages
99. Plants

DOWN
1. Bridge
2. Exist
3. Powerful particle
4. Country singer Tammy
5. Comic ____ (cartoon)
6. Simple Simon's desires
7. Naughty child
8. On edge
9. Fundamental
10. On a par
11. Bo's number
12. Skill
13. Thirst quencher
14. Diva's forte
15. Broadway light
16. Browns from the sun
23. "____ of Eden"
24. Diminish
26. Disaster code
30. Game fish
31. Bellowed
32. Blunders
33. Consider
34. Author Bombeck
35. Most smudged
36. Foot appendage
37. Luster
38. Offered
39. Evict
40. Caresses
42. Played the trumpet
43. Mist
46. ____-de-camp
47. Emissary
48. Excursion
50. Norton and Maynard
51. Expiate
52. Like some pigeons
54. Recruitment
55. Angry
56. Waist accessory
57. Corset support
58. Prudent
61. Comfort
62. Mild oath
64. Wide smile
65. Cantor and Tarbell
66. Understand?
69. Cord
70. Inscribe
71. Tell it to the ____
74. Cleansing cake
75. Feline
76. Fritter away
77. Loves excessively
78. Foundation
79. Old sailor
80. Eastern ruler
81. Sand hill
82. Social climber
83. Epidermis
84. Storage tower
85. Imperfection
86. Urges
88. Disfigure
89. Actor Wallach
90. ____ de Janeiro

95

PUZZLE 108

ACROSS

1. Kind of bar
6. Embroidery thread
11. Has a tantrum
16. English landowner
17. Lasso
18. Escaped the notice of
20. Fugitive
21. Organic compound
22. Cat
23. Rooter's shout
24. Flat cap
26. ". . . don't go near the ___"
28. Sn
29. Son of Aphrodite
31. Matterhorn song
33. ___ Royal Highness
34. Shed
35. Played again
37. Benefactor
39. Craves
41. Playing marble
43. Rhythm
45. Eternity
46. Means
50. Tricked
52. Clare Boothe Luce play, with "The"
56. Coney Island attraction
58. Halve
60. Clarke's "Rendezvous With ___"
61. Capek play
62. Commencement
64. Demolish
66. Comic DeLuise
67. Hard job
69. Movable barriers
71. Release
73. "Now I lay me down to ___"
75. Neck backs
77. Table vegetables
78. Negative word
80. ___ and onions
82. On the ___ (fleeing)
83. Thin
87. Overalls material
89. "The ___ of Flatbush"
93. Sacred
94. Zero in
96. Library book
98. Irritate
99. Balm for an aching head
100. "Peter Gunn" star Stevens
102. Make over
104. Chinese truth
105. American Indian
107. Boundary
109. Esprit de corps
111. Allen and McQueen
112. Make happy
113. Takes the soapbox
114. Growing out
115. Lieu
116. More modern

DOWN

1. Kind of dance
2. Writer
3. "___ Abner"
4. Native of Riyadh
5. ___ decimal system
6. ___ of speech
7. Paid attention
8. Morsel for Mr. Ed
9. Meat dish
10. Conductor Caldwell
11. Game official
12. Affirm
13. "My ___ Sal"
14. Magazine employee
15. Doddering
16. More painful
19. Car blemishes
25. Baseballer Carew
27. Yachtsman Turner
30. Pago Pago's land
32. Yoga position
34. Trivial
36. Part of TNT
38. Fend off
40. Plant a crop
42. Existence
44. Make merry
46. Pub game
47. On a par
48. TLC giver
49. Actress Dey
51. Underworld leader
53. "Call Me ___"
54. Overact
55. Monikers
57. "Full ___ Jacket"
59. Insurgent
63. Lukewarm
65. Lawful
68. Singer Rogers
70. "___ Days in May"
72. Hearsay
74. Pea's house
76. Spanish miss
79. Garden flower: 2 wds.
81. Bolted down
83. Leg fronts
84. Find
85. Football team
86. Narrow inlet
88. Grown boys
90. Spin
91. Phone user
92. Blackthorns
95. Actress Vera
97. Dud
100. Newsman Huntley
101. Young sow
103. Had on
106. Actress Gardner
108. Ms. West
110. Uncooked

PUZZLE 109

ACROSS

1. Weighty book
5. Circuits
9. Wine barrel
13. Prophet's presage
14. Colorful fish
16. Not fer
17. "____ of the Flies"
18. Ice pinnacle
19. Defense org.
20. Beetle
21. Buffoon: hyph.
23. Time spans
25. Zilch
26. "Fawlty ____"
28. Sentence
32. Zola
33. Gay ____
34. Poetic night
36. Antimacassar
37. Old World snake
38. Provable
39. WWII area
40. Levees
41. Small pack animal
42. More dulcet
44. Grofe's "Grand ____ Suite"
45. Gene component
46. Shakespeare's Kate
47. Revelers
52. Martinique, e.g.
55. Met solo
56. Adult insect
57. Bristol's county
58. Kind of suit
59. Biblical prophet
60. Prolific popular composer
61. She, in Siena
62. Snick's companion
63. On a voyage

DOWN

1. Snitched
2. Melville novel
3. Lehar operetta, with "The": 2 wds.
4. Abolish
5. Weepers, proverbially
6. Imitators
7. Henry VIII's sixth
8. One-hoss carriage
9. Roman ____
10. Seaweed product
11. Position
12. Feel in one's bones
15. CAT device
21. Flicka's mom
22. Pheasant brood
24. Slippery
26. Mal de ____
27. Leaves out
28. Cavort
29. Bonanza yield
30. Shakespeare's Windsor ladies: 2 wds.
31. Nerve: prefix
33. Explorer Zebulon
35. Inert gas
37. Dietary supplement
38. Tommy of Broadway
40. Contradict
41. Excludes
43. Printing goofs
44. Fancy car finish
46. Musical transition
47. Labyrinth
48. Olympian Cupid
49. Tajo and Ebro
50. Amo, ____, amat
51. Gus or Madeline
53. Tradition
54. Sicilian town
57. Alias inits.

MIDDLE OF THE ROAD

PUZZLE 110

Place the correct missing letters into the diagram to form words reading down. Then read the filled-in letters across from left to right to complete the sentence started below. Be careful—some of the words are tricky!

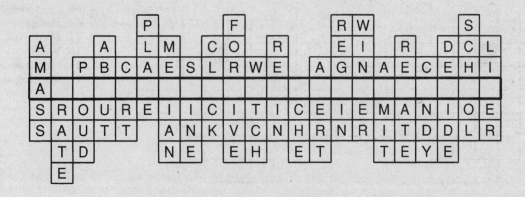

PUZZLE 111

• ONE OF OUR GREATEST •

ACROSS
1. Cloudy
4. Moon-buggy acronym
7. Takes the title
8. Mimicked
10. Circle segments
11. Paddled
16. ____ as an owl
17. Yankee side
19. Conscious (of)
20. Home of youthful 24 Across
23. Breezy
24. Our 16th chief executive
26. King's title
27. Drink on tap
28. Greets
30. Kind of walker
33. Golf mound
34. Buzz
36. Little pies
38. Remnants
39. One who is: suffix
40. Lament
41. Sloth or envy
43. Officeholders
44. ____ Saud
45. "The ____ and the Pendulum"
46. Payable
47. Story
50. Get together
52. Confederate soldier
53. Baxter and Bancroft
55. Ring name
57. Fished for slippery ones
60. Explosion
62. Shirt accessory
65. Maiden name of 24 Across's wife

67. Emancipation Proclamation's target
69. Lofty
70. Coat material
72. Foreign
73. Doles
74. Hard to find
76. Comes close
77. Suitor
78. Do in
79. Ill at ____
80. Sault ____ Marie: abbr.
81. Compass pt.

DOWN
1. Soiled
2. Part of a foot
3. Editors' concerns: abbr.
4. There oughtta be a ____
5. Heroic saga
6. Tablelands
7. Fought
9. Figures in the red
11. ____ Splitter (nickname of 24 Across)
12. Possesses
13. GI's female counterpart, once
14. God of love
15. Small valley
17. Financial auditor's org.
18. Nonrenewable resource
21. Anger
22. Once named
24. Misrepresentations
25. Trapeze artists' safeguards
28. Nickname for 24 Across: 2 wds.
29. Plus
31. ____ your heart out!
32. Title of 24 Across
35. Bring together again
37. Homage
40. Slumberous Van Winkle
42. Compass pt.
48. Grant's opponent
49. Building wings
50. Little lamb's owner
51. Printers' measures
52. Horsemen
54. Marble likeness
55. Member of the bar: abbr.
56. Downcast
58. Verve
59. Cowgirl Evans
60. Milwaukee's specialty
61. Vases
63. ____ de France
64. Subways' opposites
66. Transactions
68. ____ Veneto
69. Badger
71. Mild oath
73. Villainous
75. Hurricane center
77. Quilting event

ACROSS

1. Writer Buchwald
4. Likely
7. Neither's companion
8. Widemouthed jug
9. Make a choice
12. Shapeless mass
14. Songstress Horne
15. "(31 Down), my children, and you shall hear of the (19 Across) (84 Across) of ____": 2 wds.
19. See 15 Across
23. Pester
24. Landed property
26. Crazy bird
27. Jump
28. Weird
29. Forget-me-____
30. Town map
33. Greek vowel
35. Ran, as colors
37. Faucet
40. Be sick
41. Unusual
43. ____ carte: 2 wds.
44. Recipe amount: abbr.
45. Rapid
47. Give the news
49. Start a battle
52. Good-bye: Fr.
54. Three: prefix
55. "One if by land, and two if by ____"
56. Charged particles
57. Actor Asner and others
58. Franklin's kite tail attachment
59. Penny
61. Cry of discovery
64. Cloth belt
65. Drunkard
66. Occurrence
69. Injure
73. Asian nurse
75. Cautioned
77. Diva Callas
78. Early North American settlements
82. War of Independence
84. See 15 Across
85. Actress Gabor and others
86. Had a snack
87. "A phantom ship, with each mast and ____ . . ."
88. First woman
89. Curvy letter
90. Crimson

DOWN

1. Irate
2. Actor's part
3. Treasure find
4. Impressed greatly
5. Quaker settler
6. Mountain path
8. Inventor Whitney
9. October birthstone
10. Window glass
11. Salad fish
13. Assail
16. Trim short
17. Highway: abbr.
18. Organ of hearing
19. Run into
20. Departed
21. Car engine covering
22. Explosive: abbr.
25. Make a knot
30. Any hero of 82 Across
31. See 15 Across
32. High mountain
34. ____ longa, vita brevis
35. Enemy in 82 Across
36. Made an exit
37. Roofing liquid
38. Strong beer
39. Mama's mate
42. Medals
46. Chore
48. Chief Norse god
50. Third letter
51. Foster brother of King Arthur
53. Federation of 78 Across: abbr.
54. Boston ____ Party
59. Singer Perry ____
60. And others: abbr.
62. Fells a tree
63. One of Frank's wives
64. Singer Lawrence
65. Animal pouch
67. Make a mistake
68. Opposite of SSW
69. Bonnet
70. Opera solo
71. Mob scene
72. Lion's neck hair
74. Mount for 15 Across
76. Capital of Delaware
77. Pondered
79. Bites gently
80. Slayer of Castor
81. Always, in poems
83. Bathe

PUZZLE 112

• UNITED WE STOOD •

PUZZLE 113

ACROSS

1. "____ Little Indians"
4. 3 Down wear
8. Actor Raymond
12. Unclose, poetically
13. Scheme
14. "Un Bel Di," e.g.
15. Stitch
16. Dress up
18. Certain autos
20. Burros
21. Goal
22. Tibetan monk
24. Stop
26. Look like
30. Baseball-bat wood
31. Hunts
32. Spanish river
33. Certain lures
35. Criticizes
36. Lubricates
37. Make leather
38. Drink noisily
41. Indian leader
44. South Carolina trees
47. Fr. possessive
48. Actress Sten
49. Plunder
50. Building wing
51. Genuine
52. Manage
53. Tiny

DOWN

1. Ready the salad
2. Fencing sword
3. City for 41 Across: 2 wds.
4. Exhaust
5. Charity
6. Mr. Reiner
7. Native: suffix
8. Fragrant evergreen
9. Author Leon
10. Shine's mate
11. Stadium cheers
17. Shiny fabrics
19. Picnic crasher
22. Lascivious looks
23. Inquires
24. Possesses
25. Cleo's snake
26. Stagger
27. Just minted: 2 wds.
28. Sass
29. Dawn goddess
31. Game bird
34. Standard
35. Kurosawa epic
37. Sapor
38. Mast
39. Primrose or Penny
40. Forearm bone
41. Glop
42. Links locale
43. Man, for one
45. Cable station
46. Excessively

PUZZLE 114

ACROSS

1. Stinging insect
5. Singer Boone
8. Gives a thumbs-down
12. "____ each life . . ."
13. Mr. Onassis
14. Step ____!: 2 wds.
15. Romberg opus, with "The": 2 wds.
18. That girl
19. Philippine island
20. Always, poetically
21. Farmer's locale
23. Seraglio room
25. Actor Michael et al.
27. Mordecai's niece
31. Singer Laine
32. Aviation prefix
33. King Juan ____
36. It's about time!: 2 wds.
38. Gorilla, e.g.
39. Nailed obliquely
40. Saratoga, e.g.
43. Middle Devonian
45. Flipped item
48. Ms. Kelly, in Monaco: 2 wds.
51. Republic of Ireland
52. Clear
53. Fresh way to start
54. ____ off (miffed)
55. Prior, to a bard
56. Whirlpool

DOWN

1. Hope
2. Chip in a chip
3. More durable
4. Vegetable case
5. Juries
6. Culturally pretentious
7. Go quietly
8. Taro's yield
9. Actress Bancroft
10. Agreeable
11. Agent: suffix
16. She, to Henri
17. Cincinnati nine
22. ____ Gay
24. "____ of Two Cities": 2 wds.
25. New Deal org.
26. Neighbor of Ga.
28. Cape
29. Vocal hesitations
30. Corrupt
34. Oil cartel
35. Peaceful
36. "____ of Honey": 2 wds.
37. Chinese society
40. Small barracuda
41. ____-dieu
42. English river
44. Elbe tributary
46. Like some tea
47. Like morning lawns
49. Sparks or Beatty
50. Actress Charlotte

PUZZLE 115

ACROSS
1. Opens one's big mouth
6. Threat
11. Send payment
12. Holiday event
13. Reno business
14. Toted
15. Seine feeder
16. Racetrack
18. Joke
19. Wind dir.
20. Lash
21. Network
22. Organic compound
24. Lives
26. Goes to bed
28. Aver
31. "____ Fall in Love"
34. Anent: 2 wds.
35. Puzzle abbr.
37. Across, to Keats
39. Sch. gp.
40. Methods
41. Apiary unit
42. Felt sorry for
44. Hit solidly
46. Builds
47. Senior
48. Advises, in Glasgow
49. Marsh plants

DOWN
1. Cook, in a way
2. Abate
3. Fr. girlfriend
4. Receptacle
5. Bar furnishing
6. Baseball's Molitor
7. Work unit
8. Teased
9. Imagine
10. Cliff projections
12. Golfer Gary
13. Romaine
17. Spice of life
20. Circus performer
21. Come up
23. Heraldic border
25. Convince
27. Walks
28. Ladle
29. Whole
30. Boxed
32. Worked
33. Cuts
36. Actor Ed
38. Eric the ____
40. Prohibition foes
41. Secrete
43. Rocks
45. Pub brew

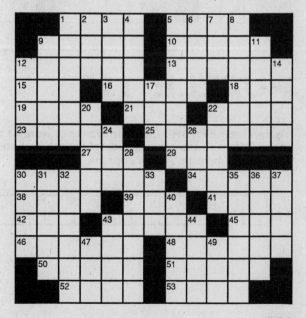

PUZZLE 116

ACROSS
1. Hide of the hare
5. Feeler
9. Fido's friend
10. In the know
12. Harm
13. Tape
15. Goal
16. ____ days (youth)
18. Actress Wray
19. Employs
21. Child's game
22. Location
23. Sub
25. Keep an eye on
27. Mauna ____
29. Sign of assent
30. Remainder
34. High time
38. Augury
39. Bill
41. Eternally
42. Fortune
43. Russian co-op
45. Before, poetically
46. Complete
48. Waiting room
50. Aedes, e.g.
51. Pouncing jump
52. He-sheep
53. Ms. Adams

DOWN
1. Saddle knob
2. ____ Marie Saint
3. Gams
4. 10/31 word
5. Masterpiece
6. Thunderstruck
7. Lake, in Arles
8. Gain
9. Rear
11. Poetry Muse
12. Smear
14. Colorist
17. On the ____
20. Gannet
22. Move obliquely
24. Was victorious
26. Head
28. Starlet
30. Tree trunk
31. Included in
32. Missive
33. Dine
35. Make up for
36. Woolen fabric
37. Corner aloft
40. Southern beauty
43. Jack-in-the-pulpit
44. Uproarious
47. Ms. Claire
49. One: prefix

PUZZLE 117

ACROSS

1. ____ d'Azur
5. Slight slip
10. Antitoxins
14. Football field
15. Ram constellation
16. Suave Sharif
17. ____ store
19. Exist
20. Prior to
21. Seasons on the Riviera
22. Spain and Portugal
24. Raced
25. Muslim priest
26. Mind over ____
29. Inert
33. Bay window
34. Encounters
35. Injure
36. Presidential tenure
37. Spanish mother
38. Fluid rock
39. Singleton
40. Book units
41. Gratified
42. Heating device
44. Doddering
45. Substitute spread
46. In a hopeless situation
47. Having more volume
50. Sicilian volcano
51. Beatles' "And I Love ____"
54. Against
55. Augment with pictures
58. British gun
59. River to the Oise
60. Bard of ____
61. Sprinkler attachment
62. Slightest
63. Confined

DOWN

1. System of rules
2. Ended
3. Adhesive ____
4. Guido's highest note
5. Near to the end
6. Ready for battle
7. Pizzas
8. Coin of the Orient
9. Rough guess
10. Awe-inspiring
11. Eastern prince
12. ____ Shankar
13. Vicinity
18. Drive back
23. Sacks
24. Stalk
25. Roman roads
26. Power unit
27. Combat locale
28. All in
29. Passover dinner
30. Famous Italian violin
31. Type of orange
32. Commerce
34. Cartoon Mr.
37. Fabric
38. Lean
40. Wan
41. French Upper House
43. Antiseptic
44. "77 ____ Strip"
46. Amazes
47. After whip or eye
48. Aware of
49. Colorado Indians
50. "Lohengrin" heroine
51. Possess
52. Short squarecut jacket
53. Charter
56. Recline
57. Knock

PUZZLE 118

Keyword

To find the KEYWORD fill in the blanks in words 1 through 10 with the correct missing letters and transfer those letters to the correspondingly numbered squares in the diagram. Approach with care—this puzzle is not as simple as it first appears.

1	2	3	4	5	6	7	8	9	10

1. C H A R __
2. R __ N T S
3. R O U __ E
4. __ U I T E
5. C L __ N G
6. W R __ S T
7. S T E E __
8. T __ M E S
9. __ A T E D
10. S T R __ W

ACROSS

1. Contrary girl
5. Competent
9. Attract
13. Worth
14. Steno collection
15. French river
16. Amphitheater
17. First HRE
19. ____-Coburg
20. Show position
21. More obtuse
22. Fraternity letter
23. Contended
24. Ms. Verdon
25. Hits solidly
27. Feather scarf
28. Slightly open
32. Cape Cod sights
33. Father of Regan
34. One: prefix
35. Bronx-cheer source
37. Actress Sally
38. Eskimo vehicle
39. Tapestry
40. Agreements
41. Existence
42. Atom
43. Robert ____ Stevenson
44. Danish king of England
45. Old English letter
46. Dep.
47. Darts
48. Appear
50. Wager
51. Flowering shrub
52. Baseballer Slaughter
54. Flees
55. Cry of triumph
58. Source of mistreatment
61. Large nail
63. Espied
64. First Christian Roman emperor
66. Didn't exist
67. Certain Iroquoians
68. Back of the neck
69. Building beams: hyph.
70. Boring routines
71. Architect Christopher
72. Actor Cooper

DOWN

1. Corday's victim
2. ____ Great: 2 wds.
3. Norse character
4. Pro vote
5. Garden pest
6. Wild hog
7. Nobleman
8. Building addition
9. Actress Durbin
10. Carriages
11. Ms. Boleyn
12. Smaller, in Glasgow
13. Bud holder
15. Merganser
17. Mating game
18. Name of 8 English kings
20. Mason's co-worker
23. Climbing plants
24. Aims
26. Emanations
27. Sugar vegetables
29. Month's namesake: 2 wds.
30. Concerning
31. Blue ____ Mountains
33. Aboveboard
35. Name of 2 English kings
36. Eat away
37. Goethe play
38. Actress Berger
40. Affectations
41. Dips out
43. Ora et ____ (pray and work)
44. Weather region
47. Oddball
49. Disorderly states
53. Butterfly catchers
54. Fine fabric
56. Winkler or Fonda
57. Army insects
58. Maple genus
59. Brian ____
60. Army group
61. Polaris, e.g.
62. Conduit
63. A Leeward Island
65. Vane dir.
66. Peruke

PUZZLE 119

• RULERS •

103

PUZZLE 120

ACROSS

1. ___ and hearty
5. Different
10. Put away
14. Ardor
15. Depart
16. Evergreen
17. Impart
18. Noble Italian family
19. Villainous look
20. Devote
22. Path
24. Prying
25. Of few words
26. Forgive's mate
29. Rule-breakers
33. Had a bite
34. Singer Reese
36. Carpenter's tool
37. Shoshones
39. Waken roughly
41. Speed
42. Jeans
44. Swerves
46. Fireworks flop
47. RR supports
49. Horse operas
51. ___ off (angers)
52. ___ boy!
53. Stick
56. Went to
60. Untruthful one
61. Throw away
63. "___ Descending a Staircase"
64. Satanic
65. Sacrificial site
66. Saber's kin
67. Actor Grant
68. Decade segments
69. Tear

DOWN

1. Maintained
2. Away from aweather
3. Touch down
4. Conclusion
5. Russian olive
6. Quick to anger
7. Abhor
8. Night prior
9. Save
10. Speak incoherently
11. Stadium level
12. Billfold bills
13. Existed
21. Campus girl
23. Kind of test
25. Pursue
26. Bad serve
27. Aquatic mammal
28. Actor Christopher
29. Hints
30. Avoid
31. Happen repeatedly
32. Winter coasters
35. Adores
38. Like some advice
40. Raceway horses
43. Agent: suffix
45. Make replete
48. Room to maneuver
50. Leathermaker
52. Floral essence
53. Actor Guinness
54. Opera star
55. '60s musical
56. Nick and Nora's pooch
57. Take in
58. Sir Anthony ___
59. Legal document
62. Dark brew

PUZZLE 121

WORDS WITHIN

Two clues are contained in each line below, one for the three-letter answer you place on the blanks, the second for the complete 5-letter word.

1. Where actors play, you'll find a stub,   S _ _ _ E
2. And get an average in the sub.   S _ _ _ E
3. Gain a victory in your pigs,   S _ _ _ E
4. And find a hole for nasty digs.   S _ _ _ E
5. A measurement of wire in grin;   S _ _ _ E
6. A seed case in fine porcelain.   S _ _ _ E

ACROSS

1. Lids
5. Bring about
10. Monk's garb
14. Sheltered
15. Steve or Woody
16. French friend
17. Sea gull's kin
18. Raises
19. Thaw
20. Regional dialect: 2 wds.
23. Orient
24. Belonging to us
25. Economizes
28. Feeler
33. English coins
34. Jousting weapon
35. Meadow
36. Fencing sword
37. Actress Carter
38. Moss starter
39. Always, to poets
40. Firm
41. Courageous
42. Deprecates
44. Oklahoma native
45. Social insect
46. Bard
47. Alabama hit tune: 4 wds.
54. Twinge
55. Caesar or Cicero
56. Dirk
57. Oriental food staple
58. Use
59. City in Judah
60. Polish river
61. Units of force
62. Learning

DOWN

1. Makes lace
2. Butterine
3. South American country
4. Statement
5. Affectionate gesture
6. Vigilant
7. ____ Bator
8. Antitoxins
9. Harbor
10. "I Am a ____"
11. Portent
12. Wither
13. Allow
21. Detest
22. Pretty
25. Go fast
26. Wigwam
27. Lethargic
28. Cabs for hire
29. Camelot lady
30. Purify
31. Depart
32. Diner
34. Happy air
37. Practiced medicine
38. Offer of marriage
40. Warbled
41. Hisses
43. Texas lawman
44. Aromas
46. Partake
47. Uttered
48. Formerly
49. Sly
50. Federal agents: hyph.
51. Disconnect
52. Rip
53. Present
54. ____ and con

PUZZLE 122

• ABOUT THE SOUTH •

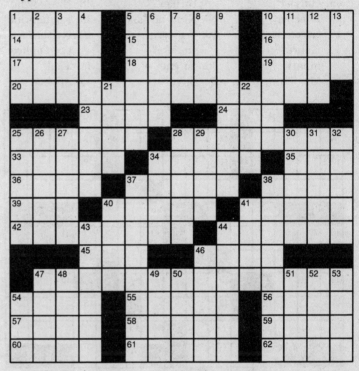

BLOCKBUILDERS

PUZZLE 123

Fit the letter blocks into the diagram to spell out the name of a famous singer-actress.

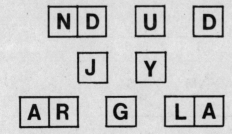

PUZZLE 124

ACROSS

1. Elaborate ceremony
5. Harriet Beecher ___
10. Green stone
14. Hebrew month
15. Mr. Truman
16. Cornelia ___ Skinner
17. Robin Cook thriller
18. Kind of daisy
19. Western Indians
20. Serene
22. Spin
24. ___-de-sac
25. Actor Alda
26. Not prepared
30. Leave O'Hare, e.g.
34. Milk producer
35. Diner offerings
37. Christmas
38. Brief swim
39. Foundation
40. Neither's accomplice
41. Tied
43. Spoken
44. Hollywood statuette
46. Subscription continuation
48. Tension
50. Like an optimist's view
51. Poetic time of day
52. Table protector
55. Feeling gratitude
60. Aviation prefix
61. Uproar
63. Regal title
64. Place
65. Normal
66. Gymnast Korbut
67. Goals
68. Suspicious
69. Navigation hazard

DOWN

1. Treaty
2. Scent
3. Papa's mate
4. One of Santa's team
5. Ought to
6. Cab
7. Russian city
8. Type of wit
9. Monocle
10. Trip
11. ___ girl!
12. Waist-watcher's regimen
13. To be, to Caesar
21. Wharf
23. Tibetan animal
25. Hun king
26. Cow's feature
27. Unsophisticated
28. Mature
29. Per annum
31. Pound portion
32. Raft
33. Commuters' boat
36. Red ___ beet: 2 wds.
39. Bragging
42. On edge
44. Beasts of burden
45. ___ swims: 2 wds.
47. Sorrow
49. Almost
52. Story
53. Rider's control
54. Miffed
55. Genuine
56. Rime
57. Scraping tool
58. Prod
59. Page
62. Function

PUZZLE 125   TRIANGLE QUOTE

Each letter in the quotation is represented by a number. To determine that number, count the number of triangles in the symbol next to the letter. Next, place that letter on the correspondingly numbered blank at the bottom to reveal the Triangle Quote.

$$\overline{}_{3}\ \overline{}_{10}\ \overline{}_{9}\ \overline{}_{6}\ \overline{}_{1}\ \overline{}_{6}\ \overline{}_{8}\ \overline{}_{4}\qquad \overline{}_{10}\ \overline{}_{2}\ \overline{}_{8}\qquad \overline{}_{3}\ \overline{}_{7}\ \overline{}_{2}\ \overline{}_{8}\ \overset{V}{\overline{}_{5}}\ \overline{}_{8}\ \overline{}_{2}$$

F   I   R   M   S

E   A   V   L   O

106

PUZZLE 126

• IN CHARACTER •

ACROSS

1. Payoff
7. Triangular sail
10. Meg's sister
13. British Museum marbles
18. Cure-all
19. Old capital of Myanmar
20. Swiss painter
21. Broad comedy
22. Claim
23. Justices of the peace
25. Released
26. Pinochle combination
27. Arabian gulf
29. List shortener: abbr.
30. Chute sled
31. "___ tu"
32. Minor Prophet
33. Mo. summer hours
34. Blackboard pads
37. "___ Daughter"
39. Contrive
41. Actor Hackman
42. Mother
44. Swab
45. Third generation relatives
47. Stout
48. Moslem month
50. Church seats
51. U.S. fur trader
52. ___ go bragh
53. Eastern women's quarters
54. Newspaper head
56. Paper art
59. Austrian composer
61. Novel
62. Racehorses
64. Bishopric
65. On ___ (carousing)
67. Darling: Fr.
69. Intimidate
71. Old card game
73. Headland
74. River to the Black Sea
76. Starts alterations
78. Move out of
80. Russian city
81. Deeds
83. Adult insect
85. "___ de Castro"
86. Shuttlecock
87. Morse code word
88. Volunteer smoke-eaters
91. Violinist Bull
92. Globe
93. Actor Jannings
94. Leopard's kin
95. French painter
98. Expense allowance
100. Permit
101. ___ noire
103. Pismire
104. ___ tetra
105. Islamic commander
107. Simple
108. Jason's ship
109. Speed check
111. Property rater
113. Antenna
115. Sra. Peron
116. South African
117. Wedding words
118. Burger ballad
119. Lone Star State
120. Finis
121. Corral
122. Sports palaces

DOWN

1. Orange juicer
2. Sleuth Queen
3. Diamond star
4. Dismissed
5. Outfit
6. Reverie
7. Battle star
8. Netman Lendl
9. Tavern
10. Epithet of Athena
11. Literary star
12. Certainly!
13. Exudes
14. Big
15. Nobel star
16. Rocks
17. Composer Rorem
20. Young cats
24. Animal relief organization
28. Evaded
30. Path
32. Egyptian snake
33. Spy gp.
35. Shouts again
36. Arias
38. Din
40. Neckline garment
43. Males
46. Japanese statesman
48. Arguments
49. In the ocean
50. Thought: Fr.
52. Scottish uncle
55. Be obliged
57. Crystal-lined stones
58. Taj Mahal site
60. Batters
63. Judgelike
66. Treeless flatland
67. Musical syllable
68. Ethnic
70. Join metal
72. Actress Claire
75. Aristocratic
77. Day of rest: abbr.
78. Organ adjusters
79. Wobble
81. Brouhaha
82. Grumble
84. Of a bookbinding design
88. Soft felt hats
89. "___ the Mood for Love"
90. Retrieve
91. Pindaric
96. Goat wool
97. Supplies
99. "Giant" ranch
102. Croatian physicist
106. Teacher's degree: abbr.
107. Fashion
108. English queen
109. Soak flax
110. Hail!
111. Actor Vigoda
112. Drink daintily
114. Eternally, in poems

PUZZLE 127

ACROSS
1. Rudiments
5. "___ in Toyland"
10. Edges
14. Chair
15. Bedeck
16. Great Lake
17. Otherwise
18. Western prop
19. Beauty spot
20. Certify
22. Thought out
24. Jump
26. "Krazy ___"
27. Long banner
31. Turns inside out
35. Charisma
36. ___ Haute
38. Chop out weeds
39. ___ and crafts
40. Mexican sandwiches
41. Jab with the elbow
42. Born
43. Dish of mixed greens
44. Horseman
45. Last six lines of a sonnet
47. Louisiana birds
49. Large rodent
50. Malt kiln
51. Brought to mind
56. Head parts
60. Father of Cain
61. Be
63. Underground tree part
64. Ginger cookie
65. Wash out suds
66. Sea eagle
67. Pots and ___
68. Spirited horse
69. Profound

DOWN
1. On a cruise
2. Waistband
3. Actors in a play
4. Pittsburgh footballers
5. Small chicken
6. Commotion
7. Oaf
8. Gaelic
9. Tennis shoes
10. Distant
11. Press clothes
12. 5,280 feet
13. Kernel
21. Garment joint
23. Rescue
25. Flower part
27. Looks over quickly
28. Valuable canasta card
29. Fees
30. News summary
32. Valerie Harper role
33. Bus fare
34. Prophets
37. Cowboy show
40. Telltales
41. Envisioned
43. Close tightly
44. Danger
46. Hobos
48. Endured
51. Coarse file
52. Writer Ferber
53. Actor James
54. Doorway out
55. Have a feast
57. Folk knowledge
58. "The ___ Ranger"
59. Footfall
62. Opposite of NNW

PUZZLE 128   Across and Down

Place the answers to the clues into the Word Squares below so that the same words read both across and down.

A.

1. Mountain lion
2. Atop
3. Burrowing animal
4. Once more

B.

1. The one here
2. Search
3. Peruvian Indian
4. Male deer

108

ACROSS

1. Sudden increase
5. Precious
9. Novice
13. Picnic dish
17. ___ prima
18. Follow
19. Intention
20. Greater Antilles island
21. School purchase
24. ___ State (Nebraska)
26. Turkish city
27. Birds of prey
29. Russian city
30. Overjoy
32. Wild ox
33. Geologic layer
35. 17th-century card game
38. Rolling Stones tune
40. Gather hastily
44. Comrades
45. Sword
46. Industrialist
47. Bronze Age trumpet
48. Alphonso's wife
49. Pierce
50. Daughter of Leda
51. Salt: pref.
52. Mythical bird
53. Mockery
54. Dull surface
55. Play a trick on
56. Sacred chest
57. "Iliad" locale
58. Impudent
59. Kind of meat
60. Chance
62. Puppeteer Krofft
63. Austere
64. Mysterious
65. Valletta's land
66. Onion
67. Aurora
70. Ladd film
72. Bologna coins, once
73. Actress Theda et al.
74. Mickey's ex
75. Food fish
76. Dependable
77. Weathercock feature
78. Nonsense
79. Formicary dweller
80. Yellow Sea bay
81. Alacrity
82. King of the Huns
83. Portrait painter
85. Declines
86. "Backdraft" crime
87. Parrots
88. Chinese: pref.
89. Commence
92. Laborer of yore
94. Wilde heroine
96. Colorado mount
99. Harney Peak's locale
102. Forger
105. Supporter
106. Mars
107. Seed coat
108. March date
109. Disc jockey Rick ___
110. Ms. Thompson
111. Holly tree
112. Throne

DOWN

1. Science rm.
2. Governor Grasso
3. Trammell of baseball
4. Green Bay team
5. Elapid snake
6. German vessel
7. Chinese shrub
8. Bronte character
9. Masonic doorkeeper
10. Wells and Harper
11. Entertainment, for short
12. Furniture wood
13. Egyptian amulet
14. Pear-shaped instrument
15. Seth's brother
16. Struggle
22. Moola
23. Printer's mark
24. Despondent
25. Lennon song
28. Author Parent
31. Restaurant
33. Mass of loose rock
34. Harpoon
35. Strauss work
36. Feudal estate
37. Sewell classic
39. Straight
40. Like potato chips
41. Joan Jett's band, with "The"
42. Remarkable person
43. Libido
45. Haunt
46. Golfer King
49. Branch
50. Until: Sp.
51. ___ d'oeuvre
53. Cordwood measure
54. Stores
55. Round dances
58. Bar or fork
59. Southern fruit
61. Schism
62. Julie Andrews role
63. King of Judea
65. Marathon measures
66. Stroke
68. Convex molding
69. Sheet material
70. Lustrous mineral
71. Whet
72. Masters
73. Belgian balladeer
76. Flatfish
77. Assurance
80. Russian money
81. Healthy, in Hidalgo
82. Moon goddess
84. Lopez and Kerrigan
85. Son, to Pierre
86. Humanities
88. Puerto Rican dance
90. Implied
91. Leg part
92. Ms. Macpherson
93. Store sign
94. Coaster
95. Ancient kingdom
97. Depend
98. New Zealand island
99. Adverse
100. Fools
101. George's brother
103. Celestial altar
104. Presidential inits.

PUZZLE 130

ACROSS
1. Subside
6. Narrative
10. Resorts
14. Lox's partner
15. Idol
16. Forage
17. Cabinet
19. Strongbox, of old
20. Newspaper section
21. Read, to Jacques
22. Inert gas
23. ___ En-lai
25. Threaten
26. Put forth
29. Portions
32. Memorizes
34. Scandinavian god
35. Mystery writer
38. Innocent one
39. Lullabies
41. Jot
42. RR depot
43. Turkey, in Tegucigalpa
44. Intrepid
46. Interceptor missile
48. Parade
49. Steep slope
52. Musical work
54. Fishing vessel
55. Sherlock's find
57. Female
60. Quirk
61. Thief
64. Lotion ingredient
65. Tangible
66. Anxieties
67. Bulrush
68. Yellow fish
69. Consciousness

DOWN
1. Eban
2. John Donne, e.g.
3. Epochs
4. Beverage
5. Deer
6. Dog Star
7. Acidity
8. Vanished
9. Emmet
10. Black piano keys, sometimes
11. Cleanse
12. Elbow
13. Attitude
18. "Alice" character
22. So be it
23. Rein
24. Female lobster
25. Moss or coffee
26. Misfortunes
27. Throne
28. ___-Veda (Hindu songs)
30. Wedding-vow word
31. Fruit drink
33. Mark
35. Needy
36. Auricular
37. Every
40. Grape
41. Cleopatra's maid
43. Meat
45. Australian bird
46. Sponsored
47. "The Odd ___"
49. Glacial ridge
50. Bruce Dern film
51. Hiawatha's craft
53. Fencing dummy
55. "Mermaids" star
56. Dillydally
57. Ollie's partner
58. Towel word
59. Gaelic
61. Theater sign
62. Maybes
63. Tuition

PUZZLE 131   SKELETON KEY

Can you guess the one letter of the alphabet to be put into the same place in each of the 4-letter answers to change them into 5-letter words? Do not rearrange the order of the letters. First fill in column A with the answers to the clues. Then insert the Skeleton Key letter to complete column B.

		A.	B.
1.	Sacred	___ ___ ___ ___	___ ___ ___ ___ ___
2.	Quarrel	___ ___ ___ ___	___ ___ ___ ___ ___
3.	Possess	___ ___ ___ ___	___ ___ ___ ___ ___
4.	A lot	___ ___ ___ ___	___ ___ ___ ___ ___
5.	Military group	___ ___ ___ ___	___ ___ ___ ___ ___
6.	Nimble	___ ___ ___ ___	___ ___ ___ ___ ___
7.	Fly high	___ ___ ___ ___	___ ___ ___ ___ ___
8.	Retain	___ ___ ___ ___	___ ___ ___ ___ ___
9.	All even	___ ___ ___ ___	___ ___ ___ ___ ___
10.	Skewer	___ ___ ___ ___	___ ___ ___ ___ ___

ACROSS
1. Duet numbers
5. Servant
9. Debussy's "La ____"
12. ____ of office
13. "Wheezy ____"
14. Previous, to poets
15. "____ B"
17. Narrow inlet
18. Sound system
19. National song
21. Sailor
22. Dodecanese island, to Mikos
23. Great joy
26. Certain wools
29. Particle
30. Craze
31. Merited
32. Detective
35. Frighten
37. "Maybe This ____"
38. "Eight to the ____"
39. Despot
41. Spews
45. Court
46. Beach Boys hit
48. "Long ____ in Alcala"
49. "Dedicated to the ____ Love"
50. Stuff
51. Olivia Newton-John hit
52. "____ Mister Callaghan"
53. "____ We Go Again"

DOWN
1. Hurl
2. Mr. Disney
3. Sioux Indian
4. Summer clothes
5. "The Toy Drum ____"
6. Prefix meaning up
7. Took a breath
8. Actress Blythe
9. "Help ____"
10. "____ Canal"
11. Quantity of paper
16. "Goober ____"
20. Prefix meaning three
23. "____ Bad John"
24. "Lindy ____"
25. Beach Boys hit
26. Singer Eartha ____ Kitt
27. "____ Day Will Come"
28. "____ You in September"
30. "The ____ Teller"
33. "____ Cruise"
34. Type of cab
35. Madras dress
36. Critical test
38. Suit
39. "____ Off the Blue Canaries"
40. Indian discipline
42. "Ah! So ____"
43. Nicholas or Peter
44. "____ Old Saturday Night"
47. Ruff's mate

ACROSS
1. Ultimate degree
4. Tuesday of movies
8. Chomp
11. "We ____ Not Alone"
12. Brainchild
13. Nullify
14. "Bull Durham" actress
17. Caught wind
18. Actress Gold
19. "Married to the ____"
21. Bit for Silver
22. Squealer
25. "The ____ Eastwick"
30. Biblical hunter
32. Use a shuttle
33. 1984 David Lynch fantasy
34. Captained
37. "A ____ Leaf"
38. French preposition
39. Cargo weight
41. Another time
44. Female relative
48. "Batman" actor
52. French girlfriend
53. "Moonstruck" actress
54. Note to a reader: abbr.
55. "Woman in ____"
56. Face flankers
57. "____, Georgio"

DOWN
1. Crosby, Stills & ____
2. Verifiable
3. "____ Cockeyed Wonder"
4. "Rear ____"
5. Begleys
6. Actress Salonga
7. Patriotic org.
8. Concludes
9. Hubbubs
10. Acting award
13. Joined
15. Provide with weapons
16. Nanking nanny
20. Stings
21. Musical group
22. Thing in law
23. Query
24. Skater Babilonia
26. Macadamize
27. Solar-system member
28. Countdown ender
29. "A ____ Good Men"
31. "Rabbit Redux" author
35. Magician Jillette
36. Blood givers
40. Zilch
41. Slightly open
42. Up, as for adventure
43. Sour substance
45. Glimpse
46. Sheep shelter
47. Baseball's Slaughter
49. Rapper Vanilla ____
50. Chinese tea
51. "Take ____, She's Mine"

PUZZLE 134

ACROSS
1. Appraise
5. Stuffy
10. Imitator
14. Crowbar
15. Asylum
16. Makes a hole in
18. Scarface Al
19. Pass
20. Ground-meat dishes
22. Atop
23. Canadian Indian tribe
25. Demand
27. Adam's mate
28. ____ judicata
29. Ado
30. Scoff
31. Clothes hanger
32. Chosen
34. African republic
35. Certain South Africans
36. Young boy
37. Unit of gem weight
38. "____ Rosenkavalier"
39. Piece of asparagus
42. Carroll or Josephine
43. Send another way
47. Loan
48. Hub
49. Shaver
51. Hill dweller
52. Town
53. Craters
54. Pitch
55. Shooting scripts
58. Enclosures
59. Mexican coin
60. Infidel
61. Laborers
63. More uncommon
64. Petite
65. Commutes
66. Operate
67. Peeled
70. Virtue
71. Daydream
75. Debtor
76. Repair
77. ____ julep
78. Article
79. Code item
80. Guide
81. Vamp Theda
82. Stop!
83. Harangues
85. Countrified
87. Hails
89. Type of bee
90. "As ____ goes, so goes . . ."
91. Deserves
92. Ellipsis symbols
93. Wades
94. Goddess of hope

DOWN
1. Peacefulness
2. Bard's river
3. Referee's count
4. Established
5. Crowd's yell
6. Back road
7. Reproductive units
8. Minor
9. Beg
10. More competent
11. Needy
12. Gay Nineties, e.g.
13. American patriot
14. Collar fold
17. Disjoin
18. Rectify
21. Notes
24. Divest
26. Hideout
29. Headliner
30. Definite
31. Matadors' quests
33. Covered
34. Rice wine
35. Arctic masses, for short
37. Freight
38. Impressions
39. Slit
40. British coins
41. Come in
42. Type of acid
43. Wrecks
44. Absolute
45. Gibe
46. Miscalculation
48. Radium discoverer
50. Inaugurates
52. Lessened
56. Fresher
57. Incorporeal
58. Versifier
59. Gasp
62. Revise
63. Carry on
65. Improvements
66. Contrives
67. Venetian traveler
68. Medal
69. Recompense
70. Honey
71. Pine's kin
72. Georgia city
73. Injections
74. Certain votes
76. Looms
77. Boys and men
80. Confined
81. Thrill
82. Used to be
84. Excessive
86. ____ Muni
88. Chat

DOUBLE TROUBLE

PUZZLE 135

Not really double trouble, but double fun! Solve this puzzle as you would a regular crossword, EXCEPT place one, two, or three letters in each box. The number of letters in each answer is shown in parentheses after its clue.

ACROSS
1. Stagger (5)
4. Bundle (5)
7. Use a strainer (4)
10. Mature (3)
11. Mistake (5)
12. Maritime (5)
13. Clip (5)
15. Wearies (5)
16. Centers (5)
17. Nuisance (4)
19. Stopwatch (5)
21. Warning buzzer (5)
23. Peered (6)
25. Gift (7)
28. Stride (4)
29. Makes a speech to (9)
31. Cleaner (4)
32. Abut (6)
34. Oceans (4)
35. Crimson (3)
36. Monarchs (5)
38. Wren's home (4)
40. Bell sound (4)
42. Fresh-water duck (4)
44. Further down (6)
47. Play backer (5)
48. Exile island (4)
50. Remove rind from (4)
51. Irritable (5)

52. Close-packed (5)
53. Uncommon (4)

DOWN
1. Whip (4)
2. Impulse (4)
3. Inexpensive (5)
4. Diaphanous (5)
5. Bower (5)
6. Black or Sherwood (6)
7. Earnest (7)
8. Friendly act (5)
9. Stories (5)
14. Adding ammo again (9)
18. Stirred (the fire) (6)
20. Affected deeply (9)
21. South American beast (6)
22. Furnished weapons (5)
24. Feminine garb (5)
26. Signal device (6)
27. Recorded (5)
30. Actor Connery (4)
33. In a humorous way (8)
37. Spirited horse (5)
39. More sharply inclined (7)
40. "Inferno" author (5)
41. Swallow (6)
43. Ethan or Steve (5)
45. Fleshy fruit (4)
46. Author Gardner (4)
49. Foundation (4)

BLOCKBUILDERS

PUZZLE 136

Fit the letter blocks into the diagram to spell out the name of a famous composer.

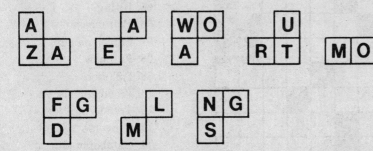

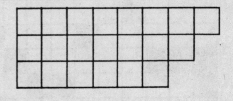

PUZZLE 137

• HOW THE WEST WAS WON •

ACROSS

1. "Days of Wine and ___"
6. Humbled
11. Handle roughly
14. Famed mission
15. Lithe
16. Task
18. Class
19. Western outlaw: 3 wds.
21. Break a fast
22. Shade of green
24. Atelier item
25. Genetic molecules: abbr.
27. Feminine suffix
28. Molts
30. Data banks
32. Letter before upsilon
33. Paper measures
37. Geraint's beloved
38. Denver athlete
40. Baby food
41. ___ on it!
42. Yarn measure
43. Can
44. GPs' org.
45. Autos
46. Western spreads
48. Cicatrix
49. Mauna ___
50. Distress signal
51. Feather's mate
52. Pep-rally shouts
53. One: prefix
54. "___" Pete Maravich
56. Garden intruder
57. Attorney Melvin
59. Otic organ
60. Singer Page
61. Praying figure
63. ___ Cruces
64. Cinch
67. Moon of Saturn
69. ___ voce
71. 601, in 61
72. Western frontier military outpost: 2 wds.
75. Kind of terrier
77. Zodiac ram
78. Festoon
79. Expect
80. "___ and don'ts"
81. Actress Debra
82. Moves, with a riff

DOWN

1. Stormed
2. New York city
3. Road west: 3 wds.
4. Ostrich's kin
5. Fair: hyph.
6. Rustic homes
7. Kind of arch
8. Stratagem
9. Building wing
10. African VIP of yore
11. Nudge
12. Seed coat
13. Join
16. Nebraska city
17. Nobelist Hermann
20. Kicker's aid
23. Told tall tales
26. Trig functions
28. ___ Paulo
29. Actor Tab
31. Sass
32. Farm vehicle
34. Western native: 2 wds.
35. Papas' mates
36. Boom or sprit
38. Publisher Bradlee
39. On this side: prefix
41. Rhone feeder
42. California mount
45. Steak or car
46. French king
47. Actor Linden
48. Gobs
50. Helices
52. Eyewash
55. Make lace
56. Sail support
58. Singer Lenya
60. Obvious
62. Actress ___ Alicia
63. Longest French river
65. Biting
66. Pub measures
67. Barcelona bull
68. Rainbow
69. Pollution
70. Wood sorrels
72. Trend
73. Converse
74. Oklahoma city
76. Thunderstrike

PUZZLE 138

ACROSS

1. Quit
5. Packs firmly
10. Frosted
14. Sole
15. Be ready for
16. Rant
17. Baseball failures
18. Gala
19. Boding
20. Male siblings
22. Idle
23. Prior to
24. Center points
26. Cuts
30. Fatty fruit
34. Sawing frame
35. Black bird
37. Brooch
38. In a violent frenzy
39. Strictness
40. Martial ___
41. Debtor's ink color
42. Hang
43. Chosen
44. Chair
46. Voter's ticket
47. Formerly
48. Tavern
49. Binge
52. Hull clinger
57. Times
58. Island
60. Attired
61. Professional robe
62. Search for water with a stick
63. Roof overhang
64. Gush forth
65. Detain
66. Graceful bird

DOWN

1. Untidy person
2. Sightseeing journey
3. Hep
4. Bother
5. Candles
6. Knowing
7. "Eyes of Laura ___"
8. Hole in the ground
9. Pig's home
10. Wry
11. Arrived
12. Always
13. Fender nick
21. Present!
22. Representation
24. Advantage
25. Higher than
26. Not blurred
27. 4-base hit
28. Wear down
29. Request
31. Month for taxes
32. Likewise
33. Beginning
35. Metal fastener
36. Era
39. Bars
40. Entirely
42. Employ
43. Receive for labor
45. Teeter-totter
46. Malt grain
48. Light wood
49. TV units
50. Support
51. Anger
52. Stadium
53. Scores on serve
54. Pincer
55. Melted rock
56. Paradise
58. Sum
59. Foot digit

HALFTIME

PUZZLE 139

Pair off the groups of letters to form ten 6-letter names of birds.

GRO PAR CAN PIE _____ _____

ARY FAL USE OLE _____ _____

ROT ORI KOO CUC _____ _____

KEY TUR PIG CAN _____ _____

EON CON TOU MAG _____ _____

115

PUZZLE 140

To complete this Circular puzzle fill in the answers to the Around clues in a clockwise direction. For the Radial clues move from the outside to the inside.

AROUND (Clockwise)

1. Comedienne Lillie
4. Bump headfirst
7. Taste
10. Type of sister
13. Trivial
19. Conveyed
25. Charming
26. Magical incantation
27. Actor Michael ____
28. "____ They Sail"
30. Overplay
31. Daddy Warbucks's charge
33. Modify
34. Piece of music
35. Son of Zebulun
36. Legal right
37. Bandleader Brown
38. Vichy, e.g.
39. French contraction
40. Conger

RADIAL (Out to in)

1. Foreshadowed
2. Notable time
3. Facing the pitcher
4. Indian coin
5. Cuckoo
6. Holy city
7. Show scorn
8. Possessive pronoun
9. Vexation
10. Old hat
11. Eyeball
12. Reveals
14. Drag one's feet
15. Group of rooms
16. White-tailed fliers
17. Em and Eller
18. Abate
20. Designated
21. Make a home run
22. Liver pastes
23. Bert's friend
24. "Divine Comedy" author
29. Apple cider girl
32. ____ at ease

116

PUZZLE 141

ACROSS
1. Water between continents
6. Messy one
10. Couple
14. Portion
15. Conceal
16. Get up from bed
17. Small pies
18. Completes
19. Unemployed
20. ___ sauce
21. "How do I love ___?"
23. Truly
25. Chair part
26. Owed
27. Polo hammer
30. Consider
32. Also
35. Opera solos
36. Water body
37. Under
39. Breton or Highland Scot
40. Paving material
41. Exist
42. Put in one's stake
44. Wholly
45. Competitor
46. Had been
47. Rows
49. Hate
50. Imp
51. Character
52. Four-leaf ___
55. Greek letter
56. Congeal
59. Speak wildly
60. Likeness
62. Profession
64. Always
65. Chilly
66. Consumed
67. Cautious
68. Totals
69. Disburse money

DOWN
1. Makes a choice
2. So long!
3. Mysterious
4. Deed
5. Settles down snugly
6. Bed linen
7. Job
8. Unusual
9. Next to
10. Group of lions
11. Secretary, e.g.
12. Small land mass
13. Slender grass
22. Beret
24. Without feeling
25. Chalkboard
27. Central American parrot
28. Activity center
29. Sings with a swing
30. Passes out cards
31. James ___ Jones
32. Animated
33. Variable stars
34. Resided
36. Twinkler
38. Upper crust
43. Dispense
45. Describes
48. Continent
49. Speck
50. "___ Which Way But Loose"
51. Rips
52. Rowing team
53. Melted rock
54. Excessively
55. Brave
56. Gorge
57. First garden
58. Care for
61. Massachusetts cape
63. Knock

Build-A-Quote

PUZZLE 142

Fill in the diagrams by putting the lines of letters VERTICALLY into their squares. The letters in each line must remain in the same order. The lines are given in jumbled order. When finished, you will be able to read a saying ACROSS the rows in the diagram.

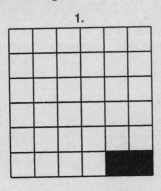

1.

E R O H T L
I H E R E
G E T D Y
B T M A H L
H E C E R A
T G Y H E F

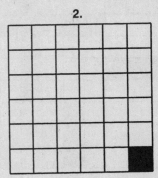

2.

L B T T F
L F T N E A
H O E H I A
A S R O F L
A A T A M T
F I E N O L

PUZZLE 143

ACROSS

1. Pose a question
4. Lose footing
8. Chair
10. Fresh-water ducks
12. Against

13. Give a new title to
15. Road sign
17. Turn down
18. One of LBJ's beagles
19. Take out, in printing
20. Desert animal
23. Biblical law-giver
24. The Greatest et al.
25. Rather
26. Avenues: abbr.
27. Grocery
30. Dog variety
32. Ages
34. Singer Della
35. Time gone by
36. Enjoy a book
37. Cut wood

DOWN

1. Snug ____ bug: 2 wds.
2. Transmit
3. Actress Jackson
4. Play a guitar
5. Ogle
6. Writer Fleming
7. Concordes, e.g.
9. Church offerings
11. Grin
14. Former spouses
16. Lubricate
19. Brayer
20. "Monday, Monday" singer
21. Change
22. Husband, e.g.
23. Damage
25. Belled the cat
27. Flat-topped hill
28. God of love
29. O'Hara's home
31. Duffer's gadget
33. Ply a needle and thread

PUZZLE 144

ACROSS

1. Poker stake
5. Hair decoration
8. Removes earth
12. Conceited
13. Fruit beverage
14. Thought
15. At any time
16. Mr. Skelton
17. Banner
18. Spa
20. Puts off

22. Fib
23. Before
24. Person who alters clothes
27. Moved swiftly
31. Possess
32. Mature
33. Delicate
37. Take on
40. Fish eggs
41. Mimic
42. Have membership
45. Gazed fixedly
49. Declare frankly
50. Large deer
52. Cloak
53. Manipulates fraudulently
54. Born
55. Sycamore
56. Fruit of the blackthorn
57. Make lace
58. Pit

DOWN

1. Assert
2. Church part
3. "Family ____"
4. Join, as in a class
5. Exchange in trade
6. Lyric poem
7. Married
8. Disagree
9. Unoccupied
10. Cog
11. Hangs unevenly
19. ____ Grande
21. Epoch
24. Toddler
25. Wonder
26. Roadside hotel
28. Paving substance
29. Self-esteem
30. Condensed moisture
34. Be half asleep
35. Vast time frame
36. Governor
37. Woven container
38. Choose
39. Responds
42. Taverns
43. Morally wrong
44. Company symbol
46. Exceptional
47. Fencing sword
48. Something done
51. Grassland

PUZZLE 145

ACROSS

1. Baltic or Red
4. With-it
7. Gallup ___
8. Kind act
10. Eject
11. Nimble
12. Fantasizes
14. Exist
16. Wealthy
18. Mongrel
19. Society girl, for short
22. Untruth
23. Craving
24. Spanish cheer
25. Make a sweater
27. Highway measure
29. Take into custody
33. Breakfast food
35. Throb
36. Follow
37. Avoid
38. Jewel
39. Sizzling

DOWN

1. Tart
2. Alternatively
3. Communion table
4. Crone
5. Bad
6. Insurance document
7. Pea's home
8. Enthrall
9. Follies
13. Dairy product
15. Coastal bird
17. ___ apparent
19. Comedian DeLuise
20. Aristocracy
21. Be suitable
26. Garbage
28. Soothe
30. Reverberate
31. Close
32. Finger count
34. Total

PUZZLE 146

ACROSS

1. Valuable item
6. Wrath
9. Chat
12. Round of gunfire
13. Born: Fr.
14. North American Indian
15. Tartan
16. Most tranquil
18. Noise
20. Employs
21. Acorn producer
23. Starchy tuber
24. Analyze
25. Grows up
27. Olympic athlete Owens
29. Precede
31. Fools
35. Load of goods
37. Female horse
38. Christmas tune
41. Diving bird
43. Immediately
44. Stratford-on-___
45. Merciful trip?
47. Facts
49. Bellows
52. Fib
53. Little
54. Prevent legally
55. Find a sum
56. Be mistaken
57. Poor

DOWN

1. Horned viper
2. Actor Mineo
3. Shirker
4. Corrupt
5. Morning show
6. Revenue
7. Back
8. Snakelike fish
9. Conjecture
10. Bewildered
11. Seamstress Ross
17. The Guggenheim, e.g.
19. Military officer
21. Clumsy person
22. Gone by
24. Fire residue
26. Minute component
28. Scrub
30. Guy's date
32. Command
33. Paid athlete
34. Stitch
36. "The Rockford Files" actor
38. Lily
39. Evade
40. Propelled a boat
42. Singer Carpenter
45. Water pitcher
46. Snout
48. Be in the red
50. Stick
51. Secret agent

119

PUZZLE 147

• **LATERALLY SPEAKING** •

ACROSS
1. Used
4. Touches on
9. Emperor
13. Toil
15. Adjust again
16. Puerto ____
17. Actress Barbara
18. Combine
19. Pindarics
20. Dining-room furniture
22. Mimics
23. Spooky
24. Yalies
25. Cotton thread
28. Motorcycle attachment
31. Zodiac sign
32. Booty
33. Noisy clamor
35. Mary Lincoln, nee ____
36. Platform
37. Icelandic poem
38. Wind dir.
39. Edible root
40. Starchy tuber
41. Pistol or sword: 2 wds.
44. Ripening agents
45. Mop
46. Inactive
48. ____ beam
50. Divert
55. Hebrew month
56. Communion plate
57. 57, in Roma
58. Carol
59. Thoughts
60. Tug at
61. Soap frame
62. Hostess Mesta
63. Oahu wreath

DOWN
1. Is beholden to
2. Lombardy town
3. Slave Scott
4. Bower
5. Secure, at sea
6. Patron
7. Watch over
8. Norm: abbr.
9. ____ of Capricorn
10. Horsewoman's seat
11. Maple genus
12. Flagmaker Betsy
14. Genuflected
21. Apiary inhabitants
22. Pub drink
24. Brink
25. Tardy
26. Fetters
27. Concerns apart from the main point: 2 wds.
28. Horde
29. "Othello" heavy
30. Amendment to a document
32. Celebrity
34. Dozes
36. Pierce
37. Fervently
40. ____ Lake City
42. Abides
43. Pitcher's handle
46. Perfect
47. Obtuse
48. Eye part
49. Century plant
50. Marquis de ____
51. Roman road
52. Grandparental
53. Spanish movie
54. Singer Dee
56. "Great Expectations" character

PUZZLE 148

ESCALATOR

Place the answer to clue 1 in the first space, drop a letter, and arrange the remaining letters to answer clue 2. Drop another letter and arrange the remaining letters to answer clue 3. The first dropped letter goes into the box to the left of space 1 and the second dropped letter goes into the box to the right of space 3. Follow this pattern for each row in the diagram. When completed, the letters on the left and right, reading down, will spell related words or a phrase.

1. Austere
2. Encouraged
3. Uncouth
4. Procession
5. Window curtain
6. Mimicked
7. Capture
8. Steady gaze
9. Relax
10. Bali, for one
11. Watch faces
12. Boys
13. Peril
14. Impressive
15. Haul
16. Abrade
17. Area
18. Ann or Cod

120

PUZZLE 149

• FAB FOUR TUNES •

ACROSS

1. Blockades
5. Holy women: abbr.
9. Himalayan monarchy
14. Busy as ____: 2 wds.
15. Waste allowance
16. Declaim
17. Shakespearean king
18. English river
19. "____ all a good night": 2 wds.
20. Beatles' song: 4 wds.
23. Singer Tormé
24. Donkey
25. Turkish title
29. Blemish
32. Snare
36. Poplars
38. Social insects
40. Pub offering
41. Beatles' "Lucy in the ____": 3 wds.
44. Sunday lecture: abbr.
45. Singe
46. Warm again
47. Revise for print
49. Caustic substances
51. Silt
52. Lubricate
54. Mr. Boone
56. Beatles' song: 3 wds.
65. Emit
66. Beach blanket?
67. Region
68. U.S. electrical engineer Nikola
69. Actress Sommer
70. Source
71. Dirks
72. Beams
73. Lodging places

DOWN

1. Indonesian island
2. Brother of Cain
3. Actual
4. Vassal
5. Banal
6. Warbles
7. Saarinen
8. Fret
9. ____ Ark
10. Hemingway
11. Tablets
12. Aleutian isle
13. Singer Russell
21. Muscat natives
22. Mongol
25. Obsolete
26. Inquired
27. Swiss author Johanna
28. Cut
30. Framework
31. Blackbird
33. Hindu queen
34. Robert and Alan
35. Nuisances
37. "____ Dallas"
39. Fuses
42. Fodder
43. Exclamation
48. Take baby steps
50. Plucky
53. Concepts
55. South American mountain range
56. Obtains
57. Beasts of burden
58. River to the Humber
59. Belgian river
60. Spanish room
61. Mata ____
62. Strong metal
63. Gas sign
64. Dines

PUZZLE 150

INSIDERS

Scrambled in each of the words below is a short word related to the subject.

For example: BECOME (BeCOMe) = COMB

IN THE BATHROOM

1. BUTTER _____
2. OPERAS _____
3. CHORTLE _____
4. TAMER _____
5. SHRUBS _____
6. WHOLE-WHEAT _____
7. SWEATSHIRT _____

121

PUZZLE 151

ACROSS
1. Skedaddled
5. Bomb
9. Sports enthusiast
12. Adore
13. Airship
14. Rescue
15. Poems by Keats
16. Fabric from flax
17. Site
18. Grimm monster
19. Coach Parseghian
20. Warn
21. Withdraw
23. Walking stick
25. Contend
26. Stringy
27. Prohibit
30. Cut the grass
33. Donate
34. High card
35. Mellow
36. Sincere
39. Choler
40. Under the weather
41. Itemize
42. Pretended
44. Was ahead
45. Patsy
46. Knight's title
47. Seethe
48. Backslide
52. Task
55. Triumph
56. Study
57. Own
58. House surroundings
60. Flying toy
61. To shelter
62. Saw
63. Eye lasciviously
64. Heavy weight
65. Sulk
66. Pianist Duchin

DOWN
1. Deluge
2. Henry Cabot ___
3. Turn outward
4. Merit
5. Act coquettishly
6. Actress Turner
7. Single
8. Sty
9. Passenger
10. State
11. Orderly
13. Sundance's girlfriend
14. Auction
20. Some
22. ____-de-camp
23. Jealously long for
24. Simians
26. Washer cycle
27. Night crawler, e.g.
28. Land measure
29. Necessity
30. Post
31. Gawk
32. Join together
33. Complain
37. Grad
38. Follow secretly
43. Sound of static
45. Rightful
46. Feel
47. Let loose
48. Arete
49. Used a crowbar
50. Satisfied
51. Abrasive material
52. Gab
53. Ring of light
54. Range
55. Cloak
58. Edible tuber
59. Stir

PUZZLE 152   Complete-A-Word

Fill in the dashes with the 4-letter answers to the clues to complete 7-letter words.

1. Comfort   B __ C __ U __ __

2. Burn   __ N __ __ K E __

3. Heap   R E __ T __ __ __

4. Jungle cat   C __ A R __ __ __

5. Shrub   __ __ L R U __ __

6. Small nail   __ __ A V __ __ O

7. Tart   __ O J __ __ __ N

8. Pealed   W __ __ __ __ L E

9. Modify   __ __ __ I E T __

10. Requirement A N __ __ X __ __

ACROSS

1. Very chilly
5. Hard to find
9. Bat wood
12. Audibly
14. Declare
15. Scat!
16. Steamship
17. Heap
18. Big sandwich
19. Heavy mist
20. Omit
22. Piece of lumber
23. Uttered
24. Late
25. Chubby
27. Explosion
29. Entrance
30. List of candidates
31. Use a shovel
34. Overhead
36. Play on words
37. Portion
39. Encountered
40. Medal
42. Tiny particle
43. Boxing, for one
44. Poe's bird
46. Flax cloth
48. Very big
49. Fancy house
50. Glisten
52. Night before
55. Unique person
56. Quartet
57. Of ships
59. Lot measurement
60. Capri, e.g.
61. Lock of hair
62. Seine
63. Daring
64. Leg joint

DOWN

1. Young bovine
2. Medley
3. Yearn
4. Owing
5. Swift
6. Greedy
7. Actor's part
8. Female sheep
9. Out in front
10. Apologetic
11. Head covering
13. Reverie
15. Brief
21. Sass
22. Military HQs
23. Ocean breakers
24. Do macrame
25. Telephone ____
26. Plunder
27. Speak abruptly
28. Come down
29. Water barrier
30. Mast
31. Appointment
32. Golf club
33. Jewel
35. Slim candle
38. Own
41. Came in first
43. Night noise
44. Operate
45. Representative
46. Spear
47. Motionless
48. Employed
49. Complain
50. Average
51. Ship's body
52. Smooth
53. Flower holder
54. Otherwise
56. Tiny lie
58. Noah's boat

PUZZLE 153

SPINWHEEL

PUZZLE 154

This game works two ways, outward and inward. Place the answers to the clues in the diagram beginning at the corresponding numbers.

OUTWARD

1. Shrub
3. Terrapin
5. Alter
7. Watchful
9. Undermines
11. Necromancer
13. Bus-ticket price

INWARD

14. Historical period
13. Brother in France
12. Cranky
10. Gone by
8. Team race
6. Come undone
4. Established fact
2. Deli sandwich

PUZZLE 155

ACROSS

1. Phones
6. Cat sound
9. Monster
14. Situated on a center line
15. Mature
16. Blunder
17. Incline
18. Impresario Hurok
19. Sly
20. Nag
22. "If It's ____, This Must Be Belgium"
24. Increase
25. Impudent
26. Swift
29. Ascertain
31. Water
35. Actress Arden
36. Lead performer
37. Thrown
38. Scandinavian
40. Beam
42. Make happy
43. Cat
44. Wind
46. Family
47. Paradise
48. Scent
50. Animal skin
51. Twirl
52. Sailor
54. Ax
58. Ring salesman
62. Hawaiian hello
63. Colorado Indian
65. Cognizant
66. Assembly
67. Respect
68. Hemp
69. Swarms
70. Cut off
71. Imbibed

DOWN

1. Money
2. Spindle
3. Wild feline
4. Flap
5. Glossy
6. Disguise
7. Self
8. Wallow
9. Attack
10. Sea birds
11. Dry
12. Pop
13. Card with three spots
21. Gael
23. Footed vase
25. Model
26. Barrier
27. Evade
28. Deliver
30. Organ of hearing
31. Total
32. Tremble
33. Up to the time
34. Federal man
36. Gel
37. Service charge
39. Indonesian money
41. Sweet potato
45. Tardy
48. Mimic
49. Ceremonial act
50. Before an armed conflict
51. Imitations
53. Prize
54. Knife handle
55. African succulent
56. Ripped
57. Pal
58. Four-wheel vehicle
59. Monk
60. Actress Gray
61. Stink
64. "Tea for ____"

PUZZLE 156

SQUARES

Each of the Squares below contains an 8-letter word. It can be found by starting at one of the letters and reading either clockwise or counterclockwise. In the example below, the word STANDARD is found by starting at the letter S and reading counterclockwise.

Example:
D R A
S   D
T A N

1.
U N D
Y   E
A P R

2.
A B S
S   S
E L E

3.
N G F
I   L
H S A

4.
E R O
E   B
J A M

PUZZLE 157

ACROSS

1. Licks
5. Blind parts
10. Toboggan
14. Bassoon's relative
15. Turn
16. Seam
17. Glacier fragment
18. "Sleeping With the ___"
19. Yen
20. Veranda
22. "Law and ___" (TV series)
23. Beryl and talc
27. Tahini ingredient
31. Earth
32. Pear-shaped fruit
35. Shout
36. For fear that
37. Flank
38. Geologic divisions
39. Frolics
40. Adolescent
41. Choir singer
42. Skating surfaces
43. Kind of eclipse
44. Cereal grass
45. Bridge
46. Walk like a duck
47. Harbors
49. Lessen
52. Consequences
57. Soft drink
58. Storms
61. Pick
62. Elsa's sound
63. Nominate
64. "What's in a ___?"
65. Formerly, once
66. Track events
67. Slant

DOWN

1. Attic
2. Equal to the task
3. Meager
4. Oracle
5. Coined money
6. Fabric type
7. Hail!
8. Journalist Brokaw
9. Pen
10. Mumbles
11. Actor Jack
12. Border
13. Bambi, for one
21. Slugs
22. "The ___ Man and the Sea"
24. Component
25. Files
26. "B.C." insects
27. Clip
28. Ahead of time
29. Blackboard
30. Too
32. Fanatic
33. Perfect
34. Art class
36. Native
37. Spike
39. Mellow
43. Young woman
45. Andress film
46. Seizes
47. Commence
48. Construct
49. Israeli port
50. Stooge
51. Cry of dismay
53. Vessels
54. Drip
55. Docile
56. Spurt
58. Stone
59. Ginger ___
60. Brenda or Bruce

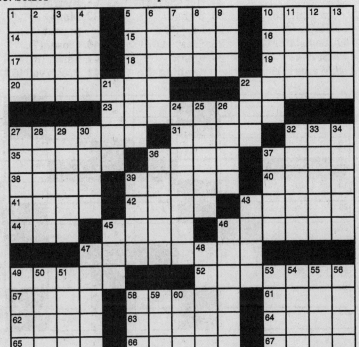

Escalator

PUZZLE 158

Place the answer to clue 1 in the first space, drop a letter, and arrange the remaining letters to answer clue 2. Drop another letter and arrange the remaining letters to answer clue 3. The first dropped letter goes into the box to the left of space 1, and the second dropped letter goes into the box to the right of space 3. Follow this pattern for each row in the diagram. When completed, the letters on the left and right, reading down, will spell related words or a phrase.

1. Bull's-eye, e.g.
2. Scrape
3. Cry
4. Wheedle
5. Spirit
6. Singer Campbell
7. Gritty
8. Frighten
9. Sheath
10. Facet
11. Glue
12. Nuisance
13. Desert vision
14. Dirt
15. Arab chieftain
16. Seek
17. Pursue
18. Singer Johnny ___

1	2	3
4	5	6
7	8	9
10	11	12
13	14	15
16	17	18

PUZZLE 159

DOUBLE TROUBLE

Not really double trouble, but double fun! Solve this puzzle as you would a regular crossword, EXCEPT place one, two, or three letters in each box. The number of letters in each answer is shown in parentheses after its clue.

ACROSS
1. Two scores (5)
4. The fifth canonical hour (5)
7. Most pristine (6)
10. Raise (4)
11. Legislator (7)
12. Sad (4)
13. Wares (11)
15. Foundation (13)
17. Pleasing (4)
18. Above (3)
19. Extreme (7)
21. Ennui (7)
24. Hot spot (4)
26. Sign (3)
27. Law (5)
28. Sassy (4)
29. Rustic dwelling (5)
30. Particular account (7)
31. Gauge (7)
32. Poet (4)
33. Discover (4)
34. Bistros (11)
37. Money payout (11)
40. Closer (7)
41. Select (6)
43. Preserved (6)
44. Old-timers (4)
45. Violated (6)
46. Twitches (4)

DOWN
1. Earlier (6)
2. Achieve (5)
3. Despotic (10)
4. Foolishness (8)
5. Devour (3)
6. Most painful (6)
7. Newspaper bigwig (9)
8. Continue (6)
9. Outdoor shelter (4)
14. Expire (3)
16. Flowering (6)
19. Iris (7)
20. Bargain (6)
21. African (4)
22. Beatty film (4)
23. Parlance (7)
24. Horse and soap (6)
25. Dare (7)
30. Inexperienced (7)
31. Beggar (9)
32. Exchanges (7)
33. Demon (5)
34. Stubborn (7)
35. Tutored (6)
36. Wound mark (4)
37. Bared (7)
38. Loose garment (5)
39. Hollow grasses (5)
42. Residence (5)

PUZZLE 160

IN AND AROUND

Place the answers to the clues into the diagram, from the outside to the inside. When you have finished, two 12-letter words will be revealed, reading from 1 to 12 on both the outermost ring and the third ring in.

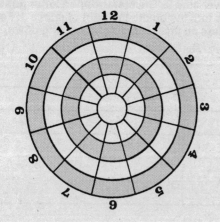

1. Jab with the elbow
2. Pile
3. Unctuous
4. Difficult journey
5. Leave out
6. Deities
7. Housetop
8. Too
9. Treaty
10. Engine cover
11. Catch sight of
12. Spool of film

PUZZLE 161

ACROSS
1. Strange
4. Unfeeling
8. At present
11. Pain
12. Toward shelter
13. Dwarf-star type
14. And so forth: abbr.
15. Coral formation
16. Unusual person
17. Singer Della
19. Unsociable people
21. Neither's companion
22. Tennis units
23. Picnic spoilers
25. Facts
26. Porky's abode
29. For each
30. Gauge
31. Ram's mate
32. Brewed beverage
33. Hopis' cousins
34. Baseball's Slaughter
35. Misplaces
37. Took a chair
38. Pitcher's pride
40. Ordeal
43. Take it easy
44. Stage part
47. Exist
48. Summer treats
49. Great Lake
50. Meadow
51. Actor Danson
52. Moose or elk
53. Tree's fluid

DOWN
1. Debtor
2. Love excessively
3. Not confined to one place, as government
4. Concerned one
5. Rah, in Spain
6. Gen. Robert E. ____
7. Lets air out of
8. Unnecessary items
9. Above
10. Conflicts
13. Not at all
18. Distress call
20. Actor Sharif
22. Swinging openings
23. Liable
24. Society-page word
25. Hindered
27. Noah's number
28. Affirmative
30. Contemplate
34. Lend an ____
36. Poetic forms
37. Guide
38. Narrow opening
39. Shoe need
41. Defined space
42. Jump
45. Unrefined metal
46. Falsehood

PUZZLE 162

ACROSS
1. Comedian Carney
4. Part of a necklace
8. Public-opinion sampling
12. Caspian, e.g.
13. Depend
14. Region
15. Something to lend or bend
16. Otherwise
17. Starring role
18. Odor
20. Spoken
22. Had lunch
24. Baseball pitch
28. More distant
32. Worship
33. Miss Gardner
34. Entrap
36. Prevaricate
37. Fist fight
40. Espied
43. Woodland paths
45. Before: prefix
46. Paradise
48. Where the action is
52. Dry
55. Force
57. Promise
58. Half: prefix
59. To the sheltered side
60. Wind dir.
61. Bridge
62. Requirement
63. Incline the head

DOWN
1. On the ocean
2. Back end
3. Tapioca plant
4. Respiration
5. Elongated fish
6. Too
7. Fabric colorers
8. Pale
9. Metallic rock
10. Meadow
11. Small boy
19. Small rug
21. Predecessor of mode or king
23. Level, to a poet
25. Slow-witted person
26. Huron's neighbor
27. Marsh grass
28. Speedy
29. Assert
30. Pro ____
31. Legal thing
35. Gratuity
38. Fit harmoniously together
39. Ancient
41. Shredded
42. "Leave ____ to Heaven"
44. Closed car
47. Egyptian river
49. Smooth
50. "____, Nanette"
51. Impressed greatly
52. Wild donkey
53. Corded fabric
54. Beatles' "____ Loser"
56. Betty Ford, ____ Bloomer

127

PUZZLE 163

ACROSS

1. Slalom necessity
5. Spice
9. Cold wind
13. Sacrifice
14. Kind of exam
15. Actor Alain ____
16. Singer Guthrie
17. "Road to ____"
18. Pitch-black
19. Tilt
20. Draft horse
22. Samuel Richardson novel
24. Throw
25. Desires
27. Crape ____
32. Swiss city
35. Apple
37. Water jug
38. Issue
40. Natural force
42. Nick
43. "Body ____"
45. Grammatical term
46. Make esteemed
48. Socialite Perle ____
50. "____ and the Swan"
52. ____ Conquest
56. Plush
61. Essential part
62. Jacob's father
63. Cuisine
64. Type of skirt
65. Brussels river
66. Author Tyler
67. Columnist Bombeck
68. Low card
69. North Sea feeder
70. Close

DOWN

1. Kind of lock
2. ____ Strait
3. Allah's religion
4. English prehistoric monument
5. Headdress for women
6. Asian sea
7. West Indian music
8. Slur
9. Curve
10. Spanish jar
11. Irritate
12. Wager
15. Powdery
21. Playwright Rice
23. "Damn Yankees" dame
26. Foil's relative
28. Investigates
29. Esau, to Jacob
30. Durocher and Tolstoy
31. Marine flier
32. Venerable monk
33. Jerusalem mufti Al-Husaini
34. Grit
36. Allot
39. Projected
41. Essential oil
44. Hippolyta and friends
47. Asian clover
49. Jimmy "The Greek" ____
51. Flemish composer Guillaume ____
53. "The Lone Ranger" star
54. Bouquet
55. Site of the Himalayas
56. Street fighter's weapon
57. Employer
58. Writer Grey
59. Eccentric
60. Temperate or Torrid

PUZZLE 164

CATEGORIES

For each of the categories listed, can you think of a word or phrase beginning with each letter on the left? Count one point for each correct answer. A score of 15 is good, and 21 is excellent.

	TV SHOW HOSTS	TOOLS	ANIMALS	SENATORS	RIVERS
M					
A					
R					
C					
H					

PUZZLE 165

ACROSS
1. Mischievous ones
5. Treaty
9. School org.
12. "Quantum ____"
13. Singer Guthrie
14. Tanker cargo
15. Juan's room
16. Time limit
18. Actor Baldwin
19. Mommy's mate
20. Sense of self
22. Egg parts
26. Tattler
29. Tooth-ailment symptom
32. Tidy
33. British rock gp.
34. Economize
36. ____ carte
37. Dutch cheese
39. Blend
40. Lock opener
41. Lost color
43. Distress letters
45. Marcel Marceau and others
48. Wedding dessert
52. Farewell
55. Taken by mouth
56. Slippery surface
57. Islamic prince
58. Actress Moreno
59. Ink stick
60. Disclaim
61. First garden

DOWN
1. Ingrid Bergman role
2. Feast
3. Faintly colored
4. ____ shuttle
5. Horse enclosures
6. Neighborhood
7. Dressed
8. Spiced drink
9. Hawaiian dish
10. Kind of foil
11. Tavern offering
17. French city
21. Fuel
23. Faucet problem
24. Cabbage
25. Remain
26. Nautical hazard
27. "M*A*S*H" star
28. Frog's kin
30. Successful song
31. Delegate
35. Paid athlete
38. Written reminder
42. Had supper
44. Get a touchdown
46. Broadway auntie
47. ____ go bragh!
49. Hot and dry
50. Actress Jackson
51. Pep
52. Drink slowly
53. Certain pilot
54. Craving

PUZZLE 166

ACROSS
1. Contend
5. Read quickly
9. Become mature
12. Summit
13. Yield
14. Gentle bear
15. Withered
16. Supported
18. Competitor
20. Forget-me-____
21. Shady plants
23. Horse's gait
26. Curved
29. Rodent
31. Pub fare
32. Rarely
34. Fred Astaire, e.g.
36. Compass dir.
37. Mr. Van Winkle
39. Majorette's wand
40. Doc Bricker of "The Love Boat"
42. Contributor
44. Male sheep
46. Request again
50. Indoctrinate
53. Elaborate solo
54. Swindle
55. Garbed
56. Waterproof covering
57. Easter-basket item
58. Friendly nation
59. Meadow mamas

DOWN
1. Container
2. Unlocked
3. Sassy
4. Strained
5. Setting
6. Core
7. Tack on
8. Sign gas
9. Theoretical
10. ____ whiz!
11. Complete
17. Decay
19. Zeal
22. Melancholy
24. Bread topper
25. Aquatic bird
26. On the ocean
27. Tear apart
28. Treeless area
30. Forbidden
33. Term or night starter
35. Relate
38. Door
41. Welcome item
43. Wanting
45. Certain mineral
47. Sketch
48. Emerald Isle
49. Sharp knocks
50. Decorate with frosting
51. Yuletide drink
52. Totally

129

PUZZLE 167

ACROSS

1. Show approval
5. Designer Bill ____
10. Race position
14. Filament
15. Indian ruler
16. Exclude
17. Area measure
18. Bustling
19. Occupying two positions
20. Deference
22. Usual
24. Impress
25. Push back
26. All-inclusive
30. Authorize
34. Rent
35. Long time
36. Bottled up
37. Affiliation
38. Coronas
41. Joke
42. Wipe out
44. Baseball stat
45. Stance
46. Porter
48. Breaks
50. Particles
52. Mariner
53. Seal again
56. Atonement
60. Lackluster
61. Taste
63. Fictional mansion
64. Speck
65. Matriculate
66. "____ Since Venus"
67. Beginning
68. Anecdote
69. Stitches

DOWN

1. Scorch
2. Cord
3. Melodies
4. Make ready
5. Piece of jewelry
6. Final
7. Pismire
8. Net
9. Mexican shawl
10. Fashionable
11. Poet Khayyam
12. Turkish money
13. And others: abbr.
21. Ram's mate
23. Yurt and tepee
25. New York players
26. Complete
27. Watery silk
28. Dinero
29. Card game with forfeits
31. Sired
32. Rental term
33. Borders
38. Pacific pact: abbr.
39. Rage
40. Kind of wind
43. Burned
45. Corsairs
47. Search groups
49. Forty-niner's aid
51. Intended
53. St. Louis team
54. Clinton's canal
55. Refer to
56. "____ Little Rich Girl"
57. Church section
58. Sport with shells
59. All ____ (interested)
62. Favoring

PUZZLE 168

FOURSOMES

In each puzzle the letters have a different numerical value from 1 to 9. Four sums of combinations of four letters are indicated by the arrows. For example, 23 is the sum of the values of the letters W, I, L, and R. Find the values of the letters and place them on the correspondingly numbered blanks to spell a word or phrase. The center letter is entered to start you off.

1.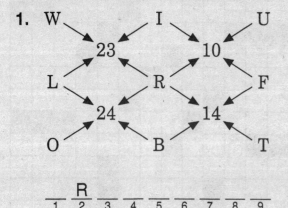

2.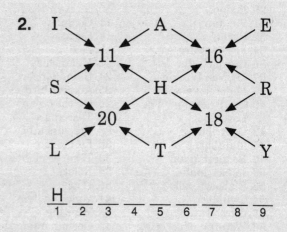

130

PUZZLE 169

ACROSS
1. Reverence
4. Quarterback's forte
8. Charter
12. Loose
13. Island farewell
15. Hearsay
16. Tongue part
17. "M*A*S*H" character
18. Broadway whisper
19. Perpetually
21. Bank container
22. Song
23. Heirloom
25. Tedious
27. Seed vessel
29. Charge
34. Morsel
37. Loss
41. Opinion
42. Active person
44. Debonair
45. Hideaways
46. Margarine
47. Mean
49. Society-page word
50. Represent
52. Cravat
54. Permit
58. Stags, e.g.
62. Bean dish
66. Light bender
68. Incline
69. Secured
70. Craze
72. Affirmative vote
73. Expiate
74. Shocks
75. Goof
76. Fender nick
77. Hindu sect member
78. New York town

DOWN
1. Change
2. Sacrifice
3. Banish
4. ___ excellence
5. Alack!
6. Pops
7. Roundtree movie
8. Trick
9. Descendant of Muhammad
10. Agrees
11. Redwood, for one
14. Vicinity
15. Composer Maurice ___
20. Rend
24. Massachusetts cape
26. Dormant
28. Covet
30. Plug
31. Idyllic garden
32. Actor Hackman
33. Recede
34. Smell
35. Part
36. "___ Wolf"
38. Diversion
39. Devour
40. Hail!
43. Reel's partner
48. Faint
51. Ignore
53. Cup handle
55. Charity
56. Benches
57. Apathy
59. Cake feature
60. Kind of board
61. Bowling term
62. Clothed
63. Dislike
64. Image
65. Pre-Easter period
67. Kitchen feature
71. Burnt wood

Codebreaker
PUZZLE 170

Each group of five letters is a word in a simple substitution code. The same code is used throughout. The clue next to each group gives you one of the real letters. The ten clues give you the ten letters used to form all the words. As a starter we'll tell you that H stands for O in all words.

1. F W M V T — one letter is K
2. G V Q W M — one letter is I
3. W H G V T — one letter is O
4. G V T W C — one letter is N
5. Z M Q V V — one letter is S
6. F V Q M T — one letter is L
7. Z H V Q C — one letter is D
8. V Q W T W — one letter is E
9. G V T Z Z — one letter is B
10. Z F G V T — one letter is A

131

PUZZLE 171

ACROSS
1. Boxes
6. Spaghetti, e.g.
11. Nun's wear
12. Olivier, for one
13. Game site
14. Form
15. Kitchen tool
17. Tape
20. Afternoon drink
23. ___ Jima
24. Of course!
26. Boy
27. Jewel
28. Actress Bernadette ___
30. Annoy
33. Shipping box
35. Excuse me!
39. Nobleman
40. Shun
41. Pay out
42. Unwanted plants

DOWN
1. ___ Na Na
2. Golfer's goal
3. Honest ___
4. One of the Beatles
5. Like some night skies
6. Ago
7. Pain
8. Surprise
9. Summit
10. "We ___ the World"
16. Skillful
17. Equip
18. Ram's mate
19. Liken
21. Hearing organ
22. Classified items
25. Teeterboard
29. Treasure ___
31. English school
32. Mail
33. TV network
34. Knock
36. Fish eggs
37. Free
38. Distance units: abbr.

PUZZLE 172

ACROSS
1. Mesh
4. James Beard, e.g.
8. Distribute
12. Rower's need
13. Hawkeye State
14. Rubbed out
15. Squirmed
17. Tow
18. Kind of flower, for short
19. Hesitate
20. Theater employee
22. "The Greatest"
23. Haul
24. View
29. Tavern fare
30. Recorded
31. ___ Allen Belt
32. Melon
34. Thread bits
35. ___ and downs
36. Charter
37. Steeple
40. Duke
41. Tall, in Tijuana
42. Noon, for instance
46. Chirp
47. Callas specialty
48. Hardwood
49. Identical
50. Soapstone
51. Named at birth

DOWN
1. Thrill
2. Cup handle
3. Illuminate
4. Havana nonpareil
5. Grip
6. Palindromic beast
7. Rage
8. Plane's milieu
9. Neutral hue
10. Social occasions
11. "Jagged ___"
16. Mirth
19. Trek
20. Provo's state
21. Song for Pavarotti
22. Once more
24. Mats
25. Imitate
26. Earhart's interest
27. Operates
28. Feed the kitty
30. Sort
33. Zurich's region
34. For fear that
36. Fragrant shrub
37. Depletes
38. Appeal
39. Part of a list
40. Go kaput
42. Floor cover
43. Division of time
44. Pearl ___ Bailey
45. Scratch (a living)

ACROSS

1. String or wax
5. Competitor
10. Attempt
14. Norwegian capital
15. In reserve
16. Wallach and Mintz
17. Consumer
18. Olympia's state
20. Canines, e.g.
22. Scottish refusal
23. Give a speech
24. Sharpens
26. Mold
27. Unexpected hit
30. Takes into custody
34. Tower
35. Nest locale
36. Tyke
37. ___ instant
38. Greek letter
40. ___ fide
41. ___ Vegas
42. Skidded
43. More malicious
45. Dealt with
47. Flirts
48. Melancholy
49. Handbag
50. Valuable violin
53. Mess up
54. Siskel's partner
58. School punishments
61. Maintain
62. Eros
63. Blacksmith's device
64. Vein of ore
65. Soaks
66. Tearful
67. In case

DOWN

1. Contest
2. Being, to Caesar
3. Away from the wind
4. "___ Exposure"
5. Noisy quarrel
6. More foolish
7. Passport permits
8. Suffer
9. Hawaiian necklace
10. Extent
11. Canadian province: abbr.
12. Tumult
13. Anglo-Saxon laborer
19. Bete ___
21. Aspire
25. Irritated
26. Idealist
27. Marsh bird
28. Of the moon
29. Wipe out
30. Singer Garfunkel
31. Rock
32. Copier powder
33. Celebrities
35. Danson of "Cheers"
39. Shrouded
40. "Field of Dreams" sport
42. Spot
44. Relax
46. Fall flowers
47. Rutabaga
49. Verify
50. Rehan and Clare
51. Office communique
52. On the summit
53. German article
55. Bacchanalian cry
56. Cincinnati team
57. Weight allowance
59. Playing marble
60. Sneaky

Piece by Piece

A humorous quotation has been divided into 3-letter pieces. Spaces between words have been eliminated. Rearrange the 3-letter pieces to reconstruct the quotation. The dashes indicate the number of letters in each word.

```
ESM  EYD  FAS  GOA  IDI  INL  ITD
MON  NOT  OES  RAS  RTA  SFA
TCE  TER  THO  UCH  UGH  YGO
```

T H O _ _ _   _ _ _ _ _ _   _ _ _ _ _ _

_ _   _ _   _ _ _ _   _ _ _ _ ,   _ _ _

_ _ _ _ _ _ _ _ _   _ _ _ _ _   _ _ _ _ _ _ _ .

PUZZLE 175

ACROSS

1. Greenish pear
5. Krupp works city
10. Early female soldier
14. Den
15. Animated
16. Sicilian resort
17. Conductor Klemperer
18. Hindu queen
19. These may be inflated
20. Children's song
23. Methods
24. River to the Seine
25. Maneuver a car
28. Entire range
31. Barrier
32. Seaman
34. Health club
37. Children's song
40. Grown boys
41. Moon valleys
42. Ruled mark
43. Biblical weeds
44. Goddesses of destiny
45. Booty
47. Secondhand
49. Children's song, with "The"
56. Verdi heroine
57. Maternally kin
58. Brainstorm
59. Let it stand
60. With weapons
61. Bird's home
62. Beginner
63. Ogles
64. Snick-or-____

DOWN

1. Ink stain
2. Imprecation
3. Location
4. Puritan statesman
5. Ahead of time
6. Thick slices
7. Trig ratio
8. Eternally
9. ____-do-well
10. Small amount
11. County in Scotland
12. Win by ____
13. Ready money
21. Nasser's gp.
22. "____ the Top"
25. '60s dance, with "The"
26. Domesticated
27. Verve
28. Fish lungs
29. Toward shelter
30. Witticisms
32. Agitate
33. Tamarisk
34. Barbecue rod
35. Corn cake
36. Sweetsop
38. Wrathful
39. ____ lamp
43. Love apple
44. Professional charge
45. Body of worshipers
46. Command
47. Say
48. Molts
49. Rapid
50. Genuine
51. Concerning
52. Title
53. Paradise
54. ____ majeste
55. Tardy

PUZZLE 176   Carry-Overs

Add and subtract letters from the ROOT WORDS to form answers to the CLUES. Start with the first ROOT WORD, subtract one letter, and rearrange the remaining letters to form the answer to the first CLUE. Carry over the letter you subtracted to the next line, add it to the second ROOT WORD, subtract the number of letters indicated, and rearrange the remaining letters to form the second answer. Continue solving in this way.

	ROOT WORDS		CLUES
1.	HORNET	−1= _____	(Something else)
2.	☐ + CORSAGE	−2= _____	(Motive)
3.	☐ ☐ + ENABLED	−3= _____	(Quick look)
4.	☐ ☐ ☐ + PURLOIN	−3= _____	(Constructor)
5.	☐ ☐ ☐ + SMITHY	−0= _____	(Mesmerism)

134

PUZZLE 177

ACROSS
1. Felon's flight
4. Agitate
8. Reviewer of books: abbr.
11. Queen ant in "B.C."
12. Undiluted
13. Bogus
14. Depressed
16. Starchy root
17. Instruct
18. More precious
20. Assembled
21. Child in "The Scarlet Letter"
22. Stop
24. Clamors
25. Pitcher's handle
28. Seed container
29. Impressionist
30. Haggard novel
31. Yeoman's yes
32. Ancient
33. Economist Smith
34. Some teeth
36. Guido's high note
37. County seat of Kerry
39. Jazzman Chick ____
42. Lagomorph
43. Tells
46. "Picnic" playwright
47. Wickedness
48. Corroded
49. Sault ____ Marie
50. Load
51. "____, though I walk through . . ."

DOWN
1. Tilt
2. Month after Shevat
3. "Tale of Two Cities" character
4. Expended
5. Cask
6. Rage
7. Blushed
8. "Tale of Two Cities" character
9. Clip
10. ____ patriae
13. Betelgeuse, e.g.
15. Per ____
19. Sunrise spot
21. Longs
22. Evian, e.g.
23. Whirligig
24. Crude verse
26. Norwegian trio
27. Sleep stage: abbr.
29. Some horsehair
33. Baseball family name
35. To the sheltered side
36. School, in St. Louis
37. Now hear ____!
38. Upbraid
40. Diminutive ending
41. Cruising
44. Model Herzigova
45. El ____

PUZZLE 178

ACROSS
1. TV spots
4. Oodles
8. "And ____ There Were None"
12. Buzzer
13. Kirghiz range
14. Latest fad
15. Wailer's formal dance?
17. Persuade
18. Bert's buddy
19. Shut
21. Foxy
23. Anesthetic gas
26. Shoe adjunct
29. Washstand item
32. Fit ____ fiddle
33. Fruity refreshers
34. Tire filler
35. Basin
36. Escort frequently
37. Energy units
38. Algonquin
39. Spud
41. Seaman
43. Cab clients
46. Simpleton
50. Horned animal
52. Nude grizzly?
54. Economist Greenspan
55. Radarscope signal
56. Cuckoo
57. Flying mammals
58. At once, to Dr. Kildare
59. Ball holder

DOWN
1. French priest
2. Letter opener
3. Stitched
4. Designer tag
5. Palm leaf
6. Grey-green mineral
7. Place for a window garden
8. Have faith in
9. Bunny's coat?
10. Goad
11. Born
16. Rosters
20. Above, to a bard
22. Interval between birthdays
24. Slave of yore
25. Strafe
26. Culminating
27. Brainstorm
28. Tootsies' act?
30. Pate topper
31. Once, once
35. Cancel, to an astronaut
37. Bobble
40. Brings home the bacon
42. Skilled
44. Wanes
45. Shaker's contents
47. Orderly
48. Bamboo stem
49. Border lake
50. Smidgen
51. Highest note
53. Narrow inlet

PUZZLE 179

ACROSS

1. Game with irons
5. Press down
9. Eban
13. Deceiver
14. Stair part
15. Street
16. Easily, in sesquipedalian style, with 34 and 52 Across
19. Use henna
20. Billow-borne
21. Saws wood
22. Dancer Astaire
23. Twirl
24. Parsley units
27. Dele not
28. Spanish cheer
31. Unsupported
32. Omnia vincit ____
33. Asian river
34. See 16 Across
37. Son of Seth
38. Mark
39. Toot
40. Sunday talk: abbr.
41. Electrify
42. Mounted trooper
43. Plunge
44. Join in the chorus
45. Blame
48. Urban blight
49. Gardening tool
52. See 16 Across
55. Actor Estrada
56. Pan-fry
57. Makes mistakes
58. Assistants: abbr.
59. Finishes
60. Comfort

DOWN

1. Elated
2. Unctuous
3. Delayed
4. Part of TGIF: abbr.
5. ____ over (helped for a while)
6. Tashkent's continent
7. Guys
8. Ariel's master
9. Pyromaniac's crime
10. Tusker
11. Bad thing
12. Tots up
14. Tricks
17. Aim
18. Least positive integer
22. The end
23. Garnet or ruby
24. Mall come-ons
25. Jet
26. Copter feature
27. Thwack
28. Simian, for short
29. Actress Hope
30. Church VIP
32. Really go for
33. Exploiting
35. Cosmos
36. Uele-Bomu junction
41. Desire
42. ____ Janeiro
43. Quackers
44. South African statesman
45. Mirrored
46. Panacea
47. Snip
48. Five-card ____
49. Spanish hour
50. Belonging to us
51. Latin being
53. Singer Janis
54. Born

PUZZLE 180

ANAGRAMS PLUS

Find ten government terms by adding one of the letters below to each word and rearranging all the letters. Each letter will be used only once. For example, STOVE + E becomes VETOES.

A C D E E E N T T U

1. ANTES + ? __ __ __ __ __ __
2. TYPED + ? __ __ __ __ __ __
3. CREED + ? __ __ __ __ __ __
4. ELDER + ? __ __ __ __ __ __
5. GROVE + ? __ __ __ __ __ __

6. CORER + ? __ __ __ __ __ __
7. SEERS + ? __ __ __ __ __ __
8. ROPER + ? __ __ __ __ __ __
9. TEARY + ? __ __ __ __ __ __
10. GRIME + ? __ __ __ __ __ __

136

DOUBLE TROUBLE

PUZZLE 181

Not really Double Trouble, but double fun! Solve this puzzle as you would a regular crossword, EXCEPT place one, two, or three letters in each box. The number of letters in each answer is shown in parentheses after its clue.

ACROSS

1. Sleeveless jacket (6)
4. Surfaced a road (5)
7. Of that kind (4)
9. Permission (8)
11. Flavorful (5)
12. Danger (5)
13. Swerved (6)
14. Refrigerate (5)
15. Purify (6)
16. Spew lava (5)
18. Shrewd (6)
20. Bend (4)
22. Young hooter (5)
24. Meeting schedule (6)
26. Unlock (4)
27. Ladies' companions (9)
29. Goal (3)
30. Bearlike (6)
32. Rub out (5)
33. Ripped (4)
34. Small map feature (5)
36. Inside information (4)
38. Affectionate (6)
39. Corner (5)
41. White water (6)
45. Coagulate (3)
46. Postpone (6)
47. Windstorm (7)
48. Frigid (3)
49. Zeal (5)
50. Guided trip (4)

DOWN

1. Make cloth (5)
2. Boat commander (7)
3. Valuable collection (5)
4. Sweater sleeve reinforcement (5)
5. Ice cream flavor (7)
6. Nervous (4)
7. Foreman (14)
8. Neighbor of Argentina (5)
10. Birch (5)
15. Haven (6)
17. City residential area (6)
19. Pollen source (6)
20. Milled wheat (5)
21. In a lavish way (11)
23. Epistle (6)
25. Decorate (5)
27. Honking birds (5)
28. Chartered (6)
31. Baseball division (6)
35. Citrus hybrid (7)
37. Telephone exchange worker (8)
38. Sound reasoning (5)
40. Crowbar (5)
42. Half quart (4)
43. Bottom section of a room wall (4)
44. Tart (4)
46. Pottery fragment (5)

(crossword grid with numbered cells 1–50)

Categories

PUZZLE 182

For each of the Categories listed can you think of a word or phrase beginning with each letter on the left? Count one point for each correct answer. A score of 15 is good, and 21 is excellent.

	NECKWEAR	SEATS	TIMEPIECES	CONDIMENTS	COUNTRIES
S					
M					
A					
R					
T					

PUZZLE 183

ACROSS
1. Harvest
5. Seed container
8. Cabbage salad
12. Utah ski resort
13. Anger
14. Great affection
15. Fasten securely
16. Knock
17. River of Germany
18. African antelope
20. "The ___ Strikes Back"
22. Little bed
23. Pinch
24. Remove
27. Ohio city
31. Hail, Caesar!
32. Epoch
33. Polite answer
37. Actor Poitier
40. Lyricist Gershwin
41. Consumed
42. Liquor containers
45. Settle a question
49. Rave
50. Owned
52. Greek war god
53. Sea eagle
54. Lamb's mom
55. Mom's admonition
56. Row
57. Raced
58. Grafted, in heraldry

DOWN
1. Hindu princess
2. Biblical kingdom
3. Eager
4. Queen's home
5. Brigand
6. ___ pro nobis
7. Rely
8. Messy
9. New Jersey city
10. State positively
11. "The Way We ___"
19. Place for a house
21. Actress Farrow
24. Dennis or Doris
25. "All About ___"
26. Bandleader Brown
28. Perfect score
29. Mine find
30. Senate vote
34. Nun
35. Annoy
36. Slice of bacon
37. Depress
38. Follower: suff.
39. Group of 10 years
42. Worry
43. Hook money
44. Actress Bancroft
46. Press
47. Fender problem
48. Villa d'___
51. Not at home, to a Scot

PUZZLE 184

ACROSS
1. Fuel
4. Remain
8. Musical symbol
12. Likely
13. In good health
14. Pit
15. Golly!
16. Uncomfortable
18. Window glass
20. Walk through water
21. Splendor
23. Applaud
25. "Charley's ___"
26. Leg bone
27. Tonic's partner
30. Hit the slopes
31. Smarted
32. Lyric poem
33. Favorite
34. Rabbit's cousin
35. Pack away
36. Flowerless plant
37. Ninnies
38. Lounge lazily
40. Pocket fuzz
41. Tease
44. "The ___ Couple"
47. Land measurement
48. Arrange
49. Court
50. Tidy
51. Singer Nelson ___
52. Seine

DOWN
1. Joke
2. Mimic
3. Hurry!
4. Glossy
5. Story
6. Everything
7. Biblical affirmative
8. Tawdry
9. Burden
10. Otherwise
11. Charge
17. Nasal sound
19. Painting, e.g.
21. Pant
22. Gospel writer
23. Butter maker
24. Spiel
26. Headliner
27. Do speedily
28. Heathen god
29. TV offering
31. Ledge
35. Male offspring
36. Swift
37. Number of states
38. Shoestring
39. Soup veggie
40. Actor Jack ___
41. Male
42. Employ
43. Bow the head
45. Female deer
46. Period

PUZZLE 185

ACROSS
1. House wing
4. Hot springs
8. Run away to wed
13. "Old Dog ___"
14. Heart of the matter
15. Wanders
16. Encourage
17. Soothing plant
18. Open
19. Honey or spelling
20. Subordinate
22. Use a van
25. Society-page word
26. Tree-held nurseries
29. Totaled
33. Kind of writing
36. Water jug
38. First person
40. Peel
41. Kick up one's ___
42. Anger
43. Featured player
44. Singles
45. Up to the time when
46. Change
48. Twit
50. Unrefined
52. Detection device
55. Shape anew
60. Show agreement
62. Centers
63. Songstress Adams
64. Lug
65. Make a neat row of
66. Slippery swimmers
67. Worshipped one
68. Great actions
69. Highland miss
70. For each

DOWN
1. Went wrong
2. Kind of beer
3. Soap ingredient
4. Black suit
5. Heap
6. On
7. Gloss
8. Worn down
9. Adore
10. Baker's need
11. Sassy
12. Id ___
13. Vat
21. Approaches
23. Loose magazine ad
24. Victory sign
27. High-schooler
28. Saccharine
30. Mended
31. Emend
32. Surrealist painter
33. Second added note: abbr.
34. Pro ___
35. Spoken
37. Otherwise
39. Comedian Brooks
41. Mideast dances
45. "Born in the ___"
47. Scratches out
49. "Gunsmoke" actor
51. "___ of Fortune"
53. Positive pole
54. Helicopter part
55. Stage part
56. Pennsylvania port
57. Ward off
58. Thought
59. Some paintings
61. First State: abbr.
62. Bounder
64. Gratuity

Spinwheel   PUZZLE 186

This game works two ways, outward and inward. Place the answers to the clues in the diagram beginning at the corresponding numbers.

OUTWARD
1. Engrossed
3. Small wagons
4. Whalebone
6. Lamp fuel
8. Sea bird
9. Snooze
11. Impair

INWARD
12. Sloping way
10. TV equipment
8. Chromosome units
7. Native metal
6. Genuflect
5. Kind of art
2. Average

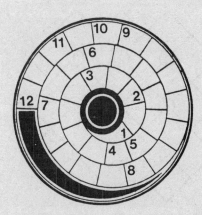

PUZZLE 187

ACROSS

1. Study hard
5. Pluckier
10. Indonesian island
14. "___ Man"
15. Wide open
16. Thunderstruck
17. Norse god
18. Talk-show host Philbin
19. Magician's rod
20. Disputes
23. Bring to court
24. Swine
25. Quarterback, at times
27. Make lace
30. Congeal
32. Ilk
33. Wed
35. Type of saxophone
37. Singer Redding
41. Settle one's uncertainty about
44. Tinged
45. Middle Eastern bread
46. Uptight
47. Hemsley series
49. Conflict
51. Abraham Lincoln's son
52. Take one's place, militarily
55. "My country, ___ of thee . . ."
57. "___ to Billy Joe"
58. Verbal controversy
65. Holly of folk music
67. Cacophony
68. Swenson of "Benson"
69. Miami county
70. Red, in heraldry
71. Bulblike base
72. In addition
73. Frozen rain
74. ___-jerk reaction

DOWN

1. Gator's kin
2. Change
3. Hear ___ drop
4. Year unit
5. Carport's relative
6. Like some cheese
7. Biblical trio
8. Heroic
9. Fonzie's "office"
10. Chat
11. Flooded
12. Scene
13. Common viper
21. Thesaurus man
22. Big ___, California
26. "Uncle Tom's Cabin" author
27. Film-crew member
28. Matty of baseball
29. Large volume
31. Italic language
32. Berry beginning
34. Bicycle part
36. Tennis call
38. Shade
39. ___ girl!
40. Shelter
42. Pores
43. Narrow groove
48. Center
50. Certify
52. "Easy Rider" star
53. Cut ___ (agree)
54. Starring roles
56. Pole
59. Actor/singer David ___
60. Heap
61. Certain plaintiff
62. Privy to
63. Monster
64. Moniker
66. Classic auto

PUZZLE 188   NINE OF DIAMONDS

Fill the small diamonds in the diagram with the 2-letter pieces in the box to form the answers to the clues. All answer words have eight letters and read clockwise around the corresponding number. Words overlap in the diagram so that a 2-letter piece may be used in more than one word.

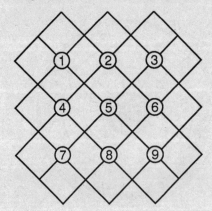

AB	AD	AN	CA	CA	CI	DE	DO
ED	ED	GI	LE	LI	MA	ME	MI
NT	OW	RE	RE	RE	RK	SH	TE

1. Fragile
2. Trusty
3. Abode
4. Disavowed
5. Corps
6. Illusionist
7. Trailed
8. Fine wool
9. Commented

PUZZLE 189

ACROSS
1. Sociologist Mannheim
5. Purpose
9. Russian jet
12. Pen name for Lamb
13. Heroic poetry
14. Metal-bearing rock
15. Shout wildly
16. Air outlet
17. Grand Coulee, e.g.
18. Famous nurse
21. Relieves
22. Therefore
25. Title of respect
28. Directed
29. Small ducks
30. Deteriorates
32. Door
33. Morning garments
34. Bad review
35. Tokyo, formerly
36. Indigo
37. Fashion town
39. Evening classes
44. Paid notices
46. Newspaper section, for short
47. Grimm character
48. Cote sound
49. Soon
50. City blueprint
51. Finger count
52. Hungers
53. Forwarded

DOWN
1. "Show Boat" songwriter
2. Asian mountain range
3. Wedding purchase
4. Turning tool
5. Amends
6. Began
7. Huey and Earl
8. This, in Tampico
9. Mild
10. Ethan Allen's brother
11. Valuable stone
19. Stories
20. Grimace
23. Pleased
24. Norwegian capital
25. Evening, to Antonio
26. Inflexible
27. Basketball's David ____
29. Quinine water
31. Pastrami seller
32. Clergymen
34. World War II general
37. Call
38. Goes bargain-hunting
40. Dreary
41. Eye
42. Algerian department
43. Latvian
44. Exploit
45. Female ruminant

PUZZLE 190

ACROSS
1. Vehicle for hire
4. Geologic periods
8. Rogue
11. In the style of
12. Expansive
13. Breezy
14. Molasses liquor
15. Impersonator
16. French cheese
17. Fix into a surface
19. Palms
21. Due
23. South African archbishop
24. Healing plant
26. Mideastern nation
28. Small rug
31. Egyptian cap
32. Kansas river
33. Compete
34. Sesame
35. Bony beginning
36. Hawk
37. Shore bird
39. Ignoble
41. Certain gong
43. Students' study materials
46. Curved arch
47. Spoiled kid
50. Author Levin
51. Quills
52. Veil material
53. Salad dressing ingredient
54. Ready
55. Pitcher
56. Monarch catcher

DOWN
1. Concern
2. Styptic
3. Trickery
4. Dodge
5. Chat
6. Peer Gynt's mother
7. Scheme
8. Avoidance
9. Soprano's solo
10. Colors
13. Support a felon
18. Pasture parent
20. Ancient letter
22. Feign
24. Nautical direction
25. Waikiki wreath
27. Large rodent
29. Feel poorly
30. ____ Aviv
32. Eugene O'Neill's daughter
36. ____ Paulo
38. Map abbrs.
40. Come in
41. Betters
42. "A Death in the Family" author
44. Buffalo's canal
45. NaCl
48. Unrefined
49. Master

PUZZLE 191

• ICE BREAKING •

ACROSS
1. Doctor's beeper
6. One Waugh
10. Masculine
14. Straighten
15. Zhivago's love
16. Basic Latin word
17. 30 Across quote, with 64 Across
20. Birthright seller
21. Tofu source
22. Stage whisper
23. Zodiac symbol
25. "____ Lay Dying"
27. Fulcrum adjunct
30. Author of quote
36. 1968 Christopher Lee film
37. Incentive
39. Detroit product
40. Ange's motive power
42. Princess of Wales
43. Less than a gallop
44. Tennis's Smith
45. Profession
47. Wonder
48. Source of quote
50. Fishing basket
52. Addams Family cousin
53. ____ Paulo
54. Amulet
58. Ending for a believer
60. Heroic narrative
64. See 17 Across
68. Wake-robin
69. Parisian suburb
70. One form of pollution
71. ____ tide
72. Fast-growing problem
73. Change for a dollar

DOWN
1. Walk back and forth
2. Cry of despair
3. Ms. Lollobrigida
4. Last
5. Ferdinand, for one
6. In addition
7. Previous title for 42 Across
8. Time period
9. Give the boot
10. Former Giant
11. Both: prefix
12. Praise
13. Villa d'____
18. Doctrine
19. Hammett's "The ____ Curse"
24. Circle segment
25. Beautiful youth
26. Bristles
27. Dog-collar extension
28. Weber-Rice musical
29. Of the soft palate
30. East
31. Fireplace structure
32. "King" Cole
33. Charged atmospheres
34. Legree's creator
35. "Monopoly" purchase
38. Own up
41. Grid position
46. TV letters
49. VIP's transport
51. Tanner of tennis
53. Alphabetical name
54. Sect
55. Employ
56. Blue-green
57. Roast variety
58. Capri or Man
59. Carpet meas.
61. Related
62. Daring deed
63. Bellicose deity
65. Popular-round starter
66. Anger
67. Biz abbr.

PUZZLE 192   Math Maze

Find your way through each math maze. Start at the top arrow and move through the boxes, across and down, but never diagonally, to the arrow at the bottom so that the sum of the numbers in the boxes will equal the total shown.

1.

1	2	1	4	6
7	7	3	1	5
9	2	4	8	1
3	4	1	2	7
6	6	2	1	2

27

2.

7	1	4	6	3
9	2	1	5	8
4	6	6	1	7
5	2	4	9	3
5	4	8	1	1

49

PUZZLE 193

• IT'S MYSTERIOUS •

ACROSS
1. Ledger word
6. Draws up
10. ____ Le Pew
14. Mountain ridge
15. Smell ____: 2 wds.
16. John to Glinka
17. Christie creation: 2 wds.
19. Take it easy
20. USN rank
21. Rainbow maker
22. French menu
23. Greek letter
24. Substance
25. Mystery writers' awards
28. Profitable
30. Shoots the breeze
31. Pre-1917 ruler
32. Moslem Gnostic
36. Nautical term
37. Sierra resort
38. Poetic cavern
39. Sly look
40. Riviera summers
41. Counterfeit
42. ____ clear of
44. Queen of mystery
45. Robespierre's foe
48. Hatfield-McCoy affair
49. Portuguese city
50. Pitfall
52. Wing
55. Trevi coins
56. Poe adventure: 3 wds.
58. Theater section
59. Rajah's wife
60. Stadium
61. Dill herb
62. Church corner
63. Director William

DOWN
1. Title for Agatha
2. Mavourneen's home
3. Good Queen ____
4. Possessive
5. Moderates
6. Black ____
7. Dadaist Jean and family
8. Pilfer
9. Canonized Frenchwoman: abbr.
10. Certain hidden treasure: 2 wds.
11. Turn outward
12. Sock
13. Go in
18. Liberal or manual
22. Bullet-size abbr.
23. ____ Irregulars: 2 wds.
24. Get stuck
25. Handy abbr.
26. Valley
27. Exultation
28. Poe's house
29. Pueblo art colony
31. "Soap" name
33. Press
34. Freedoms number
35. Bitsy's pal
37. High-schooler
41. Passe enactment: 2 wds.
43. ____ man: 2 wds.
44. Saarinen
45. Perry's secretary
46. Par ____
47. Norway in Norway
48. Oliver's "teacher"
50. Phony
51. Aloha State bird
52. Actor Walter
53. "Clair de ____"
54. Culture medium
56. Singing syllable
57. Like a bone

CRYPTO-LIMERICK

PUZZLE 194

To read this humorous verse, you must first decode it as you would a regular cryptogram.

BASIS FOR OK GXZ RGXZPSI GN YPRBSI

FSKB FOXQPKC GKS ZOV FPBA APR RPRBSI,

FASK O EGF OB GKS UGQS

BGRRSZ ASI PKBG OK GOQ

YSNGIS BAS GXZ CSKBXSJOK JPRRSZ ASI.

143

PUZZLE 195

• TAKE A LOOK •

ACROSS
1. "____ Dog" (Terhune): 2 wds.
5. Refrain word
8. WWII agency: abbr.
11. Netherlands Antilles island
13. Winter precipitation
15. Discussion group
17. Agree completely: 4 wds.
19. Ugly sight
21. Writer Hunter
22. Thong
23. Telescope ends
27. ____ the mark
30. Marconi's medium
31. Tokyo, formerly
34. "____ Wednesday"
35. Inventor Whitney
38. French city
41. Hither, thither, and ____

42. Follower: suffix
43. Still
44. Actor Majors
46. Lamb's mother
47. Signs
49. Danny and Sammy
51. "____ Joey"
52. Ordinal number suffix
53. Omit in pronunciation
56. Oklahoma city
58. Neat as a ____
60. Accomplished
61. "The Hairy ____" (O'Neill)
62. Pop
65. Dublin's land: abbr.
66. Put on (a show)
71. Wrestling surface
72. Iron source
73. Sailor

74. Swamps
76. Triumph
77. Flirts bat them
81. Order one's attire
83. War god
85. Fascinating sights
88. Revenge formula, with "An": 4 wds.
95. Therefore
96. 27th President and kin
97. Mideast currency
98. Droop
99. Likely
100. Take it very easy

DOWN
1. ____ Vegas
2. Exist
3. Postage ____
4. Lincoln's nickname
5. Golf locale
6. King, in Madrid
7. Broke a fast
8. Artist Yoko
9. ____ annum
10. "Cakes and ____" (Maugham)

12. Nautical affirmative
13. Corset item
14. Hermit
15. Shade of green
16. Cleo's snake
18. Actress Arden
19. Summer, to Simone
20. Lunar and leap: abbr.
22. Glasgow native
24. Swing a camera
25. "Apple Cider" girl
26. German article
27. Skater Babilonia
28. Canadian province: abbr.
29. Enlightening event: 2 wds.
31. Cosmetic: 2 wds.
32. ____-Jones average
33. Indefinite pronoun
35. Place for 31 Down
36. Writer Deighton
37. "____ a Living"
39. Moose's cousin
40. Body of water
45. Grommet
48. ____ de mer
50. French "ands"
54. Apart: prefix
55. Summer hrs. in NYC: abbr.
56. Highland hat
57. ____ tree (trapped): 2 wds.
58. Peach stone
59. Lyricist Gershwin
63. "Exodus" hero
64. Lair
67. Prayer finale
68. Actor Gerard
69. Historic time
70. ____ Plaines, Ill.
75. Richard Roundtree film
77. Moray
78. ____ sirree!
79. Love god
80. Sunday lecture: abbr.
81. Rank under Cpl.: abbr.
82. Regret
84. Blue
85. Inquiring interjections
86. Pro vote
87. School subject: abbr.
88. Greek letter
89. Bark shrilly
90. Newt
91. Zero
92. 20th-century Spanish queen
93. Famous Red Sox player, for short
94. Before, to Blake

PUZZLE 196

ACROSS
1. Arizona tribe
5. Supports
10. ___ vera
14. Irish island
15. Dry as ___
16. Actor Lugosi
17. Male deer
18. "It's ___" (Presley song)
20. Reaction to pollen
22. Warn
23. Makes mad
24. Edge around
25. Flight part
27. London suburb
28. Navigation device
32. Official bulletin
35. Make over
36. Chopper
37. Inherent
39. Entangle
40. Scourge of serge
42. TV reflection
44. Fed the pot
46. River island
47. Exposed
48. Stadium
50. Migration
51. Precious gem
54. ___ tell
57. Cole Porter musical

59. Ancestor of the Hebrews
60. Inner: pref.
61. Pope's headdress
62. Blackthorn
63. Actor Martin
64. Foolish
65. Look after

DOWN
1. Laughing sound
2. Unwritten
3. British government
4. Meantime
5. Forehead fringes
6. It's ___!
7. Heifer
8. Sausage type
9. Caravansary
10. Criminal's aide
11. Jacob's son
12. Dairy-case item
13. Merit
19. Button decoration
21. Summer TV offering
24. Redwood
25. La ___, Milan
26. Poison
27. Friends and relatives
29. Outstanding
30. Old saying

31. Well-known
33. Find fault
34. Sup
38. Book, in Barcelona
41. "___ My Pillow" (Little Anthony hit)
43. Life jacket
45. Short snort
49. Varnish resin

50. "Over ___" (Berlin title)
51. Made with difficulty
52. Pit
53. This, in Toledo

54. British gun
55. Sign gas
56. Slave Scott
58. ___ loss

LETTER TILES

PUZZLE 197

Can you fit these 8 letter tiles into the diagram to form 4 words reading across and 5 words reading down? In the example diagram we show how to fit 3 tiles together to form the words SAW, ONE, SO, AN, and WE.

Example:

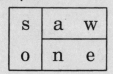

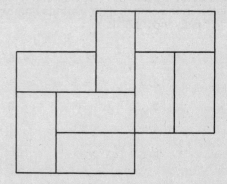

PUZZLE 198   Slant-A-Word

Words in the Slant-A-Word diagram start at the numbered squares and read Slanting Down (from upper left to lower right) and Straight Down (top to bottom). Some of the answers are 2-letter words. The first two answers have been placed in the diagram for you.

SLANTING DOWN
1. Ability
2. Cantaloupes
3. Made public
4. Written regulation
5. Billion: prefix
6. ____ and ruin
7. Ventilator
8. Very small
9. Caesar or Cato, e.g.
10. Pipe
11. Make lace
12. ____ Moto
13. Obliterate
15. Beast
16. Valuable violin
18. Narrate anew
19. French river
21. Cousin of inc.
22. Allow
24. Ave.
25. Oakland ____ (baseball team)
27. Tranquil
28. Of arteries
29. Cheerful
30. Gershwin
31. Epoch
32. Current abbr.
33. Exists
34. Ration
36. Arrested
37. Biceps band
38. Shrewdness
39. Daily log
41. Japanese or Thai
42. Memos
43. Clocks
46. Close
47. Famed tent expert
48. Unique person
50. Sea eagle
51. Board's mate
52. ____ de mer
54. Canadian prov.

STRAIGHT DOWN
1. Destructive insect
2. Deface
3. Lugosi
4. Cotton bundles
5. Actor Power
6. Become less adamant
7. Electrical measures
8. Large parrot
9. Skating arena
10. Weighty amount
11. Uproar
12. Horses' hairs
14. Let up
15. Newman role
17. Article of faith
20. Patriotic song
21. Along the side
23. Stories
24. Abalone's armor
26. Sick
27. Red or Sargasso
30. Silly
31. Author's aid
32. Graceful horse
35. Word used for another
37. Like Berg's music
38. Scribe
39. Not so bright
40. Dill seeds
42. Bedouin, e.g.
44. Cays
45. Headed
47. Sign of the future
49. Summer drinks
51. Tavern
53. Spoil

PUZZLE 199   Plus and Minus

Each group of letters below represents a 7-letter word. To "decode" them determine which letter is indicated by the "?." The remaining letters are represented by a plus number (which comes after the "?" letter in the alphabet) or a minus number (which comes before the "?" letter). For example, if "?" is F, then "-1" is E, and " + 5" is K.

1.	+ 4	+ 5	?	+ 3	−14	− 8	−10
2.	− 1	− 4	+ 9	+ 6	?	+10	+ 4
3.	− 8	+ 3	− 4	− 9	− 2	−13	?
4.	−21	?	−13	−21	− 2	− 7	− 4
5.	+11	+15	− 5	+ 6	+ 3	?	+19

THREE-D CROSSWORD

Here's a crossword with a third dimension! Each of the 3 faces (A,B, and C) is a crossword with words reading across and down. As you solve this puzzle, you'll see that some of the answers from one face continue on another face of the cube. Watch your ABC's, and you'll find that this is a real blockbuster!

A CLUES

ACROSS
1. ____ and arrow
4. Storage boxes
7. Blackbird
8. Motive
9. Crimson
10. Make angry
11. Build
13. Alcoves
16. Painful
19. Son of Jerahmeel
20. Selves
21. Ship's officer

DOWN
1. Uncovered
2. Outstanding person
3. Expansive
4. Greek island
5. Egg-layer
6. Hearing organ
12. Shape of some rolls
14. Tailed heavenly bodies
15. Rubs out
16. Plant grass
17. Beast
18. Muddy the water

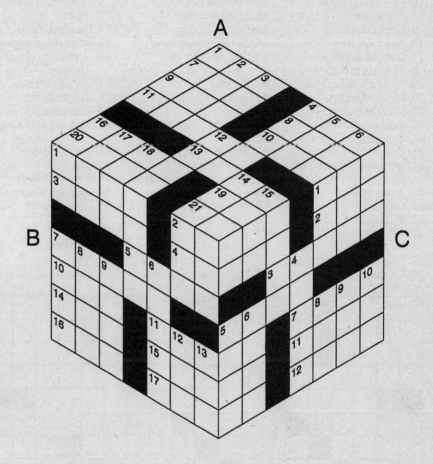

B CLUES

ACROSS
1. ____ the Red
2. Colorado's ____ Park
3. Take out
4. Adolescents
5. Loch ____ monster
7. Religious groups
10. Be indebted to
11. South American animal
14. Lair
15. Make happy
16. Actor Carney
17. Goes by car

DOWN
6. Chemical compound
7. Soft drink
8. Widemouthed jug
9. Small coin
12. The Greatest
13. Cushion

C CLUES

ACROSS
1. Wild donkey
2. Obtained
3. Levels
5. Common flower
7. Title
11. Egg-shaped
12. Olympian Spitz

DOWN
4. Snake poison
5. Ceremony
6. Mineral deposits
8. Actress Gardner
9. Disfigure
10. Antlered animal

PUZZLE 201

• JAZZ GREATS •

ACROSS

1. Sheet of quilt lining
5. Exclamations of discovery
9. Not of the cloth
13. Actor La Rue
17. Dairy-case buy
18. Electric measure
19. "Do ___ others . . ."
20. Singer Guthrie
21. Kind of party
22. Jazzman Duke
24. Los Angeles hazard
25. Gaunt
27. Comedian Louis and kin
28. Armor plates
30. Charity
31. Middle and old
32. Set fire to again
33. Lays open
35. Printer's instruction
36. Cakes and pies
39. Finishes
40. Destitute
41. Spotted pony
42. Mine output
43. Compass dir.
44. Bivalve mollusk
45. Slender sticks
46. On bended ___
47. Cougar
49. Tender spots
50. Bet
51. Narrow shoe width
52. Closes
53. Summer objective
54. Very important
57. Chemical compounds
58. Little chickens
62. Savage Olympian god
63. Three's a ___
64. Dried up
65. Insect egg
66. Sesame plant
67. Important financier
68. "Upstairs, Downstairs" maid
69. Tipsy tower's site
70. Tethered
72. Nagger
73. Field or Ford
74. Give way
75. Singing range
76. Columnist Barrett
77. Exit
79. Baseball family name
80. Adds flavorings to
83. "Open the ___, Richard"
84. Jazz drummer
87. Singer Billy
88. Competent
89. At sixes and sevens
90. Univ. sports gp.
91. Wind indicator
92. Clement
93. Scout units
94. Eastern European
95. Looked over

DOWN

1. Nonsense!
2. Utah town
3. Jazz trombonist Jack
4. Switches
5. States
6. Hang on to
7. "___ My Sons"
8. Brandy cocktail
9. Downhill racers
10. Pants visitors
11. Japanese statesman
12. Bouts
13. TV dog
14. Satchmo
15. Blackthorn fruit
16. Sty residents
23. No, to Raisa
26. Mornings: abbr.
29. Too
31. Powerful mite
32. Tears
33. Toot
34. Teacher in Siam
35. Go aloft
36. Eats
37. Locust, for one
38. Crystal-gazer
40. Supplication
41. Elements
44. London cleaning lady
45. Is willing to
46. Philosopher Immanuel
48. New Mexico town
49. Demonstrated
50. Ebb
52. Hair restraint
53. Container weight
54. School subj.
55. Song for Sutherland
56. Jazzman Morton
57. Blundered
58. Defeat
59. Jazz songstress
60. "Gorillas in the ___"
61. Remain
63. New Mexico caverns
64. Medium
67. Busy insects
68. Comes back
69. Thoughtful
71. Arranged in ascending rows
72. Ruse
73. Big snake
75. Alan and Robert
76. Part of R & R, for short
77. Yellow cheese
78. Mongolian desert
79. Mideast gulf
80. Surgical mark
81. "___ But the Brave"
82. Vehicle for a husky
85. Purpose
86. Frozen water

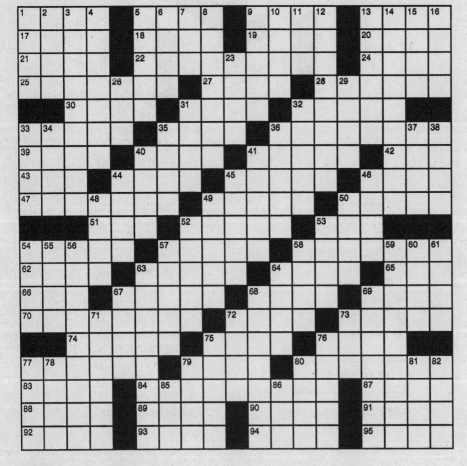

ACROSS

1. California mount
7. Word with well or way
12. Top-drawer
16. Condiment
17. Late, in Spain
18. Insect
20. "Waiter, there's a fly in my soup!" comeback, with 2 Down
22. Boxer's aide
24. Ecole counting word
25. Noted U.S. editor
26. Another comeback, with 14 Down
28. Vases
29. Pied ___
31. Percussion instruments
32. Stinger
33. Krazy ___
34. Like lawns
36. Compass pt.
37. Squalid
38. Socialist Bevan
40. Wed
42. 1980 DeLuise film
43. Ancient Syria
44. Began
45. Forlorn sound
46. Office problem
49. Teeny
50. Arthurian knight
53. Mouths: Latin
54. Made a bridge play
56. Bread spread
57. Saltpeter
59. Light tune
61. "I'm ___ cowhand . . ."
62. Nickname for a former Yankee star
64. French lass: abbr.
65. Maui salute
67. Ship's timber curve
68. Russian section
70. Succor
71. Inked
73. Franklin
74. North Atlantic sea
76. Move quickly
77. Most docile
79. Area: abbr.
80. Coolidge's veep
82. "I'm dreaming of ___ . . ."
83. He replaced Ruth
86. Iterated, as East
87. Ziegfeld
88. Importance
90. Social affair
91. Knievel
92. Simpletons
94. Eastern bigwigs
95. Autocrat
96. See 60 Down
99. Data: abbr.
100. Picasso
101. Used a dirk

102. See 51 Down
105. Raises
106. ___ Oro
107. Halts
108. Cradle call
109. Test answers, at times
110. Scope

DOWN

1. Highlander's wear
2. See 20 Across
3. Plant insect
4. Mineral springs
5. Eastern holiday
6. Noble steed
7. Tends the fire
8. Cross form
9. Chi-chi
10. Moron
11. Answered, in tennis
12. Rural sights
13. QED word
14. See 26 Across
15. Musical deficiencies
18. Day's march
19. Arrives at
20. Luftwaffe plane
21. Hits hard
23. Viscous
27. Fairy's rod
29. First, to Juanita
30. Picked up, as an option
34. Allow
35. Ate in style
37. Mesopotamian god
39. Actress Mary
41. Golf gadget
42. Iraqi coin
44. Donny or Marie
45. Winged fruit of the maple
46. Falana
47. Seed coats
48. Time of day
50. Most brave
51. Another comeback, with 102 Across
52. Fleur-___
55. Layer
56. Bowsprit extension
58. Alter
60. Another comeback, with 96 Across
62. Eating area
63. Building parts
66. Broadcast
68. Trailers, for short
69. Light-footed

72. Integers: abbr.
73. Scrooge's expletive
75. Inquire
77. Kind of building
78. Nautical distances
80. Give entirely, as time
81. Heloise's companion
82. Judd Hirsch's "Taxi" character
83. Exterior
84. Most genuine
85. Indian people of California
86. NL team
87. Supplies with
89. Metallic sound
92. Garbo
93. Pyle
95. Whip, in England
97. Alphabetic quartet
98. Biblical prophet
100. Land-site chart
103. Small fish
104. Barker of films

PUZZLE 202

• RIPOSTES •

149

PUZZLE 203

ACROSS

1. Humbug!
4. Bowlers, e.g.
8. Maude portrayer
11. Touches
15. Dill seed
17. Fail to include
18. Post
19. Away from the weather
20. Asta's owner
21. Prevalent
22. Cartoonist Peter ___
23. Ripped
24. Alighieri and Rossetti
26. Shelley character
29. Starflower
31. Coastal bird
32. Turn right
33. Jogged
35. Kite part
37. Retained
40. Comedian Johnson et al.
44. Scrap
45. South American mountain range
47. Cross
49. Waste away
50. Speck
52. Fiend
54. Acidic
56. Kansas City to Boston dir.
57. Helen's mother
58. Wedding bigwigs
60. Mountain moisture
61. Viper
62. Beige
64. Detach
66. Worthless coins
68. Fume
70. Omelet ingredient
72. Small finches
74. Totals
77. Flurry
78. Freud's concerns
80. Reigned
81. Ireland
82. Cherry middle
83. Votes for
85. Ponds
87. French season
88. Ensile
91. Dentist's command
93. Certain quantity
94. Resident: suff.
95. Dated
97. News director on "WKRP in Cincinnati"
99. Scenes
101. Some spies
107. Ship's kitchen
110. First name in mysteries
111. ___ Chaco (South American region)
112. Actor Alda
114. Venezuelan state
115. Winged
116. Descended
117. Comment
118. Indigo plant
119. Fasting period
120. Michael, to Kirk
121. Doe, e.g.
122. Actress Sandra ___

DOWN

1. Collaborate
2. Sulawesi ox
3. Spanish explorer
4. Colonial transportation
5. Pierre's friend
6. Skirmish
7. Cubic meter
8. Tree covering
9. One, in Berlin
10. Beside
11. Walk quickly
12. Bitter herb
13. Garr of films
14. Observed
16. Does needlework
18. Style
25. Sundance's girlfriend
27. Biblical craft
28. Baltic, e.g.
30. Addendum
33. "Camino ___"
34. Feed the kitty
36. Author Primo et al.
38. Vessel
39. Amphibian
41. Stevenson novel
42. Ages and ages
43. Pace
46. Teams
48. Chanel, e.g.
51. Singer Davis
53. Pry bar
55. Pair
59. Antitoxin
63. Ruff's mate
65. Provoked
67. Take advantage of
68. Cavities
69. Mine passage
71. "Anything ___"
73. Sleuth Wolfe et al.
75. Catcher's need
76. Snick's partner
79. Weaken
84. Noiseless
86. Bristlelike part
89. Poet Frost
90. Building wing
92. Perfect score, to Mary Lou
96. French Impressionist
98. Position
100. Fitzgerald of song
101. Transaction
102. Heraldic border
103. ___ Bator
104. "___ and Janis"
105. Obtain
106. Blackthorn fruit
108. Part of HOMES
109. Ivy League school
113. Goddess of recklessness

PUZZLE 204

• AND THEY'RE OFF! •

ACROSS
1. Brooklyn team
5. Trade
9. Medicine
13. Farm unit
17. Part of QED
18. Greek poet
20. Scene of action
21. Pigeon sounds
22. Over the entire course
24. Short whip
26. Pirate ship
27. Seductive women
29. Avaricious
30. Poverty
31. "___ Marner"
32. Mayday!
33. Increased
36. Surfaced
37. Hides
41. Country negatives
42. Triple Crown jockey
46. Chopper
47. Stain
48. Algonquian
49. Lager
50. Formerly
51. Nosh
52. River bend
56. Decree
57. Dances
60. Wild ox
61. Serves
62. Blaze
63. Portly
64. French coin, once
65. Vacuum tube
67. Chops down
68. Fish story
71. Safaris
72. Open contest
74. Group of seals
75. Olympic Games site
76. ___ butter
78. Church corner
79. Gyrate
80. ___ Plaines
81. Campaign opening
85. Queen of heaven
86. Mortified
88. More unusual
89. Folkways
90. FFV name
91. Lassoed
92. Little, e.g.
94. Cartridge replacement
97. Indian queen
98. Opening number
102. Boxer sharing a manager with another
104. Payroll clerk
106. Actress Garr
107. Chopper blade
108. Small drum
109. All-male
110. Roles
111. Observed
112. Skills
113. Fuss

DOWN
1. Current events
2. Sandusky's lake
3. Fictional plantation
4. Most severe
5. Push
6. Thrilled
7. Descendant of Mohammed
8. ___ diem
9. Nerds
10. Cincinnati team
11. One: prefix
12. Racketeer
13. Entry
14. Middle
15. Crucifix
16. Notice
19. Revive
20. Spanish fleet
23. Nailed on a slant
25. Complain
28. Writer Waugh
31. Is thrifty
33. Loose, as a gem
34. Fleshy fruit
35. Suspenseful outcome
36. Equals
37. Not he
38. Sports columnist
39. Outdo
40. Fortunetellers
42. Plot
43. Figure of speech
44. German submarine
45. Plumbing joint
50. Praying figure
53. Diner
54. Deceives
55. Dwelling
56. Ellipse
58. Pigeonholes
59. Youngsters
61. Actress Dahl
63. Young pig
64. Gem surface
65. Actress Bara
66. Decides a case
68. Daughter of David
69. Longest French river
70. Actress Best et al.
72. That woman
73. Stormed
76. Pittsburgh team
77. Possessed
79. Briefest
81. Aroma
82. Mangle
83. Scruff
84. Welcomes
87. Excuses
89. Simple
91. Boca ___
92. Ward off
93. Small dogs, for short
94. Q-V connectors
95. Summers: Fr.
96. Passenger
97. Criticize
98. Persian poet
99. Capable of
100. Interpret
101. Therefore
103. One of the Stooges
105. Actress Balin

PUZZLE 205

Diagramless crosswords are solved by using the clues and their numbers to fill in the answer words and the arrangement of black squares. Insert the number of each clue with the first letter of its answer, across and down. Fill in a black square at the end of each word. Every black square must have a corresponding black square on the opposite side of the diagram to form a diagonally symmetrical pattern.

ACROSS
1. Circle segment
4. Yellow jacket
8. Capacity
10. Rye, for one
12. Baby's cry
13. Matchless
14. Forsake
16. Function
17. Rickshaw
18. Suds
19. Kick
21. Uncovered
22. Element
23. Play by ___
24. Sea bird
25. Shelter
28. Pencil part
30. State of bliss
32. Payback
33. Columnist Barrett
34. Give out for a time
35. Swipe

DOWN
1. Supply
2. Thoroughfare
3. "___ Back to Me"
4. Departed
5. Actress Meyers
6. Continuation
7. Hesitated
9. Bringer of luck
10. Restrain
11. Evil look
15. Ingest
18. Figaro's profession
19. Drum
20. Opulent
21. Obstacle
22. Colleague
23. Attain
25. Throng
26. Aroma
27. Nevada city
29. Bask
31. Snatch

PUZZLE 206

ACROSS
1. Vat
4. Type of energy
6. Hold down
9. Bonus
10. Scent
12. Tune
13. Immediately
16. Singing star
17. Vehicle
19. Incensed
21. Edible grass
22. Complaisant
26. Crony
27. Singer Greenwood
28. Bradley and Marshall
30. Remote
32. Tyke
33. Speck
36. Give off
38. Hankering
40. Marsh
42. Swab
43. Excuse
45. Study
46. Jeopardy
47. Achieve

DOWN
1. Poisonous
2. Extreme
3. Exclude
4. Caspian, e.g.
5. Functioned
6. Seedcase
7. Buffoon
8. TV science program
11. Squeal
14. Egg dish
15. Roll of bills
18. Tether
20. Make wider
23. Embargo
24. Sniggler's prey
25. Refuge
28. Criticism
29. Singer Acuff
30. Small number
31. Surrounded by
34. Burning
35. Shortcoming
37. Gymnast's perfect score, once
39. Cloth surface
41. Void
44. Triangle side

152

ACROSS

1. "____ with the Stars" (TV quiz show)
4. Proofreader's mark
6. Pewter mug with a lid
8. Clutched
9. Unusually good
11. Thin layer of ore
12. Agreement
14. Fido's warning
15. Cutthroat
17. Earsplitting
18. And no other
20. Have
21. Born
22. Becomes the owner of
24. Edible part of a nut
25. Depend (on)
27. Fine coating
28. Sand ridge
30. Football throw
31. Great Chinese structure
33. Emily or lamp
34. Wearing apparel
36. Morning ____
37. Pinafore wearer

DOWN

1. Fairy godmother's prop
2. Annoy
3. Just around the corner
4. Tranquility
5. Golf-course hazard
6. East Indian tree
7. Mild expletive
8. Group of cattle
10. "Little Sir ____"
11. Walk about idly
13. Moles' byways
14. Shaded retreat
16. Momentary brightness
17. Ship's record
19. Up to now
23. Large number
24. Haze
26. Period of time
27. Not easily moved
29. Become limp
30. Steed for a youngster
32. Springy buoyant movement
33. Trim and chic
35. Lowing sound

PUZZLE 207

Starting box on page 562

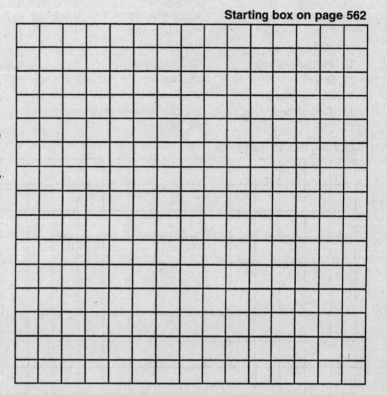

Word Math

PUZZLE 208

In these division problems, letters are substituted for numbers. Determine the value of each letter. Then arrange the letters in order from 0 to 9, and they will spell a word or phrase.

1. 0 1 2 3 4 5 6 7 8 9

```
              OAR
      ─────────────
TREE | DEEPEN
        DNNT
        ─────
        RTEE
        TREE
        ─────
        DPPN
        ZAIO
        ─────
        AEOA
```

2. 0 1 2 3 4 5 6 7 8 9

```
              HOE
      ─────────────
SMUG | GUSSET
        SMUG
        ─────
        RRJJE
        REMMO
        ─────
        HREJT
        HEGJU
        ─────
         EGE
```

3. 0 1 2 3 4 5 6 7 8 9

```
              MID
      ─────────────
NAIL | ELATED
        MDEY
        ─────
        MNLE
        IDNM
        ─────
        TOND
        DOIA
        ─────
         ELD
```

153

PUZZLE 209

ACROSS

1. Center
4. On one's way
7. Fable ending
9. Muhammad ____
10. Ridicule: 2 wds.
12. Buss
14. Choice word
15. Tam or beret, e.g.
17. TV's "____ Girl"
19. Gosh!
20. Handle
22. Stallone's nickname
23. Fitted case
25. Suggestion
26. Snooze
29. Leave be: 2 wds.
31. Honeycomb segment
32. Deface
33. Regal title
34. Betrayal
36. West or Largo
37. Broke a fast
38. Badger
39. Knight's title
40. Fruit skin
43. The long ____ of the law
46. Rope fiber
48. Coupe, e.g.
49. Double-reed instrument
50. Ledge
52. VIP: 2 wds.
54. Certain vote
55. Helmsman
56. Coloring
57. Neither's pal

DOWN

1. Dwelling
2. Yen
3. Rubbish!
4. Table wood
5. Gad
6. Tall tale: 2 wds.
7. Tom or buck, e.g.
8. Deficiency
10. Gam
11. Beach color
13. Briny
16. Kind of face
18. Sort
21. Took the bait
24. Stint
26. Skip it: 2 wds.
27. Porter or stout
28. Scheme
29. Secular
30. Stretch out
31. Municipalities
32. Sleight of hand
34. Deep cut
35. Armed conflict
41. Arrest
42. Nerd
43. Detest
44. Cheer
45. Was in session
47. Stage drama
49. Baltic capital
51. Caustic substance
53. Card game

Starting box on page 562

PUZZLE 210   CHANGAWORD

Can you change the top word into the bottom word (in each column) in the number of steps indicated in parentheses? Do not change the order of the letters, and change only one letter at a time. Proper names, slang, and obsolete words are not allowed.

1. WELL (4 steps)   2. FORE (4 steps)   3. GOOD (5 steps)   4. LAST (5 steps)

DONE   LOCK   TURN   WORD

PUZZLE 211

Starting box on page 562

ACROSS
1. Tropical tree
5. Marsh
8. Spider's lair
11. Caruso solo
12. Clamorous
14. "Make ____ while the sun…"
15. Piston packing
17. Poison cure
19. Glowing
20. "A ____ of robins . . ."
22. Muck
23. Lemon drink
24. Perch
25. Responsibility
28. Impede
31. Chess pieces
33. Born
34. Longs for
37. Tavern
38. Traveler's home
39. Kohoutek, for one
42. "____ Are My Lucky Star"
44. Protected path
46. Intention
47. Decompose
48. Ride a bike
52. Scheme
54. Point
56. Support laboriously
57. Bill
59. Shade of blue
61. Flipper
62. Elastic
66. Powerful
68. Lamprey
69. Portal
70. Level
71. 24 hours
72. Youngster
73. Peruse

DOWN
1. Pale color
2. Ancient animal refuge
3. Mortgage
4. Ships' hands
5. Compliment
6. Long, long time
7. Almond
8. Mystery story
9. Ingest
10. Lucky tournament position
13. Murky
15. Happy
16. Adjutant
18. Flop
21. Alike
26. Decade
27. Craving
29. Stir
30. Still
32. Cravat
35. Baste
36. Seed
38. With compassion
40. Atlas item
41. Look at
42. Chatter
43. Cooking fat
45. Drawing
49. Protect from attack
50. Related
51. Fasting period
53. Nothing doing!
55. Tabloid
58. Offer
60. Cupid's business
62. Nourished
63. Grassland
64. Float
65. Old card game
67. PM drink

WORD MATH

PUZZLE 212

In these long-division problems, letters are substituted for numbers. Determine the value of each letter. Then arrange the letters in order from 0 to 9, and they will spell a word or phrase.

1

0	1	2	3	4	5	6	7	8	9

```
                ERN
        RUST | SETTLER
               SLLIC
                TUILE
               SITCT
                ESLLR
               TGNIU
                SUTT
```

2

0	1	2	3	4	5	6	7	8	9

```
                TED
        EASE | KETTLES
               KILLA
                RLITE
               HTRTD
                ETDAS
               ESLRK
                TEIE
```

3

0	1	2	3	4	5	6	7	8	9

```
                ARE
        NONE | LOATHED
               RATNN
                EEHRE
               EMDTM
                HEHED
               HTAHL
                OLOH
```

155

PUZZLE 213

ACROSS

1. Spider's creation
4. Expert pilots
6. Contour
8. Health resort
11. Large body of water
13. Roe source
14. Sultan's wives
16. Taunt
17. Work dough
19. Organs of hearing
20. Expire
21. Writing table
22. Refers indirectly
24. Storm wind
26. Is able to
27. Bivouac
28. Go in
31. Relocates
32. Consumed
34. Unlock
35. Theater boxes
37. Singer Torme
38. Of warships
40. Songstress Horne
41. Scarlet

DOWN

1. No longer is
2. Sound repetition
3. Sandy shore
5. Deliver an address
7. Acquire
8. Ferocious fish
9. Go by
10. Summer beverage
12. Sewing implement
13. Sail the seven ____
15. Send by post
16. Golf pegs
18. Two, at cards
21. Of teeth
22. Swiss peaks
23. Native of Copenhagen
24. Judge's mallet
25. So be it!
27. Make do
29. English school
30. Kingly
31. Pop's mate
33. At no time
36. Rational
39. Young boy

Starting box on page 562

PUZZLE 214   QUOTAGRAM

Fill in the answers to the clues below. Then transfer the letters to the correspondingly numbered squares in the diagram. The completed diagram will contain a quotation.

1. Sameness
   ___ ___ ___ ___ ___ ___ ___ ___
   14 29 24 47 3   35 48 17

2. Wall brackets
   ___ ___ ___ ___ ___ ___ ___
   15 40 12 51 6   28 1

3. Republic
   ___ ___ ___ ___ ___ ___
   39 8   34 2   50 42

4. Adjective modifier
   ___ ___ ___ ___ ___ ___
   18 13 21 7   45 26

5. Sundry
   ___ ___ ___ ___ ___ ___ ___
   43 22 19 49 41 30 46

6. Uncompounded
   ___ ___ ___ ___ ___ ___ ___ ___ ___
   36 23 44 11 4   9   16 25 32

7. Began vigorously: 2 wds.
   ___ ___ ___ ___ ___ ___ ___ ___
   37 31 38 27 20 10 33 5

1	2	3	4	5	6	7		8	9	10		11	12	13	14	15	16	17
18	19	20		21	22	23	24	25	26	27	28		29	30	31	32	33	34	35
36	37		38	39		40	41	42	43	44	45	46	47	48	49	50	51		

ACROSS

1. Used ticket
5. Blow one's own horn
9. ____ Scotia
10. Well-balanced
12. Arabian gulf
13. One of the mob
15. Nanny, e.g.
16. Parched
17. ____ as molasses
19. Singer ____ John
21. Stout relative
22. Hamelin problem
23. Nevertheless
24. Filmy strand
26. Viola's relative
29. University in New Haven
31. Part of a circle
34. Contribute
36. Nothing
37. Witches' convention
38. Too bad!
40. Blackthorn
41. Actor Andrews
45. Discharge
48. Once ____ a time
49. Easily bent
50. City in Nevada
51. Makes a choice
52. Paradise on earth

DOWN

1. Hidden obstacle
2. Commotion: hyph.
3. Part of the eye
4. Good-natured raillery
5. Goldfinger's nemesis
6. Equip
7. Donkey
8. Obtains
10. Discomfort
11. Postpone
13. ____ Pointe
14. Characterization
16. Garret
18. Soaked through
20. Attorney's bailiwick
25. Thickness
27. "The Blue ____" (film)
28. Popeye's "goil"
30. Second person
31. Collection of notes

32. Stir up
33. Fastening device
35. Bear
37. Coagulate
39. Storage area
40. Goes wrong
42. Mimicked
43. "____ But the Lonely Heart"
44. By and by
46. Nurse a drink
47. Enjoyed a rocker

Starting box on page 562

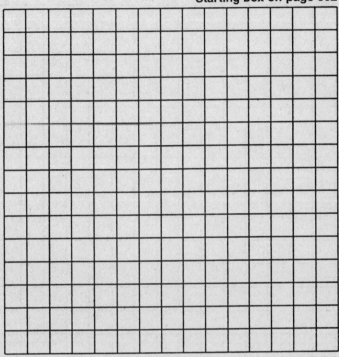

WORD MATH   PUZZLE 216

In these long-division problems, letters are substituted for numbers. Determine the value of each letter. Then arrange the letters in order from 0 to 9, and they will spell a word or phrase.

1

0	1	2	3	4	5	6	7	8	9

```
              H I M
TYPE | PATTIES
       P S Z P A
         P I M P E
         P T E I P
           Y M H H S
           Y S M I Z
             M P Z M
```

2

0	1	2	3	4	5	6	7	8	9

```
              F O G
RIOT | GROTTO
       I O G F
         E N S O T
         E O G N O
           R S T F O
           R R I E O
             E G E D
```

3

0	1	2	3	4	5	6	7	8	9

```
                T A M
MEAT | TEACHER
        H M I H R
          A E I E E
          E A G E G
            A M L C R
            A A L C R
              I L L L
```

PUZZLE 217

ACROSS
1. Animal's coat
4. Swipe
7. Reggie Jackson to 1977 Yankee fans
8. Love god
10. Bess's man
11. Trunk item
12. Actress Irene
13. Inklings
14. Sea fliers
15. Tippler
16. Tatters
17. Skirt feature
19. King Kong, e.g.
20. ____ whiz!
21. Carry with effort
23. Upshot
25. Strike sharply
26. ____ George
28. Children's game
30. Perform
31. Comprehend
33. Sousa specialty
35. Shut hard
36. Montand's street
37. Agitates
38. Shackles
41. Ostracizes
42. West Pointer
43. Accompanying
44. Constantly
45. Wild disorder
46. Sigmoid figure
47. Very likely

DOWN
1. Nonflowering plants
2. Persuade
3. Cowboy Rogers
4. Investment money
5. Muscat and ____
6. Ruby wine
7. Sharpens
9. Legal thing
10. Spicy
11. Sabot or clog
12. Hang in folds
14. Historical period
15. Snoozed
17. "Miss ____" of the comics
18. Laundry container
20. Prayer
22. Young bird
24. Aswan, for one
27. "The Best ____ of Our Lives"
29. James et al.
32. Printing measures
34. Oxidation
35. Daring exhibition
37. Take pictures
38. "Rocks"
39. Utter incoherently
40. Keatsian poems
41. Faux pas
43. Coach Parseghian

Starting box on page 562

PUZZLE 218   Quotagram

Fill in the answers to the clues below. Then transfer the letters to the correspondingly numbered squares in the diagram. The completed diagram will contain a quotation.

1. Pencil-point improvers
 __ __ __ __ __ __ __ __ __ __
 42 6 9 49 38 40 31 37 10 29

2. Tallest
 __ __ __ __ __ __ __
 21 50 12 36 33 27 15

3. Pupil
 __ __ __ __ __ __ __
 35 45 30 17 22 5 14

4. Summertime drink
 __ __ __ __ __ __ __ __
 39 43 3 48 1 19 47 28

5. Thread holders
 __ __ __ __ __ __
 44 23 16 46 32 34

6. Island salutation
 __ __ __ __ __
 7 24 18 13 4

7. Cigars
 __ __ __ __ __ __ __
 20 53 2 51 11 25 8

8. Caught you!
 __ __ __
 41 52 26

1	2		3	4	5		6	7	8		9		10	11	12	13	14		15	16		17
18		19	20		21	22		23	24	25	26	27	28	29		30	31	32	33	34	35	
36	37		38	39	40	41	42	43	44		45	46		47	48		49	50	51	52	53	

158

ACROSS

1. Honey insect
4. Fly high
5. Fewer
9. Tranquil
11. Evangelist Roberts
12. Well said!
14. Strong wind
15. Have a snack
16. Central
18. Rip
20. Restaurant
21. Shy
24. Eye suggestively
25. Shopping basket
29. Horseman
31. Cry
32. Butter substitute
33. Sum
35. Billboard
36. Heroic poem
38. Roofing liquid
39. Distress call
41. Happy
44. Take care of
48. Hawaiian dance
49. Special ability
50. Abound
51. Male deer
52. Small child

DOWN

1. Wild hog
2. Apiece
3. Great Lake
4. Bed board
5. Flight record
6. Historical period
7. ____ and pepper
8. Frozen rain
9. Pod vegetable
10. Injure
12. Loner
13. Carbine
17. Profound
19. Ventilate
20. Dairy animal
22. Wedding vow
23. Hate
25. Price
26. Assumed name
27. Rue
28. 2,000 pounds
30. Knock sharply
34. Feathery
37. Hint
39. Ballad
40. Away
42. Strong beer
43. River barrier
45. Toward the rising sun
46. Female singer
47. Flog

Starting box on page 562

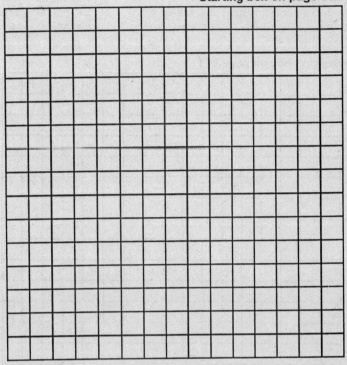

Word Math

PUZZLE 220

In these long-division problems, letters are substituted for numbers. Determine the value of each letter. Then arrange the letters in order from 0 to 9, and they will spell a word or phrase.

1

0	1	2	3	4	5	6	7	8	9

```
              F O R
      ┌──────────────
SOL   │ F R A N C S
        L N N O
        ─────────
        O F L C
        R W W L
        ─────────
        R R L S
        C N A H
        ─────────
        W A S
```

2

0	1	2	3	4	5	6	7	8	9

```
              P T A
      ┌──────────────
RUN   │ C R U S T S
        C M C R
        ─────────
        C I P T
        C R P P
        ─────────
        A M A S
        R U N
        ─────────
        U P N
```

3

0	1	2	3	4	5	6	7	8	9

```
              H U G
      ┌──────────────
DAN   │ B U S H E S
        U G I E
        ─────────
        U B G E
        D A N
        ─────────
        D H D S
        A G B B
        ─────────
        E H N
```

PUZZLE 221

ACROSS

1. Droop
4. Unruly group
7. Singer Stevens
8. Copy
9. Beginning
11. Charter
13. Pray
14. Likely
17. Airfoil
18. Have debts
20. Shade of green
21. Singleton
22. Fortune
23. Excavation
25. Mr. Buttons
26. Precise time
27. Naval diary
29. Mr. Crane
31. Keats work
32. Duffer's quest
35. Actor Steiger
37. Eyewash
38. Broke a fast
39. Quick swim
41. ___ Alamos
42. Seine
44. Scout unit
47. Pie ingredient
49. Paleo's antonym
50. Ms. Gardner
51. Moo
53. Building wing
54. Knock
55. Pekoe, e.g.
56. Pronoun
58. Touch down
60. Ship of the desert
63. Marvin or Grant
64. Stroll
65. Summate
66. Purpose

DOWN

1. Intone
2. Burro
3. Well I'll be!
4. Leatherneck
5. Started
6. Mr. Gazzara
7. Fish eggs
10. Faucet
12. Showed
13. Improve upon
15. ___ rally
16. Take up, e.g.
17. Pro
19. Merino
24. Commotion: hyph.
28. Perceive
30. Grass
32. Chum
33. Energy source
34. Outcome
36. Main meal
40. Pare
43. Tunnel fee
44. Mended, in a way
45. Dodged
46. Short snooze
48. John or Jane
52. WWII female
56. Maintained
57. Moose's kin
59. Neighbor of Fla.
61. Wonder
62. Isle of ___

Starting box on page 562

PUZZLE 222   CHANGAWORD

Can you change the top word into the bottom word (in each column) in the number of steps indicated in parentheses? Do not change the order of the letters, and change only one letter at a time. Proper names, slang, and obsolete words are not allowed.

1. LOSE (4 steps)   2. READ (5 steps)   3. WORK (5 steps)   4. TREE (8 steps)

FIND   BOOK   GOAL   LEAF

PUZZLE 223

ACROSS
1. Telephone
5. Medley
6. Power unit
10. Emerson's middle name
11. Lamb's pen name
12. Fire set intentionally
13. Northern Africa country
16. Mil. transport vessel
17. Fiddler crab genus
18. Finished
20. Year or frog
22. Cleaving tool
23. Agave plant
25. Rescue from refuse
28. Sounds of hesitation
29. Hypnotic state
30. The jig ____!
31. Beams
32. Catcher's glove
34. Stunned
36. Anger
38. Nothing
39. Tackle or guard
41. Reverie
44. Hat material
45. Fortune
48. City slicker
49. Squealer
50. Girl
51. Meeting proposals
53. Debate
55. Fish-catching birds
56. Webfooted birds
57. Appraise
58. Before: pref.
59. Politician Perot

DOWN
1. Unrefined
2. Top athlete
3. Beach resort
4. Diving bird
6. Doormat message
7. Aquatic plants
8. Ascot
9. Late
10. Mural location
13. Related to gold
14. Debt note
15. From one's forefathers
19. Beige
21. Oil
22. Rooters
24. Poisonous snake
26. Steep rock
27. Deposit
30. Bit of information
32. ____ Blanc
33. ____-de-France
34. Conjunction
35. Prepare for action
36. Wash
37. Sword handles
40. Lumps of gold
42. Fuss
43. Indicator
44. Facade
46. Results in
47. Painter Paul ____
52. Writer Levin
53. Seaweed product
54. Nevada city

Starting box on page 562

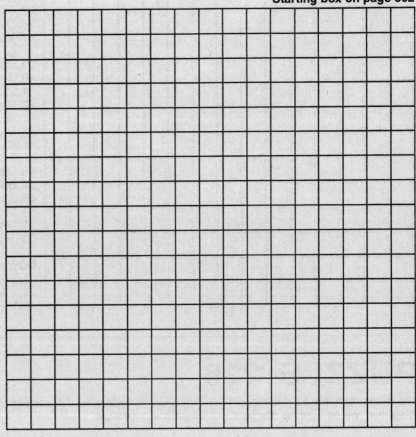

NUMBER SQUARE

PUZZLE 224

Fill in answers to the clues with 2- or 4-digit numbers, one digit per square. The heavy lines separate the answers.

ACROSS
1. Consecutive digits, in rearranged order
5. Three less than 6 across
6. Perfect square
7. Two more than 8 down doubled
9. Two more than 5 across added to 7 across
10. 6 across multiplied by 3 down

DOWN
1. 2 down multiplied by 9 across
2. One more than 6 across doubled
3. One more than 9 down halved
4. Consecutive digits, in order
8. Perfect square
9. Three less than 9 across

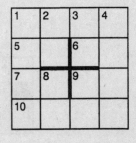

161

PUZZLE 225

ACROSS
1. Receive
4. Smooth a road
5. Pull behind
8. Cut in two
9. "____ Maria"
10. Upper limb
13. Escape
14. Changed location
16. Grassland
17. Wharf
18. Seductive woman
19. Grit
20. Have being
21. In a while
22. Highest point
23. Snake or turtle
25. Limited in scope
27. Actress Gardner
28. Feathery scarf
29. Dinner jacket
32. Self-important
36. Dollar bills
37. Valerie Harper role
39. Spleen
40. Slide
41. ____ and effect
42. Gymnast Korbut
43. Dog or cat
44. Desires
45. Fencing sword
46. One or more
47. Breakfast food
48. Finished
50. Golfer's peg
51. Witnessed
52. Japanese coin

DOWN
1. Bestowed
2. Adam's wife
3. Wood eater
4. Equal
5. Saloon
6. Kitchen appliance
7. Merged
8. Snooze
10. Texas shrine
11. Continue a subscription
12. Angry
13. Remove from a job
15. Mined matter
17. Golfer's goal
18. Kind of bar
19. Small piece
21. Exists
22. Fragrance
24. Imposed a levy on
26. Home
29. Bus fare
30. Oneness
31. Citrus fruit
32. Have
33. Lubricated
34. Egg on
35. South China, for one
38. Hovel
40. Health resort
41. Canary's home
42. Store sign
44. Rainy
45. First garden
49. Born

Starting box on page 562

PUZZLE 226 Quotagram

Fill in the answers to the clues. Then transfer the letters to the correspondingly numbered squares in the diagram. The completed diagram will contain a quotation.

1. Challenges   39 17 33 13 7

2. Flower necklace   27 41 6

3. Slacks   10 23 20 25 14 30 12 38

4. Spouse   1 8 31 11

5. Bridle part   4 34 37 21

6. Aim   16 2 35 9 22

7. Weary   36 18 3 28

8. Lad   29 24 5

9. Uncertainty   19 32 40 26 15

1	2	3	4	5		6	7		8	9	10	11	12	13	14	15
	16	17	18	19		20	21		22	23	24	25	26	27	28	
29	30	31	32	33	34		35	36		37	38		39	40	41	

PUZZLE 227

ACROSS
1. Humble ____
4. Eddie Murphy, e.g.
7. Actor Holliman
8. Unity
9. Vagrant
11. Table spread
13. Posed
14. Viper
17. Guido's high note
18. Squealer
20. Author Buscaglia
21. Longing
22. Before, of yore
23. Ginger drink
25. Finish
26. Observe
27. Suitable
29. Summer drink
31. Formerly named
32. Owned
35. Gloomy
37. Cozy room
38. Hail!
39. Sunburned
41. Gang
42. Sack
44. Author Conroy
47. Used to be
49. Shoshonean Indian
50. Freudian term
51. Oriental sauce
53. Lid
54. Effort
55. Flock member
56. Certain railways
58. Steadfast
60. Slip
63. Charge
64. Sour
65. Ancient
66. Moist

DOWN
1. Component
2. Author Levin
3. New Haven tree
4. Made of mohair
5. Away from the ocean
6. To a ____
7. Greek letter
10. Chum
12. Mineral deposits
13. Certain horses
15. Ocean
16. Warsaw's locale
17. Needle aperture
19. Expanse
24. Fencer's need
28. X
30. Pinna
32. Bad actor
33. Pledge
34. Reduce in value
36. Coming-out parties
40. Information
43. Emeralds, e.g.
44. Seabird
45. Concurred
46. Type of poodle
48. Scatter seed
52. Of course!
56. Prepare for print
57. ____ Zeppelin (rock group)
59. Celestial sight
61. Statute
62. Rapper/actor ____ Cube

Starting box on page 562

STEP BY STEP

PUZZLE 228

In five steps change each word one letter at a time into a new 5-letter word so that by the fifth step each letter has been changed. Do not rearrange the order of the letters. You do not have to change the letters in order.

Example: Heard, Hears, Heads, Heeds, Seeds, Sleds

1. APACE

____
____
____
____
____

2. CREEL

____
____
____
____
____

3. CLING

____
____
____
____
____

4. LEAST

____
____
____
____
____

163

PUZZLE 229

ACROSS

1. Twig broom
6. Ballet composer Vittorio ____
7. Queen of the gods
11. "____ They Sail"
12. Kind of hat
14. Fluffs, as hair
16. Click beetle
17. Significant event
19. Winged
20. Termini
21. Let fall
22. WWII naval base islands
24. Cancel
27. Crimson Tide
31. Punish with an arbitrary penalty
32. Taxes
36. Rationalizing adage, with "A"
42. Left
43. Splinter
44. Mind finds
45. Slackening
46. Matched groups
47. Among
49. Confused
53. Spirit
54. Erring
56. Temperament
57. Bakery machine
62. Wagner works
63. Habituate
64. Fe
65. Waterwheel
66. Jabbed

DOWN

1. Very dry, as champagne
2. "____ kleine Nachtmusik"
3. Stiff hair
4. Elevator man
5. Distance indicators
7. Holbrook and March
8. Maternally kin
9. Boca ____
10. Correct
12. Equal
13. War god
15. Farm building
18. Race part
21. Deceives
22. Streetcar
23. "Do-____" (song)
25. Sour substance
26. ____ majeste
27. Smudges
28. Medicinal plant
29. Anti-DWI group
30. Eastern general
32. Ivan or Peter
33. Fictional monster
34. Being: Lat.
35. Room in a casa
37. Mil. address
38. Last puzzle piece
39. Covered with certain vines
40. Pre-Easter time
41. Work units
47. Actress MacGraw
48. Le ____, France
49. Shot and shell, for short
50. Famous basso
51. Chemical compound
52. Houston player
53. Ogles
55. Alda or Paton
58. Privy to
59. Heal
60. Pennsylvania port
61. Peruse

Starting box on page 562

164

ACROSS

1. Young bear
4. Track circuit
7. "Born in the ____"
8. Have being
9. Crimson
10. Small fry
13. Strongbox
16. Sixty minutes
17. Fib
18. Singleton
19. Everything
20. Hive insect
21. Mr. Hingle
23. Spinning toy
26. Halter
28. Jump
29. Hairpiccc
31. Paddle
32. Corny
34. Born
35. "The ____ Valley"
36. Have a meal
37. Before, in poems
38. Modern
40. Plead
41. Animal hair
43. Skating surface
45. Drink slowly
46. Comic Rickles
47. Fly alone
48. Canvas shelter
49. Occur
51. Haggard heroine
53. Apple cider girl
54. Atmosphere
55. Speck
56. Jewel

DOWN

1. Heal
2. Function
3. Naughty
4. Lion's den
5. Upper limb
6. Vigor
10. Sandal
11. Sharpen
12. Regret
13. Bed board
14. Be sick
15. Hat material
20. River boat
21. Kind of luck
22. Monkey
24. Proprietor
25. Wharf
26. Comedian Newhart
27. Beatles song
28. Successful show
30. Golly!
32. Golf gadget
33. Dust cloth
39. Broad
40. Warped
41. Rasp
42. Atop
44. Anti
45. Soak up
47. Petty quarrel
48. Semester
49. Concealed
50. Commotion
51. Droop
52. Hurry

Starting box on page 562

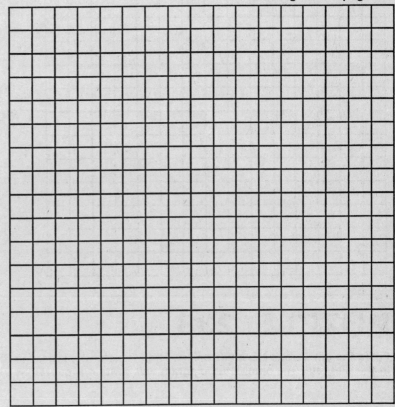

Changaword

Can you change the top word into the bottom word (in each column) in the number of steps indicated in parentheses? Do not change the order of the letters, and change only one letter at a time. Proper names, slang, and obsolete words are not allowed.

1. **SHOE** (3 steps)   2. **PAST** (4 steps)   3. **COCK** (5 steps)   4. **TREE** (7 steps)

BOOT   YEAR   TAIL   TOPS

PUZZLE 232

ACROSS
1. Mispronounce
5. Molten rock
9. Region
10. Took advantage of
11. Georgia fruit
13. Hollow stalk
14. Water vapor
16. Twelve months
17. Trademark
19. Front of a ship
23. Deposits, as eggs
25. Bowling alley
26. Actress Burnett
27. Kidded
28. Disdain
30. Make a speech
32. Relieve
34. Avid
36. Scorch
37. Snare
38. Expectation
39. Sole
41. Defect
44. Jerks
48. Stratum
49. Cash
51. Actor Guinness
52. Ripped
53. Engage gears
54. Sheep mothers

DOWN
1. Drink like a dog
2. Angers
3. Chair
4. Walk restlessly
5. Entice
6. Cruising
7. Swerve
8. Append
12. Actor Holbrook
15. Grinding tooth
16. String toy
18. January birthstone
19. Story outline
20. Lawn tool
21. Individual
22. Marry
24. Motto
26. Demure
27. Bottle
28. Strike with the open hand
29. Be concerned
31. Answer
32. Fire residue
33. Writer Tolstoy
35. "And pretty maids all in ____"
40. Sweet potato
41. Store correspondence
42. Dregs
43. Curved monument
45. Memo
46. Recognize
47. Withered
48. Scottish cap
50. Word of permission

Starting box on page 562

PUZZLE 233   Quotagram

Fill in the answers to the clues below. Then transfer the letters to the correspondingly numbered squares in the diagram. The completed diagram will contain a quotation.

1. Spin
   ___ ___ ___ ___ ___
   15 30 6 27 1

2. Spectacle
   ___ ___ ___ ___ ___
   13 34 3 25 11

3. Narrate
   ___ ___ ___ ___ ___ ___
   18 10 35 21 5 28

4. Arab chief
   ___ ___ ___ ___ ___
   24 9 31 2 14

5. Shabby: hyph.
   ___ ___ ___ ___ ___ ___ ___ ___ ___
   20 33 29 4 17 26 8 19 22

6. Rash
   ___ ___ ___ ___ ___
   16 12 7 32 23

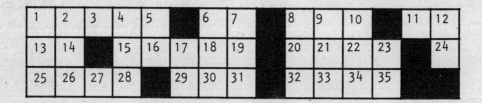

PUZZLE 234

ACROSS
1. Knob
5. Beatles movie
9. Sent through the Post Office
11. Medley
12. Defy
15. Convenes
16. Mispronounce
17. Long ago
19. Fido's doc
20. Flap
21. Propane, for one
24. "___ as a Stranger"
25. "Where the Boys ___"
26. Enclosure
27. Shred
28. Observe
29. Pitch
30. Ski course
33. Set
34. Stubborn
38. Cistern
40. Give
42. Chat a while
43. Small lump
46. Energy
47. Short sleep
50. Pharaoh or red
51. Goof
52. Lamb's mom
53. Regret
54. Envy, for one
55. Hodgepodge
57. Fatigue
58. Salesperson
60. Fanciful
64. And
65. Guarantee
66. Final
67. Sort

DOWN
1. Zilch
2. Cheer for a matador
3. Study
4. Nervous
5. Garden tool
6. Raise
7. Word-for-word
8. Wall announcement
9. Bricklayers
10. Climber's mountain
12. Applaud
13. Conceal
14. Ages and ages
15. Apportion
18. Caviar
21. Snatch
22. Feels poorly
23. Stain
31. Building site
32. Central
33. Acquire
35. Nah!
36. Again
37. Adhesive, for one
38. Ice-cream flavor
39. Suitability
41. Add greater value
42. Rogue
43. Office piece
44. Paintings
45. Steep tea
48. Atmosphere
49. Pare
56. Reporter's question
57. Twitch
59. Spoil
61. Vine
62. Swab
63. Take to court

Starting box on page 562

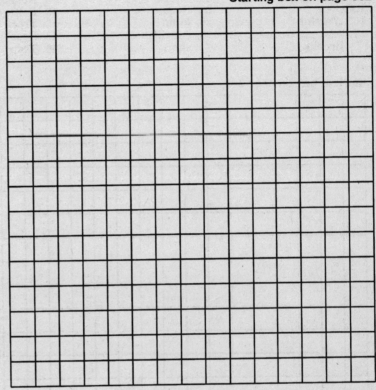

WORD MATH   PUZZLE 235

In these long-division problems, letters are substituted for numbers. Determine the value of each letter. Then arrange the letters in order from 0 to 9, and they will spell a word or phrase.

1

0	1	2	3	4	5	6	7	8	9

```
              REV
REINS | THEATER
        EGSIH
        AHNETE
        GGAEH
         GVRER
         IEVSS
          ANNNI
```

2

0	1	2	3	4	5	6	7	8	9

```
            LAC
ART | CREATE
      CUOL
      UUPT
      UPOE
       ECLE
       ESRP
        EAP
```

3

0	1	2	3	4	5	6	7	8	9

```
              NEE
LEND | DEMAND
        MNKA
        NINRN
        NUMMI
         NINAD
         NUMMI
          NKUK
```

PUZZLE 236

ACROSS
1. Broadway's Billy
5. Hill dwellers
6. Was in the Indy 500
11. Yard parts
12. Ooze
16. Worship
17. "A ___ Grows in Brooklyn"
18. Then's mate
19. Poet Marianne
20. Merchant
22. Guided
23. Emcee Griffin
24. Zipped
26. Require
28. Mind
29. Brazilian city, for short
31. Big top, e.g.
32. Constitution segment
35. Had IOUs out
36. Cub Scouts unit
37. Musical pair
38. Cozy spot
41. Kitties
42. ___ and potatoes
44. Buddy
45. Echoed
49. Felt poorly
52. Track-meet unit
53. Brother of Eris
56. Trap
57. Aerate
58. Lone
59. Soda fountain implement
60. Satanic
61. Hand out hands

DOWN
1. Actor George
2. Pip
3. Range animal
4. Respect
6. Run into on purpose
7. Hubbub
8. Lost heat
9. Went wrong
10. Gest
12. Said "I'm cold" in body language
13. Moray
14. Prior to, to Prior
15. Apiece
18. Weight allowance
21. Downing Street number
24. Moved, with jazz
25. Favorite
27. Clamor
28. Chick's mom
30. Unusual
31. City structure
32. Fills with wonder
33. Encountered
34. Brando film, with "The"
35. "___ of Africa"
37. Greenback
39. County or hot
40. Make lace
41. Work with oils
43. Ribbed
44. Make the grade
45. Gun (the motor)
46. First lady
47. Stir site
48. Impelled
50. Period
51. Morning moisture
54. Charles Lamb
55. Market

Starting box on page 562

PUZZLE 237   CHANGAWORD

Can you change the top word into the bottom word (in each column) in the number of steps indicated in parentheses? Do not change the order of the letters, and change only one letter at a time. Proper names, slang, and obsolete words are not allowed.

1. **MEAT** (4 steps)   2. **DILL** (5 steps)   3. **SHOE** (6 steps)   4. **TRUE** (7 steps)

BALL   WEED   HORN   GRIT

PUZZLE 238

ACROSS

1. European mountain
4. Antiquity
7. Alums
12. Famous hostess
17. Feathered stole
18. Author of "Ligeia"
19. Utmost extent
20. Ancient Hebrew measures
21. Hirschfeld creation
23. Images
25. Answers
27. God of love
28. Dir.
29. Cut of meat
31. Temperature tester
32. Frosted
33. Explosives: abbr.
34. Inspires with reverence
35. Haw's partner
36. Specks
37. Hull
38. Drew
40. Cariou and Deighton
41. Arab
44. Poetic contraction
45. Actress Rita et al.
46. Mexican ponchos
47. Novelist Stephen
50. Soprano Gluck
51. Sugar vegetable
52. Annoy
53. Dutch painter
54. Lawn nuisance
56. Raison d'——
57. Hill builder
58. College girl
59. Greases
60. Remitter
61. Wavers
63. Expletive of old
64. Guitarist Paul
65. Placid
66. Polluted
67. Washington city
71. Natalie Cole's dad
72. Math term
73. School gp.
74. Lament
75. Word of sorrow
77. Dickens, e.g.: abbr.
78. Baseball stat
79. Article
80. Hazel or butter
81. Merit
82. Rising
85. Flapjack
88. Helms
91. Fit to be tied
92. German river
93. Dutch commune
94. —— Muni
95. Swelling
96. Ratty
97. Cub Scout group
98. —— Joaquin

DOWN

1. First 3 of 26
2. Mauna ——
3. Turned aside
4. Heroic poetry
5. Circle
6. Signified
7. Skim
8. Edges
9. Electrical unit, for short
10. Orders
11. Metric measures
12. Playwright Hart
13. Flightless bird
14. Incredible luck
15. Italian city
16. Burros
22. Strains
24. Turf
26. —— de plume
29. Chou En- ——
30. Possess
32. Charged particles
33. Liberian tribe
35. Pronoun
36. Rabble-rouser
37. Saucy
39. Golf appurtenance
40. Kin or skin
41. Religious districts
42. —— Haute
43. Glacial ridge
45. Pleased
46. Olden tax
47. Converses
48. Rajah's mate
49. Option

50. God of war
51. Like Kojak
54. Center
55. Iranian coin
56. Certain breeze: 2 wds.
58. Penny
60. Small legume
62. Socials
63. Eternities
64. Meadow
66. Betrothed
67. Featured
68. Rags
69. Misspeak
70. Tree
72. Termagants
73. Grand —— (Evangeline's home)
75. Point of view
76. Gruesome
77. Presidential nickname
78. Nail board
81. Great Norse tales
82. Pieced out
83. Not bad, in Scotland
84. Ancient garden
86. Obscure
87. Enzyme suffix
89. Small inlet
90. Progeny

PUZZLE 239

ACROSS

1. Telegraphs
6. Toil
11. Disconcert
16. Connecting channel
17. Foolish
18. Hidden stores
20. Exchange views: 2 wds.
22. Sharp reply
23. —— Baba
24. Brightens up
25. "—— There"
27. "—— and Peace"
28. Retreats
30. Aykroyd
31. "Exodus" author
32. Soft drink
33. Showed contempt
35. Artery
37. Convenient
38. —— buggy
39. Totes
40. National flower
41. Occupant
44. Location
45. Rummy variety
48. Make joyful
49. Starch source
50. Expect
51. Provided sustenance
52. Beget
53. Miser
55. Joker, for one
56. High, rocky hill
57. Indigo plant
58. Leveret
59. Mother-of-pearl
60. Temporary substitute
62. Rouse from sleep
63. Profession
64. Sob
65. Short staff
66. Major-——
67. Made tractable
69. Shoe parts
70. Erin
74. Spoil
75. Nothing more than
76. Past
77. Nova
78. Sea eagle
79. Hindu god of destruction
80. Kansas city
83. Compass reading: abbr.
84. Signified approval
86. Be in high spirits: 3 wds.
89. Fanciful visions
90. Rub out
91. Past and present, e.g.
92. Confess
93. Farm buildings
94. Gluts

DOWN

1. Pilfered
2. Fine white fur
3. Doze
4. —— tone
5. Shrill
6. Napery
7. Erelong
8. Belfry occupants?
9. Single
10. Spas
11. Fields
12. Max or Buddy
13. Play division
14. Appear: 3 wds.
15. Messenger
16. Large amounts
19. Wander
21. Dodge
26. By way of
29. Sober
31. Advocate strongly
32. —— Grande
34. Germanic letter
35. Bring into agreement
36. Not in control: 3 wds.
37. Sharpen
40. Completely absorbed
41. Trial runs
42. American writer
43. Prejudiced: hyph.
44. Spanker or jib
45. Evergreen fruit
46. —— Haute
47. Viper
49. Ricochet
50. Employ
53. Break suddenly
54. George and Charles, e.g.

55. Christmas songs
57. Got older
59. Cognomen
61. Hammer part
62. Abate
63. Small crowns
65. Decanters
66. Work hard: 2 wds.
67. Tendency
68. —— australis
69. Race the engine
71. Military command: 2 wds.
72. French city
73. Attire
75. In the center of
76. Lily plants
79. Half: prefix
80. Close tightly
81. In addition
82. On the ocean
85. Weir
87. Assam silkworm
88. Canadian province: abbr.

PUZZLE 239

PUZZLE 240

ACROSS

1. Proper's partner
5. Zip
9. Pack cargo
13. Float
17. Slugger Jim
18. Kind of vaccine
19. Tryon's "Harvest ——"
20. Patronage
21. Unfold
22. Carte-du-jour word
23. Surround-ed by
24. Yip
25. Luncheon entree: 2 wds.
28. Aquatic birds
29. Barcelona bear
30. Bon ——
31. Resin
32. Vigilant
35. So be it!
37. High-spirited steeds
42. Minstrel songs
43. Menda-cious one
44. Spoil
45. Asian nurse
46. Summer, to Jeanne
47. Sherry's kin
48. Major artery
49. Do kitchen work
50. April event
52. Burden
54. Seed covering
55. Israeli statesman
57. Donate, to a Scot
58. Of Aare, e.g.
60. Ridge
62. Certain horses
65. Movement
68. Intimation
69. Madrid melodies
70. Stopper
72. Oriental sash
73. Piece of news
74. Wedelns
75. Sweat for
76. Stuck-up one
77. Lesser Antilles
79. Contribute a share
80. Tricks
81. —— Vissi, Greece
82. Lineman
83. Tec Spade
84. "The Paper ——"
87. "East of the Sun and ——": 4 wds.
94. Swinging cadence
95. Inverness girl
96. Lightly cooked
97. Sailors' saint
98. Brink
99. Lioness of "Born Free"
100. Handed stealthily
101. Willis of basketball
102. Fright
103. Permit
104. Shade trees
105. Time past

DOWN

1. Ship's stem
2. Ready
3. Summer treats
4. Trusted advisers
5. S. American fox
6. —— horse
7. Alliance acronym
8. Sparkle
9. Command-ments verb
10. Weighty book
11. Overlook
12. United
13. English novelist: 2 wds
14. Actor John
15. Glacial snow
16. Chiding sounds
26. Some N.Y. hrs.
27. Very long time
28. August hue
31. Actress Turner
32. Brewed beverages
33. Slat
34. Instructive event: hyph.
35. Ether
36. Netman Wilander
37. Knitting stitch
38. Religious services
39. Pollutants
40. Absorbed
41. —— butter
43. Folk knowledge
44. Cowboy competi-tion
47. Sassy
48. Mine ingresses
51. Cathedral site
53. Ms. De Mille
54. Pulsate
56. Large nail

59. Caution
60. Fashion-
able
61. Actress
Moreno
63. Rainbow
64. Shoo, cat!
66. Woodwind
instrument
67. Bird
beaks
69. Lost

71. Cinnabar
or bauxite
75. Approve
76. Like
July
78. Drone
79. Emmet
80. Scottish
explorer
82. School
paper
83. Molts

84. Bass or
treble
85. Animal
pelt
86. Pond plant
87. Promenade
88. She, in
Roma
89. Autumn

90. In good
shape
91. Edible
spreadable
92. Part of an
ephah
93. Stem part
95. Writer
Tolstoy

PUZZLE 240

PUZZLE 241

ACROSS

1. Money lender
5. "And pretty maids all in ____"
9. Roughen
13. Poet's black
14. Florida city
15. Singer Cantrell
16. Make a start
19. Laws
20. Philadelphia team
21. Bright color
22. Author Leon ____
23. Ship position
27. Scrape
28. Overhead railways
31. Brief
32. Musial of baseball
33. Excuse
34. Refuse to yield
37. Roof feature
38. Duct
39. Asian country
40. Pub quaff
41. G-men
42. Most bizarre
43. Aquatic bird
44. Fix beginning
45. Pie ingredients
48. Work compensations
53. Entirely
55. Part
56. Made of a cereal grain
57. Plane starter
58. Czech river
59. Kitty
60. Chimney sweep's concern

DOWN

1. Implores
2. Assist
3. ____ bene
4. Nautical unit of speed
5. Functioned
6. Cheerleaders' shouts
7. Violinist Bull
8. Playing the horses
9. Blocks
10. Lug
11. ____ of Cleves
12. Apartments
14. Frequently
17. Trimmed with mink
18. Pour
22. Czar's edict
23. Uncertain
24. Relating to a bristle
25. Architectural bay
26. Anglo-Saxon laborer
27. Phases
28. Escape
29. Actress Riefenstahl et al.
30. Egyptian president
32. Malicious
33. Pool
35. Union-optional factory
36. Ontario lake
41. Guitar feature
42. Synthetic fiber
43. Mr. Fudd
44. Whittles
45. Hair style
46. Push
47. Stick
48. Mil. officers
49. Biochemist's letters
50. Conception: pref.
51. Wallaroo
52. Name for a leopard?
54. ____ de Cologne

ACROSS

1. Snow coaster
5. Evidence
10. Highlander
14. Salad fish
15. Madagascar mammal
16. Bark cloth
17. "—— against my father's house . . ." (Judg. 9:18): 5 wds.
20. Auto fuel
21. Read fast
22. Pile up
23. Observed
24. Point
26. Lid latch
29. Greek Aurora
30. Golf mound
33. Killer whales
35. "Unto —— and to his wife . . ." (Gen. 3:21): 2 wds.
38. "—— peace . . ." (1 Pet. 1:2): 4 wds.
41. Kennedy aide
42. Chipped in
43. Married
44. Ike's area: abbr.
45. Hardy heroine
46. "—— Miniver"
47. New Testament book
50. Kitchen range
54. Ananias
55. Fall behind
58. "——, because they . . ." (1 Tim. 5:12): 2 wds.
62. So be it!
63. Map addition
64. Mrs. Leonowens
65. Simple
66. Gluts
67. Encounter

DOWN

1. Male deer
2. Roman Diana
3. Finishes
4. 24 hours
5. Location
6. Showed a film again
7. Sign
8. Of us
9. Workweek finish: abbr.
10. Plant stalk
11. Miracle site
12. Musical work
13. Spigots
18. Vane dir.
19. Plant juice
23. Left room
24. Stir: hyph.
25. ". . . what shall —— unto them?" (Exod. 3:13): 2 wds.
26. Pigs
27. Dart
28. Alarm
29. Jack Sprat could ——: 2 wds.
30. Jibes
31. Gladden
32. Anglo-Saxon workers
34. Japanese coin
36. Extinct bird
37. Proba-bilities
39. Employer
40. Fish snares
46. Males
47. —— Semple McPherson
48. Jargons
49. Refrain word
50. Pretense
51. Not wild
52. Above
53. Grape plant
54. Endure
55. Ruled mark
56. Tops: hyph.
57. Small fly
59. Soldiers
60. Genetic initials
61. Highlands cap

PUZZLE 243

ACROSS

1. Ceramic square
5. Chitchat
8. Heating fuel
11. Ship's master: abbr.
15. Pindar poems
16. Ginger beverage
17. Baseball's Mel
18. Sandarac
19. Uncluttered
20. Guy's date
21. Surprised cry
22. Handyman's clamp
23. Roof edges
25. Soak up gravy
27. Cowboys' ropes
29. Slumbers
31. Broad
33. Makes comfortable
34. Debatable
36. One of two
38. Dog's foot
41. Blow a horn
43. Calf meat
44. No longer is
47. "Rock of ___"
49. Looped rope
51. Occupant
53. Furious
55. Not tight
57. Elude
58. Sagebrush State
60. Tally
62. Actor Lugosi
63. Ball holder
64. Plate
66. Remain
68. Impresario Hurok
69. Moved obliquely
71. Moved through water
73. ___ Antoinette
76. Smell
78. Santa's transport
82. Accumulates
84. Spinning toy
86. Actor Kovacs
87. Carpet fluff
88. "Honor ___ Father"
90. Footed vase
92. Lofty
93. Brink
94. Society-page word
95. Four-in-hand
96. Aware about
97. Prophet
98. Commercials
99. Conceit
100. Robin's home

DOWN

1. Musical pitches
2. Flawless
3. Go
4. Regard highly
5. Choke
6. Word of sorrow
7. Under
8. Sticky stuff
9. Sportsman
10. Portico
11. Sturgeon roe
12. Opera highlights
13. Fake jewelry
14. Lock of hair
24. Garment stain
26. Baked dessert
28. Staggered
30. Shortly
32. Gets rid of
35. Implement
37. Pass the ___
38. "___ Your Wagon"
39. Approve
40. Make fabric
42. Cogged
44. Fords
45. ___ -Saxon

46. Commit robbery
48. R.R. locale: abbr.
50. ____ Canals
52. Cribbage card
54. Whirlpools
56. Has a meal
59. Support
61. Statutes
65. Splashed in mud
67. New Haven university
69. "____ Carrie"
70. Period
72. "The Seven Storey Mountain" author
73. Man and boy
74. Ammonia compound
75. Kitchen stove
77. Itinerary
79. Meaningless
80. Gold materials
81. Spartan serf
83. Sicilian peak
85. Prude
89. Affirmative answer
91. Recent: prefix

PUZZLE 244

ACROSS

1. Johann Sebastian ___
5. Swab
8. Stuffing herb
12. Sound repetition
13. Historical period
14. City in Oklahoma
15. Saharalike
16. End of an argument
18. Butterfly snare
19. Lair
20. Intoxicating
21. Hint
23. Animal hair
24. Pale
26. Carriage
27. Gear tooth
30. Enjoy a book
31. Wheel center
32. Possess
33. Ran into
34. Tint
35. Wall painting
36. Actor Young
37. Renown
38. Neck wrap
41. Make a mistake
42. Distant
45. Snoop on
47. Jason's ship
48. Arrow poison
49. Tavern
50. Antitoxins
51. Bog fuel
52. Naughty
53. Sewing juncture

DOWN

1. Legume
2. Unit of farmland
3. Small talk
4. Brick trough
5. Confused fight
6. City in Algeria
7. Fathers
8. Stitcher
9. Wild ox of Sulawesi
10. Encircle
11. Small whirlpool
17. Ruffian
19. Press for payment
22. Went in front
23. White lie
24. Upper limb
25. Catch sight of
26. Regret
27. With no worries
28. Eggs
29. Congeal
31. Embrace
32. Buzz
34. Record player
35. Deface
36. Welcome
37. Palm leaf
38. Small cut
39. Ice-cream holder
40. On the ocean
41. Sicilian volcano
43. Taj Mahal site
44. Wander
46. Penpoint
47. Donkey

PUZZLE 245

ACROSS
1. Mouser
4. Like a diamond
8. Status
12. Ring great
13. Fencer's weapon
14. Verve
15. Avoid
17. Actress Curtin
18. Marking devices
19. Predicted
21. Senator Symington
23. Personal quirk
24. Liberate
28. Precipitous
32. A Gershwin
33. Ankle bones
35. Bovine utterance
36. Storybook deer
38. Spring back
40. Journal
42. Actor Conway
43. Ill-fated vessel
47. Renter's concern
51. First person
52. Neophyte
54. Withered
55. Amend copy
56. Old horse
57. Lip
58. Refuse
59. Lennon's wife

DOWN
1. Musical Mama
2. Dismounted
3. Meticulous
4. Dillydallying
5. Quick to learn
6. "Donovan's ___"
7. Station
8. Discard
9. Word of woe
10. Zola novel
11. Was informed
16. Or ___!
20. Disposition to laugh
22. "Born in the ___"
24. Chest bone
25. Historic time
26. Felon's flight
27. Goof
29. Flightless bird
30. Ages and ages
31. Pea pack
34. Movie site
37. Points a finger at
39. Augury
41. Taunted
43. Soviet news agency
44. Brainstorm
45. Sailors
46. Hand over
48. ___ Domini
49. Young or Connery
50. Hence
53. Card game

181

PUZZLE 246

ACROSS

1. Large pot
4. Sports-shoe feature
9. That girl
12. Register
14. Unwilling
15. Fatherland
16. Wild animals
17. Concur
18. Let fly
19. Nomination
21. Dotes on
23. Zeroes in on
24. Water tester
25. Western resort ranches
27. Wisconsin products
31. Filleted
32. Hearing organ
33. Garbanzo, e.g.
35. Handicaps
36. Workers
38. Prejudice
39. Ripen
40. Picnic spoiler
41. Faiths
42. Missions
45. Tumbler
46. Tack on
47. Smelting waste
48. Piazzas
51. Office needs
55. Malt liquors
56. One who stares
58. Radiate
59. Legend
60. Lilac color
61. Flank
62. Husbands
63. Rims
64. Corded fabric

DOWN

1. Hankering
2. Genuine
3. Reputation
4. Maintains
5. Symbols
6. Deserve
7. Ingested
8. Auditoriums
9. Tart
10. Employ
11. Building extensions
13. Ten-year periods
15. Sneakers
20. Equaled
22. Female rabbit
25. Evade
26. Beneath
27. Coins
28. Owned
29. Poems about heroes
30. Benches
31. Large snake
34. Burro
36. Good-looking
37. Ampersand
38. Long-eared dogs
41. Smack
43. Jack up
44. Excitement
45. Scowls
47. Singer Winwood
48. Underside of the hand
49. African plant
50. Sea bird
51. Strike forcibly
52. Turkish title
53. Heckle
54. Measure
57. Roam about

182

PUZZLE 247

ACROSS
1. City in Arizona
5. Davenport
9. Demean
14. Crude metals
15. "And pretty maids all in ___"
16. Kind of eel
17. Put into jeopardy
19. Pickling solution
20. Aloof
21. Married
22. Director Howard
23. Skin
24. "Peyton ___"
28. Golf hazard
30. Coarse file
34. Subside
36. Inventor Whitney
37. Dalai ___
38. Stove part
39. Smallest
41. Boxer Barkley
42. Actor Lahr
43. Nibble
44. Disregard
46. German river
47. Bird's crop
49. Leases
50. Pier pests
52. Winter danger
54. Barn divisions
57. Chose
62. Routine
63. Hitter's delight
64. Actress Cara
65. Thought
66. Diva's tune
67. Pickle-picker Piper
68. Three winning numbers
69. Pepper variety

DOWN
1. Anchor
2. Aquatic flier
3. Perches
4. Tennis star
5. Artillery barrage
6. Far East
7. Loving
8. Extreme admiration
9. "Forever ___"
10. On the edge
11. Desertlike
12. Balanced
13. Green-___ (jealous)
18. Blundered
21. Elk
23. Friends
24. Explore
25. Even
26. Bitter
27. Court divider
29. Cowboy's rope
31. Producer Spelling
32. Knowledgeable
33. Window sections
35. Chooses
40. Corn units
45. Avarice
48. ___ schnitzel
51. Affect
53. Spotless
54. Watercraft
55. Weight allowance
56. Encourage
57. Aspect
58. Fiddler on the reef?
59. Grow weary
60. Sinful
61. Transaction
63. Ignited

183

PUZZLE 248

MOVIES AND TELEVISION

ACROSS
1. Lorenzo ____ of "Falcon Crest"
6. "Sooner or ____"
11. Simpleton
16. Like ____ from the blue
17. Clean a videotape
18. "____ Gay"
19. "____ Cry Wolf"
20. Wrong
21. "____ Gold"
22. Mintz of "The Goldbergs"
23. "____ Living"
25. Slippery fellows
27. "The Three Faces of ____"
28. "____ Street"
30. Gambler's stake
31. Computer operator
32. Comic Philips
33. Charles Dutton series
34. Fool
36. Scarlett's home
39. "She ____ Him Wrong"
40. Watered silk
44. "Havana" actress
45. "____ Kind of Wonderful"
46. Lionel ____ of "Hart to Hart"
48. Free
49. "Days of ____ and Roses"
50. Comedian Laurel
51. Always, to a bard
52. "____ Shade"
54. Rich Little, e.g.
55. TV host Garroway
56. Sleuth Wolfe et al.
57. Grace Kelly film, with "The"
58. "____ Three Lives"
59. "Just the ____ of Us"
61. Forever
62. Lamb's sound
64. Actress Veronica ____
67. Of an age
69. "War of the Worlds" narrator
72. Mr. Vigoda
73. Prepare a film for TV
74. "____ the End of Time"
75. "____ Max"
77. Franklin ____ of "The Jeffersons"
79. Dutch painter
81. Actress MacMahon
83. Crimes
84. Large antelope
85. "Weeds" actor
86. Feel
87. "Revenge of the ____"
88. Silver or Scout

DOWN
1. Superman's love
2. Rudy and Walter
3. "____ Crazy"
4. Falstaff's quaff
5. "Islands in the ____"
6. "____ of Life"
7. "This Is the ____"
8. Skater Babilonia
9. "Bare ____"
10. Adjust a VCR clock
11. "A Fine ____"
12. Yoko ____
13. Film parts
14. Ms. Oyl
15. Michael ____ of "Dynasty"
24. ____, amas, amat
26. "____ Miserables"
29. Actress Young
30. Tops
31. "Once ____ a Horse"
33. "Tony ____"
35. "____ for All Seasons"
36. "Casbah" actress
37. "Staying ____"
38. "Pale ____"
39. Doorbell sound
41. "____ in Danger"
42. Actor Christopher ____
43. Miscalculated
45. "The ____ of Madelon Claudet"
46. Nana portrayer
47. Roofing material

184

49. He played Laura Palmer's father
50. Bridge
53. Memo
54. Military letters
55. "___ M for Murder"
57. "Those Redheads from ___"
60. Actor Beatty
62. Barbara ___ Geddes
63. Comedian Sherman et al.
64. Shoestrings
65. "This ___ All"
66. "The Wonder Years" character
68. Climbed
69. "The ___ of War"
70. "The Life of ___ Zola"
71. Health, to Bardot
73. Highlands language
74. Watch over
76. Exploit
78. Raised railways
80. Play it by ___
82. "Salem's ___"

PUZZLE 248

PUZZLE 249

ACROSS
1. Bear's youngster
4. Obligation
8. Men's party
12. Milky gem
14. "___ Smith and Jones"
16. Bee abode
17. Timbre
18. Slogan
19. Toward shelter
20. Finishes
21. Mimic
22. Constructor
24. Wise
26. Trust
27. Love
29. Carpenter's need
30. Guy's date
33. Publish
34. Pal
35. Self
36. Defeat
37. Dish
38. Saucy
39. Question
40. Chowder ingredients
41. Military headquarters
42. Of course!
43. File
44. Thick soup
45. Wealthy
46. Mailed
47. "Her ___"
49. Pub drink
50. Memo
54. Saharalike
55. Pertaining to ships
57. Vile
58. Finger ornament
59. Orange orchard
60. Skelton and Buttons
61. Birthday dessert
62. Pitcher
63. Born

DOWN
1. Pigeon house
2. Atop
3. Dance orchestra
4. Mar
5. Run away to marry
6. Chew
7. Make lace
8. Weak and unsteady
9. Ceramic slab
10. State
11. Horse command
13. School studies
15. Anybody
23. Colleague
25. Type of gallery
26. Alex Haley's book
27. Woke up
28. Data storage platters
29. Hobo
30. Silly persons
31. Concur
32. Great amount
33. Romp
34. Conflict of views
37. Putting
38. Associate
40. Baby bed
41. Hamburger roll
44. Potato parer
45. Chain of hills
46. Serf
47. Operatic solo
48. Bracelet part
49. Promise
51. Kiln
52. Ocean movement
53. In addition
54. Part of a circle
56. Have being

PUZZLE 250

ACROSS
1. Grimm meanie
5. "The ___ Kings"
10. Spy's message form
14. Dessert choice
15. Toppings for toast
16. So be it!
17. Take care of
18. Heaps
19. Constrain
20. Selfishness
23. Impudent
24. Supporter
25. Entertains
28. One who supplies bonds
33. Have a ___ to pick
34. Lox holder
35. Altar words
36. Invitations
37. Mislays
38. Yokel
39. Raw metal
40. Cut back
41. Hither
42. Balconies
44. Degrees
46. Brew
47. Bucket
48. Commander in chief
54. Soft mineral
55. Accommodate
56. Cook book
58. Jai ___
59. Bet backer
60. Fifty-fifty
61. Manipulate
62. Grinding mineral
63. Ship

DOWN
1. Frequently, in poems
2. Kind of club
3. Tolled
4. Supports
5. Motorized bikes
6. Skirt style
7. Dissolve
8. South African Dutch
9. Becomes inflexible
10. Rustic houses
11. Disregard
12. Disclaim
13. Objective
21. Hint
22. Telephone
25. Monk
26. Ripple-patterned fabric
27. Beneath
28. Foundations
29. Like vintage wine
30. Runners' distances
31. Revere
32. Centering points
34. Caliber
37. Cut
38. Goblets
40. White
43. Rotten
44. Sweet roll
45. Masculine pronoun
47. Bagpipe player
48. Strong breeze
49. Gusto
50. Biblical man
51. Body of water
52. Advance
53. Presage
54. Bill
57. Share ___ share alike

187

PUZZLE 251

ACROSS

1. Authentic
6. Baseballer Musial
10. Novelist Bagnold
14. Boxing site
15. ___ -de-camp
16. Canter
17. Comedian Arnold ___
18. Lose one's temper
20. Actor Knight
21. Sharpen
23. Adolescent
24. Use a pitcher
25. Stretch across
27. Atoll pond
30. Gentlemen
31. Spigot
34. Audibly
35. France's capital
36. Honest ___
37. Street fight
38. Oregon's capital
39. Shoo!
40. Auto fuel
41. Clergyman
42. Hoist
43. Wind dir.
44. Charge against property
45. Gaudy
46. Actress Lucille ___
47. Chicago location
48. Expectations
51. Admonish
52. Urban railways
55. Completely
58. Fiend
60. Chair
61. Type of china
62. "Goodnight" girl
63. Whetstone
64. Lager
65. Comforted

DOWN

1. Enormous
2. Johnson the funnyman
3. Show the way
4. Stopping place
5. Mr. Bumstead
6. Cavalry sword
7. Pinball foul
8. Hubbub
9. Up-to-date
10. Pixyish
11. Person, place, or thing
12. ___ facto
13. Venison source
19. Assemble
22. Attila, e.g.
24. Sulk
25. Warning signal
26. Prudish
27. Member-at- ___
28. Assumed name
29. Cook one's ___
30. Beauty shop
31. Tortilla sandwiches
32. Humiliate
33. Trivial
35. Group of judges
38. Boat's canvas
39. Soft- ___ (flatter)
41. Mismatch
42. Mrs. Bumstead
45. On behalf of
46. Singer Midler
47. Filled cake
48. Talk over
49. Butter substitute
50. Mastermind
51. Decline
52. Arden and Plumb
53. Ruled mark
54. Snow toy
56. Waste away
57. Trouble
59. Mesozoic, e.g.

188

ACROSS
1. Brief note
5. Sluggish
9. Grovel
12. Lined up
13. Complete
15. Viva voce exam
16. Adjacent
18. Watch the birdie
19. Pipe fitting
20. Bullfight cheers
21. Manufacture
23. Greek war god
24. Put up with
25. Talks back
28. Crony
29. Tree juice
32. Layers
33. Wild pigs
34. Lupino of filmdom
35. Hawkeye portrayer
36. Do the electric slide
37. Skunk's defense
38. Fasten
39. Bo or John
40. Thwart
41. Wimbledon unit
42. Mirrors
43. Exchanges
44. Stirs up
46. Monty Hall's transaction
47. Skimpy
49. Endure
50. Canine mother
53. Pleasant
54. Repels
57. Grills
58. Choice
59. Building site
60. Fuel
61. Hodgepodge
62. Charity

DOWN
1. Sail support
2. Huron's sister lake
3. Method
4. See red?
5. Fashions
6. Misplaces
7. Character Campbell on "Andy Griffith"
8. Lump
9. Hit with a barrage
10. Direction from Illinois to Ohio
11. Joy
14. Oration
15. Store sign
17. Reams
22. Pasture animals
23. On the ocean
24. Hut
25. Quarrels
26. Kate's friend
27. Diverts attention
28. Crispy containers
30. Revere
31. Components
33. Uncovers
36. Exhaust
37. ____ office
39. Raised platform
40. Brazilian parrot
43. Tantalizes
45. Mine shipments
46. Dings
47. Obstacle
48. Italian tower town
49. Party cheese
50. Dip spice
51. Actor West
52. Queens nine
55. City on the Danube
56. Healthy place

PUZZLE 252

PUZZLE 253

ACROSS
1. Astronaut Shepard
5. Golfer Snead
8. Ago
12. Cuts into cubes
14. Buckeye State
15. Mature
16. Move heaven and ___
17. Ponder
18. Ireland, to a poet
19. Recorded again
21. Ability
23. Edit
24. Evade
25. Soften
28. Concluded
30. Marine bird
31. Heal
33. Fishing gear
37. Actor Wallach
38. Ready, ___, go
39. Sopping
41. Daisy ___
42. Confusion
44. Otherwise
46. Hotel
47. Cowboy's rope
49. Erected
52. Hold dear
54. Carpenters' needs
56. Pass by
57. More than
60. Feast
61. Difficult journey
63. Verne's captain and namesakes
65. At any time
66. Snake sound
67. Line ___ (baseball term)
68. Famous loch
69. New York summer hrs.
70. Simmer

DOWN
1. Lemon refresher
2. Falsifier
3. "God's Little ___"
4. Entrapped
5. Shake
6. Feel ill
7. Shed feathers
8. Musical opener
9. Vented
10. Backbone
11. Teepee
13. Embarrass
14. Sign
20. Pound portions
22. Wide-awake
25. Consider
26. ___ Stanley Gardner
27. Blue dye
29. Current events
32. Western Indians
34. Arab leader
35. Path
36. Transmit
38. Scorches
40. Weird
43. Couple on the run
45. Of greatest duration
48. Boil
50. Antelope
51. Michaelmas daisies
52. Animated
53. Great ___ (large dogs)
55. Floating zoos?
56. First address
58. Give off
59. Wander
62. Disencumber
64. Darn

PUZZLE 254

ACROSS

1. Worker
5. ____ Ababa, Ethiopia
10. Circular sections
14. Cosmetic ingredient
15. 1984 Grand Prix champ Niki ____
16. King Leonardo, e.g.
17. Home of William Jennings Bryan
20. Vapor
21. Shopper's quest
22. Barrel
23. Rickey ingredient
26. Ego
28. Delay
31. After-bath sprinkle
33. George Eliot's Marner
36. Lagers
38. Anthropologist Margaret ____
40. ____ Domingo
42. Oakland County seat
45. Primp
46. Georgia school
47. Apartment payment
48. German town
50. " . . .able to ____ tall buildings . . ."
52. Movie theater monogram
53. Club fee
55. Small drink
57. 1 or 11, in blackjack
60. Pitch-adjusting device
62. Billy Joel's forte
66. Wyatt Earp's domain
70. So be it!
71. Loosen
72. Actress Merrill
73. Choice for diners
74. Flower
75. Celebrity

DOWN

1. Dutch painter
2. Landed
3. "And Then There Were ____"
4. Transferable design
5. "____ the King's Men"
6. Anchorman Rather
7. Presses for payment
8. Inspirations
9. Expensive furs
10. In that way
11. Venture
12. Industrial fuel
13. Hosiery hazard
18. Overlook
19. Savor
24. Talking-doll word
25. Choose
27. Panache
28. Northern native
29. Then: Fr.
30. French author Jean ____
32. Bactrian
34. Ire
35. Smelled bad
37. Place
39. Chopped
41. Atop
43. Urge
44. Scorch
49. Pekoe holder
51. Hemingway's nickname
54. Book back
56. Obeys
57. Cartwright son
58. Arrive
59. Sir Anthony ____
61. Director Preminger
63. ____ were
64. Darling dog
65. Glacial ridges
67. African antelope
68. Yang's opposite
69. Anthem poet

PUZZLE 255

ACROSS
1. Price
5. Understands
9. Go in
14. World's fair
15. Run in neutral
16. Home of the Dolphins
17. Night activity
19. Uncover
20. Finale
21. House greeneries
23. Schlep
24. April 1st star
25. Salary
27. Beauty center
29. "Star ____ Banner"
34. Chef's garb
35. Retiring
36. Roman tourist spot
37. Shimmer
38. Actor Holbrook
39. Terrible tsar
40. Ringside official
42. Panhandler's find
43. Shorthand
44. Show about the "Enterprise"
46. Despises
47. Green soup
48. Mailman's mount, once
49. Fair to middlin'
52. Danger
55. Montana of football
58. Thunderstruck
60. Acrobatic trick
62. Tenth president
63. Kitty food
64. Early Peruvian
65. Superfluous
66. Mrs. Truman
67. Look like

DOWN
1. Yield
2. Yoked animals
3. Exceeded 55 mph
4. Before gun or banana
5. Actor Matt ____
6. Perfect
7. Secluded valley
8. Before Oct.
9. Dorothy's auntie et al.
10. ____ Dirt Band
11. Poi base
12. Give forth
13. Ready for plucking
18. Place-setting component
22. Health resort
24. Hippie slogan
26. Picnic crasher
27. Separate
28. Fragrance
29. "Jaws" subject
30. Ernie or Gomer
31. Embankment
32. Linda or Maurice
33. Flintstone pet
34. Go-betweens: abbr.
35. Mule or loafer
41. Hwy.
43. The ____ of time
45. Bowl cheer
46. Mobs
48. Trousers
49. Location
50. Jet black
51. ____ of the earth
53. Moby Dick's pursuer
54. Writer Grey
55. Fonda of films
56. Thrice minus twice
57. Cheese-shop choice
59. Time period
61. Third word of "America"

192

PUZZLE 256

ACROSS
1. Sum up
6. Barn sound
11. Large
14. Dodge
15. Spooky
16. Opposite of WSW
17. Pretend
18. Mail-order book
20. Conductor Fiedler
22. Animals' homes
23. Identical
25. Upright
28. Place for a jeans patch
29. Desert wear
30. Ugly thing
32. Drilled
34. Racetrack bet
39. Gospel
42. Washington bills
43. Depicted
45. Garret
46. Front-porch item
49. Teacher's gp.
50. Historian's concern
54. Slow creature
55. Catch one's breath
56. Farewell
58. Quit talking
60. Screech
63. Popular ski resort
66. Conceit
67. Statue base
68. Inscribed stone
69. Home room

70. Lend ____ (listen)
71. Now

DOWN
1. Electrical unit
2. Night before
3. Twin-hulled boat
4. Idolize
5. Confined
6. Protected
7. Closest
8. Table scrap
9. Narrow inlet
10. Spill the beans
11. Commence
12. Harden
13. Honkers
19. Mighty tree
21. "____ Jude"

23. Saw type
24. Overhead
26. Firewood measure
27. Three voices
30. Outlined
31. Musical key
33. Means justifier
35. Young sow
36. Dozed
37. Goes for it
38. Songwriters' gp.
40. God of love
41. Fighter Spinks
44. Stoker character

47. Mitch or Glenn
48. Between chicken and king
50. Walked back and forth
51. Saying
52. Squelch
53. Wooden peg
55. Relish
57. Sky bear
59. Upright pole
61. Was victorious
62. Crack pilot
64. Guido's note
65. Negative vote

193

PUZZLE 257

QUOTEWORD

A quotation reads clockwise around the outside squares of this diagram. To find the quotation, work the puzzle as a regular crossword, filling in the remaining blank squares with the letters given below.

A A B B F H H I N N N O O P R T T T T U

ACROSS
14. Guido's note: 2 wds.
15. Greek letter
16. Noise
17. Individual
18. Group: abbr.
19. Part of a mosque
21. New York hours: abbr.
22. Asian body of water: 2 wds.
24. Wind dir.
25. Of a cereal
27. Railroad station abbr.
28. "The Tender ___"
31. 6 feet, 5 inches
33. ___ King Cole
35. Bell sound
38. Time period
39. Beach soil
40. Want
43. Comedian Louis
44. Encountered
45. "___ will be done"
46. Before: Latin
47. Neither's partner
48. Vietnamese holiday
49. Dance step
50. Shade tree
51. Skin
53. Power type
56. Frank's ex
57. Parisian place
60. I smell ___: 2 wds.
62. Baseball stats.
63. Arabian gulf
64. Is in debt
65. Lima's country
66. Skirt bottoms
67. Markdown time
68. ___ Willie Winkie
69. ___ and doughnuts
70. Gnat
72. Actor Knight
73. Morose
74. Uncle: Sp.
76. WWI army: abbr.
78. "To ___ with Love"
79. Eavesdropping device
80. Language of Northern Thailand
82. Commotion
83. Takes control forcibly
85. Hurt
86. Sprite
87. Of sound mind
89. Patriotic group: abbr.
90. European
91. Ego
92. Work unit
95. Fleshy
97. Nationality suffix
99. Summoning
103. First woman
104. Saline solution use
107. US security group
108. ___ Paulo
109. ___ -dye
110. Green or pekoe
111. Enemy

DOWN
1. Yale alum
2. Stood for office
3. Makes mistakes
4. Spotted cats
5. Palindromic word for child
6. Suitable
7. Fog
8. Strong
9. Indian region
10. With regard to: 2 wds.
11. Administrative power site
12. Dawn goddess
13. Anger
20. Poisonous snake
23. Once around track
25. Ancient
26. Snooze
29. Fish eggs
30. Emmet
32. Some
34. White metal
36. Came in
37. Sailor's assent
39. Nova
40. Appendage
41. Riatas
42. Mesozoic, e.g.
46. Carpenter's tool
49. Old-fashioned
50. ___ Knievel
52. Speedy
54. Zinc coin of Denmark
55. Make fun of

56. Nabokov book
57. Cringe
58. Amazed
59. Cost
61. "___ You Lonesome Tonight?"
63. Fall bloom
69. Animal enclosure
71. Cutting implement
72. Scale notes
73. Measured land
75. Actress Lupino
77. FBI man: abbr.
78. Roads
79. Constricting snake
80. Confederate general
81. Entire
84. Uncle ___
85. Foxy
88. Scream upon seeing a mouse
90. Strong metal
91. Baste
93. Yeast-caused action in dough
94. Chew
96. Ardent
98. Actor Connery
100. By way of
101. Simpleton
102. Sticky substance
104. And so forth: abbr.
105. Astern
106. Great Lakes' ___ Canals

195

PUZZLE 258

ACROSS

1. Filth
5. Scheme
9. Now hear ___!
13. "___ the Night"
17. Aroma
18. Fishing cord
19. Bombast
20. Sign gas
21. Different
22. Rich Little, e.g.
23. Irish river
24. Great ___
25. "The Four ___"
27. Repair
29. Restaurant employee
31. Ascot
32. Breeze
33. ___ Lang (Superboy's girlfriend)
34. Yet
37. Snack
38. Co-owners
42. Ore vein
43. Be overly fond
44. "___ and Prejudice"
45. Digit
46. Wedding vow
47. Oolong
48. Lances
50. "___ in Yonkers"
51. Endure
54. Telescope glass
55. Skeleton parts
56. Diamond gal
57. Imbibed
59. Pod vegetable
60. Sell tickets illegally
63. Leda's seducer
64. Power
69. Rocky crags
70. Huts
72. Faraday term
73. Director Spike ___
74. Copy
75. Gay
76. Minister to
78. Oracle
79. Used logic
81. Bitter
82. Believes
83. Tailless amphibian
84. Southern bread
85. She lays around the barn
86. Of late
89. Never ___ (don't bother)
90. Flip-flops
94. Grieve
95. Unfold
97. James et al.
99. New York canal
100. Wearing shoes
101. Fare
102. Ruckus
103. Soar
104. Sodas, in the Midwest
105. Winter vehicle
106. News
107. Trees' fluids

DOWN

1. Accomplishes
2. Inert
3. Singer Ponselle
4. Viaduct
5. Carpenter's smoothing tool
6. Facial features
7. United
8. White ants
9. Style
10. Firm
11. Wayside respite
12. Wine attendants
13. Cherokee, e.g.
14. Orderly
15. Actor Franchot ___
16. Unique person
26. Black gold
28. Chemical suffix
30. Contribute a share
32. Punster
33. Hideaways
34. Skirt feature
35. Commotion
36. Worshipped one
37. Clipper
38. Practical jokes
39. English town
40. Bette Midler role
41. Congeals
43. Dole
44. Hammer part
47. Expedition
49. Board
50. Borrowed sum
52. House wings

53. Pirate Teach
55. Existed
58. Sprightly
59. Urge
60. ____ apple
61. Make do
62. Neighbor-
     hood
63. Cut
     cabbage
     for slaw
65. Hue
66. Mirth
67. Swarm
68. Towel title
70. Upper House
     members
71. Criterion
75. Earth's
     satellite
77. Poet's before
78. Transmitters
80. Spirited
     horses
81. Cargo
     weight
82. Study
84. Languished
85. Waste
     producer
86. Coarse file
87. Lover of
     Narcissus
88. Cleave

PUZZLE 258

89. Apportion
90. Cease
91. Solo for Sills
92. Speak
     imperfectly
93. Looks
96. Buddy
98. ____ de Oro

PUZZLE 259

ACROSS
1. Artist Chagall
5. Civilian clothes
10. Feds
14. Block
15. Ram sign
16. Patriot Nathan ____
17. Petty tiff
18. Howls
20. Disney specials
22. A.k.a.
23. Cato's years
24. Hillside dugout
26. Implied
29. Twin-hulled boat
34. Computer type
36. Fishing spears
37. Go quickly
38. Vegetable containers
39. Mountain ridge
41. Show up
42. One ____ time
43. Musician Getz
44. Gas choice, once
46. Gingham dog's pal
49. Hollywood names
50. Biblical weed
51. College gp.
53. Quechuan
56. Seattle eleven
60. Attempt something dangerous
63. Memory's route
64. Mine, in Amiens
65. Type size
66. Garnishment
67. Church court
68. Stage awards
69. "Rosebud," e.g.

DOWN
1. Opposite of fem.
2. Stringed instrument, in Italy
3. Bring up the ____
4. Marsh reeds
5. Georgia city
6. Of the heavens
7. If the shoe ____ . . .
8. Duffer's need
9. Neighbor of Leb.
10. Muse of comedy
11. Hawaiian isle
12. Logan or Cinders
13. Promontory
19. Heats up
21. Atop
24. Keep ____ (persist)
25. Bread with lox
26. Paris cigar sign
27. Author Loos
28. Water channel
30. Booster rocket
31. Harper TV role
32. Pointer
33. Requisites
35. Bayou denizen
40. Competition
41. Boos
43. In short supply
45. O.T. book
47. Napoli's land
48. Political pact
52. Joyce Carol ____
53. Construction beam
54. "Nautilus" captain
55. Thicken
56. Examine
57. Bemoan
58. On bended ____
59. ____ packing
61. Hedda Hopper's topper
62. Numero uno

PUZZLE 260

The answers to the clues can be found in the diagram, but they have been camouflaged. Their letters are in the correct order, but sometimes they are separated by extra letters which have been inserted throughout the diagram. You must black out all the extra Camouflage letters. The remaining letters will be used in words reading across and down. Solve Across and Down together to determine the correct letters where there is a choice. The number of answer words in a row or column is indicated by the number of clues.

	1	2	3	4	5	6	7	8	9	10	11	12	13
1	S	T	C	L	N	I	M	E	B	G	I	S	T
2	A	J	R	O	E	M	A	G	R	B	I	O	E
3	R	A	A	G	L	A	L	D	K	O	D	U	R
4	S	B	U	P	O	S	Y	R	A	O	R	U	M
5	C	L	V	I	N	G	B	E	I	D	E	R	T
6	H	E	S	S	H	I	B	E	E	T	R	I	A
7	I	M	H	I	F	E	S	A	D	E	S	S	O
8	E	Y	R	X	A	N	E	E	A	R	E	S	T
9	S	I	Q	T	U	E	R	N	N	A	N	U	T
10	Z	P	I	E	B	L	H	L	G	I	D	E	E
11	B	E	G	I	N	T	O	M	E	N	N	S	S
12	A	S	H	C	O	O	P	S	L	E	W	D	T
13	D	O	T	S	K	B	E	A	L	O	D	S	N

ACROSS

1. Ascend • Main point
2. Bouquet • Caviar
3. Dust cloth • Young man • " ____ Town"
4. Channel marker • Fortify
5. Type of peach • Sea duck
6. Dame Myra ____ • Spain and Portugal
7. Underworld
8. Period • Closest
9. Rigid • Macadamia, e.g.
10. Tablet • Golly!
11. Israeli statesman • Signs of the future
12. Strong wood • Poultry pen • Allow
13. Specks • Rosary ____

DOWN

1. Fallen ____ • Spoiled
2. Competent • Mexican money
3. Subjugate • Correct
4. Military science branch
5. Actor Chaney • Year, to Juan
6. Suppose • Hit
7. Perhaps • Lasso
8. Poor grade • ____ mater
9. Ornamental trim • Show backer
10. Supreme being • Sea eagle
11. Choler • Split
12. Biting • Publishes
13. Semester • Certify

PUZZLE 261

ACROSS

1. Table extender
5. Singer Vicki ____
9. Music's George M. ____
14. Jazzy Fitzgerald
15. Busy as ____
16. Give a speech
17. Coiffure need
19. Horse control devices
20. Did dinner
21. Best in the blabbermouth department
23. Nonsense
24. Continues a subscription
26. Sounds a horn
28. Sign gases
31. English elopement green
34. Thai money
37. Ireland, to a poet
39. Bread grains
40. Wings
41. Alley components
42. Roman 152
43. One who inherits
44. Made like a monkey
45. Banana coverings
46. Leftover pieces
48. Female
50. Blackthorns
52. Complete
56. Cleo's killer
58. Accurate
61. No, to a Scot
62. Divest
64. Gun-sight marker
66. Toil
67. Carry
68. Against
69. Trifled
70. Health resorts
71. Parcel

DOWN

1. "The Merry Widow" composer
2. Please
3. Not of this planet
4. Few and ____ between
5. Tenor Enrico ____
6. Be next to
7. Time out
8. Restore to good health, for short
9. Swell thing
10. Norwegian coin
11. Beautician's concern
12. ____ time (never)
13. Hatching place
18. Pitney's partner
22. Laws
25. Intestinal
27. Certain part
29. Kind of tide
30. Tendon
32. Astronaut Armstrong
33. Sale condition
34. Exclamations of disgust
35. Fish sauce
36. Beautician's sticky stuff
38. Accomplish again
41. Intense light gun
45. Window parts
47. Burst
49. Disorders
51. Denominations
53. Stupid
54. Singer Bonnie ____
55. Supernatural
56. Helper: abbr.
57. World War II battlefield
59. Cut to fit
60. Little bit
63. "____ Got the World on a String"
65. Stage hog

200

PUZZLE 262

ACROSS
1. Spanish jar
5. Word of despair
9. Riga resident
13. Cheerful
15. Scrabble piece
16. Winglike
17. Penitence
19. Masculine
20. Article
21. Chemical suffix
22. Vital element
24. Neighbor of Mass.
25. Long time
26. Debate side
28. Possessive pronoun
30. Satisfied
33. Public transportation, in London
34. French resort
36. Blanched
38. Cavort
39. Foolish people
41. French actor Jacques ___
42. "All ___ Eve"
44. Piano novelty
45. Part of a list
46. Bandleader Skinnay ___
48. Buddy
49. "___ the ramparts . . ."
50. Computer screen initials
51. Dublin darlin'
53. Water holder
57. Procured
58. Motive
61. Mine, in Paris
62. Regret
65. Western defense gp.
66. Spouted vessel
67. Aquatic mammal
68. British weapon
69. Elevator pioneer
70. The auld sod

DOWN
1. Killer whale
2. Big cat
3. Bring the plane in
4. Pismire
5. Military command
6. Fifty-two, to Caesar
7. Shampoo additive
8. Has a feeling
9. Wailing
10. Zest
11. Soft mineral
12. One grew in Brooklyn
14. Quartet with one absentee
18. Six outs make one of these
23. Detergent
24. Remorse
26. Explore
27. Navarro of the silents
29. Dish up
31. Make happy
32. Stop
33. La-la preceder
35. Darkroom equipment
37. Gloomy
40. Old West watering hole
43. Wear out
47. Teenage must
52. Preminger of the director's chair
53. Fires
54. Amo, amas, ___
55. What you sign when you borrow
56. Salamander
58. Prefix for freeze or dote
59. Champagne cooler
60. Insignificant
63. Famous architect
64. Pigged out

PUZZLE 263

ACROSS

1. Twenty quires
5. As well
9. New York district
13. "____ on the Wild Side"
17. Japanese language
18. Sacred song
19. School hops
21. Mangle
22. Same: Lat.
23. Textile fiber
24. Misbehave
25. ____ majesty
26. Navy engineer
28. Moth
30. ____ Anne de Beaupre
31. Onetime
32. Slip-ups
33. Shenanigans
36. Social travelers
39. History Muse
40. Slow-witted
43. Light brown
46. Black gold
47. Slumbered
48. Panoramas
50. Suite
52. Objective
54. Sets aside
56. ____ numerals
58. Actress Nettleton
59. Schoolbooks
60. Barcelona misters
62. Picnic drinks
64. Canoe blade
65. Calendar cycles: abbr.
66. Bis!
68. Guard
71. Cigarette residue
74. Lid
75. Sortie
77. Disdain
82. Kids' wheels
84. Mouth, slangily
86. Crania
87. Behind: Fr.
88. ____ tartar
91. Plant disease
92. Choppers
93. Conch, e.g.
94. Smash sign
96. "____ John" (Hirsch sitcom)
97. Laundry machine
99. Military cap
100. Prime
102. Itty-bitty
105. Ultimate goal
109. Tramp
112. Yup's opposite
113. "The Tempest" spirit
115. Artist's workplace
116. Jai ____
117. Expel
119. Small cases
121. Extinct bird
122. Fluff
123. Continue, in music
124. Tropical plant
125. Pendant
126. Sluggish
127. Cast off
128. Joie de vivre
129. Desires

DOWN

1. Pay increase
2. Sea duck
3. Lend ____
4. Gibberish
5. ____ rule (generally)
6. Fancy fabric
7. Snub
8. The end
9. Glistens
10. Grampus
11. Nightclub
12. Japanese city
13. Disorganized
14. Environs
15. Preoccupied
16. Patella site
18. Magician's word
20. Disburse
27. Before, to bards
29. Send with
34. Cry of pain
35. Hawser holder
37. Small taste
38. Month after Ab
41. Break off
42. Vase-shaped jugs
43. Historic times
44. Middle
45. Speckled horse
47. Web spinner
49. Draft agcy.
51. Papa horse
53. Shout
54. Coast Guard women
55. Bitterns
57. Lineman
59. Tippler
61. Twenty
63. Helix

67. Goddess of plenty
69. "____ Bede"
70. Akin
71. With property
72. More bruised
73. Pretentious
76. Place for Picasso
78. Conservative
79. Abscond
80. Diva Gluck
81. Russian ruler
82. Modeled
83. Giggle
85. Affectation
88. Masticate
89. Iterated
90. Fish ____
93. Out of sight
95. Black Sea port
98. Coty and Clair
100. Of rainfall
101. Army insect
103. Hubs
104. Female relative
106. Revere
107. Put a ____ (curb)
108. Picots
109. Corridor
110. Medley
111. Clobber
114. Moon goddess
118. Prompt
120. Stopover spot

PUZZLE 264

ACROSS

1. ____ committee
6. Israeli mountain
12. Halley's ____
17. Hang loosely
18. Ancient Greek region
20. Make amends
21. Carnation locale
22. Robert B. Sinclair film
24. Mischievous one
25. Cruising
27. Scribble idly
28. Bishop's domain
29. Barks at the moon
31. Recluse
33. Formerly named
34. Dry
35. Sacred
37. British transport
39. Swell
41. Tender
42. Star in Aquarius
44. Pester
48. Sums
51. Lone Star State
53. Put up with
54. Producer Lesser
55. Commentary
57. Multiplication word
59. This, in Barcelona
60. Short fiber
62. Diploma
64. College residence
65. Seaweed
66. Comedian Kovacs
67. Simpleton
69. Fleur-de-____
70. Borge's instrument
72. City in Alabama
74. Recruit
76. Lady of Spain
78. "The King and I" locale
79. Gale
80. Balkan
82. Eager
84. Poker pot
85. Add liquor to
88. Forage vetch
90. Damaged: abbr.
92. Rice wine
95. Feel poorly
96. Radio interference
98. Dismissed suddenly
100. Senator Aspin
101. Comic strip character
104. Sublease
106. Cassia family shrub
107. City in Florida
108. Zeus' daughter
109. Sharp
110. Doghouse
111. Compensator

DOWN

1. Improvise
2. Theater piece
3. Comic strip
4. Unlock, to poets
5. That, in Giverny
6. Type of film role
7. Flagrant
8. Communications giant initials
9. Comic strip character
10. Taro root
11. Costa Rican seaport
12. Jean Toomer work
13. Nebraska Indian
14. Code man
15. Enrol
16. Snicker
19. English forest
23. Slumber
26. Crafty
30. Kind
32. Formerly, formerly
34. Declared
36. Not fatty
38. Aphorism
40. Hirt and Jolson
41. Informer
43. Constrained
45. Comic strip
46. New
47. Dutch cheeses
49. Run easily
50. Night twinklers
52. Mister, in Madrid
54. Fasteners

56. Fish-eating eagles
58. Capital of Manche
61. Wooly
63. Eyelashes
68. City
71. Prospector's find
73. Cupid
75. Tool sets
77. Mountain ridge
81. Well done!
83. Rio ____
84. Years of life
85. Slippage
86. Made public
87. Adhere
89. Unadorned
91. Tout
93. New Hampshire city
94. Chemical compound
96. Food fish
97. French river to the Vilaine
99. Trickle
102. Opposite of SSW
103. Dancer Miller
105. Historical period

PUZZLE 264

PUZZLE 265

MOVIES AND TELEVISION

ACROSS

1. Actress Jane ____ ("Dear John")
5. "Love Me Tender" actress
10. Mineo and Viscuso
14. ____ vera
15. Mara of "Robin Hood of Texas"
16. "Dies ____"
17. "That Funny Feeling" actor
19. PBS science series
20. Vic Damone film
21. "What's Up, ____?" (Streisand)
23. "____ This Town on Fire" (Chuck Connors film)
24. Please greatly
27. Mistake correctors
29. "____ Baba Goes to Town"
31. "Tony ____" (Sinatra film)
33. Part of RSVP
34. Anchorman Rather
35. Bruce Dern film
37. "Let ____ Write My Epitaph"
41. Hera's son
43. "____ of the Night"
45. Carry on
46. "Inherit the Wind" actor
48. Luncheon entree
50. Thing, at law
51. "____ for the Lamps of China"
53. Emphatic affirmative, to Juan
54. "____, Giorgio" (Pavarotti film)
55. Frontiersman
59. Author Alexander
61. Gardner of "Seven Days in May"
62. "The ____ and Only" (Winkler film)
63. Egg repositories
66. Dick Van Patten role in "Mama"
68. Matt Helm portrayer
72. The Stooges, e.g.
73. Chemical compound
74. Exercise a franchise
75. And others: abbr.
76. Donna and Robert
77. Pennsylvania city

DOWN

1. Calloway et al.
2. Top-heavy
3. Mike Stivic portrayer
4. "____ Without a Cause"
5. Hipster's home
6. Susan Hayward film
7. Eur. land
8. Omit in pronouncing
9. Opera heroes
10. "____ of Innocence"
11. "____ for Everyone" (Cardinale film)
12. Wimbledon champion
13. Theater furniture
18. "The Best ____ of Our Lives"
22. "Mildred Pierce" author
25. Conti and Hanks
26. Radiates
28. "____ Burn"
29. TV's "____-12"
30. Julie Christie role in "Doctor Zhivago"
32. Walter ____ Disney
36. Actor Christopher ____ ("The Nightcomers")

38. "The Great Lie" actress
39. Film critic James ____
40. Eliot of "The Untouchables"
42. Highlander
44. Actor La Rue
47. Hawaiian city
49. Rigg of "A Little Night Music"
52. Generous owner
55. A votre ____
56. Wimbledon winner
57. Actress Shire of "Rocky"
58. Sergeant Velie of "Ellery Queen"
60. Audacity
64. Grayish monkey
65. Snick-or- ____
67. Photography director Polito
69. Noshed
70. "____ Kelly" (Mick Jagger film)
71. "The Ghost and ____ Muir" (Tierney film)

PUZZLE 266

ACROSS
1. Dutch export
5. Go by
9. Sioux
13. Dickens character
14. Actress DuBois
15. Caspian Sea feeder
16. S'well song?
18. Semester
19. Printers' measures
20. Miguel's cheers
21. Except
23. Caustic substance
24. ___ voyage!
25. Portico
26. Sugary song?
31. Mel's waitress
34. Like a ghost story
35. Orangutan
36. Theater section
37. Enjoys a paperback
39. Till the cows come home
40. Elsie's hello
41. Faction
42. Primp
43. Rainy day song?
47. New York district
48. "Much ___ About Nothing"
49. Inquire
52. Arm of the Indian Ocean
55. Roman 1059
56. Charlotte of television
57. "___ Ben Adhem"
58. Song for a newborn?
61. Footloose
62. Simplifies
63. Competent
64. Fling
65. Mast
66. Changed color

DOWN
1. ___ Ford Range (Antarctica)
2. Feathery
3. Ascended
4. ___ in the moon
5. Nurture
6. Sandy's replies
7. Actor Erwin
8. Greeters
9. Billy the Kid, for one
10. Timber
11. Paddles
12. New Haven trees
14. Cantaloupe
17. "___ Gillis"
22. Prying
25. Shanty
26. ___ in the hole
27. Asiatic alliance: abbr.
28. Roof overhang
29. "En garde" weapon
30. Gull
31. Diva Gluck
32. Downtown Chicago district
33. Dr. Frankenstein's helper
37. Modifies
38. Repeat
39. Bitter vetch
41. Plum
42. Substitute
44. Editions
45. Actor Matthau
46. Bleeps out
49. "The Sheik of ___"
50. Luxurious fur
51. Typed
52. Finn's boat
53. Spanish river
54. Female deer
55. Desert sight
59. Gavel sound
60. Rotten

PUZZLE 267

ACROSS
1. Bring up
5. Smash
9. Army officer
14. Taj Mahal city
15. Bustle
16. Sleepless
17. Winter-nose nipper
19. Implied
20. Sticks like glue
21. Bowlers' knockdowns
23. Charged it
25. Rocker David Lee ____
26. Some Louisianans
30. Hibernia
32. Begum's mate
35. Praying figure
36. Thickens
37. Metric measures: abbr.
38. Costa ____
39. Course
40. Famous cookie maker
41. Query
42. Danish pianist
43. Actor Martin
44. Grazing ground
45. Old Norse poem
46. Alarms
47. Sign gas
49. Computer food
51. Spanish city
54. Herring's kin
59. Jogged
60. Scrubby northern trees
62. Grenoble's river
63. Lotion additive
64. Ladder part
65. James or Perry
66. Word of disgust
67. Buffalo Bill

DOWN
1. Rani's mate
2. Old oath
3. Crafty
4. Take in
5. Scatters
6. Untied
7. Madison Avenue products
8. Witticisms
9. Women guards
10. Mark time
11. Rock driller
12. Migrant worker
13. Soaks flax
18. Facade
22. Commonplace
24. Overwhelmed
26. ____ Gables
27. Rebel
28. Impudent child
29. Actress Merkel
31. Fixed routine
33. Car compartment
34. Beasts of burden
36. Crib filler
39. Circuit
40. ____ glance
42. Expand
43. Cliff formation
46. Tent pegs
48. January, to Juan
50. English racetrack
51. Lamp
52. Soprano Ponselle
53. Slightly open
55. Floppy item
56. Toward
57. Craving
58. Spot
61. In the manner of

PUZZLE 268

ACROSS

1. Small monkey
5. One-horse carriage
9. "____ Attraction"
14. Author unknown: abbr.
15. Dresses up
16. "That's ____"
17. Belted
18. Alpine city
20. Bell tower
22. Betrayer
23. Call it a day
24. Some breads
25. Spanish queens
27. Spins
30. Violinist Isaac ____
32. Scamp
33. Extreme
34. Mountain pool
38. Sagging
39. Factions
40. Lamb's "Essays of ____"
41. Impudent
42. Nat "King" ____
43. Curl with an iron
44. Cancel
46. Squanders
47. Rubbernecker
50. Fume
51. Sickly
52. Kind of drop or shoe
54. Contrary
58. Symphonic piece
61. Lamb's home
62. Present theatrically
63. Diving bird
64. British prep school
65. Slave
66. Rocky pinnacles
67. Pew

DOWN

1. Touches for an out
2. J, F, or K: abbr.
3. Hied
4. Arguer, at times
5. Fence stairs
6. Sharpens
7. Rep.
8. River to the North Sea
9. Hesitate
10. Medical gp.
11. Bus fare
12. Sporting facility
13. Accommodates
19. Street shows
21. Mayberry gas-station attendant
26. Ladder spaces
27. Do up in fancy paper
28. Mouse's escape
29. Stravinsky
30. Edge
31. Trap, in a way
33. Vaya con ____
35. Hit the ground
36. Frost
37. Toddlers' time-outs
39. "Harum ____"
43. Biblical land
45. Rue the day
46. Conestogas
47. Rustle
48. Maman's sister
49. Maestro Dorati
50. Grooming tool
53. Fuse
55. Reminder
56. Greek portico
57. Yurt
59. Id's kin
60. Bronx attraction

PUZZLE 269

ACROSS
1. Saunter
6. Java's neighbor
10. Huge
14. Unbroken
15. Warning
16. Last mo.
17. Escape
18. South African coin
19. Jungle VIP
20. Summer fruit drink
21. Florence the nurse
24. Lures
26. Desisted
27. Valiant of comics
29. Where to say "I do"
31. Cape or shoe
32. Most choice
34. ____-Magnon
37. Type of ink
39. ____ du Diable
40. Jokester's payoffs
42. Palmas or Vegas
43. Unassuming
46. In ____ veritas
47. Makes a recording
48. Assembles
50. Having a handle
53. Search
54. "To Kill a ____"
57. Horned viper
60. To be, in Paris
61. Mavourneen's home
62. Songstress Gorme
64. Almost there
65. Celebration
66. Cattails
67. Chef's measures: abbr.
68. Went over fifty-five
69. Syrupy

DOWN
1. On the ocean
2. Hollow form
3. Warblers
4. Topper
5. Heavenly
6. Bjorn and kin
7. Hong Kong nanny
8. Pre-Easter time
9. Charges with a crime
10. Ill-bred
11. Escapee's ruse
12. Took without asking
13. ____ down (softened)
22. Old road to Rome
23. Bard's below
25. Years, to Brutus
27. Silvers of comedy
28. Columnist Barrett
29. Rhone city
30. Dregs
33. Person Friday
34. "My Little ____"
35. Go into a rage
36. Bears, to Pedro
38. Treasured violin
41. Forum greetings
44. Zippers
45. Guam, for one: abbr.
47. Captors
49. Commuters
50. Catkin
51. Written messages
52. Toss out
53. Penalized
55. Firm hold
56. ____ the bullet
58. Aspect
59. Mosquito, for one
63. Evergreen

211

PUZZLE 270

ACROSS
1. Minus
5. Equal
8. Nursery item
12. Actor Baldwin
13. Pub quaff
14. Top-notch
15. Consumer
16. Nothing
17. Pry
18. Refused
20. Molecule component
22. Spoke impiously
26. Succinct
29. Mao ____-tung
30. Actress Meyers
31. Lampreys
32. Heartache
33. Mix
34. Feel poorly
35. Gawain, for one
36. Linen item
37. Sameness
40. Diamond quorum
41. Cleaned
45. Thug
47. Wooden peg
49. Seize
50. Musician Clapton
51. Actress Gardner
52. Fencing sword
53. Interlock
54. Chum
55. Comedian Foxx

DOWN
1. Praise
2. Other
3. Observed
4. Writers
5. Bamboo eater
6. ____ Baba
7. Setback
8. Indian craft
9. Apartment sharer
10. Powerful people
11. Hive denizen
19. Diminutive being
21. Article
23. Blizzard
24. Pennsylvania port
25. Damaging information
26. Suitor
27. Check
28. Peoria's location
32. Bug
33. Dishonest lawyer
35. Offspring
36. Actor Gilliam
38. Small songbird
39. Perfect
42. Record
43. Added to
44. Legal document
45. Lapis lazuli, e.g.
46. Mine find
48. Actress Marie Saint

PUZZLE 271

ACROSS

1. Velvety
5. Encountered
8. "Little ___ of Horrors"
12. Not working
13. Mine find
14. Citrus fruit
15. Diving bird
16. Pale
17. Mine entrance
18. Curl
20. Poems
22. Went in
24. ___ Alamos
27. Hearing organ
28. Drain
32. Fugitive
34. Advance
35. Pause
36. "My Gal ___"
37. Actor Knight
38. Lowered in rank
41. Large kettle
44. Curtain
48. ___ Canal
49. College cheer
51. Very dry
52. Close
53. Consumed
54. Stubborn creature
55. Paves
56. Sweet potato
57. Prayer ending

DOWN

1. River dregs
2. Stench
3. Iceberg
4. Taut
5. Cut the grass
6. Pencil top
7. Choir voice
8. Defame
9. Pelt
10. Leave out
11. Favorites
19. Tennis shoe
21. Snuggled
23. Playing marble
24. Tennis shot
25. Belonging to us
26. Canonized lady
29. Humor
30. Actress Arden
31. Blushing
33. Fireman's equipment
34. Perched
36. Musical composition
39. Eel
40. Theater production
41. Penny
42. Location
43. Fibber
45. Lily
46. Stack
47. Garden of ___
50. Garment part

213

PUZZLE 272

ACROSS

1. Portable bed
4. Certain traffic sign
8. Dietary fiber
12. Impersonate
13. Walk through water
14. Advertising emblem
15. Small truck
16. Dollar bills
17. Aroma
18. Church officer
20. Fret
22. Classified items
24. Shallot's kin
28. Matures
31. Youth
34. Small game cube
35. Paint layer
36. Globe
37. Sets
38. Goof
39. Sponge
40. Endure
41. Detect
43. Fathom
45. Example
48. Erode
52. Robin Cook book
55. Steep cliff
57. "We ___ Not Alone"
58. Word-of-mouth
59. Lieutenant
60. Princess's irritant
61. Existed
62. Mounds
63. Pitcher handle

DOWN

1. Bats' abode
2. Milky gem
3. Care for
4. Saber
5. Change into leather
6. Lyric poems
7. Irritant
8. Inflated
9. Actor Cameron
10. In the past
11. Neither's follower
19. Sunrise direction
21. Eternity
23. Store
25. Perception
26. Greases
27. Sparrow's abode
28. Experts
29. Pierce
30. Obtain
32. Gay Nineties, e.g.
33. Declines
37. ___ club (chorus)
39. Vast amount
42. Progression
44. Rims
46. Type of jazz singing
47. Cleveland's water
49. Cod or Horn
50. Length x width
51. Decade unit
52. Female elephant
53. Mine yield
54. Disfigure
56. Summer fruit drink

PUZZLE 273

ACROSS
1. Football's Sayers
5. Melancholy
8. Moist
12. Actor West
13. Pastry dessert
14. Clinton's canal
15. Blue gem
17. Period before Easter
18. Author Fleming
19. Begs
21. Begin
24. Tempo
25. Quote
26. Economize
30. Fuss
31. Musical pitches
32. Acorn source
33. Nullified
35. Flower holder
36. Feels unwell
37. Trousers
38. Entwine
41. Actor Vereen
42. Verbal
43. Horse-drawn vehicle
48. In person
49. "___ Little Bluebirds"
50. Look over
51. "___ of Thunder"
52. Use a needle and thread
53. Bovine group

DOWN
1. Oxygen, for one
2. Nabokov heroine
3. Race circuit
4. "The ___ Strikes Back"
5. Rotate
6. Telecast
7. Intensified
8. Remove
9. District
10. Heed
11. Household animals
16. Bowler, e.g.
20. Young woman
21. Mark of an injury
22. Ocean movement
23. On the peak of
24. Skeleton parts
26. Gathers
27. Sorrel horse
28. Wide-ranging
29. Supplements
31. Follow
34. Birds of prey
35. Disappear
37. ___ annum
38. Divulged
39. Song for Carreras
40. Military branch
41. Forehead
44. Flabbergast
45. Receive a high grade on
46. Needlefish
47. Cease

PUZZLE 274

ACROSS
1. Get along
5. Sheep's cry
8. Retreat
11. Matured
12. Hounds
13. Tailless primate
14. Lag behind
15. Freudian entities
16. Certainly!
17. Builds
19. Fire remnant
21. Caspian or Adriatic
22. Sailor
23. Scold
26. Control knob
29. Stagger
32. Mine find
33. Senior citizen
35. Respectful fear
36. Cultivate
38. Bubbly beverage
39. Barrel
40. Billion years
42. Musician's job
44. Fling
46. Basement
49. Steeped beverage
50. Have on
52. Steamy appliance
54. Vocation
55. Goofs
56. Amiable
57. Regret
58. Ruby
59. Grab

DOWN
1. Rogue
2. Boogeyman
3. Bosc or Anjou
4. Borders
5. Swamps
6. Past
7. Resource
8. Sunrise
9. Foil's kin
10. Not far
12. Elements
18. Surrender
20. Disfigure
23. Decompose
24. "Just the Way You ___"
25. Create
27. Bustle
28. Account books
30. Wool producer
31. Support
34. Banister
37. Female rabbit
41. More modern
43. Sparkle
44. Celestial body
45. South American country
46. Witty one
47. Opera solo
48. Sway back and forth
51. Sooner than
53. Born

ACROSS

1. Ingested
6. Small fry
9. Citrus drink
12. Hierarchy
13. Goof
14. Faint
15. Thong
16. Edible mollusk
18. Index
20. Loud sleeper
21. Unfold
25. Gritty
26. Was obligated
27. Fanatical
29. Fetch
30. Metal bar
31. Merry
34. Scour
35. Grant
36. Fresco
39. Closest
41. Nail polish
43. Two, in Genoa
44. Claims
46. Braved
50. Zip
51. Prayer
52. Venice's locale
53. Shoat's home
54. Caustic
55. Strained

DOWN

1. Hairpin curve
2. Ham it up
3. Sailor
4. Jovial
5. Katmandu's locale
6. Earl Grey, e.g.
7. Heavenly bodies
8. Passage
9. Embellish
10. Had supper
11. Manicurist's board
17. Weight
19. Carried
21. "My Life as a ____"
22. Palindromic animal
23. Former GI
24. Heathen
28. Filleted
30. Forbidden
31. Gosh!
32. Classified items
33. But
34. Approached
35. Originate
36. Averages
37. Dark
38. Gathering
40. CPA's inspection
42. Tax
45. Notice
47. Operated
48. Chicago trains
49. Pigment

PUZZLE 276

• PUT UP YOUR DUKES •

ACROSS
1. Retired for the night
5. Papa
8. Impolite
12. Unique
13. Monetary penalty
14. Individuals
15. Be sold
19. Confuse
20. Among
21. Code deviser
23. Pistol
27. French connections
30. Citrus cooler
31. Hospital workers: abbr.
34. Above
35. Seaman
38. Sailor's hail
39. Domesticated animals
40. Floaters
41. Frighten
42. Corn center
44. Submit
47. Phooey!
50. Is able
51. Crimson
52. Daniel ____ Lewis
55. Turkish general
56. Records, for short
57. Unclose, poetically
58. Greek letter
59. Decimal unit
60. Cinnabar, e.g.
61. Crazy
62. Republican's rival: abbr.
63. Numerals
66. Maiden
67. Interoffice notes
69. Theater passage
73. Standard
77. Stove chamber
78. Attractive
81. Scent
82. Cushion
83. Policeman
84. Barley beard
85. Fingerless gloves
88. Make a speech
90. Verdi opera
91. Scattered grain
93. Precarious
100. Fairy tale writer Andersen
101. Cry of dismay
102. Diva's forte
103. Formerly, in the past
104. Table part
105. Dye

DOWN
1. Circle segment
2. Scrooge's exclamation
3. Distinctive time
4. Bear's home
5. Racket
6. Ampersand
7. ____ Moines
8. Curtain fixtures
9. Dishonorable
10. The First State: abbr.
11. Opposite of WNW
13. Momentary craze
16. Joke
17. Flightless bird
18. Female deer
19. "People ____ Funny"
21. Person
22. Peculiar
23. Jump
24. Street or road: abbr.
25. Butterfly snare
26. Medics: abbr.
27. Old French coin
28. Boxing decision: abbr.
29. Bashful
32. Neither's partner
33. Orchestral work: abbr.
36. Wane
37. Fire residue
38. ____ Pasha
41. Totaled
42. Bay of Naples island
43. Beginning
45. Scent
46. Himalayan nation
47. Singer Boone
48. Era
49. Used clothes
50. Wooden shoes
53. Supped
54. Sweet potato
64. Charged atom

PUZZLE 276

65. ____ Bernardino, California
66. Precious stone
67. Wipe
68. Actress Bartok
70. Actress Lupino
71. Opposite of NNE
72. Actor Chaney
73. "To Have and Have ____"
74. Keats poem
75. Reagan's nickname
76. "____ Miniver"
78. Torrid
79. Parrot
80. Radiate
83. Bounder
86. Wedding vow
87. Scottish lid
89. Take five
90. Classified items
91. That woman
92. Rowing blade
93. Actor Holbrook
94. Tavern fare
95. Old horse
96. Cereal grain
97. Swiss canton
98. Can metal
99. Bonnet

PUZZLE 277

ACROSS

1. ____-color (risque)
4. Had bills
8. Zip or area
12. Composer Gershwin
13. Ripped
14. Milky stone
15. Texas cow
17. Brew
18. Born
19. Daggers
20. Prize
22. Absent
23. Woven
24. Prolonged
27. Tavern
28. Langston Hughes works
30. Hyson or oolong
31. Young frog
33. Actor Harmon
34. Loving
35. Migratory flocks
37. Tinge
39. Consumer lures
40. Body of a dismantled ship
41. Amulet
46. Still
47. Actor Baldwin
48. I
49. Avian domicile
50. Over
51. ____ Zeppelin

DOWN

1. Moisten
2. To's companion
3. Groupie
4. Different
5. Romanced
6. Botch
7. Retreat
8. Managing
9. Short musical dramas
10. "____ Eyes"
11. Wapitis
16. No-see-um
19. Spanish noblemen
20. "____ Christie"
21. Bits of good fortune
22. Jewel
23. Young fox
24. Golfer Trevino
25. Present
26. Shaggy ox
28. Corn bread
29. Timeworn
32. Pouch
33. Clutter
35. Strong winds
36. Mandate
37. Dilute
38. Surly
41. Faucet
42. Carte or king
43. Diner owner
44. Mature
45. Doze

PUZZLE 278

ACROSS

1. Evening
6. Mist
11. Supper
12. Shut
14. Job-hunter's need
15. Shake
16. Pretend
17. Heathen
19. Yale alumnus
20. Competition
22. Scottish cap
23. Worry
24. Aimed
26. Sweet treat
27. Cot
28. Lend an ___
29. Governed
32. Notices
36. Leave out
37. Knight's title
38. Actress Mia ___
39. ___ and downs
40. Fast
42. Stripe
43. Fool
45. Loosening
47. Marvelous
48. Position
49. Garden tool
50. Uptight

DOWN

1. Sibling's daughters
2. Arch
3. Wildebeest
4. Rope fiber
5. Handled
6. Beat it!
7. Blueprint
8. Decay
9. Behind, in a boat
10. Screamed
11. Play
13. Divinity
18. Look for excitement
21. Himalayan country
23. Charges
25. Scarlet
26. Lion, e.g.
28. Spookiest
29. Circular
30. Judge
31. Organized
32. Scoop
33. Backwoods refuges
34. Daze
35. Officer, for short
37. Half-goat, half-man
40. Hoarfrost
41. Palm fruit
44. Shake
46. Japanese title of respect

PUZZLE 279

ACROSS
1. Cherry stones
5. Cover
8. Window ledge
12. Sandusky's water
13. Expert
14. Factual
15. Flapjacks
17. Dancer Moreno
18. Mother sheep
19. Expunged
21. Self-respect
24. Actress Barrymore
25. Appraise
26. Memo
27. Favored pupil
30. "____ Got a Secret"
31. Fictional book
32. Pilsner
33. Jewelry stone
34. Complete
35. Brook
36. Wallet stuffers
37. Ride a bike
38. Type of drum
41. Tree juice
42. Release
43. Blimps
48. Baseball team
49. Needle feature
50. Skid
51. Recipe direction
52. Skelton or Buttons
53. Slippery

DOWN
1. Vim
2. Retirement plan letters
3. Sn
4. Withdraw
5. Body of water
6. Frost
7. Defector
8. Fodder
9. Showy flower
10. Pear-shaped instrument
11. Graphite
16. Wonderment
20. Film spool
21. Snob
22. Carry on
23. Article
24. Birds of peace
26. Thanksgiving month
27. Reimbursed
28. Mother Bloor
29. Reveal
31. "____ Nanette"
35. Rest
36. Playful aquatic mammal
37. Chum
38. Decades
39. Leave out
40. Kind of skirt
41. Winter vehicle
44. Voter's yes
45. Bullring shout
46. Naught
47. Agent 007, e.g.

222

ACROSS

1. Industrial center
5. Upon
9. Gorilla
12. Concept
13. Threesome
14. Sunburn color
15. Clay
16. Place for a wedding banquet
17. Joke
18. Senior
20. Cheer
22. Owing
23. Male sheep
24. Fellow
27. Detail
30. Ignore
33. Grow older
34. At no time
36. Born
37. Warty amphibian
39. Arid
40. Decade
41. Decompose
43. Inexperienced
45. Trace
47. Nonmetallic chemical element
51. Sorrow
52. Pleasant
54. Matriarch
55. "___ a Wonderful Life"
56. Epochs
57. Foil's kin
58. Nitrogen or oxygen
59. Temporary shelter
60. Split

DOWN

1. Race distance
2. Adored one
3. Precede
4. Hebrew letter
5. Olympics participants
6. Flat receptacle
7. Corn or olive
8. ___ bear
9. Dispute
10. Podded vegetables
11. Advantage
19. Wreck
21. Cross
24. Gym pad
25. Gone by
26. Proximity
28. The night before
29. Most cheerful
31. Charge
32. Desire
35. Authentic
38. Canine
42. Canon or dogma
44. More extensive
45. Branch
46. Particle
47. Examine
48. Shawl
49. Premonition
50. Require
53. Fury

PUZZLE 281

ACROSS
1. Good friend
4. Deed
7. Boxer Sugar ____ Leonard
10. Departure
12. Vittles
14. Be in hock
15. Otherwise
16. Musical sound
17. Give the go-ahead to
18. Spare
19. Morays
21. 24 hours
24. Attempt
25. Glass ____
28. Grizzly
30. "____ of Eden"
34. Self-importance
35. Moderated
37. Regret
38. Village
40. Ship's mast
41. Chess pieces
42. Diamond call
44. Color changer
46. Faulty firecrackers
48. ____ Victoria
52. Tippler
53. Radiate
57. Considerate
58. Green vegetable
59. Springboard leap
60. Air pollution
61. Cigar residue
62. Caustic substance
63. Porky's pad

DOWN
1. Rind
2. Wheel holder
3. "Mona ____"
4. Fore and ____
5. Dove sound
6. Like a ____ of bricks
7. Rock 'n' ____
8. Astonishes
9. As of now
11. Care for
13. Woodland animal
20. Look at
22. Actor Vigoda
23. Bread ingredient
24. Step
25. Modern engine
26. Gone by
27. Surprised exclamation
29. Egyptian cobra
31. Provide with weapons
32. "A Boy Named ____"
33. Five plus five
36. Arid
39. Show silent approval
43. Utilized
45. Lodge members
46. Bambi's mom et al.
47. Ogden's state
49. Gets ready to shoot
50. Granny ____
51. Nervous
52. Health facility
54. Unit of thickness
55. Wall climber
56. Popular shirt

ACROSS

1. Defeats
6. Dog's pest
10. Indian rule
13. Type of frequency
14. Mower or tennis
15. Manicurist's tool
16. West Indies chain
18. Fancy
19. Offspring
20. Pastel color
21. Deteriorate
23. Confined
24. Parisian parent
25. Drill again
28. Noble
32. Verbal examinations
33. Kansas senator
34. Tender
35. Hobgoblin
36. Made public
37. Pilot's stunt
38. Heaven on earth
39. Grant
40. Expire
41. Representative
43. More obtuse
44. Foam
45. Beneficial
46. Certain Muslim
49. Diana, to Eugenie
50. "This ___ House"
53. Andean shrub
54. Indian Ocean republic
57. Honest
58. Mideastern country
59. Proportion
60. Newsman Koppel
61. Bullets, e.g.
62. Val Kilmer film, with "The"

DOWN

1. Catches
2. Wallaroo
3. Yemen seaport
4. Baking pan
5. Afternoon shows
6. Spark stone
7. Thin
8. Cote parent
9. Replied
10. Frees
11. Sheltered
12. Actress Stapleton
15. New York resort area
17. Feast
22. ___ y plata
23. South Pacific language
24. Fray
25. Like a judge
26. Undermine
27. Breakfast roll
28. Swarm
29. Pens
30. Began
31. Outcast
33. Food regimens
36. Professor's milieu
40. Aerobics attire
42. Paunch
43. Bell sound
45. Fertilizer
46. Edinburgh native
47. Famous diamond
48. ___ tea
49. Seth's father
50. Eight: pref.
51. Cave
52. Cupid
55. Chair part, sometimes
56. ___ Paulo

PUZZLE 283

ACROSS

1. Garden veggie
5. Algae
9. ___ mater
13. Tater
17. Provoke
18. Zola novel
19. Son of Adam
20. Zhivago's love
21. Neighborhood
22. Not a repro.
23. New England st.
24. Old oath
25. Fahrenheit measure
28. Big ape
30. Furniture wood
31. Grit
33. Cartoon bear
34. Is important
38. Ancient Egyptian deity
40. Pursue
43. Scoop
44. Lax
46. Cold or ginger
48. Highlander
49. Idyllic spot
51. Persian kings
53. Jug
55. Camp bed
56. Mr. Castro
58. Loud kiss
60. Hopi sacred dancer
62. Mountain pass
64. Trapshooting
66. Place for a massage
67. Stockpile
71. Dormant
73. Floated down the river
77. Pasture
78. Sighs of satisfaction
80. Treasury agent Ness
82. Fancy trim
83. Valid
85. Actress Arlene ___
87. Former Egyptian president
89. Burnish
90. Energy source
92. ___ off (annoys)
94. Settings
96. Faded
98. Short-billed rail
100. Torero's accolade
101. Hoards
104. Mules and burros
110. ___ vera
111. Buckeye State
113. Cab
114. Off-Broadway trophy
115. Blowers
116. Ring
117. Radiate
118. Literary never
119. Boxer's weapon
120. Cuddled
121. Evans the cowgirl
122. Swing about

DOWN

1. Annoying child
2. Irish land
3. Before J.H.S.
4. Cozy's place
5. Swimmers' gear
6. "___ Mia"
7. Squadron
8. One of the wise men
9. Emphasizes
10. Thai language
11. Chinese porcelain
12. Bother
13. Horse-drawn vehicles
14. Leoncavallo opera
15. Caspian feeder
16. Word from the crib
26. Munches
27. Emulate Kool Moe Dee
29. Mythical bird
32. Native of Copenhagen
34. Skirt length
35. Mirrored
36. Cheers
37. Swindles
39. Falcon
41. Ere long
42. Ms. Kett
43. Mil. concern
45. Army wear
47. Legumes
50. Guitar part
52. Location
54. Voucher: abbr.
57. "Whatever ___ wants ..."
59. Ship bottoms

61. Transport
63. Weight
65. Lawsuit
67. Luncheonette specials
68. Word on Mexican mail
69. Large pots
70. Steps to a river
72. Hubbub
74. Empty
75. Old French coins
76. Society girl
79. "____ a Lady" (Tom Jones hit)
81. Low-grade iron ore
84. Serious
86. Brother of Marie Antoinette
88. Anklebones
91. "Norma ____"
93. Mexican Mrs.
95. Mechanical headaches
97. Consomme
99. Played the part
101. Fisherman's spear
102. Jai ____
103. Boot
105. Volga feeder
106. Leaf angle
107. Eve's boy
108. Substitute
109. Waterless
112. Wisc.'s neighbor

PUZZLE 284

• JUST DESSERTS •

ACROSS

1. Busy as ____
5. Taken by mouth
9. Sunscreen ingredient
13. Soothing creams
18. Hairstyling tool
19. Relocate
20. Olympic prize
21. T.S. ____
22. Humiliation
24. Speechify
25. Girl: Fr.
26. Timetable term: abbr.
27. Bullfight cheers
28. Stalwart people
30. Very: Fr.
31. Type of code
32. "You ____ There"
33. Rue
36. "Gay" city
37. Evaluate
39. "____ the season . . ."
42. Foreigner
43. Milkshake additive
44. Prophets
46. El ____, Texas
47. Baseball-team count
48. Pepper's partner
49. Permit
50. Unclothed
51. Label
52. Well-kept used cars
56. "Carmen," for one
57. Compass point: abbr.
58. Plenty
59. Caravan stopover
60. Shred
61. Alex Haley book
63. French health resort
64. Auto wreck
65. Monastery head
66. Hurl
67. For both sexes
68. Overhead trains
71. Type of stock certificate
72. Pinup picture
74. Leopard, e.g.
75. Bards
76. Sprinted
77. Fail to include
78. Statistics
79. Geologic divisions
80. Diamond weight
82. Sherlock's find
83. Los Angeles player
84. Finale
85. Subdue
86. Spirit of a culture
88. Solitary people
89. Ulna's locale
90. Slander
91. Remove rind from
92. Hospital volunteer
97. Yard
98. Elderly
101. Sectors
102. Dined
103. Very simple
105. Bias
106. All
107. Kitty contribution
108. O'Hara plantation
109. Bulls: Sp.
110. Loch ____ monster
111. Bring up
112. Actor Ladd

DOWN

1. Throb
2. Boxing match
3. Thompson of "Dead Again"
4. Subside
5. Egg dish
6. Heavy cords
7. Rara ____
8. Actress Remick
9. Reads thoroughly
10. Maxim
11. Tub or mat
12. Actor Baldwin
13. Prior to
14. Identical
15. "____ Marlene" (song)
16. Double agent
17. Canonized women: abbr.
20. Demi or Roger
23. Actress Sophia ____
28. Legal wrong
29. Feedbag fillers
30. "A ____ Grows in Brooklyn"
31. Mediterranean island
33. Yells
34. Inventor Howe
35. Victorian ornamentation
36. Dims
37. Coral structures
38. ____ and crafts
39. Win the prize
40. French river
41. Carbonated drink
43. Stores
45. Fairylike
46. The Mamas and the ____
48. Actor George C. ____
50. "WarGames" locale
53. Film
54. Twinges
55. Custom
58. Circles
60. Welcome

PUZZLE 284

62. Newspaper notices, for short
63. Actress Verdugo
64. Newswoman Roberts
65. Oak product
66. Divvy up
67. Author of "The Stranger"
69. In a while
70. Lead actors
71. German admiral (WWI)
72. Stuff
73. Dye
78. Copenhagen native
80. Irregular wheels
81. Dispositions
82. Sear
83. "____ Doone"
85. Lovers' meetings
87. Itty-bitty
88. Attorney
89. "A Bell for ____"
90. Locales
91. Fettuccine, e.g.
92. Playbill listing
93. Woody's son
94. Approach
95. High schooler
96. Talk wildly
97. Country road
98. Iridescent gem
99. Italian money, formerly
100. Campus bigwig
103. Pitcher handle
104. Depot: abbr.

PUZZLE 285

ACROSS

1. Pause
5. Ice mass
9. Iraqi, e.g.
13. Shine
17. Nurse
18. Composer Stravinsky
19. Philippine port
20. High point
21. Style of the '60s
22. Absent
23. Row
24. Persuade
25. Rummage
27. Habit
30. Computer input
32. Sailor
33. Tokyo waistband
34. Hen
37. Hurried
39. Mates
43. Actress Adams
44. Star
45. Part of the crew
47. Legume for sprouting
49. Comic Kovacs
50. Staff
51. ___ barometer
52. Music hall
53. Lab burners
55. Hairpin curve
56. Odysseus's faithful dog
57. Shucks!
58. Pale-faced
61. Ooze
62. Canyons
66. Greek letter
67. Group of three
68. Strictest
69. Directly
72. "___ Only Just Begun"
73. Comic Carvey
74. Jungle knife
75. Nerve network
76. Many times
77. Juanita's river
78. Afflict
79. Jacob's son
81. Subsidiary
87. Handle
91. Factory
92. Eugene O'Neill's daughter
93. Potpourri
95. Pace
96. Word-of-mouth
97. Ladder part
98. Pugilist's weapon
99. Earth goddess
100. Emeralds, e.g.
101. Gaelic
102. Reputation
103. Movie spool

DOWN

1. Airwave buffs
2. Gaul friend
3. Actress Turner
4. Grilling
5. Gulf
6. Self-esteem
7. Reagan and Howard
8. Hailed
9. Thespian
10. Harness piece
11. Snoozing
12. Desert garb
13. Christening
14. Neutral color
15. Eros
16. Ancient Persian
26. Small low island
28. Scoundrel
29. Adjoin
31. Full steam ___!
34. Speaker's platform
35. Wife of Bragi
36. Eat
38. Writer Fleming
39. Kind of headache
40. Demure
41. Be entitled to
42. Portico
44. Luau attire
45. Austrian psycho-analyst
46. Sullivan and Murrow
48. Ship's off.
49. Trimmed
52. Mountain nymph
53. Place for an icicle
54. Ring site
56. Skirt style
57. Blacktop

58. Kennel comment
59. Wedge
60. Circle dance
61. Imp
62. Carouse
63. Great!
64. Laborer, of yore
65. Saxophonist Getz
67. Author Dreiser
68. Hardened
70. Ancient manuscripts
71. Prune
72. Prosperous
75. Eliminate
76. Caesar's breakfast
78. Proverb
80. Behave theatrically
81. Los Angeles blight
82. St. Patrick's domain
83. Mollusk
84. IV
85. Taverns
86. Lamb's pen name
88. Swiss river
89. French novelist
90. And others: Lat.
94. Doctrine

PUZZLE 285

PUZZLE 286

ACROSS
1. Blue
4. Green fruit
8. Horse's gait
12. Actor Wallach
13. Hubbubs
14. Talk wildly
15. Playwright Tennessee ____
17. Smashing serves
18. Lend an ____
19. Emphasize
21. Donations
23. Holmes's creator
25. Resin
26. Condensation
27. Revises
31. Baseball stat
32. ____ tube
34. Actress West
35. Classroom items
37. Large deer
38. Tart
39. Sour compounds
41. Volume
42. Small donkeys
45. Roll of bills
46. Tibet's location
47. Workers
52. Crooked
53. Always
54. Pinch
55. Advantage
56. Youth
57. Plaything

DOWN
1. Stitch
2. Actress MacGraw
3. Predicaments
4. Burrow
5. Apple cider girl
6. Pop's mate
7. Composition
8. Copied
9. Competition
10. Kitchen appliance
11. Try out
16. ____ Vegas
20. Office worker
21. Ripened
22. Entice
23. Cozy room
24. Possessed
26. Dancing spot
28. Brazen
29. Follow
30. Look for
33. Chicago trains
36. Martial art
40. Key
41. Saloon
42. Paul Bunyan's blue ox
43. Secondhand
44. Boxer's arena
45. Frayed
48. Hail
49. Quilting ____
50. ____ Grande
51. Secret agent

232

Some of the clues in this crossword are Triple Play clues. They consist of three words separated by commas. The answer to a Triple Play clue is a word that can precede or follow each of the three words to form a common phrase, name, or compound word. For example, the answer to "Shelter, Income, Payer" is TAX (tax shelter, income tax, taxpayer).

ACROSS

1. Red, Stock, Shed
5. Jet, Point, Back
8. Tennis great
12. Division term
13. Like Willie Winkie
14. Julia Child, e.g.
15. Advertising sign
16. White, Seal, Grass
18. Elbow, Monkey, Bacon
20. Eye, Out, Down
21. Land piece
22. Mind, Task, Piece
25. John, Cotton, Bar
28. Milky, Farer, Lay
29. Author LeShan
30. Sierra Madre gold
31. Peter, Cake, Fry
32. Rocker Ocasek
33. "____ the ramparts . . ."
34. Port, Brush, Line
35. Up, Board, Tomato
37. Dormant
39. ____ Moines
40. Cap
41. Island, Basket, Egg
45. North, Dream, Cheese
49. Canal of song
50. Bread, Pepper, Starch
51. Billboards
52. Marine bird
53. Large amounts
54. Hold, Tip, Nail
55. Pearl, Poppy, Sesame

DOWN

1. Chair, Tip, Wax
2. Dilly
3. Oklahoma Indian
4. Trump, Duck, Sutherland
5. Dolph, Semi, Heart
6. Moray
7. Off, Shirt, Totaler
8. Head, Heart, Back
9. Splinters
10. Mud, Peck, Wet
11. Salamander
17. Foul, Mate, Pen
19. Bean, Milk, Sauce
22. Hunt, Sand, Anchor
23. Abridge
24. Rat, Track, Human
25. Chilly
26. Locality
27. Exposure, Lights, Hemisphere
28. Price, Cry, Horse
31. Bull, Fall, Money
34. Dote, Trust, Septic
35. Coat type
36. Wealth
38. Merits
39. Thick
42. Frog, Shoe, House
43. Irish Free State
44. Sever
45. Out, Riot, Stamp
46. Ranch noise
47. Call, Bob, Nip
48. Confusion

PUZZLE 288

ACROSS

1. Beehive State
5. Gentle person
9. Pal
13. Constitutional
17. Red-tag event
18. In charge of
19. Alley Oop's girl
20. Buffalo's lake
21. Columnist Bombeck
22. Lucy's partner
23. Ringing sound
24. Helm position
25. Thin
27. Utterly
30. Throw
32. Monk
33. Pay dirt
34. Pyromaniac's crime
37. Booty
39. Samson's lover
43. Gobble (down)
44. Exceedingly
45. Dutch export
46. Steal
48. Passing by
50. African tree snake
51. Actor Hunter
52. Quarreled
53. Separator of sorts
54. Gluck's forte
56. Principle
57. Golf term
58. Confucian golden rule
59. Foe
62. Audible
63. More suspicious
67. Sign of the zodiac
68. Oar
69. Repartee
70. Jackie's second
71. Drills
72. Spot
73. Former Italian bills
74. Bayou natives
76. Spasms
77. Thunderclaps
78. Humorist Burrows
79. March sister
80. Every
82. Honest!
88. Cool-headed
92. Take it easy
93. Carol
94. Eternities
96. Woe is me!
97. Loafing
98. Grecian instrument
99. Father
100. Astronaut Sally ____
101. Oaf
102. Time past
103. Lath
104. Stratum

DOWN

1. Employs
2. Canvas cover
3. ____ mater
4. Salad delicacy
5. Veinlike deposits
6. Hail, to Caesar
7. Screen
8. For a short while
9. Hooded snake
10. Owl sound
11. Forearm bone
12. Southern flower
13. Sneaky animal
14. Singer Guthrie
15. Place
16. On an even ____
26. Father's boy
28. Canine comment
29. Trickle
31. Deplete
34. Struck silent
35. Function
36. Side of bacon
38. Energy unit
39. Dressmaker's aid
40. Exile island
41. Comic Johnson
42. Rime
44. Sight
45. Gentled
47. College deg.
49. Postpone
50. Ski slope bump
53. Chills
54. Exclaimed
55. Hero's award
57. Doldrums
58. Belgrade native
59. Long time
60. Undercover cop
61. Arab prince
62. Land measure

63. Cad
64. Hip bones
65. Countess's spouse
66. Blended whiskeys
68. Earnestly
69. Military woman: abbr.
71. Hope and Newhart
72. Ramble
75. Occasion for spring break
76. Boston Harbor jetsam
77. Proportion: abbr.
79. Skirmish
81. Investment
82. Baby's bed

83. Decorate again
84. Norwegian seaport
85. Timeless toy
86. Mister, in Munich
87. Elbow grease
89. Latin abbr.
90. Miami's county
91. North Sea feeder
95. Sharp-shooter's gp.

PUZZLE 288

PUZZLE 289

ACROSS

1. "___ Alibi"
4. Asian range
8. Improvise
13. Cabbagelike veggie
17. Pleased the cook
18. Polenta grain
19. Sky dragon
20. Heed
21. Mel Gibson film
23. Star in Cygnus
24. Cherished
25. Candid
26. City on the Meuse
28. Squirm
30. Storms
32. Perjurers
33. Halt!
34. Not taped
35. Some canines
36. Unkind remark
40. Fruit cooler
41. North Dakota town
42. Stains
43. So that's it!
44. Cranes
46. Chatter
47. Yuletide
48. Greek war god
49. Follow
50. Panama or Suez
51. Help
54. Caper
55. Powered bicycles
56. Tour of duty
57. Slice
58. Forsaken
59. Prospects
60. Snazzy
61. Oriental taxi
65. One of the Gershwins
66. Boxes
67. Certain rockers
68. Tokyo, once
69. Noisy insects
71. Periods of time
72. Stun
73. Parasites
74. Gourmet cooks
75. Facets
76. Zodiac twins
79. Japanese verse
80. MP's concern
81. Mild cheese
82. Circa
84. Humorous verse
88. Singer Turner
89. Slip
90. Air-show maneuver
91. No, in Edinburgh
92. Charon's river
93. Gloss
94. Kirghiz tent
95. Government agcy.

DOWN

1. Sunday dinner
2. Airport info: abbr.
3. Gunslinger's weapon
4. Pasture measures
5. Cut of meat
6. Circle part
7. Hints
8. Calculating snakes?
9. Sediment
10. Byway
11. Polar abundance
12. Quail
13. Alaskan bear
14. Encourage
15. Jacob's wife
16. Bronte's governess
22. Fencer's foil
27. "Othello" villain
29. Mythical birds
30. Tall flower
31. Staff assistant
32. Sweet singers
33. Composed
35. Side
36. Sea or pepper
37. Pat or Daniel
38. In the lead
39. Knells
41. Chief
42. Reinforce
45. Squalls
46. Pierce

236

47. Scruffs
49. Linden and juniper, e.g.
50. ___ out (falls asleep)
51. Tomato jelly
52. Cowgirl Belle ___
53. Moses' mountain
54. Layers
55. Ridicules
57. Dinnerware item
58. Chain components
60. Bargains
61. Regretfully
62. Banner
63. Woodworking tool
64. Troubles

66. Pelt
67. Glimpse
70. Pinnacle
71. Blanch
72. Fashion designer
74. Invoke
75. Cleaned
76. Acquires

77. Correct
78. Lots
79. Longing
80. Eros
83. Humbug!
85. Debtor's note
86. Top
87. Parrot

PUZZLE 289

PUZZLE 290

ACROSS

1. "___ No Angels"
5. Palo ___, California
9. Wail
13. Otherwise
17. Prayer ending
18. Give temporarily
19. Telephone ___ code
20. Sulk
21. Extinct reptiles
23. Must-have
24. Presidential office shape
25. Pub potion
26. Summit
28. Nags
30. Yaks
33. Bound
35. Hammer's target
36. Enchant
40. Judge
42. Labors
45. Cow's sound
46. Target
48. Shut with force
50. Orderly
51. Footed vases
53. Method
55. Part of the eye
57. Hit the slopes
58. Blur
60. Marshal Wyatt ___
62. Royal wand
64. "Hollywood Squares" host
68. Ardor
71. Vietnam's continent
72. Grew dim
76. Martian ship
77. Poet Ogden ___
79. Decree
82. Sleuth Wolfe
83. Light source
85. Sword fight
87. Actress Raines
88. Transgression
89. Primp
91. Vaselike jug
93. June 21, for one
96. Decorate
98. Novelist Bellow
100. Term of affection
101. Floated
104. Sign of crying
106. Jewish cleric
110. Caesar's city
111. Bind securely
113. Full underskirt
116. Actor Guinness
117. Correct
118. Char
119. Remove
120. Sunset direction
121. Crystal-ball gazer
122. Nervous
123. Wineglass feature

DOWN

1. Money rolls
2. Send forth
3. Gambler's town
4. No more!
5. ___ carte
6. "Skip to My ___"
7. Painting cloth
8. Beginning
9. New York team
10. Pay dirt
11. Bawl
12. Burdened
13. Feeling
14. Most beautiful
15. Box
16. Morays
22. Big Dipper member
27. Relief
29. Took a chair
31. Satchels
32. Coin opening
34. Cold-cut shop
36. Ostrichlike birds
37. Standard
38. Pitch
39. Tier
41. Bog
43. Actress Veronica ___
44. Ado
47. South American animal
49. Isinglass
52. Tree fluids
54. Delete
56. Ego
59. Bridle part
61. Vanity
63. Blueprint
65. Kermit's kin
66. Result
67. Puts to sea

68. Tooth substance
69. A long way off
70. Occasionally
73. Mr. Arnaz
74. Idle of Monty Python
75. Finished
78. Chops
80. Dimwit
81. Parable
84. Flawless
86. Suede or kid
90. Insect egg
92. Regret
94. Indian garment
95. Pamphlets
97. Thaws
99. Backslide
101. No-win situation
102. Function
103. "Truth or ___"
105. Clarinet feature
107. Floating vessel
108. Roast
109. Piece of news
112. Mystery author Grafton
114. Running game
115. Attempt

PUZZLE 290

PUZZLE 291

ACROSS

1. Taunt
5. Lays out
9. Trade
13. Shampoo
17. African antelope
18. Asian nurse
19. Sea eagle
20. Capri or Man
21. Gondolier's song
23. Wildcatter's find
25. Drafts
26. Breakfast flake
28. Monks
29. It's fit for pigs
30. Carry
31. Mammoth
32. Tom Jones's homeland
35. Dinner beverage
36. Hole in a volcano
40. Scurried
41. Elvis's title
42. Enchantress
43. June honoree
44. Legendary birthplace of Zeus
45. Former
46. Lambaste
47. Somewhat: pref.
48. Turtle, e.g.
50. Shadowboxes
51. Incursion
52. Cooler cooler
53. Cutlass
54. Greek letter
55. Side
58. Peep
59. Dappled
63. Song by The Kinks
64. What's good for the ___ ...
65. Source
66. Tip of Italy
67. Purpose
68. Blueprints
69. Slime
70. Fell on ___ ears
71. Salad green
73. Metal thread
74. Price for a thought?
75. Trims
76. Geologic time spans
77. Rose fruit
78. Stir to action
81. Elation
82. Blackouts
86. Potluck contribution
88. Complicated matter
90. Aggravate
91. Skater Heiden
92. Singer Guthrie
93. Remove
94. Son of Seth
95. Mortgage
96. Eye suggestively
97. Nanook's vehicle

DOWN

1. Mongolian desert
2. OPEC nation
3. Polar explorer
4. Pardoned
5. Borgnine film
6. Cookie man
7. Sidekick
8. Kit and caboodle
9. Calyx part
10. Architect Christopher ___
11. Picnic pest
12. Scented
13. Trickier
14. Aboard ship
15. Garble
16. Skirts' borders
22. Performs
24. Church instrument
27. French street
30. Clue
31. Throws
32. Revolve with a hum
33. ___ -de-camp
34. Bound
35. Sagacious
36. Scandinavian bay
37. Keats's offerings
38. Gold fabric
39. Redact
41. Garden green
42. Cliff
45. ___ and choose
46. Germ
47. Snooty one
49. Singer Turner
50. Watch or cheese
51. Exclaimed
53. Sparkled
54. Hockey arena

PUZZLE 291

55. Air passage
56. Defeat
57. Actor Guinness
58. Barbecue necessity
59. Shade of purple
60. Egyptian sun god
61. Bank transaction
62. Challenge
64. Looked angry
65. Hides
68. Ordinary writing
69. Neither animal nor vegetable
70. Takes off
72. Entertains
73. Suffering
74. Pocket bread
76. Put into office
77. Wit
78. Land measure
79. Squall
80. Christiania, today
81. Fluent
82. Eye
83. Objective
84. Actress Sommer
85. Plant
87. Prospector's find
89. Fury

PUZZLE 292

ACROSS

1. Make tea
5. Deteriorate
10. Art style
14. Parking-lot sight
15. Saltpeter
16. German river
17. Ratio phrase
18. Goes on a cruise
19. Notoriety
20. Direct
21. Joel Chandler Harris character
23. Let it stand
25. "___ the best is good enough"
26. Wandered
29. Beg
32. Northern highway
33. Stringed instrument
34. Gardening tool
37. Legendary orchardist
41. "___ You Ready?"
42. Employs
43. Pocketbook
44. Flees
46. Gentle
47. Author Horatio ___
50. Apiary inhabitants
51. Legendary lumberjack
55. Israeli dance
59. Indigo
60. Crowd sounds
61. Infuriates
62. Demolish
63. Swell
64. Straight
65. Gifts for dad
66. Peruvian mountains
67. Singer Fitzgerald

DOWN

1. Release money
2. Trick
3. Kett of comics
4. Logger
5. Followed
6. Laughing
7. Of the ear
8. Small valley
9. Scots Gaelic
10. Protect
11. Colorful lizard
12. Take exception
13. Give it ___
22. River inlet
24. Volunteer State: abbr.
26. Indian king
27. Trumpeter swan genus
28. Yearn
29. Flute and clarinet
30. Cuts off
31. Building wing
33. Expansive
34. Flock
35. Looped platinum wire
36. River in Hesse
38. Actor Brynner
39. Dueling sword
40. Jonathan Edwards tune
44. Outlaw Starr et al.
45. Globe
46. Past and present
47. Detached
48. Hawaiian veranda
49. Semblance
50. Flat-bottomed vessel
52. Sky bear
53. Part of speech
54. Scotland ___
56. Russian city
57. Genuine
58. Movie dog

PUZZLE 293

ACROSS

1. With: Fr.
5. ____ music
10. Godiva's title
14. Flat bean
15. Brutal
16. Succulent plant
17. Ready copy
18. Stair part
19. Hindu deity
20. Onager
22. Lent's end
24. Gams
25. Golfer Irwin
26. Gawks
28. Waterfall
32. Kingly
33. Garden pest
34. "____ any drop to drink"
35. Change for a five
36. Fiend
37. Yield
38. Heavy weight
39. St. Tropez summers
40. Whets
41. American grapes
44. Aquatic birds
45. Objective
46. Belle's dance
47. Links locales
50. Apers
54. Forsaken
55. Foolish
57. On the briny
58. Surrounded by
59. "____ on Sunday"
60. Joust
61. Actor Andrews
62. Cog sites
63. Mall happening

DOWN

1. Fish sauce
2. Pitcher Blue
3. Radiate
4. Flowering trees
5. Indifferent gestures
6. Salutes
7. Once, formerly
8. Opposite of WNW
9. Menace
10. Actress Louise ____
11. Perched
12. Pigeon's kin
13. 12 months
21. Rind
23. ____ mode
25. Nimbi
26. Columbus's birthplace
27. Middleman
28. Arrives
29. In re
30. Enciphers
31. Very: Fr.
32. Univ. org.
33. Titanium, e.g.
36. Running down
37. Hipsters
40. Sacred
42. Schedule
43. Triumphed
44. Heists
46. Gaffe
47. Pleased
48. Italia's capital
49. Paddy's land
50. Vena ____
51. Largest continent
52. Inform
53. Cloy
56. Society-page word

243

PUZZLE 294

ACROSS
1. Circle piece
4. Car fuel
7. Realtor's sign

PUZZLE 295

ACROSS
1. Matures
5. Headquarters
9. Likely
12. Cab
13. Actor Alda
14. And not
15. Space traveler
17. Foot digit
18. Slippery creature
19. Clinically clean
21. Swears
24. Before, poetically
25. ____ Baba

(Puzzle 294 clues)
9. Pine Tree State
11. Frost
12. Come
14. Corkscrews
16. Writing tool
17. Compete
18. Transmit
19. Staircase segment
21. Hair divider
22. Movie shark
23. Sandwich spread
24. Ripen
25. Aided
28. Small talk
30. Happy as a ____
32. T-bone or porterhouse
33. A Great Lake
34. Bark
35. Snoop

DOWN
1. Fire residue

(Puzzle 295 clues)
26. Ancient
28. Teams
32. Haughty one
34. Up to now
36. Fiddle-playing Roman emperor
37. Large rabbits
39. Intelligence
41. ____ Abner
42. Exclamation of surprise
44. Royal residence
46. Dilapidated: hyph.
50. Moo
51. Mine product
52. Wet-weather garments
56. In the past
57. Mosaic piece
58. Group of three
59. Family room
60. Cook slowly
61. Transmit

DOWN
1. "One Day ____ Time": 2 wds.
2. Auto fuel
3. Outside
4. Fathers
5. Prohibit

(Puzzle 294 DOWN)
2. Cheer
3. Talon
4. Long-nosed fish
5. Make public
6. Anonymous critic
8. Operates a car
9. Spouse
10. Happening
13. Finish
15. Small drink
18. Taste
19. Tall tales
20. Score
21. Buddy
22. Poke for Ali
23. Steve Martin role
25. Pile
26. Hearing organs
27. Trickle
29. Afternoon affair
31. Door opener

(Puzzle 295 DOWN continued)
6. Sorrowful exclamation
7. Fry quickly
8. Goes in
9. Against
10. Swimming or car
11. Sapling
16. Butter substitute
20. Bridle strap
21. Money
22. Forearm bone
23. Crafty
27. Morning moisture
29. Diamond State
30. ____ the Red
31. Foot bottom
33. Necklace piece
35. Hint
38. Bermuda ____
40. Powder ingredient
43. Be ready for
45. Plunders
46. Highway
47. Impulse
48. Type of sign
49. Egyptian river
53. Modern
54. ____ Pan Alley
55. Turf

PUZZLE 296

ACROSS
1. Lassos
7. Liabilities
12. Open up
13. Ms. May
15. Florida attraction: 2 wds.
17. Beach color
18. Copycats
19. Author Fleming
20. Ancient kingdom
22. Govt. power agcy.
23. The Venerable ____
24. Arnaz, father and son
26. Mystery awards
28. Edicts
30. Position
32. Gam and Moreno
36. Green and jasmine
37. "That he is mad, ____ true . . ."
39. Memo
40. Egyptian cobra
41. Fragrance
43. Aunt or uncle: abbr.
44. Florida launch site: 2 wds.
47. Egg dish
48. Rewrite
49. Eliminate
50. Merchant

DOWN
1. Bumpy, as a road
2. Take a breath
3. Stadiums
4. Water tester
5. Thomas ____ Edison
6. G. Washington ____ here
7. Abase
8. Building wings
9. Sheep bleat
10. Neater
11. Golfers J.C. and Sam
14. Serf
16. Turning back
21. Gold-mad king
23. Bowl
25. Collection
27. Bonn native: abbr.
29. Discounted: hyph.
30. Bagel seed
31. Knocker
33. Steamy hot
34. Comfortable: 2 wds.
35. Vendor
36. Mexican snack
38. Elegant
41. "Easy ____"
42. State
45. Guido's note: 2 wds.
46. Miss Gabor

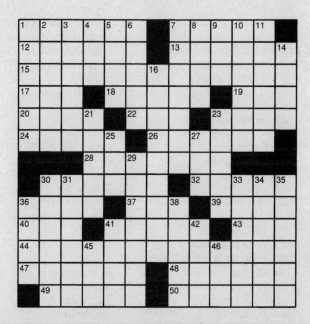

PUZZLE 297

ACROSS
1. Pal of Tarzan
4. Fix a ms.
8. Skirmish
12. Levy
13. Legends
14. Sole
15. Lamb's mom
16. Hymn ending
17. Whit
18. Rank
20. Temper
22. Sam or Remus
24. Waist decoration
25. Spike
26. Gambling town
27. Wonder
30. ____ a boy!
31. Yard enclosure
32. "All the King's ____"
33. Sock tip
34. Titled woman
35. Fail, on Broadway
36. Guys' mates
37. Quarrels
38. Take gladly
41. Property right
42. Kidney or lima
43. Double-reed instrument
45. Toddler
48. Verge
49. ____ estate
50. Time period
51. Golf gadgets
52. Mail
53. Cozy room

DOWN
1. Noshed
2. Cat's foot
3. Aerobics
4. Make very happy
5. Rounded roof
6. Incense
7. Inclination
8. Fire starter
9. Crucifix
10. Before: pref.
11. 12 months
19. Entire
21. Healing plant
22. One
23. European alliance: abbr.
24. Curves
26. House sellers
27. Had a value
28. Solder
29. Concludes
31. Flutter
35. Service charge
36. Hereditary factors
37. Meadow
38. Assist in crime
39. Give up
40. Actor Nicolas ____
41. Bank deal
44. Spelling, for one
46. Pay dirt
47. Light brown

245

PUZZLE 298

• HARD AND FAST •

ACROSS
1. Bog fuel
5. Volcanic scoria
9. Spanish muralist
13. Palomino feature
17. Actress Logan
18. Turkish pound
19. Irish island gp.
20. Crazed
21. Egyptian god
22. TV award
23. Archaic story
24. Imitated Destry
25. Fun spot in Queens
28. Chasm
29. "My country,
____ . . ."
30. 40-day period
31. Wire measure
32. Prop for a witch
35. Biggers's sleuth
37. Party supplier
41. Clay piece
42. Toboggan
43. Chime
45. Sharpen
46. Peer Gynt's mother
47. Prehistoric ruin in England
49. ____ Alonzo Stagg
50. Scolded
52. British composer
53. Detonation
54. Hat or dog
55. Harness parts
57. Mate
58. Brazilian dance
61. Lugosi
62. Woodwind
66. Actress Patricia
67. Famed London site
70. ____ de la Paix
71. Diva's specialty
72. Sculls
73. Holiday, for short
74. Make the grade
75. Raincoats for rancheros
77. Minor argument
78. Sags, as a flower
79. "____-Tiki"
80. Scottish hillside
82. Topsy's friend
83. To the left, aboard
86. Hoover Dam area
92. Pedestal part
93. Glacial snow-field
94. Rocker Billy
95. Bulwer-Lytton girl
96. Singer Clapton
97. Actress Revere
98. So long!, in Soho
99. Predatory bird
100. Go down
101. The seven ____ of man
102. Exude
103. Do a lab job

DOWN
1. Succulent fruit
2. Sailor's saint
3. One of the Waughs
4. Shirt type
5. Lots
6. Succotash bean
7. Arnie's group
8. "Zorro, the ____"
9. French novelist
10. Perpendicular
11. Foolhardy
12. Explosive
13. "I dreamed I dwelt in ____"
14. Chinese port
15. Shakes the head
16. Makes do
26. Aspire
27. Bard's night
28. River island
31. Cock or bull
32. Tell secrets
33. Ploy
34. Part of an ephah
35. Piece of soil
36. Layer
37. Zoo enclosure
38. City on the Tevere
39. Slaughter of baseball
40. Take a nap
42. ____ lively!
43. Parisian parent
44. River to the Danube
47. Long portico
48. Arabian porter
51. Tracy's "Bad Day ____"
53. Lively party
55. Title for Fritz
56. Linen vestments
57. Boot liners
58. Photo
59. Space prefix
60. Water-supply carrier
61. Cote sounds
62. Obnoxious kid
63. Mr. Roberts
64. Evict
65. Promontory
67. Pine
68. Facilitate
69. Doctors' gp.
74. Van Cliburn, for one
76. Spicy
77. Actor Mineo
78. Ohio R. state
80. Carried
81. Old Norse poems
82. Brilliance
83. July drinks
84. ____-mutuel
85. Norse god
86. Opera's Sir Rudolph
87. Dutch city
88. Roasted, in Rouen
89. Pair of oxen
90. Heavy load
91. Shipshape
93. Govt. agcy.

ACROSS

1. Christie sleuth
7. Actress Worth
12. FDR follower
15. Nova Scotia
16. "____ a Hot Tin Roof": 2 wds.
17. Summers pour Suzette
19. Christie mystery: 3 wds.
22. Noshed
23. Bread pieces
24. Stroller: hyph.
25. Body fluids
27. Shout
28. Ascribes
29. Money in Minsk
31. South African village
32. Neck artery
35. Korean soldiers
36. Holiday nights
40. Hole driller
41. "The ____ Horse" (Christie mystery)
42. "The ____ Murders" (Christie mystery)
43. Song for Sills
44. Gadgets
47. Town in Venezuela
48. At the center of
49. Oh, dear!
50. Uproar
52. Annoyance
54. Gang or mob ending
55. Christie mystery
56. Chose
58. Mature
59. French author and family
62. Obtains
63. Condiment
67. Good speaker
68. Vacuum tube
70. Neither's partner
71. Christie mystery: 3 wds.
74. Black, in Boulogne
75. Edward ____ of the silents
76. Inflicts
77. Minn. neighbor
78. Chinese weights
79. Hospital workers

DOWN

1. Half a '60s singing group
2. Intense
3. Harder to find
4. Teaching deg.
5. Canards
6. Worm getter: 2 wds.
7. Eaves dripper
8. Badger cousin
9. Biblical verb endings
10. ____ de plume
11. Puzzles
12. Christie sleuth Poirot
13. Summer ermine
14. ____ Haute
18. Fast fliers
20. Handle
21. Clothes, in Castilla
26. Fragrance
28. Out of sorts
30. Shoshonean
31. Tropical nuts
32. Charley horse
33. High home
34. Forays
35. Control-tower device
37. Crooked bone joint
38. "Christ Stopped at ____"
39. Leaves in a hurry
41. Propelled a punt
45. Author Joyce Carol
46. Hands over the reins: 2 wds.
47. Hymn endings
51. Japanese apricot
53. Staggers
54. Caviar source
55. Glowing gas
57. Malayan boat
58. Queens, in Quimper
59. Right away
60. Directional signal
61. Circle sections
62. Question
64. Indian coins
65. English philosopher
66. Part of a mane
68. Phoenician seaport
69. Off-white
72. Merino comment
73. Ending for auction or profit

PUZZLE 299

• CHRISTIE CAPER •

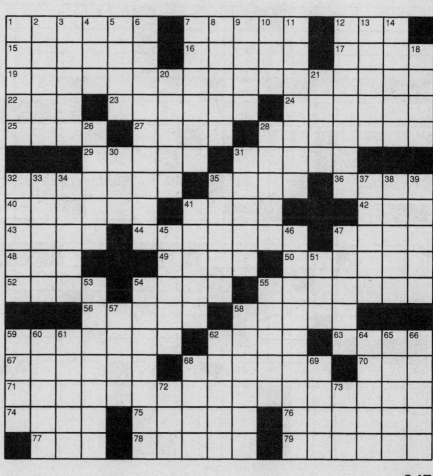

PUZZLE 300

• ON THE DOWNBEAT •

ACROSS

1. Sponges
7. Glad ____
11. Ocean shore
17. Come forth
18. Constructed
19. Caper
20. Spangler Arlington Brugh
22. Covered carriage
23. Shoshonean Indian
24. Everything
25. Of gold
27. Coltrane's horn
28. Chess opening
32. Falls behind
33. Bounds
34. Sault ____ Marie
35. Long story
39. Mine contents
40. Humble
42. Yearned
44. Senior
47. Tasseled hat
48. Gambling inits.
50. Moved cautiously
51. Cumberland ____
53. Hockey position
55. Sugary suffix
56. Chess opening
63. Author Levin
64. Dick Van ____
65. Layer
66. Core group
68. Booming letters
69. D.C. gp.
72. Furies
76. Baker, at times
78. Explosive
81. Zodiac sign
82. Kingly title
83. Raincoat, for short
85. Oxygen isotope
86. Tumble
87. Chess opening
90. Bible book: abbr.
93. Jazz opening
94. Resort town
95. Pa's bro
96. Complete
98. ____ Defense (chess opening)
103. Shrewdness
104. Employing
105. Meeting program
106. Narrow-minded teacher
107. "Jane ____"
108. Vermont horse

DOWN

1. Waxy
2. Latin I word
3. Remedied computer defects
4. Garbo and others
5. Wading bird
6. Tennis unit
7. Chess opening
8. Feel poorly
9. Betray self-satisfaction
10. Swaggers
11. Edits film
12. Follow
13. Operated
14. No ifs, ____, or buts
15. Scholastic sports gp.
16. Trois moins un
18. Verse form
21. Dickens title part
26. Proportional
28. Berg's kin
29. Wilson or Hines
30. Shade tree
31. Donkey
35. Luckman or Caesar
36. Inert gas
37. Silly sorts
38. Summed
41. Horn blast
43. KP worker
45. Humpty-Dumpty
46. Grated
49. Boy
52. Links org.
53. Type of rummy
54. "____ bin ein Berliner"
56. Cheap thrills
57. Teheran resident
58. Lawyer Ralph
59. Lure
60. Atlas abbr.
61. Ray or particle
62. Ms. Claire
67. "Norma ____"
69. Northern Israeli
70. Rock throwing
71. Modern digs
73. Deflected
74. Congers
75. Food fish
77. Noteworthy
79. "L'etat, c'est ____"
80. Majors or general
84. Grand Imperial ____ de Paris
86. Wheel cover
87. Enchantress
88. Miserable
89. Batted ball
90. Pile
91. Fairy-tale word
92. Poker variation
97. Miss Hogg
99. Healing goddess
100. Early morning time?
101. Tooth doctors' gp.
102. Bobbsey Twin

PUZZLE 301

• AGAINST THE GRAIN •

ACROSS

1. Spring or winter crop
6. ____ Na Na
9. Stake
12. German composer and organist
16. Eagle's home
17. Despicable person
18. "Butterflies ____ Free"
19. Chef's wear
21. Whirlwind on the Gobi
23. Porous rock
25. Elementary: abbr.
26. Annie's pooch
27. Mr. Kefauver
28. Join together
29. Fret
31. ____ Aviv
32. Sniggler's quarry
33. Terminates
34. Degrades
37. Going astray
39. Author Bret
42. Betelgeuse and Sirius
44. Uses a bucket
48. Muslim rulers
50. Small bill
51. More irked
52. Alias for Madame Dudevant
55. "Harper Valley ____"
57. Western lily
58. Alencon or Chantilly
59. Juicy fruit
60. Fish sauce
64. Abraham's nephew
65. Pretend beach edifice
71. "Stella ____"
73. Gangster's gun
74. Shops
75. Divans
76. Satiates
78. Pollute
79. Amazes
82. Cover again
85. Rents
88. Jackie's second
89. Shore bird
90. Tiff
94. "____ Believer"
95. Gladiator's milieu
97. Across: prefix
99. Blackbird
100. Typewriter character
102. '65 Taylor-Burton movie, with "The"
104. Songstress Della
105. Golf mound
106. Greek goddess of recklessness
107. Actress Papas
108. Word before chic or bien, for Pierre
109. Bitter vetch
110. Blushing
111. Bakery treats

DOWN

1. Hornets' kin
2. Core
3. Kovacs or Pyle
4. First or band follower
5. Hardy heroine
6. Tea biscuits
7. Track events
8. Type of ant
9. Diamond feature
10. Chalkboards' adjuncts
11. Framework for stretching cloth
12. Game fish
13. Proper
14. Tiara
15. Sharpened
20. Beatty and Sparks
22. London goodbye
24. Market for a hero
30. Aqueduct filler
33. Mild oaths
35. Ice floe
36. Like the Rosetta
37. Before, to Longfellow
38. Hoopster's organization: abbr.
39. Witch
40. Soul, to Monique
41. ____ Speedwagon
43. Connection word
45. Cyprinid fish
46. Journey part
47. Hit show sign
49. Vends
51. Antony and Chagall
53. ____ Miguel
54. Play division
55. Sty
56. Small bit
59. British father
60. Classifieds
61. Thai language
62. Helper for Santa
63. School group
65. Posed
66. Sweetsop
67. Afternoon TV fare
68. Prefix for angle or color
69. Football's Dawson
70. New York clock zone: abbr.
72. Straight-grained timber
73. Vaporized material
76. Cornelia Otis
77. Having sawlike notches
80. Dory adjuncts
81. Manufacture
83. Separated slowly
84. Tear violently
85. Charlatan
86. Colonial insect
87. Slender candle
91. Type of tiger or airplane
92. Concerning
93. Enervates
95. Counterpart of Mars
96. Soft drinks
97. Autocrat
98. ____ and image
101. Language suffix
103. Pensioner's nest egg: abbr.

PUZZLE 302

ACROSS
1. Mast
5. Toddlers
9. Extra, as a tire

10. Amphitheater
12. Broadcasted
13. Certain opera singer
14. Charge
15. Used a bench
17. Prefix for angle or sect
18. Otherwise
20. Rented
22. Mixes
24. Lurch
27. Chums
31. Refreshing drink
32. What's ___?
34. Civil War general
35. Appraised
37. Shade of green
39. Steeple
40. Nile or Avon
41. Rip
42. Fawn, for one

DOWN
1. Persuasive line
2. Peels
3. "Where the Boys ___"
4. Crimsons
5. Shred
6. Miner's quest
7. Big tops
8. Night noise
9. Secure
11. Dry
16. Straighten
19. Compass point: abbr.
21. Snake
23. Soft-hearted
24. Jalopies
25. Conform
26. Bind again
28. Existing
29. Prying tool
30. Prophet
33. Sentence part
36. Age
38. Fish story

PUZZLE 303

ACROSS
1. Scottish headwear
4. Knocks lightly
8. Dalmatian marking
12. Pub brew
13. Buckeye State
14. Record
15. Pitching must
17. Location
18. Weep
19. Heeds
21. Jets
24. Owing
25. Fireplace item
26. ___ Tin Tin
28. Composition
32. Washington's bill
33. Summit
35. "Three men ___ tub": 2 wds.
36. Examinations
39. Chest bone
41. Cut off
42. Paddle
44. Grooms
46. Letter carrier
50. Sea bird
51. Opera solo
52. Went away
56. Shout
57. Dry
58. Soap ingredient
59. Antlered animals
60. Decays
61. Craving

DOWN
1. Restaurant bill
2. Pie ___ mode: 2 wds.
3. Notes
4. Thief
5. Exclamation of surprise
6. Medicine unit
7. Firm
8. Alabama and Alaska
9. Peel
10. Not closed
11. Brewed drinks
16. Long time
20. Take to court
21. Plan
22. "The ___ Ranger"
23. Rest one's feet
27. Neither's partner
29. Without a sound
30. Unknown writer: abbr.
31. Sharp barks
34. Fruit seed
37. Adds up
38. Mr. Snead
40. Rye and white
43. Sonar's kin
45. Make a mistake
46. Step
47. Verbal
48. Smooth as ___
49. Rome's fiddler
53. Deep hole
54. Sight organ
55. Lion's lair

Codeword is a special crossword puzzle in which conventional clues are omitted. Instead, answer words in the diagram are represented by numbers. Each number represents a different letter of the alphabet, and all of the letters of the alphabet are used. When you are sure of a letter, put it in the code key chart for easy reference. Three letters have been given to start you off.

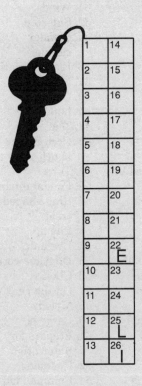

Code key chart:

#		#	
1		14	
2		15	
3		16	
4		17	
5		18	
6		19	
7		20	
8		21	
9		22	E
10		23	
11		24	
12		25	L
13		26	I

Main grid (■ = black square):

6	5	26	14	■	24	8	25	6	8	■	18	8	6	3
18	8	12	22	■	8	25(L)	26(I)	22(E)	12	■	22	21	12	22
8	1	8	21	■	18	25	26	3	8	■	3	26	7	12
16	22	9	22	■	3	7	21	3	■	6	3	8	24	6
22	21	22	■	12	26	3	■	6	18	10	■	■	■	■
■	■	13	23	26	19	■	17	22	3	■	21	8	3	■
6	7	23	21	16	22	■	8	12	10	■	11	22	12	6
8	9	8	2	22	■	9	23	9	■	18	8	6	3	8
21	7	3	22	■	2	26	12	■	18	8	23	18	22	21
26	21	22	■	7	18	3	■	21	26	25	22	■	■	■
■	5	22	24	■	9	8	9	■	16	8	18			
24	8	3	11	22	■	1	21	8	10	■	6	3	26	21
22	15	11	26	25	8	21	8	3	22	■	3	26	9	22
8	25	22	6	■	6	22	20	22	21	■	22	20	22	6
14	22	22	4	■	11	22	22	9	6	■	14	22	6	6

Place the answer to clue 1 in the first space, drop a letter, and arrange the remaining letters to answer clue 2. Drop another letter and arrange the remaining letters to answer clue 3. The first dropped letter goes into the box to the left of space 1 and the second dropped letter goes into the box to the right of space 3. Follow this pattern for each row in the diagram. When completed, the letters on the left and right, reading down, will spell related words or a phrase.

	1		2		3	
	4		5		6	
	7		8		9	
	10		11		12	
	13		14		15	

1. More friendly
2. Less cooked
3. Unusual
4. Hold back
5. Having prongs
6. Nurse
7. Jitters
8. Lucky number
9. Nights before
10. Frightened
11. Honeys
12. Epochs
13. Received jointly
14. Peruses
15. Risk

251

PUZZLE 306

ACROSS
1. Breakfast food
5. Glance at
9. Thong
14. Tie game
15. Story
16. Show to be true
17. Eat elegantly
18. Aware of
19. Swiss song
20. Long story
21. Masked mammal, for short
22. Occident
23. Youngster
25. Charge
27. Out-of-date
30. Red
34. Deed
35. Kind of pudding
38. Big tank
40. Anger
41. Lamp dweller
42. Imitate
43. Majors or Marvin
44. End products
46. Lair
47. Races at full speed
49. Deflect
51. Choose
52. Information
54. Shopper's paper
57. Minute particle
59. Pace
63. One-year record
65. Popular sandwich
66. Pop
67. Say
68. Burden
69. Surrounded by
70. Aspired
71. Dog and cat
72. Allows

DOWN
1. ____ and ends
2. Opera solo
3. Vivid flavor
4. Perspires
5. Shop's supply
6. Birchbark
7. Choir voice
8. Light gas
9. 007, for one
10. Garden tool
11. Went by bus
12. Streets: abbr.
13. Animal skin
24. Still
25. Gem surface
26. Epoch
27. Bucket
28. Farm units
29. Brew
30. Nasal cavity
31. Wind
32. Sidestep
33. Slender candle
36. Representative
37. Nuisance
39. Camper's home
44. Tear
45. Occupied a bench
48. Turn
50. Feudal tenant
52. Ring-shaped treat
53. Pile up
54. Eye hair
55. Division word
56. Click
57. On the peak of
58. Melody
60. Large book
61. Prepare for publication
62. Cushions
64. Commanded

PUZZLE 307   FAN WORDS

Place the 5-letter answers to the clues into the fan to discover an 8-letter word reading across the shaded area. As an added help, pairs of answers are anagrams (1 is an anagram of 2, 3 is an anagram of 4, etc.).

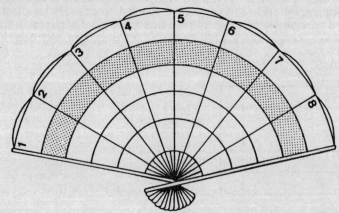

1. Pacific, for one
2. Lake vessel
3. Malign
4. Paper quantities
5. Small buoy
6. Soaring
7. Greek giant
8. Contaminate

PUZZLE 308

• IN TIPTOP SHAPE •

ACROSS

1. Game of chance
6. Wax: pref.
10. Forehead
14. Assert strongly
18. City on the Missouri River
19. Sleeping
20. West Indian city
21. Church part
22. Biblical weeds
23. European capital
24. Valuable thing
25. "____ a Song Go Out of My Heart"
26. ____ about
27. Robust
28. Colorless gas
29. Marsh
30. "____ for Love" from "Singing in the Rain"
34. Diamond-setting method
35. "For ____ Eyes Only"
36. Spouse's family
38. Resuscitate
41. Solid
42. Held tight
45. French beverage
46. Humiliate
47. Slender
48. Accomplishing
49. Mixed, in color
50. Superlative
51. Explosion
52. Blob
53. Knowledge
54. Rocker Adam
55. Smugly moral person
56. Automobile event
57. Having less fat
59. Conceited
60. European blackbirds
61. Wheeled shopping basket
62. Stationing
65. Exams
66. Hare-and-tortoise contest
67. Mineral spring
70. Work
71. Well-being
73. Fail-safe
74. Revolve
75. Church recess
76. Stories
77. Trigonometric function
78. Sao ____, Brazil
79. Despicable person
80. High nest
81. Fontaine's partner
82. Healed

83. Formal, as clothes
85. Painful
86. Sonoran Indians
87. Shipshape
95. Deneb or Betelgeuse
96. Moldings
97. "Topaz" author
98. Composer of "Rule, Britannia"
99. Japanese ethnic group
100. Mountain ridge
101. Ensnare
102. Rebelled
103. Evening: pref.
104. Approaches
105. Actor Auberjonois
106. Ruled
107. Wallet stuffers
108. Strike out
109. The heavens: pref.
110. Endures

DOWN

1. "A ____ Livin' to Do"
2. Certain Arabians
3. Fortune-telling card
4. Treatment-giver
5. Treaty group: abbr.
6. Liquid server
7. Village in southern Italy
8. Bettering
9. Horace poem
10. ____ nova
11. Violinists use it
12. Standing up
13. Oasis
14. Beast
15. Certification
16. Here and there
17. Solar plexus
20. Kitchen tool
27. Possess
28. Astringent
31. Rescue
32. Silly one
33. Agma
37. Passover feast
38. Incarnation of Vishnu
39. Black, poetically
40. Very spacious
41. Snake tooth

42. Universities' cousins: abbr.
43. Pond pad
44. Numero ____
47. Reclined
48. Kachinas, e.g.
49. Piece of land
51. ____ bushy-tailed
52. Vader
55. "Peter ____"
56. Takes it easy
58. Sooner than, to a bard
59. Bench tool
60. Skirmish
61. Part of TLC
62. Two-by-four
63. Specter
64. Support
65. Ankle bones
66. Undersized one
67. Tater
68. Heap
69. "And giving ____, up the chimney . . ."

72. Musical sense
73. No-work jobs
74. Healing places
77. Waves
78. Persian sprite
80. Lumber tree
81. Actress-author Anita ____
82. Healing agts.
84. Walks proudly
85. Snow gear: var.
86. Anonymous critic
88. Gay
89. Utopian
90. ____ Dame University
91. Praying figure
92. Fetters
93. Beginning
94. Wants
95. "Mens sana in corpore ____"
101. Refrain syllable
102. Entire

PUZZLE 309

• KITCHEN CAPER •

ACROSS

1. Witty remarks
5. Vault
9. Musical finale
13. Glance at
17. African lily
18. Cloak
19. On a vacation
20. Place for doves
21. Carnival attraction
22. Ovid's years
23. Coty or Enriquez
24. Function
25. Ruin personal chances
28. Cheapskate
29. Wapiti
30. Thrust
31. Asian desert
32. Bolivian city
35. Wild hog
37. Water carriers
41. Golf mavens
42. Spume
43. Pseudonym
44. Intimidate
45. Sonoran bear
46. Chess piece
47. Belle of the West
48. Ionian Sea gulf
49. Hire
51. Biblical dancer
53. Cornflower
54. Meld
56. "___ Homme" (French song)
57. Antitoxin
59. Carpet
61. Gathered
64. Lumberjack's cry
67. Paved surface
68. Frenzy
69. Biblical Syria
71. Taradiddle
72. Swiss river
73. Garlic section
74. City map
75. Pool
76. Door opening
78. Check
79. Artist's need
80. Hospital department
81. Roman sun god
82. Solution: abbr.
83. English race track
85. Cordon bleu awarder
92. Dejected
93. Rack for fodder
94. Aquatic bird
95. Russian log hut
96. Hinged closing
97. Fireman's need
98. Imitator
99. Son of Isaac
100. Spur on
101. Jug
102. Stout's Wolfe
103. Dune material

DOWN

1. Artist Chagall
2. Medley
3. Brouhaha
4. "The Shell ___"
5. Showy elegance
6. English composer
7. Punkahs
8. Concise poem
9. Billiard shot
10. Has unpaid bills
11. Man from Odense
12. Sailor's assent
13. Reporter
14. That's the way the ___
15. Tamarisk tree
16. At no time, to a bard
26. Comedian Olsen
27. Dory's adjunct
28. Patio planters
31. Growl
32. Sally, Dick, and Jane's dog
33. Sky bear
34. Invent an alibi
35. Scare word
36. Acorn droppers
37. Silent one
38. Buenos ___
39. Memo
40. Ruth, king of ___
42. Typeface
43. Make amends
46. French kings
47. Incline
48. Styptic
50. Sir Geraint's wife
52. Astound
53. Fedora feature
55. Actor Flynn
58. French state
59. Journey
60. Topnotch
62. Roof overhang
63. Catalan artist
65. De Valera's land
66. Virginia ___
68. Sate
70. Stood for office
73. Gab
74. Louisiana's bird
75. Golf clubs
77. Punctual
78. Korean soldier
79. Reference book: abbr.
81. Solemn
82. Dome or physics starter
83. Turkish general
84. Chunk
85. Black bird
86. Seine feeder
87. No way, Jose!
88. Active one
89. Peak in Thessaly
90. Firth of Lorn port
91. Praise highly
93. Guevara

ACROSS

1. Rabbits' moves
5. Alliance
9. Drift sideways
13. Brink
17. Actor Baldwin
18. Khayyam or Sharif
19. Center of activity
20. Actress Skye
21. Hacienda kid
22. Beginner
23. Cake finisher
24. Wading bird
25. Reed or Mills
27. Dark rye bread
30. Gulf of Aden country
33. General Thumb
34. Landbound bird
35. Faulty
37. Alan Greenspan's expertise: abbr.
39. "____ Man in Havana"
41. Provoke
45. Blunder
46. Reconnoiterer
48. Type of tide
51. Melody
52. Piccadilly brews
54. Within: pref.
55. "M*A*S*H" setting
57. Be indisposed
58. Tennis star Yannick ____
59. Down and out
61. Frolics
63. Skillful
65. Skyrockets
68. Apartment fee
69. Business
72. Copper or bronze
74. Kilkenny native
77. Actor Gulager
78. Headdress
81. Smear
82. Part of HOMES
83. Pitch in
85. Tribe
86. Building support
88. Chess pieces
89. Picasso's tripod
91. Athens vowel
93. Apiece
94. Carpenter or fire
95. Playmate
97. Indignation
99. Takes the cream off
101. Brakes suddenly
107. Illustrious
110. Ecclesiastical mantle
111. Lombardy lake
112. Uniform
115. Reject
116. Ripener
117. Dill
118. Pianist Peter ____
119. Fe
120. Numerous
121. Ranger or wolf
122. Army color
123. Serf

DOWN

1. Workman
2. Potpourri
3. Victorian thrillers
4. Tea cake
5. Crock
6. March sister
7. Nag
8. Rainbow-colored fish
9. Musical Alvin
10. Cajun fare
11. Declare
12. Swiss capital
13. Dog's treat
14. Castle, in chess
15. Concerning
16. Ground corn
26. Iowa town
28. "Alley Oop" kingdom
29. Rascal
31. Unorthodox
32. Peter of Herman's Hermits
35. Comic Orson ____
36. Folksinger Guthrie
38. Artists' models, often
40. ____ Speedwagon
42. Ships' officers
43. Component
44. Snigglers' quests
47. Hurly-burly
49. Curved line
50. "Dragon Seed" author
53. Strawberry's field?
56. Blvd.
60. Southern sweet potato
62. Unrepeated
64. Able
66. Carrot-tops
67. Say aloud
69. Soreness
70. Beagle's bane
71. Actor Mineo
73. Luminous outlines
75. Legal claim
76. Temporary shelter
79. Film Norma
80. Remedy
84. Spicy
87. Sparse
90. Refrain syllables
92. Teen star Meyers
96. Home-grown
98. Revise
100. Hollywood production
101. Con game
102. Forum garb
103. Candid
104. "____ Nanette"
105. Grace ending
106. Perpetually
108. Harrow's rival
109. Finished
113. Important period
114. San Franciscan hill

PUZZLE 310

• CHANGE OF PACE •

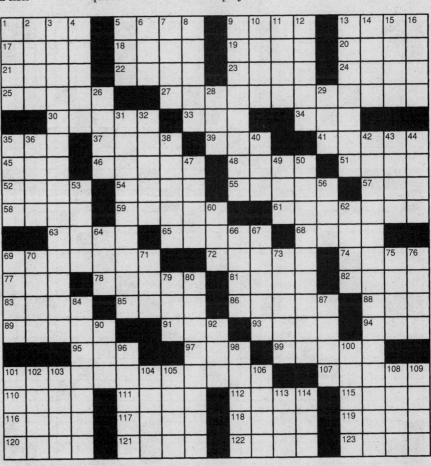

255

PUZZLE 311

• CHARACTER STUDY •

ACROSS

1. Petty crook, slangily
6. Obelisk
12. Aphrodite's boy
16. Lifelong occupation
17. Tennis ____?
18. Early Teutons
20. TV's Hannah Miller
22. Rhea or emu
24. Globe
25. Abhor
26. Emulated Marceau
28. Fink
29. African nut
31. French wine region
32. 1978 Peace Prize winner
33. River in "Kubla Khan"
34. Actress Verdugo
36. Tokyo, formerly
37. Clerical headwear
38. An Astaire
39. Hallow
41. Named
42. Having less color in the hair
43. Steins
44. Bobby or knee-length
45. "Out on ____"
46. Lessen
48. Siouan tribe
49. Equestrian guidance
52. Type type
53. Garbo
54. Judy of "Laugh-In"
55. Witness
56. Spanish abstract painter
57. Portrayer of Gigi and Lili
59. Eskers
60. Priest's garment
61. North Dakota city
62. French valley
63. Brooks of "Spenser: For Hire"
64. Northern Atlantic fish
66. Flays
67. Quarries
68. Rosie's fastener
69. Book part
70. Singer Vicki
71. Catapult
73. Poets
74. White-flowered trees
78. Batman's sidekick
79. Ribbed vertically
80. Pigeon pea
81. Stringent
82. Alum
83. Fake jewel
84. Lunches
86. English poet Alexander ____
87. Mien
88. Computer link
89. Pallette and McCarthy
91. VI times CLXVII
92. Limited
94. Portrayer of Mrs. Loman
97. Mesh
98. Battery poles
99. Eskimos
100. Flirt
101. Modern painting
102. Actress playing Ed Brown's landlady Della

DOWN

1. Took risks
2. "Exodus" hero
3. Require
4. Conger chaser
5. Stream overflows
6. Actor who plays Michael in "The Godfather"
7. Employed
8. Harplike instrument
9. Place for parking
10. Enlivens
11. Dwelt
12. Stilt's kin
13. Byway
14. Hubbell teammate
15. Singer of "Goldfinger"
16. Daredevil's damsel Landis
19. Paper fastener
20. Bantered
21. Lyric poem
23. Anesthetic gas
27. Nick
30. Lively, to Muti
32. Alaska city
33. "1776" role
35. Keen
37. Choreographer in "Smile"
38. Rebel
40. Period
41. Raccoon's relative
42. Trombonist Miller
44. Food fish
45. Indonesian islands
46. Nimble
47. Mini-series Mamie Eisenhower portrayer
48. Welles or Bean
49. Black terns
50. Outfits
51. Bizarre
52. Part of a Latin trio
53. Old World mammal
54. "Dressed to Kill" pursuer
57. ____ and onions
58. Change
59. Extend beyond
61. Know-it-all
63. Irish cry
65. Unyielding
66. Bash
67. ____ on the back
69. Place of drudgery
70. Schedule
71. Bach's instrument
72. Water wheels
73. Infielder
74. Repaired chairs
75. Boost
76. Gelatins
77. Valentino role
79. Amount of cotton
80. Summary
83. Authority
84. German woodcut artist
85. Alone, for Monique
88. Shift
89. Snorri story
90. Dirk
93. Spanish king
95. Inferior
96. Greek letters

DOUBLE TROUBLE

Not really double trouble, but double fun! Solve this puzzle as you would a regular crossword, EXCEPT place one, two, or three letters in each box. The number of letters in each answer is shown in parentheses after its clue.

ACROSS

1. Pursue (5)
3. Create (7)
8. Contorts (6)
12. Cover (3)
13. Side by side (7)
14. Flamboyant (6)
15. Valise (4)
17. Hollow (4)
18. Century count (7)
19. Everlasting (7)
21. Dance (5)
22. Blood vessel (4)
23. Fraud (4)
24. Extracts (5)
28. Harvest (4)
30. Date (6)
33. Calm (6)
34. Pigment (5)
36. Restricted (7)
38. Merit (4)
39. Go up (6)
41. Auto shelter (6)
43. Dossier (4)
44. Sinew (6)
45. Hint (4)
46. Catch (3)
48. Car (5)
50. Sermonize (6)
53. Income (7)
56. In a little while (4)
58. Rib (5)
59. Agitates (5)
60. Ancestor (7)
62. Ship's wheel (4)
63. Play division (5)
64. Put back to normal (8)
65. Damp (3)

DOWN

1. Goblet (7)
2. Calm (6)
3. Taxi (3)
4. Hardship (6)
5. Nasty (4)
6. Pillar (4)
7. Collection (3)
8. Dorothy's house-mover (7)
9. Gale (4)
10. Lead performer (4)
11. Horse (5)
16. Wait on (5)
18. Ferrigno's role (4)
20. Baseball-team count (4)
21. Jab (4)
23. Weariness (7)
25. Assess (4)
26. Pier (5)
27. Aged (6)
28. Meal (6)
29. Swiftly (5)
31. Rebuke (5)
32. Edge (3)
33. Pop (4)
35. Propose (6)
37. Rip (4)
40. Bunk! (8)
42. Type (5)
45. Family (4)
47. Subside (5)
49. Payable (3)
50. Think (6)
51. Nut (6)
52. Military hat (6)
53. Relaxes (5)
54. Weakness (4)
55. Sea bird (3)
56. Takes to court (4)
57. Aware of (4)
60. Pro (3)
61. "___ Sky at Morning" (3)

PUZZLE 313

• REEL THEM IN! •

ACROSS
1. College building, for short
5. Objet ____
9. Hoax
13. Outlay
17. Succulent lily
18. Caesar's road
19. Threesome
20. Aleutian isle
21. Night swoopers
22. "____, vidi, . . ."
23. Frolic
24. NT Book
25. Paper-wrapped dish
28. Cubic meter
29. Fleming or Holm
30. Bundle of hides
31. Kodiak, e.g.
32. Lunch spots
35. Dunaway or Emerson
37. Magnificent
41. Scion
42. Charabanc
43. Hawk
44. Spanish boy
45. Taxing initials
46. Sally's job in "Me and My Girl"
49. Theater sign
50. Associates
52. Bradley and Sharif
53. Desert evergreen
55. Nebraska Indian
56. Barrel part
57. London apartment
58. Wind instrument
60. Chickadee State
61. Encourage
64. Destiny
65. Porgy's place
67. Conifer
68. Space chimpanzee
70. Pindaric works
71. Dust cloth
72. Mythical war god
73. Guarded
75. Occupied
77. Secret meeting
78. Vigilant
79. Cotton-cleaning machine
80. Total
81. Milan's La ____
83. Place lacking privacy
89. Mayfair farewell
90. Enameled tinware
91. Maestro Klemperer
92. Complain bitterly
94. Baker's need
95. Legend
96. Smirk
97. Millay or O'Brien
98. Henri's dad
99. Scheme
100. Sunrise
101. Stunt

DOWN
1. Small amount
2. King of Norway
3. French menu word
4. More unkempt
5. Mideastern audience chamber
6. Egyptian sun disk
7. Split
8. Devious
9. "77 Sunset ____"
10. Yield
11. Targets
12. Thick mass of hair
13. Skipper
14. Something else to do
15. Recipe verb
16. Bulrush
26. Contains
27. Hasten
28. Sunday talk: abbr.
31. Harris's Fox
32. Fashionable
33. Prefix for dynamic or space
34. Disoriented one
35. Fidget
36. Rowan
37. Ethiopian language
38. Cannes seasons
39. About
40. Diffident
42. Snack
43. Rascals
46. Cleaving tool
47. Recurring themes
48. One from Muscat
51. Hall-of-Famer Mel
53. Aloft's antonym
54. Skirler's cap
56. Surfeited
57. Peeper
58. Ran away
59. Sole
60. Created
61. Say grace
62. Binds
63. Formerly, formerly
65. Wild Bill ____
66. Time abbreviations
69. Ship's route
72. Plated
74. Blue Eagle letters
75. Offer
76. Open
77. Ore car
79. Hunt for leftovers
80. Fleeced
81. Traffic sign
82. Grotto
83. Aspiration
84. Gymnast Korbut
85. Virginia willow
86. Ragout
87. Arabian gully
88. Operatic Jenny ____
90. Medicine measure: abbr.
93. Asian language

ACROSS

1. Noisy
5. Soaks
9. Facility
10. Brainstorm
11. Forest-doctor's specialty: 2 wds.
15. Summer TV fare
16. ____ Angeles
19. Sound receiver
20. Actress Dawber
23. Australian bird
24. Willow family members
28. Frozen water
29. Complain excessively
30. Pea holders
31. Fill the truck
33. Born
34. Lusterless
36. Cardinal color
37. Self
38. Vane direction
39. Disprove
41. Once more
43. Primary
44. Grape drink
45. Fall flower
47. Energy
48. Deeply engrossed
50. Apply friction
52. Also
53. Biblical garden
56. Squeaky-door remedy
57. Oceans
59. Dispatch
60. ____-tse
61. Summer drink
62. Baffled
64. Windy curve
65. ____ Moines
66. Dolores ____ Rio
67. Pigpen
68. Craze
70. Certain fruit producer: 2 wds.
76. Verbal
77. A Great Lake
78. Look after
79. Observed

DOWN

1. Permit
2. Rowing implement
3. Employ
4. Forest denizen
5. Omen
6. "____ on a Grecian Urn"
7. For each
8. Speak
12. Oozes
13. Russian mountain range
14. Pastoral
16. Give, for a time
17. Actor Sharif
18. Syrup providers: 2 wds.
20. Evergreen features: 2 wds.
21. Top cards
22. Come together
24. Longfellow, for one
25. Out of the ordinary
26. Fish eggs
27. Epic tale
30. Tree clippers
32. Cornus tree
35. Beauty's partner
38. Recoil
40. Small amount
42. Ventilate
46. Regrets
47. Having a liking for
48. Street
49. Assistant
51. Cave denizen
52. Golf mound
54. Orient
55. Inquisitive
58. African region
59. Share 50-50
63. Diner's card
68. Shape
69. Imitates
70. Folding bed
71. Raw metal
72. Is able to
73. Exist
74. Fib
75. Males

PUZZLE 314

• TRUNK AND ARMS •

259

PUZZLE 315

• FORE! •

ACROSS
1. Shoal
5. Squat: Fr.
10. Ties
15. Singe
19. Folk singer Jenkins
20. Fiddler's need
21. City in Portugal
22. Hindu deity
23. Use a swizzle stick
24. Michaelmas daisy
25. Carolina rails
26. War god
27. Overly diversified
31. Actress Susan and kin
32. English city
33. Islet
34. Single: pref.
35. Certain horses
37. Scottish river
38. Grimalkin
41. Alcohol abstainer
45. Plucking tool
47. Swelling: suff.
48. Deposited
49. Lieu
51. Grecian theaters
52. Soak, as flax
53. Spat
55. Contrite
56. Gloom, in literature
57. Japanese volcanic mountain
58. Bustle
59. Rusted
60. Make public
61. Treating gently
69. Morsel for Dobbin
70. Communications medium
71. Golf's Sutton
72. Thus far
73. Exhaust
76. Madras wear
77. Honor
79. Indignation
80. Give temporarily
81. Yeast
82. Slave
83. At no time: Ger.
84. Trespassers
86. Slugger's feat
90. North Sea feeder
91. Dutch city
92. Made a whirring sound
94. Reverential fear
95. Sue ____ Langdon
96. Group: Fr.
97. Baseball's Fingers
101. Got things going
108. French river
109. Imbecile
110. "One ____ the Life of Ivan Denisovich"
111. Early Peruvian
112. Uproar
113. Roman magistrate
114. Overact
115. Sign gas
116. Pitch
117. Thoroughfares
118. Charged
119. Jokes

DOWN
1. Remainder: Sp.
2. Rocker John
3. Poet T. S. ____
4. Send to the minor league
5. Passage
6. Blushing
7. Italian wine center
8. Actress Angeli
9. Revealed
10. ____ Antilles
11. Skirts
12. Preserves with brine
13. Proof word
14. Moved nonchalantly
15. Art
16. Actor Rhodes
17. Bitter: Fr.
18. Destroy
28. Part of A.D.
29. ____-do-well
30. Republic of Ireland
35. Braid
36. Melange
37. Gone
38. Acquiesce
39. Neighborhood
40. Nicholas, e.g.
41. Pentateuch
42. Ancient Syrian city
43. Puritan colonist
44. City on the Mississippi
45. Italian commune
46. Don Diego de la Vega's alias
49. Bantu language group
50. Journey
53. Caesar, e.g.
54. Redact
55. French composer
56. Lulu
59. Duck for down
60. Actor John ____ (Shirley Temple's ex)
62. Rice or Reed
63. Grazer's delight
64. Merchandise
65. Wild Asian dog
66. Competing
67. Unearthly
68. Range rambler
73. Glided
74. Johnnycake's relative
75. Chalet feature
76. Term of respect
77. Singer Lesley ____
78. Song: Ger.
81. Savior
82. Sewing aid
85. Baseballer Bucky ____
86. Court: abbr.
87. Knight's superior
88. Military acronym
89. Hardening
92. Witness
93. Bordoni and Cara
95. Glacial crest
96. Parallel line
98. String: Lat.
99. Disguise: abbr.
100. Actor Richard and kin
101. Classify
102. Huey, Dewey, and Louie
103. Shortly
104. Dullard
105. Blade: Ital.
106. Actress Sue ____
107. Singer Coolidge

PUZZLE 316

ACROSS

1. Make points
6. Marsh
11. For each
14. Potato, e.g.
15. Wigwam
16. Chopper
17. Island greeting
18. Boxing locale
19. Nothing
20. Mirth
21. Scarlet
22. Dapper
24. Charity
27. Umpire's call
28. Magician's speech
31. Twists
36. Consume
37. Get free
39. Airplane maneuver
40. Prevaricates
42. Hail!
43. Old stringed instrument
44. Glut
45. Program
48. Bo's number
49. Magnifies
51. Certify
53. Water tester
54. Mind
55. Abyss
58. Tease
60. Spool
64. Research room, for short
65. Ascended
67. Tough
68. 100 square meters
69. TV knobs
70. Wrath
71. Seine
72. Binge
73. Rock

DOWN

1. Male deer
2. Select
3. Double-reed woodwind
4. Warm again
5. Epoch
6. Leading actors
7. Existed
8. Mimicked
9. Males
10. Type of butter
11. Gasp
12. Leave
13. Count on
23. Coral island
25. Actor Marvin
26. Wife's title: abbr.
27. "A Chorus Line" song
28. Throb
29. Korean, e.g.
30. Molars
31. Grottoes
32. Store sign
33. Path
34. Lugs
35. Weary
38. Pen
41. Benches
45. Crackerjack pilot
46. Pat gently
47. Had lunch
50. Wanderers
52. Despot
54. Fat
55. Family
56. Rabbit relative
57. Help
58. Bellow
59. Capri or Man
61. "Cogito ____ sum"
62. Paradise
63. Harplike instrument
66. Tear
67. Possesses

Tiles

PUZZLE 317

Imagine that these tiles are on a table, each showing a 2-letter combination. Can you rearrange these tiles visually to form a 10-letter word?

PUZZLE 318

ACROSS
1. Gaol
5. Blue-green
9. ____ Halen (rock quartet)
12. Lounge
13. Official language of Pakistan
14. Self
15. Norway's capital
16. Swamp croaker
18. Actress Cicely ____
20. Singer/dancer Abdul
21. Civilian dress
23. High point
26. Quiet sound
29. ____ Palmas
30. Maple or corn
31. Badly
33. Greet
34. Authors Rice and Tyler
35. Monopolize
36. Zuider ____
37. Abound
38. Merrier
40. Thresholds
42. Detecting device
46. Most clever
49. Price
50. Everyone
51. Gander or cob
52. Paradise
53. Upper atmosphere
54. ____ corner
55. Lose control

DOWN
1. Absorb
2. Glowing
3. Wrongs
4. Darkness
5. Clumsy old boat
6. Spews
7. Politician Stevenson
8. Dilly
9. Mexican seaport
10. Gone by
11. Holiday potion
17. Cast about
19. Zeroes
22. Actress Wray
24. Silent
25. Fencer's sword
26. Quarrel
27. Whet
28. Frankly
30. Wiser
32. Send money
33. Tofu ingredient
35. Bother
38. Shine
39. Scarcer
41. Kind of bean
43. Baby's first word?
44. Egyptian sun god
45. Let
46. Used to be
47. Type
48. Five-and-____ (Woolworth's creation)

PUZZLE 319

CATEGORIES

For each of the categories listed, can you think of a word or phrase beginning with each letter on the left? Count one point for each correct answer. A score of 15 is good, and 21 is excellent.

	APPLIANCES	SEATS	MYTHOLOGY FIGURES	MATH TERMS	TYPES OF BOATS
A					
R					
O					
S					
E					

CODEWORD PUZZLE 320

Codeword is a special crossword puzzle in which conventional clues are omitted. Instead, answer words in the diagram are represented by numbers. Each number represents a different letter of the alphabet, and all of the letters of the alphabet are used. When you are sure of a letter, put it in the code key chart for easy reference. A group of letters has been inserted to start you off.

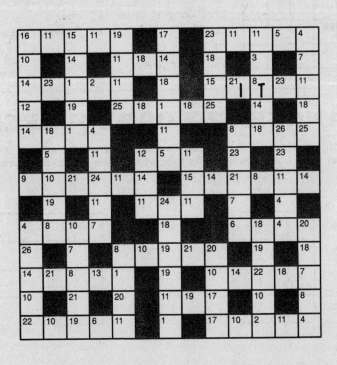

CODEWORD PUZZLE 321

PUZZLE 322

• TRICOLOR •

ACROSS

1. Design
5. Avian abodes
10. Anthracite
14. Of the atmosphere
15. Clear sky
16. Nimbus
17. Have a riotously good time
20. Miscellaneous
21. German novelist
22. Director Strasberg
23. Ailing
24. Demure
26. Spelling contest
27. Voice contempt
28. Repute
32. Confronts
35. TV serial
37. "I'm dreaming of ____"
39. Ten of Shakespeare's plays
40. River to the English Channel
41. "Auld Lang ____"
42. Tibetan gazelle
43. El ____ Campeador
44. Cob's mate
45. Joan of ____
46. Grant
49. Multitudes
53. Blind adoration
55. Rarely
58. Coup d'____
59. First zodiac sign
60. British princess
61. Dressing gown
62. Service chaplain
63. Pianist Myra

DOWN

1. Pontifical
2. Charter
3. Get up
4. Words for Nanette
5. Stinging herb
6. Actress Barrymore
7. Molt
8. Asian holiday
9. Sign of a hit
10. Sugar source
11. Belonging to us
12. Mars
13. Put on cargo
18. Italian port
19. For what reason
24. Towers
25. Arizona Indian
26. Light brown
27. Inferior grade of black tea
28. Chose
29. Lesser: prefix
30. Algerian port
31. Demolish: var.
32. Lipids
33. Askew
34. Detective Charlie
35. Descendant
36. Small bone
38. Margin
43. U.S. dramatist
44. Greek letter
45. Austrian psychiatrist
46. Supply satisfaction
47. Shackles
48. Units of force
49. Weeder
50. Aware
51. Strikebreaker
52. ____-beche
53. In the same place: abbr.
54. Asian nurse
56. Shag
57. Heavenly altar

PUZZLE 323   ANAGRAM WORD SQUARES

Rearrange the letters in the words shown to form new words, then place them in the diagrams so that they form words reading across and down. The first word across will be the first word down, the second word across will be the second word down, etc.

1. SAGE
   PARE
   GEED
   ERST

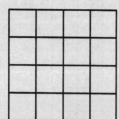

2. PERU
   SETT
   POST
   ROBS

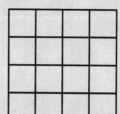

3. COLA
   SELL
   ERIC
   LODI

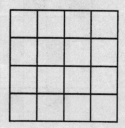

264

ACROSS
1. Falls behind
5. Pipe type
8. Jail money
12. Unemployed
13. Stadium sound
14. Actress Skinner
15. Principal
16. Grow older
17. Split
18. Envoy
21. Gift for Dad
22. City in Ohio
26. Wading bird
29. Gamble
30. Anger
31. Say with certainty
32. Container
33. Individuals
34. Unruly crowd
35. Juvenile game
36. Rendezvous
37. Add salt
39. Irish or Black
40. Precarious state of affairs
45. Type of jerk
48. Coach Parseghian
49. Encourage
50. Perfume
51. Primary color
52. Oklahoma city
53. Posted
54. No's counterpart
55. Collections

DOWN
1. Kind of bean
2. Cain's father
3. Readily fluent
4. Statesman
5. Expunge
6. Heroic story
7. Molter
8. Chuck or Ken
9. Summer drink
10. Lodging place
11. Child
19. Transgression
20. Cereal grass
23. Wee
24. Crude metals
25. Hornet's home
26. Show-offs
27. Bacchanalian cry
28. Singer McEntire
29. Sack
32. First month
33. Juicy fruits
35. As well
36. Hot beverage
38. Set out
39. Food fish
41. Algonquian language
42. Completed
43. Pace
44. ___ and evens
45. Distress call
46. Verse form
47. Actor Ameche

CANCELLATIONS

The names of eleven trees and a saying are hidden in the diagram. Taking one letter from each box, cross off the 6-letter trees from the across rows. Then cross off the 5-letter trees from the down columns. The leftover letters, one in each box, will reveal the saying, reading left to right, row by row.

ACROSS
1. _____
2. _____
3. _____
4. _____
5. _____

DOWN
1. _____
2. _____
3. _____
4. _____
5. _____
6. _____

	1	2	3	4	5	6
1	L H	I	B	E	R
	A C B A	A U L R	C D M L
2	S	N	R	E	D	F
	E L P I S A N U C E E A
3	B	O	P	Y	H	A
	D O A R L N E S D A N P
4	E	C	M	N	A	R
	V W A E L E C E U R L T
5	W	L	L	V	R	E
	Y R H I I N L H O E S W

265

PUZZLE 326

• TEAMWORK •

ACROSS

1. Velvety bryophyte
5. Koh-i-noor weight unit
10. Substructure
14. Perry's creator
15. Protein acid
16. Stratford- on-____
17. West Coast nine: 2 wds.
20. Deadly reptile
21. Pub drinks
22. Intl.-aid org.
23. Culture medium
24. Portent
26. Fancy dance
29. 100 square meters
30. Mount Viso, e.g.
33. Expunges
36. Loud report
38. Before
40. Canadian nine: 3 wds.
43. Inquire
44. Venture
45. Add salt to
46. Second sight inits.
48. Comedians Bob and ____
49. Insignificant
50. Legal claim
52. Part of UAR
55. Sadr or Enif
57. Ship's pole
58. Shoshonean
61. Midwest nine: 3 wds.
65. Bunny's cousin
66. Benefit
67. Lyra component
68. Roman date
69. Dance-music makers
70. Mild cheese

DOWN

1. Arizona city
2. Minerals
3. Hit with the hand
4. Matched group
5. Kind of lily
6. Moslem prince
7. Frames
8. Collection
9. Rocky hill
10. Fruit
11. State positively
12. Tender
13. Printers' measures
18. Child's game
19. Refrigerant
23. "____ Sprach Zarathustra"
24. Spoken
25. Dining-out needs
26. Greek letter
27. Got up
28. Songbirds
29. Dublin theater
31. Rental agreement
32. Comedian Richard
34. Last bit
35. Gaze steadily
37. Haw's opposite
39. Hireling, to Scott
41. Algerian city
42. Lintel support
47. Does better than show
51. Writer Levin
52. Plant insect
53. Train tracks
54. Life's imitator
55. Food fish
56. Become bored
57. Sibelius's bird of Tuonela
58. Previously owned
59. Roman garment
60. Test, briefly
61. Greek letter
62. Gift of ____
63. Eggs
64. "The ____ of St. Agnes"

PUZZLE 327   CODE RING

Ten common English words are given in code. The letters of each word have been shifted on the Code Ring a certain number of spaces. For example, to decode FYNNW, try shifting each letter 1 clockwise and you find GZOOX; next try shifting each letter 2 clockwise and you find HAPPY. The code is different for each word below.

CODE RING

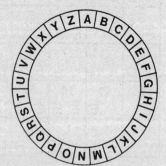

1. Q P P A N _____
2. L M T K X _____
3. Q F Y P I _____
4. H W F F Q _____
5. Q D M T G _____
6. X G V N C _____
7. P F O N S _____
8. Q Y C L X _____
9. I S E E F _____
10. C I R F A _____

PUZZLE 328

ACROSS
1. Evergreen trees
5. Vegetarian, e.g.
9. Rec. measure
12. Revise for publication
13. Israeli city
14. Regret
15. Or ___!
16. Certain horse
18. Looked suggestively
20. Bean or brim
21. British nobleman
23. Jockey's cap and shirt
26. Those being recognized
30. Gambling city
31. Ginger drink
32. Titled
34. Half a score
35. Jump
37. Thick brown syrup
39. Indian pole
41. Snug retreat
42. Close by
44. Captivates
48. Cloudy
51. Castle trench
52. Used to be
53. Chills
54. Heap
55. Type measures
56. Unwanted plant
57. Heap

DOWN
1. Think
2. Out of work
3. Get up
4. Sound system
5. Reverie
6. Sorbet
7. Time periods
8. Small sea gulls
9. Any combination of three
10. Light source
11. Tent stake
17. Animal's burrow
19. Procure
22. Citrus fruit
24. Leg joint
25. "My Three ___"
26. Cease
27. Butter replacement
28. Tidiness
29. Chosen
33. Dart
36. Cohort
38. Postal requirements
40. Large parrot
43. Fad
45. Irritate
46. Gander, e.g.
47. Goulash
48. Have debts
49. Moving truck
50. "Curly ___"

PUZZLE 329

ACROSS
1. Viper
4. Parrot
9. Took by the hand
12. "Norma ___"
13. Defense
14. Woodchopper's tool
15. ___ fruit
17. Actor Brynner
18. Singer Turner
19. Live
21. Flee
23. Edmonton's locale
25. Scarce
26. Indian, e.g.
27. Bawl
28. Overcharged
29. Acquired
32. Hill or Baker
33. Ear part
34. Kind of checkers
37. Director Lynch
38. Author Bret ___
39. Freshwater fish
40. Kind of nest egg
41. Healed
46. "A Few Good ___"
47. Call forth
48. Negative vote
49. Greek letter
50. Passe
51. Prosecute

DOWN
1. Canine comment
2. ___ Paulo, Brazil
3. Irk
4. Bar Harbor's state
5. "M*A*S*H" regular
6. Spanish hero
7. Mr. Vigoda
8. Bombastic one
9. Tier
10. Jump for joy
11. Singer Reese
16. Wait
20. Runic W
21. Hesitation sounds
22. Thai language
23. Severe
24. Actress Olin
26. Football's Taylor
28. Scoffed
29. Rules
30. Kimono sash
31. Newscaster Koppel
32. Fire or army follower
33. Baikal or Titicaca
34. Ape
35. Lagomorphs
36. Persian
37. Jackknifed
39. Jab
42. Ms. Peron
43. Camp bed
44. ___ de toilette
45. Color

PUZZLE 330

ACROSS
1. Changes residence
6. Diva's showpiece
10. Become restless
14. Worship
15. Budget entry
16. Forum wear
17. Tourist court
18. Tease
20. Exist
21. Simpleton
23. Motionless
24. Unreliable person
25. Annoying one
27. Meal
30. Like a pancake
31. Small child
34. Luck of the ____
35. Shack material, perhaps
36. Function
37. Electrical unit
38. Author Stephen
39. Dart along
40. Humorist George
41. Accuse
42. Fly effortlessly
43. Conducted
44. Kentucky Derby, e.g.
45. Fitting
46. Large book
47. Annoyance to a farmer
48. Valuable possession
51. Exhibition
52. Train section
55. Hurry
58. Rope loop
60. Leave out
61. Legumes
62. Join together
63. Clockmaker Thomas
64. Canopy
65. ____ colony

DOWN
1. "I Remember ____"
2. Scent
3. Cast a ballot
4. Sooner than
5. Illiberal
6. Suit of mail
7. Actual
8. Writing fluid
9. Supped
10. Remarkable feat
11. Actor Franchot
12. Composer Stravinsky
13. Log float
19. Boxers' weapons
22. Cereal grain
24. Endure
25. Aircraft
26. Facility
27. Competitor
28. Wear away
29. Heaped
30. Picture border
31. Dutch flower
32. Stage whisper
33. Discourage
35. Singer Slick
38. Chowder base
39. Stream
41. Clear soup
42. Adult
45. Golf instructor
46. Choppers
47. Bureau
48. Minor prophet
49. Ditto
50. Revue scene
51. Comedian Laurel
52. To ____ a phrase
53. Nick Charles's dog
54. Film holder
56. Likely
57. Told you so!
59. Single thing

PUZZLE 331

Dial-A-Grams

These challenging cryptograms are in a number code based on the familiar telephone dial. Each number represents one of the letters shown with it on the dial below. You must decide which one. A number is not necessarily the same letter each time.

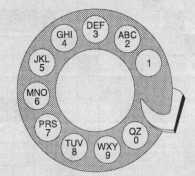

A. 28 24784 26 35374268 934447
3766 663 4863733 263 74989
86 896 4863733 768637.

B. 968 74273 9687 24784329 9484
28 53278 6463 6455466
684377.

PUZZLE 332

ACROSS
1. Singletons
5. In favor of
8. Lean-to
12. Traveler Marco ___
13. Reverent dread
14. In this place
15. Toying
17. Precipitation
18. Black liquid
19. Combines
21. Money vaults
24. Slender
25. Rotate
26. Illegal ticket sellers
30. Historic time
31. Sudden outpouring
32. Large tub
33. Fingernail care
35. Withered
36. Palm fruit
37. Threaded nail
38. Sandy wasteland
41. Mongrel
42. Opera solo
43. Early nights
48. Money drawer
49. Disencumber
50. Thrash
51. Picnic pests
52. Catch sight of
53. Slippery

DOWN
1. Choose
2. And not
3. Inventor Whitney
4. Relent
5. Blonde
6. Possess
7. Adjust
8. Prawn's cousin
9. Warmth
10. Great Lake
11. Lairs
16. ___ Palmas
20. River at Cairo
21. Flower stalk
22. Atmosphere
23. Footballer Tarkenton
24. Frighten
26. Mumbles angrily
27. Eternally
28. Scarce
29. Soupy meat dish
31. Dueling status symbol
34. High hopes
35. Writer
37. Source of light
38. Facts
39. Ireland, in poetry
40. River sediment
41. Yield
44. Compete
45. Born
46. Girl
47. Pigpen

PUZZLE 333

ACROSS
1. Mugs
5. Snatch
9. Health resort
12. Milky gem
13. Impolite
14. 2,000 pounds
15. Had on
16. Mild oath
17. Likely
18. React to a nose tickle
20. Pepper grinder
22. Canvas shelter
24. Grinding tooth
27. Bonnet
30. Gather a crop
32. Wheel cushion
33. Ventilate
34. Church musical instrument
36. Born
37. Notion
39. Christmas season
40. Flit socially
41. Send payment
43. Chair
45. Shapeless mass
47. Hikes
51. Building wing
53. Desire
55. Painful
56. Honey insect
57. New York canal
58. Recognize
59. Mischievous
60. Seance sounds
61. Drains of strength

DOWN
1. Dairy animals
2. Atop
3. Remove rind
4. Frozen rain
5. Foliage
6. Carpet
7. First man
8. Darken
9. Putting off
10. Explode
11. Hill insect
19. Naught
21. Building site
23. River at Lisbon
25. Region
26. Hollow grass
27. Crowning glory
28. Military assistant
29. Shivered
31. Artists' boards
35. Close at hand
38. Be under the weather
42. Steeple
44. Chores
46. Actress Theda ___
48. ___ Lisa
49. Actor's object
50. Takes stitches
51. Wane
52. Meadow
54. Pinch

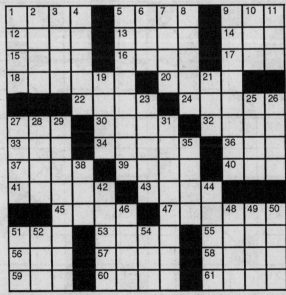

269

PUZZLE 334

Wordbenders

The answers for this crossword puzzle might be just around the bend! Solve the puzzle as you would a regular crossword. The clues for the words which bend in the diagram are listed under the heading BENDERS.

BENDERS

1. Please step ___ of the bus
2. Raise
8. Jokes
9. Makeup
17. Agreeable
18. Looking glasses
28. Femme fatale
29. Silhouette
30. Smarter
32. ESP communication
43. Songstress Fitzgerald
49. Grassy area

ACROSS

1. Eagle's claw
6. Sorcery
10. Pertaining to tenths
13. Bric-a-brac stand
14. Brick carrier
19. Total
21. Mother sheep
22. Cry noisily
23. Sooner than, to bards
24. Meal
25. Wayward
26. Atmosphere
33. Cry of triumph
34. Like better
36. Pluck eyebrows
38. Large cask
39. Struggle
40. Small drink
41. Soak hemp
42. Mineral spring
44. Domestic pigeon
50. As a rule
51. Lower leg
52. Southpaw

DOWN

3. Lyric poem
4. Take-home pay
5. Lively dance
6. Scratch
7. Malt beverage
11. Windlass
12. Club participants
15. Have debts
16. Behavior
19. Dressmaker
20. Footed vase
27. Restless desire
29. Upstart
31. Sideways
35. Regret
37. Postal code
44. Merriment
45. Inquire
46. Government levy
47. Sick
48. Caustic solution

Wordsworth

Fill in each row and column of the Wordsworth diagram with at least two words. The number of answer words in a row or column is indicated by the number of clues. Words are not separated by extra squares, so all the squares will be filled in when the diagram is completed.

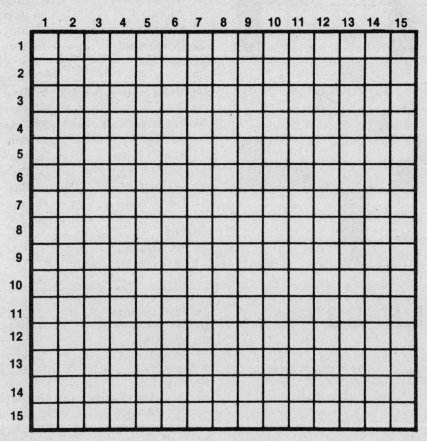

ACROSS

1. Prophet • Goals • Melt • Exclamation
2. Truce • Yucatan buddies
3. Dishonest • Rage • Aerie
4. Netherlands city • Main course
5. Mars • Actor Burr • Culture medium
6. Wetland • Long-distance messages
7. Cheer • Sect • Pushed
8. Star • Singer Miller • Former Peruvian coin
9. Tailor's tool • Stage • Clothes
10. Quibble • Issue • Wigwam
11. Alda • Confused • Stadium
12. ____ race • Loner • Gear
13. Fury • High note • Nev. city • Preserve
14. Finished • Tidied the yard • Hill builder • Decade
15. Adolescents • Jazz great Fountain • Begrudge

DOWN

1. Church rite • Vitamin A source
2. Goof • Hilo hello • Go
3. Overact • Shankar • Glen: abbr. • Golly
4. Brawls • Endurance • Sea eagle
5. Questioner • Pot plant • Tiers
6. Roman road • Honor • Drink
7. Sailor blouse • Bore • Mr. duck
8. Like some eggs • French map word • Soak flax
9. Oolong • Shed • Destroy: var. • Ancient Persian
10. Refuge • Mr. Arcaro • Ancient Moslem coin
11. Alter • Grain • Expiate
12. Earn • Asphalt • Concerns
13. Maturing device • Bestowed • Run
14. Biblical book • Fuse • Actor David
15. Fall blossoms • Snout • Spy

PUZZLE 336

ACROSS
1. Gather crops
5. Kind of hill
8. "____ Is Not Enough"

PUZZLE 337

ACROSS
1. Fort Knox hue
5. Affected actor
8. Fish-tale teller
12. Vicinity
13. Winning serve
14. Certain singer
15. Having frills
16. Walked all over
18. Picnic crasher

---

9. Smears
12. Borscht need
13. Say yes
14. Troublemaker
16. Imperfection
18. Spin
21. "It Happened ____ Night"
22. French hat
23. Do the twist
25. Total up
26. Come forth
28. Music for two
30. Goal
31. Christmas song
33. Sinister
37. Run off to wed
38. Baseball team
39. Golf peg
40. Put up with

DOWN
1. Mr. Reiner
2. Vane direction: abbr.

---

19. Stage settings
20. Beehive State
22. Intensify
26. Hollowed
28. Fast plane
29. Verse form
30. Last word of a hymn
31. Golf standard
32. Naval diaries
33. Each
34. Draw a bead
35. Hat for Antoine
36. "____ Pulver"
38. Garden walk
39. Drink of the gods
41. Dory propeller
44. Washes
47. Heal
48. Otherwise
49. Deep groove
50. Laos's locale
51. Woodland animal
52. Get the point
53. Athletic group

DOWN
1. Festive affair
2. Algerian port
3. Speakers
4. Actress Doris
5. Deck door

---

3. High card
4. Little
5. Go with the flow
6. Find fault constantly
7. Sod
10. Fit in
11. Spirit session
15. Join together
17. Very small
18. Lose weight
19. Severe test
20. Adam's paradise
22. Like Leroy Brown
24. Passionate
27. Fracas
29. Slow run
32. Unclose, in poems
34. By way of
35. Sign
36. Actor Marvin

---

6. Unit of farmland
7. Stroll
8. Mistake
9. Sick
10. Had a bite
11. Reel's partner
17. Convene
19. Downcast
21. ____-gallon hat
23. Charity residence
24. Sidle
25. Aerie, e.g.
26. ____ Cod, Massachusetts
27. Presage
28. Traffic tie-up
31. Lobster claws
32. Give permission to
34. Like good wine
35. Grill's mate
37. Tube or sanctum
38. Fake gems
40. Quiz choice
42. Solo melody
43. Paper measure
44. Was ahead
45. Dark beer
46. Utilize
47. "____ Ballou"

PUZZLE 338

ACROSS
1. Ask earnestly
4. Flow
8. Appends
12. Sailor's consent
13. Comfort
14. Rake
15. Moderated
17. Majority
18. Higher than
19. Sections
20. Came to terms
23. Author Serling
24. Silent one
25. Pharaoh's tomb
29. Toddler
30. Bed linen
32. "____ on a Grecian Urn"
33. Cardigan
35. Transfer of ownership
36. Metal container
37. Huffed and puffed
39. Small pulpy fruit
42. Game on horseback
43. Cooking fat, sometimes
44. Latest thing
48. Colleen
49. Different
50. Word of suffering
51. Picnic spoilers
52. Range player
53. Fresh

DOWN
1. Club
2. Potato bud
3. Solitaire
4. Irritate
5. Sculled
6. Employer
7. Wine-colored
8. Naval squadron
9. Entryway
10. Fine dirt
11. Matched groups
16. Longfellow output
19. Anchorage
20. Biblical book
21. Radiance
22. Judge
23. Blended whiskey
25. Part of MPG
26. Castle defense
27. Not busy
28. Tour de force
30. Stop for a while
31. Rooster's mate
34. On the other side
35. Deceive
37. Sheriff's men
38. Modify
39. South American weapon
40. Brilliance
41. Take ten
42. Wan
44. Preceded
45. Have as property
46. Caviar
47. Early day wetness

PUZZLE 339

ACROSS
1. Boxing punches
5. Ollie's pal
9. Lamb's dam
12. Anagram for race
13. Poor boy
14. Type of cabin
15. Leap ____
16. Real
18. Move about
20. Organ for vision
21. Percolates
24. Fate
28. Bellowed
31. ____ West (life jacket)
32. Military tune
33. Id's companion
35. Hairstyle feature
36. Tavern drink
37. Sign a received check
39. Left
41. Of a region
42. Droop
44. Chicago footballer
47. Interrogate
52. Buck
54. "Born in the ____"
55. Conglomeration
56. Large land mass
57. Above, to a poet
58. Hide
59. Related

DOWN
1. Blue songbird
2. Mavens
3. Spoiled child
4. Grave
5. Feminine pronoun
6. Country singer Ritter
7. Zodiac sign
8. Snooping
9. Actor Wallach
10. Conquered
11. Female gamete
17. Senator Kennedy
19. Decay
22. Zuider ____
23. Lawn tool
25. General Bradley
26. Rowboat adjuncts
27. Distribute
28. Hart
29. Aura
30. Shut's opposite
34. Song from "A Chorus Line"
35. Skunk
38. Smear
40. Curvy letter
41. Lithe
43. Surmounting
45. Plus
46. Wading bird
47. Status ____
48. Apply
49. Hearing organ
50. Castor bean product
51. "But ____ for Me"
53. Incensed

PUZZLE 340

ACROSS
1. Nursery bed
5. Trade
9. That man
12. Sharpen
13. Zoo enclosure
14. Lyric poem
15. Border on
16. Cute
18. Writing instrument
19. Tavern order
20. Tennyson, e.g.
21. Broad valley
23. Fast plane
25. Abyss
27. Play on words
28. Fire fuel
31. Dictatorial
34. Hive dweller
35. Droop
36. Gold or copper
37. Hog's home
38. Retina cell
39. Supermarket section
42. Armed conflict
43. Knock
46. Mackintosh
49. Nimbus
50. Street: abbr.
51. Desire
52. Gossip topic
53. Tokyo money
54. Brewery product
55. Profound

DOWN
1. Guy
2. Morning attire
3. Flood
4. Wager
5. Weighing device
6. Walk in the water
7. Gone by
8. _____ capita
9. Vagrant
10. Not working
11. Run into
17. Capable
19. Nearly
22. Baseball bat wood
23. Protrude
24. Captivate
25. Vehicle for hire
26. Color
27. Greedy person
28. Well-read
29. Eggs
30. Thicken
32. Sugar _____ Leonard
33. Hamilton bill
37. Break a commandment
38. Provide food
39. Cart
40. Roof feature
41. Property right
42. Carry on
44. Toward shelter
45. Magnificence
47. Young bear
48. Mineral source
49. Concealed

PUZZLE 341

ACROSS
1. Enclose
5. Traffic problem
8. Innocent
9. Generous
13. Deduce
14. Disturb
15. Allow
16. Mingle
18. Obsolete
19. Muscle spasm
20. Electric fish
21. Predict
25. At the stern
28. Diva's forte
29. Large snake
30. Concept
31. Stop sign color
32. Adversary
34. Bagel topping
36. Center of the solar system
37. Small engine
40. Track transaction
41. Cat's foot
44. Teach
46. Foolish
48. Nullified
49. Famous
50. Actress Remick
51. Sprouted

DOWN
1. Diminish
2. Fissure
3. Roman greeting
4. Student driver's certificate
5. Kind of dance
6. Endure
7. Iron, e.g.
8. Zilch
9. Loose
10. Mouse's cousin
11. Eroded
12. Conducted
17. Refrigerator
19. British brew
20. Pass by
21. _____ and wide
22. Mine product
23. Purge
24. Hang limply
25. Fruit beverage
26. Marsh
27. Make lace
30. Country hotel
33. Excursion
34. Certain train
35. Make a speech
37. Troops
38. "_____ to Joy"
39. Harbor boat
40. Garden section
41. Liver paste
42. Over again
43. Unite
45. Golfer's gadget
47. Neither here _____ there

CRYPTIC CROSSWORD

PUZZLE 342

British-style or Cryptic Crosswords are a great challenge for crossword fans. Each clue contains either a definition or direct reference to the answer as well as a play on words. The numbers in parentheses indicate the number of letters in the answer word or words.

ACROSS

1. Four-footer and six-footer run off to get married (8)
5. Inspects Europeans, we hear (6)
9. Stupefied pet given a pick-me-up (9)
11. Lenin sullied sheets (5)
12. Eye article and get real angry (6)
13. Damages in court groups (8)
15. Fellow I heal with treatment of the hands (8)
16. The woman's error in this place (4)
19. Volcano blowing up. Neat! (4)
20. Five is total for nobleman (8)
23. Quit or got hired again (8)
24. Stick king in underground pipe (6)
27. Company maintaining radical belief system (5)
28. Penny lodged in excessively fat piece of wood (9)
29. Pen was first fashioned (6)
30. The "Moonstruck" actress over there is a world leader (8)

DOWN

1. Confront a $100 fee (6)
2. Put it here, holding church offering (5)
3. Fastening light can loosely (8)
4. Color piece of paper with pen's contents (4)
6. Sing about Yale student? That's a gas! (6)
7. Happy about one northern land (9)
8. Nun hiding in dark (8)
10. Agreement with shrink (8)
14. Mistake I'd put in stress (8)
15. Supreme skill holding on to monk's community (9)
17. Steer car carelessly into porches (8)
18. Ammunition and dollars stolen (8)
21. Pay no attention to rocky region (6)
22. Stock expert becomes more insolvent (6)
25. Consider oral method (5)
26. Ritzy new shop (4)

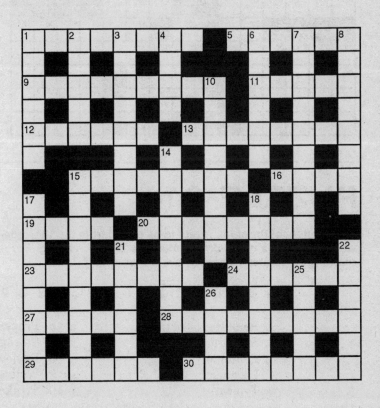

275

PUZZLE 343

ACROSS

1. Seed
5. School dances
9. Mississippi or Missouri
14. Apiece
15. Of an epoch
16. Expunge
17. Aleutian island
18. ___ avis
19. Ziti, e.g.
20. Hepburn film
23. Aft
24. Comedian Laurel
25. Tree
27. War of words
32. Acclaim
36. Irish Rose's sweetheart
39. Foray
40. Peter Sellers film (with "The")
43. First letter of a name: abbr.
44. Comedienne Martha ___
45. Shabby
46. Second-time vendition
48. Barnyard sound
50. Adam's grandson
53. Glided on ice
58. Bob Hope film (with "The")
63. Sensational
64. Possess
65. Serf
66. Wear away
67. Paradise
68. Mix
69. Western
70. Tear
71. Golf pegs

DOWN

1. Lariat
2. Pledges
3. Group of eight
4. Eskimo settlement
5. Egrets
6. Algiers city
7. Helen's abductor
8. Slope
9. Fret
10. Teheran's country
11. Immense
12. Noted Italian family name
13. Raise
21. Angry
22. One who walks in water
26. Sound of laughter
28. Scottish hillside
29. Swiss river
30. Made a knot in
31. Swirl
32. Arabian title
33. Ice-cream holder
34. San ___ Obispo
35. Movie dog
37. Inlet
38. Article
41. Fad
42. Japanese city
47. One who loans
49. Rise
51. Else
52. Hue
54. "___ of robins"
55. Sip
56. Tennessee ___ Ford
57. Henna users
58. Singer Laine
59. Emanation
60. Jog
61. Assistant
62. Level

PUZZLE 344   Two at a Time

All 26 letters of the alphabet are to be pulled from the 13 words—two at a time! The remaining letters in each word will form a new word, sometimes by rearranging. For example, in the first word take out O and E, rearrange the letters, and you have the word TURTLE.

A B C D E̶ F G H I J K L M N O̶ P Q R S T U V W X Y Z

1. Roulette Turtle
2. Straight
3. Example
4. Lacquer
5. Typical
6. Property
7. Storage
8. Reviews
9. Waltzes
10. Trinket
11. Blasted
12. Jostled
13. Fixedly

276

ACROSS
1. Moist
5. Malone of "Cheers"
8. Fight between families
12. By mouth
13. Nabokov novel
14. Comfort
15. Info
16. Employ
17. "King Kong" actress
18. Followed
20. Appear
22. Artist's purchase
26. More tender
29. Sphere
30. Attorney's charge
31. Hemsley sitcom
32. Grande or Bravo starter
33. At a distance
34. Guy's counterpart
35. Emergency letters
36. Zest
37. Math
40. Territory
41. Menu listing
45. Bunyan's ox
47. Neither's partner
49. Dubuque's state
50. Loaf
51. Demo or limo
52. Poems
53. Low digits
54. Greek vowel
55. Bird's home

DOWN
1. Extinct bird
2. OPEC delegate
3. Spouse
4. Nursery enclosure
5. ___ Arabia
6. Newspaper revenue source
7. Great conductor
8. Less
9. Winter wear
10. "Born in the ___"
11. "L.A. Law" actress
19. Corn serving
21. Recede
23. Clamor
24. Stool
25. Man of the hour
26. Narrative
27. Actor Sharif
28. Trustworthy
32. Infatuation
33. Public sale
35. Andress role
36. Card game
38. Kilmer opus
39. Cotta or firma beginner
42. Went by car
43. Female sheep
44. Bridge position
45. Bridle part
46. Fuss
48. Feedbag morsel

ACROSS
1. Ms. Hayworth
5. ___-Wan Kenobi
8. Thick slice
12. Enthusiastic
13. Frying vessel
14. Marco ___
15. Bill of fare
16. Intimation
18. Flying vehicle
20. Skulk
21. Fodder in storage
23. Money risked
24. Poetic Muse
25. Automobile
26. Oxygen
29. Speed
30. Piece of land
31. Fairy-tale beginning
32. Cin. to NYC dir.
33. Bear's lair
34. Muffles the sound of
35. Pool of money
36. Most recent
37. Reject
40. Chinese "bear"
41. Taken into custody
43. Aleutian island
46. Sit for an artist
47. Moray or lamprey
48. Drop of sadness
49. Extend across
50. 100 square meters
51. Ireland, poetically

DOWN
1. Aries
2. "___ Got a Secret"
3. Coated steel
4. Praise excessively
5. State one's belief
6. Curse
7. Roadside stop
8. Tuckered out
9. Solitary
10. Alan ___ of "M*A*S*H"
11. Library component
17. Consumer
19. Of yore
21. Withered
22. Khomeini's country
23. Flying mammal
25. Not pro
26. Aardvark, e.g.
27. Chills champagne
28. Remainder
30. Rent
31. Make obsolete
33. Rickles and Knotts
34. Homo sapiens
35. Primp
36. Soup spooner
37. Sucks the strength of
38. Item onstage
39. ___ Major (the Big Dipper)
40. Jury member
42. Pekoe or oolong
44. ___ chi (yoga's relative)
45. Vase

PUZZLE 347

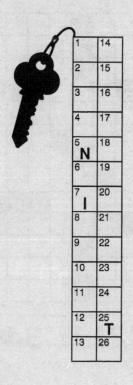

CODEWORD

Codeword is a special crossword puzzle in which conventional clues are omitted. Instead, answer words in the diagram are represented by numbers. Each number represents a different letter of the alphabet, and all of the letters of the alphabet are used. When you are sure of a letter, put it in the code key chart and cross it off in the alphabet box. A group of letters has been inserted to start you off.

Code key chart:

1		14	
2		15	
3		16	
4		17	
5	N	18	
6		19	
7	I	20	
8		21	
9		22	
10		23	
11		24	
12		25	T
13		26	

Alphabet box:

A ⊘	N
B	O
C	P
D	Q
E	R
F	S
G ⊘	T ⊘
H	U
I ⊘	V
J	W
K	X
L	Y
M	Z

Grid:

21	11	19	17	■	21	4	13	17	10	■	13	17	1	21
17	8	17	13	■	6	24	23	3	17	■	17	9	7	25
18	23	21	21	■	24	13	15	17	21	■	18	23	8	23
14	18	23	25	25	17	13	■	21	25	17	23	19	17	13
■	■	■	■	13	23	20	■	■	10	23	9	■	■	■
21	26	13	7	17	3	■	23	12	23	13	■	2	13	11
2	17	23	4	17	■	11	5	17	13	■	14	18	23	10
18	23	16	17	■	25	24	5	17	1	■	13	23	7	5
23	8	17	13	■	23	25	11	2	■	25	17	5	21	17
20	17	21	■	22	24	21	20	■	12	24	25	25	17	1
■	■	■	10	23	5	■	■	2	17	5	■	■	■	■
21	6	24	7	13	25	21	■	13	17	23	18	7	16	17
11	24	21	25	■	7	4	26	11	13	■	11	1	11	13
1	7	17	26	■	5	23	7	8	17	■	15	11	5	15
21	2	13	20	■	15	13	17	17	1	■	11	18	17	11

(Inserted letters in grid: T at 25, I at 7, N at 5)

PUZZLE 348

Escalator

Place the answer to clue 1 in the first space, drop a letter, and arrange the remaining letters to answer clue 2. Drop another letter and arrange the remaining letters to answer clue 3. The first dropped letter goes into the box to the left of space 1, and the second dropped letter goes into the box to the right of space 3. Follow this pattern for each row in the diagram. When completed, the letters on the left and right, reading down, will spell related words or a phrase.

	1		2		3	
	4		5		6	
	7		8		9	
	10		11		12	
	13		14		15	
	16		17		18	

1. Adventurous
2. Wheat, e.g.
3. Pealed
4. Fold
5. Frighten
6. Speed
7. Seasoned
8. Passed, as cards
9. Palm fruit
10. Echo
11. Babble
12. Sassy
13. Male bees
14. Knots
15. Performs
16. Tyrant
17. English dinnerware
18. Model

PUZZLE 349

ACROSS
1. Pastime
5. Strides
10. Makes do
14. Enthusiasm
15. "___ Hall"
16. Cousin's mother
17. Diplomacy
18. Track
20. Scorched
22. Graceful horse
23. "A Boy Named ___"
24. Ventured
26. Tennis shoe
28. Equipped with guns
31. Cobb and Detmer
32. Branch
33. Colander
35. ___ kebab
39. Plumber's problem
41. Accesses
43. Hit by The Village People
44. Scientist Newton
46. Slow mover
48. Walk
49. Hack
51. Talent
53. Largest penguin
57. Having auricles
58. Princess's bane
59. Rewrite
61. Indian rulers
64. Violinmaker Antonio ___
67. Bit
68. Mesabi deposits
69. Mont ___ (Alpine pass)
70. Beige
71. '60s teens, in London
72. Rye disease
73. Sow

DOWN
1. Procures
2. Wings
3. Hawaiian nut
4. Capture
5. Cape jasmine
6. Actress Alicia
7. Early Peruvian
8. Layers
9. Intersecting line
10. ___ de Cologne
11. Russian city
12. Result
13. Navigate
19. Minds
21. Cupid
25. Exploits
27. Pale
28. Syrian stream
29. Miscalculates
30. Baltic feeder
34. Day's march
36. Rudeness
37. Food fish
38. Geologist's angle
40. Tempo
42. Indian lute player
45. Felt concern
47. Turkish coin
50. Dress part
52. Tightens
53. ___ Downs
54. Paris subway
55. Whittled
56. Waterway
60. Strong taste
62. Where the Shannon flows
63. Tater
65. Beast of burden
66. Brazilian resort

Guesstimates

PUZZLE 350

Here's an opportunity to practice your "guesstimating" skills. Allowing 5 seconds for each one, look carefully at each box below and try to guess how many letters or numbers are contained in it.

1.

2.

3.

279

PUZZLE 351

ACROSS
1. Sour
5. Molten rock
9. "Charlotte's ___"
12. Pub potables
13. Mideast native
14. Fiesta cheer
15. Provo's state
16. Wallet
18. Subject
20. Combat of honor
21. Pied Piper follower
23. Wore away
27. Elbowed
31. "The Way We ___"
32. ___ out (barely make)
33. Rent
36. Recline
37. Golf hazard
39. Not as smooth
41. Earnings
44. Purchase
45. Entryway
47. Swipe
51. One involved in a cause
55. Jack rabbit
56. Paddle
57. Bill of fare
58. Kitchen appliance
59. Have
60. Gambling machine
61. Cool!

DOWN
1. Tightly drawn
2. Choir voice
3. Harvest
4. Casual pullover
5. Researcher's room
6. Very dry
7. Merit
8. More capable
9. Romance
10. Building wing
11. Fourposter, e.g.
17. Gush
19. Phone
22. Golfer's gadget
24. Cold-cut shop
25. Pennsylvania port
26. Bambi, e.g.
27. New York football team
28. Gumbo vegetable
29. Circus animal
30. Smidgen
34. Underwater boat, for short
35. Australian birds
38. Tablets
40. Constrictor snake
42. Wanders
43. Alpine song
46. Nevada gambling town
48. Overhanging roof edge
49. District
50. Ash Wednesday to Easter
51. Bill and ___
52. Uncooked
53. Decorative vase
54. Groove

PUZZLE 352

ACROSS
1. Sew
6. Happen
11. Spoiled
12. Advanced
14. Aim
15. Blue
16. Trim
17. Rant
19. Collection
20. Slippery swimmer
21. Critic Siskel
22. Area
23. Had the leading role
25. Hues
26. Affirmative
27. Football's Marino
28. Mouselike animal
31. Withers
35. Prompts
36. Goals
37. Wing
38. Globe
39. Slopes
40. Goals
41. Andes climbers
43. Slips away from
45. Itemize
46. Chauffeur's attire
47. Thick
48. Poppy and sesame

DOWN
1. Automobile hood, in London
2. ___ the Hun
3. Stair
4. Hamilton bill
5. Menu options
6. Martini garnish
7. Pine fruit
8. Boor
9. In ___ (together)
10. Ruler
11. "The Sun Also ___"
13. Is overly indulgent
18. In addition
21. Got bigger
22. A metal
24. Cereal grains
25. Bitumens
27. Maidens
28. Berate
29. Pitched
30. Discount
31. Seed
32. Left or right
33. Honeysuckle family shrubs
34. Fresh
36. Passageway
39. Platform
40. Roof part
42. Male
44. Contend

280

CODEWORD

Codeword is a special crossword puzzle in which conventional clues are omitted. Instead, answer words in the diagram are represented by numbers. Each number represents a different letter of the alphabet, and all letters of the alphabet are used. When you are sure of a letter, put it in the code key chart for easy reference. Three letters have been given to start you off.

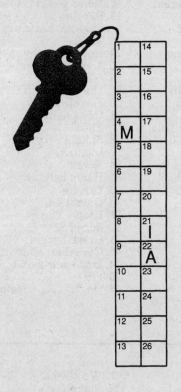

Code key chart:

1	14
2	15
3	16
4 M	17
5	18
6	19
7	20
8	21 I
9	22 A
10	23
11	24
12	25
13	26

Grid clues (partial): A I M given at squares 22, 21, 4.

Quotagram

Fill in the answers to the clues below. Then transfer the letters to the correspondingly numbered squares in the diagram. The completed diagram will contain a quotation.

1. Witticism — 4 32 24 35

2. Blackjack: hyph. — 17 22 36 39 7 41 42 37 14

3. "Picnic" author — 3 23 40 6

4. Lad — 20 34 5 12 49

5. Author from Salem — 13 21 27 33 30 18 44 25 9

6. Make less severe — 45 10 29 38 26 15 48 1

7. Lucky — 19 31 16 2 47 28 8 46 43 11

Diagram squares 1–49.

281

PUZZLE 355

• PLUMAGE PUZZLER •

ACROSS
1. 27th president
5. Overzealous actor
8. Rhine feeder
11. Phone code
12. Part of QED
14. Mineral spring
15. Grizzly or Kodiak
16. Birds of ___ flock together
18. Jogs
20. In that place
21. Theater employees
23. ___ Speedwagon (rock group)
24. Native of Stockholm
25. Unhappiness
28. Head flanker
29. Geologic time period
30. Singer Cole
32. Exclamations of contempt
35. Fountain in Rome
37. Sooner than, poetically
38. Lizette and Della
39. Physicist Enrico ___
42. Devil
43. "...___/And called it macaroni."
45. Swiss archer
48. Old card game
49. Combination school
50. Large continent
51. Road curve
52. Days of yore
53. Plant part

DOWN
1. Actor Hunter
2. Exist
3. Uses funds for self-interest, with 26 Down
4. Covered with pitch
5. Warms
6. Sounds from Sandy
7. Daisy ___
8. Arthur of the courts
9. Mimicker
10. Unusual
13. Spud
17. Norse god of thunder
19. Pay dirt
21. Take advantage of
22. Trade
23. Howard or Ely
25. Mayday letters
26. See 3 Down
27. Undulate
29. Female sheep
31. "My Country ___ of Thee"
33. Sphere or cycle beginner
34. Revolt
35. Hanoi holiday
36. Lariats
38. Quick
39. Rasp
40. Son of Seth
41. Greek letters
42. Comedian Mort ___
44. Little one: suff.
46. Fib
47. On the ___ (fleeing)

PUZZLE 356

ACROSS
1. Brief quarrel
5. GI's food
9. Mars or Pluto
11. Dressing gown
12. Pantry
13. Soon
14. Pie ___ mode: 2 wds.
15. Truly
17. Give the ___ (agree)
18. Greasy liquid
19. Humble
22. Outdo
25. Cover
27. Sty
29. Prisoner
32. Singleton
33. Kind of opera
34. Meeting program
37. Smaller
38. Fail to remember
39. Otherwise
40. Ale cousin

DOWN
1. Twisting ski course
2. Procession
3. Also
4. Golf gadget
5. Baby bed
6. Sharpen
7. Woodwind
8. Make one's way
9. Scheme
10. Threesome
16. Pen point
20. Slip by
21. Set of tools
23. Porous cleaner
24. Sore
26. Unhearing
28. Tidy
29. Dot of land
30. Carol
31. Church service
35. Tar
36. Before, to a poet

PUZZLE 357

ACROSS
1. Type of admiral
5. ___ and wear
9. Sharp rebuke
13. Shoo!
17. Unemployed
18. Gam or Moreno
19. Actress Lange
20. Reporter Lois ___
21. Untidiness
22. Blue-pencil
23. Overwhelmed
24. Steel component
25. Noses
27. Relax
29. Makes wet
31. Building sites
33. Topers
35. Baby's place?
36. Babbles
40. Hart
42. Under stress
46. Disencumber
47. Family car
49. Quantity of paper
51. "___ Abby"
52. Milky gem
54. Flower component
56. Barber's action
58. Biblical priest
59. Fiend
61. Roamed
63. Elate
65. Cashew or acorn
67. Stormed
69. Gaming cube
70. Hangs loosely
74. Collar extension
76. Red-ink items
80. Humorist Burrows
81. Ogle
83. Adored
85. Divide
86. Coin opening
88. Percolate
90. Multiplication word
92. Meadow
93. Mr. Kissinger
95. Mend socks
97. District
99. Moray
101. "___ Gynt"
103. Memo
104. Handled
108. Horned mammal
110. Rosier
114. "___ Lang Syne"
115. Purposes
117. Information
119. Storm wind
120. ___ of Wight
121. Wild plum
122. Landed
123. Pennsylvania port
124. Shakespearean king
125. New Haven trees
126. Speed contest
127. Peruse

DOWN
1. Borders
2. Utopia
3. Too
4. Outcome
5. Grapples
6. Help
7. Mix
8. Loathes
9. Break into small pieces
10. Moo
11. Imitated
12. Piano component
13. Slid
14. Heed
15. Soon
16. Hamilton bills
26. Toddlers
28. Turf
30. Gym pad
32. Passover meal
34. Dioceses
36. Urge
37. Mature
38. "___ Bede"
39. Taste
41. Pealed
43. Exigency
44. Shopper's delight
45. ___ go bragh
48. Maritime
50. Gentle
53. Lengthy
55. Lawful
57. Settled a bill
60. Void's partner
62. Bus stop
64. Esoteric
66. Casual shirts
68. Imp
70. Hyphen's kin
71. Equal to the task
72. Sign gas
73. Kernel
75. Tart fruit
77. "___ Ha'i"
78. Waste allowance
79. Corset stiffener
82. Gather
84. Adorn
87. Trampler
89. Mangles
91. Glut
94. Still
96. Seine
98. Book of accounts
100. Rental contract
102. Navigational device
104. Kite adjunct
105. Trick
106. Logan or Fitzgerald
107. Pickle spice
109. Festive
111. Take a chance
112. Charles Lamb's alias
113. Marsh grass
116. Female parent
118. Twitch

PUZZLE 358

ACROSS
1. "___ Time Next Year"
5. Took a chair
8. Church seats
12. Cognizant
14. Court in love
15. Suez ___
16. Cleansing agent
17. Mr. Linkletter
18. Stadium
19. Piece (out)
20. Wobbles
23. Stag party guests
24. Relaxed
26. Purple gem
28. Erelong
30. Fire or tag
31. Gem shape
35. Lead-tin alloy
39. Little devil
40. Payable
42. Self-pride
43. Lop: 2 wds.
47. Shipping problem
51. Heap
53. Talk enthusiastically
54. USO clubs
58. Man at the gate
62. Part of "to be"
63. Glossy finish
65. Color
66. Wandered
68. Your and my
69. Framework
71. Signs of future times
72. Tatter
73. Stand for Manet
74. Pork fat
75. Ram's mate
76. Hodgepodge

DOWN
1. Cavalry sword
2. Roused
3. Mothers of fillies
4. Historic time
5. Smack flies
6. Blood channel
7. Indian poles
8. Golf term
9. Foe
10. Diminishes
11. Tilt
13. Prolong
15. Palace
21. Scent
22. Gather a crop
25. Roofing liquid
27. Chop down
29. Sign of assent
31. TV's "___ Tac Dough"
32. Down-under bird
33. Prone
34. London local
36. Afternoon social
37. "The ___ and I"
38. Fish delicacy
41. Bobble
44. Decide
45. W.C. ___
46. Kind of collar
48. Lessen
49. Unwilling
50. Berry of "Mama's Family"
52. Repeat performance
54. December song
55. See 21 Down
56. Nary a time
57. Brave's mate
59. The things here
60. Governs
61. Hollers
64. Yen
67. Termination
70. Stage hog

PUZZLE 359   ESCALATOR

Place the answer to clue 1 in the first space, drop a letter, and arrange the remaining letters to answer clue 2. Drop another letter and arrange the remaining letters to answer clue 3. The first dropped letter goes into the box to the left of space 1 and the second dropped letter goes into the box to the right of space 3. Follow this pattern for each row in the diagram. When completed, the letters on the left and right, reading down, will spell a name.

1. Like some peanuts
2. Distributes
3. Boys
4. CB nickname
5. Pilgrim John
6. Skinny
7. East
8. Bury
9. Sea swallow
10. Flow swiftly
11. Fall flower
12. Rip
13. Biblical dancer
14. Small animals
15. Shade trees
16. Rocks
17. Memos
18. Pedal digits

FOUR-MOST   PUZZLE 360

All of the four-letter words in this crossword puzzle are listed separately and are in alphabetical order. Use the numbered clues as solving aids to help determine where each four-letter word goes in the diagram.

4-Letter Words

Agha
Agra
Ante
Ares
AWOL
Beef
Cars
Dens
E. Lee
Ella
Emma
Erse
Fool
Glad
Glum
Hint
Laic
Lain
Lark
Late
Lint
Loam
Loge
Lore
Oral
Pete
Pray
Roil
Role
Ruse
Sees
Skin
Sled
Stan
Swig
Tale
Tile
Wool

ACROSS

15. Mistake
19. Fable teller
20. Golf prop
21. Baby tenders
23. Shade tree
24. Brother of Electra
26. And so on: abbr.
28. Heel
29. Obliterations
34. Edgar ___ Poe
40. "Head of the ___"
44. Spanish rooms
45. Picnic drink
47. Snow runner
48. Golfer's concern
49. Fishing lure
53. Pub drink
56. Strong defense
59. Guido's note: 2 wds.
60. Carved stone
64. Racing official

DOWN

1. Greek philosopher
2. Actor Moore
3. Concur
4. Slangy agreement
5. On the same side
6. Manners of walking
9. Creatures
10. Before, to a poet
16. Record letters
22. Paper measures
25. Mollusk
27. Agatha Christie book
29. Make happy
40. Barton or Bow
46. Actor Jim
47. Wheel parts
49. Warning device
50. More modern
51. Cream of the crop
52. Has a tantrum
53. Play division
61. Ending for mountain or musket
63. Resort

RAPID READER   PUZZLE 361

Can you find the nine other 5-letter words that are written backwards in the lines below in 4 minutes or less? Underline each word as you find it as we have done with JEWEL.

```
T N R U O Y R O V I N O B L E W E J A R
G N I E S U O M L O T V R E P A C P L A
L A G N I R U O S S A L F E E L S I A B
O F R A W D Y E L A D A E N K O R O L P
D N I M A L A Y O R L I K A L W O R G E
```

PUZZLE 362

ACROSS

1. Mast
5. Winter vehicle
9. In favor of
12. Sound judgment
14. Idol
15. Impact
16. Avoid
17. Derive
18. Ploy
19. Anguish
20. Requirement
22. Domesticated
23. Gait
24. Stopper
26. Delicate hue
29. Crustacean
33. More adept
34. Attempt
36. "___ Good Cop"
37. Lyric
38. Solo
39. Movable barrier
40. Actress Arden
41. Rope
42. Held a position
43. Revived concept
46. Guard
47. Otherwise
48. Chump
49. Delay
52. Slope
53. Hairpiece
56. Song for Callas
57. Milky-white gem
59. Wear away
61. Cautious
62. Tumbled
63. Thames, e.g.
64. Snoop
65. Card after a deuce
66. Shine

DOWN

1. Large quantity
2. Equine sport
3. Chills and fever
4. Purge
5. Ewe or ram
6. Heavy metal
7. Bungle
8. Football's Shula
9. Purple fruit
10. Ascended
11. Felt obligated to
13. Focus
15. Gloats
21. Lamprey
22. Old boat
23. Stalk
24. Carpenter's tool
25. Ear part
26. "___ Moon"
27. Overhead
28. Frozen precipitation
30. Words of congratulation
31. Insert
32. Sounding like an oboe
34. Plunge
35. Unit of weight
38. Exclamation of concern
39. Left
42. Seasoning
44. Transmit
45. Building wing
46. Amount
48. Loiter
49. Cuts
50. Snare
51. Breezy
52. Rattling sound
53. Interlaced
54. Concept
55. Microbe
57. Frequently, to a bard
58. Each
60. Tease

PUZZLE 363   Step by Step

In five steps change each word one letter at a time into a new 5-letter word so that by the fifth step each letter has been changed. Do not rearrange the order of the letters. You do not have to change the letters in order.

Example: Heard, Hears, Heads, Heeds, Seeds, Sleds

1. FLOAT

2. PAPER

3. PERCH

4. SHARE

ACROSS

1. Pianist Templeton
5. Texas river
10. Make known
14. Luna ____
15. Cherish
16. Actress Martha
17. Mr. Marquand's Mr.
18. Addition to a document
19. Once ____ a time
20. Lehar work
22. Beethoven's "____" Overture
24. Baseball's Otis
25. Takes potshots
26. Strad or Amati
29. Ms. Keaton
30. Fjord
31. "American ____"
35. Letter after zeta
36. Marsh grass
37. Old auto
38. Linnet and thrush, e.g.
41. Ms. Faye
43. Long-limbed
44. Fractures
45. Amphitheaters
47. Ciao, for now: hyph.
48. Padre
49. Deep-voiced band instrument: 2 wds.
53. Sword handle
54. Ridicule
56. Bronte's Jane
57. Capri or Man, e.g.
58. Licoricelike flavoring
59. Pink table wine
60. Villainous look
61. Goes it alone
62. RBI, e.g.

DOWN

1. Bullets, to a GI
2. Chicago section
3. Feminine suffix
4. Beethoven's Ninth
5. Singer Dolly
6. Prepares for publication
7. Musical end
8. Mined find
9. Woo with music
10. Severinsen's instrument
11. Lit. signature: 3 wds.
12. City in France
13. Imparted
21. Issue
23. Cotton and sloe
25. Croons
26. Competes
27. Division word
28. "Good Earth" heroine: hyph.
29. "My Heart Belongs to ____"
31. Kin of floes, for short
32. Opera tune
33. Nape site
34. She-deer
36. Frank and Nancy
39. Welcoming one
40. Prohibits
41. Part of B.A.
42. Guides
44. Sews loosely
45. Pop up
46. Moon valley
47. Poet Torquato
48. Rock-star Collins
49. Surety bond
50. Indian peasant
51. Sky Bear
52. Encounter
55. Artist Yoko

PUZZLE 364

• FACE THE MUSIC •

SUBSTITUTIONS

PUZZLE 365

In these addition problems, letters are substituted for numbers. When the letters are placed in order from 0 to 9, they spell a 10-letter word. The same code is used in all three addition problems.

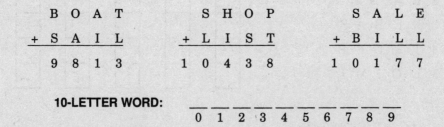

```
    B O A T          S H O P          S A L E
  + S A I L        + L I S T        + B I L L
  ─────────        ─────────        ─────────
    9 8 1 3        1 0 4 3 8        1 0 1 7 7
```

10-LETTER WORD: __ __ __ __ __ __ __ __ __ __
         0 1 2 3 4 5 6 7 8 9

PUZZLE 366

ACROSS
1. Pale
4. Music and painting
8. Mineral spring
11. Caused to stick in mud
13. Ring
14. Male deer
15. Strike
16. Poet Millay
17. Pillar
18. Splash
20. Followed
22. Landlord's concern
24. Sea birds
25. Guides
28. Sweet O'Grady
30. Ventilate
31. Merit
33. Stockpile
37. Hawaiian neckwear
38. Total
39. Prompter's concern
41. Meadow
42. In a difficult position
44. At any time
46. Actor Mineo
47. Ms. Doone
49. Classify by kind
52. Military teachers
54. Claw
56. Father
57. Land masses
61. Mineral sources
62. Author Levin's namesakes
65. Spaces
66. Dispatched
67. Wrap
68. Send back
69. Time period
70. Singer Adams
71. Mayday!: abbr.

DOWN
1. Sniveling guy
2. Song for Callas
3. Prickly weed
4. Mimics
5. Cardinal color
6. Sunbathe
7. Bluish-gray rocks
8. Improperly took
9. Turns white
10. Elderly
11. Editors' reading: abbr.
12. Put off
14. Small upright piano
19. Made comfortable
21. Get up
23. Misspeak
25. ____ and pepper
26. Row
27. New York canal
29. Single time
32. Persian Gulf state
34. In addition
35. Scorch
36. Stop
38. Decorate
40. Asian range
43. Born first
45. Keg
48. Go to bed
50. About the sun
51. Traps
52. Concerned one
53. Place for contests
55. Usher's beat
56. Sit
58. Verne's captain
59. Raised platform
60. Fast jet: abbr.
63. ____ Steiger
64. Mr. Baba

PUZZLE 367   GUEST STAR

Unscramble the letters of each group below to form a 5-letter word and place the word into the correspondingly numbered column reading from top to bottom. There are no plurals. Next, rearrange the top 5 letters for the first name and the bottom 5 letters for the last name of our Guest Star.

1. G A U S E
2. H M N P Y
3. R E B A Z
4. T R U S B
5. D O I M I

GUEST STAR: __ __ __ __ __ __ __ __ __ __

288

PUZZLE 368

ACROSS

1. Lose feathers
5. Talon
9. Became older
13. Vex
17. Imitator
18. Wealthy
19. Folk knowledge
20. Biblical garden
21. Storm
22. Contribute a share
23. Hog fat
24. Repair
25. Component
27. Run briskly
29. Homer epic
31. Not any
32. Melt
33. One-spots
34. Father: Sp.
36. Masticate
37. Send
41. Historic times
42. Scalp growth
43. Hunting shoes
44. Great anger
45. Atmosphere
46. Moral wrongs
47. Taunt
48. Network
49. Baby's outfit
51. Rank
52. Consecrate
53. ____ Vegas
54. Chairs
55. Ocean
56. Electronic speed check
59. Remains
60. Hard cheese
64. Ireland, in poems
65. Cake layers
66. Fly high
67. Woodsman's tool
68. Electrical unit
69. Valleys
70. Fishing bait
71. ____ Stanley Gardner
72. Occult
74. Actor Penn
75. Liberated
76. Bonnets
77. Pile
78. Clothed
79. Stable compartment
81. Curtsies
82. Useful cats
85. Sports group
86. Beige
88. Work on copy
90. Wicked
91. Rouse
92. Mineral springs
93. Minstrel's instrument
94. Actress Moreno
95. Crude metals
96. Poultry herb
97. Defeats at bridge
98. Great many

DOWN

1. Female horse
2. October birthstone
3. Fabled
4. Slight earthquakes
5. Hoisting machine
6. Carpet fluff
7. Perform in a play
8. If or not
9. Permit
10. Butting animal
11. Make a mistake
12. Inscribe in honor of
13. Lax
14. Thought
15. Grant temporary use
16. Finale
26. Opposite of WSW
28. Unprocessed
30. Camera eye
32. The one here
33. Rebelled
34. Ring
35. Opera highlight
36. Sugar source
37. Amphibians
38. Deep mud
39. Spring flower
40. Spreads hay to dry
42. Strikes
43. Flogs
46. Night twinkler
47. Cafeteria utensils
48. Happy
50. Enthusiasm
51. Toothed wheels
52. Brewed beverage
54. Tempered iron
55. Counterfeit
56. Quantity of paper
57. Military group
58. Scoops of ice cream
59. Mr. Marner
60. Maize
61. Stunt man
62. Wheel rod
63. Hollow grass
65. Undiplomatic
66. Cleanser
69. Make a phone call
70. Ermines
71. Blackboard pads
73. River through London
74. Use a needle
75. Winter ill
77. Residence
78. Sheep shelters
79. Scorch
80. Seize
81. Boast
82. Catcher's glove
83. Religious observance
84. Cabbage salad
85. Pair
87. Auditor: abbr.
89. Payable

289

PUZZLE 369

Cryptic

British-style or cryptic crosswords are a great challenge for crossword fans. Each clue contains either a definition or direct reference to the answer, as well as a play on words. The numbers in parentheses indicate the number of letters in the answer word or words.

ACROSS

1. An aptitude for discovery with a drop in calmness (11)
10. Put drive in our boy to become a doctor (7)
11. Most frightful bug lies trapped in sight (7)
12. Watch stunt, i.e., to escape from ropes (5)
13. Al's Lumber redesigned shelters from bad weather (9)
14. Sandra's embracing select group of enthusiasts (8)
16. Saint with emanations wanders off the path (6)
18. Writer has corn supply in the Southeast (6)
20. Superman's chest rumbles oddly and sleeps (8)
24. Noisy and glamorous with a change of face (9)
25. Most tragic return of Havana export (5)
27. Thing with horns runs a mile mad (7)
28. Do irons get recasted under protection (7)
29. Cowboys in art composition (11)

DOWN

2. Regret beheading the bird (5)
3. First Lady has to repose on high (7)
4. Need rust spoil teeth? (8)
5. Sounds like fruit weights (6)
6. Highest of all, in examination (7)
7. Painters in dire straits (7)
8. Published incorrect ID uses (6)
9. Fabulous archer Rocky et al. (8)
15. In aria, blends are not constant (8)
17. Embarrassed Crosby by being around drinker (8)
18. After a short time, two editors withdrew (7)
19. Flower's undergarment? (7)
21. Queen goes around bounder on the roadway (7)
22. America's northern balance is most positive (6)
23. Musical work in lines on a tablet (6)
26. Rightly nag or complain (5)

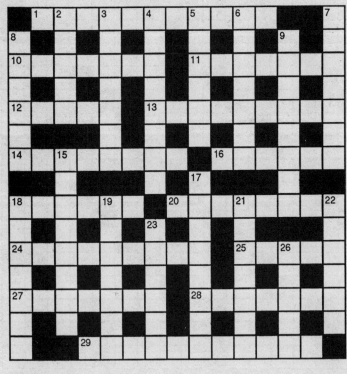

290

PUZZLE 370

• FEBRUARY DAYS •

ACROSS
1. Sod
5. Highland girl
9. Footballer Starr
13. Winter ill
14. "___ and Psyche"
15. Prove false
16. February events
18. Some ed. insts.
19. Antonym's ant.
20. Wild ox of Sulawesi
21. Ratings
22. December event
24. Scurry
27. Arab chieftains
30. They, in Thiers
31. Winter vehicle
32. Woolly she
34. Castle ditch
35. More cunning
37. Despot
38. Tennis term
39. Chew the fat
40. Chambers
41. Charred
43. Expert
44. January events: 2 wds.
47. Piscine group
50. Winning margin
51. Type of doll
54. Happy as ___: 2 wds.
55. Add antifreeze to
57. Repairs socks
58. Thought: Fr.
59. The Bard of ___
60. Primates
61. Headland
62. Body of a church

DOWN
1. Labels
2. "The ___ American"
3. Destroy
4. Turkish hat
5. Look to for support: 2 wds.
6. Quiver missile
7. Fountain treats
8. Draft org.
9. Looked good on
10. "When I Was ___ . . .": 2 wds.
11. NASA's Sally
12. Hardy girl
15. Estopped
17. Author Grey et al.
21. TV's Pyle
22. Editor's notation
23. At a distance: prefix
24. Does a tailor's work
25. "A Lesson from ___"
26. Blackboard
28. Give new turf
29. Hindu teacher
31. Pull up a chair
33. Once, once
35. Bombard
36. Actress Cheryl
37. Coal units
39. Robbers
40. Indian coin
42. Oak seeds
43. Glues
45. Derogatory
46. Roman calendar date
47. Actress Thompson
48. Applaud
49. Tortoise's foe
51. Derby winner ___ Ridge
52. Asian sea
53. Mr. Hackman
55. Triumph
56. Went swiftly

FAMILY TIES

PUZZLE 371

Each group below contains four unrelated words. Without rearranging the letters, change one letter in each of the words to form four related words.

1. Hair _____   Snob _____   Fleet _____   Ruin _____

2. Hulk _____   Pig _____   Tangy _____   Reef _____

3. Late _____   Middle _____   Cells _____   Hasp _____

4. Defy _____   Wee _____   Hoist _____   Dame _____

5. Fully _____   Pond _____   Mark _____   Speed _____

6. Peach _____   Coy _____   Some _____   Have _____

PUZZLE 372

DOUBLE TROUBLE

Not really double trouble, but double fun! Solve this puzzle as you would a regular crossword, EXCEPT place one, two, or three letters in each box. The number of letters in each answer is shown in parentheses after its clue.

ACROSS

1. School marks (6)
4. Simpson of TV (4)
6. Grouch (4)
9. TV dolphin (7)
10. Actress Anderson (4)
11. Golf cup (5)
12. Oust from office (6)
13. Portrayal (11)
15. Mideast nation (4)
17. Opposed (4)
18. Far-flung newsman (13)
22. Arthur's place (7)
26. NFL team (7)
27. Greek letter (7)
29. Stevens of opera (4)
30. Ames and Spinks (5)
32. Taught (8)
34. Domestic duck (5)
36. Switch positions (3)
37. Explosive device (11)
41. Utah range (6)
45. Places (5)
46. Drysdale or Mattingly (3)
47. Low stool (7)
48. Loblolly, for one (4)
49. Spouse (4)
50. Smooths (6)

DOWN

1. Beam (4)
2. Church part (4)
3. Recklessness (11)
4. Fair-haired (6)
5. Skilled worker (7)
6. Vault (5)
7. News medium (5)
8. Swiss capital (4)
9. Winter scourge (3)
14. Movie judge (6)
16. Without design (6)
18. Cattle pen (6)
19. Live (6)
20. Individual (6)
21. Lure (6)
23. North or South (7)
24. Misplaced (4)
25. ____ off (angry) (4)
28. Sonata movement (5)
31. Javelin (5)
33. Inappropriate (10)
35. Realm (7)
37. Leave (6)
38. "Over ____" (5)
39. Chevy ____ (5)
40. Growing out (5)
42. New (5)
43. Sailors (4)
44. Matched group (3)

PUZZLE 373

BLIPS

Using the letters listed below, place one letter in each circle to form nine 3-letter words reading from top to bottom. Use each letter only as many times as it is listed.

A B D D E G G I M M O T Y

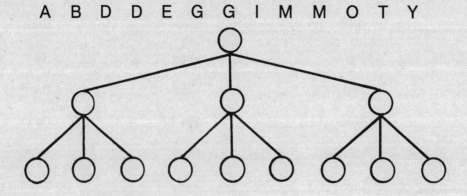

Codeword is a special crossword puzzle in which conventional clues are omitted. Instead, answer words in the diagram are represented by numbers. Each number represents a different letter of the alphabet, and all of the letters of the alphabet are used. When you are sure of a letter, put it in the code key chart for easy reference. Three letters have been given to start you off.

Code key chart:

1	14
2	15
3	16
4	17
5	18
6	19
7 K	20
8	21
9	22
10 I	23
11	24
12	25
13 N	26

Grid:

11	24	12	5	■	■	12	23	15	■	■	6	16	21	20
10	6	7	16	■	■	18	10	11	■	■	24	26	16	13
23	24	24	15	■	15	19	11	24	14	■	15	10	7	16
23	11	16	16	14	10	16	■	15	11	16	18	15	7	16
■	■	■	10	13	13	■	19	10	5	■	■	■	■	■
■	■	2	24	14	■	■	■	9	4	10	25	■	■	■
23	7	12	14	■	14	12	17	24	4	■	5	16	12	13
12	10	6	16	■	12	3	12	1	16	■	12	14	7	16
15	16	16	18	■	21	24	5	16	15	■	3	11	16	22
■	■	6	16	18	20	■	■	■	17	16	12	■	■	■
■	■	■	1	10	15	■	21	24	24	■	■	■	■	■
18	24	1	11	12	13	24	■	11	16	10	13	3	7	16	15
15	11	16	16	■	3	12	8	16	7	■	11	12	8	16
16	12	18	16	■	■	18	24	6	■	■	12	20 K	10 I	13 N
1	7	24	6	■	■	15	22	24	■	■	5	16	7	6

TWO-A-CROSTIC

PUZZLE 375

Use each 2-letter combination in the box below once to form the 6-letter answers to the clues. Place these words in the diagram reading from top to bottom. When completed, the top and bottom rows will spell out the title of a famous film. Rearrange the circled letters to find a related film.

BA	CK	EL	EM	ER	ES	EX	HO	IC	IE
IN	LE	LI	MB	MO	NA	NT	OT	PI	RE
RK	RU	SC	SQ	ST	TA	TI	TO	UE	WL

1. Native ability

2. Funny joke

3. "___ lama sabachthani?" (Matt. 27:46): 2 wds.

4. Begin a journey

5. Holy place

6. Zodiac sign

7. Bury

8. Eye part

9. Strange

10. Smitten

Diagram columns numbered 1 2 3 4 5 6 7 8 9 10.

RELATED FILM: _____

PUZZLE 376

ACROSS
1. Acting crew
5. Implore
9. Hawaiian greeting

11. Furious
12. Cone-producing trees
13. Thin coins
14. Luster
16. Book leaf
19. Suds
23. Epoch
24. Towel word
25. ____ mode: 2 wds.
26. Small shot
28. Give off
29. Stadium
31. Get up
34. Bow and ____
38. Hired helpers
39. Float
40. Finishes
41. Raced

DOWN
1. Small hat
2. Actress MacGraw
3. Male offspring
4. The ones here
5. Publish
6. Ewe's mate
7. Consumed
8. Sure!
10. Fireplace residue
11. Thoughts
15. Upper crust
16. Vigor
17. Exist
18. "My ____ Sal"
20. Deli meat
21. Inventor Whitney
22. Rodent
24. Groups of cattle
27. Alights
28. Noblemen
30. Pester
31. Haggard heroine
32. Brown
33. In addition
35. Tear
36. Lyric poem
37. Marry

PUZZLE 377

ACROSS
1. Attic
5. Fruit pastry
9. Viper
12. Mideast prince
13. Affirm
14. Enemy
15. Father
16. Bill of fare
17. High mountain

18. Precipitous
20. Tape
22. Reply
24. Candidate
28. Foolish
32. Citrus fruit
33. Sound system
35. Cried
36. Flood
37. Manor
40. Narrow passage of water
42. Bowie, for one
47. Saloon
48. Tardy
50. Redolence
51. Self
52. Field
53. College official
54. Make lace
55. Flit
56. Ditto

DOWN
1. Not as much
2. Leave out
3. Dismiss
4. Elm, e.g.
5. Highlands hat
6. Reluctant
7. Take up again
8. Armistice
9. Remote
10. Vended
11. Energy
19. Throe
21. Command
23. Born
24. This minute
25. Mine find
26. Chart
27. Bury
29. Have being
30. Marsh
31. Little one
33. Tippler
34. Hard journey
36. Rag
38. Greens dish
39. Small crown
40. Long story
41. Horse gait
43. Bows the head
44. Inkling
45. Froth
46. Sea bird
47. Wager
49. Dine

DOUBLE CROSSER

Fill in the missing letters in this crossword diagram, making sure that no word is repeated. Then write the missing letters entered in the numbered boxes on the correspondingly numbered dashes below (1-39) to spell a quotation.

R	⁹S	P		S	P	R	Y			F	³⁶	A	T
E	P	E	¹⁷	¹L	U	³⁴			L	I	M	B	O
B	A	N	G		R	E	²⁴	L		I	¹⁸	P	U	T
U	⁶	N		S	³⁷	A		P	A	³⁵		A	T	¹⁴
³⁰	T	A	C	C	A	²⁹	O		M	O	¹²	R		
		A	²⁷	M		R	A	P		I	T	C	²¹	
A	M	A	T	I		W	E	L	L		L	²⁰	R	E
¹³	A	D		P	L	A	G	U	²⁶	S		A	¹⁶	R
L	I	²⁵	E		A	⁵	A	M		M	²²	L	B	A
E	D	E	⁸	³³	E	²³		²		I	T			
		N	E	S	S		O	V	E	R	A	⁴	L	S
M	E	³⁹		³¹	E	L		³	R	K		O	A	K
E	³²	U	¹⁵	E		¹¹	L	S	E		A	C	¹⁰	E
S	I	R	E	³⁸		T	A	T	S		S	A	G	E
S	T	⁷	W			S	²⁰	A	Y		P	L	O	¹⁹

1 2 3 4 5 6 7 8   9 10 11   12 13 14 15 16 17 18 19

20 21 22 23 24 25 26 27   , 28 29 30   31 32 33 34 35 36 37 38 39 .

HOP, SKIP, AND JUMP

What is the longest word you can find in the row of letters below, starting with any letter and picking out letters, moving only from left to right? You may hop, skip, and jump over any number of letters, but once you choose a letter you may not backtrack. A word of 4 to 6 letters is good; 7 to 9 letters is very good; a word with 10 letters is excellent.

O J C B R Y Z O T A X H I C E N R U H O K O F S D

PUZZLE 380

ACROSS
1. Male deer
5. Streetcar
9. Lhasa's land
11. Mechanical man
13. Nimble
14. Cognizant
15. Crimson
16. Poisonous snake
18. Heavy weight
19. Get to
21. Pre-Easter season
22. Use a razor
24. Straight and limp
27. Self-assurance
30. Military address: abbr.
31. Court divider
32. Faucet
34. Hackneyed
36. Rub out
38. Water tubes
39. Challenges
40. Tidy
41. Animal hide

DOWN
1. Main player
2. Striped cat
3. Stay
4. Harden
5. Snare
6. Tier
7. Ease up
8. Dope
10. Instruct
12. Camper's home
17. Form
20. Question
21. Hawaiian souvenir
23. Cast a ballot
24. Thin strip of wood
25. Chef's garb
26. Din
28. Gaze
29. Artist's stand
31. Bird's home
33. Nuisance
35. Pekoe or oolong
37. Knock

PUZZLE 381

ACROSS
1. Distant
4. On the peak
8. Ray
12. Mine product
13. Barbie, for one
14. Goad
15. Office worker
17. Public disturbance
18. Paddles
19. State as true
21. Freight vessel
23. Largest continent
24. Grooves
25. Brass instruments
29. Dined
30. Coast
31. Short sleep
32. Hare's opponent
34. Sicilian volcano
35. Unusual
36. Happy songbirds
37. Gobi, e.g.
40. Confront
41. Paradise
42. Huge animal
46. Matured
47. Snakelike fishes
48. Afternoon party
49. Camera eye
50. Egyptian river
51. Desire

DOWN
1. Enemy
2. Provide with weapons
3. Newsman
4. Worship
5. Playthings
6. Mexican cheer
7. Fun and games
8. Sack material
9. Great Lake
10. Excited
11. Dole out
16. Falls behind
20. Green fruit
21. Unruly child
22. Car
23. Got up
25. Unlucky number
26. Plea
27. Army vehicle
28. Resorts
30. Fly high
33. Movements in style
34. Apiece
36. Trivial error
37. Business transaction
38. Rim
39. Witnessed
40. Dropped
43. Flower garland
44. Born
45. Beige

PUZZLE 382

ACROSS

1. Ring winner, for short
6. Doug Henning's forte
11. Keep
13. Neighbor of the United States
14. Drink fruit
15. Trash
16. Weep
17. Glossy fabric
19. Owned
20. Bus-rider's desire
22. Spigot
23. Lampreys
24. Bit of wood
26. Jostles
27. Tavern
28. Astronaut Grissom
29. Beef fat
31. Most wise
34. Defeatist's word
35. Wire measure
36. Cooking fat
38. Frothy brew
39. "Les ____"
41. Cultivate
42. Black birds
44. Capital of 13 Across
46. Last letters
47. Nearsighted one
48. Trivial
49. Lash marks

DOWN

1. Traverse
2. Brave guys
3. Kettledrum
4. Provide with a crew
5. Hogs
6. Primary
7. Pismire
8. Reap
9. Models
10. Deck items
12. More shipshape
13. Snip
18. Gob
21. Lama land
23. Painter's stand
25. Cistern
26. Ewer
28. Horse's gait
29. Deli meat
30. Irregular
31. Knight's title
32. Mighty desert
33. Small shovel
34. Bounce
35. Feel nostalgic for
37. Honeys
39. Growl
40. Ragout
43. Conceit
45. Driving mound

PUZZLE 383

ACROSS

1. Dune material
5. Entreaty
9. "I ____" (1960s TV show)
12. Again
13. Street
14. Score, of sorts
15. Only
16. Reciprocate
18. Breaking down
20. Each
21. Obtained
22. Rubbernecks
25. Clare Boothe Luce play, with "The"
28. Breathe
29. Past
30. Cathedral seat
31. House wing
32. Marched
35. Luscious mushroom
37. Sinew
38. Nutria, for one
39. Play the ponies
40. Indonesian island
44. Ragtime dances: hyph.
47. Journey
48. Meadow
49. Pennsylvania port
50. Give relief
51. Rep.'s opposite
52. Borge, for one
53. Hustled

DOWN

1. "____ Like It Hot"
2. Declare
3. Evil emperor
4. River-bottom mud remover
5. Etching
6. Yearn
7. Nosh
8. Clever ones
9. More twinkling
10. Photo
11. Still
17. Glean
19. Charged particle
22. Stitch
23. Perry's creator
24. Vend
25. Scottish inventor
26. Fictional bad guy
27. Night ray
28. Blushing
30. Corral
33. Beautiful poems
34. Enclosed, as house plants
35. Fall flower, for short
36. Speaks movingly
38. Friction match
40. Twirl
41. Snare
42. ____ and shine!
43. Copied
44. Ancient
45. Born
46. Epoch

PUZZLE 384

DOUBLE TROUBLE

Not really double trouble, but double fun! Solve this puzzle as you would a regular crossword, EXCEPT place 1, 2, or 3 letters in each box. The number of letters in each answer is shown in parentheses after its clue.

ACROSS
1. Schedule of charges (5)
4. Write (6)
6. Capital of Ohio (8)
10. Temperature gauge (11)
12. Ill-prepared (7)
13. Wedding band (4)
14. Actor Guinness (4)
15. Petty quarrel (4)
16. Fibbing (5)
17. Vatican chapel (7)
19. Occur (6)
22. Persia, today (4)
23. Stop signal: 2 wds. (8)
27. Speckled horse (4)
28. Waistcoat (4)
30. Mislay (4)
31. Go before (7)
33. English county (5)
34. Performed in a play (5)
35. Less tidy (8)
38. Legal thing (3)
40. Place (3)
41. Facts and figures (4)
42. Roman war god (4)
44. Sound of lightning (7)
46. Commendable (12)
48. Daunt (10)
49. Over there (3)
50. Welles role (4)

DOWN
1. More readily (6)
2. Naming (7)
3. Any (4)
4. Uncertain (10)
5. Roman road (4)
6. Responded in turn (9)
7. Bait (4)
8. With intensity (5)
9. Keeping occupied (7)
11. Yarns (5)
15. Iberian land (5)
18. Forward freight (9)
19. Angel's instrument (4)
20. Skin opening (4)
21. Atonement (7)
24. Flowering shrub (5)
25. Specter (5)
26. Prepared to drive a golf ball (4)
29. Nervous fear (11)
32. Practically hopeless (9)
36. Oaf (4)
37. Rub out (5)
38. Change the color of (6)
39. Leveling wedge (4)
42. Mrs. Washington (6)
43. "Auld Lang ___" (4)
45. Destroyed (5)
46. Entreat (4)
47. Labor (4)

PUZZLE 385

PICTURE PAIRS

Some of these designs match up as pairs, and some designs have no mates. Can you discover the designs that do not match in 3 minutes or less?

298

PUZZLE 386

ACROSS

1. "Brandenberg Concertos" composer
5. Transaction
9. Proper
13. Equivalent
15. Diva's forte
16. Learning
17. Florence Nightingale, e.g.
18. Five-dollar bills
19. Large continent
20. Sample
21. Brink
22. Aerie
23. Goof
25. Ardor
27. Rotate
30. Above
33. Microbe
36. Single
37. Bowling article
38. Chemical element in salt
40. Drink slowly
41. Having apprehension
43. To and ____
44. Pilfers
46. Metallic rock
47. ____ Vegas
48. Alternately
49. Type of club
50. Animal skin
51. Listen to
53. Fish eggs
55. Field of study
58. Book page
61. Less intense, as color
65. Thailand, once
66. Domesticated
67. Similar
68. Israeli seaport
69. At a loss
70. Embankment
71. Await decision
72. Lease
73. Work table

DOWN

1. Twisted
2. Turquoise's kin
3. Mongrels
4. Hurry along
5. Strongbox
6. Dry
7. Tarry
8. Artist's stand
9. Calculated
10. Thorny flower
11. Eye part
12. Beef or pork
14. Lascivious look
24. Thick cords
26. Eager
27. Throw
28. Bring together
29. Drive back
31. By the route of
32. Register
34. Hunter's gun
35. Wall painting
38. Scoff
39. Largest amount
41. Skedaddle
42. Wrath
45. Feeling guilt
49. Lubricate
50. Rang
52. Church platform
54. October birthstone
55. Stat's kin
56. Japanese staple
57. Garner wages
59. So be it!
60. Action
62. Dwell
63. Supplements
64. Stench

Insert-A-Word

PUZZLE 387

Insert a word from Group B into a word from Group A to form a longer word. Each word is used only once. For example, if the word FAR appeared in Group A and THE appeared in Group B, the answer would be FATHER (FA-THE-R).

GROUP A	GROUP B	
1. DETER	CALL	1. _____
2. TRIES	PILL	2. _____
3. HEN	POND	3. _____
4. SET	LAY	4. _____
5. SOPS	AVE	5. _____
6. RESENT	CAN	6. _____
7. TIER	HERB	7. _____
8. SAGE	RAT	8. _____
9. PIES	EAT	9. _____
10. DEED	OUCH	10. _____

PUZZLE 388

ACROSS

1. Dogie
5. Shakespeare, often
9. Clay house
14. Engine track
15. Small case
16. "___ is an island"
17. Cartoonist Peter ___
18. Singer Diana ___
19. Humdingers
20. Dusk, to Longfellow, with 54 Across
23. Being, in Barcelona
24. "___ Sematary"
25. Cager Larry ___
27. Starch
30. Villa d'___
34. Bit part
35. Costa ___
37. Spanish hero
38. Serling TV series
42. Singer Cole
43. Spanish women: abbr.
44. Tanker
45. Thailand, once
47. Roman road
49. Drowses
50. Double curve
52. Spirit
54. See 20 Across
61. Classify
62. Dry watercourse
63. Affront
64. Nimble
65. First garden
66. Painted metalware
67. Allotted
68. Marionette man
69. Ruth's kingdom

DOWN

1. Crosspatch
2. River of Switzerland
3. Fluff
4. Piece of broccoli
5. Hat for Picasso
6. Makes up for
7. Oxidize
8. Spoon's pal, in rhyme
9. Battery terminal
10. Give
11. Hebrew measure
12. Tree rind
13. Printers' measures
21. Bestows
22. Era
25. Iranian religion
26. "___ a man with seven . . ."
28. Originate
29. Band engagement
31. Dress down
32. Prongs
33. River of Germany
34. Cardboard boxes: abbr.
36. Keyless, in music
39. Kind of coffee
40. Map abbr.
41. Some Israelis
46. Interfere
48. Book lover
51. Destrier
53. Prone
54. Jason's vessel
55. Brad
56. Sheep
57. Art style
58. Shine
59. Island dance
60. Waste allowance
61. Flit about

PUZZLE 389   Escalator

Place the answer to clue 1 in the first space, drop a letter, and arrange the remaining letters to answer clue 2. Drop another letter and arrange the remaining letters to answer clue 3. The first dropped letter goes into the box to the left of space 1, and the second dropped letter goes into the box to the right of space 3. Follow this pattern for each row in the diagram. When completed, the letters on the left and right, reading down, will spell related words or a phrase.

1. Shriek
2. Fright
3. Speed contest
4. Involve
5. Bay
6. African river
7. Elaborate
8. Make reparation
9. Observe
10. Of an Indian group
11. Beaten path
12. Fibber
13. Law provision
14. Gravy
15. Highest cards
16. Produce
17. Outline
18. Wagon

ACROSS

1. Young boy
4. Quarrel
8. Desire
12. Smell
14. Comfort
15. Runner
16. Seep
17. Or ___!
18. Exhibition
19. Get ready
21. Meddle
23. Paradise
24. That man
25. Reclining
29. Ogled
34. Poke
37. Peruse
39. Operate a car
40. Iraqi
42. Spare
44. Out of the wind
45. Dug for ore
47. Eye drop
48. Culmination
49. More unhappy
51. Avow
54. Burst
56. File
59. Shrewd
62. Says from memory
65. Expect
66. Sweetheart
68. Achy
69. Cent
70. ___ and crafts
71. Bad
72. Rim
73. For fear that
74. Sprite

DOWN

1. Noose
2. Love
3. Catnapped
4. Fortune teller
5. Ashen
6. Beast of burden
7. Incisors
8. Twist
9. Land measure
10. Approach
11. Hear a lawsuit
13. Parry
15. Butted
20. Some
22. Be under the weather
26. Anger
27. Following
28. Fence entrances
30. Time period
31. Irk
32. Tied
33. Feat
34. Traffic snarls
35. Operatic solo
36. Dance orchestra
38. Sketch
41. Cot
43. "You ___ There"
46. Sheriff's assistant
50. Decay
52. Circle part
53. Lift up
55. Foot lever
57. Franklin ___
58. Danger
59. Amazed
60. Warbled
61. Prong
62. Ship deserters
63. Once, once
64. Ego
65. Simian
67. Before, to a poet

Bits and Pieces

Can you identify these two-word dog breeds from the Bits and Pieces shown in the boxes? The first word of each breed is always on the top and the second on the bottom.

1.
```
A I N
R N A
```

2.
```
O C K
A N I
```

3.
```
F G H
U N D
```

4.
```
E N C
O D L
```

5.
```
R I S
E T T
```

6.
```
A L A
A M U
```

PUZZLE 392

Diagramless crosswords are solved by using the clues and their numbers to fill in the answer words and the arrangement of black squares. Insert the number of each clue with the first letter of its answer, across and down. Fill in a black square at the end of each word. Every black square must have a corresponding black square on the opposite side of the diagram to form a diagonally symmetrical pattern.

ACROSS
1. Donkey
4. Opposite of NNE
7. Seance sound
10. Mel ____ of baseball
11. "Ode ____ Nightingale"
12. Boxing great
13. Antique car
14. Jam fruit
16. Spencer or Dick
18. French thoughts
19. Against
20. Ogles
21. Crown's cousin
23. Shapes
25. "The ____ Ranger"
29. Pacific isle
30. Fall flower
31. Citrus fruits
33. Brewed beverage
34. German exclamation
35. Sixth sense letters
36. Newspaper employees: abbr.
37. Pod inhabitant
38. Draft organization: abbr.
39. Deli bread

DOWN
1. Main artery
2. Rear of a ship
3. Weasel
4. Remain
5. Bribe
6. More cautious
7. Indy 500 participant
8. Bitter plants
9. Seeds
15. Standards of perfection
17. Fruitcake ingredient
20. ____ Vegas
22. Likenesses
23. Slapstick comedy
24. Nebraska city
26. Aquatic mammal
27. Poor
28. Wipe out
29. Kind of opera
30. Vipers
32. Road curve

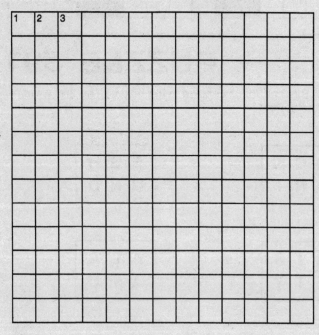

PUZZLE 393

ACROSS
1. Chick's mother
4. Turf
7. Mature
8. ____-bits
9. Blow a horn
11. Lengthy
12. Agreement gesture
14. Jump on one foot
15. Slippery one
17. Small barrel
18. More intelligent
20. Turn right!
21. Mold
23. Except
24. Declare
26. Is able to
27. Countdown starter
29. Potter's material
31. Divan
34. Goal
35. Use needle and thread
36. Golf mound
37. Female sheep

DOWN
1. Bonnet
2. Self-esteem
3. Sign gas
4. Halt
5. Possess
6. Canine
10. Foot digit
11. Ship's diary
13. Morning moisture
14. "And I Love ____"
16. Illumination
17. Preserves
19. Body of water
21. Earth's star
22. Munch
23. Inlet
25. Word of consent
26. Arrived
28. Facial feature
29. Tabby
30. Recline
32. Not many
33. Wonderment

302

ACROSS

1. Former soldiers' org.
4. Exclamation of regret
6. Female horse
7. I see!
10. Heap
11. Sped
13. Cavort
15. Ennui
17. Milan greeting
19. Examination
20. Actress Betty ___
24. Prepare dough
26. Loathe
27. Make cherished
28. Station, in Paris
29. Cupid
30. Border
31. Actress Pola ___
33. Singer Damone
35. Owed
36. Circle fragment
38. Furious
40. Puff up
42. Thick rug
46. Arrived
48. Out of control
50. Rice dish
53. "I ___ a Symphony"
54. Alaskan peninsula
56. Slowly, in music
57. Muslim leader
58. Camera glass
59. Make poisonous
61. Small missile
63. Condescend
64. Twist
66. ___ Diego
67. Part of the foot
68. Out of the weather
69. Actress Lupino

DOWN

1. Temptress
2. Special talent
3. Male witch
5. Appearing
7. Expert
8. Row of shrubs
9. Decorate
11. Seaport on the Don

12. Pertaining to some blood vessels
14. Song of thanksgiving
15. Ray of light
16. Constructed
18. Paddled
19. Bangkok native
21. ___ and breakfast
22. Fall behind
23. Before, in poetry
25. Remove stickiness from
32. Extending to
34. Frog sound

37. Desert animal
39. Fiend
40. Mound of snow
41. Pitched
42. Mineral spring
43. Secreted
44. In the manner of
45. Token of defiance

47. Female title
49. West Virginia river
51. Locates
52. Area of the retina
55. Tel Aviv resident
60. German article
62. Cornered
65. Entreaty

Starting box on page 562

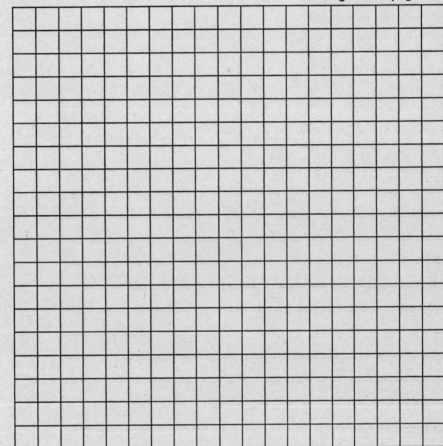

MISSING TRIOS   PUZZLE 395

For each number below, fill in the same 3 missing letters (not necessarily in the same order) to complete a 7-letter, 6-letter, 5-letter, and 4-letter word. The Missing Trio is different for each number below.

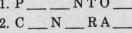

1. P __ __ N T O __   __ __ __ P E R   C __ __ R __   __ __ T __
2. C __ N __ R A __   __ E __ T __ R   __ I T __ __ __   __ I __ __ __
3. C __ __ C __ I T   B __ Y __ __ D   T __ __ __ R   N __ __ __ __
4. __ E S __ __ R E   B O __ __ H __   __ O __ __ H   __ __ S __

PUZZLE 396

ACROSS

1. Entranced
5. Sass
8. Fragrance
9. Wag's stock in trade
10. Station
12. Crow's kin
13. Kitchen VIP
15. Labyrinth
16. Bronze element
18. Wow
20. Mongrel
21. Actress Balin
22. Fateful phrase: 2 wds.
23. Sweet potato
25. At that time
26. Camp bed
27. Via
28. Chocolate source
30. Keep at bay: 2 wds.
33. Prop for Dali
34. Small lizard
37. Emmet
40. Mast support
42. Very pale
44. Ocean
45. Old Fr. coin
46. Clucker
47. Even match
49. "____ Sloopy" ('60s song): 2 wds.
51. Prod
52. Deli offering
53. Floor
55. Beelzebub
58. Owl sound
59. Vendition
60. Conclusion
61. Ragout

DOWN

1. Actor Steiger
2. Fruit drink
3. Cinema snack
4. Boy Scout unit
5. Beautiful
6. I Like ____
7. Mighty weapon
9. "All That ____"
11. Theme
12. Stropped item
14. Game of chance
15. Fabricated
16. Signal
17. Squeal
18. Pickpocket
19. To ____ his own
20. Complete disorder
24. Low
25. Pauley's show
29. Polish
31. Chosen quantity
32. Leeds apartment
34. Lamb work
35. Ongoing dispute
36. Faucet
37. Bat wood
38. Mr. Webster
39. Makes harmonious
40. Make a goal of: 2 wds.
41. Lacrosse number
43. Up to ____: 2 wds.
48. Classify
50. Shade of green
53. Andress film
54. Heavy weight
56. Stout, e.g.
57. Freshly coined

Starting box on page 562

PUZZLE 397   CHANGAWORD

Can you change the top word into the bottom word (in each column) in the number of steps indicated in parentheses? Do not change the order of the letters, and change only one letter at a time. Proper names, slang, and obsolete words are not allowed.

1. **BACK** (4 steps)   2. **JUNK** (5 steps)   3. **HEAD** (5 steps)   4. **LIFE** (5 steps)

SEAT   YARD   LINE   BOAT

ACROSS

1. Beach material
5. Hunts for game
7. Official paper
10. Always
11. ___ avis
13. Communists
14. Heroic narrative
16. Sea eagle
17. Countries
20. Inventor Whitney
21. Steal from
22. Feels blindly
25. Psychological safety valve
29. L.A. team
30. Building site
31. Baseballer Charlie
32. Bent down
34. Pacific sea
36. Old French fabric measure
37. Indonesian island
38. Fathers
40. Algerian city
41. Coming to a point
43. Cream of the crop
44. Night twinkler

DOWN

1. Horse goads
2. Upper limb
3. ___-do-well
4. Hereditary ruler
6. As the crow flies
7. Oil well towers
8. Baking compartment
9. Yield
12. Greek marketplace
15. Ever and ___
16. Actress Martinelli
17. ___ de plume
18. White poplar
19. Overflowing
20. Snakelike fish
21. Amplify vibrantly
23. Jacob's twin
24. Dallas campus: abbr.
26. Bataan native
27. Haughty
28. Atlantic fish
33. Foot levers
34. Hindu gown
35. ___ Bator
37. Destructive beetle
39. Barbecue rod
42. Greek letter

PUZZLE 398

Starting box on page 562

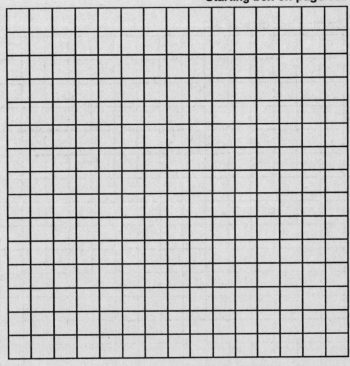

Word Math   PUZZLE 399

In these long-division problems, letters are substituted for numbers. Determine the value of each letter. Then arrange the letters in order from 0 to 9, and they will spell a word or phrase.

1

0	1	2	3	4	5	6	7	8	9

```
              ARM
MARE | SUMMARY
       SSABE
       LLUR
       MARE
       SEEYY
       ELPAP
       UESY
```

2

0	1	2	3	4	5	6	7	8	9

```
              KID
LIDS | CLASSIC
       CCLEL
       FFKCI
       KLSFI
       EKDBC
       EBLAC
       KBSB
```

3

0	1	2	3	4	5	6	7	8	9

```
              CON
ART | ATOMIC
      AAII
      NCI
      NTI
      MPC
      YYP
      OC
```

305

PUZZLE 400

ACROSS

1. Chapeau
4. Past
5. Chef
9. Just out
10. Alamo, for one
12. Alder tree
14. Makes possible
15. Hawaiian food
16. Operated
17. Of course!
18. Recede
19. Samovar
20. "Bobby Shaftoe's gone to ___ . . ."
21. Cider fruit
23. Conniving
25. Illuminated
26. Building site
29. Curved moldings
31. Excavation
33. Eskimo knife
34. Standard
35. Lyricist Gershwin
38. Tennis need
39. Crude metal
40. Optical illusions
42. Negative vote
43. Armored
44. Weeding tool
46. Ancestor of the Hebrews
47. Motel of old
48. Teacher's favorite

DOWN

1. Alps crosser
2. Mature
3. Pull along
5. TV frequency
6. Globe
7. Unctuous
8. Athlete's vulnerable spot
10. Tangle
11. Double curve
12. "Planet of the ___"
13. Judges' gowns
14. Blows
21. Natives of Alaska
22. Chart shape
24. Not as old
27. Adversary
28. Coronet
30. Glowing coal
32. Playing card
35. Little devil
36. Irritate
37. Riyadh dweller
41. Lunched
44. Ball-and-socket joint
45. Singleton

Starting box on page 562

PUZZLE 401 {KEYWORD}

To find the KEYWORD fill in the blanks in words 1 through 10 with the correct missing letters. Transfer those letters to the correspondingly numbered squares in the diagram. Approach with care—this puzzle is not as simple as it first appears.

1	2	3	4	5	6	7	8	9	10

1. T O __ E R
2. S L __ N G
3. B __ O W N
4. C H I L __
5. __ O L I O
6. G __ O V E
7. S P __ K E
8. __ A S T E
9. B R A V __
10. __ A V E N

PUZZLE 402

ACROSS
1. Cadence
5. Love god
6. Czech river
10. Dismounted
11. Craving
12. Pumpkin for Nicholson?
16. Baby's nurse
20. Roe
21. Aim
22. Give off a special light
23. Reserve
25. Ogle
26. Posed
28. Solo
29. Laborer
30. Bang
32. Do needlework
33. Surfacing material
36. Sites
38. Soccer great
39. "Cheers" psychiatrist
41. Singer/guitarist Clapton
42. Jason's ship
43. Off-center
45. Advance
46. Chihuahua currency
47. Building addition
48. Drink cooler
50. Oscar Madison, e.g.
53. Bridge position
57. Ensemble
59. Italian monk's title
60. Owns
63. Extinguish
64. Peruvian Indian
65. Attack
67. Cleopatra's nemesis
68. Consider
69. Leg cramp for Chase?
73. Furnish
74. Crab larva
75. Nervous

76. War god
77. Gael

DOWN
1. Pinnacle
2. Singer Guthrie
3. Entwine
4. Landed property
6. Unconventional
7. Remainder
8. Exit
9. Lease income
12. Wisecrack
13. Prayers
14. City in Normandy

15. Indeed
16. In the manner of
17. Harnesses' parts for Short?
18. Large continent
19. Warmth
24. Papal contribution for Jennings?
27. Soft mineral
31. Disposition
34. Similar
35. Indentation
37. Yule hymn
38. Green vegetable
40. Long time

44. Eat quickly
48. Footnote abbr.
49. Sugar source
51. Visionary
52. Struck
54. Winglike
55. Lip
56. Category
58. Hoover, e.g.

60. Laurel's cohort
61. Suffer
62. Actor Walter of "Fanny"
66. Crooned
70. Days past
71. Irresponsible person
72. Tobacco oven

Starting box on page 562

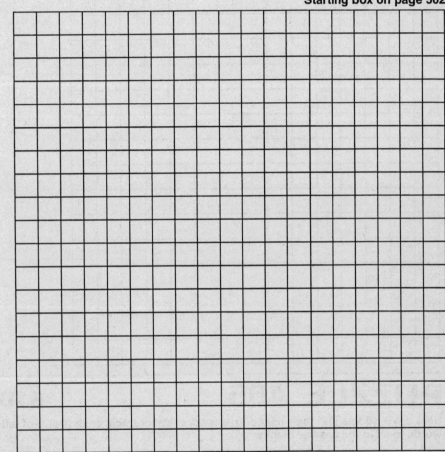

COMMON CODE   PUZZLE 403

The set of numbers represents a letter pattern for certain words. How many words can you think of which use this pattern? If a number is repeated, the same letter is repeated. For example, the letter pattern 12232 has three different letters, with the same letter in the second, third, and fifth positions; it could be GEESE, PEEVE, etc.

1 2 2 3 4 2

PUZZLE 404

ACROSS

1. Pester
4. Tank filler
7. Flying mammal
10. General Bradley
12. Tear
13. Geologic time division
14. Remove from print
15. Tumult
16. Atmosphere
17. Swiss canine
22. Ski slope covering
23. Spinning toy
24. Broadway sign
25. ___ de Janeiro
27. Sailor
30. Large canine
33. Ice-cream treat
34. Say further
35. Suitable
38. Conger
40. Manner of walking
42. Herding canine
47. Emulate a bunny
48. Pasture sound
49. Journey
51. Lyricist Gershwin
52. Ancient
53. Withered
54. ___ Aviv
55. Born: Fr.
56. Lair

DOWN

1. Gesture of agreement
2. Actor Leon ___
3. Parties
4. Snatch
5. ___-de-camp
6. Basketball, e.g.
7. Endure
8. Extremely dry
9. Paving substance
11. Harness straps
18. Neither here ___ there
19. Tango number
20. Designer Kamali
21. Of bees
26. Individual
27. Melancholy
28. Greek H
29. Fruit drink
30. Brownie's org.
31. Less polite
32. Terminated
35. In the past
36. Chum
37. Leans
39. Fish garnish
41. Weary
42. Drill
43. October gem
44. Actor's goal
45. Morse or zip
46. Republic of Ireland
47. Strike
50. Writing tool

Starting box on page 562

PUZZLE 405

RIDDLE ME THIS

Here are 5 riddles and their mixed-up answers! Unscramble each group of letters to form a word. Use those words to fill in the answer blanks.

REHA   RBAE   EOSOG   RSYPA   ROPLA   ROSDO   NATZRA   OTSL

1. What grows down as it grows up?   __ __ __ __ __

2. What allows people to walk through walls?   __ __ __ __ __

3. What is big and white and found in Florida?   __ __ __ __ __ __ __ __ __ __ __ __ __ __ __ __ __

4. Who was the first swinger?   __ __ __ __ __ __ __

5. What do you get if you cross a rabbit with a lawn sprinkler?   __ __ __ __ __ __

308

PUZZLE 406

ACROSS
1. Gone by
5. New York canal
9. Finished
10. Idolize
11. Weighty book
12. Demolish
13. Sister's daughter
16. Yearn
17. American Indian
19. Health resort
22. Land measure
23. Saloon
26. In a group
28. Give sparingly
29. Covered soup dish
31. Deleted
33. Article
34. Forsakes
38. Church seat
39. Additional
40. Inlet
41. Sheep
42. Genuine
45. Garret
49. Perceived with the ear
51. Greek god
53. Wrong
54. Vein of ore
55. Stubborn one
56. Was aware of

DOWN
1. Cooking vessel
2. Shakespeare's river
3. Trucker's rig
4. Forest member
5. Biblical garden
6. Wander
7. Anger
8. Moray
10. Noted boxer
14. Winter garment
15. Engrave
16. Observed secretively
18. Mine find
19. Scatter
20. Verse
21. Generation
23. Domineering
24. Malt brew
25. Crimson
27. Glossy paint
28. Actor Andrews
29. Topple
30. Colorado brave
32. Steal
35. Ribbon loop
36. Space
37. Tree home
42. Race-track fence
43. Gaelic
44. Classified units
46. Chat
47. Press
48. Yield
49. Amateur radio operator
50. Flightless bird
52. Stitch

Starting box on page 562

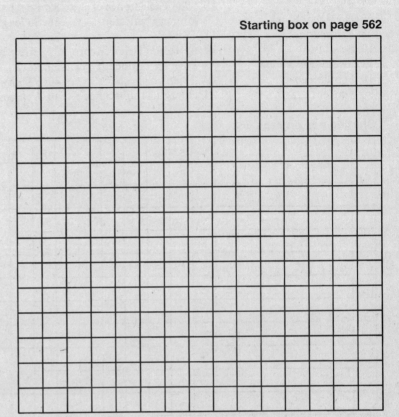

QUOTAGRAM

PUZZLE 407

Fill in the answers to the clues below. Then transfer the letters to the correspondingly numbered squares in the diagram. The completed diagram will contain a quotation.

1. Opulent
$\overline{21}$ $\overline{46}$ $\overline{32}$ $\overline{1}$

2. Maxim
$\overline{3}$ $\overline{22}$ $\overline{48}$ $\overline{56}$ $\overline{14}$

3. Juvenile
$\overline{44}$ $\overline{27}$ $\overline{49}$ $\overline{7}$ $\overline{10}$

4. Cavernous
$\overline{37}$ $\overline{54}$ $\overline{5}$ $\overline{13}$ $\overline{23}$ $\overline{15}$

5. Housing
$\overline{16}$ $\overline{53}$ $\overline{19}$ $\overline{36}$ $\overline{12}$ $\overline{50}$ $\overline{26}$

6. Cover-up
$\overline{29}$ $\overline{33}$ $\overline{4}$ $\overline{20}$ $\overline{41}$ $\overline{17}$ $\overline{39}$ $\overline{51}$ $\overline{30}$

7. Ultimately
$\overline{38}$ $\overline{45}$ $\overline{18}$ $\overline{42}$ $\overline{9}$ $\overline{2}$ $\overline{34}$ $\overline{43}$ $\overline{35}$ $\overline{8}$

8. Preferential treatment
$\overline{25}$ $\overline{11}$ $\overline{40}$ $\overline{55}$ $\overline{47}$ $\overline{6}$ $\overline{24}$ $\overline{31}$ $\overline{52}$ $\overline{28}$

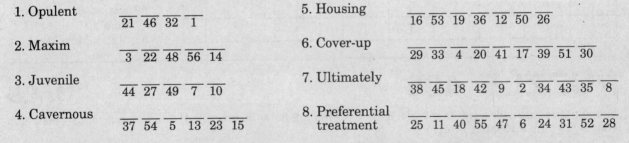

PUZZLE 408

ACROSS

1. Phase
5. Household task
6. Exotic utopia
10. Sordid
11. Sweater mishaps
13. Football coach Walter ___
14. Severe trial
16. "The Persistence of Memory" painter
17. Teased
19. Actress O'Brien-Moore
20. Fleetwood Mac hit
22. Delany or Plato
23. Hourglass substance
25. Author
27. Islamic chieftain
28. This: Lat.
29. Buchanan of "One Life to Live"
30. Asian nursemaid
32. For the time being
35. So long!
36. Sphere prefix
37. Birds' beaks
39. Rarae ___
40. Variety of a language
45. Apartment payment
46. More hackneyed
47. Little pitchers have big ones
48. Goddess of peace
49. Apportion
51. Determine
53. Vestige
54. Virginia estuary

DOWN

1. Pillow cover
2. Theater award
3. Unit of work
4. Human being
5. Fellow
6. Certain college class
7. Concerning
8. Load cargo
9. Advanced in years
10. Contact lens solution
12. Bando and Maglie
13. Jeweler's weight
15. Charter
16. Committed
18. Playwright
21. Aromatic seed
24. Small drink of liquor
25. "___ Every Woman Knows"
26. Holiday or candle
31. Convent attire
32. Egyptian ruler
33. Return
34. Portents
38. New Delhi dress
41. Italian coins, once
42. Paris seasons
43. Penny
44. Formal agreement
47. You're something ___!
49. Wing-shaped
50. Eat, as an ice-cream cone
52. Male sibling, for short

Starting box on page 562

PUZZLE 409

TILES

Imagine that these tiles are on a table, each showing a 2-letter combination. Can you rearrange these tiles visually to form a 10-letter word?

310

ACROSS

1. Crescent
4. Playmate
5. Bulky
8. Acerbic
10. Exercise
11. Comedienne Taylor
13. Moyers or Blass
14. "The ___ of Rosie O'Neill"
16. Dossier
17. Horror-movie sound effect
19. Pleat
20. By way of
21. Penguin's cousin
22. Menacing
24. Primitive dwelling
25. Deli order
26. "Odalisque" artist
28. Relative
29. Macadamia, e.g.
30. Solder
31. Encircled
35. Bear in mind
36. Sizzling
38. Pile
39. Phil's wife
40. Boat blade
41. Brewer's need
42. Thickness
43. Bring in
44. Thirsty

DOWN

1. Isolated
2. Jockeys
3. Infirmary
5. Physique
6. Cuba or Puerto Rico
7. Hairstylist's substance
9. Much loved
12. Uplifting
13. Cheat
15. Cruise
16. Referee's call
18. Violent whirlpool
19. Fake, in France
22. Excepting
23. Adversary
24. Applause
26. Gentle
27. Courtship
28. Hold
30. All in
32. Apothecary's measure
33. Mission
34. Funny Phyllis
35. Recuperate
37. Batty
38. Bounce

PUZZLE 410

Starting box on page 562

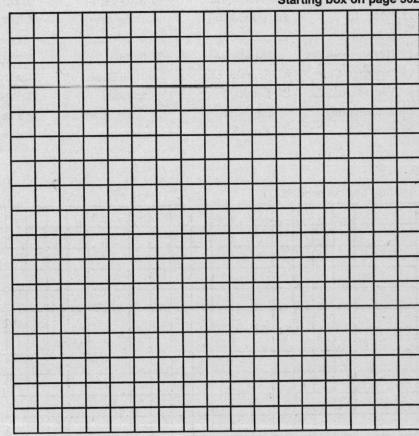

Changaword   PUZZLE 411

Can you change the top word into the bottom word in each column in the number of steps indicated in parentheses? Change only one letter at a time and do not change the order of the letters. Proper names, slang, and obsolete words are not allowed.

1. COOL (5 steps)   2. DULL (5 steps)   3. HEAD (5 steps)   4. STAY (5 steps)

WARM   KEEN   TAIL   QUIT

PUZZLE 412

ACROSS

1. Asian nurse
5. Lollobrigida
6. Have half ____
8. Some strikes
12. Goop
16. Without principles
17. Narrow passage
18. "Brother, Can You Spare ____"
19. Before: pref.
20. Pompous
22. Famous designer
23. Secretes
24. Krung ____ (Thai capital)
25. Native: suff.
26. Too much: Fr.
30. ____ Rong (racehorse)
31. Soprano Lily
33. Semitic language
35. Actor Ken
36. Does nothing
40. Having digits
41. Gentleness
42. Hindu god
45. Brain membrane
46. Indifferent
47. "____ the World Ends"
48. Mild oath
49. Bone: pref.
51. Smell ____
52. Joint
54. 1958 Oscar winner
55. C.S. Lewis lion
56. Bread spread
57. Leather straps
59. Secluded place
60. Purses
63. Kind of shrub
64. Actress Albright
65. Ultimate

DOWN

1. Turkish rulers
2. 1932 Rodgers/Hart song
3. Author Loos
4. Attendants
7. Scribble
9. Legal documents
10. Title
11. Luge
12. Welcomes effusively
13. Poet Sidney ____
14. Successful
15. Equal
20. Embark
21. Yugoslav president
24. Lean
26. Stepped
27. Sought office
28. Ancient Greek coin
29. Yearns deeply
30. Portray
32. Condition
33. Confused
34. Recent: pref.
35. "____ be in England . . ."
37. Civil wrong
38. Brother's sib
39. Famous Sioux
43. Contends
44. Century plant
45. Sugar-coated candy
48. Tool
49. Synthetic fabric
50. Tolerates
51. Eager
52. Geom.
53. Safety acronym
58. Navigators Islands, today
61. Guys' dates
62. Kind of singing

Starting box on page 562

ACROSS

1. Respect
4. Coll. prerequisite, usually
7. Sly mammal
8. Bind
9. Warty creatures
12. Tone
14. Stuff
16. Chimney grime
17. Mosaic piece
18. Ashy
19. Gaze
21. Solid
22. Instructor
24. Fortune
25. Discourage
27. Set of two
29. Waste
32. Crop
33. Performs
35. Rabbit
36. Castle ditch
37. Glossy
39. Twist
42. Olive or corn
43. Cry of discovery
44. Married
45. Kitten's cry

DOWN

1. Astern
2. Court
3. Precise
4. Condition
5. Support
6. Golf term
10. Leak
11. Auction
12. Sail upward
13. Contain
15. Encounter
16. Box
20. Sovereign
21. Inn
23. Spinning toy
25. Ready to pick
26. Soil
27. Scheme
28. Breezy
30. Flat-bottomed boat
31. Heavenly body
32. Tot
34. Mist
37. Female pig
38. Hasten
40. That woman
41. Marble

PUZZLE 413

Starting box on page 562

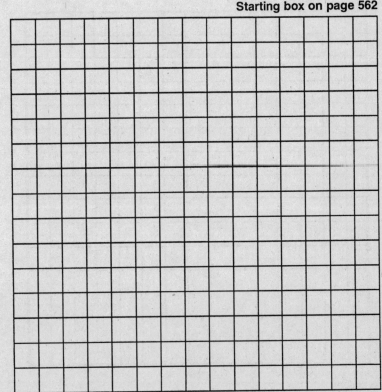

Word Math

PUZZLE 414

In these long-division problems letters are substituted for numbers. Determine the value of each letter. Then arrange the letters in order from 0 to 9, and they will spell a word or phrase.

1 | 0 | 1 | 2 | 3 | 4 | 5 | 6 | 7 | 8 | 9 |

```
              I R K
        ┌──────────────
BELL  │ R A S H E R S
        R I E A N
        R S K K R
        H K E B A
        N K B A S
        I E E N S
        K L R S
```

2 | 0 | 1 | 2 | 3 | 4 | 5 | 6 | 7 | 8 | 9 |

```
                T U G
          ┌──────────────
NAGS   │ S U S T A I N
          S E A I E
          U X G A I
          A A S N E
          N A S I N
          I S S S S
          N E H A
```

3 | 0 | 1 | 2 | 3 | 4 | 5 | 6 | 7 | 8 | 9 |

```
                E K E
          ┌──────────────
NINE   │ A N I M A T E
          A T M K E
          A M A L T
          T K L L M
          A E M T E
          A T M K E
          S Y L M
```

PUZZLE 415

ACROSS
1. Upper limb
4. Price
8. Flog
10. Female singer
11. Arab chieftain
12. Food plan
13. Foxy
16. Lyric poem
17. First woman
18. Greek porticoes
20. Victory symbol
21. Gull-like bird
23. Hobo
24. Decimal unit
25. Pungent
27. Boat paddle
29. Cleanser
30. Small rodents
31. Plaything
32. Governs
33. Weep
35. Rub out
37. Raced
41. Malt beverage
42. Went out with
43. Eggs
44. Building site
45. Affirmative answer
46. Wharf
47. Eager
49. Anglo-Saxon laborer
50. Antitoxins
51. Meshed fabrics
52. Danger color

DOWN
1. Mr. Fortas
2. Dislodge
3. Young girl
4. Military student
5. Martini garnish
6. Guide a car
7. Youngster
9. Family ____
13. Denude
14. Burden
15. Sweet potato
18. Wandered
19. Ruined
22. Unpleasant
24. Lock of hair
26. Dove's sound
28. High card
30. Ponders
32. Charge per unit
33. Four-leaf ____
34. Go to bed
36. Beam of light
38. Social grace
39. Occurrence
40. Challenges
41. Cry of despair
46. Ink writer
48. Father

Starting box on page 562

PUZZLE 416   Quotagram

Fill in the answers to the clues below. Then transfer the letters to the correspondingly numbered squares in the diagram. The completed diagram will contain a quotation.

1. Highly pleasing ___ ___ ___ ___ ___ ___ ___ ___ ___ ___
                    3 33 18 16 48 45 7 25 39 17

2. Selection, as   ___ ___ ___ ___ ___ ___ ___ ___ ___ ___
   for office   34 12 15 46 27 36 40 19 6 21

3. Expertise: ___ ___ ___ ___ ___ ___ ___
   hyph.   8 5 38 11 23 26 1

4. Seaplane float   ___ ___ ___ ___ ___ ___ ___
                    29 4 42 35 20 10 47

5. Ice-cream   ___ ___ ___ ___
   holder   32 24 13 2

6. Born   ___ ___ ___
                     9 30 28

7. Series of tests ___ ___ ___ ___ ___ ___ ___
                    37 41 22 44 14 31 43

1	2		3	4		5	6	7		8	9	10	11		12	13	14		15
16	17	18	19	20	21	22	23		24	25		26	27	28		29	30	31	32
33	34	35		36	37	38	39	40		41	42	43	44	45	46	47	48		

314

ACROSS

1. Saloon
4. Forbidden
6. Printing mistake
8. Submissive
9. Sale term
11. Conversation
12. Baby-sit
14. Crafty
15. Spike
17. Stare open-mouthed
18. Prudish
20. Actor Carney
21. Chinese beverage
22. Tie stain
24. Half quart
25. Withered
27. Professional charges
28. Prima donna
30. Duelist Aaron
31. Fourth of a bushel
33. Toward the setting sun
34. Simpletons
36. Actions
37. Female sheep

DOWN

1. Tree covering
2. Camel's-hair coat
3. Church court
4. Hard journey
5. Evict
6. Slippery
7. Demeanor
8. Man or boy
10. Break suddenly
11. Moved stealthily
13. Grimier
14. Distorts
16. Mortgages
17. Cooking fuel
19. Gym pad
23. Journey
24. Saucy
26. Level
27. Commotion
29. Etching fluid
30. Honey insects
32. Leg joint
33. Broad
35. Modern

PUZZLE 417

Starting box on page 562

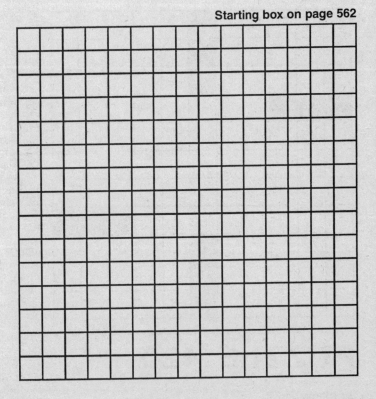

Word Math

PUZZLE 418

In these long-division problems, letters are substituted for numbers. Determine the value of each letter. Then arrange the letters in order from 0 to 9, and they will spell a word or phrase.

1

0	1	2	3	4	5	6	7	8	9

```
                  N I L
STEER | S P L A T T E R
        A I R T T N
        A T I G R E
        A T L N G A
          R P I S R
          S T E E R
          A R L N P
```

2

0	1	2	3	4	5	6	7	8	9

```
                C U T
DOTE | O U T P O U R
       O W U W C
       O W N U U
       R D E P U
       O T R N R
       O T P E T
           C O
```

3

0	1	2	3	4	5	6	7	8	9

```
                 S T A
CATS | T A C T I C S
       T H A G S
       T I I B C
       H T K C F
       B I C C S
       B I G I S
         B A F
```

315

PUZZLE 419

Diagramless crosswords are solved by using the clues and their numbers to fill in the answer words and the arrangement of black squares. Insert the number of each clue with the first letter of its answer, across and down. Fill in a black square at the end of each word. Every black square must have a corresponding black square on the opposite side of the diagram to form a symmetrical pattern.

ACROSS
1. Build
6. Dinette furniture piece
11. Trap
12. Hautboys
13. Small knife
14. Dampen again
15. Credit
17. Foot part
20. WWII agcy.
23. November U.S. event: 2 wds.
26. Affirmative
27. Remove
28. Crinkled fabric
30. Extra
33. Axman
37. Western resort
38. Each
39. Speak like a Southerner
40. Sandwich

DOWN
1. Sixth sense: abbr.
2. Pt. of a cell
3. Sound receiver
4. Bring into being
5. More concise
6. Ripped
7. Encourage
8. The "It" girl
9. Grant's opponent
10. Hour designation: abbr.
16. Detective Sam
17. Vine
18. Born
19. Roads: abbr.
20. Pindar's output
21. Mrs. Nixon
22. See 26 Across
24. Sister's son
25. Arm-holder
28. Gloat
29. Fishing gear
30. Widely used: abbr.
31. ___ avion
32. Word of discovery
34. Marry
35. Work unit
36. Seeded bread

(Grid: first row filled with E R E C T)

PUZZLE 420

ACROSS
1. Ill-mannered man
4. Map book
9. Health resort
12. Lyric poem
13. Selected
14. "___, We Have No Bananas"
15. Indian hatchets
17. Rodent
18. Prayer end
19. Dessert topping
21. Fermented juices
23. Dispatcher
25. Says further
26. Branch
27. Car fuel, for short
28. Silverware item
29. Wood-chopping tool
32. Prize
33. Chinese fabric
34. Throb
37. Wait on
38. Decree
39. Thick slice
40. Umbrella rod
41. Moderate
46. Sun
47. Sinned
48. Watched
49. Summer, in France
50. Metal plates
51. Before, before

DOWN
1. Army bed
2. Fuss
3. Claims
4. Pains
5. Comparative word
6. Depressed
7. Request
8. Court sitting
9. Pancake topper
10. Quiet
11. Fall flower
16. Iowa city
20. Likely
21. Sway
22. Ms. Lupino
23. Coastline
24. Rain bonnet
26. Quarrel
28. Hit hard
29. Landing field: 2 wds.
30. Roman 45
31. Make do
32. Curved line
33. Scorch
34. Poem
35. Fool
36. Book of sacred writings
37. Snow vehicles
39. Detailed description, as of a building, for short
42. Silkworm
43. Married woman's title: abbr.
44. Seaman
45. Female sheep

PUZZLE 421

ACROSS
1. Mountain ____
4. "Welcome" site
7. Spring blossom
9. Spelunker's place
10. Riches
12. "The Dirty ____"
13. Wee one
14. Type of coffee
16. Shiny fabric
17. Beat a tattoo
19. Anger
20. ____ to a customer
21. NYC mayor Beame
22. Tennessee's Howard
24. Bare
27. Swing the camera
28. Mimic
29. Domingo, for one
30. Hold sway
33. Billy ____ Williams
34. Timid
37. Surplus
38. Fish
40. Color
41. Zodiac beast
42. Anonymous John
43. Choir voice
45. Meerschaum, e.g.
46. Information
48. Annoy
49. Serenity
51. Commandeer
53. Foot part
54. Story
55. Rent
56. Football-great Grange

DOWN
1. ____ of Worms
2. Geology span
3. Untamed
4. Labyrinth
5. Hail, to Caesar
6. Incline
8. Hit the jackpot: 3 wds.
9. Dinner call: 4 wds.
10. Alcott's were little
11. Employ
12. Samba, e.g.
13. Bass horn
15. By way of
16. Misplaced
18. Criticize
22. Uncover
23. Zenith
25. Mr. Coward
26. "A ____ Grows in Brooklyn"
31. Wine fruit
32. Appellation
34. Loan or tiger
35. "The Incredible ____"
36. Heretofore
38. Put 2 and 2 together
39. Mr. Webster
44. Girasol
45. Treaty
47. Slightly open
48. Chilled
50. Before, to Blake
52. Porter

Starting box on page 562

QUOTAGRAM   PUZZLE 422

Fill in the answers to the clues below. Then transfer the letters to the correspondingly numbered squares in the diagram. The completed diagram will contain a quotation.

1. Comprehended
$\overline{11}\ \overline{16}\ \overline{14}\ \overline{51}\ \overline{28}\ \overline{1}\ \overline{18}\ \overline{39}\ \overline{5}\ \overline{50}$

2. Winter holiday
$\overline{2}\ \overline{19}\ \overline{42}\ \overline{46}\ \overline{48}\ \overline{38}\ \overline{40}\ \overline{23}\ \overline{33}$

3. Miss the grade
$\overline{25}\ \overline{20}\ \overline{12}\ \overline{32}$

4. Osier
$\overline{34}\ \overline{49}\ \overline{13}\ \overline{6}\ \overline{44}\ \overline{29}$

5. Toiletry item
$\overline{36}\ \overline{26}\ \overline{41}\ \overline{21}\ \overline{3}\ \overline{10}\ \overline{43}\ \overline{27}\ \overline{8}\ \overline{37}$

6. Misplacing
$\overline{31}\ \overline{4}\ \overline{24}\ \overline{15}\ \overline{47}\ \overline{17}$

7. Fiftieth state
$\overline{22}\ \overline{9}\ \overline{45}\ \overline{30}\ \overline{7}\ \overline{35}$

1	2	3	4	5	6		7	8		9		10	11	12	13	14	15	16	17	
18	19	20	21		22	23	24		25	26	27	28		29	30	31	32	33		34
35	36	37		38	39	40	41	42	43	44	45		46	47	48	49	50	51		

317

PUZZLE 423

ACROSS

1. Maul
4. Smoking implement
5. "Memphis ____"
6. Affirmative response
9. Hong Kong counterpart
10. Withstand
11. Keep ____ (keep away)
15. Write
16. Favoritism
17. French city
19. Dignity
21. Infant
24. Fuel
27. Redraft
28. Wind instrument
29. Naughty child
30. Study
31. Assurance
33. Just barely
35. European shrub
37. Otherwise
38. Dregs
41. Wizardry
45. Designate
48. Nevada city
49. Mature
50. Cube
51. Wound covering
53. Sch. type
54. Ornamental shrub
55. Mexican snack
56. Apportion
58. Soft mineral
60. God of love
62. Afternoon beverage
65. Regards seriously
68. Living quarters with stables
69. Entertain
70. Nova Scotia's Grand ____
71. Dexterous
72. Hereditary unit
73. Peculiar

DOWN

1. Covered with hair
2. Poise
3. Tiny
4. Nut
5. Diminish
6. Japanese currency
7. Baby bird
8. Pretentious
9. Chart
10. Furthermore
12. Drink slowly
13. Texas city
14. Vagrant
18. Indian official
20. Eat elegantly
22. Wild pig
23. Abominable Snowman
24. Caustic remark
25. Chemical group
26. Twinge
32. Steering-control post
34. Proximate
36. Prepared
39. Pennsylvania port
40. Swivel
42. Romance in verse
43. Ancient Peruvian
44. Function together
45. Noble title
46. Eternal
47. Discourse
52. Seacraft
53. Green Bay athlete
57. Also
59. Illuminator
61. Colored
62. Brownish gray
63. Formerly, formerly
64. Consumed
66. Female sheep
67. Correct
71. Gone by

Starting box on page 562

ACROSS
1. Bank vault
5. Merry
8. Region
9. Dark bread
10. Lion's cry
11. Red root vegetable
12. Pillar
13. Hair ribbon
14. Maine tree
15. Diaper fastener
16. Bell sound
17. Under
21. Thoroughfare
24. Flying mammal
25. Pigeon sound
26. Presses clothes
27. Belonging to us
28. Spin
30. Cushion
31. Box top
32. Swapped
33. Unique
36. Guided trip
37. Conclude
38. Cotton bundle
39. Moose
40. Frigid
41. Egg-shaped
43. Paying passenger
44. Atmosphere
45. Ajar
46. Jogged
47. Take a break

DOWN
1. Malay skirt
2. Got up
3. Deed
4. Organ of hearing
5. Flourished
6. Affirmative vote
7. Still
11. Skeleton part
12. Half quart
13. Storage drawer
14. Crusted desserts
15. Household animal
16. Lion's lair
17. Saloon
18. Etching fluid
19. Ripped
20. Contain
21. Drinks through a straw
22. Snare
23. Went by bus
24. Young flower
27. Grease
28. Factual
29. Armed conflict
31. Young boy
32. Narrated
34. Prison room
35. Printing fluid
36. Natural ability
38. Drills a hole
39. Get as wages
40. Sleeveless coat
41. Rowing blade
42. By way of
43. In favor of

PUZZLE 424

Starting box on page 562

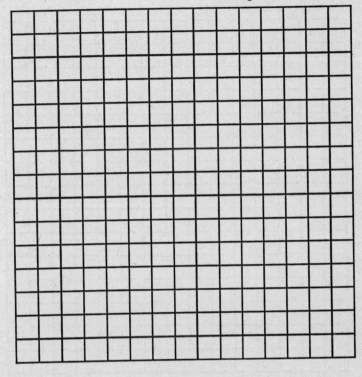

Word Math

PUZZLE 425

In these long-division problems, letters are substituted for numbers. Determine the value of each letter. Then arrange the letters in order from 0 to 9, and they will spell a word or phrase.

1 | 0 | 1 | 2 | 3 | 4 | 5 | 6 | 7 | 8 | 9 |

```
                N I T
P I E D | D E N O T E
          E H I Z
          Y Z I Z T
          Y I Y N O
            Y T O Y E
            Y N O O T
              Y D Z N
```

2 | 0 | 1 | 2 | 3 | 4 | 5 | 6 | 7 | 8 | 9 |

```
                N O R
D O T E | C E N T E R
          D O T E
          T R E O E
          T N C N T
            T N R U R
            N U T E O
              D I C S
```

3 | 0 | 1 | 2 | 3 | 4 | 5 | 6 | 7 | 8 | 9 |

```
                S I T
P O S E | B A L L O T
          A S T L
          O I P H O
          O S T O A
            O B L T T
            O T A I T
              S S O H
```

PUZZLE 426

ACROSS

1. Fellow
5. Make lace
8. Jack rabbit
9. Shade
12. Naught
13. Aquatic flier
14. Too
16. Second telephone
18. Aquatic rodent
20. TV ____
21. Asian body of water
22. Colorado park
26. Yucatan Indian
28. ____ de Cologne
29. Saloons
30. Pant
31. Shade tree
32. Expunge
34. Writing tables
37. Prayer ending
38. Writer Fleming
40. Neighbor of Peru
43. Texas city
47. Nevada city
48. Dismounted
49. Fully cooked
50. Scarlet
51. Oriental grain
52. Vast expanse
53. Groan

DOWN

1. Treasure boxes
2. Mata ____
3. Italian river
4. Hammerhead
5. Schoolbook
6. Singer Garfunkel
7. Little piggies
9. Smoked pork
10. Eskimo knife
11. School papers
12. Ardor
15. Gumbo vegetable
17. Born
19. Sprinted
23. Receptions
24. Comfort
25. Eat the evening meal
26. Masculine
27. "____ and the Man"
29. Sleeping place
30. Goose's mate
32. Flightless bird
33. Back end
35. Young cat
36. Old saying
37. Dull pain
39. Agrees silently
40. Sicilian volcano
41. Singleton
42. Actor Steiger
43. Agricultural home
44. Mixture
45. Costa ____
46. Caviar

Starting box on page 562

PUZZLE 427   Quotagram

Fill in the answers to the clues below. Then transfer the letters to the correspondingly numbered squares in the diagram. The completed diagram will contain a quotation.

1. Truthfulness

    ___ ___ ___ ___ ___ ___ ___
    39 35 9   22 11 34 31

2. Invention

    ___ ___ ___ ___ ___ ___ ___ ___
    23 41 37 5   20 29 17 21

3. Totters

    ___ ___ ___ ___ ___ ___ ___ ___
    26 38 8   32 36 12 6   25

4. Finished

    ___ ___ ___ ___ ___
    40 13 16 24 1

5. Threw (dice)

    ___ ___ ___ ___ ___ ___
    28 2   30 4   15 10

6. Western bars

    ___ ___ ___ ___ ___ ___ ___
    14 27 3   19 33 18 7

1	2	3	4	5	6	7	■	8	9	10	■	11	12	13	14
15	■	16	17	■	18	19	20	■	21	22	23	24	25	26	27
28	29	30	31	■	32	33	■	34	35	36	37	38	39	40	41

PUZZLE 428

ACROSS
1. Vague
4. Pronoun
7. Chowderhead
9. Instruct
11. Item of furniture
13. Having just used up
15. Sink's option
17. ___ chowder
18. Proprietor
19. "Three Faces" woman
20. Assist
21. Statute
22. Insect pest
23. Journey for the "Enterprise"
25. Password
26. Fastened
28. "___ the King's Men"
29. Sans mixer
31. Pleased
33. ___ rata
34. Use scissors
36. Hold in check
37. Actor Jim ___
39. Egg on
40. Uncooked
43. "Sleepy Time ___"
44. Recede
45. Drop in on
47. Decorate
48. Hodgepodge
50. Take up a collection
52. Regular procedure
54. Sultan's wives
55. Nephew's sister
56. Pale
57. Beverage "for two"

DOWN
1. Tip one's hat
2. Author Levin
3. Crowds
4. Appear to be
5. Owns
6. Yodeler's delight
7. Anchor a vessel
8. Part of the U.S.
9. Part of a car purchaser's deal
10. Wolfman's cry
11. Ragout
12. Low couch
13. Coquette
14. Miss Merkel
16. Assembled
17. Mouser
22. Liquid measures
24. Remain informed about
25. Droop
27. Was gutsy
30. Male turkey
32. Crossword part
35. Braid
36. Temperate
38. Dutch ___ disease
39. Sapphire, for one
40. Soar
41. Donkey
42. "A Date ___ Judy"
45. Weathercock
46. Melt
47. Now's partner
49. Spades, e.g.
50. Size of type
51. Historical period
53. Golf gadget

Starting box on page 562

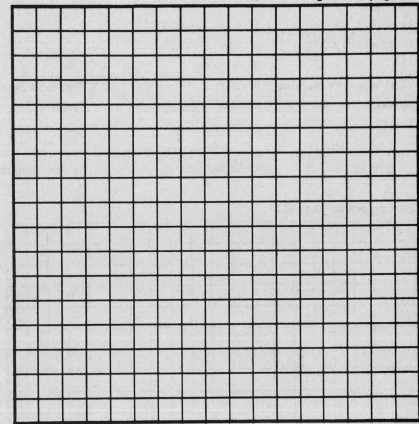

Changaword
PUZZLE 429

Can you change the top word into the bottom word (in each column) in the number of steps indicated in parentheses? Do not change the order of the letters, and change only one letter at a time. Proper names, slang, and obsolete words are not allowed.

1. **POLE** (4 steps)

2. **WORK** (5 steps)

3. **RING** (6 steps)

4. **DROP** (7 steps)

MAST

TOIL

BELL

FALL

PUZZLE 430

ACROSS

1. Muslim pilgrimage
5. Melville romance
6. Lanes
8. Lincoln's Secretary of War
11. Arid
12. Speaker's platform
16. Left
17. Montpelier's neighbor
18. Shafts
19. Basements
21. Business letter opening
22. Handy fellow
27. Author George ____
28. Dam city on the Nile
29. Wild plum
33. Leans
34. African tree
35. "____ You Like to Take a Walk?"
36. Misplace
37. Dart
38. Actress Burstyn
39. "March King"
44. Loudness measure
45. Inexpensive cigars
46. Tub ablutions
48. "To fetch her poor dog ____"
49. Verve
50. Folk knowledge
51. Allows
52. Keenly
56. Painful spots
57. Sage
58. ____-do-well

DOWN

1. Beer ingredients
2. Part of a Latin trio
3. Spanish dance
4. St. ____ (yellow wildflower)
7. Knife sharpeners
9. Caen's river
10. Seines
12. Actress Tyne ____
13. Singer Guthrie
14. Afghanistan's neighbor
15. Spanish muralist
17. Propensities
18. Atomic particle
19. Hundred-dollar bill
20. Rose of ____
21. Mast
22. Congeal
23. Hodgepodge
24. Boo
25. Prevent, legally
26. Lines of mowed grass
29. Flies alone
30. "Little ____" (comic strip)
31. Bullring cheers
32. Poet St. Vincent Millay
34. Throb
35. "All that ____ or seem/ Is but a dream within a dream" (Poe)
37. Heirs, sometimes
39. Conemaugh Dam's neighbor
40. Type of type: abbr.
41. Timber wolf
42. Inventor Sikorsky
43. Loblolly or Scotch
44. Rank
46. Actor Lugosi
47. Sir Guinness
53. Part of HOMES
54. ____ majesty
55. Belgian river

Starting box on page 562

322

PUZZLE 431

ACROSS
1. Applaud
5. Military assistant
6. Actor Harrington
9. Use the eyes
12. Pare
13. Reign
14. "Peter ___"
15. Occur: 2 wds.
20. Function
21. ___ rummy
22. Separated
24. Departed
25. Flipper
26. Cravat
28. Religious group
29. Treaty
30. Spouse
33. Eyelid swelling
36. Openwork fabric
37. Over again
38. Weeding tool
39. Harbor
40. Apple-cider girl
41. Pulls behind
42. Inventor Whitney
43. Unique person
44. House plant
45. Cooking fuel
46. Fewer
47. Apple center
48. Baby-sit
51. Upper limb
52. "Much ___ about Nothing"
53. Bosc
56. Railroad station
58. Long fish
59. Jet-engine housing
60. Ready, set, go!: 3 wds.
65. "___ Maria"
66. Corrode
67. Comfort
71. Strong desire
72. Still
73. Opera song
74. Pre-Easter season

DOWN
1. Bottle top
2. Fib
3. Cooling drink
4. Animal skin
6. Young dog
7. Completely
8. British drink
9. Goad
10. Orient
11. Vane direction: abbr.
13. Lease payment
16. Mature
17. Kith and ___
18. Restaurant
19. Heroic poem
23. Social insect
24. Not dry
26. Diplomacy
27. Frozen water
28. Baste
29. Helen's abductor
30. Pine Tree State
31. South American mountains
32. Sign of weeping
33. Songstress Dinah
34. Village
35. Affirmative answer
36. "Whatever ___ Wants"
39. Wooden nail
41. School semester
43. Ancient
44. Go ___ broke
47. Auto
48. Atlas chart
49. False god
50. Memo
53. Saucy
54. Always, to a poet
55. Clay, today
56. Pigeon
57. Adam and Eve's home
59. ___ the piper
61. Attempt
62. Color
63. Superlative suffix
64. Ring
68. Exist
69. Moral transgression
70. Have supper

Starting box on page 562

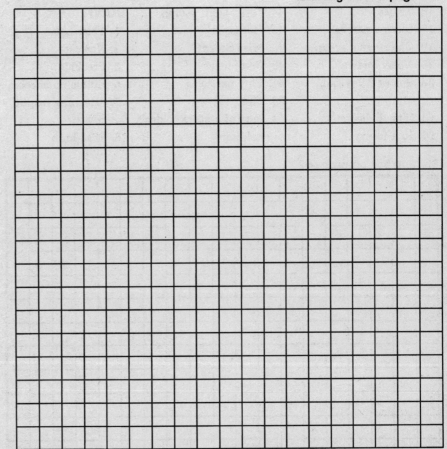

STEP TO THE RIGHT

PUZZLE 432

Using the word ACCOMPLISHMENT, form as many words of at least 3 letters as you can by stepping from the left to the right. Start each word with any letter in ACCOMPLISHMENT; each successive letter in the word must be to the right. Do not use the same letter twice by "sitting" on it. For each new word you may again go back and use letters even if they have been used in other words in your list. Proper names and hyphenated words are not allowed.

ACCOMPLISHMENT

PUZZLE 433

ACROSS

1. Possessed
4. City in 39 Down
6. Actor Sebastian ____
8. Watering place
11. Its ancient name was Lutetia
13. Beneficial
14. Splendid
16. Tribes
17. Clark's partner
19. Chairman's group
20. Noisy quarrel
23. Son of Rhea and Mars
25. City divisions
26. In a frenzy
28. These make a bank account grow
30. Leeward island
32. Urged insistently
34. Do a host's job
35. Use up
38. Heavy luggage piece
42. Choice at an ice-cream parlor
44. "____ Doll" (song)
45. Harasses
48. Miss Storm
49. Confidence
51. Tiny particles
53. Chop
54. Part of a stockholder's holdings
55. Chateaubriand
57. Swiftly
58. Put away for a rainy day
60. Quite a few
61. ____ flush
63. Actress Joan Van ____
64. Grapevine traveler
66. Fishing rod
67. Kid or cat follower

DOWN

1. This: Latin
2. Not care ____
3. Preclude
5. Edible mushroom
7. "Burning bright" creature
8. Flies high
9. "On Golden ____"
10. Paid notices
12. Used a toothy tool
13. Rejoicing
15. Citrus fruit
16. Foundation garments
18. Replaces
19. Flirts with the eyelashes
20. Pealed
21. Hebrew measure
22. Made fabric
24. Kind of loser
25. Sagacious
27. Ukraine capital on the Dnieper
29. ____ no store by (disbelieve)
31. Natural height
33. Something unpleasant, to a teen
35. Laundry problem
36. Slippery ____
37. Appeal
39. Western state
40. Luxor's river
41. Recognized
43. Center of attention in rhinoplasty
46. Little children
47. Smudge
49. "____ Heaven for Little Girls"
50. Risque
52. Taste
54. Gaff or boom
56. Excite
57. Medical gp.
59. Mr. Runyon
62. Broadway role for Gwen Verdon
65. Corded fabric

Starting box on page 562

ACROSS

1. Young sheep
5. Seance sound
8. Wash the floor
11. Lily plant
12. Stir
13. Flank
14. Inattentive
16. Remnants
17. Practice
18. Sign up
20. Turkey or cat
22. Talked back to
25. Hail!
26. Sample
27. List of practices to be avoided
31. Lease payment
33. Scatter rug
35. Letters
36. Caper
38. Neptune's reign
40. Legume
41. Conventional
43. Globe
44. Gully
47. Sniggler's quarry
49. Pennsylvania city
50. Sundae ingredient
55. Norm's drink, on "Cheers"
56. San Franciscan hill
57. Additional
58. Donkey
59. Cry noisily
60. Rectangular pilaster

DOWN

1. Take it on the ____
2. ____ Baba
3. Shrine
4. Bunks
5. "Norma ____"
6. TV spots
7. Sits
8. Skirt type
9. Gambler's concern
10. Annoyance
13. Rarely
15. Minus
19. Comedian Sparks
20. Home of ancient Irish kings
21. Baking chamber
23. Objective
24. Twitch
28. French emperor
29. Upright row
30. Thick slice
32. Smaller
34. Oolong, e.g.
37. Against
39. Actor McCowen
42. Controls
44. Singer McEntire
45. Mars
46. Contends
48. Writer Bombeck
51. Dove's murmur
52. ____ tide
53. Columnist Buchwald
54. ____ culpa

PUZZLE 435

ACROSS

1. Sandal or pump
5. Mountain pass
8. Barbecue item
12. Regulations
13. Spanish river
14. Campaign
15. Actor Guinness
16. Noah's craft
17. Miscalculates
18. Awards
20. Obliterates
22. Vim
23. Curb
24. Convoys
27. Secret agent's forte
31. Sailor's affirmative
32. Dove's comment
33. Postpones
37. Most arid
40. Turn right
41. Sprinted
42. Indicating more than one
45. Engraved
49. Knowledge
50. ____ Vegas
52. Honey factory
53. Border
54. Chicago trains
55. Eve's garden
56. Legal document
57. Beam
58. Mailed

DOWN

1. Bang
2. Sound
3. Was in the red
4. Flee
5. Understands
6. Ventilate
7. Fireplace tools
8. Soft and smooth
9. Paddles
10. Land measure
11. Minus
19. Permit
21. Tear
24. Craze
25. Soap-making ingredient
26. Snakelike fish
28. Rapper ____-T
29. Votes against
30. Earned
34. Came to terms
35. Word of assent
36. Dealer
37. Suitable for formal wear
38. Squealer
39. Foot parts
42. Begged
43. Ore deposit
44. Impulse
46. Camouflage
47. Flat
48. Shallow hollow
51. ____ carte

PUZZLE 436

ACROSS
1. "The ___ Wolf"
4. Pounds
9. Chum
12. Ashen
13. Bide time
14. Cold cube
15. Pretend
16. Rued
18. Not our
20. Attorney's field
21. Prayer endings
24. Illuminate
28. Portable stove
31. Open delight
32. Refreshing drink
33. Sam ___ of "The Maltese Falcon"
35. Nest egg letters
36. Semester
38. Otis invention
40. School paper
42. Genuflected
43. Trail behind
45. Marsh grasses
48. Do as a bear does
53. Adverse review
54. Confusion
55. Ventures
56. Yale or Whitney
57. Droop
58. "___ Little Sixteen"
59. Room for relaxation

DOWN
1. Police acronym
2. Every
3. Pismire munchers
4. Cylindrical containers
5. Respect
6. Nitpick
7. "That ___" (Thomas series)
8. Take by theft
9. Excavation
10. Tennis shot
11. Was in front
17. Branch
19. Little devil
22. Back of the neck
23. Hunt
25. Sparkled
26. Guy in white
27. Shred
28. Loathe
29. Poems
30. Utopia
34. Hillary's conquest
37. Masculine
39. Pub drink
41. Lawns
44. Chew on, as a bone
46. Cowgirl Evans
47. Rotate
48. Owns
49. Journalist Wells
50. Swampy place
51. "You ___ There"
52. Pipe joint

327

PUZZLE 437

ACROSS
1. Crosby's pal
5. Felines
9. Tree trunk
13. Incline
17. Amino or lactic
18. Civil disorder
19. Enthusiasm
20. Sector
21. Devour a book
22. Fragrance
23. Salacious
24. Pickle herb
25. Responds hysterically
27. Roman army unit
29. Painter's stand
30. Carols
31. Abilities
32. Concurs
33. Hero
34. Fail to mention
35. Courts
36. Gamble
39. Failure
41. Small pincers with long jaws
43. Epoch
46. Sinister
48. East's opposite
50. Prepare for publication
51. Unit of a data transmission rate
52. Spirit in a bottle
54. Pirates, e.g.
56. Deletions
58. Blemish
60. Eating utensil
62. Sink beneath a weight
63. Fast felines
67. Belfry denizens
69. 747, e.g.
73. Corn, peanut, and vegetable
74. Source of sugar
76. Aggravate
78. Pitcher
79. ___ Aviv
80. Tolerates
82. Printed mistake
84. Female bighorn
85. Tinter
86. Rock to and fro
88. Incense
90. Small flower
93. Arouse
94. Store events
97. Rakes
98. Beast
100. Spanish and black
102. Play sections
103. African lily
104. Rosary component
106. Grotto
107. Pesters
108. Spinners' works
109. "Better ___ than never"
110. Think-tank product
111. Satiate
112. For fear that
113. Scratches out
114. Portable shelter

DOWN
1. Dwell
2. Pacific or Indian
3. Keyboard instrument
4. Vortices
5. Arrow shooter
6. Benefit
7. Hammer, for one
8. Brook
9. Demean
10. Margarines
11. Grassy spread
12. Complete
13. Speed trackers
14. Revolt
15. Fracas
16. Makes dull
26. Association
28. Grasp
29. Easily bruised items
32. Main arteries
34. Haunted
35. Bob ___ of The Grateful Dead
36. Ask earnestly
37. She raised Cain
38. Soft metal
40. Encountered
42. Card or crisis
43. Corn spike
44. Lament
45. Classified items
47. Citrus fruits
49. Spigot
51. Brass horn
53. Have a snack
55. Disorderly crowd

57. Drain
59. Notch in a board
61. Scull
63. Folding bed
64. Speed
65. Plumbing joint
66. Descendant
68. Surreptitious
70. Dread
71. Novel
72. Sooner than
75. Crossest
77. Occurrences
80. Sailor's affirmatives
81. Compete in a freestyle
83. Unwritten
85. Stylish
87. Land fit for cultivation
89. Extract
90. French dollar, once
91. Kind of train
92. Expenditure
93. Social climbers
95. Sidestep
96. Lucky number
98. Helm position
99. Security problem
101. Bench
103. Leather worker's device
105. Grazed

1	2	3	4		5	6	7	8		9	10	11	12		13	14	15	16
17					18					19					20			
21					22					23					24			
25				26			27		28					29				
	30							31					32					
		33				34					35							
36	37	38		39		40			41		42					43	44	45
46			47		48			49		50					51			
52				53		54			55		56			57				
		58		59		60				61			62					
63	64	65				66			67			68		69		70	71	72
73					74			75		76			77		78			
79				80					81		82			83		84		
		85					86		87			88		89				
90	91	92				93							94			95	96	
97					98					99		100						101
102				103					104		105				106			
107				108					109						110			
111				112					113						114			

PUZZLE 438

ACROSS

1. Traffic sign
5. Actor's role
9. Gift-box trim
12. Type of history
13. Bouquet
14. Wonder
15. Musical symbol
16. Handbag
17. Accounting term
18. Liquefy
20. Bird food
22. Obi
25. Theatrical fare
28. Forefather
32. Fascinated
33. Shad delicacy
34. Manipulate
35. Eden dweller
36. Brush's kin
38. Regarded with contempt
41. Grimace
43. Certain deer
44. Without dilution
46. Corrode
49. Liable
51. Information
54. Nautical call
56. Hint
57. Hemsley series
58. Zilch
59. At the ____ of one's rope
60. Robert ____ ("The Brady Bunch")
61. Large primates

DOWN

1. Father's boy
2. Jog
3. Promise
4. Gratify
5. Cooking vessel
6. Excitement
7. Deteriorates
8. Cornered
9. Dresses
10. Be indebted to
11. Soaked
19. Existed
21. Notable time
23. Nailhead
24. Rubber pipes
26. Change residence
27. Matured
28. Curves
29. "High ____"
30. Bound
31. State of inactivity
37. Honey maker
39. Norm
40. Lizard
42. Radio device
45. Gentle
47. Market
48. Timbre
49. High card
50. Joke
52. Palmer's peg
53. Additionally
55. Affirmative

ACROSS

1. This girl
4. Paid athlete
7. Units of time
9. Don't spill the ___
11. Scared
13. Root vegetable
14. Damage
15. Mexican money
17. Oriental sauce
18. Noticed
20. Dove's comment
21. Comedian Rickles
22. Sound a horn
24. Mets, e.g.
26. Kettle or Barker
27. Military off.
28. Minimum ___
30. Applications
32. Female fowl
33. Tub
35. Pop
37. Ocean
38. Pie nut
40. Corn on the ___
42. Preacher
44. Husky, like a voice
46. Wide-awake
47. Freezing rain
48. Foxy
49. Commercials

DOWN

1. Couches
2. Cheer
3. Important time period
4. According to
5. Kidnapper's demand
6. Leek's relative
7. ___ and cheese sandwich
8. Drink daintily
9. Commuter vehicle
10. Secret agent
12. Ship's floor
13. Beep
16. Therefore
19. "Oh, Pretty ___" (Orbison tune)
21. Escorted
23. Nitpick
25. Overhead trains
28. Ferret
29. At any time
30. Beehive state
31. Holy
32. Mends
34. Room-cooling device: abbr.
36. Portions
37. Mineral spring
38. Cooking vessel
39. Negative responses
41. Wager
43. Attempt
45. ___ carte

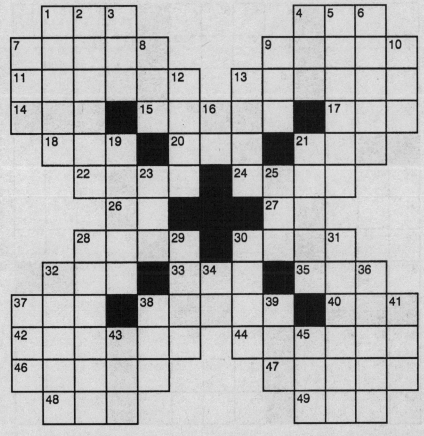

PUZZLE 440

ACROSS
1. Sizzling
4. Tykes
8. Boxing punch
12. Make a mistake
13. Buckeye State
14. Motored
15. Actor Vigoda
16. Prayer ending
17. Had debts
18. Russian rulers
20. Type
22. Perched
23. Grimaced
27. Bongo, e.g.
29. Bundle
30. "You ___ My Sunshine"
31. Cup handle
32. Fetes
33. Game cube
34. Adam's mate
35. Again
36. Breeze
37. Takes personal offense at
39. Red, White, or Black
40. Years of life
41. French heads
44. Metal containers
47. Gambling city
50. Hockey surface
51. African lily
52. Actor Jannings
53. Pay dirt
54. Plays the horses
55. Fool
56. Convent dweller

DOWN
1. Warmth
2. Spheres
3. Holds dear
4. Breakfast bread
5. Electric unit
6. Attachment
7. Daughter's husband
8. Bankrupted
9. Base
10. "___ on a Grecian Urn"
11. Marry
19. Male herd animal
21. Dregs
23. Transfers of ownership
24. Energy source
25. Emerald Isle
26. Land title
27. Forest creature
28. Rant
29. Exchanged playful remarks
32. "Our ___"
36. Tiny
38. Relieves
39. Fur wrap
42. Unbleached color
43. Detected
44. Taxi
45. Malt brew
46. "Thou shalt ___ . . ."
48. Australian ratite
49. Sip

PUZZLE 441

ACROSS
1. Finder's exclamation
4. Leaning tower locale
8. Mat
11. Scratch
12. Dropper's word
13. Song for one
14. Delight
16. Capri, e.g.
17. Begin
18. Shows ennui
20. Jewel
22. Nimble
25. Admired
28. Revolt
29. In favor of
30. ____ Aviv
32. On the ____ (escaping)
33. Unattended
36. Hoped
39. More achy
40. Hawaiian wreath
41. Creature
44. Train station
48. Escaped
50. Cherish
52. Lubricates
53. "____ We Got Fun"
54. Sprinted
55. Harden
56. Went on horseback
57. Some railways, for short

DOWN
1. Electrical units
2. Cease!
3. Space
4. Printed ad
5. Debtor's note
6. Energetic
7. On the ocean
8. Perhaps true
9. Everything
10. Female rabbit
13. Scorch
15. Jason's ship
19. Combat
21. Congregated
23. Starring role
24. "Nightmare on ____ Street"
25. Singer Guthrie
26. Chime to announce visitors
27. Morning moisture
29. Faux ____
31. "____ Abner"
34. Requires
35. Baseball stat.
37. Tranquil
38. Hurries
42. Celebrity
43. Peter, Paul, and Mary, e.g.
45. Unadulterated
46. Kind of test
47. Decades
48. Mist
49. Bend the truth
51. Outcome

333

PUZZLE 442

ACROSS
1. Jogged
4. Supervisor
8. Ready, willing, and ____
12. Ginger drink
13. Grandma Moses
14. Actress Fay ____
15. School reading matter
17. Man Friday
18. Surplus
19. Pay
21. Southernmost Great Lake
23. Tingly
26. Opera highlight
29. Tennis star
31. Weeding tool
32. GI's identification
34. Actress Lansbury
36. Stopover spot
37. Inner being
39. Customer
40. Pine Tree State
42. Actress Carter
44. Here's to you!, for one
46. Deacon
50. Like Snow White
52. Stored wealth
54. Molecule
55. Belonging to us
56. ____ Juan
57. Comic Carvey
58. ____ moss
59. Fast jet

DOWN
1. Fixed charge
2. Trebek of "Jeopardy!"
3. Subsequent
4. Well-dressed elephant
5. Yoko ____
6. Sleeps loudly
7. Welfare
8. Be ready for
9. Too big for his ____
10. Youth
11. Storm center
16. Pick up the check
20. Demeanor
22. "Othello" villain
24. Cavity
25. Fifty-two weeks
26. Take ____ view of
27. Miss Barrett
28. Starter
30. Patriot Nathan ____
33. Befuddled
35. Water birds
38. False
41. Marilyn's real name
43. Fewest
45. Call it quits
47. Nonexploding fireworks
48. Greek love god
49. Apartment fee
50. Passing fancy
51. "One Day ____ Time"
53. Period of time

334

PUZZLE 443

ACROSS

1. ____ the way
5. Steiger and Serling
9. "____ Joey"
12. Singer Guthrie
13. New York canal
14. ____ Grande
15. Elvis's home
17. Asner and Ames
18. Airedale's appendage
19. Valuable item
21. Bring goods into the country
24. Suit to ____
25. Chars
26. Primps
28. ____ and feather
29. Belfry dweller
30. Young boy
32. Rag
35. Greek isle
37. Billy or nanny
38. Window covers
39. Bunnies' kin
41. Hit, as a fly
42. Age
43. Ring up
48. Tear
49. Mild oath
50. Son of Seth
51. Word from Scrooge
52. Love too much
53. Cincinnati nine

DOWN

1. Fall behind
2. Make a mistake
3. Pie ____ mode
4. Physician
5. Kindled again
6. By mouth
7. Noise
8. Tranquilize
9. Gave, as an award
10. ____ -de-camp
11. Like Peep's sheep
16. Wet behind the ____
20. Observe
21. Believer: suff.
22. Butcher-shop purchase
23. Sentence grouping
24. Actor Carney
26. Golf score
27. Fill up
29. Wager
31. ____ Moines
33. Foot part
34. Tried a sip
35. Bloke
36. Newsman Dan ____
38. Native of Stockholm
39. Bandleader Alpert
40. Opera highlight
41. Bed part
44. Conceit
45. Singleton
46. Give silent consent
47. Curvy letter

335

PUZZLE 444

• MOVIES AND TELEVISION •

ACROSS

1. Sherilyn ___ of "Twin Peaks"
5. Brownies' org.
8. Actor Torn
11. Appellation
15. Mars: pref.
16. Native of Melmac
17. Worldwide workers group: abbr.
18. Actor Sharif
19. Robbie ___ of "Lucas Tanner"
20. Washington city
22. Petty of "A League of Their Own"
23. "Full ___ Jacket"
25. He was, to Cato
26. Valentine or Carpenter
27. Trickle
29. "___ Place"
32. Early women's movement word
35. "Open ___ Night"
36. "___ Window"
37. Actor Mineo
40. Woe!
42. Minus
45. Waterston or Donaldson
46. Wrath
47. Seaweed
48. "The Maltese Falcon" actress
50. TV dog
52. Sandra or Ruby
54. Comedian Soupy ___
56. Court divider
57. Marx Brothers film
60. "The ___ Wild"
62. Carson's replacement
65. "The Greatest"
66. Carrere of "Wayne's World"
68. "Super ___"
69. John Hurt film
70. "___ in White"
71. Beatles film
73. See 82 Down
75. Posed for a portrait
76. Jerry ___ of "Pantomime Quiz"
78. "Cheers" barfly
80. Gary Burghoff role on "M*A*S*H"
83. Look after
85. "___ Derringer" (TV series)
89. Vouch
90. "___ of Living Dangerously"
93. "___ American Graffiti"
94. Tippi Hedren film
95. Audio receiver
96. Sandwich bread
97. Actor Kincaid
98. Williams or Griffith
99. Burro
100. Ladd film
101. "___ at Sea" (Laurel & Hardy film)

DOWN

1. "Animal ___"
2. Great Lake
3. "Empty ___"
4. "___ a Stranger" (de Havilland film)
5. Fuel for KITT on "Knight Rider"
6. Like a film character in 20 Across
7. Off yonder
8. John or Tex
9. Under the weather
10. "The Loves of Edgar Allan ___"
11. Lloyd ___
12. Love, in Madrid
13. Actress Winningham
14. Moran or Gray
21. Hines/Davis film
24. Nicholas ___ of TV's "The Commish"
26. Harvey ___ of 79 Down
28. Actress Joyce of "Roc"
30. "___, Giorgio" (Pavarotti film)
31. Philippine volcano
32. "Mighty ___ a Rose"
33. Small French land mass
34. Alec or William
37. TV series starring 51 Down
38. Emma on "Kate & Allie"
39. Tommy ___ Jones
41. "Graf ___"
43. "___ Search"
44. "___ Gold"
49. Actress Rose of "Temperatures Rising"

336

PUZZLE 444

51. Actress Ward of 37 Down
53. Williams or Rolle
55. "____ to Noon" (British film)
57. Actress Rita ____
58. "Grand ____ Opry"
59. "Family ____"
61. Sweeney of "Anything Goes"
63. Actress Peeples
64. Cereal grain
67. Model/actress Carol ____
72. Bernadette ____
74. "A ____ White Season"
76. "____ King Live"
77. Alejandro ____
79. "____ Family"
80. ____ avis
81. Bard's waterway
82. Bogart film, with 73 Across
84. Angelica ____ (Barbara Carrera's "Dallas" role)
86. Writer/director Ephron
87. Riding whip
88. Hankerings
90. Hot beverage
91. "____ Anybody Seen My Gal?"
92. Legal thing

337

PUZZLE 445

ACROSS
1. Residence
6. Tumult
9. Spanish cheer
12. Strength
13. Baby's seat
14. Obscure
15. Lone Ranger's pal
16. Get better
18. Notices
20. Less wealthy
21. Dentist's customer
25. Impertinent
26. October birthstone
27. Anxious
29. Toe count
30. Designates
31. Peccadillo
34. Duped
35. Texas city
36. Purse handle
39. Separated
41. Young biddies
43. Snaky fish
44. Cold-blooded animal
46. List of candidates
50. "Where the Boys ____"
51. Zilch
52. Babel almost had one
53. French sea
54. Messy home
55. Take an oath

DOWN
1. Ordinarily disposed
2. Halloween greeting
3. Have
4. Particular
5. Eat away
6. "____ Baba and the Forty Thieves"
7. Moist
8. Combats
9. Smells
10. "Days of Our ____"
11. Corundum
17. Lion's cry
19. Slink
21. Kettle
22. Chimpanzee
23. Light brown
24. Cultivated
28. Magic lamp dweller
30. Diners' protective wear
31. Morose
32. Skating surface
33. Biblical land
34. Diplomacy
35. Weeping tree?
36. Shoo!
37. "____ Goes Another Love Song"
38. More mature
40. Waistcoats
42. Narrow cut
45. Tarzan portrayer
47. Reverential fear
48. Pekoe
49. Be wrong

ACROSS
1. Father
5. Mindful
10. Watchdog gp.?
14. Has debts
15. Carried on
16. Break (of a habit)
17. In a vertical manner
20. "Venus de ___"
21. Religious images
22. China flaw
24. Early French king
26. ___ bodkins
29. Biddies
30. With ___ breath
31. Plenty, poetically
32. "___ Maria"
33. Shove
34. Rio de la ___
35. ___ Authority
39. Devoured
40. "Lord, ___ I?"
41. Greek letter
42. Diva Gluck
43. Quebec peninsula
45. Loire tributary
46. "Born in the ___"
47. Nuts
48. In accompaniment
49. Simpletons
51. Potter's need
52. Made at the same time
58. Oil cartel
59. Separated
60. Painting subject
61. English spa
62. Scandinavian
63. Plow or storm

DOWN
1. Kind of music
2. Reverence
3. Certain attractor
4. Salad molds
5. Florence's river
6. Paper ball
7. Bird: pref.
8. Cookbook item
9. Drew out
10. Dive or song
11. I, for one
12. Football's Hubbard
13. At least one
18. Fraternal member
19. Destiny
22. French estate
23. Discloses
24. TV's Peggy
25. Disbelief
27. Is overly fond of
28. Influencing
30. "___ Stop"
31. House wing
33. Write
34. Gentle touch
36. Teacher's org.
37. Notice
38. Contend
43. Meter reader
44. Syrian city
45. Fred and Gracie
47. Busy one
48. French river
50. Engrave
51. Actress Jackson
52. Corn core
53. WWII agcy.
54. Row
55. B&O and Short Line
56. Japanese plant
57. Use a needle

PUZZLE 446

PUZZLE 447

ACROSS
1. Cigar remains
6. At a distance
10. Once more
14. Norman Vincent ___
15. Vice cubes?
16. Mrs. Dithers of "Blondie"
17. Storage spot, often
18. "___ each life some rain . . ."
19. Mine extracts
20. Broadway
23. Promise to pay
24. Related maternally
25. Dictator
29. Patio, in Greece
32. Poplar
33. Ancient Italians
38. Manhandle
39. To have: Fr.
40. Soprano's song
41. Safe bet
43. Apply tempera
44. Elihu ___
45. Fountain treat
46. Viper
50. Smith or soldier
51. Unwelcome one
59. Story line
60. Enthusiastic
61. Swiss mathematician
62. Lois of comics
63. Telegraph
64. No way!
65. Potato buds
66. Low card
67. London sights

DOWN
1. Pit -___: hyph.
2. Son of Adam
3. Despise
4. Famed essayist
5. Cross ___
6. Farewell, to Fifi
7. Locate
8. Play part
9. Old cars
10. Future oak
11. Water wheel
12. Upright
13. What haste makes
21. Decompose
22. Oolong and hyson
25. Water barriers
26. Jacob's twin
27. Horse prod
28. Soccer name
29. Sly of music
30. Branch of math
31. Your and my
33. Satan's work
34. Actor James
35. Like the Gobi
36. 1492 ship
37. Satisfy
39. Eureka!
42. Novice
43. Flavorful
45. Transgression
46. Granny Smith, e.g.
47. Procrastinate
48. Bee type
49. Kefauver
50. Hot drink
52. Famed caricaturist
53. Claim
54. Diamond number
55. Regretful one
56. Part of T.A.E.
57. Abound
58. Timetable abbrs.

PUZZLE 448

ACROSS

1. ____ to (confront)
7. Grain beards
11. Place for a gnu
14. Breakfast juice
15. True: Fr.
16. Pulpy fruit
17. Understood
19. Bandleader Brown
20. Customer
21. Bridge concern
23. Pie nut
25. "The ____ Night"
26. Went quickly
28. Looked happy
32. Final missile-launch period
37. Story
38. Navy man: abbr.
39. Pertaining to pleasure
42. Once named
43. Hollow stem
45. New Zealand
47. Absconded
50. Vigoda and Burrows
51. Pedro's nap
55. Neckwear
58. Emphasize
62. Record
63. Tip of Italy
64. Game official
66. Lemon drink
67. Ballet garment
68. Trimming tools
69. Wise
70. Tennis divisions
71. Extent

DOWN

1. Become clouded
2. Originated
3. Neophyte
4. Get on board
5. Cry of disgust
6. Chick's sound
7. Shun
8. Squeeze
9. Edict city
10. TV offering
11. Certain African
12. Microwave, e.g.
13. Hops kiln
18. "The Raven" author
22. "The Thrill ____ All"
24. Eur. country
27. ETO leader
29. Grounds expert
30. Robert ____
31. Bambi, e.g.
32. Singer Vikki
33. Old Greek theaters
34. Eccentric
35. Court
36. Opposite of SSE
40. ____ jiffy
41. Fidel's country
44. Medicinal measure
46. Rainy-day money
48. Highest-quality goods
49. Pasture grass
52. Actor George C. ____
53. Convex molding
54. Exist
56. Part of op. cit.
57. Succinct
58. Beehive State
59. Knob
60. Esoteric
61. ____ out (supplemented)
65. Dutch city

PUZZLE 449

ACROSS
1. Armadillo
5. Arizona river
9. French nobleman
14. Fail to win
15. Black, poetically
16. City on the Missouri
17. Forceful
19. African river
20. Book part
21. Choice
23. Cut a molar
25. Pay
26. Rabbit ___
28. Functional
32. Switch around
37. Roman official
38. Everything
39. Crown
41. Actor Johnson
42. Jigsaw-puzzle unit
45. Temporary
48. City on Puget Sound
50. Halt
51. Complains
54. "Peer Gynt" girl
58. Very important
62. Author Gertrude
63. ___ Rogers St. Johns
64. Retribution
66. Distributed, as cards
67. Miss Adams
68. Water testers
69. Kovacs or Ford
70. Kind of store: abbr.
71. Former, formerly

DOWN
1. Inclined, as a ship
2. Ceremony: Fr.
3. Easy ___
4. Come back in
5. Set
6. Wading bird
7. Friendless one
8. Slant
9. Clear-cut
10. Left out
11. Creche figures
12. Lieutenant Kojak
13. Deserve
18. "Merry Widow" composer
22. Large bird
24. Part of QED
27. Agitated state
29. Billfold item
30. ___ Bator
31. Pre-Easter period
32. Enthralled
33. Essay writer
34. Author Waugh
35. Needlefish
36. Ages in history
40. B'way group
43. Italian violinist
44. Issue
46. Perceive
47. Impersonate
49. River islet
52. Adored
53. Shoe material
55. Pavarotti, e.g.
56. White and wild
57. "___ of robins . . ."
58. Constructed
59. European river
60. Unkind
61. Shear
65. Understand

342

PUZZLE 450

ACROSS

1. Was in debt
5. Not hers
8. Goad
12. Hill's opposite
13. Commotion
14. Lima's locale
15. Garage approach
17. Fad
18. Bother
19. Reserved
21. Bride's walkway
24. Actor Bridges
25. City properties
26. Excessive praise
30. Fleecy female
31. Schemes
32. Stag's mate
33. Ahab and Nemo
35. Cat call
36. Ilsa's ex
37. Suggests
38. Comment
41. Aries
42. Parched
43. Feelings
48. Blaze
49. Gab
50. Sherlock's discovery
51. ___ off (annoys)
52. Spot
53. Transmitted

DOWN

1. Unusual
2. Clash of arms
3. Yale grad
4. Demons
5. Falcon's cousin
6. Crete's highest mountain
7. Forage crop
8. Brussels or alfalfa
9. Crag
10. Desire
11. Was sorry for
16. Before, in poems
20. Feeling one's ___
21. Actor Guinness
22. Ames locale
23. Pace
24. Empty
26. Flutters
27. Serene spot
28. ___ beer
29. Evergreens
31. Duo
34. Barters
35. Apes
37. Fedora
38. Huck Finn's transport
39. Huron's neighbor
40. Marsh
41. Lasso
44. Actress West
45. Bullfighter's cheer
46. Sister
47. Place

PUZZLE 451

ACROSS
1. Irritate
6. Snare
10. Tears
14. Book
15. Commuted
16. Spoken
17. Place in a row
18. Religious image
19. Mentally healthy
20. Marry
21. Ridicule
23. Delicate
25. Mountaintop
26. Lion's tresses
27. Dormant
30. Guards
34. Long-plumed heron
35. Related on mother's side
36. College cheer
37. Small bottle
38. Worries
39. Own
40. Shade tree
41. Krupa and Kelly
42. Graded
43. Newsman
45. Fondle
46. Peach stones
47. Marquis de ____
48. Leatherneck
51. Eastern desert
52. Bard's before
55. Ardor
56. Path
58. Place of worship
60. Painful
61. Pollster Roper
62. Night lights
63. Mind
64. Believe
65. Stain

DOWN
1. Erode
2. Portrayal
3. Eager
4. Decade
5. Component
6. Ruse
7. Pop music
8. Commotion
9. Necklaces
10. Redder
11. Eastern land
12. Breathe rapidly
13. Weaver's reed
22. Cereal grain
24. Kitty food
25. Pare
26. Cold cuts, e.g.
27. Prying bar
28. Spry
29. Hobo
30. Scoff
31. Enraged
32. Roof edges
33. Shacks
35. Sea birds
38. Shackled
39. Hounds' quarry
41. Wide smile
42. Glowing
44. Stated
45. Taxi
47. ____ and Gomorrah
48. Interlock
49. Medicinal herb
50. Infrequent
51. Contest
52. Short jacket
53. Pealed
54. Scottish Gaelic
57. Corrida cheer
59. Flower garland

PUZZLE 452

ACROSS
1. Israeli dance
5. "___ at Sea"
10. French cleric
14. Love god
15. Onto
16. Follow
17. Lip
18. Code name
19. Carney and Garfunkel
20. Ginger ___
21. Highway fare
22. Playwright Edward
23. Chow ___
25. Expunger
28. Exactly: 3 wds.
30. Grissom's agcy.
31. ___ was saying: 2 wds.
34. Slipped
35. Showy bird
36. Rds.
37. Shells out
38. Passover feast
39. And others: abbr.
40. Common abbr.
41. Mrs. Eisenhower
42. NCO, for short
43. Wriggly fish
44. Writer James ___
45. Thoroughfare
46. Fix one's bearings
48. "___ Fan Tutte"
49. Did a blacksmith's job
51. Ostrich
53. Comic Caesar
56. Miss Horne
57. Scallion's cousin
59. Built
60. Retired
61. Hidden supply
62. Arrow poison
63. Tunisian rulers
64. Musketeer
65. First man

DOWN
1. "For ___ jolly good ...": 2 wds.
2. Spoken
3. "White Christmas" actress: 2 wds.
4. Donkey
5. Singer Vic ___
6. G.I. hooky
7. "The Blue Angel" actress: 2 wds.
8. Hesitation sounds
9. Take in
10. "___ of Two Cities": 2 wds.
11. "Funny Girl" actress: 2 wds.
12. Nibble
13. Other
21. Bound
22. Wise ___ owl: 2 wds.
24. Summers, to Henri
26. Street show
27. Ancient harp
28. Kind of home
29. Speak pompously
32. Arena, for one
33. Small land mass
35. Muscular males: hyph.
38. Herb
39. Roman loans
41. Cleaning woman
42. Zeno's porch
45. Angry exhibitions
47. Studies
49. Piece of concrete
50. Daughter of Zeus
52. Laughter syllables: 2 wds.
54. Concept
55. Believe
57. Wood sorrel
58. ___ King Cole
59. Actress Farrow

PUZZLE 453

ACROSS
1. Having a high temperature
4. Crowd
7. Banana treat
12. Heart of Dixie
14. "Remember the ___!"
15. Discounts
16. Diamond weight unit
17. Shed feathers
18. Mouth part
20. Pester
21. Opposite of NNW
22. Buttes
24. Russian plane
26. Took a chair
27. Plunder
29. Flies alone
32. Welcome
33. Singer Frankie ___
35. "Night and ___"
36. Dripping
37. Comes closer
39. Comedian Knotts
42. Confederate soldier, for short
44. Distress
45. Accurate
46. The Red ___ (Snoopy's foe)
48. Give forth
50. Conscious
51. Stumbled
52. Leased again
53. Yes vote
54. Bitter vetch

DOWN
1. Injures
2. Butter substitutes
3. ___ of contents
4. Doorway rug
5. Egg dish
6. Foundation
7. Baglike structure
8. Blueprint
9. Wyoming city
10. Picture mentally
11. Toddler
13. Hitter's stick
19. Golfer's standard
22. ___-Dixon line
23. Heroic stories
25. Acquire
26. Fa follower
28. Move by leverage
29. Witnessed
30. Intimidate
31. Sidelong
34. Modern
35. Cheerless
38. Main artery
39. Heavy curtain
40. External
41. Requires
43. Tiresome person
45. Bellboy's reward
46. Saloon
47. Butterfly snare
49. Gaming cube

ACROSS

1. Suez, e.g.
6. Insult
10. Neck or cut
14. Love
15. Rose or Seeger
16. Queen of heaven
17. Intrigues
19. Among
20. Makes do
21. Food scrap
22. Typist's turf
24. Brunched
25. Dos and don'ts
26. In unison: 2 wds.
29. Very small
30. Embroider
33. Indirect
35. Colleen's land
36. Fad
37. Kind of curve
38. Isolated
39. Light-hearted
40. Stubborn
42. Society page word
43. Give up
44. Pile up
45. Tete-a-tetes
47. Pedro's river
48. 4th of July event
50. ___ Plaines
51. Author Harte
55. Wrought ___
56. Fall guys
59. Ordinances
60. Kind of bag
61. Writer Loos
62. You are something ___!
63. Official stamp
64. Blooper

DOWN

1. Bistro
2. Aleutian island
3. Aardvark feature
4. Curves
5. Hawaiian garland
6. Fifth wheel
7. Latvian
8. Shoshonean
9. Reverberate
10. Irritate
11. Reprieves
12. Mr. Sevareid
13. Ford the stream
18. Famed
23. Go by air
24. ___ of Cleves
25. Washer cycle
26. High nest
27. Cornfield figures
28. Muddy
29. One of the senses
31. Sea eagles
32. Milk or tumble
33. Look over
34. Abides by
35. Writer Kazan
38. Gunpowder, for short
40. Hates
41. Cultivate
43. Rascal
46. Medieval guild
47. Force back
48. Rug surface
49. Asian sea
50. Census information
51. Lead singer of U2
52. Shower
53. Luncheon ending
54. Russian ruler
57. Cedar Rapids college
58. Chitchat

PUZZLE 454

PUZZLE 455

ACROSS
1. Behind schedule
5. Scandinavian
9. Border
12. Tel ___
13. Muse of poetry
15. Prefix for circle or final
16. Pepper picker: 2 wds.
18. Indigo source
19. Fraternity letter
20. Loosen
21. Shed: hyph.
23. Take on help
24. Straw, black, or blue, e.g.
25. Fill-in for a sovereign
28. Pod vegetables
29. Paw feature
32. Classical mall
33. Actor George
34. Freudian topic
35. Big bash
36. Bedouins
37. Don Juan's mother
38. Days of yore
39. Maternally kin
40. English poet
41. "Agnus ___"
42. To ___ (exactly): 2 wds.
43. East Indian fig tree
44. Plaster supports
46. Register
47. Be lethargic
49. Volcano's apex
50. Chicken-to-be
53. Event at Le Mans
54. Seesaw girl: 2 wds.
57. Seeks information
58. Scowl
59. Roof extension
60. Army security guards: abbr.
61. Court items
62. Revival word

DOWN
1. Northern native
2. Prayers
3. Small monkey
4. Actress Brent
5. Make an exit
6. Soar skyward
7. Scruff
8. Somme summer
9. Children's barnyard story: 2 wds.
10. Radiate
11. Venus de ___
14. City on the Loire
15. German state
17. Spanish queen
22. At one time
23. Sister of Zeus
24. American naturalist
25. Flared up
26. Equal, in Paris
27. "The Three Bears" intruder
28. Chatter
30. Booster rocket
31. Baker's ___
33. Dundee hillsides
36. Sacred songs
37. One of the Hebrides
39. Diner sign
40. Office machine
43. Gaffes
45. Inspires with wonder
46. Thesaurus author
47. Small drink
48. Grate
49. Canadian tribesman
50. Holland export
51. Yielded
52. Dancer Verdon
55. ___ Arbor
56. Affirmative word

PUZZLE 456

ACROSS
1. Fuel
5. Lifetimes
9. Tijuana treat
13. Land measure
14. Ordinary
16. Idol
17. Take off
18. Chemist's counterweights
19. Excursion
20. Decade number
21. Phase
22. Barters
24. Deletion
26. Uttered
27. Common verb
28. Tailor's guide
31. "___ New World"
34. Free-for-all
35. Auricle
37. Roof edge
38. Stops
39. Citrus fruit
40. Night before
41. Tends tables
42. ___ and dined
43. Short trips
45. "Sanford and ___"
46. Discontinues
47. Firearm
51. Place of worship
54. Wilted
55. Native of: suffix
56. Frost
57. Musical study
59. American lake
60. Kiln
61. Handed out
62. Blend
63. Departed
64. Tavern orders
65. Puts into operation

DOWN
1. Hindu social class
2. Iron-ore pigment
3. Sports area
4. Escorted
5. Get-up
6. Incline
7. Emerald Isle
8. Fr. holy woman
9. Harangue
10. Sour
11. Morse ___
12. Singles
15. Domains
21. Certain
23. Ritual
25. Rescue
26. Smelling ___
28. Hides
29. Check
30. Identify
31. Quilting or honey
32. Yell
33. Declare
34. Damsels
36. VIP carpet color
38. Manipulated
39. Fuzz
41. Abate
42. Golf club
44. Apologize
45. Pieces of paper
47. Move furtively
48. Skirt panels
49. Practical
50. Lacks
51. Noisy bird
52. Busy place
53. Hymn ending
54. Double
58. Pekoe, e.g.
59. Australian bird

PUZZLE 457

ACROSS
1. South African of Dutch descent
5. Pierce
9. Queen of Carthage
13. Concerning: 2 wds.
14. A Beatle
15. "Hallelujah, I'm ___!": 2 wds.
16. Frank Loesser's transport: 4 wds.
19. "Sanford and ___"
20. Soprano Gluck
21. Notable pond
22. Invitational initials
23. Country stopovers
24. Pacesetter in a shell
27. Cracker spread
28. Title of A. Christie or M. Hess
31. Disposed
32. Galway Bay island group
33. ___ for one's money: 2 wds.
34. Hope route: 3 wds.
37. Pollster Roper
38. Not final
39. Geometric solid
40. Chicago trains
41. Bill
42. Irregular
43. Cut with an ax
44. Author of "Double Indemnity"
45. Levels
48. Juno
49. Pocket flap
52. Burt Bacharach knows it: 5 wds.
55. Martial god
56. Soft, twilled fabric
57. River to the Baltic
58. Impolite
59. Wear's partner
60. Agile ruminant

DOWN
1. Hines or Pinza
2. Trygve Lie's birthplace
3. Buckinghamshire town
4. Noisy quarrel
5. Actor Terrance
6. Breezy farewell: hyph.
7. Pianist Tatum
8. English poetess
9. Roald and Arlene
10. Footnote abbr.
11. Beach sight
12. Muscat's locale
14. Crack a poser
17. Circular file
18. Chair material
22. Musical form
23. Kerman native
24. Bender
25. Gnome
26. Is peripatetic
27. Lively
28. Legal claim
29. Outbreak
30. Foe
32. Kind of flu
33. Part of a stage
35. Road sign: 2 wds.
36. ___ Way, ancient Roman highway
41. Kind of ray
42. Miles or Vaughan
43. Hole for an anchor cable
44. ___ Franck
45. Deneb or Vega
46. By way of, for short
47. Rex or Walter
48. Dance done in a circle
49. Fuss: hyph.
50. In a dither
51. Emcee Parks
53. Following Mon.
54. Daily run

PUZZLE 458

ACROSS

1. Journal
4. Taunt
8. Rent
11. Mickey's ex
12. Orchards
14. Scourge
15. Favorite
16. Regret
17. Nurse's helper
18. Chairs
20. Arabian chieftains
22. Yemen seaport
23. Elongated fish
24. Black eye
27. Stops
31. Tops
32. Most secure
34. Bullfight cheer
36. Mild cigar
38. Triumph
39. Satisfied
41. Barbie's friend
42. Sound system
45. Marsh plant
46. Vacation locale
48. Spirited
50. OSS's successor
51. Newts
52. Provide food
54. Warms the oven
58. Be concerned
59. On land
61. Larry and Curly's buddy
62. Ripened
63. Farmer, sometimes
64. Time of note
65. British brew
66. Pitcher
67. Mesh

DOWN

1. Reindeer herder
2. Above
3. Portal
4. Merchants
5. Ladies
6. Currier's partner
7. Decade number
8. Den
9. Finishes
10. Twentieth letter
12. Slide
13. Guides
14. Dips water out of a boat
19. More rational
21. Track events
24. Pillage
25. Golf courses have 18
26. Silly
27. Burning
28. Philosopher Descartes
29. Carries
30. Winter precipitation
33. Reverent
35. Small whirlpool
37. Actor Davis
40. Get up
43. Coronets
44. Tenderer
47. Performed
49. Anesthetic
51. Eat away
52. Tweety Pie's home
53. Length x width
54. Exclamation of relief
55. Last word in prayer
56. Raced
57. Chair
58. Feline
60. Observe

PUZZLE 459

ACROSS
1. Joke response
5. Get lost
10. Holes in one
14. Smell ____
15. Garlic-bulb section
16. Adore
17. Corrode
18. Western movie
19. Sketched
20. Rulers
22. Links features
24. Location
25. Listen to
26. Pay up
29. Dregs
33. Gold: Sp.
34. Author Jong
36. Food shops
37. Cave dwellers
39. Ladder rung
41. ____ Scotia
42. Les ____-Unis
44. "____ We All?"
46. Part of MPH
47. Short and pudgy
49. Black birds
51. Easter flower
52. Shredded
53. Prompt
56. Certain horses
60. Woeful word
61. Earn
63. Of speech
64. Sassy
65. Mountain ridge
66. Irish republic
67. Golf gadgets
68. Unadorned
69. Act

DOWN
1. Tortoise's foe
2. Cuckoopint, e.g.
3. Door clasp
4. Bear witness
5. Children's vehicles
6. Writer Boothe Luce
7. Spoils
8. "____ Maria"
9. Joined
10. City officials
11. Apple's center
12. Level
13. Stitches
21. Annoy
23. Attack
25. Throw
26. Sensible
27. Muse of poetry
28. Whole
29. Terrifying
30. Run off to marry
31. Actor David ____
32. Russian rulers
35. Rome's country
38. Clothing designers
40. Attached securely
43. Rotate
45. Small pie
48. "The ____ and the Sea"
50. Prohibited
52. Hackneyed
53. Entranced
54. General Robert ____
55. Female horse
56. Journey
57. Part of HOMES
58. Hard to find
59. Winter toy
62. Paleozoic or Mesozoic

ACROSS

1. Takes off
6. African nation
10. Bath or Vichy
13. Cognizant
14. Italian capital
15. Saga
16. Gauge
17. Type of school: abbr.
18. Back of the neck
19. Discover
21. Binds
22. Require
23. Modify
25. Menu item
29. "Li'l ____"
31. Tender
32. Leguminous plant
34. Ms. Kett
37. Halted
39. Sells
42. "Jane ____"
43. Smooth
45. Part of a monogram: abbr.
46. Obliterate
48. Upper House
50. Party givers
52. "____ of Duty"
54. Fourposters
55. Blocked
60. Load
61. Irish land
62. Having auricles
64. Singer Burl ____
65. Family
66. Steeple
67. ____ diem
68. Toe counts
69. Adolescents

DOWN

1. Hoover or Aswan
2. Was indebted to
3. Destiny
4. Worry
5. Calm
6. ____ de menthe
7. Christmas, e.g.
8. TV sitcom
9. Belittle
10. Castle locale?
11. Uttered shrilly
12. Top pilots
15. Amuse
20. Singer Della ____
24. Run into
25. Curvy letter
26. Memo
27. Helen's home
28. Puts down
30. Uncover
33. Lyric poems
35. Singer Turner
36. Landed
38. Cheeky
40. Come after
41. Sault ____ Marie
44. Experienced
47. View
49. Author Hemingway
50. Hoist
51. More unusual
53. Baking needs
54. Radar-screen sight
56. Anger
57. Record
58. Great Lake
59. Actor Bruce ____
63. ____ Moines

PUZZLE 460

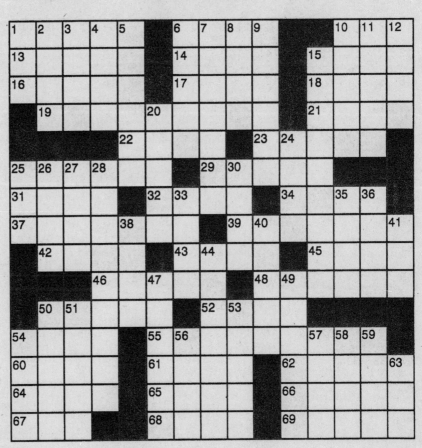

353

PUZZLE 461

ACROSS

1. Commotion
4. Shower alternative
8. Boring
12. In person
14. Bind again
15. Hawaiian island
16. Ogle
17. Go in
18. First man
19. Expanse
21. Passion
23. Angrier
25. Of higher rank
28. Vistas
30. Primped
32. For each
33. On a cruise
35. Make a speech
36. Algerian seaport
38. Bakery offerings
40. Clumsy boat
41. Sunders
43. Abominable Snowman
44. Attempt
45. Finders, sometimes
47. Sign up
50. Nocturnal sound
51. Aquatic fliers
52. Taunt
54. Abates
57. Against: pref.
60. Peeler
62. Provo's state
64. Flower necklaces
65. Inventor Howe
66. Lab burner
67. Dutch cheese
68. Buck or doe
69. Total

DOWN

1. "___ in the Family"
2. Food regimen
3. Done
4. Actor Kingsley
5. Perfume ingredient
6. Row
7. Cowboy, at times
8. Lodgers
9. Boy
10. Exclamation of discovery
11. Busy sound?
13. Wipe out
14. Refuge
20. Cheat
22. Bread spread
24. Compositions
26. Dramatizes
27. Answer
28. Baseball's World ___
29. Cowardly
30. Chatter
31. Like morning grass, sometimes
32. Kind of meat
34. Byron's before
37. Favoritism
39. "Sing You ___"
42. Very dry
46. Harvested
48. Grassy area
49. Publication
51. Spooky
53. Bargain hunter's delight
55. Kett of comics
56. Beach covering
57. Beer's kin
58. Writer Buntline
59. Pedro's aunt
61. Organ of hearing
63. Possessed

354

PUZZLE 462

ACROSS

1. Actor Bert ____
5. Arrived
9. Lump
12. Lily plant
13. Less vivid
14. Melody
15. Complain
16. Come about
17. Locale
18. Make beloved
20. Reticent
22. Feels
24. Child
25. Camper's shelter
26. Office workers, for short
30. Blubbers
33. Biting
36. Place of combat
37. Era
38. Attacks
40. Feat
41. Snatches
43. Protagonist
44. Elm or oak
45. Solemn
47. Mystery writer Gardner
49. 2,000 pounds
50. Hums
53. Related
58. Begin a paragraph
60. Kiln
61. Ham it up
63. Pennsylvania port
64. Lairs
65. Actress Hayworth et al.
66. Mature
67. Football player
68. Stage
69. Sighted

DOWN

1. Frilly fabric
2. Alda and Ladd
3. Multitude
4. Regrets
5. Auto
6. Dismounted
7. Flat-topped hill
8. Puts up
9. Hindu intellectual
10. Unusual person
11. Pinto or lima
13. Mothers
14. Rag
19. Chemical suffix
21. Bits
23. Hoard
27. Approach
28. First word in fairy tales
29. Glut
30. Droops
31. Monster
32. Rosary unit
34. Actress Charlotte ____
35. Weary
38. John Jacob ____
39. British trucks
42. Wands
44. Offers
46. Comes in
48. Actor Chaney
51. Creepy
52. Long-billed bird
53. Went by bus
54. Tied
55. Remain undecided
56. Give off
57. Love excessively
59. Youth
62. Touch lightly

355

PUZZLE 463

ACROSS

1. Attired
5. Festival
9. Crowds
13. Possess
14. Auctions off
15. In a frenzy
16. Component
17. Appeals
18. South of France
19. Breakfast food
21. Radiates
23. Diva's solo
25. Yes
26. Famous
29. Separated
34. Jogged
35. Make amends
38. Type of race
39. Again
41. Luges
43. Flirt's action
44. Fathers
46. On the up and up
48. Iron or Bronze
49. Ingested
50. Expires
52. Timeworn
55. Sandwich shop
56. Student's bane
61. Cuddle
65. Acme
66. Sudden fear
68. Wind
69. Jump
70. Overact
71. Psychic parts
72. Being: pref.
73. Wood cutters
74. Of sound mind

DOWN

1. Fashionable
2. Delayed
3. Declare
4. Humble
5. Set
6. Toward shelter
7. Andean animal
8. Appraise
9. Papa's mate
10. Skip
11. Portend
12. Hits the slopes
14. Medical-kit items
20. Zone
22. Close
24. Coral reef
26. Remove
27. Craze
28. Idle
30. Church bench
31. Pseudonym
32. Stove
33. Little kids
36. Formerly named
37. Moved sideways
40. Lilliputian
42. Quiet
45. Winter white
47. Legend
51. Zodiac fish
53. Bounds
54. Stage play
56. Ring of light
57. Clear
58. Pork or beef
59. Public exhibition
60. Comprehend
62. Roman robe
63. King of the jungle
64. Different
67. "____ My Turn"

ACROSS

1. Skirt edges
5. Emulates M.C. Hammer
9. Among
13. To the sheltered side
14. Skilled
15. Puccini work
16. Man or Wight
17. Bench
18. Christmas song
19. Takes back
21. Peaceful
22. Endure
23. Gentle tap
24. Student
27. Idol
29. With it
32. Aladdin's helper
33. Dove sound
34. Market
35. Goes to
38. Tableland
40. Cave
41. Reel's partner
43. Slants
44. "___ You Need Is Love"
45. Move up
46. Stallion
47. Congeal
48. Kind of meat
50. Helix
53. Specific
58. Tied
59. Gymnast's move
60. Knob
61. Neighborhoods
62. Play part
63. Negative answers
64. Bridge position
65. Exposed
66. Blind part

DOWN

1. Head covering
2. Alternatively
3. Thaw
4. Psychic
5. Scamp
6. Assists in crime
7. Malleable
8. Fixed
9. Detached
10. Pierre's mother
11. Press
12. Cowgirl Evans
15. Pacific, e.g.
20. Stranger
21. Thread holder
24. Flower part
25. Before
26. Dock
28. Flatfoot
29. Cads
30. Make very happy
31. Addition word
32. Festive
34. Bustle
36. Bore
37. Distress call
39. Coral island
42. Progress
45. Peruses
46. Occur
47. Wonderful
49. Banishment
50. Cabbage salad, for short
51. Diminish gradually
52. Summer treats
54. Taverns
55. Collected
56. Thought
57. Trial
59. To-and-___

PUZZLE 465

ACROSS
1. "Lord ____"
4. Play by ____
7. Drink chiller
10. Noble horse
12. Miss ____ of "Dallas"
14. Boast
15. Actress Theda ____
16. Launder
17. Pit
18. Spare
20. Male bee
22. Roll-call response
24. Prophet
25. Like some winter weather
27. Moniker
30. Ascot
31. Skipper's direction
33. Cutting tool
35. Ovum
36. Good: Fr.
37. Wire measure
38. Black cuckoo
39. Moved briskly
43. Layer
44. Walk
46. Run out
48. Of the mouth
49. Engagement
50. Poe's bird
52. Mongol
55. Vacant
56. Occupation
60. Wicked
62. "____ My Dead Body"
63. Stuffed
64. Nerve network
65. Actress Arthur
66. Turn to the right
67. Danger color

DOWN
1. Boxing move
2. "Dies ____"
3. Harpo or Groucho
4. Pipe joint
5. Malt beverage
6. Inlet
7. Golf club
8. Songwriter Porter
9. Cote denizen
11. Wash
12. Card game for two
13. Make esteemed
14. Line segment
19. Stagger
21. Tear
23. Ogle
24. Traveled on foot: Scot.
25. Omens
26. Truthful, for short
28. Light providers
29. Expel
30. Beverage for two
32. Earned
34. Actor Ron ____
39. Upset
40. Factories
41. Ecstatic
42. Info
45. Canine name
47. One of the apostles
50. Talk wildly
51. Vicinity
53. State positively
54. ____ of passage
55. Hair style
57. Scrap
58. Had lunch
59. Sandra or Ruby
61. Caused

PUZZLE 466

ACROSS
1. TV show with ***
5. Venus de ___
9. Tete-a-tete
13. District
14. Actor Jeremy
16. Job
17. Impression
18. "Bolero" composer
19. ___ go bragh
20. In addition
21. Percentage
22. Occurrences
24. Rubdown
26. Clip
27. Actress Arden
28. Humbly
32. Trite
35. Earring places
36. Fish eggs
37. Turnpike charge
38. Cut in two
39. Actress Turner
40. Ump's call
41. Guide
42. Wrapping material
43. Does well financially
45. Box top
46. Corny actors
47. Tapers
51. Turn over a new leaf
54. Rendezvous
55. Building addition
56. Butter substitute
57. Harden
59. Become dim
60. Food regimen
61. Sups
62. Phrase of comprehension: 2 wds.
63. Consumes
64. Nuisance
65. Emcee Parks

DOWN
1. "Call Me ___"
2. Field of action
3. Dispatches
4. Fedora
5. Desert phenomenon
6. Teed-off
7. Affection
8. Countdown ending
9. Crawls
10. Trumpet
11. Came to earth
12. Hamilton bills
15. Slim
21. Talk wildly
23. Contends
25. Market
26. Solemn
28. Inspires
29. Snare
30. ___ Ranger
31. Twelve months
32. Red sign
33. Excursion
34. Female voice
35. Ogles
38. Stopped the flow of
39. Actor Alan
41. Mast
42. Lonesome tree
44. Uses a camera
45. Most recent
47. Minds
48. Rent agreement
49. Church official
50. Frozen rain
51. Went by train
52. Novelist Kazan
53. Stand on your own two ___
54. Sand hill
58. ___ and tuck
59. White lie

359

PUZZLE 467

ACROSS
1. Rounded roof
5. Playing marble
10. Scratches
14. Special nights
15. Columbus's 1492 starting point
16. Indian nurse
17. Instrument in Bonn
20. Explosive charge: abbr.
21. Architectural curve
22. Loosen
23. City on the Oka
24. Cribbage cards
26. Colorless gas
29. Actor Betz
30. Former Myanmar capital
33. Smell ____
34. Excuse
35. Mal de ____
36. Well-tempered item
40. Antlered animal
41. Pursue
42. ____-Aryan
43. Draft inits.
44. Exit ____
45. Closet item
47. Flying prefix
48. Like Yul or Telly
49. Out of practice
52. Famous Scottie
53. Trouble
56. Italian instrument
60. Mimic
61. Oncle's mate
62. Traipse
63. Condition
64. Celerity
65. Green pegs

DOWN
1. IOU
2. "Hansel and Gretel" prop
3. "____ the Press"
4. Guess: abbr.
5. Most distant point
6. Courtroom pounder
7. Opposite of aweather
8. Heavy weight
9. Road curve
10. Water carriers
11. Amo, amas, ____
12. Hindu queen
13. Smithy item
18. Tooter
19. Citizens
23. Promise
24. Believing
25. Urbi et ____
26. Toyland visitors
27. Russian mountains
28. Small nails
29. Holder
30. In the midst of
31. Cape ____
32. Vim
34. Crockett's last stand
37. Test or door
38. Burn slightly
39. Back
45. Divided, in a way
46. Jai ____
47. Distress call
48. Sew
49. Small quarrel
50. Type of measure
51. Teen follower
52. Very thin
53. Lilylike plant
54. Nose or swan
55. Individuals
57. ____ a boy!
58. Short snooze
59. Crumb

360

PUZZLE 468

ACROSS
1. Tastes
5. Pant
9. Blackboard marker
14. Zone
15. Medicinal plant
16. Mortal
17. Great
19. Remain
20. Enroll
21. Falls behind
23. Ruby or Sandra
24. Scottish Gaelic
27. Snug retreat
29. First-rate
33. Long, angry speech
37. ___ carte
38. Celtic land
40. Kind of energy
41. Joins
43. Tall stories
45. Former Yugoslav VIP
46. Occurrence
48. Sounds a horn
50. Motor coach
51. Vacation spot
53. Midday
55. Lumber
57. Matched set
58. Court
61. Jump
63. Squeeze
67. Smithy's item
69. Revolving gate
72. Act part
73. Toledo's lake
74. Spanish rahs
75. Cent
76. Rush-hour prize
77. Current events

DOWN
1. Secure
2. Persia today
3. Confined
4. Glossy fabric
5. Fuel
6. High in pitch
7. Earth
8. Nutty pie
9. Vehicle's framework
10. Wheel part
11. Among
12. Put cargo aboard
13. Cap or deep
18. Archer's projectile
22. Obtain
25. Reprieve
26. Fanfare
28. Quick pace
29. Slender candle
30. Martini garnish
31. Glass sections
32. Wading bird
34. "Her ___"
35. Individual fact
36. Worn away
39. Pry
42. Winter white
44. Porch, in Athens
47. Transport of old
49. Cuts
52. Water tester
54. Poseidon's son
56. Palm fruits
58. Kind of waist
59. Formerly
60. Kitchen appliance
62. Innocent
64. Cleo's river
65. Yarn quantity
66. Dame Myra ___
68. Wayside tavern
70. Creek
71. Clear after deductions

361

PUZZLE 469

ACROSS
1. Cat's foot
4. ___ roe
8. Vow taker
13. Hay unit
14. Flow freely
15. Lofty nest
16. Toward the mouth
17. Penetrating preposition
18. Delay
19. Often-white garment
22. TV's Danson
23. Indisposed
24. Gloomy
27. Wood covering
30. At any time
31. Pungent taste
32. Name
34. Baste
38. Rock-star Cooper
40. Interval
42. Roman official
43. Fragrant woods
45. Gist
47. Yellow cheese
48. Recognized
50. Fostered
52. More weighty
54. Type of steer
55. I love: Lat.
56. Small member of the party
62. Bulky
65. Work
66. "Othello" character
67. Paper unit
68. Pit
69. Colorless
70. Brewers' ovens
71. Consequences
72. Tokyo currency

DOWN
1. Young salmon
2. Jai ___
3. Reception dessert
4. Tumbled
5. ___ Kong
6. Mat or mobile
7. Doze
8. Neon, e.g.
9. Steep, as flax
10. Give a speech
11. Canadian athlete
12. Blend
13. Short haircut
20. Pub brew
21. Calendar abbrs.
25. Apportion
26. Bouquet carriers
27. Singer Jerry
28. Oklahoma city
29. Slangy toupee
31. Tic -___-toe
33. Forbid
35. Yule or even ending
36. Dressed
37. Border
39. Sea birds
41. Witticism
44. Prophet
46. Champagne feature
49. Twist
51. Regret
52. Midwestern city
53. Drills
55. In addition
57. Lunchtime for some
58. Coat with gold
59. Infrequent
60. Actor Richard
61. Director Reiner
63. Catch
64. French connections

PUZZLE 470

ACROS
1. Ant of rock
5. Struck hard
10. ___ Kett
14. Actor Lugosi
15. Arctic explorer
16. Graceful bird
17. Abba ___
18. Edition
19. Shredded
20. Poker holdings
22. Glistened
23. Sticky stuff
24. Robber
26. Part of PG
31. Printed mistakes
34. Dote on
35. Twin crystal
37. Sunflower State: abbr.
38. Beams
39. Twofold
40. Stone chest
41. High note
42. Sharpener
43. Three-card ___
44. Merchant
46. Marooned
48. Wells ___
50. Catchall abbr.
51. Mexican sauce
53. It will beat 20 Across
59. Musical work
60. Courtyards
61. Roads: abbr.
62. ___ Arnaz
63. Principle
64. Small arrow
65. Netman Arthur
66. Result
67. ___ butter

DOWN
1. Actor Vigoda et al.
2. Obligation
3. Winglike
4. Directors
5. Tap
6. Grid
7. Kiln
8. Reliance
9. Needle hole
10. Swimmer Williams
11. Pair of peas in a pod
12. Mountain lake
13. Actress Bancroft
21. "Pompeii" heroine
22. Beget
25. Underworld
26. Trims
27. Allan- ___: hyph.
28. It beats 53 Across
29. ___ Gemayel
30. Byways
32. Sample food
33. Fed the kitty
36. Dray
39. Netman Bjorn ___
40. Table grapes
42. Zeus's wife
43. Arithmetic, for short
45. TV collie
47. Recount
49. Frequently
51. Bar mixer
52. Gorillas
54. Samovars
55. Stead
56. Beehive State
57. Withered
58. This: Sp.
60. Broke a fast

363

PUZZLE 471

ACROSS

1. Demolish, in England
5. Entranced
9. Retails
14. Asian lake
15. ___ Cinders
16. Music hall
17. Thickens
18. Afrikaans
19. Liquid measure, abroad
20. Opposite of WSW
21. Indigo plant
22. Make amends
23. Needlework unit
27. Soap ingredient
28. Before, poetically
29. Sphere
32. Shortly
34. Surface measure
35. Covered walk
36. Needlework unit
40. Dill herb
41. Diving bird
42. Seth's son
43. Expanse
44. Bridle part
45. Literary scraps
46. Needlework unit
52. Accept formally
55. Vestments
56. ___ mode
57. Boat hoist
58. Falsehood
59. Hebrew instrument
60. Roman magistrate
61. Radiate
62. Anglo-Saxon laborer
63. Passover feast
64. Impudence
65. Appear

DOWN

1. Stormed
2. Sports mecca
3. Oregon capital
4. Old railroads
5. Film do-over
6. Ladd and Hale
7. Braid
8. Scorekeepers
9. Comfort
10. TV's dingbat
11. Apollo's mother
12. Abandoned
13. Snick-a- ___
24. High up
25. In ___ (harmony)
26. ___ bien
29. German king
30. Fabulous birds
31. Humbug!
32. Sensible
33. Olive genus
34. Question
35. Biblical mountain
36. Owns
37. Shower
38. Exits
39. Canvas shelter
44. Resentful
45. Possessions
46. Barrel spigot
47. Beast of burden
48. The Devil (Koran)
49. Cup, in Crecy
50. Duplicate
51. Seraglio
52. Soft drinks
53. Miami county
54. Roman poet
59. Roman bronze

ACROSS
1. Find fault
5. Church service
9. Biscuit
13. ___ avis
14. Howdy!
15. Bacchanalian cry
16. Imitator
17. Close, in verse
18. Egg repository
19. Black suit
21. Unpleasant sights
23. Performs
25. ___ polloi
26. North Carolina native
29. Old World
33. Ad campaign, for short
34. Neighbor of Tibet
36. French refusal
37. Paddles
38. Hemmed
39. "Family ___"
40. N.Y. summer hrs.
41. Foundation
42. Speckled horses
43. Kidder
45. Slight advantage
47. "___ Joey"
48. Proofreading word
49. More insolent
54. Desire greatly
58. Corridor
59. A Bronte
61. Mere
62. Ellipse
63. Rope fiber
64. Part of TV
65. Ballpoints
66. Low card
67. Flock mamas

DOWN
1. Monks
2. Arctic native
3. ___ code
4. Sail supports
5. Chess pieces
6. Toward shelter
7. Make laugh
8. Bad sport
9. French artist
10. Concluded
11. Misplace
12. "___ Do It"
14. Quickness
20. Reverberation
22. "Body and ___"
24. Transmits
26. Swap
27. Main artery
28. On the up and up
30. Tatum ___
31. Sixteen ounces
32. Termini
33. Bard
35. Mexican coins
38. Soonest
39. Minor comment
41. Bill
42. Miss Perlman
44. Trances
46. Antiknock fluid
49. Karate blow
50. Own
51. Gusto
52. Arab prince
53. ___ and shine
55. Recognized
56. She: Fr.
57. Dark breads
60. Minstrel's song

PUZZLE 473

ACROSS

1. Do the backstroke
5. Scratch
9. Irish dramatist
14. Pisa's river
15. Zhivago's girl
16. Rebelled
17. Navy craft
19. Poe's bird
20. Express excitement
21. Redcaps
23. ___ capita
24. "___ Rita"
25. ___ de menthe
29. Least hypocritical
35. Riverbank
36. Grizzly
37. Fourth mo.
38. Designer Cassini
39. Hebrew lawgiver
41. French cheese
42. Moving truck
43. Lump of ice
44. Rhymers
45. Taking by intimidation
48. Condor's habitat
49. Actor's hint
50. "___ Magic"
52. Liberal
56. In the center
61. Thoughts
62. Navy craft
64. Scoundrel
65. On high
66. Eye part
67. Cafe patron
68. Budget item
69. Spreads to dry

DOWN

1. Marquis de ___
2. English architect
3. Academy: abbr.
4. Garment varmint
5. Shut
6. Cake tiers
7. "You ___ My Sunshine"
8. Distort
9. Navy craft
10. Spellbinder
11. Adoration
12. Consumer
13. "The ___ Club"
18. Indian coin
22. Killer whales
25. Garlic section
26. Take a break
27. Tournament
28. Actress Tilly
30. Norwegian dramatist
31. Society-page word
32. Auricular
33. Malice
34. Curl
39. Muffles
40. Kimono sash
41. ___ vivant
43. Navy craft
44. Linguini, for one
46. Do to do
47. Asian ape
51. Entice
52. Prefer
53. Actress Best
54. Brave deed
55. Russian king
57. Court order
58. Irish republic
59. Arthurian lady
60. Scottish lake
63. Shoshoni

ACROSS

1. Applaud
5. Track events
10. Seed cover
14. Jack rabbit
15. Courtyards
16. Whittle
17. Roman road
18. African mammal
19. Paid athletes
20. Titleholder
22. Special ability
24. Years upon years
25. Father
26. Bathhouse
29. Farewell act
33. Friendship
34. Painter Rivera
35. Book: abbr.
36. Go by car
37. Sonata movement
38. Vena ____
39. Develop
40. Red cosmetic
41. Fence portals
42. Turtle
44. Monopoly buys
45. ____ dixit
46. Kennel adjuncts
47. Omit
50. TV captain
54. Out of the wind
55. Put into office
57. Cable
58. Back end
59. Hindu queen
60. Jai ____
61. Trend setters, for short
62. Saber
63. Holler

DOWN

1. Vogue
2. Wood strip
3. Locale
4. Seep into
5. Yacht haven
6. Group character
7. Actress Moran
8. Roofing metal
9. Cape Verde island
10. Winesaps
11. Undercooked
12. Potential steel
13. For fear that
21. Small horse
23. Pisa's river
25. Scandinavian
26. Gold weight
27. Spanish friend
28. One who waits
29. Scorch
30. Ellipsoidal
31. Fiction work
32. Pane material
34. Wet thoroughly
37. Revels
38. "When the ____, the mice ..."
40. Lasso
41. Dinner bell
43. Jungle cats
44. Pursued
46. Sports car
47. "Animal ____"
48. Margarine
49. Interpret
50. Game of chance
51. Annoy
52. Unwritten
53. Trompe l'____
56. Statute

PUZZLE 475

ACROSS
1. Bursts
5. Russian emperor
9. Converse
13. Baseballer Tommie ———
14. Fry lightly
15. Wharf
16. Strip of wood
17. Had title to
18. Bugbear
19. Zone
21. Ginger cookie
23. Mortar mixer
24. Gruff
26. Ship's men
28. Likely
30. Blow a horn
31. Synagogue scrolls
34. Exclude
35. Mops
37. Check receiver
38. On a cruise
40. Espies
42. Saxophonist Getz
43. Hull
45. More reliable
47. Old English money
48. Spring festival
50. Moon goddess
51. FDR's successor
52. Muscle condition
53. Come forth
55. Rowing blade
57. Serb
59. Water bottle
62. Prayer
64. Iowa colony
66. Sinful
67. Ripened
68. Wearies
69. Congers
70. Overdue
71. Whirlpool
72. Housemaid's ———

DOWN
1. Go by
2. Stare at
3. Atlanta thorough-fare: 2 wds.
4. Brief fight: hyph.
5. Shooting marble
6. Gloria Swanson film: 2 wds.
7. Sun god
8. Edit
9. Navy noncom: abbr.
10. Michael Landon series: 3 wds.
11. Of flying
12. Hatrack
14. Woes
20. Sow wild ———
22. Brace
25. Daytime serials
27. Epochs
28. Degrade
29. Turkish title
32. Listens
33. French legislative body
36. Play a guitar
39. Quartet member
41. New York Indians
44. Camera eye
46. Strange: Sp
49. Empathize
54. Hellene
55. Milky gem
56. Water growth
58. During
60. Emery board
61. In addition
63. Orange drink
65. Duke of Elchingen

PUZZLE 476

ACROSS
1. Hazel, for one
5. Cartwright son
9. ____ -o'- shanter
12. Bohemian
13. Tree seed
15. Quaker word
16. Control
17. TV, etc.
18. Rabbit ____
19. Instance: Fr.
20. Woe is me!
21. "Merchant" role
23. Madison Ave. folks
25. Unfilled
26. Expect
27. Virginia family
28. Seize
31. See 3 Down
32. Premier
33. Plaza cheer
34. American Beauty, e.g.
35. Parking site
36. Duos
37. Falstaff's quaff
38. Bridges
40. ____ a ghost of a chance
41. U.K. milit. gp.
42. Annoys
43. Hiding place
44. Kelps
46. Singer Page
47. "____ and Cleopatra"
49. French stoneware
50. Blue
53. Oven
54. Small cases
56. Opening
57. "Pan" pirate
58. Theatrics
59. Remus, to Romulus
60. Row
61. Turkish title
62. ____ Capp

DOWN
1. Artist Chagall
2. Location
3. W.S. quote, with 9 Down and 31 Across
4. Power prefix
5. W.S. hero
6. Indian, e.g.
7. Plants
8. ____ Lanka
9. See 3 Down
10. Flying prefix
11. Tableland
14. Italian seaport
15. Aquatic flier
20. Between
22. Kiln
24. Cowgirl Evans
25. Parks et al.
26. ____ in one
27. Big cats
29. Unattended
30. Tops
31. Soft-shell ____
32. Chip
36. Discretion
38. Initial
39. Pleaded
40. Derbies
43. He said, "Et tu, Brute!"
45. Legends
46. First: Lat.
47. Ditto
48. Thread: pref.
49. Pacific battle island
51. Waterless
52. Disagree
55. Due's follower
56. School gp.

PUZZLE 477

ACROSS

1. Morsels
5. Fellows
10. Jewels
14. Land measure
15. Hilo porch
16. Medicinal plant
17. Mannerless one
18. Startle
19. Cat that roars
20. Give for safekeeping
22. Blockhead
24. Deadly snakes
25. English lavatory
26. Claims
29. Coaches
34. Nose and pine
35. Great deeds
36. Mrs. Nixon
37. Copied
38. Sprite
39. Parched
40. Meadow
41. Actor Lloyd
42. Expensive
43. Does
45. Derby entrants
46. Mr. Carney
47. Luau dance
48. Sentence-parser's subject
52. Ohio town
56. Jacob's son
57. Goatee
59. World Series unit
60. Baal
61. Tag
62. Ireland
63. Extremely thin
64. Clean the slate
65. Grade

DOWN

1. Baseballer Ruth
2. Religious image
3. Jogging gait
4. Toothed
5. Grips
6. Ceases
7. Literary collection
8. Cowboy's chum
9. Feign
10. Gasoline unit
11. ____ Kazan
12. Place for heather
13. Dispatch
21. Applies
23. Miss Lane
26. Head part
27. Pith helmet
28. Lend ____: 2 wds.
29. Waco's location
30. Downpour
31. Tools for duels
32. Peep show
33. Rungs
35. Movie
38. Easy to carry
39. Alien
41. Standard
42. Aria
44. TV's "____ Feud"
45. Jump over
47. Takes on
48. Smooth-talking
49. Make over
50. Shakespeare's river
51. Bring up
53. Scarlett's home
54. Pass over
55. Hawaiian goose
58. Arabian garment

PUZZLE 478

ACROSS
1. Capital of Italia
5. ___ aves
10. Magnitude
14. Revise
15. Deteriorate
16. Honk
17. Taboo
18. Stun
19. Sicilian sizzler
20. Rained lightly
22. Drips
23. Elderly
24. Johnnycake ingredient
26. Noble domain
30. Pie producer
34. Fresh air
35. San Diego athlete
36. Make bigger: abbr.
37. Reddish-brown color
38. Julie Andrews role
39. Writer Grey
40. Before, in poetry
41. Models
42. Appraiser
43. Uninhabited
45. Take off
46. Walking aid
47. Criticize
48. Spicy
51. Decisive time
56. Director Kazan
57. Game
59. Pilaster
60. Astronaut Shepard
61. Ascended
62. Final letters
63. Gold cloth
64. Jim Nabors role
65. Being: Lat.

DOWN
1. Divide
2. Smell
3. Short skirt
4. From ___ (completely)
5. Truly
6. Ready for war
7. Street
8. Carpenter's tool
9. Shoe width
10. "Remington ___"
11. Particle
12. Clobber
13. Greek vowels
21. "The Twilight ___"
22. Idle
24. Skirt types
25. Poet Pound
26. Put to sleep
27. Sky blue
28. Summer bloomers
29. Canadian province: abbr.
30. Gay ___
31. Lasso
32. Spiritual
33. Aware
35. Glue
38. Sound of pain
39. Shoot
41. Romp
42. Gambling town
44. Gasoline measure
45. Snakebird
47. Intrinsically
48. Enthusiasm
49. Singer Fitzgerald
50. "Anna and the King of ___"
51. Speed
52. Fog
53. Wallet items
54. Shoshonean Indians
55. Destroy
57. Slump
58. Paid player

PUZZLE 479

ACROSS

1. Part of GBS
5. Ms. Astaire
10. Wheel track
13. Elegant
14. Obscure
15. Unlocked
17. Vulnerable:
    4 wds.
19. WWII battle
    site: 2 wds.
20. Refrain
    syllable
21. Suit to ___:
    2 wds.
22. Preferably
24. Actor Savage
25. British sword
26. Swirled
29. Avowed
32. Diving birds
33. Hindu queen
34. Anger
35. Planted
36. King of
    Judea
37. Tied
38. Dancer
    Miller
39. Straightedge
40. Choose by
    vote
41. Added spices
    to
43. Coquettes
44. Prod
45. Taxis
46. Sponger
48. History Muse
49. Skill
52. Greek portico
53. Troubled:
    3 wds.
56. Guided trip
57. Percolate
58. Solitary
59. Peaks: abbr.
60. Jerks
61. "En garde"
    weapon

DOWN

1. Espy
2. Sixty
   minutes
3. The
   Charleses'
   dog
4. Which
   person
5. Lessened
6. Removed
7. Ms. Adams
8. River to the
   Drina
9. Hugged
10. Pulpits
11. Imprisoned,
    slangily:
    3 wds.
12. The T of TV
16. And not
18. Nostrils
23. Competent
24. Helsinki
    native
25. Mister: Sp.
26. Lanchester
    et al.
27. "Lorna
    ___"
28. Destitute:
    3 wds.
29. Risked
30. Build
31. Hollows
33. U.S. Grant's
    foe: 3 wds.
36. Ravenously
37. Yale
    students
39. Went by car
40. Arm joint
42. Sweetens
43. Denomina-
    tions
45. Timepiece
46. Chicago zone
    inits.
47. Molecule
48. Oland role
49. Upon
50. Director
    Clair
51. Coatrack
54. Teachers' gp.
55. Pub potion

PUZZLE 480

ACROSS

1. Mist
6. Married
9. Suspension
13. Boscs, e.g.
14. Bambi, for one
15. Quickness
16. Mr. Palmer
17. Singer Fitzgerald
18. Music and dance, e.g.
19. Little girl ingredients: 3 wds.
22. Distress call
23. Bard's before
24. Pied Piper follower
27. Tiny amount
28. Arabian garments
31. Cuckoo
32. Mideast land
34. God of war
36. Lovely, as a complexion: hyph.
41. Edible root
42. Greek goddess
43. Consumed
44. Ewes' mates
46. Promise
47. Reap's partner
48. Flightless bird
50. ___ Paulo
51. Table spices: 3 wds.
58. Bridge
60. Lost
61. Legal contract
62. Hourglass material
63. Hold on property
64. French river
65. Very: Fr.
66. Something to lend or bend
67. Blundered

DOWN

1. Health spots
2. Incan country
3. Tolled
4. Song for Pavarotti
5. Belgian river
6. Joins together
7. Lampreys
8. Curtain
9. Typewriter part: 2 wds.
10. Weight allowance
11. Play division
12. Consenting word
14. Names
20. Stage whisper
21. ___ Levin
24. Ecstatic
25. Close, poetically
26. Headdress
27. Exclamation of disgust
29. Regions
30. Asian treaty inits.
33. Negative exclamation
35. River duck
37. Orders
38. Person from Reno
39. Hang
40. Crow's cry
45. Musical note
49. "___ of Two Cities": 2 wds.
50. Scoff
51. Lucid
52. Largest continent
53. Something other
54. Contemporary
55. Two of a kind
56. Serf
57. Musical instrument
58. Fast plane
59. Golf score

373

PUZZLE 481

ACROSS
1. Speedy
5. Rotund
10. Buckeye State
14. Actress Jackson
15. Biblical tower site
16. Author Ayn
17. Offset
20. Flap
21. Mine yields
22. Pastry items
23. Poke
24. Calf's cry
26. Hide
29. Game plan
32. Follow secretly
33. City in Cornwall
34. Sphere
36. Illegal: hyph.
40. Sack
41. Expunge
42. Lab burner
43. Abates
45. Pact
47. Soup vegetable
48. Chow
49. Hindu supreme spirit
52. ____ and sciences
53. Debate side
56. Retaliatory actions
60. Inkling
61. Malign
62. Batons
63. Olympic site
64. Humors
65. Space agcy.

DOWN
1. Reality
2. Sulawesi ox
3. Defy
4. X
5. Merle of movies
6. Opened to view
7. Wanes
8. Coral or Red
9. Building wing
10. Showy
11. Chop
12. Arrow poison
13. Advantage
18. Ripped
19. Cashew nut
23. Name in soccer
24. Dern of films
25. Parrot fish
26. Short pencil
27. Waterway
28. Riva ____
29. Iron
30. Terra ____
31. English river
33. Express gratitude to
35. Donkey sound
37. Begrudge
38. Arboretum specimen
39. Necessity
44. Tilts
45. Adds up
46. Singer Diana
48. Released
49. Pain
50. Struggle
51. Actor Paul
52. Pulpit desk
53. Malay canoe
54. Cardinal and scarlet
55. Greek peak
57. "Nightmare" street
58. ____ Grande
59. Samovar

PUZZLE 482

ACROSS
1. Bulk
5. Talk
10. Scout's exploit
14. Italian city
15. Atmospheres of places
16. Egyptian skink
17. Anatole France novel: 3 wds.
19. Baal
20. English drink
21. British statesman
22. Open ___
24. Put up with
26. Restrain
27. ___ Yutang
28. Raging
32. Celerity
35. The Campbells, e.g.
36. Poison
37. Love, in Madrid
38. Drudge
39. Attachment
40. Used in "Three Coins in a Fountain"
41. Birthday dessert
42. Gay ___
43. Cross
45. Snead's need
46. Writer Murdoch
47. Hold dear
51. Notify
54. Increase
55. Letter from Athens
56. Labor
57. Li'l Abner's mother: 2 wds.
60. Woman's magazine
61. Ham it up
62. ___-beche
63. Brewer's ingredient
64. Shut out
65. German river

DOWN
1. Having a dull finish
2. Pale
3. Place of another
4. Knight's title
5. Dishearten
6. Whimpered
7. Actress Moran
8. Indian mulberry
9. Slapstick Kops
10. Henry James novel: 2 wds.
11. Icelandic classic
12. Esau
13. Robertson or Evans
18. Spooky
23. Attention
25. Rays found in sunlight
26. Barrel part
28. Quench
29. Genus of cetaceans
30. Exigency
31. Dancer Kelly
32. Stop
33. Arab leader
34. Carolina rail
35. "A Touch of ___"
38. Penny-pinched
42. Like a pub brew
44. Deviate
45. "Father of the Military Academy"
47. ___ Rica
48. Pestered
49. Author of "On the Beach"
50. Epic writer
51. Article
52. Lopez's song
53. Glut
54. Snooty one
58. Soul: Fr.
59. American Indian

375

PUZZLE 483

ACROSS
1. Country road
5. Josip Broz
9. Indulgence period
14. Maestro Stravinsky
15. Caesar's nemesis
16. Thoughts: Fr.
17. Strong emotion
18. Small oceans
19. Gold measure
20. Where ___ you going?
21. Biblical king
22. Rene's friend
24. Mouths
25. Roman emperor
28. Cuckoo
30. Average grade
31. Greek statesman
36. Bus expenses
39. Type of jacket
40. Hawaiian seaport
41. ___ du Diable
42. Quick
44. Part of i.e.
45. Milk: Fr.
47. Portuguese India, once
48. Ebb and neap
50. Cretan monster
52. Spade
53. Crumb
54. Greek philosopher
59. Unmoving: abbr.
62. WWI army: abbr.
64. Prohibit
65. Mine output
66. Rented
68. Virginia ___
70. Sicilian hot spot
71. Emulate Cicero
72. Celtic language
73. Train runway
74. Fisherman
75. Binds
76. Alcoholic beverages

DOWN
1. Spring garden bloom
2. Greek marketplace
3. New
4. Anagram for ree
5. Tracing paper
6. Epitome
7. Social beverage
8. Greek mountain
9. Brief bathing suit
10. Ancient mountain in Crete
11. Roman emperor
12. Outfit
13. This: Sp.
21. Epochs
23. French revolutionary
26. Frozen water
27. Looms
29. "___ bin ein Berliner"
32. Always, to Longfellow
33. Fibbed
34. Different
35. Tipplers
36. Newman's milieu
37. Turkish regiment
38. Horse holder
42. Playing marble
43. Baseballer Gehrig
46. In addition
48. Mountain lake
49. "___ Yankee Doodle . . .": 2 wds.
51. Merchant
52. Animals' protective plates
55. Corpulent
56. Sum
57. Comedian Kovacs
58. Marine animals
59. Brogan, e.g.
60. Car part
61. Asian lake
63. Guitar part
67. Summer, in the Riviera
69. Assam silkworm
70. Historical period

376

PUZZLE 484

ACROSS
1. Tooth
6. Useful thing
11. Eng. TV network
14. Cognizant
15. English novelist
16. Bet
17. Tough guys: hyph.
18. Las Vegas regulars
20. Maintain security
22. Chirp
23. Biblical prophet
25. Willow tree
28. Probability
29. Recent: prefix
30. Of a city official
32. Robert Urich role
34. Guide a ship
39. Creative persons: 2 wds.
42. Granada ladies
43. Intellectual
45. " . . . have your cake and ___": 2 wds.
46. Agrees
49. Adjective ending
50. Kind of test
54. Rarin' to go
55. Times of day: abbr.
56. Water buffalo
58. "The ___ Boy" (Jerry Lewis film)
60. Artificial lake
63. Deadbolts
66. Lyric work
67. Circular
68. Holy place
69. Forget-me-___
70. Silvery fish
71. Annoyances

DOWN
1. ___-jongg
2. Be in debt
3. Satirizer
4. Vicinities
5. Budget item
6. Merchant ship
7. Aquatic animal: 2 wds.
8. "Cheers" man
9. Dutch town
10. Research
11. Extort money from
12. Opened
13. Vesicles
19. Pair
21. Brown kiwi
23. Prank
24. Civil War general
26. Periods
27. Ecstatic review
30. African snake
31. Queues
33. No, in Edinburgh
35. Tibetan gazelle
36. Things made by man
37. Contaminate
38. ___ Park, Colorado
40. Gaelic
41. Space org.
44. Long gaiter
47. ___-well: hyph.
48. Numerical prefix
50. Baseball's Hank
51. Belief
52. Mosaic piece
53. River in Scotland
55. ___ in one: 2 wds.
57. Miscues
59. Affront
61. Famous radio monogram
62. Possessive
64. Krazy ___
65. Near grads

377

PUZZLE 485

ACROSS
1. Ship of the desert
6. Rules
10. Deception
14. Make good
15. "Dies ___"
16. Where the Truckee flows
17. Clark's partner
18. Aquatic flier
19. Baker's need
20. Assists: 3 wds.
22. Orderly
23. Sufficient, to poets
24. Diner
26. Navy man
30. Pointer
32. Algonquin
33. Noted clinic
35. Titled
39. Consideration in streamlining
41. Regarding that matter
43. Louisiana inlet
44. Jacob's twin
46. Costly
47. Increase
49. Usually
51. French farewells
54. Like ___ of bricks: 2 wds.
56. ___ Hashana
57. Later
63. ___ boy!: 2 wds.
64. Lure
65. Nip in the bud
66. Bewilder
67. Relative of 18 Across
68. Color again
69. Observed
70. Table parts
71. Refuse

DOWN
1. Summon
2. Suit to ___: 2 wds.
3. Cut
4. Wife of Geraint
5. Tenant
6. Printing process, for short
7. Sunken yard
8. Alert
9. Letter writer
10. Toward the bow
11. Riverbank
12. Close, to Whittier
13. "___ Python's Flying Circus"
21. Wind: prefix
25. First-rate: hyph.
26. Strike-breaker
27. Assam silkworm
28. High nest
29. Previously
31. Church list
34. Overwhelms
36. Swimmer's event
37. Latin abbr.
38. Fishing boat
40. Feast, Oahu style
42. Wit
45. Cushioned upholstery
48. Actress Sanford
50. "___, Christian Soldiers"
51. Originate
52. Loco
53. Edition
55. Heads: Fr.
58. Cab levy
59. State with conviction
60. Decorate again
61. Prohibitionists
62. Fr. holy women

378

PUZZLE 486

ACROSS
1. Diamond decision
5. ___ stick
9. Expense
13. Egyptian goddess
14. States positively
16. Sulawesi ox
17. Barnum & Bailey specialty: 2 wds.
20. Take notice of
21. Country road
22. Signs up
23. Manufactured
24. Blyth and Miller
25. "___ Fair"
27. Fragments
28. Feather stole
31. Backbone
32. Gats
33. Trickle
34. Confined
35. United
36. Big-top performers
37. Sleeve lurkers
38. Drove too fast
39. Embankment
40. Three times, in prescriptions
41. Nobleman
42. Passenger
43. Scoff
44. Takes to court
45. Sprouts
48. Privation
49. Youngster
52. Lives dangerously: 3 wds.
55. Toward shelter
56. Pie portion
57. Level
58. Uncouth one
59. "___ in the Attic"
60. Conquer

DOWN
1. Poses
2. Arthur of tennis
3. Inferno
4. Opposite of WNW
5. Colorful march
6. Sheeplike
7. Actor Hackman
8. Association: abbr.
9. Hauls
10. Story opener
11. Disillusioned
12. Russian news bureau
15. Perfumes
18. In seventh heaven
19. Hotels
23. Prides' prides
24. Gave assistance
25. Kind of capsule
26. "Burning bright" creature
27. Goof
28. Courageous
29. Fuel tanker
30. Church part
31. Shoo!
32. Lariat user
33. Exploits
36. Craftiest
38. Teeter-totter
41. Favored ones
42. Moves hurriedly
43. Batman's enemy
44. Wet
45. Use a mop
46. Aura
47. Muffin topper
48. Italian resort
49. Hold dear
50. Imitates
51. Hollow
53. Asian holiday
54. Johnny ___

PUZZLE 487

ACROSS
1. Ready
5. ___ Park, Colorado
10. Farm structure
14. Eve's mate
15. Nautical direction
16. Harvest
17. Arm or leg
18. Char
19. Rajah's wife
20. Delaying
22. Vindicate
24. Positive responses
25. Fish-eating duck
26. Coater
29. Godsend
33. Misplace
34. Courage
35. Kin: abbr.
36. Pitcher's aims
37. Classifies
38. Tar
39. You, in Bonn
40. "___ Boomer"
41. North American Indians
42. Military rank
44. Some baseball hits
46. Slightly cooked
47. Hoods' pieces
48. Spanish city
51. Lawmakers
55. Lotion ingredient
56. Elected
58. Bad
59. Scottish group
60. Rub out
61. Fee
62. "Citizen ___"
63. Stormed
64. Cabbage dish

DOWN
1. Guys' dates
2. Mine entrance
3. Baby's first word
4. Illuminates
5. Simpler
6. Rotates
7. Chinese society
8. Work unit
9. Irons, at times
10. Metal fasteners
11. Teheran's country
12. Hanker
13. Mayberry denizen
21. Soap ingredient
23. Part of a three-piece suit
25. Bed boards
26. Sheen
27. Danny DeVito role on "Taxi"
28. Star flower
29. French headgear
30. Enraged
31. Not even once
32. Actress Sharon ___
34. Singer Lena ___
37. Pirate
38. Jokers
40. Noggin
43. Lorne or Graham
44. "The Eagle Has ___"
45. Philippine native
47. Silly creatures
48. Short nail
49. Spanish jar
50. Lend
51. For men only
52. Racetrack shape
53. Singer Coolidge
54. Lot
57. Mouths

PUZZLE 488

ACROSS
1. Coasted
5. TV host Philbin
10. Gab
14. Part of TLC
15. Play the ham
16. Lasso
17. Upon
18. Dine
19. What ____ is new?
20. Dwelling house
22. Exchanges
24. Blockhead
25. Root vegetable
26. Consider
29. Coax
33. Mine product
34. Singing voice
36. Willow and birch
37. Misters
39. Challenged
41. Coastal fliers
42. Lucky number
44. Paris subway
46. Native: suff.
47. Lifted up
49. James ____ of "Gunsmoke"
51. Arden and Brenner
52. Small insect
53. Horse color
56. Funny people?
60. Asian mountain range
61. Free
63. Threesome
64. Chow ____
65. Mr. Fudd
66. Cadence
67. Ditty
68. Hollow grasses
69. Morays

DOWN
1. Begone!
2. Overdue
3. Heavy metal
4. Rely
5. Attributed
6. Change
7. Can eater
8. "____ a Gift"
9. Hunting dog
10. Beast
11. Grasp
12. Church part
13. Summer shirts
21. Come upon
23. Nap
25. Artist's cap
26. Sheriff's group
27. Bay window
28. Courage
29. Meditated
30. Lofty nest
31. Fender scars
32. Snaky letters
35. Calls
38. Cutting
40. Kitchen gadgets
43. Hub
45. Food scraps
48. Bank employee
50. Vex
52. Thought
53. Malone and Spade
54. Butter substitute
55. Weather forecast
56. Apple, e.g.
57. Sandusky's lake
58. Small brook
59. Tipplers
62. Spanish cheer

PUZZLE 489

ACROSS
1. Hit
5. Bend
9. "Jack ____ could eat no . . ."
14. Relaxation
15. Tree trunk
16. Maine college town
17. Stratum
18. Glacial ridges
19. Dapper
20. Idaho license-plate slogan
23. Western Indian
24. Exist
25. Pennants
29. Fly high
32. Identical
36. Secluded
38. Diva's number
40. "____ Abner"
41. "____ in Pennsylvania"
44. Printers' measures
45. Be weak-minded
46. European nation
47. Female ruffs
49. Island off Scotland
51. Arab title
52. Faux ____
54. Legal matter
56. Tennessee license-plate slogan

64. Teheran native
65. Mine passage
66. Hay bundle
68. Fires
69. Sever
70. Russian mountain range
71. Keep ____ on
72. At no time, to poets
73. Danza of "Taxi"

DOWN
1. Ready
2. Stray
3. Cruising
4. Word
5. Concerning
6. Diana and Betsy
7. Applaud
8. Idol
9. Submarine detector
10. Chatters
11. Newspaper section, for short
12. Before: pref.
13. Playthings
21. Evicted
22. Tax
25. Cook, sometimes
26. Sierra ____
27. Divert
28. State executive: abbr.
30. Of a cereal grain
31. Southern constellation
33. Coeur d'____
34. Chop finely
35. Senior
37. Conceited person
39. Take into custody
42. Ear: pref.
43. "____ a Camera"
48. Energetic
50. Come
53. Licoricelike flavoring
55. Chemical compound
56. Passport endorsement
57. North African port
58. Shoestring
59. Attain
60. Singer Adams
61. Be adjacent to
62. Poi source
63. Pep
67. Cathedral city

382

• GIRL MEETS BOY •

ACROSS

1. Hoofbeat sound
5. Sky sight
10. Short drive
14. Uncivil
15. Auriculate
16. Historic Irish hill
17. Winglike
18. Painter Max
19. Body of poetry
20. Leader of the Gunpowder Plot: 2 wds.
22. Happening
23. Barcelona bravos
24. Radio closer
25. See eye-to-eye
27. Gregorian, e.g.
31. Fog
32. Kind of beet
33. Cinnabar or galena
34. Rogers and Bean
35. Ponti's wife
36. Skidded
37. Creed
38. Holds sway
39. Strong-man Charles
40. Deliberately paced
42. Elegance
43. NBA shot
44. Thai language
45. Laissez-___
47. Ellington hit: 2 wds.
52. Otherwise
53. "Call Me ___"
54. Malay craft
55. Sweeps sweep it
56. Bookbinder's tool
57. Thanks ___!: 2 wds.
58. Dancer Tommy
59. Whitty and Hess, e.g.
60. Little one

DOWN

1. Rugged peak
2. Oner
3. Singer Anita
4. Goes on stage
5. Comic Herman: hyph.
6. Carefree adventures
7. Composer Thomas
8. Headland
9. August hrs. in NYC
10. Spielberg
11. Cutout toys: 2 wds.
12. Laundry item
13. Publisher Conde
21. Hard ___! (helmsman's cry)
22. Once
24. "Good Earth" heroine
25. Came up
26. Wild Bill Hickok portrayer: 2 wds.
27. Healed
28. Years and years
29. Netman Jimmy
30. Diane Keaton film
31. Derby feature
32. Dover delicacy
35. Lie in ambush
36. Refuse to budge: 2 wds.
38. Celtic character
39. Actor Bates
41. Safety: Fr.
42. ___ in (adds two cents)
44. Aver
45. Gala event
46. Baseball surname
47. Sweeping tale
48. Economist Smith
49. Paris airport
50. Appear
51. Tardy
53. Like Carroll's hatter

COMBOS

Form a longer word by joining two of the words below and adding an "F" at the beginning. For example, an "F" in front of AIRY and LAND forms "FAIRYLAND."

AIRY	EAR	IN	LIGHT	ORE
ALE	ED	INCENSE	LOCK	OUT
ALL	END	IRE	LOTS	RAG
AM	ERAL	LAG	ON	RANK
ARM	EVER	LAND	OR	RANT
ATE	I	LASH	ORB	RIG

PUZZLE 492

• BEASTLY BEGINNINGS •

ACROSS
1. Chose
6. Be fresh
10. Be a big mouth
14. Electron tube
15. Medicinal plant
16. Operatic slave
17. French painter
18. Mountain lake
19. Archie, e.g.
20. Consequences
23. Skating arena
24. Charged particle
25. Evensong
29. Hardens
32. Basketballer Gilmore
33. Toothpaste container
35. Draft animals
37. Walk heavily
38. Actor Rathbone
39. Garment union: abbr.
40. Sports group
41. Highways: abbr.
42. White heron
43. Stone monuments
45. Daubs
46. Find fault constantly
47. Seize
49. Unconditionally
55. Soft drink
56. Footless animal
57. Cause to get out of bed
59. Winglike
60. Split
61. Neighbor of China
62. Contradict
63. Ball holders
64. Back of a ship

DOWN
1. Unusual
2. Dock
3. Roman robe
4. Dutch cheese
5. Longings
6. Glossy fabric
7. Alas!
8. Carolina rail
9. Guard
10. Capital of Louisiana
11. Charge against property
12. Summer beverages
13. Prohibit
21. Evergreen
22. Memo of a debt
25. Expansive
26. Gardner et al.
27. Brown ermine
28. Of coloring matter
29. Wading bird
30. Spare
31. City drain
33. "Soap" family name
34. Take advantage of
36. Burmese nature spirits
38. Blow-hard
42. Sets sail
44. New Guinea town
45. Animal pouch
47. Orchard
48. Carnival attractions
49. Songwriter Porter
50. Comedian King
51. Andy Taylor's son
52. Booty
53. Bait
54. River to the North Sea
55. Bounder
58. Beige

PUZZLE 493   Categories

Can you think of a word or phrase for each of the categories listed beginning with each letter on the left? Count one point for each correct answer. A score of 15 is good, and 21 is excellent.

	INSECTS	SUPER-NATURAL BEINGS	ROYAL TITLES	BODY PARTS	FIELDS OF STUDY
L					
E					
A					
S					
T					

PUZZLE 494

ACROSS

1. Treaty
5. Votes against
9. Lay odds
12. A few
16. Jai ____
17. English horn
18. Rather than, to poets
19. Weary
20. Heart
21. Peak
23. Rub out
24. Indeed, to poets
25. Dried grass
26. Title
27. Scene of action
28. Moistureless
30. Traps
31. Mosquito bite
32. Bandleader Shaw
34. Clique
35. Actor Holbrook
36. Sewing junction
39. Female domestic
40. Ham it up
42. Turkish general
43. "What Kind of Fool ____"
44. In the past
45. Bandleader Kenton
46. Men
48. Pindarics
49. Solon
51. Seabird
52. Bakery stoves
53. Middle
55. Toward land
58. Spring bloomer
61. Gym pads
63. Run machinery
67. Mimicked
68. Metal money
70. Picnic pests
71. Distant
72. Crate
73. Drama division
74. Seabirds
76. Songstress James
77. Quick cut
79. Car fuel
80. Terminus
81. Tempered iron
82. Scruffs
84. Story
86. Sail support
87. Spurred
88. Rani's dress
89. Pigs' home
90. Roll of money
93. Fall flower
94. Dawdle
96. Equine mother
97. Tempest
98. Lend a hand
99. Listen
100. English composer
101. Egg layers
102. Dehydrate
103. Head: Fr.
104. Perfume

DOWN

1. Walk restlessly
2. Lotion ingredient
3. Lapel flower
4. Cravat
5. Migrant
6. "____ Named Sue"
7. Second person
8. Early filmmaker
9. Rays of light
10. Great Lake
11. Half score
12. Warning horns
13. Summer cooler
14. Flat-topped hill
15. Dutch commune
19. Actress Garr
22. Make lace
25. Hasten
27. Book of maps
29. Disencumber
30. ____ tetra
31. Poultry herb
32. Candlenut trees
33. Vehemence
34. Wise
35. Passageways
37. So be it!
38. Fail to hit
40. English school
41. Flightless bird
45. Footfall
47. It might have been!
48. Finished
50. Sour
51. Mother's mother
52. Metal sources
54. Sends forth
56. Sharpened
57. Selects
58. Bar bills
59. At the time of
60. Kentucky city
62. Lao-____
64. Later
65. London art gallery
66. Of an age
68. Pent
69. Wood sorrels
70. Actress Baxter
75. Illuminate anew
76. Greek vowel
78. Beeping devices
81. Undercover agent
83. Hair treatment
84. Late
85. Altar constellation
86. Cubic meter
87. Villa d'____
88. Mix
89. Venetian blind strip
91. River through Florence
92. Moose
93. Bat wood
94. Unhappy
95. Golly!
96. Chinese communist hero

PUZZLE 495

ACROSS
1. Hands out hands
6. Squander
11. Charcoal or lead item
12. Toted in a vehicle

13. Give assent
14. Labor groups
15. Zodiac lion
16. Religious denomination
18. Prescribed amount
19. Turkish coin
21. Enameled tin
23. Set
24. Inscribed pillar
26. Required
28. Peanut ____
30. Dwell
32. Feudal figures
36. Fr. gala dance
37. Warble
39. Soccer great
40. Greek letters
42. Elevator man
44. Animal foot
45. Bear witness
47. Flatter
49. Takes a snooze
50. Obliterated
51. Rough Rider Roosevelt
52. Gluts

DOWN
1. Skullduggery
2. Bis
3. High card
4. Pot covers
5. It comes down hard
6. Washed-out
7. Like the Sahara
8. Curly, e.g.
9. Became taut
10. Mr. Ford
11. Flags
12. Meat portion
17. Satisfied
20. Priestly robes
22. Slithery fellows
25. Goddess of strife
27. Profound
29. Simpletons
30. Baby's toy
31. Joyful
33. Rest
34. Blazes
35. Basted
36. Beauty's suitor
38. Taunts
41. Beginning
43. Antitoxins
46. "I ____"
48. Hep one

PUZZLE 496

ACROSS
1. Illinois city
7. Appraised
12. Slip giver

13. Wears away
15. Cavil about: 3 wds.
17. Naval off.
18. Hunts and pecks, e.g.
19. Afternoon social
20. Certain sch.
22. Mineral spring
23. Shape
24. Doctrine
26. Essential-oil compounds
28. Most proximate
30. Sainted Archbishop of Canterbury
32. Pains in the neck
36. "Graf ____"
37. ____ Alamitos
39. Kenton or Laurel
40. Southern constellation
41. "I'm a ____" (Beatles)
43. Pub drink
44. Worry needlessly: 2 wds.
47. Intertwine
48. Prime suspect?
49. Church council
50. Guides

DOWN
1. Conquer
2. Manifest
3. Sunflower State native
4. Append
5. Departed
6. Donkey sounds
7. Set free
8. Carney and Linkletter
9. Pull
10. Redactor
11. Discourages
14. Phony
16. Predominant
21. Thick
23. Parties
25. Curling mark
27. Recipe abbr.
29. Permitted
30. Stage areas
31. Almost
33. Solid as a rock
34. Higher
35. Shows scorn
36. Knowing
38. Certain Slavs
41. Loopy
42. Send running
45. Vied for political office
46. Shoshonean

386

• HOLIDAY MEAL •

ACROSS

1. Amiss
4. Mr. Carney
7. Sweet surprise
9. Nourished
12. Exclamation of triumph
13. Tiny red fruit
19. Affirmative answer
20. ___ Khan
21. Mom's sister
22. Division word
23. Chess pieces
24. Spiffily dressed
26. Color shade
29. Isle of song
31. Low-down joint
33. Hilarious
35. Caesar, for one
38. Stomach: pref.
39. Holiday highlights
41. Novice
42. Assn.
43. Scot's night
44. Bar bill
46. Card game
47. Formal eating
50. Squashed
53. Current unit
54. Discretion
55. Fowl organ
57. Spud
59. Pro's partner
60. Hold up
62. Newsman Rather
63. Bravo!
65. Advocate strongly
67. Gobblers
71. ___ on (prodded)
73. Postpone
75. Battleship to remember
76. Invited one
77. Make euphoric
80. French summer
81. Bias
83. Time period
85. Actor Mineo et al.
87. Related
88. Coop occupant
91. ___ Alamos
92. November desserts
96. Actress Arden
97. Permit
98. Eagle's nest
99. Like steak tartare
100. Snooze

DOWN

1. Sphere
2. Lawyer's charge
3. Distant
4. Villain's cry
5. Discarded cloth
6. November holiday meal
7. Explosive initials
8. Three: pref.
9. Holiday meal, e.g.
10. Needle feature
11. Lair
13. Service affairs
14. Lane groove
15. Some
16. Business abbr.
17. Greek letter
18. Steeps
25. High, musically
26. "Ben ___"
27. Actress Merkel
28. Windup
30. Turncoat
31. Past
32. Biblical ointment
33. Cooling device
34. Nevertheless
36. Parched
37. Actor Johnson
39. Cribbage marker
40. American's uncle
43. Walk in
45. Wand
48. ___ Hill (San Francisco)
49. Under the weather
51. Used a chair
52. Fairy-tale author's inits.
55. Skirt inset
56. Small child
57. Dance step
58. Cheers for a matador
59. Something to chew
61. Hobo
62. Tint
64. N.Y. time
66. Slippery fish
68. Actress Charlotte ___
69. Carson
70. Wind dir.
71. Actor Richard et al.
72. Pistol
74. File
78. Fraternity letter
79. Shade tree
81. Join the Aspen set
82. Fib
83. House wing
84. Caviar
86. Bath, e.g.
87. Mimic
89. Ms. Gabor
90. Just purchased
93. Barbie's friend
94. Lyricist Gershwin
95. Tuck's partner

PUZZLE 498

ACROSS
1. Moderately hot
5. Lamb's cry
10. Butter substitute

11. Right away
12. Home for a hornet
13. Pantry
14. Buccaneer
16. Financial gain
18. Plead
21. Long time
22. Nibbled
24. "____ Maria"
25. Find a sum
26. Mortarboard attachment
28. Place of worship
30. Flunked
33. At a distance
36. Disregard
37. Impolite
38. Camping shelters
39. Winter vehicle

DOWN
1. Came in first
2. Malt beverage
3. Answer
4. Theme
5. Spoiled child
6. Folk knowledge
7. Finish
8. Had dinner
9. Rocky crag
11. Cliche
15. Tease
16. Pod vegetable
17. Fishing pole
18. Shy
19. Adam's wife
20. Congeal
23. Road covering
27. Wound mementos
28. Coagulate
29. Belonging to that woman
30. Tantrum
31. Get older
32. Country hotel
34. Lemon drink
35. Crimson or scarlet

PUZZLE 499

ACROSS
1. Director Reiner
4. Comparative word
8. Breaks
12. Atmosphere
13. Had on
14. October birthstone
15. Reed instrument
17. Depend
18. Property
19. Move back and forth
21. Frigid
22. Atlantic and Indian
26. Animal tissue
29. Actor Carney
30. From head to ____
31. Doily material
32. Noah's vessel
33. "____ Like It Hot"
34. Fire residue
35. Droning sound
36. Females
37. Calls
39. Swindle
40. Hill insect
41. Husky
45. Male swans
48. Union Pacific, e.g.
50. Region
51. Capri or Wight
52. Pub order
53. Lively dance
54. Related
55. Animal's lair

DOWN
1. Speed contest
2. Lubricates
3. Naughty child
4. Jerky movement
5. Hive product
6. "Where the Boys ____"
7. CBS or ABC
8. Small canyon
9. Gorilla, e.g.
10. Chum
11. Tricky
16. Increase
20. Play part
23. Minute particle
24. Alaska seaport
25. Observed
26. Flutter
27. Swift blow
28. Reverberate
29. Upper limb
32. Vienna's locale
33. Underwater detection method
35. Coop mother
36. Like certain sweaters
38. Of the nose
39. Spicy dish
42. Highway
43. Bargain event
44. Biblical garden
45. Auto
46. Mine output
47. Busy as a ____
49. Inquire

388

CODEWORD

PUZZLE 500

Codeword is a special crossword puzzle in which conventional clues are omitted. Instead, answer words in the diagram are represented by numbers. Each number represents a different letter of the alphabet, and all of the letters of the alphabet are used. When you are sure of a letter, put it in the code key chart and cross it off in the alphabet box. A group of letters has been inserted to start you off.

Code key chart:

#		#	
1	B	14	
2		15	
3		16	
4		17	
5		18	
6		19	
7		20	
8		21	
9	R	22	R
10		23	
11		24	
12		25	
13	O	26	

Alphabet box:

A~~B~~CDEFGHIJKLM N~~O~~P~~Q~~R STUVWXYZ

Codeword grid (numbers):

```
13  9 21 15 21 25 24  ■ 26 16  8 17 17 24 22
 2  ■ 17  ■ 15  ■  9  ■ 13  ■  9  ■ 12  ■  8
 6  8 15 19 24  ■  8 25 12 22 24  ■ 20  8 17
21  ■ 22  ■  8  ■  6  ■ 22  ■  ■ 24  ■ 23
16 24  8 11 16 24  7  ■  2 18 12 21 22 24  2
16  ■  ■  3  ■  ■  ■ 17  ■  8  ■
 8  3 17  ■  1 14  3  8 14  ■ 11 21 16 24  2
 7  ■ 22  ■  8  ■ 13  ■ 21  ■  ■  ■ 12
24  4  8 15 24  ■  2 18 12  8  7  ■ 11 13 22
 ■ 20  ■  3  ■  ■  ■  ■ 21  ■ 26
 6 10 13 13  2 24  ■  6  8  2 24 11 12 16
22  ■ 17  ■  8  ■  ■  8  ■  8  ■  7  ■ 12
24 19 19  ■ 26  8  6 24 22(R)  5 24 24 22  2
24  ■  2  ■ 21  ■ 23  ■ 13(O) ■  8  ■ 24  ■ 24
23 21  7  7 24 17  2  ■  1(B) 24 10 21 17 15  2
```

Piece by Piece

PUZZLE 501

A humorous quotation has been divided into 3-letter pieces. Spaces between words have been eliminated. Rearrange the 3-letter pieces to reconstruct the quotation. The dashes indicate the number of letters in each word.

```
AGO  AMA  DIL  FWI  GOL  ING  ISB  ISP
LAY  LSH  MAN  NWH  ODL  OIS  OSE  OSS
OUA  OWY  RAN  SHO  THH  WHO  WME
```

_____ ___ _ ____ __ _ _____
         ,
_____ ____ ___ ____ _____ __
__ ____ ___ _____
____ _____ ____ ____ _.

PUZZLE 502

DOUBLE TROUBLE

Not really double trouble, but double fun! Solve this puzzle as you would a regular crossword, EXCEPT place one, two, or three letters in each box. The number of letters in each answer is shown in parentheses after its clue.

ACROSS
1. Membership lists (7)
5. Artist Picasso (5)
7. Suffragist Carrie Chapman ____ (4)
10. Supervision (10)
11. Gull's cousin (4)
12. Cleans feathers (6)
13. Unmoving (5)
15. Urgent recklessness (11)
17. Donkey (3)
19. Standard of measurement (9)
21. Wife of Abraham (5)
23. Storms (5)
24. Perplexing (9)
28. Coat of arms shield (10)
30. Flattened marine menace (9)
31. Feel (5)
32. Snare (4)
33. Spill over (4)
34. Of Florida (10)
37. Carpet nail (4)
38. Most meaningful (11)
41. Capital of Iran (7)
43. Evergreen trees (4)
44. Jargon (5)
46. Bell alarm (6)
49. Bed canopy (6)
50. Deities (4)
51. Abundance (8)

DOWN
1. Ancient Italian (5)
2. Theater platform (5)
3. Royal fur (6)
4. Guard (6)
5. Father: Latin (5)
6. Most flaxen-haired (8)
7. Last straw (6)
8. Pick up the check (5)
9. Tautness (7)
14. Aromatic seasoning leaves (8)
16. Loathsome (9)
17. Evaluate (6)
18. Crusader's foe (7)
20. ____ Moines (3)
22. Cabins (4)
25. Needlefishes (4)
26. French sailor (7)
27. Sprain application: 2 wds. (7)
29. Made a bird sound (7)
30. Require as a condition (9)
32. Prepares for a fight (6)
35. Baby bird (8)
36. Oratory (8)
38. Monetary gain (6)
39. Wooded area (6)
40. Auto racer Al ____ (5)
42. Western farm (5)
45. Things for sale (5)
47. Moral wrong (3)
48. Scottish monster's lake (4)

[Crossword grid with numbered cells: 1 2 3 4 5 6 7 8 9 / 10 11 12 / 13 14 15 16 / 17 18 19 20 / 21 22 23 24 25 26 27 / 28 29 30 / 31 32 33 / 34 35 36 37 / 38 39 40 41 42 / 43 44 45 46 47 48 / 49 50 51]

PUZZLE 503

EXPLORAWORD

How many words of four or more letters hidden in the word below can you find? A letter may be used more than once only if it appears more than once in the word. Proper names, contractions, plurals, and foreign words are not allowed. Our answer may differ from yours.

KEYBOARD

A humorous quotation runs clockwise around the edges of this diagram. To find the quotation, work the puzzle as a regular crossword, filling in the remaining blank squares with the letters given below.

$$E \quad G \quad I \quad L \quad O \quad O \quad R \quad R \quad R \quad S \quad S \quad T \quad T \quad T \quad W$$

ACROSS
14. Wow!
15. Conductor's asset
16. Callow youth
17. Oleo ingredient
18. I love, Ovid's way
19. Innocence
21. Dancer Reinking
22. Drafted, as a contract
24. Wand
25. Nursery time-out
27. "Fish" star Vigoda
29. Droop
30. Was aware of
32. Church projection
34. Whole
36. Purpose
38. ___ Antilles
41. Londoner's boob tube
43. Producer ___ Lloyd Webber
45. Billboard blurbs
46. However
48. Stain
49. JFK's predecessor
50. Bonfire residue
51. Shapeless mass
53. False front
56. Add comfort to
59. Half: pref.
60. Puny
61. Old-fashioned
64. Kiln
66. Hollywood biggies
68. '50s toy fad
69. "Lend Me a ___" (Broadway play)
71. Fraud
72. Red-covered cheese
76. Paddock
77. Vespasian's people
79. Actress Montez
80. Assuredly
83. Tennis call
84. Youngster
87. Odic contraction
88. London lunch spot
90. Merman and Kennedy
92. Ancient Antioch's location
94. Palace seat
96. Learn through the grapevine
97. Sault ___ Marie
99. Cryptograph
101. Movie Idle
102. On the ___ (fleeing)
104. Whack
106. Calico pet
107. Colonial insect
108. Invalidate
111. Daunt
113. Derring-do
116. Self-importance

117. Hesitation sounds
118. Carbon dioxide, e.g.
119. Cover-girl Carol
120. Prompt

DOWN
1. Sassafras drink
2. Millionaire's daughter
3. Bacteriologist Walter
4. Ingest
5. ___ Stage, in D.C.
6. Slipped by
7. Florist's vehicle
8. Poet Millay
9. Sing, in the Alps
10. Fuzzy-sounding tree
11. Spirit
12. Baneful box's curious keeper
13. Ratite bird
20. Swears
23. News
26. Inclined
28. Camptown racer
31. Beatty

33. Nevada town
35. Fishing site
37. "___ Miserables"
39. Subsides
40. Guideline
42. Weight lifter
44. Requisite
47. Author Wolfe
49. Calligrapher's expense
52. Buffalo
54. Studio stand
55. Shaft of light
57. Hail!
58. Badger's abode
60. Tussaud's medium
62. Surpass
63. Peeper
65. Neither's companion
67. Scrumptious
70. Furl
71. Bowler
73. Decimal point
74. Touched down
75. Scrunch
78. Clutter

81. Calais summer
82. Superficial
85. Circle segment
86. Bishop's district
88. Columned porch
89. One: pref.
91. Epochal
92. Bounding main
93. Palindromic gal
95. Kelly of "The Black Stallion"
98. Romantic meeting
100. Fictional Frome
103. Carriage
105. Flyleaf
107. Comic Johnson
109. Yuk!
110. Beg. of the weekend
112. Paint or part lead-in
114. Biblical priest
115. Quantity

391

PUZZLE 505

ACROSS

1. Corny actors
5. Extend, as a subscription
10. Snow coaster
14. Part of QED
15. "A Bell for ____"
16. ____ d'Azur
17. Lawn tool
18. Asp
19. Scarce
20. Bullfight cheer
21. Allows
22. Protected from the sun
24. Hollywood luminaries
26. Tread
27. Cupid's weapons
29. Come out again
33. Spools
34. Ties
35. Eternity
36. Spoken
37. Remains undecided
38. Tense
39. Pack or pie
40. Elegance of behavior
41. Piece of pie
42. "____ I Wander"
44. Supplication
45. Highway
46. Domain
47. Meets the sandman
50. Ooze
51. Mine yield
54. Paddles
55. Lum's partner
57. Indigo
58. Fit of pique
59. Din
60. Bottle part
61. Lyric poems
62. Recorded magnetically
63. Colors

DOWN

1. Brave one
2. Asian sea
3. Prepares
4. Sault ____ Marie
5. Wild ones
6. Prepares copy
7. Siestas
8. Wind dir.
9. Woolen fabrics
10. Clean carrots
11. Burden
12. Raison d'____
13. Act
21. Statutes
23. Garment edges
25. Bridge fee
26. Mails a letter
27. Odor
28. Summer TV show
29. Wash lightly
30. Cash on hand
31. Scoop out
32. "____ Laughing"
34. Part of a Santa costume
37. Agreeable
38. River duck
40. ____ suey
41. Enfold
43. Pulls away by force
44. Looked closely
46. Baseball's Pee Wee
47. Fair
48. Cry from the crow's-nest
49. Famed canal
50. Small cut
52. Oriental staple
53. Large deer
56. Feather scarf
57. "Night ____ Day"

PUZZLE 506

Escalator

Write the word that fits clue 1 in space 1. Then drop one letter of that word and rearrange the remaining letters to answer clue 2. Drop another letter and rearrange to answer clue 3. The first dropped letter goes into the box to the left of space 1 and the second dropped letter goes into the box to the right of space 3. Follow this pattern and fill the diagram. When completed, the letters on the left and right, reading down, will spell the first and last names of a famous person.

1. Sail
2. Snap
3. Garden tool
4. Spring holiday
5. Guide
6. Golf mounds
7. Gulch
8. Artless
9. Lode
10. Mounted soldier
11. Wading bird
12. Speed contest
13. Rat or rabbit
14. Drift
15. Lease
16. Cooks' wear
17. Flavor
18. Box

PUZZLE 507

• ABBREVIATED •

ACROSS
1. Like a worthless tire
5. Launder
9. Indian state
14. Cruising
15. Reverberation
16. Puppeteer Lewis
17. Infielder
19. ___ plexus
20. Sonnet conclusion
21. Faded away, with "out"
23. Brake suddenly
25. Salamander
28. Compass pt.
29. Ad libitum
33. Embroidery silk
35. Wimp
38. Formal song
39. Ore vein
40. Fence stakes
41. Animals' docs
42. Asian lake
43. Diva Gluck
44. Belief
45. 12th President
47. Chinese tea
49. Bitter vetch
50. Durham
54. Songstress Jackson
56. Laborer
60. Enjoy the taste of
61. Strawberry dessert
63. Greek marketplace
64. Serbian folk dance
65. Hastens
66. Coin factories
67. Kernel
68. Formerly, of old

DOWN
1. Edible fish
2. Tennis champion
3. Some August babies
4. Pub game
5. Actor Jack
6. Deed
7. Boutiques
8. Chinese province
9. Allege
10. Radio beam
11. Auction
12. Romanian city
13. Russian space station, once
18. Heads: Fr.
22. Amphibians
24. Punitive
25. Key of Beethoven's "Eroica"
26. Actress Robson
27. Present time
30. Songstress Cara
31. Metric quart
32. Endures
34. Underestimate
36. Shade tree
37. Arrive
40. By word of mouth
44. Fortuneteller's card
46. Tara residents
48. Souped-up car
51. Puts on the line
52. Resort lake
53. Cubbyhole
54. Star followers
55. Bard's river
57. Lion's den
58. Supplements
59. Relaxation
60. Actor Waterston
62. Violinist Bull

Rhyming Trios   PUZZLE 508

Three words that rhyme with three related words are given below. Can you determine what the three related words are? Try reading aloud to solve this one!

Example: Neigh   Tune   Arch   (Answer: May, June, March)

1. Face	Spruce	Grey	_____
2. Weaver	Shale	Teal	_____
3. Whip	Goat	Finer	_____
4. Toe	Burly	Carry	_____
5. Shone	Sock	Shoulder	_____

PUZZLE 509

ACROSS

1. Unruffled
5. Sped
10. Poet
14. Region
15. Give the slip to
16. Woodwind
17. Bearing
18. Jane Fonda's brother
19. Donated
20. Associate
22. Beak
24. TV's Lange
25. Actor Chaney
26. Railroad eating cars
28. Amuses
32. Yield
33. Poem
34. Parking ___
36. Chemical compound
40. Moors
42. Lawn tools
44. Rescue
45. Goddesses of destiny
47. Drain for the second time
49. Guided
50. Memo
52. Rubber tips on pencils
54. Roman or birthday
57. Uproar
58. Fuss
59. Consume
61. "The ___ Worker"
65. Chamber
67. Wise lawgiver
69. Train track
70. Sea eagle
71. Eat away
72. Geological stages
73. Examine
74. Strings of pearls
75. Withered

DOWN

1. Tenting ground
2. Opera melody
3. Look askance
4. Mickey of baseball
5. Contrite one
6. State positively
7. "___ Ballou"
8. Bible locale
9. Mock
10. Marsh
11. Subside
12. Wanderer
13. Ownership papers
21. Comedian Crosby
23. Wait patiently
27. Headland
28. Tip one's hat
29. Concept
30. Air opening
31. Gaze fixedly
32. Mediterranean island
35. Supplement
37. Story
38. At any time
39. Beatty film
41. Dispatch
43. Canned fish
46. Shoe bottom
48. Two of a kind
51. Taunter
53. Lures
54. Proofreader's mark
55. Worship
56. Midday periods
60. Spanish bull
61. Fashion
62. Be concerned
63. Untruthful one
64. Otherwise
66. Assembled
68. Cut (off)

PUZZLE 510

Cryptic Trivia

An interesting bit of trivia is in a substitution code (different letters are substituted for the correct ones).

MH K TVY DNVJUYJ BYSYVCP LTNVJ OKV NBYJ NL KB

ONZD YVYUWP KB CDY CMVP DNOOMVWIMUJ, DY ETNGJ

DKSY CT YKC CDUYY DNVJUYJ HTUCP LTNVJB TH

LTCKCTYB TU CET DNVJUYJ YMWDCP-HMSY LTNVJB TH

DKOINUWYU JKMGP ANBC CT OKMVCKMV DMB EYMWDC.

ACROSS

1. Tree covering
5. Befitting royalty
10. Sere
14. Yoked animals
15. Choice
16. Knob
17. Away from the wind
18. Gestured in greeting
19. Saga
20. Assign to an inferior position
22. Church official
23. "Chances ____"
24. Mineral deposit
26. Raunchy
30. Occupy completely
34. Foolish
35. Soft rock
37. Doberman's doc
38. Do housework
39. Composite-family plant
40. In this place
41. Able was I ____...
42. Beethoven's choral symphony
43. Whittle
44. Renovate
46. Dog's owner
47. At any time
48. Wrestling feat
49. Steam bath
52. Ways through
57. Fork part
58. Browned bread
60. Docile
61. Blue-pencil
62. Discarded material
63. Fail to include
64. Makes damp
65. Mink's relative
66. Caresses

DOWN

1. Wild hog
2. Wheel rod
3. Virginia ____
4. Leg joint
5. Bounty
6. Gladden
7. Hand over
8. Munched
9. Showed the way
10. Horn
11. Thoroughfare
12. Not busy
13. Forest denizen
21. Actor Gordon
22. Advantage
24. Restrainer
25. Exclusively
26. Polo player
27. Accustom
28. Acid neutralizers
29. Industrious insect
31. Plain
32. Tennis start
33. Beef animal
35. More rational
36. Box-office winner
39. Urgent
40. Possesses
42. PBS science show
43. Preserves produce
45. Creeds
46. Man's title
48. Adhesive
49. State of vexation
50. Adjutant
51. Military group
52. Bygone
53. At the summit
54. Recreational pursuit
55. Discharge
56. Lays
58. Duo
59. Type of grass

Quotagram

Fill in the answers to the clues. Then transfer the letters to the correspondingly numbered squares in the diagram. The completed diagram will contain a quotation.

1. Fiftieth state
$\overline{32}\ \overline{7}\ \overline{2}\ \overline{10}\ \overline{38}\ \overline{26}$

2. Renter
$\overline{23}\ \overline{17}\ \overline{34}\ \overline{1}\ \overline{39}\ \overline{27}$

3. Reminiscences
$\overline{14}\ \overline{12}\ \overline{6}\ \overline{18}\ \overline{16}\ \overline{3}\ \overline{36}\ \overline{41}$

4. Buddy
$\overline{37}\ \overline{22}\ \overline{28}\ \overline{5}\ \overline{25}\ \overline{40}$

5. Moxie
$\overline{4}\ \overline{20}\ \overline{24}\ \overline{8}\ \overline{11}$

6. Soup vegetables
$\overline{19}\ \overline{29}\ \overline{33}\ \overline{13}$

7. Suave
$\overline{30}\ \overline{9}\ \overline{21}\ \overline{15}\ \overline{31}\ \overline{35}$

PUZZLE 513

• CIVIL WAR DAYS •

ACROSS

1. Dancing party
5. Lodge man
10. Shoots
14. ___ fixe
15. Worship
16. Emanation
17. Civil War event
20. Hit hard
21. Yugoslav immortal
22. Perceive
23. Haughty one
26. Angel Clare's love
28. Tent type
31. Out of the wind
33. Tell
37. Folding money
38. Equals
40. Biblical brother
41. Civil War event
45. Vicious volcano
46. Turkish harem
47. Employ
48. Stop
51. Hollow
52. Thrice: prefix
53. Proximate
55. Tennis bouts
57. Heavenly Altar
60. Region
62. Alcott's "___ Cousins"
66. Civil War celebrity
70. River on the Manchurian border
71. Man from Malaya
72. Knowledge
73. Greek letter
74. Made of mesh
75. Farm animals

DOWN

1. Protection for rompers
2. "___ Bede"
3. Apollo's mother
4. Latvia residents
5. Daisy ___ Yokum
6. Commotion
7. Soap or shoe
8. Electron's path
9. Gender
10. Fast friend
11. Possessive
12. Genuine
13. Sensible
18. Delaware River Indian
19. Be bested
24. Bread spread
25. Complaints
27. Bridge thrill
28. Presented
29. Join
30. Hammer heads
32. Blundered
34. Estimation word
35. Verb form
36. Church officer
39. Ancestors
42. Profit
43. ___ sugar
44. Dave Winfield, e.g.
49. Burn
50. Highland wear
54. Singer Della
56. Move obliquely
57. Desert dweller
58. Tony played by Sinatra
59. Touch on
61. Mine passage
63. Warm look
64. Rollcall response
65. Small mounds
67. Period
68. Rebel Tyler of 1381
69. Some

PUZZLE 514

Dart Game

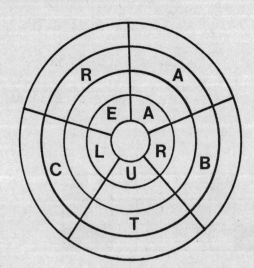

Form five words, reading from the center of the diagram outward, by adding the letters given below to complete the 5-letter words. Each letter will be used only once and each word begins with the center letter.

A E G K L N O P T U Y

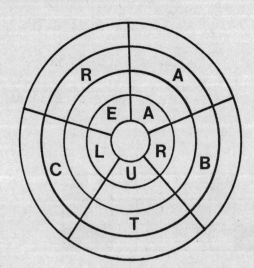

396

DOUBLE TROUBLE

PUZZLE 515

Not really double trouble, but double fun! Solve this puzzle as you would a regular crossword, EXCEPT place one, two, or three letters in each box. The number of letters in each answer is shown in parentheses after its clue.

ACROSS
1. Strength (6)
4. Bible hymn (5)
7. Bounds (5)
10. Kind of card (5)
11. Fabulous author (5)
12. Ragout (4)
13. Bureaus (8)
15. Intone (4)
17. Mr. Musial (4)
18. Triumphant ones (7)
20. Aquatic mammals (6)
22. Weds (7)
25. Missing (6)
27. Inert element (5)
28. Empty (5)
29. Up and around (6)
32. Aquatic mammal: 2 wds. (7)
34. Consecrates (7)
35. Takes a cut (6)
37. Argot (5)
39. Mr. La Rue (4)
40. Authority: hyph. (5)
42. Replying (9)
46. Mimics (5)
48. Mr. Allen (4)
50. Disputes (6)
51. Sonic boomers (4)
52. Recording (6)
53. Topers (4)

DOWN
1. Tangy condiment (7)
2. Heart (4)
3. Tennis calls (4)
4. Church official (6)
5. Bargain opportunities (5)
6. Swabs (4)
7. Most insignificant (5)
8. Bother (6)
9. Cob and pen (5)
14. Church events (8)
16. Fort Knox holdings (6)
19. French rooms (6)
21. Squid appendages (9)
22. Disfigure (3)
23. Jason's ship (4)
24. Giving a post-wash wash (7)
26. Vault site (4)
28. Indonesian island (4)
30. "____ the season . . ." (3)
31. Letters of triumph (4)
33. Elia work (5)
34. Kicks (5)
35. Rebuffs (5)
36. Bolt adjuncts (7)
38. Alighting (7)
41. Downy (4)
43. Sports (5)
44. Drumming Starr (5)
45. Invited ones (6)
47. Kin of aves. (3)
49. Harvest (4)

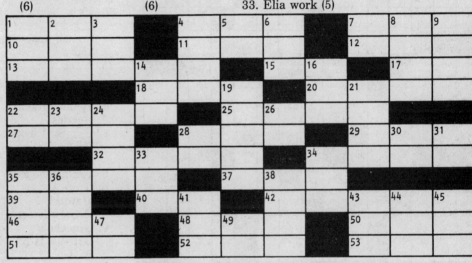

HOW MANY TRIANGLES?

PUZZLE 516

This diagram is filled with triangles large, small, and medium. Try to count them all. There are more triangles here than you may think!

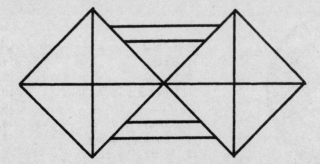

PUZZLE 517

• HAPPY TRAILS •

ACROSS
1. Ark traveler
5. Purloin
10. Being
14. General's assistant
15. Bridge score
16. 9 inches
17. Ms. Horne
18. Inquired
19. British tribesman
20. Happy ____
22. Ms. Lindstrom
24. Before
25. Big ____
26. Baseball Commissioner "Happy"
28. Elec. measure
31. Hindu deity
33. "To ____ with Love"
34. Place for salami
36. "Neither snow ____ rain . . ."
37. Capital of Minorca
41. Happy ____
45. Alma ____
46. Quilter's gathering
47. Food for titmice
48. Arab's cloak
50. Ms. Heche
52. Santa Fe et al.: abbr.
53. Comics' Happy ____
57. Literary monogram
59. After Mar.
60. Marble
61. Happy-____
65. Hardy heroine
67. Cuomo
69. Topee source
70. Ages
71. Irish islands
72. Vow
73. TV's "Happy ____"
74. French upper house
75. Want

DOWN
1. Spanish room
2. Hurries
3. ____ St. Vincent Millay
4. Repasts
5. Taking the lead
6. Chore
7. Wapiti
8. Hebrew letter
9. Groucho's tattooed lady et al.
10. Supernatural power
11. Sensational speech
12. Part of Pierre's oath
13. Come in
21. Neighbor of Ger.
23. Cicero's soul
26. S. Amer. Indian
27. Little bits
28. Man minus a rib
29. Flattop
30. Land map
32. Aver
35. Perfect
38. Happy ____ (bar feature)
39. Unique person
40. Profits
42. Journey above the Earth
43. Commandments number
44. Chicken coop
49. Certain lizards
51. House addition
53. Despised
54. "Aida," e.g.
55. Fifi D'____ of "Silk Stockings"
56. Knowing
58. Lazy ____
61. Lollabrigida
62. Shoreline recess
63. Swiss painter
64. Football meas.
66. Draft letters
68. Also-____

PUZZLE 518   Spinwheel

This game works two ways, inward and outward. Place the answers to the clues below in the diagram beginning at the corresponding number.

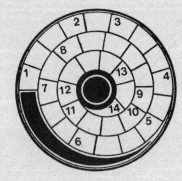

INWARD
1. Extra
3. Stories
5. Gave a sidelong look
7. Naive
9. Always
11. Eastern religion
13. Actor Howard

OUTWARD
14. Average
12. Pedigree item
10. Basin
8. Exchange
6. Line winders
4. Make joyful
2. Knocks

PUZZLE 519

ACROSS
1. Hen fruit
4. T-men
8. Recoiled
13. Indian dress
14. Mr. Roberts
15. Ahead of time
16. Mideast land
17. Disastrous
18. Came up
19. Comedian Buttons
20. Affect
22. Thickly populated
25. Sock part
26. Creepy
29. Mandate
33. Outpouring
36. Barrel
38. Pre-holiday nights
40. Actor's quest
41. Misplaces
42. Nuisance
43. Downwind
44. Lollapalooza
45. Major artery
46. Burdened
48. Hands out hands
50. ____ Jersey
52. Blockade
55. Bridles
60. Ratite bird
62. Photo finish
63. "Claire's ____" (Rohmer film)
64. Hearty brews
65. Perfume ingredient
66. Amend copy
67. Climbing plant
68. Equals
69. Rickles and Adams
70. Find a sum

DOWN
1. Auriculate
2. Mark
3. Sloe ____
4. Cattle food
5. New York canal
6. Flit
7. Winter forecast
8. Garment assembler
9. Mata ____
10. Golf club
11. Or ____!
12. Tint
13. Dear follower
21. Chess pieces
23. Cleared
24. Meet a bet
27. Religious image
28. Let up
30. Oust
31. At all times
32. Relax
33. Health resort
34. Make dull
35. Surface measure
37. Withered
39. Terminal: abbr.
41. Recluse
45. Mr. Baba
47. Inserts
49. Resources
51. Roused
53. Cold
54. Rectify
55. Scold
56. Feminine suffix
57. Vega or Sirius
58. ____-European
59. Bonn veto
61. Manipulate
62. Weatherman's visual aid
64. Ms. Gardner

Escalator

PUZZLE 520

Place the answer to clue 1 in the first space, drop a letter, and arrange the remaining letters to answer clue 2. Drop another letter and arrange the remaining letters to answer clue 3. The first dropped letter goes into the box to the left of space 1 and the second dropped letter goes into the box to the right of space 3. Follow this pattern for each row in the diagram. When completed, the letters on the left and right, reading down, will spell related words.

1. Pebbles
2. Big
3. Genuine
4. Boyfriend
5. Travels
6. Corrupts
7. Allotment
8. Teach
9. Fuss and fume
10. Endured
11. Place
12. Fruit drinks
13. Though
14. Pasture sound
15. Slug
16. Washed lightly
17. Dehydrates
18. Faction

PUZZLE 521

ACROSS
1. Exclamation of surprise
4. Small amount
7. Refrain syllable
10. Buddy
11. Exist
12. Big spender's bankroll
13. Schedule information: abbr.
14. Employs logic
16. Treat for Cheetah
18. Hollywood luminaries
20. Proverbial slowpoke
24. "___ Came Running"
25. A ___ in the bucket
26. Frees from dependence
28. Lodes
29. Changes
31. Ropers' ropes
34. Under the weather
37. Frozen dessert
38. Actor O'Brien
39. Born
40. Domesticated animal
41. Hesitation sounds
42. Acquired

DOWN
1. Copy
2. Bowler or beret
3. Selma's state
4. Mends, in a way
5. Vicinity
6. Judge Roy and Orson
7. It takes ___ to tango
8. Operated
9. Paid notices
15. Carpentry tool
17. Stadiums
18. Compass direction: abbr.
19. Foot digit
21. Ascending
22. Charged particle
23. Certain records: abbr.
27. Skier's incline
28. Waistcoats
30. Rip
31. Rim
32. High card
33. Gel
35. Horoscope sign
36. Tennis call

PUZZLE 522

ACROSS
1. Wound mark
5. Mr. Laurel
9. Depends (upon)
11. Burned brightly, briefly
13. Delivery person of yesteryear
14. Breadwinner
15. Afternoon social event
16. One of the seven dwarfs
18. Lyric poem
19. Author Ferber
21. Lubricate
22. Gusted
23. Get away
25. Cheryl or Alan
26. "My country ___ of thee"
27. Nonsense
28. Elderly
30. Bill of ___
33. Condor or bittern
34. Firework flop
35. Historic times
37. "We ___ the World"
38. "Yankee Doodle ___"
40. Past
41. Prejudiced
43. Headman
45. Follows
46. Most senior
47. Precious stones
48. Saucy

DOWN
1. Withdraw formally
2. Does a household chore
3. Goal
4. Peruse
5. Make laugh
6. Old salt
7. Mr. Schwarzenegger
8. Required
9. Ceremony
10. Pries
11. Sense
12. Sketched
17. Bakery output
20. Emulated Richard Burton
22. Wash
24. Assist
25. Ship's record
27. Enigma
28. Ventilating
29. Famed rock musical
30. Vie for election
31. Dealer
32. Most learned
33. Ruth of diamond fame
34. Fathers
36. Classify
38. Sandra and Ruby
39. Canine's sharp cry
42. Total
44. Summer drink

PUZZLE 523

• WELL-SEASONED WORDS •

ACROSS

1. Muslim leader
5. Rooters
9. Levantine ketch
13. Son of Noah
17. Bishop Desmond ____
18. Heroic tale
19. Government gumshoe
20. Actor Rhodes
21. Baseballer Slaughter
22. Part of NB
23. Western New York city
24. Chile con ____
25. ". . . ye pay tithe of ____"
29. Eras
30. Beclouds
31. Treat badly
32. Of a heart valve
35. Bundles
37. Sends forth
38. Prussic and boric
39. Passover feast
40. Oozes
41. AL or NL positions
44. Swindles
45. Caesar or Waldorf
46. AMs, to a poet
47. "____ in the Money"
48. Chemical suffix
49. Actress White
50. Future-predicting card
51. Abraham slept here
52. ____ Hawkins Day
53. Seasoning
54. Copland and Burr
55. "Sugar and ____"
61. High-tech
62. Pharmaceutical salts
63. Nanny and billy
64. Manacles
65. Tiny
67. Fragrant seasoning
68. Crimson or vermilion
71. Prefix meaning distant
72. Portals
73. Daniel or Pat
74. Seeger or Rose
75. Road curve
76. More coquettish
77. Danish islands
78. Rogue
79. Tree knots
80. Oasts
81. Clowning around
82. Not abundant
84. Rels. of twps.
85. Labor for breath
86. ". . . but when it is grown, it is ____"
93. Mountainous
94. Ditty
95. Slept like ____
96. ____ avis
97. Poker pot
98. Senior
99. Use a stopwatch on
100. Verve
101. A drupe
102. "Rosebud," e.g.
103. Oddball
104. Work station

DOWN

1. Part of a list
2. Actor Paul ____
3. Fell like ____ of bricks
4. Dijon and Indian
5. Licorice-tasting seasoning
6. Animals without limbs
7. Actress Naldi
8. Read quickly
9. King's "____ Lot"
10. Geometric concerns
11. "____ Do That"
12. Seasoning
13. Private eye
14. Injures
15. WWII's Pyle
16. Bearing
19. More intrusive
24. Sects
26. Asian rulers
27. Lazed
28. Cuts
32. Seasoning
33. Religious image
34. Prong
35. Slugged
36. Call it ____
37. Architect Saarinen
39. Smooth fabric
40. Value
41. Vive ____!
42. French coin, once
43. Touch, e.g.
45. Family car
46. Fountain treats
47. Cautions
49. Buddy and Max
50. Score
51. What makes waste
52. Don't make a ____
53. Thin boards
54. Century plant
55. Hit
56. Skin openings
57. Adored ones
58. Michaelmas daisy
59. Snow houses
60. Not anybody
65. Rum-seasoning ingredients
66. Geology suffixes
67. Word before ball or husk
68. Do-fa connectors
69. Short jacket
70. Chinese leader
72. Furze
73. Lightweight wood
74. Added a certain seasoning to
76. Spicy flavoring
77. Strain
78. Jot
79. Supermarket worker
80. Bussed
81. Rock's Mick ____
82. Classic Western
83. Prefix meaning five
84. Palo ____, California
85. Troll
86. Ensnare
87. Relate
88. ____ Grosso, Brazil
89. Music critic Downes
90. Chest rattle
91. Some undergarments
92. Submerged

401

PUZZLE 524

ACROSS
1. Soft substance
5. Bandy words
9. Book and candle's go-with
13. Seal and whale groups
17. Mary Lamb's brother
18. City near Phoenix
19. Crystal gazer's words
20. Songstress Adams
21. Square or fair
22. Very simple
24. "Arrivederci ____"
25. Scarf
27. Bovine cry
28. Explode
29. Damage
30. City on the Rhine
31. Lot item
33. Totally exhausted
36. Great ____
37. He rode Topper
42. Noteworthy achievement
43. Scepter
44. Any
45. "The ____ of Frankenstein" (1964 film)
46. Actor Devine
47. Neighbor of Mo.
48. Building addition
49. Farewell: Latin
50. Shaft
51. Martini ingredient
52. Frozen rain
53. Wife of Menelaus
54. Actor Holbrook
55. Postpone
56. "____ Joey"
57. Waits
60. ". . . ____ in the house that Jack built"
61. Actor Madison
62. River bottom
65. Dutch cheese
66. Flax fabric
67. Take the dirty dishes away
68. Work with concrete
69. Songstress Logan
70. Smooth
71. Party-dress feature
72. ____ code
73. Rudolph, e.g.
75. Essence
76. Doc, e.g.
77. Be human
78. Crones
79. Prohibit
80. "The Mysterious Stranger" author
84. Ms. Renking
85. Dorothy's home
88. Sign of an angel
89. Unworried and casual
93. ____ hoop
95. Lendl or Nagy
96. Danube color
97. "Butterflies Are ____"
98. Cornelia ____ Skinner
99. Capone's nemesis
100. Apiary creatures
101. Sense
102. Vain show

DOWN
1. A Turner
2. Fish sauce
3. Fibber
4. ____ Jane
5. Daub
6. Bog fuel
7. Donkey
8. Burr
9. Ox's kin
10. Psychic's letters
11. Wreath
12. Actor Marvin
13. Alpaca's site
14. Effluvium
15. Darkens
16. Stool
23. First-rate
26. Forefront
28. Bikini top
30. TV's "Break the ____"
31. Another 73 Across
32. Summit
33. From a distance
34. Songstress Horne
35. 1980 Kenny Rogers hit
36. Flubber's word
37. West of TV
38. Smooth
39. Face shape
40. It flowed over Ripon Falls
41. Secluded valley
43. Lament
44. Golfing great
48. Sportscaster Mel
51. Cooking fuel
52. Virtues number
53. Statesman John Milton ____
54. Macho fellow
55. 1982 film
56. Shove
57. Frat party beverage
58. Unemployed
59. Famous Surrealist
60. Onions garnish it
61. Blast of wind
62. Actress Theda
63. Eternally
64. Turn a ____ ear
66. Ogle
67. Male singer
68. Mont-de-piete
71. Cease broadcasting
74. Library
75. Mob
76. August or Rather
78. 19th President
79. Bakery product
80. Watery
81. Tidal ____
82. Alack
83. Charged particles
85. On bended ____
86. Self-propelled: prefix
87. Slender
89. Recede
90. Kin of 57 Down
91. "Sioux City ____"
92. Wrath
94. Horned viper

ACROSS

1. Add weight to the dice
5. Card player's term
10. French headquarters in 1912
15. "My Name Is ____"
19. Mysterious Gardner
20. What time does, it's said
21. Wind may do this to rocks
22. Skirt length
23. Beams boastfully
26. Stack
27. Percussion instruments
28. Fortuneteller's phrase
29. For fear that
31. Patronymic suffix
32. Shackles
34. Classic lang.
36. ____ la Paix
38. Canea resident
41. Got a long hit
45. Waited
48. Hawk leashes
49. Prefix with port or form
50. Grand ____ (Evangeline's home)
52. Verso's opposite
53. ____ ears
54. Desert
56. Calf meats
58. Prefix or suffix meaning lizard
59. At hand
61. Former Secretary of State
62. Runts
64. Amin
65. Influenza
67. Drive and reverse
69. Anent
70. Teachers' gp.
71. Alcott family name
73. Cameo role
74. Part of USNA
76. Complement of to
79. Sound defeat
80. Esse
82. Turkish inn
86. Little suffixes
87. Waited on hand and foot (with "to")
89. Exchange for Powers
91. Hang-glide
92. Robinson role
94. Pranks
95. Tea cakes
97. Spoon-bender Geller
98. Strike breakers
100. Kind of maniac
101. Unit of electrical capacity
102. Author St. Johns
104. Important chair
106. Enable
108. C_6H_5
109. Small dams
111. For example
112. Lessing
114. Printemps month
116. Cartoon's Le Pew
118. Neural network
121. Alters the caliber
125. Competent
127. Little Big Horn
130. Ancient Mid-Eastener

131. A, for one
132. Apportion
133. Whale film
134. First place
135. Movie acrobatics
136. "____ Days and Mondays" (Carpenters song)
137. Look for

DOWN

1. Bank or wing
2. It's near Paris
3. Astringent
4. Notwithstanding
5. From ____ (ever since)
6. Fir product
7. Detroit gp.
8. Twice DXXVI
9. Attention-getting sounds
10. Rescind
11. Timetable abbr.
12. Seethe
13. Viper
14. Prepares to drive
15. Elec. unit
16. Emulates Adam
17. Crossbar
18. Manner
24. Pester
25. Assists
30. Lachrymose drop
33. Bar of wood
35. Plains structure
37. Charges
38. Trolley sound
39. See 33 Down
40. Chou ____
42. Antelopes' playground
43. 500 locale: abbr.
44. Back to the ____
46. Piano exercise
47. Andrea ____
49. Musical syllable
51. Actress Verdugo
55. What the last drink's for
56. Clothes, in Roma
57. Obsequious
60. Rate of movement meas.
62. Snooped
63. Coal deposit
66. Bois de Bologne, e.g.
68. Parisian priests
72. Term of endearment
75. Missionary Bartolome de ____ Casas
76. A base
77. Psychotherapist Wilhelm
78. Irish dramatist
81. Mother of pearl
83. Joan of Arc's last residence

84. Bird with a worm
85. Error's counterpart
88. House components
90. Football defender
93. Double-reed instrument
95. Bones or buck
96. Hindu terms of respect
99. Nasty one
101. Hall
103. Early cars
105. Constructs
107. Author Gail ____
108. Way to be sitting
110. Gush
113. Bean
114. Role for Lucy or Angela
115. Sleeping
117. Twin of the Bible
119. Romanov ruler
120. Miss Logan
122. Word to the waiter
123. Noun suffix
124. State: abbr.
126. Poetic dusk
128. Pewter ingredient
129. The Greatest

PUZZLE 525

• POKER FACE •

403

PUZZLE 526

• THE WORK FORCE •

ACROSS
1. Covers with turf
5. Mrs. Truman
9. Play the lead
13. Dune buggy
17. Notion
18. "Vissi d'___"
19. Rubik's toy
20. Forearm bone
21. Gangster's gal
22. Indo-European
23. Freshly
24. Stare and grin
25. Some office workers: 2 wds.
29. Before
30. Fish eggs
31. Hammock holder
32. Salesperson
35. Roaster
37. Washington workers
41. SRO makers
42. Have being
43. Kind of wrestling
44. Siamese
45. Ostrich cousin
46. Assert
47. Sticky situation
48. Teenagers
51. Tapered splicing pin
52. "Platoon" role
54. Dragon of song
55. Net gurus: 2 wds.
60. Give up
61. Perfume
62. The loneliest number
64. On dits
67. Bauxite is one
68. ___ the Man
69. Atlantic state: abbr.
70. Motorist's club: abbr.
71. Krazy ___
72. Plural suffix
73. Eatery output
74. Cinematic bigwig
78. Proceed along
80. Restaurant employees
81. "___ Rhythm": 2 wds.
82. Revolutionary
83. Bridle part
84. Some educators: 3 wds.
92. Ladder part
93. "___ Girl"
94. Makes mistakes
95. Bacchanalian cry
96. Folklore monster
97. "Charley's ___"
98. Artifice
99. Singer Stevens
100. Forest denizen
101. Nancy Lopez's gp.
102. Fortuneteller
103. Eskimo transport

DOWN
1. Nerd
2. Reputation
3. Corner store, for short
4. Trays
5. Recipe word
6. Mr. Gardner
7. Depots: abbr.
8. Strict
9. Startle
10. Air
11. Aided in crime
12. Alert again
13. Dancer Prowse
14. Robert ___: 2 wds.
15. Chemical suffixes
16. Golfer's goal
26. Safe vessel
27. Slammer occupant
28. Power group: abbr.
32. Feast provider
33. Boundary
34. Musical study
35. Threatening words: 2 wds.
36. "Ernani" composer
37. Addition
38. Baseball's Mel
39. College cheer
40. Bro's sibling
42. Shuns
43. Trading centers
46. Grant portrayer
47. James or Owens
48. Tall lily plants
49. Frequently
50. Eerie sighting, for short
53. Unmoving
54. Kicked, in a way
56. Certain milit. man
57. Plastic ingredient
58. Calgary event
59. Move stealthily
63. Building additions
64. Talk
65. Nasser's gp.
66. ___ Tse-tung
67. Scull
71. Hamburger topping
73. May honorees
75. Archeologist
76. Yuck!
77. Of the ribs
78. Popular rock group, with "The"
79. Certain fishermen
80. Presidential title: abbr.
82. Terra ___
83. Lower
84. Enormous
85. Concerning: 2 wds.
86. Suspend
87. Word with blue
88. Irish Gaelic
89. Fiendish
90. Midler movie, with "The"
91. Gardener's purchase
92. Hot or fishing

• SPLISH SPLASH •

ACROSS
1. Bollard
5. Curtain ____
9. Convex molding
14. Cloth strainer
19. Fluish
20. Locale
21. Amazon, e.g.
22. Praying figure
23. Harold of the comics
24. Stuff
25. Alabama's eleven
27. Out of class
29. Obi
31. Woodpecker type
32. Fib
33. Churchill's sign
34. Evict
36. Energy
38. Insect egg
39. Rattletrap
40. Expert on Persian culture
42. Lodge member
44. People of today
46. Culture media
47. Letter writer
50. Footlike part
51. "____ of the Lost Ark"
53. Face with stone
55. Sunk in a bog
59. Past
61. Sirius
63. Naval
65. Lobby
67. Overlay
68. Bargain event
69. Mine entrance
70. Franchot ____
71. "On the Beach" author
73. Big bandage
74. Far: prefix
75. Bettor's interests
76. Spikes of 77 Across
77. Maize
78. Pastor
80. Atomic submarine
82. Stamp
84. Posed
85. Advantage
86. Role for Hoffman
88. Sawbuck
90. Prize piece
92. Aquatic class
94. To the left
97. Marks of disgrace
101. Mexican money
102. Sirenian
104. Dorothy's state: abbr.
105. Uncooked
107. Tex. school
108. Flippant
109. Owns
110. Print measures
111. Flags
113. "My Friend ____"
115. Redford
117. Weakened

120. Tennis star
122. Continent
123. Ecole pupil
124. Northern home
125. "____ little pig went . . ."
126. Let
127. Reimburse
128. Jewish ritual
129. Owns, in the Bible
130. Prophet

DOWN
1. Djakarta, once
2. Titanic's undoing
3. Carson book
4. River of England
5. "____ Flower"
6. Sched. abbr.
7. Smallest amount
8. Tibetan priest
9. Of a band
10. Man: Latin
11. Roman poet
12. Dud
13. Sink ____
14. Dawn backed him up
15. Skill
16. Author Norman
17. Wooden ____
18. Brews
26. ____ of the world

28. Spreading rumor
30. Mineral springs
35. Bethlehem product
37. Punt pusher
39. Falter
41. FDR act
42. Places wrongly
43. Silver State: abbr.
45. Ms. Moore
48. Harbinger
49. Rest
52. Type of engine
54. Powder
56. Synge drama
57. Iago's wife
58. Discover
59. German city
60. ____ gold
62. Cravat
64. Responds
66. Savings
68. Elves
72. Drag
73. Sun
77. Southern constellation
79. Greek seaport

81. Short article
82. Prophet: Latin
83. "What's in ____?"
87. Swab
89. WWII agcy.
91. Donny's sister
93. Quartet
95. Bringing up
96. Having left a will
97. Shish kebab holder
98. Mexican roll-up
99. Foot part
100. Famous Broadway restaurant
103. Take into custody
106. Golf club
108. Turkish officer
111. Card
112. Peddled
114. School subj.
116. Cage parts
118. Little ____
119. ____ is me!
121. Greetings

PUZZLE 528

Here is a puzzle with more than the expected crossword challenge—and rewards. Each clue involves a pun or some form of nuttiness. Look out for traps! With a little practice, you will soon catch on to these tricky clues and enjoy the extra challenge.

ACROSS

1. Petticoat junction
5. Subject of "Bartlett's"
10. Losing fifty bawls back to mop up
14. Unwanted leaf from the Bible
15. It's mint to make you drunk
16. Nathan was from hearty stock
17. Like a cancelled stamp
18. Able to outfox a fox
19. Part an actor knows backwards
20. Fake pearls?
22. Punishes with candy?
24. What a landlord is apt. to do
25. Silk stocking district
27. Hit and run?
29. Rings again
33. What's on your mind?
34. Monkey see, monkey do
35. Carries on
37. Current event
41. Net result
43. Saved phone money
45. Adams madam

46. Daisy loses it and tells
48. It's a gas to be so lazy
50. A number of thing
51. That's the chance you take
53. Hangs around
55. There, I've said it again
59. Coat tree?
60. Fall girl
61. Leveled with the London demolition crew
63. Oldfangled
67. What Peter and Florence have in common
69. It's a long story
71. All of you in Dixie
72. It hurts to be cut by one of your own glass
73. ylbiduA
74. Devil, mostly
75. Result of being kept in stitches
76. Miss the litter basket
77. Brief claims to fame

DOWN

1. Raise objections

2. Life of Riley
3. Some place
4. Run interference?
5. Short nighties
6. Come up with something Sherlock might come up with
7. A name by any other name
8. Caused another hitch in your military career
9. Stretch out a banquet
10. Haggard woman
11. Half the town in Washington
12. Herb and Lily take their medicine
13. Road bed
21. One thing you can't take lying down
23. Behaved in a racy manner
26. Brighten the corner where you are
28. Yes, Virginia, I venture to say you were the first
29. Violent age
30. One of the finer points of fencing
31. He's really little trouble
32. Ventures into the world as an ex-batter
36. Place an E on top forever
38. Subject of "The Pagan Love Song"
39. Dandy's companion
40. They tempt the beginning golfer
42. He was completely underwhelmed by the tortoise
44. Price of a return trip
47. He wouldn't give you the right time
49. A tankard of ale, bottoms up
52. They're grand for bands
54. Tattler-taler
55. Brings in the sheaves
56. Cut up
57. U.S. Keystone
58. Wandered up
62. Sign out
64. Put an egg in the nest?
65. It's a mistake
66. Wings, but no birds
68. The poem's over
70. What a long arm it has!

PUZZLE 529

• TEE PARTY •

ACROSS
1. Morse code bits
5. Had feelings
10. Drummer's "ride"
14. Dorothy's pup
18. Nang Xian nurse
19. White poplar
20. Conceits
22. Pavlov
23. Track tests
25. Wall Street reading, once
27. Forceful fellow
28. U of the UN
30. Long-running soap
31. Shad output
32. Less available
34. Solder
36. Moderated
39. Snoopy's Red foe
40. School segment
44. Reigns
45. Jute sacking
46. Garden apparatus
47. Minuscule
48. Philip Roth novel
50. Diamond St.
51. Motivate
53. "Master Melvin"
54. Fiction
55. Errand of mercy
57. Oklahoma city
58. Happiness
60. Enthrallment
61. Toothed tools
62. Congers
63. Creative folk
64. Scriptural anise
65. With intelligence
67. Cutting tools
68. Actor Louis ____, Jr.
71. River duck
72. Casino employees
73. Bop
74. Marble
75. Luscious desserts
77. Fleur-de-____
78. Collins novel, with "The"
80. Haggard novel
81. France or England
83. Rinse
84. Plexus
85. Covenant
87. Spurs
88. Was patient
89. In pieces
90. Memorable ship
91. Cairngorm cap
92. "The ____ of San Vittorio"
95. Hoard
97. Costa del Sol town
102. Traveler's chit
104. Speechless
106. In the know about
107. Double-deal
108. He threw to Chance
109. Reykjavik reading
110. Hammer head
111. Villa d'____
112. Crib calls
113. Peregrinate

DOWN
1. Computer fodder
2. "Lucky Jim" author
3. Scenery chewers
4. Most flimsy
5. Menu
6. Rose's stage hubby
7. Move around
8. Old measure
9. Obliterate
10. Ravi's tool
11. Frigg's hubby
12. Auditor's objective
13. Furniture material
14. Spine lines
15. Indy setting
16. Snack food
17. Five to a fin
21. Lees
24. ____ the boards
26. Critics
29. Grouse spouse
33. Firenze flow
35. Build a nest
36. In the hold
37. Climber's goal
38. Blabbermouths
39. Ajuga
40. Bank employees
41. Nimble
42. Weird
43. English horns
45. Growls
46. Credenzas
49. Apennine nation
50. Infant wear
52. Tolls
55. Montgomery of ____
56. Apr. collector
59. "The Most Happy ____"
60. Little onion
61. Gambles
63. Expanse
64. Actress Dixon
65. "____ of Love"
66. Fuzzy fruit, in France
67. Chap on a break
68. Thugs
69. Jacques's aunt
70. Boss ____
72. Eye-catching
73. Unfit for service
76. Bugged
78. Cheap
79. Iambic measure
82. Engine openings
83. Raised
86. Oxeye relative
87. Shoot the breeze
88. George Herman's sobriquet
90. Dull finish
91. Bind
92. Fielding play
93. Shore bird
94. Specify
96. Food division
98. Jahan built here
99. Italian islands
100. Castor's mother
101. Seth's father
103. Senor Guevara
105. Eggs

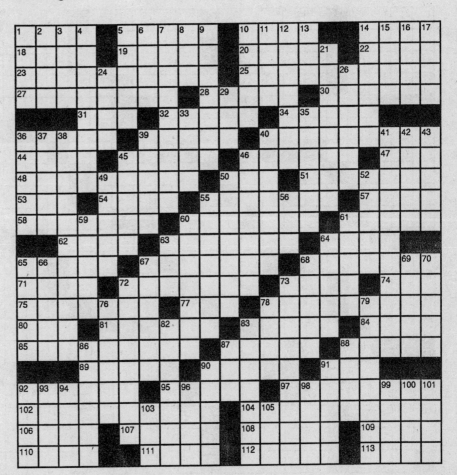

PUZZLE 530

• GREENHOUSE GREATS •

ACROSS

1. ____-in-the-pulpit
5. Plus-side item
10. Friend of Porthos
15. Altercation
18. Irish islands
19. English author
20. Disney dog
21. Malicious
23. Composer Bartok
24. Joined
25. Ohio politician Mark
26. Pop
27. Coarse hominy
28. River of Asia
29. Supplicates
30. Hit solidly
32. Angler's boot
34. Large-billed cuckoo
35. Neglect
36. House of Stuart heirloom?
42. Certain sib
43. Single
44. Tenn. athlete
45. Silver salmon
47. Classifieds
50. Chilled
51. Had aspirations
54. Joshua's protector
56. Memphis god
57. Pipe joint
58. Skin openings
59. Mexican border state
60. One of the Hebrides
61. ____-el-Amarna
62. Winglike
63. County or catbird
64. Complained, dogwise
66. Scottish viol(et)ist
70. "____ beloved . . ."
73. Author Tolstoy
74. Family member
75. Balaam's vehicle
78. Radius's partner
79. With pluck
82. Feasts
83. Sodom emigre
84. Sty fare
85. Bay window
86. Playwright Jean
87. Ball
88. Ecru
89. Parisian tec
90. Kramden's vehicle
91. Beast of burden
92. Hawaiian dish
93. Nichols play
99. My ____ back
102. Hindu goddess
103. Fortified
104. With bated ____
105. Stuff
106. 2006, Roman style
107. Singer James
111. Farm building
112. Accent
114. Danger
115. Undiluted
116. Within: prefix
117. Embankment
118. Actress Massey
119. Dividing word
120. Sibilant letter
121. Woolf work, with "The"
122. Ancient book
123. ____ and the Ants

DOWN

1. Holmes's weapons
2. ____ of expertise
3. Peaceful
4. Purple-flowered perennial
5. Fleet
6. Tars
7. Titan's planet
8. Fulda feeder
9. Spread hay
10. Goddess of widsom
11. Like Lear's story
12. Artist Holbein
13. Universal: prefix
14. Toledo blade?
15. Dammar and elemi
16. Convex molding
17. Broader
22. Draw out
29. Room or point
31. Exchange premium
33. "____ I Love Her"
36. Silent
37. "____ Vanya"
38. Actor Tom
39. Poet Merriam et al.
40. Turf
41. Narcissus's admirer
46. Thole occupant
47. Surmounting
48. Hamlet, e.g.
49. Bony herring
51. Tiffany decor?
52. Kind of tradition
53. Persian sprite
54. Bellows
55. One opposed
56. Briar
58. Bucket
59. Indian soldier
63. Aroma
65. Proponents
66. Encase
67. Away from aweather
68. Principal
69. Old Norse letter
70. Kind of bowl
71. Ms. Raines
72. Soon
75. Poplar tree
76. Cobbler's concerns
77. Trite
80. "Exodus" name
81. Sheetlike silicate
82. Mr. Arnaz
86. Astronaut Grissom
87. Florist's favorite
89. Source
90. Rafter
91. Because: It.
92. Celestas' kin
94. Etna
95. Icons
96. Musket accessory
97. U.C. campus site
98. Sarsaparilla
99. ____ Prevost
100. Stretch
101. Pods
105. Vena ____
106. City in Uruguay
108. Incline
109. So long
110. Unit of matter
113. Lilliputian
114. Movie, for short

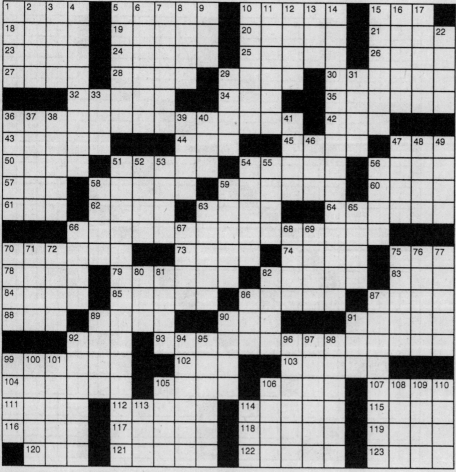

PUZZLE 531

ACROSS
1. Only
5. Craze
8. Car fuel
11. Pioneering
12. Fuss
13. Regret
14. Model
15. Camper's light
17. Flex
18. Mountain
19. Peruse
20. Hairy ox
22. Tweak
24. Possessed
27. Musicians' booking
29. Faulty
32. Actress Arden
33. Unskilled
35. Seine
36. Steel
38. Fasten
39. Carefree
40. Ajar
42. Paid athlete
44. Weathercock
46. Orange drink
48. Nail
52. Shifty
54. Serenity
55. Child
56. Gents
57. Awry
58. Be indebted to
59. Layer
60. Require

DOWN
1. Method
2. Level
3. Prepared
4. Building wing
5. Autumn
6. Conform
7. Put on
8. Salutation
9. Atmosphere
10. Transmit
11. Point
16. Neaten, as a hedge
18. Related
21. Limber
23. Liquid
24. Shorten
25. Hail!
26. Explode
28. Acquire
30. Ocean
31. Pigpen
34. Briar
37. Mimics
41. Belly button
43. Portly
44. Turn down
45. Declare
47. Refuse
49. Scoundrel
50. Got a perfect score
51. Morning moisture
53. Elf
54. Kitchen utensil

PUZZLE 532

ACROSS
1. Casks
5. Flirt's attempt
9. Poet McKuen
12. Satanic
13. Ready
14. "___ to Joy"
15. Bristle
16. Gems
18. Folklore creatures
20. Yawn-causing
21. River in France
23. Colorful parrot
26. Stuffing
30. ___ avis
31. ___ Angeles
32. Mountain range
34. Table part
35. ___ boy!
37. Zoo creatures
39. Williams and Muni
41. Get one's feet wet
42. Asian nursemaid
44. Snuggle
48. Tubular pasta
51. ___ cream
52. Deck member
53. "___ Ben Adhem"
54. Alcohol lamp
55. Sure!
56. Standard
57. Court items

DOWN
1. Waistcoat
2. State
3. Former Yugoslav leader
4. Ski race
5. Urgent
6. Intention
7. Dashed
8. Antitoxin
9. Attendance check
10. Not even
11. ___ Moines
17. Winged
19. Type of bean
22. Bequeath
24. Sector
25. Gossips
26. Certain joint
27. Roster
28. Calms
29. Garden flower
33. Kick or walk
36. ___ mater
38. Abate
40. Lucifer
43. Vagrant
45. Carry
46. ___ and Fontanne
47. Pitchers' stats
48. Beam
49. Frost
50. Conjunction

409

PUZZLE 533

ACROSS
1. Hit with the hand
5. Dined
8. Cease
12. Pit
13. Raced
14. Cover with asphalt
15. Always
16. Make a mistake
17. Portent
18. Pattern
20. Playful water animals
22. Ocean
23. Allow
24. Lamps
27. Work-force reduction
31. Exist
32. ___ is me!
33. Take out
37. Alter
40. Feel unwell
41. "___ Miss Brooks"
42. Rough-edged
45. Splendid repasts
49. Military acronym
50. Sprite
52. Dinghy
53. Sugar source
54. Observe
55. Not working
56. Organs of vision
57. Driving mound
58. Serene

DOWN
1. Lean-to
2. Adore
3. Beverages
4. ___ the thought!
5. Sports structures
6. Roof material
7. Sign up
8. Irregular
9. Domesticated
10. Above
11. Animal enclosures
19. Obtain
21. Afternoon party
24. Boy
25. Displeasure
26. Set
28. Possess
29. Heavy mist
30. Charge
34. Philadelphia footballers
35. Even score
36. First-born
37. Stimulating beverage
38. Tint
39. Mideast language
42. Hurry
43. Absent
44. Departed
46. Cola
47. High
48. Plant part
51. Actor Marvin

PUZZLE 534

ACROSS
1. Behave
4. Den
8. War god
10. Change
12. Largest continent
13. Sermon giver
15. Mustangs
17. Dos Passos novel
18. Guy's date
19. Arduous journey
20. Mr. Ford
23. Thick
24. ___ up (invigorates)
25. Actor Chaney
26. Bard's always
27. Awe
30. Blue-pencil wielder
32. Love god
34. Long look
35. ___ Ridge (1972 Derby winner)
36. Paradise
37. Poetic time

DOWN
1. GP's org.: abbr.
2. Singer Johnny
3. The Kingston ___
4. Place for a carnation
5. Woeful word
6. ___ in the bag
7. Tax filing
9. Certain NCOs, for short
11. Pete and Billy
14. Roue
16. Actor Mineo
19. Like filet mignon
20. Dueling weapon
21. Acts
22. Fairy
23. Baseball's Drysdale
25. Actress Sophia
27. Sported
28. Great Lake
29. Wander
31. Slight amount
33. ___ Jose

ACROSS
1. W. state
4. Equal portion
8. Chums
12. In favor of
13. City in Russia
14. Above
15. Newspaper section
18. Legal matter
19. Home on the range
20. Embers
23. Asterisk
24. Vessel
25. Store
26. ____ Grande
29. Dow-Jones item
32. Lamprey
33. Greek god of war
34. Matinee ____
35. Talking horse
36. Battlefield
37. Auctioned again
40. Mature
41. Additional payment to a shareholder
46. Simians
47. Epochal
48. Grassland
49. Be loving
50. Remove, in printing
51. Lock opener

DOWN
1. ____ and running
2. King: Fr.
3. Coastal flyer
4. Sharpens
5. Circle parts
6. Hawaiian wreath
7. Aircraft carriers, informally
8. Composition
9. Palm leaf
10. Theater box
11. Graf ____
16. Mountain ridge
17. Springs
20. French friar
21. Ocean fish
22. Tow
23. Drew back from fear
25. Tattered
26. Went by car
27. Religious image
28. Sooner State: abbr.
30. "Cheers" employee
31. Weary
35. Code man
36. Nimble
37. Library sign
38. World's fair, e.g.
39. Printer's direction
40. Grandparental
42. Anger
43. Large deer
44. Born
45. Time period

Quotagram

Fill in the answers to the clues. Then transfer the letters to the correspondingly numbered squares in the diagram. The completed diagram will contain a quotation.

1. Cave $\overline{29}\ \overline{25}\ \overline{33}\ \overline{10}\ \overline{20}\ \overline{4}$

2. Slightly mad $\overline{34}\ \overline{24}\ \overline{16}\ \overline{9}\ \overline{22}$

3. Minute-man's unit $\overline{18}\ \overline{1}\ \overline{15}\ \overline{13}\ \overline{31}\ \overline{27}\ \overline{7}$

4. Nictitate $\overline{6}\ \overline{30}\ \overline{28}\ \overline{26}$

5. Sorrowing $\overline{23}\ \overline{11}\ \overline{35}\ \overline{2}\ \overline{5}\ \overline{14}$

6. Dried alfalfa $\overline{38}\ \overline{36}\ \overline{3}$

7. Knickknack $\overline{37}\ \overline{21}\ \overline{17}\ \overline{8}\ \overline{12}\ \overline{19}\ \overline{32}$

PUZZLE 537

ACROSS
1. Certain paintings
5. Anatomical pouches
9. Enervate
12. Malayan canoe
13. Horse's gait
14. ____ carte
15. Line of juncture
16. Recorded proceedings
17. Part of a journey
18. The two
20. Fortify
22. Hunting expedition
25. Stout
26. Pastry
27. Agreement
32. Month before Nisan
34. Doze
35. Prefix for a trillion
36. Joined metal plate again
39. Sign for Aries
40. Spoiled
41. Go on and on
43. Crystal
46. Greek peak
47. Lowe or Reiner
48. Egyptian queen of the gods
50. French military cap
54. Era
55. Singing voice
56. At all times
57. Nevertheless
58. "The ____ in Winter"
59. Fetid

DOWN
1. Harvest goddess
2. Choler
3. Mauna ____
4. Brazilian dance
5. Assigned, as to a post
6. Curved structure
7. Portable bed
8. Unchangeable
9. Spanish room
10. Actor Guiness
11. Bellboy
19. Grampus
21. Tear
22. Sail holder
23. Military assistant
24. Worry
25. Slander
28. Slave leader Turner
29. Croat's neighbor
30. River to the Caspian Sea
31. Identical
33. Umbrella parts
37. Feudal tenant
38. "____ Boot"
42. Manufacturer
43. Dismal
44. Theatre section
45. Encourage
46. Sarge's dog
49. Mr. Baba
51. Topsy's friend
52. Female swan
53. Annoy

PUZZLE 538

See page 21 for solving directions.

CODEWORD

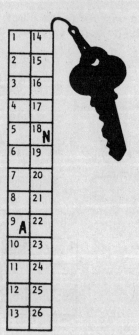

CRISS-CROSSWORD

The answer words for Criss-Crossword are entered diagonally, reading downward, from upper left to lower right or from upper right to lower left. We have entered the words RENE and REF to show you how.

TO THE RIGHT

1. M. Descartes
2. Storm
3. Machine part
4. Think
5. Ship part
6. Lace loop
7. Joker
9. Type set
11. Greek letter
14. Intone
15. Monaco worker
17. Secular
18. Opera song
20. Poker stake
22. Hospital worker
24. ____ Grande
26. Timid
28. Flower part
31. Seth's brother

32. Drink slowly
34. Milit. address
35. Certain NCO
36. Egyptian cobra

TO THE LEFT

2. Ump's kin
3. River craft
4. Reddish purple
5. Do a slow burn
6. Dance step
7. Port, e.g.
8. Datum
10. End
12. Sp. aunt
13. Poi source
15. Parlor game
16. Tabriz native
19. Mispronounce
21. Undeceived by

23. Taxing inits.
25. Shoshonean
27. Windy City
29. Leavening
30. Homeric

33. Knock
34. Totally
35. Agent
37. Actor Torn

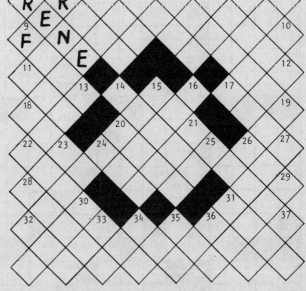

CIRCLE SUMS

Each circle below, lettered A through F, has its own number value from 1 to 9. No two circles have the same value. The numbers shown in the diagram are the sums of the circles which overlap at those points. For example, 10 is the sum of circles B and C. Can you find the value of each circle?

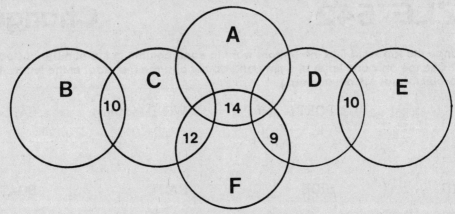

PUZZLE 541

ACROSS

1. Pop
5. Expunge
10. "Green Eggs and ___" (Seuss)
13. Rich soil
14. Mediterranean island
15. "Rose ___ rose . . .": 2 wds.
16. Poet Pound
17. Shankar's instrument
18. Like a dime
19. Thick
21. Henri's negative
22. Deception
23. Lean
25. Willing
28. Skill
31. Mop
33. "Song of the South" uncle
36. Hollywood unit
38. Southern swamp
41. VP Burr
43. Pipe bend
44. Linguistic currency
45. June VIP
48. Peter or Paul
49. Backus role, vocally
50. Swaddle
52. Actor Ron
53. "___ each life . . ."
55. Baghdad's land
57. ___ of Gaunt
60. Hipster's home
62. Desert plant
66. Cut ___ (dance): 2 wds.
67. Channels of communication
69. Melville's captain
70. Sweeping shot
71. Of a region
72. Window ledge
73. Moose's kin
74. Politician Mark
75. Woe ___!: 2 wds.

DOWN

1. Luge
2. Seep
3. Mend, in a way
4. Compile
5. Printers' measures
6. Lancaster film, with "The"
7. Choir voice
8. Actor Arnold
9. Lend an ___
10. "___ the Merrio": hyph.
11. Continent
12. Type of cat
18. Get ___ out of (optimize): 2 wds.
20. Loop loopers
24. ___ Jima
26. Exist
27. Carte du jour
28. Kind of horse
29. Provide ammo anew
30. Self-service place: suffix
32. Underneath
34. Russian edict
35. Actor George
37. Board
39. Tampa native
40. Otherworldly: var.
42. Modern gaslight
46. Understood
47. Disfigure
51. Prove profitable
54. Puccini work
56. Seemingly
57. Mock
58. Mr. Roberts
59. Large piece
61. Mideast port
63. Greek letters
64. Placid
65. Competent
67. ___-jongg
68. In the style of: 2 wds.

PUZZLE 542   Changaword

Can you change the top word into the bottom word in each column in the number of steps indicated in parentheses? Change only one letter at a time and do not change the order of the letters. Proper names, slang, and obsolete words are not allowed.

1. DECK (4 steps)   2. PORT (4 steps)   3. WIND (5 steps)   4. SAIL (5 steps)

HAND   SIDE   RAIN   BOAT

CODEWORD

Codeword is a special crossword puzzle in which conventional clues are omitted. Instead, answer words in the diagram are represented by numbers. Each number represents a different letter of the alphabet, and all of the letters of the alphabet are used. When you are sure of a letter, put it in the code key chart for easy reference. Three letters have been given to start you off.

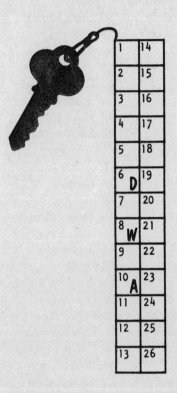

1	14	2	15
3	16	4	17
5	18	6 D	19
7	20	8 W	21
9	22	10 A	23
11	24	12	25
13	26		

Grid (Across reading):

23	10	6	9		3	10	18	19	17		2	9	1	20
21	13	25	12		9	14	10	20	9		10	24	14	9
14	9	17	25		14	21	26	21	6		17	9	25	17
9	12	10	1		9	20	10	14		3	9	6	9	1
			9	12	12			9	20	10				
1	20	10		10	5	9	1		10	4	4	9	10	12
20	7	12	25	8		20	10	14	16		10	17	17	9
10	12	10	11		6	25	13	21	9		10	26	21	1
13	25	22	21		25	17	9	1		10	12	25	1	9
1	9	1	20	9	20		1	10	8 W A 1		5	9	20	
			14	9	1			10 A 7	10	D				
1	8	10	17	16		15	19	25	6		11	25	6	9
20	10	12	10		3	19	12	26	9		21	20	9	12
21	6	9	11		9	10	13	9	12		1	7	10	13
12	21	1	9		9	8	9	12	1		1	25	17	1

COMMON COMBOS

The answer for each group can either precede or follow each of the given words.

Example: Rubber, Wagon, Brass, Stand (**Answer:** Band)

1. Station   Chuck   Train   _____
2. Station   Civil   Lip   _____
3. Office   Cash   Alarm   _____
4. Sand   Silver   Double   _____
5. Chili   Blue   Face   _____
6. League   Rich   Finger   _____
7. Butter   Weed   Tooth   _____

PUZZLE 545

ACROSS

1. Reciprocating wheel
4. Biblical king
8. Superlative suffix
11. Rowed
13. Little one
14. Moderate
15. Ill will
16. Last word in prayer
17. Gabor and Peron
18. Splash
20. Dish-dryers
22. Rent
24. Elude
25. Antics
28. Ocean crosser
30. Actress Gardner
31. Radiate
33. More recent
37. ___ annum
38. Stir
39. Some railroads
41. Wrath
42. Curl
44. Heavy reading
46. Falsehood
47. Concluded
49. Repaired
52. Risk-taker
54. Hum
56. Harsh
57. Concentrated
61. Harbinger
62. Between
65. Emends
66. Golfer's warning
67. Spice or club
68. Descartes and Lacoste
69. Picnic nuisance
70. Prophet
71. Morning moisture

DOWN

1. "Li'l Abner" cartoonist
2. Operatic highlight
3. Courage
4. Featured performers
5. Goal
6. Hawaiian guitar, for short
7. Relating to the pre-Easter period
8. Having roof overhangs
9. Dated
10. Hardy heroine
11. CIA's forerunner
12. Put off
14. Take care!
19. Lessened
21. Bakery features
23. Samuel's mentor
25. Army officer: abbr.
26. State firmly
27. Peel
29. List notation
32. Small particle
34. Unrestrained
35. Great Lake
36. Marsh plant
38. Lou Grant portrayer
40. Citrus fruit
43. Placid
45. Strange
48. Sleep fantasies
50. "___ Laughing"
51. Required
52. Devil
53. Prevent
55. Horseman
56. Parlor piece
58. Baseball team
59. One-pot meal
60. Double curve
63. Actress West
64. Frozen water

PUZZLE 546   Shuffle

Two 7-letter words with their letters in the correct order are combined in each row of letters. To solve the puzzle separate both words. There are no extra letters, and no letter is used more than once. Helpful hint: the two words are related.

Example: SOLVEDTIEREARN (SOLveDtIerEaRn) = SOLDIER, VETERAN

1. BOFULQOUEWERTS   _____   _____
2. COMNANNDERUCST   _____   _____
3. AZONOLIMOALGYS   _____   _____
4. WEALATMHEANRAC   _____   _____
5. CANTOMPHOEMSES   _____   _____
6. WEARSEANPAOLNS   _____   _____
7. PVEORRTICANODA   _____   _____

CODEWORD

Codeword is a special crossword puzzle in which conventional clues are omitted. Instead, answer words in the diagram are represented by numbers. Each number represents a different letter of the alphabet, and all of the letters of the alphabet are used. When you are sure of a letter, put it in the code key chart for easy reference. Three letters have been given to start you off.

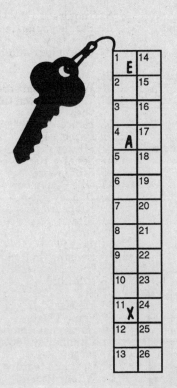

Code Key Chart

No.	Letter	No.	Letter
1	E	14	
2		15	
3		16	
4	A	17	
5		18	
6		19	
7		20	
8		21	
9		22	
10		23	
11	X	24	
12		25	
13		26	

Diagram (numbers; ■ = black square)

■	2	4	17	■	20	22	3	8	■	9	3	21	15
8	4	11	1	21	■	22	6	26	25	■	1	26	3	1
4	5	3	1	6	■	3	26	1	4	■	6	3	5	1
10	4	21	8	1	■	8	1	21	21	■	26	25	5	5
■				4	10	1	7	■	8	1	21	8	12	■
■		14	5	4	18	1	■		4	21	18	■		
19	1	4	6	■	2	7	3	10	■	1	16	1	13	8
7	1	6	8	21	■	4	6	21	■	21	4	7	4	15
21	8	1	1	5	■	3	6	1	24	■	23	4	6	1
■			4	3	26	■		4	17	4	21	1	■	
■	10	5	4	12	21	■	19	25	10	1	■			
21	5	1	26	■	5	1	4	26	■	4	5	8	4	7
15	1	4	26	■	4	7	3	26	■	13	1	4	21	1
1	4	23	1	■	6	3	6	1	■	15	4	5	1	26
21	8	1	7	■	26	1	1	7	■	10	1	4	■	

STEP BY STEP

In five steps, change each word below, one letter at a time, into a new 5-letter word, so that each letter has been changed. At each step form a new word, changing only one letter. Do not rearrange the order of the letters. You do not have to change the letters in order. Different answers are possible.

Example: Heard, Hears, Heads, Heeds, Seeds, Sleds

1. APACE	2. WHILE	3. MAKER	4. SCARF
_____	_____	_____	_____
_____	_____	_____	_____
_____	_____	_____	_____
_____	_____	_____	_____
_____	_____	_____	_____

PUZZLE 549

• FEATHERY FAIR •

ACROSS
1. Cries
5. Isle of Man native
9. Rajah's mate
13. Vicki Lawrence TV role
17. Realtor's map
18. "Lohengrin" heroine
19. Tiny particle
20. Israel's airline
21. Coleridge's bird
23. Voracious bird
25. When Dracula sleeps
26. Phase
28. Debs or Ionesco
29. Vocalized pauses
30. Pig
31. Funnyman Johnson
32. Pay TV
35. Activist
36. Imposed a tax on
40. Paris airport
41. Walter Lantz's cartoon bird
43. "We ___ not amused"
44. Thompson of "Back to the Future"
45. Crave
46. Lean-to
47. "Picnic" playwright
48. Touchable
50. Fed the kitty
52. Zeal
53. Philosopher Immanuel
54. Snooped
55. Barter
56. Fanatic
58. Pager sounds
59. Frosh headgear
62. Villain's forte
63. Maize
64. Astor or Steenburgen
65. Expert
66. ___ diem
67. Laughing jackass (Aussie bird)
70. Salesman's auto
71. Run-of-the-mill
73. On the briny
74. Jeweler's weight
75. Broadway musical
76. Shirt ornament
77. ___ tai (rum drink)
78. View
81. Suffix for gang or young
82. Troubled gulf
86. "My Little ___" (W.C. Fields flick)
88. Bird of a Christmas song
90. Fish from a can
91. Notion
92. Northern Indian
93. Robert ___
94. Cookie
95. Furnish
96. Darkens a little
97. Origin

DOWN
1. Nail
2. Earthenware pot
3. "Three Men and a ___"
4. Dignified
5. Bacteria
6. Sunscreen additive
7. Sibilant letter
8. Roped
9. Indy entry
10. On
11. Neither's partner
12. Dipped
13. Unites
14. Wings
15. "Buddenbrooks" author
16. Der ___
22. Recap, e.g.
24. ___ space
27. Ground cover, for short
30. Kick
31. Inquired
32. Stable youngster
33. Territory
34. One of four and twenty
35. Over
36. Was stiff and sore
37. Taylor-Burton film, with "The"
38. Hence
39. Bambi's kin
41. Mickey's creator
42. Senator Kefauver
45. Stiff breeze
47. OPEC member
49. Donkey put-on
50. Hippodrome
51. Bite
52. Off
54. Jaunty
55. Evening, in Roma
56. "___ Man" (1984 cult film)
57. State
58. Yahoos
59. Vamp Theda
60. Columnist Bombeck
61. Chimney sweep's target
63. Garment feature
64. Wilbur Post's horse
67. Talent
68. Lessen
69. Seized illegally
70. Field flowers
72. Glacial mass
74. Writer John Dickson ___
76. Lieu
77. Allots
78. Treads the boards
79. Avoid
80. ___ colada
81. Observed
82. Demure
83. Eric of "Nuns on the Run"
84. Author James ___
85. Exigency
87. HST's successor
89. Meyers of "Kate and Allie"

418

ACROSS

1. Literary drudge
5. Small town
9. Coptic bishop's title
13. Pertaining to grain
18. Spectacle snake
19. Hard blow
20. 1/1000 of a dollar
21. Winglike
22. "Partridge in ____ tree"
23. Femur and tibia
24. Revered one
25. Metric wt. units
26. N to S
30. Channeled
31. Zeno's lecture-hall
32. 22nd Greek letter
35. Offspring
36. Actress Joanne
39. Fasteners
43. Door features
46. Best ____ tucker
49. Footnote abbr.
50. State
51. "____ Lost" (Milton poem)
53. Roof repairman
55. SE to NW
59. Tired from walking
60. Sommer
61. Adolescence
62. Int.-seeker's purchase
64. Agnew
66. Full house
70. Disfigurement
74. Silver tellurides
79. E to W
82. Plainsong
83. In shirtsleeves
84. Japanese port city
85. Occipital ridge
87. Fatty matter
88. Director
90. Co-op's kin
91. Prescription abbr.
92. Tim McCoy's horse
93. Time divs.
94. Iris covering
97. Composes quickly
102. NW to SE
111. Godspeed
112. Shade of blue
113. Restaurant listing
114. Awaken
115. London University co-founder
116. South African dollar
117. On the sheltered side
118. Swiss philosopher
119. Destroy, '80s style
120. Other
121. Sparks et al.
122. Endings for front and arm

DOWN

1. Old Oraibi tribesman
2. Sibling-rivalry victim
3. Places where things get stuck
4. Gem weight unit
5. Bet takers familiarly
6. Put out of office
7. Designate again
8. Rasp
9. Former dictator
10. Await
11. Sounds
12. Distribute
13. W to E
14. It's a sin to tell ____
15. Ceylon palm-tree
16. School in England
17. Stack TV role
18. Part of a wheel
27. Prod
28. Kook
29. Santa ____
32. Kind of hanger
33. Lacked a choice
34. Svevo
37. Soviet revolutionist
38. Pools
40. Similar
41. Front or equation
42. Discern
44. Small talk
45. S to N
46. "____ Ronald"
47. "Dies ____"
48. Brit. decoration
51. Vb. tense
52. Caught sight of
54. Title for Alfonso
56. Dunkable delight
57. Sensual
58. Pucker
63. Steep slope
65. Plant-growth chems.
66. Pouch
67. Moral
68. South American plain
69. Bandleader Lester
71. Summoner
72. Cruiser launched by "GWTW" author
73. Fodder grasses
75. ____ La Douce
76. Perplexing
77. Duck down
78. Dipper components
80. Early form of ship
81. Half a fly
86. PBS science series
88. 17th-century shows
89. Matty, Felipe, or Jesus
92. Made more compact
95. ____ nous
96. "Let's Make ____"
98. Violinist
99. White poplar
100. Undomesticated
101. "Ethan ____"
102. For my ____
103. Bouquet
104. Latvian capital
105. Curling goal-marks
106. Sunburns
107. "Ye ____ Gift Shoppe"
108. Resign
109. Functions
110. Squiggly one

PUZZLE 550

• AS THE CROW FLIES •

PUZZLE 551

ACROSS
1. Inner or test
5. Actress Raines
9. On a roll
12. Befuddled
13. Be in the van
14. Neighbor of Miss.
15. Sassy
16. Author William
18. Sea eagles
20. Tool's mate
21. Viper
24. Sao Salvador
28. "The Cat in the ___"
30. Phobia
32. Building wing
33. Before, to Blake
34. "___ Gantry"
36. 1051, to Pliny
37. Maui necklace
38. Rozelle of the NFL
39. Adherent
40. Ling Ling, e.g.
43. "The Magnificient ___"
45. Tread the boards
47. Epic tales
50. Composer George
55. Influence
56. "Exodus" hero
57. Republic of Ireland
58. Merit
59. Chairman ___
60. Proof word
61. Colors

DOWN
1. Record
2. ___-friendly
3. Composer Leonard
4. Consumed
5. Sprite
6. Meadow
7. Praise
8. Improvise vocally: 2 wds.
9. Solo of "Star Wars"
10. Corrida shout
11. Sailor
17. Parrot
19. Ump's ruling
22. Seaweed
23. Soprano Emma
25. Actress Mariel
26. Troubles
27. Landed
28. Aid
29. Length x width
31. Nerve network
35. Clergy members: abbr.
41. "___ Kapital"
42. Pines (for)
44. Let up
46. Tease
48. Berne's river
49. Antonyms' antonyms: abbr.
50. Leg
51. Tudor or Modern
52. ___ Grande
53. Dander
54. Clear

PUZZLE 552

ACROSS
1. Morse for one
5. ___ propulsion
8. Plays a role
12. Filled with reverence
13. Yes vote
14. Work hard
15. Confuse
17. Musical sound
18. Foot part
19. Smelled to high heaven
21. ___ one's stack
23. Edges
24. Rip
25. Customary
29. Kind of breakfast meal
30. ___ by association
31. Crafty
32. Adjective for a small town: hyph.
34. Allot
35. Poker stake
36. Champion
37. Take a trip
40. Tap gently
41. Lasso
42. Copycat
47. Prayer end
48. Doze
49. Vein of ore
50. Clutter
51. Golly ___!
52. Broke a traffic law

DOWN
1. Taxi
2. Be in debt
3. Morning dampness
4. Rewriter
5. Green stone
6. Lidded organ
7. What Ivan was
8. Declare to be true
9. Meal preparer
10. Prong
11. Coaster
16. Not high
20. Send forth
21. Lima or pinto
22. Tardy
23. Lift up
24. Also
25. Rushing headlong
26. Consumer
27. Choir voice
28. Soap ingredient
30. "___ with the Wind"
33. Safe places
34. Iron and gold
36. Ten-gallon or hard
37. Streetcar, in London
38. Italy's capital
39. Monkeys
40. Meerschaum
43. Actress West
44. Peak
45. Lyric poem
46. Fiery color

ACROSS

1. Oval stadium
5. Spreads hay
9. Move a camera
12. Heckelphone's kin
13. Silkworm
14. Golden-ager's insurance payoff: abbr.
15. Cast
16. Neighborhood
18. Torrid
20. Enmity
21. Young hare
25. Spigot
26. Worldwide workers group: abbr.
27. Sandarac tree
29. Put on cargo
32. Crony
33. Loris
35. Japanese statesman
36. Plant disease
38. "Enterprise" officer
39. Neither hide ____ hair
40. Land of ____
42. Despoiled
44. Hereafter
47. Flower plot
48. Peace of mind
50. Talking bird
54. Model T
55. Honor card
56. Promissory notes
57. Biblical pronoun
58. Sicilian volcano
59. Large casks

DOWN

1. Horsefly larva
2. Kimono adjunct
3. Conquered
4. Forgetfulness
5. Wavered
6. Sea bird
7. Opera star
8. Canonized person
9. Cuing
10. Japanese aborigine
11. Headland
17. Inlets
19. Unwritten
21. Facial features
22. Shem's son
23. Freewill
24. David's daughter
28. Swedish turnip
30. Oklahoma Indian
31. News
34. Hit notice
37. Sightseeing trip
41. Male duck
43. Fess up
44. Reality
45. Western state
46. Egress
49. Hostel
51. "It Had to Be ____"
52. Convent dweller
53. Onager

ACROSS

1. "____ Lucia"
6. South Sea island
11. Makes dough
13. Warrior's defense
14. Foot part
15. Phoned
16. Place
17. It gets dressed
19. Tarradiddle
20. Ocean mineral
22. Kapek play
23. James or Julian
24. Vault
26. Tropical birds
28. Part of a B-29
30. Scottish water sprite
32. Disorder
35. Portion
36. Lead-in for angle or corn
38. Ruminant
40. Great skill
41. Commands, formerly
43. Le dernier ____
44. School book
46. Overjoyed
48. Restaurant patrons
49. Made over
50. Scoff
51. Merchandise

DOWN

1. Omits
2. Yearly
3. Cuddle
4. Make a doily
5. Certain drinks
6. Herringlike fish
7. Not be in the pink
8. Laid-back
9. Oily compounds
10. Summed
12. Box
13. Beetle
18. Walks clumsily
21. ____ d'hote
23. Howled
25. Soda
27. Machine part
29. Headdresses
30. Rhee, for one
31. Country home
33. Military zone
34. Tranquil
35. Challenges
37. Roman way
39. Carnival attractions
41. German title
42. Seattle ____
45. Ruby or Sandra
47. Ohio college town

PUZZLE 555

DOUBLE TROUBLE

Not really double trouble, but double fun! Solve this puzzle as you would a regular crossword, EXCEPT place one, two, or three letters in each box. The number of letters in each answer is shown in parentheses after its clue.

ACROSS

1. Bestow (6)
3. Count of jazz (5)
6. Kitchen gadget (8)
10. Actors' goals (5)
11. Torn (4)
12. Artillery piece (6)
13. Evening prayer (6)
15. Bell (4)
17. Trig function (4)
18. Kind of boom (5)
20. Fervent (6)
22. Widespread (9)
24. Ebbs (5)
25. Climb, in a way (4)
27. Harvest goddess (3)
28. Property owner (10)
30. Solar disk (4)
31. "____ of Kong" (3)
32. Dozen cost (4)
33. Storm (7)
35. Come into (7)
36. Defeat utterly (4)
37. Less refined (6)
39. Letter closer (5)
42. Porcupine (8)
45. Yellow-brown pigment (6)
47. Dory rope (7)
49. ____ pro nobis (3)
50. Irritable (5)
51. Elizabeth or Mary (5)
52. ____ Carlo Menotti (4)

DOWN

1. Better (7)
2. Naive (7)
3. Unveil (4)
4. Confess (4)
5. Thames school (4)
6. Give the once-over (4)
7. Fleeting (9)
8. Privy to: 2 wds. (4)
9. Sea eagle (4)
14. Private (8)
16. Kind of rifle (6)
19. Reykjavikian (9)
21. Renegade (8)
22. Loud cries (6)
23. Schoolchild chore (6)
24. Entire (5)
25. Forms (6)
26. Meaning (6)
29. Cotton fabric (6)
34. Uttered (7)
35. Native (8)
37. Pie part (5)
38. "____ Irae" (4)
40. Impervious to light (6)
41. Bearlike (6)
43. Peach State (7)
44. Indian home (5)
46. Negative vote (3)
48. Sea swallow (4)

PUZZLE 556

COMMON CODE

Each set of numbers below represents a letter pattern for certain words. How many words can you think of with each pattern? If a number is repeated, the same letter is repeated. For example, the first letter pattern 12232 has three different letters, with the same letter in the second, third, and fifth positions: it could be GEESE or PEEVE. The number in the parentheses after each pattern is the number of words our expert listed for that pattern.

A. 1 2 2 3 2 (5)   B. 1 2 1 1 3 (15)   C. 1 2 3 3 2 (5)   D. 1 2 1 3 1 4 (3)   E. 1 2 3 2 2 4 (5)

BRICK BY BRICK

PUZZLE 557

Rearrange this stack of bricks to form a crossword puzzle. The clues will help you fit the bricks into their correct places. Row 1 has been filled in for you. Use the bricks to fill in the remaining spaces.

ACROSS

1. Acetic or boric
   Paramour
   Grimalkins
2. Urn
   Battery cell
   Margarine
3. Sinful
   Sturdy cloth
   Without
   dilution
4. Dispatches
   again
   Colorists
5. "My country, ____
   of thee . . ."
   Elector
6. Tan shade
   Auto
   Mouselike
   animals
7. Intense
   Paddle
   Air
8. Male heir
   Rower
   Sol
9. Admittance chit
   Sup
   Art ____
10. Anthony and
    Barbara
    Printers'
    measures
    Trimmed
11. Short jackets
    Animal hair
12. Cut
    Advisors
13. ____ off to you!
    Palmlike tree
    Spring flower
14. Pointed arch
    Void
    Cozy place
15. Lively
    Baseball's Bucky
    and family
    "Anything ____"

DOWN

1. Allege
   Class
   Seek bargains
2. Lair
   Shirk
   Pen
3. Egyptian goddess
   Dice
   Roman way
4. Expunged
   Israeli parliament
5. Zilch
   Nuisances
6. Cheryl and Alan
   Type of bran
   Dripped
7. Count-
   down-enders
   Rogue
   Provoke
8. Wernher ____
   Braun
   Family in
   "Barnaby
   Rudge"
   Kate's anathemas
9. Newspaper worker
   ____ Cruces
   "Maid of the ____"
10. Pay
    Ran into
    Accomplishments
11. In no case
    Lower form of
    humor?
12. Regulate
    Flitting
13. Toward shelter
    Also-ran
    Name-brand
    cookie
14. Race
    Infer
    Mound
15. Tipplers
    Council
    Concordes

BRICKS

SON / TIC	DDL / ■EA	■VO / MEL	INT / TER	ORS / RIS
ERS / ■■■	NS■ / ETO	VAS / EVI	SUN / ECO	■PA / KET
GES / ENT	E■ / M■N	O■ / PER	LES / ODY	EST / OES
ER■ / T■D	R■ / AMI	M■ / A■I	CAR / AR■	END / TIS
RED / ■■■	LEO / EAT	NOD / ENI	E■E / T■D	CAM / AVI
SSO / S■Z	EL■ / D■O	ENS / NS■	EDE / ■■■	SCI / HAT
E■A / L■D	PA■ / FUR	T■N / S■G	RES / ■■■	S■T / ■VO

DIAGRAM

	1	2	3	4	5	6	7	8	9	10	11	12	13	14	15
1	A	C	I	D	■	L	O	V	E	R	■	C	A	T	S
2															
3															
4															
5															
6															
7															
8															
9															
10															
11															
12															
13															
14															
15															

423

PUZZLE 558

• CHOO-CHOO •

ACROSS

1. Choo-choo charge
5. Penthouse location
9. Fashionable
13. Molt
17. So be it
18. Oppositionist
19. Crazy
20. Chaste
21. Choo-choo employee
23. Flightless bird
24. Desire
25. Errare humanum ____
26. Modernist
27. Irish republic
29. Choo-choo unit
31. Gentleman
32. Crazed
33. Charity
34. Brace
37. Agenda
38. Gratis
39. Dander
42. Comparison word
43. Playwright O'Casey
44. Refuges
45. Argument
46. Silkworm
47. Monkeys
48. Inflections
49. Large volume
50. Choo-choo unit
52. Amphibians
53. Choo-choo unit
54. Precipitation
55. Bivalve mollusks
56. Ablution
57. Shut
59. Perfume measures
60. Choo-choo unit
63. Passion
64. Track competitions
65. Tarries
66. Decompose
67. In addition
68. Ninnies
69. Flaps
70. Princely Italian family
71. Dance step
72. Space chimp
73. Lip
74. Printing machine
75. Pigeonhole
76. Hamilton bills
77. Merriment
78. Choo-choo employee
81. Try to find
82. Kook
83. FDR's successor
86. Vicinity
87. Competent
89. Choo-choo track beams
92. Desire
93. Land of the Peacock Throne
94. Right hand
95. Pod vegetable
96. Blackthorn
97. Escapes
98. Garden flower
99. Nobleman

DOWN

1. Visage
2. Famous cookie baker
3. Charter
4. Remnant
5. Sports car
6. Privy about
7. Nebraska Indian
8. Choo-choo employee
9. Office worker
10. Dwelling
11. Cold cubes
12. Choo-choo connections
13. Boot attachments
14. Toss
15. Therefore
16. Antlered animal
22. Squadron
28. Charged atom
30. Iowa city
31. Earth's star
32. Welladay
33. Sky ram
34. Tread
35. All the way
36. Choo-choo systems
37. Hammerhead
38. Snake teeth
39. Choo-choo unit
40. Eternal City
41. Water pitcher
43. Bridge
44. Pops up
47. Girlfriend: Fr.
48. British trolleys
49. Singer Gobbi
51. Final
52. Apartments
53. Small amounts
55. Montana Indians
56. Luggage
57. Bloke
58. River from Lake Baikal
59. Choo-choo station
60. Taxis
61. Topers
62. Summers: Fr.
64. Modern choo-choo track
65. Girl
68. Remove from print
69. Choo-choo unit
70. Aquatic bird
73. Envision
74. Places
75. Say
76. High schoolers
77. Red flare light
78. Handles roughly
79. Evangelist Roberts
80. Nevada city
81. Bridge coup
82. Drowses
83. Go on foot
84. Withered
85. Russian emperor
88. Car grill cover
90. ____ de Janeiro
91. Upper surface

PUZZLE 559

ACROSS

1. Howard ____
5. Title for Judith Anderson
9. Romaine
12. Ronnie Howard TV role
13. "That's ____" (Dean Martin song)
15. "The ____ George Apley"
16. Michael ____ of 7 down
17. "A ____ for Benny"
18. Leave out
19. Ozzie or Harriet
21. "____ of Babylon"
23. Richardson or Hunter
24. "At ____" (TV series)
25. "Too ____ Girls"
27. Train station abbr.
29. Joan Crawford film
32. "Everybody ____"
33. To and ____
34. TV sportscaster Bob ____
36. ____ MacGraw
37. Mel Ferrer in "The Brave Bulls"
39. Hurry
40. "A ____ to Three Wives"
42. ____ Adams of 49 Across
43. Distant: pref.
44. ____ Haden of the Hardy family films
45. Wind dir.
46. Diana ____
47. "Pretty Maids All in ____"
49. "____ Smart"
50. "____ Curie"
52. "____ in St. Louis"
55. Hitchcock thriller
56. Murphy or Fisher
58. Actor Holliman
60. "____ 21"
61. Patricia and Tom
62. Frost
63. "The Burning ____" (TV film)
64. John ____ of "The New Leave It to Beaver"
65. Side dish at Mel's diner

DOWN

1. Milburn Stone's "Gunsmoke" role
2. "Once ____ a Time"
3. "The ____ on Thelma Jordan"
4. "Once More, With ____"
5. Actor Stuart ____
6. Sherman Hemsley TV series
7. "The ____ Squad"
8. Pencil end
9. "Five ____ Back"
10. Hal Williams role on "The Andy Griffith Show"
11. "Desk ____"
14. Raines or Fitzgerald
15. "____ and Liars"
20. "____ One for Me"
22. Actress Mary ____
25. Actress Vera ____
26. Louise or Gillette
27. Carney or Linkletter
28. Crosby-Hope routes
30. "The ____ Love"
31. Actresses Fisher and Russell
32. "My Gal ____"
33. "The ____ Country"
34. "The ____ Artists"
35. "____ Here, Private Hargrove"
37. Stiller's mate
38. "Meet John ____"
41. "____ Horn"
43. Audrey of "Medical Center" and kin
45. Garbo and Bergman, e.g.
46. Frances or Ruby
48. Peck film, with "The"
49. "Wild ____ Calling"
50. Elliott Gould film
51. Emulated Rich Little
52. "The Last ____"
53. "Jackass ____"
54. Humorist Bombeck
55. Actor Reiner
57. Rather or Fielding
59. Actor Ayres

PUZZLE 560

ACROSS

1. Biblical weed
5. Characteristic
10. Comet cloud
14. Daze
15. Irish playwright
16. Iowa college town
17. Leader of the Green Mountain Boys
19. Root vegetable
20. Suave
21. Capital of Georgia
23. Table support
24. Different
25. Flower holder
28. First woman
29. Roman goddess of spring
33. Lemon drink
34. Painful
36. Dainty
37. Writing tablet
38. Twenty-five cents
40. Baseballer Mel
41. Doing routine things
43. Building sites
44. Wager
45. Gift receiver
46. Goal
47. Brave man
48. Mrs. Eisenhower
50. Time of life
52. Released conditionally
55. ____-Bethlehem
58. Tel ____
59. Still fit to be repaired
62. Great affection
63. Dialect
64. Baseballer Gehrig et al.
65. Had debts
66. "The Yellow Rose of ____"
67. Profound

DOWN

1. Mao ____-tung
2. Aleutian island
3. River to the Rhine
4. Make possible
5. Nasal speech
6. Vex
7. Totality
8. Form a thought
9. Tithe
10. Joel Grey vehicle
11. Sign of the future
12. Encounter
13. Nick and Nora's dog
18. Scottish negative
22. Crowbars
24. Rest upon
25. Lacking liveliness
26. "A Bell for ____"
27. Four-door car
28. Period in history
30. Daughter of Tantalus
31. Speak
32. Sharp argument
34. Shrill cry
35. Away
36. Household animal
39. Male turkey
42. Took away
46. ____-camp
47. Messenger
49. Deserve
50. Potent particles
51. Needlefish
52. ____ Alto
53. Claim
54. Split
55. Greek portico
56. Reed instrument
57. Chimney duct
60. Half dozen
61. Mind-reader's talent: abbr.

PUZZLE 561   ALL FOURS

How many common 4-letter words can you find in the diagram by moving from letter to adjacent letter across, down, up, backward, and diagonally? A letter may be used more than once in a word, but only after leaving it and coming back. Foreign words, abbreviations, words ending in S, and words beginning with a capital letter are not permitted.

YOUR WORD LIST

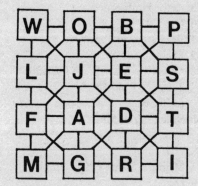

PUZZLE 562

ACROSS
1. Improvises
6. Caress
9. Danish county
12. Marketplace
13. Conceit
14. Coniferous tree
15. Choir voice
16. Blend
18. Prompt
20. Engraver's tool
21. Comedians
23. Creek
25. Pan's pipe
26. Meadow-mower
27. Oil-hauler
29. White sauterne
31. Mangle
35. Misgivings
37. Shoshonean
38. Carte
41. Sister
42. Carangid
43. Opera highlights
45. Book cover
47. At a white heat
49. Mountain nymph
52. Ike's command
53. Shelter
54. Grape conserve
55. Scion
56. Nourished
57. Sherry

DOWN
1. Cistern
2. Ripen
3. Boogeyman
4. Bows
5. Wraparound
6. Apple chemical
7. Gone by
8. Pyramid, for some
9. Burning
10. Civil War bullet
11. Course
17. Pack animal
19. Brawl
21. Spider's trap
22. Frigate bird
24. Hands on hips
27. Part of ZBT
28. Bitter vetch
30. Police unit
32. Atomic
33. Heathrow abbr.
34. Rubicund
36. Elevated
38. Mallets
39. Muse of poetry
40. Curtain material
42. Wait on
44. Psyche
46. Soup thickener
48. By birth
50. Supped
51. French preposition

PUZZLE 563

ACROSS
1. Shuttlecock
5. Enrages
9. Faulty
12. Perfume
13. Pianist Peter ___
14. Cretan mountain
15. Bitter herb
16. Philippine hardwood
17. Muffin
18. Edit
20. Malay palm
22. Podium
24. Resign voluntarily
27. Faithful
31. Opulent
32. Palace room, sometimes
33. Sioux
35. Watch
36. Bristle
38. Knightly adventures
40. Clan
42. Pennsylvania port
43. Wicked
45. High standards
49. Biblical priest
51. Use an oven
53. Trickle
54. Rubbish
55. In excess
56. Castor's mother
57. Skate
58. Raised areas
59. Sunrise direction

DOWN
1. Male swine
2. Futile
3. Cross
4. Fears
5. Indoctrinate
6. Corded cloth
7. Emerald Isle
8. Impenetrable
9. Jacob, e.g.
10. Hoosier humorist
11. Quadruped's mother
19. Roman statesman
21. Part of MPH
23. Sleep noisily
25. Cake froster
26. "___ Were Expendable"
27. Expense
28. German river
29. Birth
30. Airedales
34. Spoke
37. Hezekiah's mother
39. Heckle
41. Body joint
44. Roof edge
46. Scope
47. Tops
48. Gaiter
49. Do wrong
50. Chilean river
52. Cognizance

427

PUZZLE 564

ACROSS
1. Came to earth
5. Tilt
9. Madame Curie
14. Indian mallow genus
15. Zone
16. African antelope
17. Burgess novel, with "A"
20. Kukla's friend
21. Playwright Coward
22. Family room
23. Assayed
25. Must-have
28. Volcanic output
31. Scottish language
35. Matures
39. Jacket feature
41. Replica
42. Time frame of a Nolte/Murphy film
45. Sergeant Pepper Anderson portrayer
46. Shakespearean king
47. Canonized French women: abbr.
48. Adjusts
50. Fibber
52. Grain repository
54. Saddle part
59. Eureka!
62. Lover of Narcissus
65. Jungle vine
66. Anniversary trip
70. California border lake
71. Large ratites
72. First name in mystery
73. Proficient
74. Take ten
75. Portuguese navigator

DOWN
1. Annual Berkshire race
2. French city
3. Golden calves
4. Unvoiced
5. Crow's cry
6. "Moses und ___"
7. Sleuth Wolfe
8. ___ aback
9. Debussy's "La ___"
10. In the manner of
11. Author Ayn ___
12. Author of "Summer Brave"
13. Xanadu
18. Ship's stabilizer
19. Couturier Cassini
24. Host Garroway
26. Apiece
27. Aegean isle
29. Bridal wear
30. Gabriel, for one
32. Oaf
33. Concerning
34. British tax
35. Way off yonder
36. Away
37. Units of energy
38. Eyelid sores
40. Certain Asian
43. Abominable Snowman
44. Lobster catcher
49. "Rosebud," e.g.
51. ___-poly
53. Artist's color
55. Emulated Marceau
56. New Zealander
57. "___ Gay"
58. Alleys
59. Movie mutt
60. Climax
61. Yearn
63. Domicile
64. Heavy load
67. Comics' Alley
68. ___ income
69. Erhard's program: abbr.

PUZZLE 565   Disco

Each numbered circle has a 5-letter answer (Clue A) and a 4-letter answer (Clue B) reading in a clockwise direction. Enter the first letter of each 5-letter answer in the circle in the preceding disc. For example, in disc 1: A + LOFT = ALOFT.

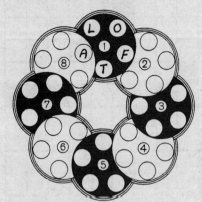

A.
1. Overhead
2. Group
3. Lading
4. Dwarf
5. Parade
6. Wire
7. Smallest
8. Lance

B.
1. Warehouse
2. Bolt
3. Jason's ship
4. Alaska city
5. Curve
6. Competent
7. Bridge position
8. Anjou or Bosc

ACROSS

1. Pencil end
5. Genesis gent
9. Plant supporter
13. Type of lore
17. Make well
18. Oscar ___ Renta
19. Copley or Garr
20. Microwave
21. Meara or Archer
22. Valley
23. Sortie
24. Rajah's wife
25. Great work
28. Spot for "happily ever-aftering"
30. Remove
31. Forerunner of jazz
33. Partake of food
34. Ambassador's place
38. Tibetan priests
40. Entrances
44. Electron tubes
45. Met every whim
47. Deteriorated
48. Cancel
49. Thirst quencher
50. Singer Clark
52. Author Anais
53. Repast
54. Less coarse
55. On the payroll
57. Bank employee
59. Atchison, ___, & Sante Fe
60. Lace or sprout
63. Radials
64. Karate blow
68. Kurosawa film
69. Baltic or Black
70. Some spies
71. Complain
72. Eager
74. Mobile home
76. From that time
77. Discourage
79. Eatery
80. Noah, for one
81. Society newcomer
83. Here's ___ in your eye
84. Sod
85. Difficult
89. Stroke of genius
95. Secular
96. Routine
98. Stuffing herb
99. Use an auger
100. Highest point
101. Chain and band
102. Xanadu
103. Redolence
104. Origin
105. Canter
106. Hardens
107. Catch a glimpse of

DOWN

1. Con game
2. Sandwich fish
3. Samovars
4. Borscht ingredient
5. 10 Downing Street, e.g.
6. Profoundly
7. Kate's cohort
8. Cob or buck
9. Banner
10. Souchong, e.g.
11. Journalist Sevareid
12. Gold-fingers?
13. Dog's foot
14. Ellipse
15. Carson sub
16. Purl's companion
26. A Ford
27. Moon feature
29. Kisser
32. Needlefish
34. Dutch treat
35. Ore source
36. ___ fide
37. Grownups
38. Procrastinator's motto
39. Mexican garments
41. Singer Tennille
42. Ashtabula's lake
43. "___ in the Clowns"
45. Walking sticks
46. Distributes
49. Weatherman Scott
51. Wild ox
54. Armada
55. More tender
56. Joanne Woodward role
58. Sibilant letter
59. Mosaic-maker
60. Actor Dillman
61. Great review
62. Apartment
63. Ohio port
65. Female deer
66. Story starter
67. Equal
70. Least
71. Momentary smell
73. Emulated Holmes
75. Zero in
76. Soup dishes
78. Collector's car
80. Congressional concern
82. Come apart suddenly
84. Trick of the ___
85. Word of woe
86. Vie at Indy
87. A ___ a dozen
88. Fly high
90. Employs
91. Hautboy
92. Laver and Carew
93. Cut short
94. Mysterious
97. "___ for the Seesaw"

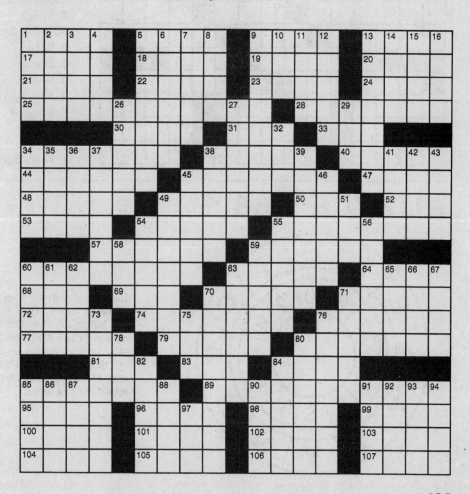

PUZZLE 567

ACROSS
1. Storm
5. Grimace
10. Aid in a crime
14. Egg-shaped
15. In what place
16. Billow
17. Dole out
18. Spooky
19. Zone
20. Advance showing
22. Coaches
24. Behave
25. Attack
26. Glide on blades
29. Saloon
30. Harvests
34. Salary
35. "____ and Peace"
36. Violin
37. Actress Meyers
38. Bonnie prince
40. Payable
41. Trifling
43. Hearing organ
44. Transmit
45. Cubic meter
46. Single thickness
47. Yelps
48. Road curves
50. Crimson
51. Room warmer
53. Deters
57. Harbor
58. With full force
60. Songstress Adams
61. Andy Taylor's son
62. Cultivates
63. Cleo's river
64. Act
65. Hackneyed
66. Footfall

DOWN
1. Play boisterously
2. Allege
3. Turnstile
4. Raise
5. Sugary
6. Munch
7. Above, in poems
8. Novelist
9. Ogles
10. Expected
11. Farm building
12. Holiday nights
13. English drink
21. Frozen water
23. High nest
25. Vats
26. Trades
27. Unit of gold fineness
28. Nimble
29. Lamb sound
31. Snake
32. Dull thud
33. Kernels
35. For what reason
36. Evergreen
38. Peak
39. Deposit
42. Handled
44. Depresses
46. Allow
47. Actor Kingsley
49. Rockers
50. Washer cycle
51. Fond wish
52. Great Lake
53. Low mountain
54. Revise copy
55. Vex
56. Ooze
57. Pea container
59. ____ carte

PUZZLE 568   Line 'Em Up

Line up the inner and outer rings to discover a 12-letter word. Use your imagination to rotate the rings so that the first letter of the word is opposite the number 1, the second letter opposite number 2, and so forth. When you have lined up the first letter with number 1 correctly, the rest of the numbers will indicate the order of the letters in the word.

430

ACROSS

1. Melon-hitting-pavement sound
6. Food
10. Cower
16. Rubberneck
18. Mideast language
21. Adversities
22. Do over a floor
23. Italian cheese
24. Israeli coins
25. Is noncommittal somewhere in Pennsylvania?
28. Pelt
29. Hard to find
30. Martinique volcano
31. Charged atoms
32. Small shark
33. "I ____ Camera"
34. Tresses
35. Change
36. Eyelashes
37. Gumshoe
38. Folk dances
39. Aromatic plant
40. Excursion
41. Claims strongly
43. Wedding-announcement word
44. Tempted
45. Sheep
46. British length
48. Indisposed
49. In the manner of
52. Nut
55. Wild hog
56. Medical photo
58. Alphabet run
59. Metal
60. Rhode Island redcap?
62. Farm measure
63. Highland attire
64. Particle
65. Modernists
66. Certain students
67. Old French coin
68. ____-relief
69. Humorous
71. Corn unit
72. Joyful
74. Young Carter
75. Coal miner
79. Kind of consonant
81. Ballesteros of golf
83. Jacket feature
84. Ed. gp.
86. Habituate
87. "If I ____ a rich man . . ."
88. Utah city
89. Remnant
90. Holding mechanism
91. Seaport in Portugal
92. Tea biscuit
93. ____ Scott
94. Printing measures
95. Alabama breakfast?
99. Climbing palm
101. Large cat
102. Roma's country
103. Prima ballerina
104. Leaning
105. Carried on
106. Certain homes
107. Dispatch
108. Hire

DOWN

1. Shrieked
2. Make a copy of beforehand
3. Turning machine
4. Indigo
5. Communication medium
6. Agricultural workers
7. Ascended
8. Hindu hero
9. Israeli diplomat
10. Birds' crops
11. Outfits
12. "But ____ on forever"
13. Virginia reel?
14. Female fan
15. Extract of a court record
17. Tried anew, as a case
19. Seneca, e.g.
20. Partner
25. Nasty kid
26. Inventor Howe
27. Some
32. Fork part
35. Competitor
36. Ringlet
38. Actress Goldie
39. Timing device
40. Hot month
42. Intended
43. Tide
44. Mendacious one
46. Cut the grass
47. Laud
50. "____ of the Flies"
51. Hairy creatures
52. Toll road
53. Blore of films
54. Ohio transportation area?
55. Wager
57. Legal point
58. New Zealander
60. Inquisitive
61. Depend
64. Earthy deposit
66. Page
68. Scottish hillside
70. Great review
71. Basic
73. Ireland
75. Ricochet
76. The outdoors
77. Atomic and electric
78. Turncoat
79. Young hare
80. Liven
81. Pulpit talk
82. Beethoven opus
83. Found
85. Does sums
87. Strife
91. Charges
92. Deprived
93. River mouth formation
95. Bundle
96. Snares
97. Mucilage
98. Jutlander
100. Link

PUZZLE 569

• URBAN ATTACHMENTS •

431

PUZZLE 570

ACROSS

1. Melt
5. Long narrative
9. Boasts
14. Hurry
15. Riding whip
16. Adjust a clock
17. Sheltered
18. Nerve network
19. Put into use
20. Nursery enclosure
22. White pigeon
24. Pasture
25. Sandy shore
28. Part of Iberia
31. Pizza
33. Slender
35. Frighten
36. Frilly
37. Washington bill
38. Fruit pastries
39. In past time
40. Chute
42. Significant period
43. Level
44. Walked restlessly
45. Constructed
47. Jalopy
48. Leafy shelter
49. Pew
51. Be human
52. Implement
54. Snappy comebacks
59. Jeans material
62. Confess
64. Deep mud
65. In the know
66. Flank
67. Brainstorm
68. Doles
69. Take advice
70. Abound

DOWN

1. Snare
2. Nut covering
3. Confused
4. Milk liquid
5. Window mesh
6. Scene of action
7. Received
8. Imitated
9. Valorous
10. Iterate
11. Cleo's undoing
12. Clot
13. Pig's home
21. Works at
23. Mind
26. Option
27. Deter
28. Sacred beetle
29. Colorful march
30. Paintings
31. Beeping device
32. Sacred image
34. Want
35. Stalk
36. Volcanic output
40. Athletic game
41. Statute
43. Reverberate
46. All
48. Steeped
50. Arrives
51. Wear away
53. Bind with rope
55. Overlook
56. Take the bus
57. Genealogy diagram
58. Ore vein
59. Canine mother
60. Ram's mate
61. Slave Turner
63. Be a rival

PUZZLE 571   Word Trails

Start at the arrow and move along the trail from letter to letter to discover a well-known saying or title in each of the diagrams. Move backward and forward along the trail. Some letters will be used more than once.

1.

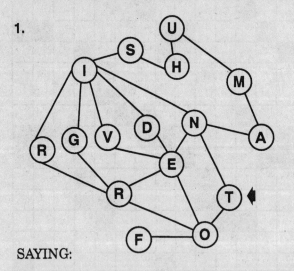

SAYING:

___ ___ ___ ___ ___

___ ___ ___ ___

___ ___ ___

2.

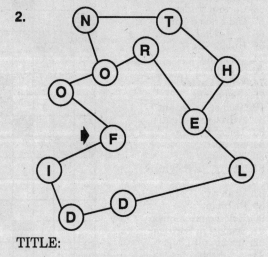

TITLE:

___ ___ ___ ___ ___

___ ___ ___ ___

PUZZLE 572

• FULL OF COLOR •

ACROSS

1. Painted metalware
5. Ms.Berger of films
10. Too-too, in Toulouse
14. Reptile feature
19. Say with heat
20. Timeless, bardic style
21. Large lump
22. Gentled
23. Feel jealous
26. Uneven
27. High-school VIPs
28. Card game
29. Mnemonic for the Great Lakes
30. Crushed
31. Sweetsop
32. Boys from Babahoyo
33. Der Alte's city
34. More skillful
36. Toast topping
37. Flabbergast
38. Track temptation
41. Rebels' hates
42. Money-minded gal
45. Thai language
46. Cold-weather ailment
47. Top
49. Layer
50. Smart-aleck's specialty
51. Strong-scented herb
52. Iditarod vehicles
53. Brief time
55. Emulates a caged tiger
56. Weapons stores
58. Freud feature
59. Sounds from Samoyeds
60. "Boys' Town" star
61. Coon's age
62. Indian symbol
63. Tot's wheels, for short
64. Has qualms
65. Lucille Ball and Billy Carter
68. Goddess of peace
69. Bivalves
70. Clotho, Lachesis, and Atropos
71. TV's Charlotte
72. Slant
73. Singe
74. Poker winners
75. Comic sketch
76. Large ruminant
77. Deep absorption
81. Thirst quenchers
82. Hefty sizes: abbr.
83. Spot for a yellow ribbon
84. Start of a soliloquy
85. Malicious
86. Barbara Cartland theme
87. Olympic vehicles
88. Spanish artist
89. Muddle
92. Not as wacky
93. Italian endearment
94. Perched
97. Salesman
98. Regal
101. Antelope's playground
102. Insist
103. Boundary between Europe and Asia
104. Spoken
105. Appendant
106. Woodland creature
107. Practical intelligence
108. Lorry feature

DOWN

1. Accounts
2. More than
3. Gams
4. Misjudge
5. Member of an Aussie pop group
6. Heating vessels
7. Salamander
8. Three: pref.
9. Insect home
10. "I'm in ___ for love . . ."
11. Secret writings
12. Address bearers: abbr.
13. Lark or lab
14. Less fun-loving
15. "Gigi" star
16. Gone wild
17. ___ majesty
18. Heaven on earth
24. Sen. Kefauver
25. Used a whetstone
30. Pergola
31. Toward shelter, to a salt
32. Recesses
33. Cream cheese's companion
34. Forewarn
35. Very fast runners
38. Illicit buying spot
39. Lightens
40. Chuck
41. ___ avis
42. Traipses
43. Brain passages
44. Embellish
47. Situate
48. Moraylike
50. Hindu fashion
52. Mamba or boomslang
53. Sizzles
54. Norms
55. Orbits
57. Gray and Moran
58. Smile broadly
59. Heralds
61. Hanker
62. Pierre's pate
63. Lilt
64. Bug
65. Risque
66. Holstein's home
67. Implants
68. Chamois's kin
69. Clog
70. Dissolves
73. Thirst for
75. Bristle
77. Promoted
78. Dazzling lass
79. "___ her poor dog . . ."
80. Copious
81. Ronstadt's "Blue ___"
85. Whodunit staple
86. Fencing ploy
87. Substantial
88. Highlanders
89. Silent-screen vamp
90. My word!
91. Patch up
92. In a huff
93. Asian sleuth
94. Chipper
95. Winged
96. Distant: pref.
98. "Father Knows Best" son
99. Signore's three
100. Putrefy

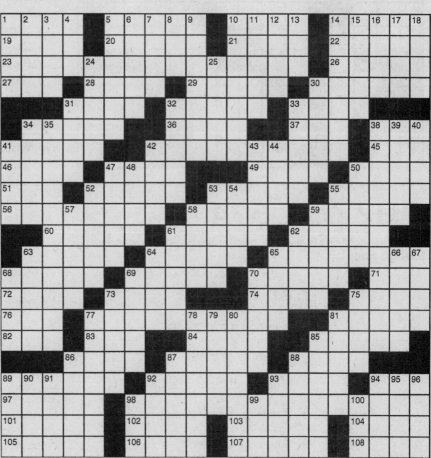

433

PUZZLE 573

ACROSS

1. Scottish cap
4. Divan
8. Display
12. Over
14. Oust
16. Story
17. Heart
18. Christmas visitor
19. Pester
20. Sign
21. Pub drink
22. Fright
24. Reciprocating wheel
26. Use a skillet
27. Procedure
30. Vassal
34. Doctorate exams
35. Yard parts
37. Enemy
38. Wipe
39. Everlasting
42. 2,000 pounds
43. Citrus drink
44. Hollow grass
45. Overweight
47. Edgy
50. Attic
51. Supply with weapons
52. "Much ____ About Nothing"
53. Certain school
54. Shoemaker's device
56. Lock openers
60. Cold-cut shop, for short
62. Artist's need
64. Way out
65. Fever and chills
66. Clan
67. Back of the neck
68. Lichen
69. Not hard
70. Cat sound

DOWN

1. Filled tortilla
2. Minute particle
3. Additional
4. "____ Street"
5. Racetrack shape
6. Dandy
7. Play division
8. Wanders off
9. Crowning glory?
10. Elderly
11. Small
13. Writing implement
15. Crisp, shiny fabric
23. Age of note
25. Church part
27. Nero, e.g.
28. Deteriorate
29. Romp
30. Be deferred
31. "____ the Fall"
32. Rope loop
33. Doctrine
35. Charges
36. Sooner than, to a poet
40. Gabriel's instrument
41. Pack up
46. Out of order
48. Differs from
49. Metallic lode
50. Ship's kitchen
53. Also
54. Large continent
55. Spiders' snares
57. Test
58. Cry of pain
59. Ragout
60. Water obstruction
61. Self
63. Exist

PUZZLE 574

Words Within

Each clue contains two parts, one for the 3-letter answer you place on the dashes, the other for the complete 5-letter word.

1. Edge in greasy dirt   G __ __ __ E

2. Poem in a Swiss song   Y __ __ __ L

3. Golfer's aid in pilot   S __ __ __ R

4. Nocturnal bird in dishes   B __ __ __ S

5. Knock in a dice game   C __ __ __ S

6. Anger in an alarm   S __ __ __ N

ACROSS

1. "Two Years Before the ___"
5. Coarsely-ground corn
9. Knight's mount
14. Solemn
15. Margarine
16. Egg-rolling time
18. Exhilarate
19. Pocket ravelings
20. Sign of worry
21. ___ King Cole
22. Mine entrance
24. Carry
26. Brooch
27. ___ to the nines
29. Hostel provisions
30. Flippant
31. Before truck or head
32. Skin aperture
33. Levels to the ground: var.
34. Colorado ski area
37. Father
38. Egypt, formerly: abbr.
39. What a blusher is compared to
40. Flowering shrub
46. Summer in Paris
47. English elevator
48. Crusted desserts
49. Unit
50. Poker hand
53. Participate in the Indy 500
54. Red or fire
55. Likewise
56. ___ to tears
57. Grassy surface of land
60. Healthy
62. Every one
63. Paddles
64. Geometric ratio
65. Eucharistic cup
69. ___ you ever?
70. Concludes
71. Feathery wraps
72. Steinbeck's "Cannery ___"
73. Disinclined
75. Termite's delight
77. Scottish feudal lord
79. Legislative body
80. ___ Stanley Gardner
81. "The Pumpkin ___" (Anne Bancroft film)
82. Longhorn
83. Cincinnati team
84. Colors

DOWN

1. Grinding tooth
2. Lessen
3. Matched pair
4. Sedition
5. Firm
6. Dismounted
7. Adult males
8. Morgan's role in "M*A*S*H"
9. Religious denominations
10. Weight allowance
11. Native of: suffix
12. Public storehouses
13. Long for
14. Dispatch
17. Leases
23. Garden moisture
25. Keats creation
28. Editor's command
29. Presage
30. Turkish coin
32. Italian restaurant staple
33. Stadium cheers
34. Encourage
35. One of three biblical brothers
36. Equal
37. Lift the hat
38. Secondhand
40. Civil disturbance
41. Consider
42. Discover
43. Cry of rage
44. ___ upon a time
45. Require
47. Impart
51. Gable's trademark
52. Curly cabbage
53. Bun
56. Caused an explosion
57. Fizzy beverages
58. Relinquishes voluntarily
59. Zealous
60. Concealed
61. Reply
62. Cry of surprise
64. Scornful look
65. Signal systems
66. Rather angry
67. Pine products
68. Jug
70. Punta del ___
71. Intrepid
74. "Facts of Life" star
76. Miner's find
78. Loft substance

PUZZLE 576

ACROSS

1. Kind of salmon
5. Pops
10. N.Y.'s Beame
13. Misplaced
17. Cupid
18. Luck of the ——
19. A —— upon it!
20. Wild ox
21. "A —— no moss": 3 wds.
25. Trifling ones
26. Arles streets
27. Samuel and Robert
28. Draft gp.
29. Seed coats
31. Initial
32. Shucks!
34. Keep one's nose to the ——
36. Actress Munson
39. Rock group inits.
40. Disparage
41. Wrath
42. Blame
43. Uproar
44. Pub brews
45. Circus worker
47. Favorites
48. Exceeded
50. WWII town: 2 wds.
51. Posed
53. Sir Anthony ——
54. Every single item: 2 wds.
57. Chance
60. Little Woman
62. Have the nerve
63. Inner ——
66. —— au rhum
69. Cotton- wood
71. Money —— object: 2 wds.
72. Seraglio room
73. Mideast gulf
74. Actor Chaney
75. Adds breadth
77. Neither
78. Fuel
79. Heliotrope
81. Top
82. Faith
84. "And thereby hangs ——": 2 wds.
85. —— -jongg
86. "An habitation of dragons and —— for owls" (Isaiah 34:13): 2 wds.
88. Scent
89. Texas town
92. Investi- gated thor- oughly: 4 wds.
96. Not —— of it: 2 wds.
97. Slave Turner
98. Fragrant compound
99. Flirt
100. Obligation
101. Self
102. Frets
103. Dam

DOWN

1. Dray
2. Melville work
3. Scrubbed the deck
4. More ——: 2 wds.
5. Errs
6. Assoc.
7. Negative prefix
8. "Man on ——" (1960 film): 2 wds.
9. People in glass houses ——: 3 wds.
10. Copies
11. Swamp
12. Test givers
13. Bert and kin
14. ". . . leave in thee —— upon another" (Luke 19:44): 2 wds.
15. Aching
16. Soviet agcy.
22. Taxing letters
23. Lawman Eliot
24. Sped
29. Ms. Francis
30. Journalist Jacob
31. Links warning
32. Decorate again
33. —— and kicking
34. Celebra- tory fete
35. "—— of Athens"
37. Bolt's partner
38. Burro
40. WWI river
42. Of the eye
46. Medicinal plant
49. Provide new troops
50. Flimflam
52. Cartoonist Peter's family
55. Hersey's bell town
56. Early Hebrew ascetic
58. Famed English site
59. Praise
61. Surgical target
64. Ms. Bancroft
65. Shopping place
66. Sack

67. Nabokov novel
68. Make the ——: 3 wds.
70. Swag
71. Matinee ——
76. Give —— (leave off for a while): 3 wds.

79. Incinerate
80. Pedestal part
81. Pushcart
83. Like many dirt roads
85. Tsetse fly
86. "When I was —— ...": 2 wds.
87. Philippine island

88. Director Preminger
89. Missives: abbr.
90. Hero source
91. Neisse's partner
93. Droop

94. Western Indian
95. Like FDR's deal

PUZZLE 576

1	2	3	4		5	6	7	8	9		10	11	12		13	14	15	16
17					18						19				20			
21				22					23				24				
25							26					27					
	28				29	30				31						
32	33				34					35					36	37	38
39				40					41				42			
43				44				45	46				47			
48			49				50					51	52			
	53				54	55				56		57		58	59	
		60		61		62				63	64				65
66	67	68			69	70				71				72		
73				74			75	76					77		
78			79			80						81		
	82	83				84					85			
86	87				88					89			90	91
92				93			94	95				
96			97			98					99		
100			101			102					103		

PUZZLE 577

ACROSS

1. Enclosure
4. French painter
9. Also-ran
14. Johnson of "Miami Vice"
17. Fabrication
18. Egg-shaped
19. Cognizant
20. Flightless bird
21. Rainbow
22. More recent
23. Corolla segment
24. Light brown
25. Organized system
27. Lump
29. Sword
31. Ethereal
32. Completed
33. Measure of length
34. Sea birds
36. Small horse
37. Saved
40. In the course of
41. Go by
42. Connection
43. Savings plan: abbr.
44. Fiver
45. Bundle of cotton
46. Canter
47. Clove hitch, e.g.
48. Lattice
50. Worries
51. Gaggle members
52. "___ Hospitality"
53. Rapture
54. Cook fish
55. Social class
58. Smacks
59. Synthetic material
63. Beame and Ribicoff
64. Miss
65. Bridge coup
66. Mesozoic or Cenozoic
67. Agent: abbr.
68. Invite
69. Stream
70. Haughty person
71. Inactive
75. Nourishment
76. Anatoly Karpov's game
77. Perch
78. Baltimore, e.g.
79. Flourish
80. Los ___
81. Use an auger
82. Moon features
85. Groove
86. Evans and Robertson
88. Yell
90. Seine
91. Indignation
92. Mortgages
93. Rich cake
94. Iced ___
95. Pie ingredient?
96. Delight
97. Charger
98. Crafty

DOWN

1. Scheme
2. Irish republic
3. Smooth peach
4. Benefactors
5. All
6. Stare
7. Had breakfast
8. Sunday talks
9. Interval
10. Is indebted to
11. Sixth planet: abbr.
12. Scraped out
13. Compare
14. Ascertain
15. General Bradley
16. Religious sister
26. Coil
28. Some
30. Bumbling insect?
32. Amount
33. Encounters
34. Former Chief Justice
35. Arabian prince
36. Buddies
37. Outbreaks
38. Love god
39. Palm fruit
41. Duo
42. Locket keepsake
45. Sad
46. Excursions

PUZZLE 577

47. Low islands
49. Tons
50. Glass bottle
51. Unit of weight
53. Sudden sound
54. Imperfection
55. Train components
56. Help
57. Removed
58. Bias
59. Trudge
60. Dwelling houses
61. Spring bloom
62. Completes
65. Coin opening
69. Woods
70. Fired
72. "I ____ Rhythm"
73. Simpleton
74. Beset
75. In favor of
76. Glazed
78. Sheriff's group
79. Thug
80. Hindu intellectual
81. Curved
82. Center
83. Spool
84. Stick around
85. Margin
87. Pasture
89. Spicy

439

PUZZLE 578

ACROSS

1. Caprice
5. Train type
9. Sway loosely
13. Gloat
17. Operatic Egyptian princess
18. Split
19. Place to rest, in London
20. At this juncture
21. Exactly the same
23. High point
24. Nobleman
25. Let
26. Knolls
28. Far less than many
30. Recede
32. Appearances
34. Insect egg
35. Venomous reptile
38. Imaginary being
40. Refuse
42. Mother, to Caesar
46. French sea
47. Conversed
49. Player in St. Louis
51. Possess
52. Apiary denizens
54. Deficiency
55. Mysterious
57. Understanding
58. Peruvian native
59. Scottish river
60. Admiration
61. Abandon
63. Babylonian war god
65. Pianos
68. Tract of land
69. Next to
72. Furtive
73. Truck part
75. Hairdo
78. Lager's kin
79. Lecture
81. Peninsula
82. Kind of sapphire
83. Herman Munster's wife
85. Pen requirement
86. Red
88. Jan, on "The Brady Bunch"
89. Stratum
91. Block
93. Cave
94. Legal thing
95. River island
97. Facets
99. Basin
101. Issues
105. Dud
107. Reigning princess, in India
111. Inform strongly
112. Without value
114. Measuring instruments
116. Alternately
117. Corner
118. Pact assn.
119. Algerian city
120. Grass stem
121. Crystal gazer
122. Belgian river
123. Trunk

DOWN

1. Lament
2. Cache
3. Impression
4. Parsonage
5. Angle starter
6. Poet Adrienne ____
7. Be of use
8. Ripened
9. Flat bottles
10. Varnish ingredient
11. Missions
12. Adorn
13. African cat
14. Erect
15. Not regular, in Edinburgh
16. Artesian, e.g.
22. Hebrew month
27. Weight
29. Enthusiasm
31. Casual
33. Trolley
35. Both: pref.
36. Recognized
37. Perfectly
39. Takes flight
41. Auricle
43. Resemble
44. Perpetually
45. Fissure
48. Heirlooms
50. Central
53. Indira's garb
55. Kwa language
56. Sniggler's catch
60. Some

440

62. Black and White
64. Public notices
66. Sort
67. Palatable
69. Masked or medicine
70. Director Kazan
71. Over: pref.
74. Assail
76. Acclaim
77. Norwegian coins
80. Purpose
81. Observance
84. Longed
86. Yield by treaty
87. Accustom
90. Equip
92. Cultivator
96. Encamps
98. Ice-cream drinks
100. Conductor's requirement
101. Water jug
102. Boy
103. Gaelic
104. Confident
106. Praise
108. Pianist Peter ___
109. Distinctive intervals
110. Old worker
113. "Do the Right Thing" director
115. Afr. kingdom

PUZZLE 578

PUZZLE 579

ACROSS

1. Crooked
6. Litter
11. Collision
16. Birchbark
17. Street show
18. Kind of cassette
19. Overlooks
20. Following
21. Studies
22. Confidant
23. Discretion
25. Active person
27. Obtain
28. Component
30. Dreary state
32. Plate scraping
33. Chiding word
34. Command to Dobbin
35. Electrical unit
38. Mrs. Yokum
40. Hindu prince
44. Mimicker
46. Brokaw or Selleck
48. Biblical term of reproach
49. Tatter
50. Wild ox
51. Animal hide
53. Place
54. Discontinue
56. Pioneering
58. Assign
60. Alpine area
62. British tax base
64. Flogged
65. Fabled bird
67. Kind of dance
68. Mongrel
69. On the agenda
73. Long-eared hounds
77. Court
78. Equipment
79. Italian money, once
80. ____ Tin Tin
81. Dodge
83. Sailing vessel
85. ____ d'hote
87. Conundrum
88. British dandies
89. Omit from speech
90. Low cards
91. Sentimental one
92. Hinder

DOWN

1. Magnitude
2. Eastern porter
3. Old-womanish
4. Polka ____
5. Tomorrow, 48 hours later
6. Treatise
7. Huck's transport
8. Kind of glass
9. Most shabby
10. Sea bird
11. ____ pigeon
12. Street: Fr.
13. Old saying
14. Opposing factions
15. Party givers
24. Aardvark's tidbit
26. Chicken-to-be
29. Castle ditch
30. Hullabaloo
31. Close-by
33. Out-of-the-way
35. Original
36. Rare violin
37. Hardship
38. Kind of face
39. Rube
41. Lacquer
42. Severe
43. Abominated
45. Hosiery shade
47. Wire measure
52. Embezzled

55. Study hard
57. Decisive event
58. Shoot the breeze
59. Apparel
61. Roomers
63. Little boy

66. Actor's signal
68. "My Mother the ___"
69. Moved swiftly
70. Pigment
71. Give shelter to

72. Endures
73. Inebriated
74. Satellite's path
75. Diacritical mark
76. Taunt

79. Garret
82. Algerian governor
84. Switch position
86. Stout

PUZZLE 579

PUZZLE 580

ACROSS
1. Printers' measures
4. Presidential dog
8. Insect stages
13. Farm structure
17. Drilling tool
18. Kuwaiti or Omani
19. "—— of Two Cities": 2 wds.
20. Redolence
21. Garden bloom: 2 wds.
24. American Beauty, e.g.
25. Regrets
26. Backward: prefix
27. —— Globetrotters
29. Saber
31. Madison Ave. execs
32. Alaskan city
33. 27th President
34. Founder of psychoanalysis
35. Locale of Fort McHenry
39. Feign
40. More crafty
41. Fable conclusion
42. Scary word
43. Unconventional one
45. Helen's abductor
46. Princely disguise
47. Moran and Gray
48. Attempts
49. Desist
50. Next to last syllable
52. Thwarts
53. Cleanses
54. Incline
55. Harnesses
56. Ohio city
57. Red stag
58. Storms
59. Moses et al.
62. Barrister: abbr.
63. Actor Stu
64. —— Boothe Luce
65. Misrepresent
66. "Yes, —— Bananas": 3 wds.
68. Lock
69. Yarn spool
70. Majors and Trevino
71. Greek tourist attractions
72. Big tops
73. Backward, at sea
76. Rowed
77. Painter Chagall
78. Biblical pronoun
79. Herbert Hoover's birthplace: 3 wds.
84. Wrongful act
85. Cruising: 2 wds.
86. Crazy
87. Varnish ingredient
88. Colorado Indians
89. Pine
90. Pennsylvania port
91. Blue Eagle letters

DOWN
1. Abate
2. Wire measure
3. Minnesota's motto: 4 wds.
4. Simulated
5. God of war
6. Secular
7. Scottish county
8. Copied and ——
9. Motorist's ploy: hyph.
10. El ——
11. Wing
12. Portuguese women
13. Reddish-brown horse
14. Baal
15. Come in last
16. Utah city
22. Abrupt
23. Object
28. Starch: prefix
29. Wild attempt
30. Texas city
31. Jimmy of tennis
32. Nasal passage
34. Michigan city
35. Habits
36. The Great Emancipator: 2 wds.
37. Loop
38. Venetian magistrates
40. Show pleasure
41. Posts
44. Burst forth
45. Snoops
46. Honored
48. Subway fare
49. Chili con ——

PUZZLE 580

50. Expression of contempt
51. Cheer up
52. Large book
53. "The Bad News ——"
55. Gapes
56. Army VIPs
58. Arkansas town
59. City near Los Angeles
60. Direction, in Scotland
61. D.C. VIPs
63. Always
64. Town ——
67. Alaskan inhabitants
68. Asian headgear
69. Persian sprite
71. Grader
72. Western resort area
73. Aleutian island
74. Worn out
75. Ripped
76. Greek mountain
77. 1,201 to a Roman
80. Summer, to Henri
81. Neither's partner
82. Strife
83. Here, in Madrid

445

PUZZLE 581

ACROSS

1. Crazes
5. —— Verde
9. Bounders
13. "Educating ——"
17. Aid in crime
18. Finished
19. Chester —— Arthur
20. Delightful spot
21. Building beam: hyph.
22. Italian republic: 2 wds.
24. Air outlet
25. Impart
27. Dunce
28. People of Pusan
30. Actress Carter
32. Great Barrier ——
34. Standard
35. Former VP
38. Happy or stick
40. "The Time Machine" author
44. One —— million: 2 wds.
45. Gettysburg general
48. Egyptian port
50. Carbon substance
51. Use profanity
53. Census
55. Exigency
57. Travel term
58. Pallid
60. Large books
62. Theft
64. Shift
66. Pay
68. Creator of Lorelei Lee
69. Pinched pennies
72. Grapevine item
74. Scapegoat
77. Diamond gal
78. Scottish shirt
80. Newspaper section
81. Ms. Albright
82. Elvers
84. Secular
86. Approaches
89. Capek play
90. Inflict
92. Liquid globule
94. Ensnared
96. Tennis term
98. Hebrew measure
100. Bandy words
101. Porky Pig's gal
105. Bog fuel
107. Obliterates
111. Came to rest
112. Bette Davis film
115. Dorothy's dog
116. Crease
117. Smell ——: 2 wds.
118. State: Fr.
119. Redolence
120. Falls behind
121. Forsaken
122. Specks
123. Make no sense

DOWN

1. Like Monday's child
2. Fr. priest
3. Transaction
4. Abandon
5. River to the Rhine
6. Mrs. Peron
7. Dispatch
8. Protection
9. Business combines
10. Clay, today
11. Cold and damp
12. Be meddlesome
13. Esteems highly
14. Concept
15. So. state
16. Tiny toilers
23. Malt brews
26. Matched pair
29. Like crudites
31. Vaulted
33. "The Marble ——"
35. Isinglass
36. Burden
37. Altman film
39. British statesman
41. Segal opus: 2 wds.
42. Meat cut
43. Remain
46. Way in
47. Author Rice
49. Ardor
52. Witnessed
54. Madagascar mammal
56. Tear or ear
59. Brooklyn athletes
61. Singer Carly
63. Anthracite
65. —— estate

446

67. Transport
69. Seattle ——
70. Layer
71. Olive ——
73. Byways
75. Swing about
76. Football unit
79. Metric measure
83. Honors
85. Contend
87. Feels regret
88. Wound mark
91. Author Kesey
93. Warning sound
95. Public speaker
97. Kind of wave
99. Criticized
101. Grow tiresome
102. Famed essayist
103. Metallic sound
104. Sphere or station
106. One of the Jacksons
108. Fountain treat
109. Harrow's rival
110. Ilk
113. U.S.A.'s neighbor
114. Grain

PUZZLE 582

ACROSS
1. End of the honeymoon
5. Buffalo ——
9. Church recess
13. Recipe instruction
17. Life of Riley
18. Diva's showpiece
19. Yahoo
20. Essence
21. Songstress James
22. "Reflections in a ——": 2 wds.
24. Customary function
25. Hone
27. Food regimen
28. Discourage
29. Guy's mate
30. Commit a blunder
31. Largest continent
33. Atoll material
36. Tortoise's racing opponent
38. —— Jim Brady
42. Blue flag
43. Foreman
44. Relieve on duty
46. Female deer
47. Sunbather's goal
48. High mountain
49. Silent Marx
50. Watering tube
51. Up in years
54. Jeweler's weight
55. Sultan's wives
56. Make a knot
57. Deck out
58. Paving liquid
59. Barber's leather band
62. Redden
63. Synopsis
67. Neighbor of Turkey
68. Impudent
69. Lowest form of wit
70. Caviar
71. Children's chasing game
72. Canonized person
73. Be concerned
74. Sound a bell
75. —— City
77. Past due
78. Songstress Bailey
79. —— -decamp
80. English bar
81. —— Aviv
82. Cattle mark
85. Actress Theda ——
86. Principal city
90. Electrically charged atoms
91. Fur: 2 wds.
94. Carbonated drink
95. Dorothy's dog
96. Germ of an invention
97. Buffalo's lake
98. Seven —— of man
99. Forward part of a ship
100. Place in hock
101. Related
102. English architect

DOWN
1. Notices
2. Garden walk
3. Hammett pooch
4. Induces crying: 2 wds.
5. Roll with a hole
6. Potential steel
7. "Dakota ——"
8. Stocking runs
9. Baseballer Doubleday
10. Bard
11. Oriental sauce
12. Rather than, to a bard
13. Howl
14. Blow a horn
15. First name in whodunits
16. —— pressure
23. Republic of Ireland
26. Comrade
28. Watch face
31. Proficient
32. Missile housing
33. Quote
34. By word of mouth
35. Peel
36. Sacred
37. Cleopatra's snake
39. Redolence
40. Sense of smell
41. Judge
43. Bundle wrapped in burlap
44. Songstress Vaughan
45. Supplicate
49. Grim
50. Injure
52. "A Yank at ——"
53. Actor Torn
54. Bread rind
55. Smoked pork
57. Comedian King

448

58. Choreographer Tommy ——
59. Position
60. Mine car
61. Violent anger
62. Newlywed
63. Certain
64. Environment
65. Lion's cry
66. Shout
68. Hairless
69. TV host Sajak
72. Uttered
73. Nightclub
74. Louisiana bird
76. Hostage payment
77. Entice
78. Energy
80. Stately dance
81. Made serious demands on
82. Fragments
83. Underground plant part
84. Contribute a share
85. Puffed
86. Spiral
87. Forum garb
88. Oktoberfest drinks
89. Bind with rope
91. Drink slowly
92. Apple cider girl
93. Back, of old

PUZZLE 583

ACROSS

1. Be lenient
6. Dancer Bob
11. Solitary efforts
16. Tallies
17. Residue
18. Mr. North
20. Cane: 2 wds.
22. Famed silversmith
23. Silkworm
24. More tidy
25. Concept
27. Jazzman Norvo
28. Bible book
30. Anne or Jeanne: abbr.
31. Iowa town
32. "—— Lisa"
33. Growing years
35. Issue
38. Flax yield
39. One, in Ulm
41. Disen-cumbers
42. All there
43. Range
46. Corn ——
47. Plays the market
50. Get word
51. Confine
53. Authentic
54. Babylonian god
55. Otic organs
56. Hints
57. Booty
58. Page
59. Yore, of yore
60. Opposite of aweather
61. "—— My Way"
62. Soothe
63. Part of AARP
65. Boxing match
66. Freight handler
68. Leftovers
69. Author MacDonald
70. College official
71. Yearns
73. Fashion anew
75. Allude
79. Kind of nail
80. Offers
81. Pismire
83. Remove
84. Strong desire
85. Biblical king
86. Metallic element
89. Bert Bobbsey's sister
90. Calm
92. Vegas thief: 2 wds.
95. Schisms
96. Uptight
97. Foreigners
98. Ecological stages
99. Paving stones
100. Metric unit

DOWN

1. In short supply
2. Civil
3. Flood boat
4. Horse control
5. Laborers
6. Observed Lent
7. Bone: prefix
8. Cook, in a way
9. Dry, of wine
10. Yukon natives
11. Bruises
12. Olive genus
13. Actress Ullmann
14. In too deep: 3 wds.
15. Peaceful
16. Perspire
19. Fort
21. Portals
26. Library
29. Shows contempt
31. Man Friday
32. Dig for ore
34. Echo's title
36. Niblicks, e.g.
37. Hue
38. Wash
40. Cuddles
42. Get cozy
43. Diapha-nous
44. Author Norman Vincent
45. Unwieldy: 3 wds.
46. Flute
47. Persia, today
48. Harass
49. Less perilous
52. Even-Steven
53. Taunt
57. March King
58. Tilted
60. Martial ——

450

61. Gee whiz!
64. Provoked
65. Foreman
67. Boat
    paddle
69. Certain
    candies:
    hyph.
70. Jeans
    cloth
71. Chasm

72. Crawls
73. River
    inlet
74. San Diego
    team
76. Fireplace
    item
77. Actress
    May
78. Leases
80. Consecrate

82. Horns
85. Small:
    suffix
86. Broadcast
87. Pottery
    kiln
88. Scotch
    base

91. Song
93. Once
    named
94. Never in
    Bonn

PUZZLE 583

451

PUZZLE 584

ACROSS
1. Church recess
5. Outline
9. Excursions
10. Unyielding
12. Outdoor party
13. Pressed
15. Johann S. ____
16. Innocent
18. Level
20. Writing fluid
21. Pod dweller
22. Feminine suffix
23. Reps.
25. Takes a break
27. Or ____!
28. Voted in
30. Took place
32. Wonder
33. Stir
34. Pretense
38. Passed a law
42. Fail to win
43. Exhausted
45. Idol
46. "____ Enterprise": abbr.
47. Statement abbr.
48. Males
49. Existed
51. Stainless ____
53. Humane gp.
54. Hi-fi
56. Rebel
58. Vapor
59. Elude
60. Exclusive
61. Noises

DOWN
1. Instep
2. Safety ____
3. Rotate
4. Got free
5. Personal
6. Italian coin, once
7. Gone by
8. Baseball team
9. Amuse
11. Demons
12. Door portion
14. Thick
15. Wait patiently
17. Plural suffix
19. Necessity
24. Frighten
25. Hollow stems
26. Tilt
27. Era
29. Old airline
31. Oklahoma city
34. Social group
35. Watering tubes
36. Items of value
37. Synopsis
38. Registered
39. Church
40. Raise
41. Spanish lady
44. Opposite WSW
50. Snares
51. Glue shut
52. Son of Jacob
53. Turfs
55. Car of old
57. Moving truck

PUZZLE 585

ACROSS
1. Spread the word
5. Social reformer Lucretia
9. Christiania, today
13. Robt. ____: 2 wds.
14. Diamond Head's locale
15. Singes
17. Analogous words: 2 wds.
18. Sheriff's insignia
19. Kind of boom
20. Abandoned: 2 wds.
23. Type of wine
24. Actor Brynner
25. Illuminated
27. Trinity member
28. Nightstick
31. Sweet-smelling
33. No matter who
34. Opposite of astern
35. Per ____
36. Tantrum
37. Gambling game
41. Flynn of films
44. Cake mixture
46. Athletes Walt and Joe
49. Foolish
50. Confederate soldier, for short
51. ____ canto
52. Enjoy a winter sport
53. Arab garments
55. Southpaw: hyph.
61. Georgia city
63. "Born ____"
64. Prod
65. Musical exercise
66. Bridge levy
67. Poet Pound
68. Brother of Jacob
69. Songstress Sumac et al.
70. Bank on

DOWN
1. River duck
2. Different
3. Viking first name
4. Yankee pitcher of yore: 2 wds.
5. Rhine tributary
6. Sworn statement
7. Siamese
8. Go west from south: 2 wds.
9. Military program: abbr.
10. Restaurateur Toots
11. Wooly
12. Devotional prayer
16. Perfume
21. Good: Sp.
22. Prank
26. Rocky hill
28. Ill-bred fellow
29. Before form or verse
30. Coloring matter
31. Banisters
32. Liberal politico: hyph.
36. "Waiting ____": 2 wds.
38. Philippine people
39. Legal thing
40. Lode load
42. Ridicule
43. Stagger
44. Potato units
45. Singer Paul
46. Picture casing
47. Car company's offering
48. Eastern calculator
54. Club ____
56. Out of
57. Tissue
58. Have a siesta
59. Justice Warren
60. June 6, 1944: hyph.
62. Just bought, in Bonn

453

PUZZLE 586

ACROSS
1. Crunchy
6. Climbing plant
11. Naughty!
14. Fill in potholes
15. Florida city
16. Actor Linden
17. Jane Pauley, formerly
19. Hook's partner
20. Act
21. Generosity
23. Beatty film
25. "Pepe ___" (Gabin film): 2 wds.
26. Sunken fence: hyph.
29. Trim the nails
31. Noted Baba
32. Nickname at Yale
33. Poetic tribute
34. Cheeky
37. Table protectors
39. Spanish tether
41. Numbers men: abbr.
42. Like some dates
44. Dale's guy
45. Before, to poets
46. Attila the ___
47. Over
48. Fox of fable
49. Heart
51. Place of worship
53. "Seems Like ___": 2 wds.
55. "Iliad," for one
59. File suit
60. Toilette items: 2 wds.
62. Dry, as wine
63. Anesthetic
64. Saarinen and others
65. Make inquiries
66. Sweet things
67. Threefold

DOWN
1. Sand or fiddler follower
2. Mr. Auberjonois
3. Yen
4. Neighbor of the Nile
5. Certify
6. Promise
7. EPA's concern: abbr.
8. Mexican dish
9. ___ Boothe Luce
10. Popular word-game
11. Gilligan's pal: 2 wds.
12. Authorization: hyph.
13. Noted Swiss artist
18. "Legal Eagles" star
22. Windblown
24. Extra order, as of toast
26. Rope fiber
27. Range in Asia
28. Duck down!: 3 wds.
30. Hear about
34. Pourer's request: 2 wds.
35. Trim away
36. River to the North Sea
38. Knievel forte
40. Pedicure site
43. Tempted
47. Songstress Franklin
48. Rest-room gadget
49. Mystery offerings
50. Ham it up
52. Underdog win
53. Mt. Pelion's neighbor
54. Ending for lob or mob
56. Equal: prefix
57. Bard's black
58. Being, to Brutus
61. Alternative words

454

ACROSS

1. Vat
4. ____ of the line
7. "The Purple ____ of Cairo"
11. Miner's yield
12. Stolen goods
14. Bad
15. Carver
17. Camera part
18. Smidgen
19. Morning juice
21. Poker pot
22. Zoot ____
23. Have supper
24. Dotted
28. Lyric poem
29. Noah's birds
30. Grow up
31. Wood-eating insects
33. King of the beasts
34. Peck film, with "The"
35. Skillets
36. Vegetable plot
39. Lend a ____
40. Slender woodwind
41. Young ones
45. Dull
46. Old times
47. Have bills
48. Witnessed
49. Join together
50. Favorite

DOWN

1. Water tester
2. Coffee pot
3. Tenderfoot
4. Make happy
5. ____ Scotia
6. Female deer
7. Narrate
8. Kiln
9. Vocalize
10. Additional
13. Companies
16. Footballer Kyle ____
20. Tears
21. Helper
22. Lucky number
23. Spot
24. Strength
25. Downpour beginning
26. Easily bruised items
27. Lair
29. Piggy-bank filler
32. Recent
33. Property
35. Faded
36. Scads
37. Up to it
38. Man about town
39. Employ
42. In what way
43. Female sheep
44. Fisherman's tool

PUZZLE 587

PUZZLE 588

ACROSS
1. Wight, for one
5. "Three Musketeers" author
10. Expectant
14. Buckeye State
15. Scent
16. Seldom seen
17. Wolverine State locale
20. Sheepish female
21. Latin hymn, with 12 Down
22. German city
23. Dining hall
24. Robust
26. County, in the Pelican State
29. Food fish
30. Bounty inits.
33. Wallet fillers
34. Bristles
35. Be under the weather
36. Cornhusker State locale
40. Nationality suffix
41. Origins
42. British gun
43. Run up
44. Rows
45. Current
47. Safeguard
48. Barcelona room
49. Valuable instrument, for short
52. TV staple
53. Mr. Durocher
56. Equality State locale
60. "Rule Britannia" composer
61. ___ Semple McPherson
62. False god
63. Grooves
64. Footballer Bart
65. Baseballer Pete

DOWN
1. Mythical Greek princess
2. Actor Robert
3. Point connector
4. Aurora
5. Deli pastry
6. Impels
7. Family members
8. Pierre's pal
9. Sooner State tribe
10. Get up
11. Nicknames
12. See 21 Across
13. Keystone St.
18. Roman date
19. Assistant
23. Varied: abbr.
24. Dislikes
25. Mideasterner
26. Warsaw citizens
27. Spicy herb
28. Resume
29. Change
30. Waste-maker
31. Connors and Douglas
32. Angle
34. A little night music?
37. Gold-imitating alloy
38. Burden
39. Movie dog
45. Legal eagle
46. ___ -ran
47. Actor Gabby
48. Ed Norton's domain
49. Blemish
50. By way of, informally
51. Overhead item
52. Eelworm
53. Venetian resort
54. Biblical man
55. Stare
57. Scientific gp.
58. Insect egg
59. Former Russian space station

ACROSS

1. Artist's home
5. Arabian garments
9. Freshen
14. Hebrew month
15. Sprightly
16. Shirk
17. Formal act
18. Stewpot
19. Judge's mallet
20. Leg joints
22. ___ firma
24. Wind up
25. ___ serpent
27. Moonshine factory
29. Haggard novel
32. Compete
34. Contracts
38. TV ad
42. Spare
43. Traffic-light color
44. Craggy hill
45. City on the Meuse
46. Bamboo shoot
47. Ronstadt, for one
49. Traveling
51. Plaza de Toros sound
52. Perceive
53. Free
56. Word of agreement
58. Wing
61. "Divine Comedy" author
63. Irreligious
67. True
69. Nimbus
71. Skedaddled
72. Egg-shaped
73. Hero
74. Rainbow
75. Dwindled
76. For fear that
77. Shipshape

DOWN

1. Adventure
2. Norse god
3. Kismet
4. Tupelos, e.g.
5. GI's address
6. Strap
7. Van Gogh's town
8. Begin
9. Amuse highly
10. Stowe's Little ___
11. Wheel hub
12. Shangri-la
13. Actress Tuesday
21. Cut
23. Brooklet
26. Mien
28. Tardier
29. Alarm
30. Four-bagger
31. Live coal
33. Outside: prefix
35. Teams
36. Expunge
37. Intelligence
39. Purple Heart, e.g.
40. Charged atom
41. Jason's ship
45. Precipitous
47. Portico
48. Family Stone member
50. Dozed
54. Slow mover
55. Musical composition
57. Lustrous fabric
58. Declare openly
59. Molten rock
60. Actor Mowbray
62. God of love
64. Pierce with horns
65. Scotto song
66. Wren's retreat
68. Resident: suffix
70. Height: abbr.

PUZZLE 590

ACROSS
1. Spat
4. Tater
8. Labyrinths
13. Eight, to Pedro
15. Tiny opening
16. Digression
17. Upon
18. Saudi Arabian province
19. Scope
20. Skirmish
22. Not so wild
24. Dancer Charisse
25. Like certain recordings
28. Ralph ___ Emerson
29. Rocker Boy
33. Phooey!
35. Kind of boom
38. Icy rain
39. Ancient Greek city
41. Of the kidneys
43. From a distance
44. Imprint
46. Bit of info
48. Wrath
49. Turkish tribesmen
51. Charged particle
53. Hosts
58. ___ Jima
61. Book page
62. Fountain item
63. Disney deer
65. Border on
67. German pronoun
68. Standard of perfection
69. Movie: Sp.
70. Spool for film
71. Not very bright
72. "Kiss Me ___"
73. Salt: Fr.

DOWN
1. Traipses
2. Musical group
3. Kind of bread: hyph.
4. Health resort
5. Put off
6. ___ Heep
7. Skin: pref.
8. Leaves the singles scene
9. ___ rule: 2 wds.
10. Metal
11. Nervous
12. Germ
14. "Fidelio," e.g.
21. Sniggler's catch
23. Sch. subj.
26. Garlic feature
27. Soft drink
30. Purifying plants
31. Apparatus
32. Raison d'___
33. "Personal ___"
34. Edmonton's prov.
36. Once ___ while: 2 wds.
37. Fierce feline
40. He loves: Lat.
42. Moon goddess
45. Side view
47. Long for
50. ___ Paulo
52. Web-footed animal
54. Negligent
55. Limb bone
56. Hindu queen
57. Nifty!
58. Footnote abbr.
59. Virginia of tennis
60. Augury
64. College degrees: abbr.
66. Shirt type

PUZZLE 591

ACROSS
1. Coil
5. Group of soldiers
10. Slightly open
14. Out of work
15. Handbag
16. Hawaiian fire goddess
17. ___-do-well
18. Wash cycle
19. Train track
20. Rock-'n'-roll followers
22. Sweetie
23. Aardvark's bit of food
24. Nickel or dime
26. Malay garment
30. Capone, for example
34. Cohere
35. ___ football
36. Chopping tool
37. Terrific review
38. Opted
39. Gyrate
40. Had a hamburger
41. "Blue ___ Shoes"
42. Bureau
43. Does
45. Card suit
46. Overdue
47. Mr. Linden
48. Insect
51. Chicago suburb
56. Summit
57. Jeweler's gold measure
59. Rush ___
60. Ceremony
61. Oil source
62. Poet Pound
63. Urgency
64. Shepherd
65. Trial

DOWN
1. Half of a panda's name
2. Czech waterway
3. Bread topper
4. Lima's locale
5. Bounce
6. Partner of peace
7. Samovars
8. Burro
9. English river
10. Pinafores
11. ___ Claude Killy
12. "It's a Sin to Tell ___": 2 wds.
13. Depend (on)
21. Qualm
22. "___ Noon"
24. Occasion
25. Formerly
26. Kind of iron
27. Winged
28. Actor Phoenix
29. Solitary
30. Wares
31. Candle
32. Be
33. Tears
35. Park or song
38. Abrupt
39. ___ Na Na
41. Climb
42. Cubicle
44. Moved (a muscle)
45. Bridle
47. Lift
48. Rural sight
49. Mayberry resident
50. Network
51. Soft cheese
52. Grind
53. Seep
54. Mine and yours
55. Mild oath
57. Greek island
58. Height: abbr.

PUZZLE 592

ACROSS

1. Musical sound
6. Soggy
10. Gold-rush town
14. Nomad
15. Lamb's pen name
16. Frosted
17. Iowa community
18. Football kick
19. Strike
20. Surprise: 4 wds.
23. Greek letters
24. Window material
25. Duel memento
28. Nobility
32. Poorest
34. Small sofa: 2 wds.
38. Pie ____ mode: 2 wds.
39. Artist's studio
42. Hit-show sign
43. Alleviate
45. More logical
47. Adds
50. College head
51. Liking
54. Jot
56. Infrequently: 5 wds.
63. Inventor Sikorsky
64. Verbal
65. Cookstove
66. Italian coin
67. Dreadful
68. Fishhook line
69. Blind a falcon
70. German river
71. Ford bomb

DOWN

1. Grumble
2. ____ sapiens
3. Elliptical
4. Tenants
5. Sketch
6. Unseat
7. Astringent
8. After-dinner candy
9. Garden walk
10. Bites
11. Florida city
12. Bills of fare
13. Margins
21. Seance sound
22. Tent caterpillars
25. Barter
26. Soft drink
27. Asian sea
29. Actress Burstyn
30. King: Fr.
31. Hail!
33. City in Taiwan
35. Old laborer
36. Neighborhood
37. Actor Rip
40. Siphon
41. Nice summer
44. Football pass
46. ____ Eve: 2 wds.
48. Comedienne Phyllis
49. Old French coin
51. Works hard
52. Actress Dickinson
53. Game tally
55. Concise
57. Drowses
58. Opera solo
59. Actress Theda
60. Change for a five
61. Leer
62. Actress Gwyn

PUZZLE 593

ACROSS
1. Artist Chagall
5. Insertion mark
10. Melt
14. Esau's wife
15. Japanese seaport
16. Hebrides island
17. Holding an advantage over: 4 wds.
20. Goofs at bridge
21. Catch cod
22. Affirm
23. Produced
25. Degraded
28. Slave Scott
29. Zoo attraction
32. Quick gait
33. New Orleans athlete
34. ____ ragged
35. Marriage-vow phrase: 5 wds.
39. Blackbird
40. Draw forth
41. Slacken
42. Rover or river
43. Pilaf base
44. Entrapped
46. Type of room
47. Was profitable
48. Office worker, for short
51. Formal surrender
54. Possessing no superiority over: 3 wds.
58. Fleur-de-lis
59. Lofty abode
60. Mucilage
61. Person from Posen
62. Hollows
63. Released

DOWN
1. ____ -jongg
2. Jewish month
3. Bawl
4. Asian water: 2 wds.
5. Like some machines
6. Fall bloom
7. Bowl cheers
8. Piece (out)
9. Mahal's first name
10. Clocked
11. Indian tribe
12. Presently
13. Lose size
18. Snowfield
19. In the habit of: 2 wds.
23. "The ____ of Frankenstein"
24. Charter
25. Sacred table
26. Singer Pat
27. Plant louse
28. Emulate Ben Vereen
29. Bellowing
30. Throb
31. Concluded
33. Apple or tomato
36. Mount ____, Va.
37. Blue-pencil
38. Chapter titles
44. Window parts
45. Unless: Lat.
46. Fragrant seed
47. Type of jury
48. Ocean craft
49. Starchy plant
50. Kind of eye
51. Belt or pone
52. Flirt with visually
53. Part of speech
55. Move restlessly
56. Born
57. Mosquito ____

PUZZLE 594

ACROSS
1. Where Katmandu is
6. Engine
11. Wine descriptive
14. Where the action is
15. ___ Boothe Luce
16. New Deal agcy.
17. Some recreational groups: 2 wds.
19. Eternity
20. Flaunt one's victory
21. Actress Bara
23. Dishonest
26. No-frills lodging
27. Marie Curie's husband
28. Lack
30. Homeric epic
31. Soar skyward
32. Ratite bird
35. Take it easy
36. Sparkle
37. Vientiane's land
38. British money abbr.
39. Painter Charles or James
40. Writer Bret
41. Haifa's locale
43. Reel
44. U.S. industrialist
46. Most excellent
47. Big volumes
48. Roman official
50. Pedro's precious metal
51. Fictional detective: 2 wds.
57. Blemish
58. Violinist Mischa
59. Made accurate
60. Wide receiver
61. Author Dahl
62. Certain harnesses

DOWN
1. Capture
2. Stray
3. Architect I.M.
4. Common connector
5. Loiterer
6. Genuine article
7. Pot for senora
8. Tight
9. Sphere
10. Recondition
11. Beloved ones
12. Lyric poem
13. Waterway
18. Actress Sommer
22. Presidential monogram
23. Missile housings
24. "Heartlight" singer: 2 wds.
25. Of a time
26. Biblical verb
27. Pain in the neck?
28. Rehearse
29. "___ kleine Nachtmusik"
31. Wings
33. Sacred composition
34. Consumer
36. Baggage
37. Like Mr. Apley
39. Laundry worker
40. The best policy
42. Fr. holy woman
43. Cashbox
44. Ski mecca
45. "Houseboat" actress
46. Villain
48. Austen title
49. Double
52. Lily plant: var.
53. Golf VIP
54. Diving bird
55. Scottish river
56. Wynn et al.

ACROSS

1. Pizzazz
6. Gossip
10. Iron oxide
14. Interim
15. Annoy
16. Against: pref.
17. Ultimately
19. Matinee ___
20. Dame Rebecca
21. Actress Vera
22. Bench
23. Mr. Doubleday
24. Mooring for a ship
25. Rouses
29. Crab or blue
31. Penny place
32. Pubescent
33. Make lace
36. Bridge coup
37. Inclines
39. Brain or duck
40. Finished edge
41. Metal refuse
42. Atomic particle
44. Entreaties
46. Hangs around
47. White-sale item
49. "The ___ Man Theme"
51. Israeli dance
52. Boars
53. Stare
57. Friendly Frenchmen
58. Turner paintings
60. Director Clair
61. Impel
62. Beasts of burden
63. Work units
64. Biblical garden
65. "Over ___"

DOWN

1. Hightailed it
2. Wash
3. Mimics
4. "___ It Romantic"
5. Soak flax
6. Intelligence
7. French city
8. Ragweed, e.g.
9. Turkish rulers
10. Increases, as pay
11. Downplay
12. Summer ermine
13. Land condition
18. Parasol
23. Subsidize
24. Exclude
25. Party
26. Mr. Gardner
27. Running nimbly
28. Beret's kin
30. Gives back
32. Children's game
34. Cupid
35. KO counts
38. Toward the rising sun
39. Ignited
41. Collection
43. Relieved (of)
45. Rents
46. Actor Hal
47. Portion
48. "Iliad" author
50. Pivot
52. Turn on an axis
53. Cut
54. Church area
55. Counterpart
56. Being
59. Calico, e.g.

PUZZLE 595

PUZZLE 596

ACROSS
1. Let go
5. Olden possessive
10. ___ mater
14. Vicinity
15. Showed a film again
16. Vault
17. Diamond star
19. Legends
20. Willy Loman, e.g.
21. Horseshoe position
23. Actor Chaney
24. Grassy plots
25. Meat processor's employee
29. Wander
30. L.A. time
33. Take to lunch
34. Daily gazette
35. ___ cubes
36. Aid a felon
37. Stipends
38. Biting insect
39. Acquired
40. Took on
41. Leg part
42. Goof
43. Parched
44. Diverts
45. Iroquoian Indians
47. Colorado Indian
48. Veiled
50. Star-shaped figure
55. Idi ___
56. Court star
58. Lion's pride
59. Eucharistic vessel
60. Ooze
61. Figurehead's locale
62. Be lenient to
63. Warmth

DOWN
1. Maxims
2. Diva's solo
3. Prisoner's pad
4. Hardy cabbage
5. Slight earthquake
6. Macho type
7. Iraq's neighbor
8. Negative vote
9. Forces into bondage
10. Poe's middle name
11. Ring star
12. Dark spot on the moon
13. Mime
18. Bit of land
22. Pitcher
24. Ran easily
25. Actor's milieu
26. Grape's home
27. Links star
28. Use a shuttle
29. Fumed
31. Ready a fish
32. Heads, in 34 Down
34. City on the Seine
37. Bugs a phone
38. African antelope
40. Win by a ___
41. Mideast bigwig
44. Bring into harmony
46. Continue a subscription
47. Wedding assistant
48. David, for one
49. Khayyam
50. Tropical ant
51. Impetuous
52. Conversational phrase
53. ___ butter
54. Hung on to
57. Criticize sharply

464

ACROSS

1. Reindeer herder
5. Dull thud
8. Drove over the limit
12. Helm position
13. Mighty whaler
15. Main artery
16. Whirring sound
17. Pianist Peter ____
18. Cirrus or cumulus
19. Apple choices
22. Hebrew instrument
23. Billy ____ Williams
24. Sword handle
26. Baseball nine, e.g.
29. ____ avis
33. Cowboy spectacle
34. Busy as ____
36. Morning moisture
37. Banana choices
41. Employ
42. In good mental health
43. Strolls
44. To be: Fr.
46. "Peter Pan" pooch
48. God of war
49. Fitness facility
51. Milano money, once
53. Orange choices
61. Actor Welles
62. City on the Ural
63. Entice
64. Ripening agents
65. Actress Sommer
66. Shamrock land
67. Borscht ingredient
68. Auricle
69. Fast planes

DOWN

1. Chemists' workshops
2. Inter ____
3. Where Quechua is spoken
4. Sheet materials
5. Bluegrass instrument
6. ____ as big as all outdoors
7. Grape refuse
8. Bond with hot lead
9. Brace
10. Small case
11. Florida county
14. ____ choy
15. Complexion woe
20. Bars legally
21. Publicity agents
24. Lift
25. Lounger
27. Consumed
28. Arab garment
30. An Astaire
31. Stinks
32. Pointed tools
33. Rake
35. "____ Scissorhands"
38. Hawaiian porch
39. ____ world of one's own
40. Allegories
45. Accompany
47. Nome's home
50. Puts to paper
52. Dye worker
53. Biblical soldier
54. Impulse
55. Phrase of comprehension
56. Iowa college
57. First name in whodunits
58. Possessive pronoun
59. Legal document
60. Contact ____

PUZZLE 597

PUZZLE 598

ACROSS
1. Ostentation
5. Sediment
9. Host Griffin
13. Opposite of aweather
14. ___ Sadat
15. African lily
16. "It" girl/oriels
19. Make lace
20. Oaths
21. Trumpet
22. Flower plots
23. Computer data unit
24. Repair, as brakes
27. Grown pike
28. Brother, e.g.
31. Parallel to
32. Shopping center
33. Rational
34. Frontier justice/toy
37. Fruit drinks
38. Nights before
39. Venezuelan statesman
40. Biddy
41. Always
42. ___ Island
43. Uttered
44. Roe fish
45. Fully grown
48. Headliner
49. Meadow
52. Songstress/dilutes
55. Prod
56. Wed secretly
57. Served well
58. English queen
59. Scoops
60. Inquisitive

DOWN
1. Agreement
2. Spanish stew
3. Main course
4. ___ diem
5. Deceives
6. Wobblies: abbr.
7. There oughta be a ___
8. Tot's vehicle
9. Sierra ___
10. North Carolina college
11. Poet laureate Nicholas ___
12. Waistcoat
14. Domicile
17. Vindicate
18. Short letter
22. Dark cherries
23. Electric lights
24. Hindu ruler
25. Avoid
26. Olive green
27. Coat
28. Wooden shoe
29. Silly
30. Start
32. Relocated
33. Golfer Sam
35. Critiqued
36. Church tables
41. Nobleman
42. Be generous
43. Napped leather
44. Paces
45. Large: pref.
46. Solar deity
47. "More ___ You Know"
48. Cease
49. Crazy
50. Rams' dams
51. Artist Warhol
53. Actress MacGraw
54. Actor Aykroyd

466

PUZZLE 599

ACROSS
1. First code word
5. Belittle
10. Rio Branco's locale
14. Ambition
15. African republic
16. At that time
17. ____ and for all
18. At close quarters
20. Command to a horse
21. "____ Lisa"
22. Goddess of peace
23. Powerful people
25. Comedian Laurel
26. Satellites
27. Satisfactory
31. Smart
32. "Gay ____"
33. Abet's partner
34. Sad cry
35. Plots
36. Highest point
37. Calif.'s ocean
38. Filmy
39. Match
40. Gym shoes
42. Dos and ____
43. Gibson and Ferrer
44. Fracas
45. Pittsburgh product
47. Depots: abbr.
48. Hoskins of "Mermaids"
51. Film spools
53. Constructed
54. All: pref.
55. Remus or Sam
56. Amino, e.g.
57. Louise of "Gilligan's Island"
58. Spud
59. Increases

DOWN
1. Eager
2. ____ Star State
3. Fronts together
4. Foamy brew
5. Detests
6. Baked and lima
7. Tolstoy heroine
8. Baseball's Fernandez
9. Bodies
10. Goddess of wisdom
11. Sleuth Charlie ____
12. French philosopher Descartes
13. Wind down
19. Declaim
21. Innumerable
24. Topers
25. More certain
26. Italian city
27. Gorges
28. In unbroken sequence
29. Ade fruits
30. First address
31. Siestas
32. Docks
35. Pay
36. "____ No Sunshine"
38. Form of trapshooting
39. Oodles
41. Aviator Earhart
42. Tradesman
44. Grave marker
45. Teamster's rig
46. Volunteer St.
47. Cult
49. Garfield's canine friend
50. Bassinet and cradle
51. Disintegrate
52. Gene component initials
53. West of Brooklyn

467

PUZZLE 600

ACROSS
1. Doilies
5. Western campus: abbr.
9. Chinese tea
12. Verve
13. Object
15. Exhibit
16. Derby winner, 1937
18. Gold fabric
19. Pose
20. Whit
21. On cloud nine
23. Bulk
24. Irritate
25. Beau
28. Fluffy
29. Swiss river
32. Narration
33. ___ operandi
34. Psychic Geller
35. Substantive
36. Student
37. Mellowed
38. Sea eagle
39. Bird in "Peter and the Wolf"
40. Winged
41. Clique
42. Baseballer Speaker
43. Actor
44. ___ acid (B vitamin)
46. Olympic site
47. Four quarts
49. To shelter
50. Turkish title
53. Russian city
54. Derby winner, 1930
57. Olive genus
58. Bed linen
59. Weathercock
60. Period
61. Blyth et al.
62. God of war

DOWN
1. Sea gulls
2. Jai ___
3. Sour
4. Snow, to Scots
5. Nth degree
6. Vouchers
7. Italian coin, once
8. Miscellanea
9. Derby winner, 1963
10. Domicile
11. Overwhelmed
14. Exultant
15. Czech, e.g.
17. Daily record
22. "___ Do It"
23. "September ___"
24. Daises
25. Old laborers
26. Mart
27. Derby winner, 1943
28. Jrs.-to-be
30. Rugged ridge
31. Jockey
33. Songs
36. Shavings
37. Oh, sorrow!
39. Capital of Manche
40. Strange
43. Skirt folds
45. Spicy stew
46. Actress Burstyn
47. Wholesome
48. Woody's son
49. Danish measure
50. At a distance
51. Departed
52. Hewing tools
55. Cry of triumph
56. Power gp.

REVELATION

PUZZLE 601

Solve this puzzle as you would a regular crossword. Then read the circled letters from left to right, and they will reveal a quotation.

ACROSS

1. Uncovered
5. Portion
9. Bribe
12. Silent-star Jannings
13. Lotion additive, often
14. Vanity
15. Buttery bean
16. Pedestrian's pavement
18. Trial run
20. Fracas
21. Ball
24. Marsh
25. Wear down
26. Fashion's slave
30. Milne character
31. Distant
32. Mary ___ Retton
33. Authorize
36. Actress Ina ___
38. Vapor
39. Hound
40. Anecdote
43. Actress Anderson
44. More attractive
46. Clothes
50. Ginger ___
51. Citrus drinks

52. French needlecase
53. Sawbuck
54. Harness
55. Grit

DOWN

1. Barbara ___ Geddes
2. Cannes chum
3. Lip
4. Ecstatic
5. Out
6. Deplaned
7. Pole
8. Swarmed
9. Make airtight

10. Leer at
11. Dawdle
17. Make one's way
19. Afore
21. Moistureless
22. High-school event
23. Ring
24. Booster
26. Favoring
27. Misfortunes
28. Loam
29. Melody
31. You betcha!
34. Grimm meanie

35. Ambush
36. Disallow
37. Script directives
39. Palfrey
40. Begone!
41. Tinware
42. Presage
43. Soup vegetable
45. Marriage vow
47. Lizard genus
48. Drab color
49. Baseball's Fernandez

469

PUZZLE 602

ACROSS

1. Supervisor
5. Hawaiian root
9. Rebuff
13. Puncture
17. Field
18. Horse color
19. Fence stake
20. Enameled metalware
21. Seasoning
22. Indefinite
24. Cleveland's lake
25. Oval
27. Toboggan
28. Occurrences
30. Convened
31. Interpret
32. Ivan the Terrible
33. Fish hooks
36. Ointment
37. Creative
41. Confederate
42. Squabble
43. Sportsman-like
44. Exist
45. Employ
46. Football kick
47. Angler's basket
48. Walked on
49. Shelter
51. Noblemen
52. Writer Stephen ___
53. Bash
54. Violent outburst
55. Central
56. Contradict
58. Pasture
59. Intolerant
62. Reclined
63. Idle chatter
64. Bargain
65. Shoshonean Indian
66. Mil. branch
67. Bait
68. Frozen-yogurt holder
69. Blackthorn
70. Sharpens again
72. Foray
73. Intends
74. Skipper's word
75. Bucket
76. Cover charge
77. Tract
80. Tennis units
81. Kind of pipe
85. In a frenzy
86. Tyrant
89. Capitol feature
90. Account
91. Zenith
92. Banish
93. Work on manuscripts
94. Molt
95. Snacks
96. Clears
97. Soaks

DOWN

1. Foundation
2. Kind of hygiene
3. Order to a stockbroker
4. Please
5. Confidence
6. Tiptop
7. Wheel: Ger.
8. Numero uno
9. Glimpsed
10. Actress Cheryl ___
11. Malt beverage
12. Architectural support
13. Guides
14. Rent
15. Dismounted
16. Quilting and honey
23. Mollusk
26. Dance step
29. Worthless
31. Huck's transport
32. Kilmer poem
33. Frenchman
34. Besides
35. Inexperienced person
36. Sweet cherry
37. Wary
38. Large, hairy spider
39. Do a laundry chore
40. Yield
42. Albacore
43. Salad ingredient
46. Fabric nap
47. Discontinue
48. Singing group
50. Profit
51. Silver coating
52. Actor Nicholas ___
54. Gall

55. Eight furlongs
56. Smear
57. Naturalness
58. Level
59. Strip
60. Harrow's rival
61. Ruby and Sandra
63. Wife of Odysseus
64. Besmirch
67. Ceramic square
68. Ammunitions chest
69. Meager
71. Persecuted
72. Assess
73. For each
75. What coffee docs
76. Strongholds
77. Signs of approval
78. Chinese nurse
79. Function
80. Young oyster
81. Expense
82. Value system
83. Overlook
84. Speculates
87. Coal size
88. Petition

PUZZLE 603

ACROSS

1. Appraises
6. Speak imperfectly
10. Drop heavily
14. Scar tissues
19. Fanon
20. Tennis star
21. Traveled
22. Jeweler's weight
23. 6 ANs
27. Party
28. Hollow stem
29. Certain Japanese divers
30. Can, for one
31. Compass pt.
32. Rapid
33. N.C. college
34. Winter vehicle
35. Towel word
36. Obstacle
37. In the manner of
38. Run into
41. 6 ONs
49. Lifeless
50. Greek vowels
51. Political cartoonist
52. Musical work
53. Brynhild's brother
54. Ripening agent
55. Wear down
56. Contradicts
57. Fancy hotel
58. Film Norma
59. City sections
60. French forest
61. 3 UNs
65. Turned by hand
68. Unusual thing
69. Polynesian warrior
70. Norwegian city
74. Apartment
75. Loiters
76. Sullen
77. Grounds
78. Thoughts
79. Porgy's love
80. "I Have ____ Here Before"
81. Bearings
82. 6 INs
86. Letters
87. Tree
88. Roman poet
89. "____ the season ..."
90. Confined space
92. Prudish
93. Kentucky fort
95. Potent pugilist
98. Partners
101. Ancient Scot
102. Momentarily
103. Snarl
104. 6 ENs
108. Attack
109. Relax
110. Actor Leon ____
111. Stranger
112. Brings up
113. Utopia
114. Sea wall
115. Name in tractors

DOWN

1. Red cosmetic
2. Wall hanging
3. Eating place
4. Exile island
5. Comprehend
6. Corset items
7. Bit of land
8. Take off
9. Princess's problem
10. Earliest ancestor
11. Civil War general
12. Pindarics
13. Through
14. Goat or grace
15. Was concerned
16. Irish islands
17. Infant
18. Mix up
24. Understand
25. Side dish
26. Tooth
32. Decree
33. Space chimp
34. Flat strip
35. Recumbent
36. Boat feature
37. Church part
38. Arrested
39. Actress Eve ____
40. Friend of Archie
41. Pretender
42. Curative: pref.
43. Slangy wherewithal
44. Esteem
45. Exorbitant
46. Swamp
47. See 77 Across
48. Exclusive controls
54. Russian cooperative
55. Pitches
56. Tiresome, to a poet
59. Dockworkers
60. Total

62. Czar's edict
63. Ridicule
64. Western Indians
65. Felony
66. Fortification
67. Dill plants
71. Wise man
72. Loaned
73. Peak in Thessaly
75. What some faucets do
76. Legal document
79. Tell
80. Top
81. 1109
83. Din
84. Vices
85. Repent
90. Fall drink
91. Naps
92. Hesitate
93. Russian coin
94. Scandinavian
95. Sandy's owner
96. Afterward
97. Peace goddess
98. Love god
99. Path
100. Actress Bonet
101. Alum
102. Truck type, for short
103. Wind
105. Victory sign
106. Owned
107. Reprobate

PUZZLE 604

ACROSS

1. Hound's quarry
5. Volume
9. Not first
13. Tied
14. Author Stephen ___
15. Follow
16. Revere's journey
17. Unlucky person
18. Guzzle
19. Garlic feature
20. Nosh
21. Cuddle
23. Pleased
25. Embroider
26. Pre-schooler's "pen"
29. Promise
33. Ignited
34. Hassle
37. Kaiser and Parker House
39. Eager
41. Fear
43. Cathedral part
44. Less
46. Creates
48. Lair
49. Lower in rank
51. Densely wooded area
53. Lassie's pal
54. Give up
55. Not as fast
59. Heir
60. Elegant
64. Own
65. Hereditary factors
67. Lowest female voice
68. Sign
69. Disintegrate
70. Ooze
71. Saucy
72. Flaps
73. Hauls

DOWN

1. Brave person
2. Excited
3. Perform again
4. Pep
5. Wide
6. Kiln
7. Single thing
8. Corn seed
9. Fireplace wood
10. Touch
11. Vend
12. Use a keyboard
14. Scoured
22. Pitcher
24. Parcel of land
25. Utter
26. Chowder ingredient
27. Stiff
28. Make amends
30. Put on
31. Clearing
32. Santa's helpers
35. Supplied with weapons
36. Ocean
38. Dispatched
40. Chewing ___
42. Protection
45. Shoe part
47. Turf
50. Goal
52. Meal
54. College girls
55. Look for bargains
56. Fancy fabric
57. Finished
58. Departed
59. Social climber
61. Potato topping
62. Fret
63. Jumps
66. Important age

474

PUZZLE 605

ACROSS
1. Peels
6. Light-switch position
9. Camp beds
13. Remain
14. Speed
16. Once ____ a time
17. Wigwam's cousin
18. Locale
19. Make over
20. Slimmest
22. Lackluster
23. Fraternal group
24. Compositions
26. Ohio port
30. Job
32. First gardener?
33. History
35. Tiny bit
39. Trainees
41. Confers holy orders upon
44. Pace
45. Plumbing part
47. Nevada city
48. Do a household chore
50. Reduce
52. Attach
56. Wicked
58. Schoolroom problem
59. Spotless
65. Uproars
66. Follow closely
67. Luncheonette
68. Thaw
69. Dimensions
70. Cafe customer
71. Swirl
72. Mesh
73. Frock

DOWN
1. Butter servings
2. Cain's brother
3. Mature
4. First garden
5. Sowed
6. Missouri mountain range
7. Wooded places
8. Enemies
9. Miss Muffet's treat
10. "Aida," for one
11. At this time
12. Snooty people
15. Partners
21. Wed secretly
25. Slide
26. Summer skin hue
27. Scent
28. Molten rock
29. Radiate
31. On the peak of
34. Poisonous serpents
36. Rower's needs
37. Neckwear items
38. Actress Bancroft
40. Yield
42. Antique
43. Male child
46. List
49. Apartments
51. Avoided
52. Fire
53. Helped
54. Rebuke
55. Grouchy
57. Personal servant
60. Primary
61. Tall-tale teller
62. Poker stake
63. Casual shirts
64. Blunders

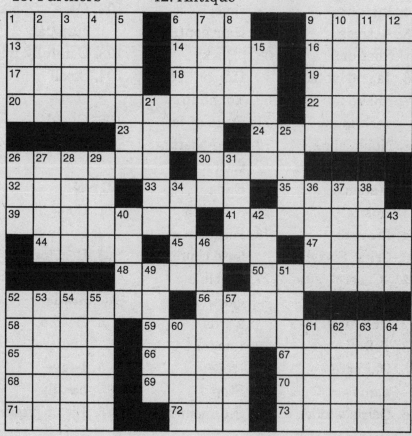

475

PUZZLE 606

ACROSS

1. Prison
5. Stimulus
9. Meager
13. Sediment
17. Ancient Hebrew dry measure
18. Gist
19. Resiliency
20. "Dare to ___ peach": 2 wds.
21. Boundary
22. Red tape: hyph.
24. Instant
25. Actress Sheridan
26. Jazz devotee
27. Choke up with mud
28. Noble aims
30. Round cheese
32. Maneuver
33. Bustle
34. Proverb
36. Critic Siskel
37. "Cheers" site
41. Stake
42. Operated
43. Tell
45. Old card game
46. Osiris's killer
47. Appear out of nowhere: hyph.
49. Arabic fruit
50. Coagulate
51. Be unfaithful to: hyph.
53. Improper
55. Commerce
56. Unit
57. Put in a box
58. Monk's title
59. Petty malice
62. Light, mild cigar
63. "Sesame" sayer
67. Hair controls
68. "Rocky Horror" role
69. Roundup
71. Style of jazz
72. Gold-bearing rock
73. Ends
75. Stomach
76. Performs a lawn chore
77. Forcible ejection: 2 wds.
79. London trolley
81. Stop
82. Sediment
83. Lewd grin
84. Angled
85. Fame
88. Drinks like a dog
89. Stitch
90. Opponent
93. In a line
94. Inadvertent omission
97. Finjan stand
98. Mathematical ratio
99. Give evidence
100. Fine carbon powder
101. Auditor: abbr.
102. Gaze curiously
103. Carefully put
104. Small shark
105. Ovoid veggies

DOWN

1. Cook book
2. So be it
3. Become friendly with: 3 wds.
4. Bard's "before"
5. Leave hastily
6. Fit of pique
7. Vase
8. Sanity
9. Priestly vestment
10. Clumsy fellow
11. Tavern
12. Reflect
13. Abandon
14. Genus of frogs
15. And others: 2 wds.
16. Deficits
23. Don or Lena
26. Eccentric wheel
29. Eat a big meal
31. Expire
32. Bill of fare
33. Has a capacity for
34. Ship's spar
35. Once more
36. Stare open-mouthed
37. Satiated and bored
38. Spanish jar
39. Forest
40. Brief letter
42. Eternal City
44. Reporter's boss
47. Kind of tar or needle
48. Military display

50. Nebula or cake
52. Small children
54. Disfigure
55. Triumvirate
57. Skirmish
58. Traveled by air
59. Fellow who's rank to lower ranks

60. Pizarro's place
61. Object
62. Hybridize
63. Rocker Ant
64. Antipodal change: hyph.
65. Subdues
66. Church part
68. Prude
70. ____ Khayyam

73. Ship's complement
74. Stages
76. Operate
78. Less hurried
80. Withstand
81. Church seat
83. Grand
84. Actress Davis
85. Grate harshly

86. Pa. port
87. Not any
88. Eye part
89. Boutique
91. Whale
92. Newts
95. By way of
96. Sticky stuff
97. Laser shot

PUZZLE 607

ACROSS

1. Belfry denizens
5. Spoiled child
9. Century plant
13. Make origami
17. Use an egress
18. Sound-system parts
20. First name in film direction
21. ___ Cinders
22. Tires
23. Local
24. Withdraw
26. Fail to hit
27. Repeated performance
29. Meat or cent
30. Regimen
31. Leg joint
32. Luster
35. Fiddlesticks
36. Gird
40. Obey
41. Singer Seeger
42. Play: Ger.
43. Long period
44. Omelet ingredient
45. Identical
46. Small branches
47. Lump
48. Kettle sound
50. Nut-bearing tree
51. Percolates
52. By birth
53. Most base
55. Globe
56. Energy
58. Harass
59. Treated with esteem
63. Allowance for waste
64. Ignited again
65. Enemies
66. End of the first line of "American Pie"
67. Belonging to you and me
68. Rabbits
69. Portal
70. Dateless
71. Annoyed
73. Margaret ___
74. Acts
75. Extra dry
76. Peaceful
77. Stannum
78. Tropical bird
81. Created
82. Threatens
86. Eager
87. Repetition
90. Gross
91. Palm seed, for short
92. Acts of relief
93. Store sign
94. Ending word
95. Hit
96. Arcade game, with "ball"
97. Relax

DOWN

1. Alcoholic beverage
2. Pin on a wheel
3. Pinball foul
4. Played the lead
5. Cold cash
6. Landlord's income
7. Pro pilot
8. Destructive insect
9. Halt, matey
10. "___ Make a Deal"
11. Lode load
12. Intrinsic elements
13. Swordsman
14. Butter substitute
15. Pinocchio, for one
16. Venture
19. Climbing plants
25. Night, to a poet
28. Playwright Simon
30. Appointment
31. Way to change a subject
32. Kind of duck
33. Elevated
34. Train drivers
35. Recollected
36. Lengthy stories
37. Observe
38. Circuit
39. Make ___ meet
41. Chum

42. Darling
45. Plant part
46. Belief
47. Mackerellike fish
49. Capital
50. Foundation
51. Heirs
54. Fished
56. Depot
57. Genuine

60. Above
61. Gadzooks!
62. Follows
64. Unusual things
65. Froth
68. Hoagie
69. Eradicates
70. D.C. VIP
72. Large game fish

73. Feminine title
74. Noise
76. Insertion mark
77. Uptight
78. Rodent
79. Molecular component
80. Cereal grain

81. Arizona town
82. Small amount
83. Vampire's garb
84. Lengthens
85. Caused to go
88. Marble
89. Quill filler

PUZZLE 608

ACROSS
1. Elapse
5. Small rodents
9. Transgress
12. Sound repetition
13. Kind of exam
14. Thirst quencher
15. Like the Mojave
16. Venture
17. Use oars
18. Sunder
19. Beast of burden
20. Basketball's Chamberlain
21. Building shape
23. Rink surface
25. Mawkishly sentimental
28. Makes possible
32. Blvd.
33. Severity
35. Emmet
36. Cushioning
38. Dizzy
40. Perform
41. Male heir
42. Tepid
45. Butt
47. Catch one's breath
51. Tint
52. Sandwich fish
53. Ethically wrong
54. Wrathful feeling
55. Smell
56. Antitoxins
57. Frantic
58. Departed
59. Playing card

DOWN
1. Bartlett, e.g.
2. Land tract
3. Leg part
4. Soaked
5. Upstanding
6. Eye part
7. Central Italian town
8. Largest deer
9. Hindu garment
10. Matinee star
11. Tailed amphibian
20. Mesh
22. Verse
24. Freight
25. Tam
26. Roe
27. Maroon
28. Faberge product
29. Young boy
30. Finale
31. Pen
34. Trespass
37. River barrier
39. Swallow
41. Intelligent
42. Fancy
43. Emanation
44. Woodwind
46. Soon
48. State positively
49. Royal title
50. Drama
52. Pull behind

ACROSS

1. Bar bill
4. Treat for Fido
8. Knocks
12. Have unpaid bills
13. "And pretty maids all in ___"
14. Dueling sword
15. Reflect
17. Apportion
18. Old King ___
19. Fall drink
20. Crowlike bird
23. 2,000 pounds
24. Barren
25. Type of pie
30. Neckwear
31. Flock of birds
32. Feel sorrow over
33. Surgeon
35. Raced
36. Unit
37. Adjusted musically
38. Be generous
41. Stretch across
43. Tattled
44. Boston Harbor's historic event
48. General Robert ___
49. Eye suggestively
50. Crude mineral
51. Gaze
52. Three-___ sloth
53. Prohibit

DOWN

1. Singer Jones
2. Dread
3. Garden plot
4. Twirling item
5. Of the mouth
6. Short letter
7. Cote member
8. Jog the memory of
9. Imitated
10. Singer Seeger
11. Prophet
16. Frosted
19. Duplicate
20. Charlie Brown's exclamation
21. Opera melody
22. Witness
23. Plumbing joints
25. Fully cooked
26. Night before a holiday
27. Fe
28. Positive
29. Give careful attention to
31. Ice-cream holder
34. Outline
35. Albacore
37. Recorded
38. Stair part
39. Excavation
40. To the sheltered side
41. Utah's lily
42. Faintly colored
44. Tyke
45. ___ Roy
46. Refrain syllable
47. Strong desire

PUZZLE 609

481

PUZZLE 610

ACROSS
1. North (Dennis the Menace portrayer)
4. Other
8. Cold cut mart
12. Corrida cheer
13. Lima or string
14. Persia today
15. Pirates' sport
17. Chore
18. Aloof
20. Fragrance
22. Synthetic fiber
25. "____ Comes Mary"
26. Omelet ingredient
27. Buck's mate
29. Bear's young
30. Apply henna to
31. Demand payment from
32. Bungle
33. Deplore
34. Use legal tender
36. John Phillips and Dennis Doherty
38. Darlings
39. Insect home
41. Principal
44. Asphalt
48. Footed vases
49. Fish sauce
50. ____ whiz!
51. Refuse
52. Cozy retreat
53. ____ up to (confess)

DOWN
1. Position
2. ____ mode
3. Certainly!
4. Decreasing
5. Smallest amount
6. Ocean mineral
7. Make bigger
8. Lyric
9. RBI's kin
10. ____ Vegas
11. Squid's camouflage
16. First garden
19. Pester
20. Drink noisily
21. Snake charmer's partner
23. More peculiar
24. Name words
25. King topper
26. Look closely at
28. Leftover
30. Cleaning crew's utensil
33. Dashed
34. Pick out
35. Inner hand
37. Violet
38. Disreputable nightclubs
40. ____ and hearty
41. Mire
42. Exist
43. Wayside respite place
45. Freudian topic
46. Modern
47. Sawbuck

PUZZLE 611

ACROSS
1. Point
4. Dance move
8. Reach
12. Infuriate
13. ___ stick
14. Roman emperor
15. Salary
17. Imitated
18. ___ meal (nourishing repast)
19. Feather accompaniment
21. Family member, for short
22. On fire
26. Actor George C. ___
29. Generation
30. Provided with nourishment
31. Drama
32. Tennis point
33. Scarce
34. Your and my
35. Morsel
36. Fool
37. Bed canopy
39. Basin
40. Sniggler's quarry
41. Pressed
45. Word of comparison
48. Juvenile
50. Delay
51. Brad
52. Can
53. "Against All ___"
54. Results
55. Harden

DOWN
1. "Family ___"
2. Baghdad's country
3. South American country
4. Enthusiasm
5. Hues
6. Breakfast item
7. Letter necessity
8. Entangle
9. Vitality
10. Exist
11. Cain's dwelling place
16. Offensive
20. Humorist Burrows
23. Off yonder
24. Zilch
25. Blissful abode
26. Locate
27. Inkling
28. Sculls' instruments
29. "Sister ___"
32. Delta, e.g.
33. Android
35. Hive denizen
36. Wall paintings
38. Canvas shelters
39. Shy
42. Betel and macadamia
43. American Indian
44. Groove
45. Tango's need
46. Owned
47. Assist
49. Male

PUZZLE 612

ACROSS

1. Scrooge's word
4. Religious group
8. Texas school inits.
11. Road sign
15. Mourns
17. Salty drop
18. "____ Horizon"
20. Skin
21. Zone
22. Sailor's saint
23. On the sheltered side
24. Capri, for one
25. More lofty
27. Bread choice
30. Declare
32. ____-relief
33. Italian number
34. Hold responsible for
37. Beatles film
39. Game bird
44. Verdi heroine
45. Only
46. Discover
47. Grassland
48. Government agents
49. Author Fleming
50. Flies like an eagle
51. Coagulate
52. Footwear
54. Humpback or right
55. Leveling tool
56. Compass point
57. TV's "Evening ____"
58. Mai ____ (cocktail)
59. Wed
62. Masts
63. Cayenne, red, and green
67. Greek god of war
68. Look hard
69. House extension
70. Scheme
71. Narrow inlet
72. Winter neckwear
73. Greenish-blue color
74. One, in Berlin
75. Princess of Monaco
77. Dix or Knox
78. Automobile pedal
79. Edgar Allan ____
80. Machine part
81. Musical composition
83. Chance
89. Theater employees
93. Hodge-podge
94. Greeting or playing
95. Minute particle
97. Terrible tsar
98. Gives a bad review of
99. Duel tool
100. Yellowfin or albacore
101. Middle Eastern bread
102. Place
103. Put
104. Poses
105. Journey part

DOWN

1. Spoiled child
2. Emanation
3. Shoe part
4. Cubic meter
5. Sniggler's catch
6. "Ernest Goes to ____"
7. Distress
8. Sarcastic comments
9. Skin spot
10. Manipulator
11. Nutmeg and thyme, e.g.
12. Assignment
13. Heraldic border
14. Lemon skin
16. Newts
19. People sleeping in portable shelters
26. Adam's wife
28. Atlas feature
29. Iraq's neighbor
31. Ostrichlike birds
34. Flying mammals
35. Kind of bean
36. Gulf in the Middle East
38. Coastal eagle
39. Norman Vincent ____
40. Lagomorph
41. ____ breve
42. Sign gas
43. Certain art museum
45. Distance unit
46. Fills with bullets
50. Portion out
51. Sailing vessel

484

53. Whichever
54. Jetty
55. Baby's food
57. Kind of tire
58. Relate
59. Roman general Antony
60. Operatic highlight
61. Kind of admiral
62. Musial or Smith
63. Greek philosopher
64. Charles Lamb
65. Position
66. Snick or ____
68. School subject
69. Always, to a bard
72. Kind of gin
73. Alley howlers
76. Be against
77. Summer cooler
78. Public transport
80. West Point student
82. Cougars
83. High school dances
84. Jai ____
85. Half a quart
86. Weakens
87. Lineage chart
88. Needle case
90. Demonic
91. Assess
92. Obstacle
96. Canadian prov.

PUZZLE 612

485

PUZZLE 613

ACROSS
1. Rainbow
4. Blunders
8. Peat ____
12. ____-jongg
13. Sediment
14. Revise copy
15. Game bird
17. Actor's part
18. Assemble
19. Cupid's weapon
20. Sprinter Lewis
22. Kind of bear
24. Bid
26. Father
27. Prompt
30. Dried plums
32. Cantaloupes
34. Sun god
35. Vapor
37. Send payment
38. Philosophers
40. Comedian Johnson
41. Creep
44. Venomous, hooded snake
46. Topnotch
47. Cordial
50. Appraise
51. Gong
52. Potato bud
53. Give out
54. ____ girl!
55. Tennis division

DOWN
1. Current measure, for short
2. Stadium scream
3. Good-natured
4. Otherwise
5. Respond
6. Leased
7. Concorde, e.g.
8. Festive
9. Fragrance
10. Farm building
11. Irish or beef
16. Michael ____ (British novelist)
19. Poisonous snake
20. Robbers' pursuers
21. Kind of hairdo
23. Hoover or Aswan
25. Kingly
27. Chums
28. Segment
29. Northern Italian town
31. Slump
33. Acquire knowledge
36. "The ____ of My Success"
38. Sugary
39. Stains
41. Feel concern
42. Meander
43. Opposed to
45. Actor Lugosi
47. National security police
48. Caustic substance
49. However

PUZZLE 614

ACROSS
1. Spinning toy
4. Writer George Bernard ____
8. Lingerie item
12. "All About ____"
13. Follow with a stopwatch
14. Mexican food
15. Pair
16. Copycat
17. Over-whelmed
18. Pay the tab
20. Close
22. Rate
24. Fragrant wood
28. Tableland
31. Huron or Erie
34. ____ Grande
35. Aroma
36. "A Boy Named ____"
37. Boys
38. Title of respect
39. Seize
40. Has given IOUs
41. Actor/ comedian Martin
43. Average
45. Afresh
48. Award
52. Iridescent gem
55. Ceramic piece
57. Mine find
58. Bagel feature
59. Store sign
60. Contend
61. Competition
62. Lack
63. Lend an ____

DOWN
1. Exam
2. "____ the Rainbow"
3. Rose of baseball
4. Frame of mind
5. With it
6. Prayer ending
7. Used to be
8. Look fixedly
9. Attorney's concern
10. Rapper Vanilla ____
11. Pea container
19. At a distance
21. High card
23. Adamson's lioness
25. Sketch
26. Assistant
27. Songstress Diana ____
28. Rolling stone's lack
29. Revise
30. Tender
32. Diving bird
33. Withhold
37. Legend
39. X
42. Parking attendant
44. Modify
46. Jacket or collar
47. ____ out (demolish)
49. Pigeon
50. Melody
51. Ogle
52. Electric unit
53. Edgar Allan ____
54. Ginger drink
56. Film director Spike ____

487

PUZZLE 615

ACROSS
1. Distress
4. Angel's headgear
8. Horse shed
12. Stir
13. Fragrance
14. Mock butter
15. Produce
17. Highway
18. Serpents
19. Wharves
20. Clandestine
23. Chef's need
24. Prayer response
25. Gizmos
29. Center
30. ____ over (collapses)
32. Before, of yore
33. Perpetual
35. Escape
36. Broadcast
37. Entertained
39. Fast
42. Teheran's locale
43. Endure
44. Mishap
48. Gape
49. Dorm inhabitant
50. By way of
51. Equal
52. Tips
53. ____ tide

DOWN
1. Joker
2. Lyric poem
3. Geologic time
4. Mustang
5. Conform
6. Building sites
7. Crude mineral
8. Unexciting
9. Healing plant
10. Raise
11. Gives silent assent
16. Gain
19. Writing tablets
20. Alike
21. Discharge
22. Give up
23. Comrade
25. Solidify
26. Snaky swimmers
27. Elm or maple
28. Poppy or sesame
30. Cable-stitch
31. Hearing organ
34. Roof support
35. Finance
37. Curved
38. House-keepers
39. Swill
40. Salary
41. Small land mass
42. Image
44. Expert pilot
45. Actress Arden
46. Bird's beak
47. Bill

ACROSS

1. Toboggan
5. Be concerned
9. Winged
12. Ashen
13. Verse forms
14. Doze
15. China's site
16. Resume
18. Perched
20. Sink
22. Poppy and caraway
25. That girl
26. Tote
28. Transmits
30. Goal
31. Faucet
33. Mountain pass
34. White
37. Feathery wrap
39. Climbing vine
40. Avarice
42. Malice
44. Pen names
46. String of pearls
49. Moos
53. Retirement plan letters
54. Blunders
55. Buffalo's lake
56. Lily ____
57. Colors
58. Camper's dwelling

DOWN

1. Belgian resort
2. ____ Vegas
3. Yale nickname
4. Sweethearts
5. Hard-shelled palm fruit
6. Uproars
7. Leases
8. Respect
9. Columnist Landers
10. Singer/musician Reed
11. Fruit beverage
17. Brainstorm
19. Lubricate
20. Creature
21. Knight's attire
23. Finger or toe
24. Work hard
25. Contains
27. Gossip
29. Secret agent
32. Own
35. Unstable
36. Cheered
38. Gorilla
41. Journal
43. Cay
45. "God's Little ____"
46. Bite
47. Cenozoic, e.g.
48. Scoundrel
50. Pay dirt
51. Triumph
52. Gel

PUZZLE 616

489

PUZZLE 617

ACROSS
1. Chicken
5. Dump
8. Stable newborn
12. Territory
13. Author Levin
14. "___ and the King of Siam"
15. Wagon
16. Island liquor
17. Chilled
18. Picked
20. Sails a ship
21. Budapest's country
23. Directory
26. Yale student
27. Green vegetable
30. Extinguished
32. Coals
34. Commotion
35. Smidgen
37. Abraham's wife
38. Soft drink
40. Scoops
43. ___ and raving
47. Bait
48. Go schussing
49. Notion
50. Pennsylvania port
51. Ink holder
52. Close noisily
53. Hornet
54. Singer Garfunkel
55. Only

DOWN
1. Visage
2. Unwritten
3. No longer are
4. Hooks
5. Police car feature
6. Walk laboriously
7. Sweet tuber
8. Sprite
9. Formerly
10. Over again
11. Tykes
19. Dinner jackets
20. Deep red
22. Stout
23. Actress Lupino
24. Sign of assent
25. Pair
27. Each
28. Baseball stat
29. Burnt wood
31. Mom's counterpart
33. Christening
36. Carnival worker
38. Slumber
39. Color
40. Gusted
41. Atmosphere
42. Purple flower
44. At rest
45. Close by
46. Amusement
48. Mineral spring

ACROSS

1. Guzzle
5. Graceful horse
9. Secret agent
12. In the distance
13. Decorate anew
14. Cravat
15. Toy for "walking the dog"
16. Grow out of hand
18. Dry, as ink
20. Brand name
21. Pilfered
24. River bottom
25. Bounded along
26. Possessed
27. Murmur
30. Columnist's entry
31. Garden veggie
32. Zilch
33. Caesar's X
34. Has permission
35. Singer/ actress Day
36. Plant
37. Draws
38. Contributor
41. Checks
42. Exclusion
44. Whit
48. Lion's lair
49. Epochs
50. Idyllic spot
51. "___ Less Bell to Answer"
52. Noblewoman
53. Marsh grass

DOWN

1. Merry
2. Controversial saucer, for short
3. Set
4. Dilemma
5. Pyromaniac's crime
6. Lease payment
7. Confusion
8. Played ninepins
9. Random try
10. Heap
11. Bellow
17. Naughty
19. Influenced
21. Skirt feature
22. Carryall
23. Begin
24. Flock sound
26. Attention getter
27. Antler
28. Military group
29. Untidy heap
31. Dog's foot
32. Louder
34. Crumb
35. Smidgen
36. Distress signal
37. Purple flower
38. Fuddy-duddy
39. Warning
40. Baseball team
41. Warty critter
43. A Gershwin
45. Keats offering
46. Shirt type
47. "Beauty ___ the Beast"

PUZZLE 618

491

PUZZLE 619

MOVIES AND TELEVISION

ACROSS

1. "Taxi" cabby
4. Scarlett's home
8. "Two Years Before the ___"
12. Zhivago's love
13. West of TV's "Batman"
14. Fragrant wood
15. Part of U.S.A.: abbr.
16. Peggy Wood TV role
17. "___ of Two Cities"
18. Heston film, with "The"
21. Compass pt.
22. Affirmative reply in 8 Across
23. "___ the land of the . . ."
24. "___ a Gift" (W.C. Fields film)
25. Musician Guthrie
27. "El ___" (Heston film)
30. "A ___ of Honey"
33. "The ___ to Bountiful"
34. "Two Mules for Sister ___" (Eastwood film)
35. Powell-Loy film
38. He played Jethro Bodine
39. Grade
40. Laconic negatives from Gary Cooper
41. They outrank jrs.
42. Honor with a party
43. Pull
44. High note
45. Beau, to Lloyd Bridges
46. Health farm
49. Heston film
55. "The Ghost and Mrs. Muir" actress
56. "A ___ Grows in Brooklyn"
57. Jackson of "Charlie's Angels"
58. Meara and Bancroft
59. River duck
60. Thought
61. "Hud" actress
62. Market
63. Mediter-ranean, to Bardot

DOWN

1. Actor Mason of "Odd Man Out"
2. Actress Dunne
3. Actor Singer of "The Beastmaster"
4. Wynette and Grimes
5. "There Is Nothin' Like ___"
6. "Nine Hours to ___"
7. "___ for All Seasons"
8. "Taxi" item
9. Moslem call to prayer
10. "___ and Pepper" (Davis-Lawford film)
11. Very, to Tati
12. "The ___ Show"
14. Small film role
19. Horse opera
20. Actor Sweet of "Gimme a Break"
24. Road to old Rome
25. Glacial ridge
26. Ceremony
27. TV's "___ Runamuck"
28. "Dies ___"
29. Rather and Dailey
30. Actor Hunter et al.
31. At a distance
32. Hallowed Fr. women
33. TV's "___ Girl"
34. TV static

36. Actor Williams of "Smooth Talk"
37. ____ ear and out the other
42. Hightails it
43. "____ and Back" (Audie Murphy film)
44. Comedienne Georgia
45. "Never ____ Anything Small"
46. "The Maltese Falcon" character
47. Actor O'Toole
48. Befuddled
49. "____ 9 from Outer Space"
50. Kidder role in "Superman"
51. Magnani or Neagle
52. Baseball's Mel and kin
53. "A ____ Soul" (Clark Gable film)
54. Actor Tamiroff

PUZZLE 619

PUZZLE 620

ACROSS
1. Kind of pear
5. Caroled
9. Sullen one
13. Be overly fond
17. Butter stand-in
18. Dueling weapon
19. Contest
20. Actor Dixon
21. Knoll
22. Ingressed anew
24. —— Beach, Fla.
25. Casters
27. Highlands language
28. Goods
29. Actress Balin
30. Baseball figure
31. Roughage source
33. Waited
36. Heroic
37. Complain
38. Bleat
41. New York heights: 2 wds.
45. Beak
46. Disburdens
47. Family member
48. Tumbler, in Bonn
49. Be verbally bold: 2 wds.
51. Cheese skin
52. "The —— Mutiny"
53. Corrida shouts
54. Council city
56. Climb, as a rope
57. Woolly ones
59. Grasslands
60. Alters
63. Celery, in Madrid
64. Dairy structure
65. Windy City area, with "The"
66. Swiss canton
67. Tall-tree site: 3 wds.
72. Chop off
73. Tennessee gridders
74. Author Bagnold
75. Islamic deity
76. Ancient guitar
77. Feds: hyph.
78. Roman 52
79. Oregon city
82. Travel kit
83. Elected official
87. District
88. Rank improvement
91. —— of contention
92. Chicken ____
93. Frenzy
94. River in NE China
95. Blaring
96. Facilitate
97. "—— of Laura Mars"
98. Kennel cries
99. Otherwise

DOWN
1. Danish physicist
2. Hodgepodge
3. Convince
4. Miner
5. Father Junipero ——
6. Chimpanzees, e.g.
7. Born a she, in Paree
8. Hereditary
9. Cockscomb
10. Diner's order
11. Crack aviator
12. Garden spot
13. Sofa
14. Above
15. Biblical weed
16. Baseball's Slaughter
23. Rail
26. Approves
28. Crave
30. Health spots
31. Tied
32. Carry on
33. Circlet
34. Brain wave
35. Certain compound
36. Small whirlpool
37. Ascend
38. Fluent in two tongues
39. Moscow panda
40. African fox
42. Indian Ocean island
43. Central
44. Bis!
50. Nudge
51. Legal matter
52. Mil. prelate
54. Coastal flyers
55. Frog genus
56. Old Ethiopian kingdom
57. Pasternak heroine

58. Apogee
59. Large spoon
60. Orch. leader
61. —— Pater (almanac)
62. Hindu sect
64. Kick
65. Choice cut
68. Egg

69. Beat
70. Without competence
71. Elastic
76. Bequeath
77. Weighty works
78. Open weaves
79. For Pete's ——!

80. Oratorio segment
81. Dregs
82. Venetian ruler
83. Cleanser
84. Implement
85. Burden

86. Advice, of yore
88. Ante
89. Beam
90. Clock marking

PUZZLE 620

495

PUZZLE 621

ACROSS

1. Honest ____
4. Gin and Hearts, e.g.
9. Overly
12. Fish eggs
13. Animated
14. Building wing
15. Speak the plain truth
21. Chooses
22. Golf mound
23. Adrift
24. Epoch
27. Diplomacy
30. Lemon meringue ____
31. Begin
33. "The Cat in the ____"
35. Fishing poles
36. Actors
38. Goof up
39. "I Like ____"
40. Income
41. ____ girl!
43. Vase
46. "____ Got a Secret"
47. Bro's sibling
48. Lawyer: abbr.
49. Actress West
50. Patriotic women's gp.
51. Sure!
52. Witness
53. Cherry center
54. Sprite
55. School subject: abbr.
56. Stayed out of sight
57. Snaky curve
58. Gentle ____ lamb
59. Decades
61. Barnyard resident
62. Lyric poem
63. Bee follower
65. Wagered
69. Collar ____
70. "Nightmare on ____ Street"
71. Three-pipped dice
72. Pointed end
73. ____ of Capri
76. Sault ____ Marie
77. Actress Lupino and others
79. Printers' measures
81. Hard journey
82. Hidden ace?
91. Be in debt
92. Sports place
93. Potato container
94. Cot
95. Ed Norton's domain
96. Evil

DOWN

1. Joan of ____
2. Feather scarf
3. Snakelike fish
4. Empty spaces
5. Pie ____ mode
6. Between
7. Adam's mate
8. Chair
9. "____ and Sympathy"
10. Ancient
11. Spanish cheer
16. Comes in second
17. Gorilla
18. Subway depot: abbr.
19. Ready
20. Sweet or sugar snap
23. Helper
24. Greek letter
25. Sunbeam
26. "We ____ the World"
28. Marked the deck, e.g.
29. ____ and feather
30. Expressionless kisser
31. Foxy
32. Prefix with cycle or dent
34. Concocted falsely
35. Competitors
36. Elapsing
37. Squirreled away
40. Portion
42. Author Gertrude ____
44. Jacked up
45. Butterfly traps
46. Notion

PUZZLE 621

47. Formulas
60. Posed
61. "For ____ a jolly ..."
62. Singer Redding
64. Inventor Whitney
66. "____ Miniver"
67. Put money down
68. Caustic liquid
69. Claim
74. Guided
75. Australian bird
77. April addressee
78. Neighbor of Md.
80. Health resorts
81. Former Russian ruler
82. Corn on the ____
83. Deep respect
84. Apple color
85. Miner's find
86. Recent
87. Opposite of WSW
88. ____ tide
89. By way of
90. Finale

PUZZLE 622

• AUTUMN OUTING •

ACROSS
1. Make a choice
4. Entice
8. 1975 Wimbledon winner
12. Pair
15. Opponent
16. Dry, like the desert
17. Down to earth
18. Corn piece
19. Gridiron three points
22. Gridiron practice game
24. Pindarics
25. ___-Margret
27. Otherwise
28. N-S connection
31. Small porch
33. Feat
36. Earsplitting
37. Gridiron final event
41. "Younger ___ Springtime"
43. Partner for alack
44. Southern constellation
45. Worthless coin
46. Somewhat: pref.
47. Out of the way
48. Flutter
49. Nero's garb
51. Moray
52. Mosaic piece
54. Long nosed fish
56. Notable periods
57. Lucille ___
58. Zodiac sheep
59. Peeve
60. Elbow poke
62. Fencing sword
66. Pleasure drive
68. Ordinarily disposed
71. Saudi, e.g.
73. ___ Marie Saint
74. Author Fleming
75. Inert
76. Peruvian Indian
77. Gridiron shape
81. Malevolent look
82. Approves, for short
83. Safe harbor
84. Mideast land
85. Ambush
89. Tyranno-saurus ___
90. Leaning Tower site
93. Gridiron catchers
97. Gridiron score
102. Gone by
103. Center
104. Province
105. Large quantity coffee maker
106. Thrill
107. Hill insects
108. Comic Foxx
109. Blended whiskey

DOWN
1. "We're ___ to see the wizard ..."
2. Luau food
3. Driving site
4. "Shane" actor
5. Coax
6. Spanish rivers
7. Author Le Shan
8. Lob's path
9. Withered
10. Ice pellets
11. Shade trees
12. Hot brew
13. Witty person
14. Crude metal
20. Noblemen
21. Behind schedule
22. Uppity one
23. Chicken and hamburger
26. Neither's companion
28. Norse king
29. Ms. Negri
30. Gridiron sack target
31. Lovers' quarrel
32. Mail
34. Gridiron acrobat
35. Docile
37. Mall events
38. Psychic Geller
39. Romance
40. Carry with effort
42. Zip
48. Blaze
50. Encore
53. Babylonian war god
55. The whole amount
57. Pickling solution
60. ___ alai
61. Cartoonist Peter ___

63. ____ se
64. Lady from Eden
65. Every individual
66. Billboard
67. Ally
69. Defendant's answer
70. Aquatic flier
72. Moisten with drippings
75. Homeric epic
78. Applies asphalt to
79. Blvd.
80. Following
86. Costa ____
87. Shakespeare's river
88. Saucy
90. Undiluted
91. Glazed
92. Herringlike fish
93. Crude
94. Freud topic
95. Heifer
96. Thing, at law
98. Boat propeller
99. "... ____ daily bread"
100. Twisted
101. Opposite of SSW

PUZZLE 623

ACROSS
1. Mesozoic, e.g.
4. English poet
9. Hemp
14. Med. sch. course
18. Cabin material
20. Fertile spots
21. School: Fr.
22. Folk-rock star
23. Kilmer phrase, with 35 Across: 6 wds.
27. Engraved gem
28. Legal claim
29. French river
30. "___ a Rock": 2 wds.
31. Goad
33. Males
35. See 23 Across: 7 wds.
46. Sea swallows
47. Eyepiece
48. Diving birds
49. Hebrides island
50. Footed vase
51. Signify the hour
52. Inhabitant: suf.
53. New Mexico resort
54. Stand
56. Vex
57. Actress Rehan et al.
58. Kind of code
59. Street or oil
61. Wait ___: 2 wds.
63. Longfellow phrase: 3 wds.
70. Elects again
71. Spurted
74. Waste maker
78. Major or Minor
79. Ponder
82. Perry's creator
83. Silkworm
84. Big bird
85. Indulge
86. ___ de France
87. Judicial decisions
88. Ringer
89. Mongol
90. Uniform in tone
92. William Bliss Carman phrase: 5 wds.
96. Paid notices
97. Calm inner spots
98. Bark sharply
99. Western resort park
103. Voice type
105. Hassock
108. Housman phrase: 5 wds.
116. Twosome gatherer
117. France's longest river
118. Teheran native
119. Exile place
120. Flying: pref.
121. Track participant
122. Consternation
123. However

DOWN
1. Harvard man's foe
2. College mil. gr.
3. Turkish general
4. 1988 Beach Boys hit
5. Sup
6. Timber tree
7. Oolong or pekoe
8. Fast jet: abbr.
9. Dwell
10. Yearn
11. Lament
12. Under the weather
13. Long fish
14. Feathered friends
15. Glacial snowfield
16. Ripening agent
17. Biblical weed
19. Monkey
24. Lowest high tides
25. "The Man ___": 2 wds.
26. Singer Simone
31. Set with feathers
32. Hitchcock film
33. Reconciles: 2 wds.
34. Hook shape
35. Theater mementos
36. Uncanny
37. Actor Borgnine
38. Type of text, for short
39. Drudge
40. Stored for future use: 2 wds.
41. Chinese philosopher Lin ___
42. Former Yugoslavian president
43. Bellow
44. Adam's grandson
45. Relax
51. Thick liqueur
55. Sun god homonym
57. Friend: Fr.
58. Restaurant offering
60. Simple
61. Ovid's "___ Amatoria"
62. Fierce cat
64. Loan sharks
65. Player-piano part
66. Diamond with a diamond
67. Actress Hagen

68. From Miami to San Juan: abbr.
69. High-pitched
72. "Dallas" role
73. Title-transfer documents
74. Warm up
75. Cunning
76. Location
77. Russian news agency
79. TV's Houston and Dillon
80. Beehive State
81. Saharan
85. Bistro
88. Terrible
89. "Happy birthday ___": 2 wds.
90. Speaks
91. Confront
93. Tender
94. Moor
95. Occult
99. Lab burner
100. Jeff MacNelly comic strip
101. Gas or sheet
102. Canyon feature
103. Seed coat
104. Ancient musical instrument
106. As recently as
107. Ear or brain part
109. New Haven tree
110. King: Fr.
111. Small snort
112. Dear: Irish
113. Pale
114. Order of animals: suf.
115. Buddhist temple

PUZZLE 623

PUZZLE 624
UNITED NATIONS

ACROSS
1. Descends
6. Lovely, graceful person
10. Mexican money
14. Storehouse
19. Removed
20. Pizzeria feature
21. Egyptian god
22. Actress Shire
23. ____ Rapids
24. Fabricated
25. Lamented
26. Build
27. 4 NATIONs
31. Haddad or Gardner
32. " . . .long, long ____"
33. Metal
34. Turkish general
37. Playwright Rice
41. Blow
44. Named
49. Revolver inventor
51. Plastic wrap
53. FDR's mother
55. Actor Peter ____
56. Party wear, sometimes
58. Long narrative
60. Funnel cloud
62. Baltic gulf
63. 4 NATIONs
67. Illustrator Ernest Thompson ____
68. Chalet feature
69. Realized
70. Latin conjunctions
71. Highlands language
73. Risers
75. Catch
77. Belgian resort
80. Singer James
82. Heraldic border
83. Conscription
86. 4 NATIONs
91. Land owned absolutely
92. Grease
93. Something to let off
94. Small tree
96. Shifted
98. Permeate
100. Keyboard word
102. Duchamp subject
103. Cubic meters
105. Condescending person
107. Bar
109. Arikara
110. Day of the wk.
112. ____ Palmas
114. Kind of kettle
116. 4 NATIONs
127. Carry
128. Potatoes' companion
129. Entrance
130. Emanated
131. Poet David ____
132. Ocean flier
133. Remodel
134. Ugandan native
135. Oceans
136. Activist
137. Understood
138. Youths

DOWN
1. Ornamental braid
2. High point
3. Nothing, in Madrid
4. Play
5. Struggle
6. Equine game
7. Nasty
8. Scottish dance
9. Rani's land
10. Shrewd
11. Small case
12. Appear
13. Rumor, in Paris
14. Everlasting
15. Starchy root
16. Hebrew letter
17. 12-point type
18. Have a sandwich
28. Amigos
29. Person
30. Cavity
34. Operation
35. Errs
36. Salt-water plants
38. Girl
39. Perry's creator
40. Worker's rewards
42. Fill
43. Fasten
45. Irish king Brian ____
46. Illicit payment
47. Plant disease
48. Sweeties
50. Experience
52. Swimmer
54. "____ Irish Rose"
57. Quarterback, at times
59. Amuses
61. Schedule
64. Inculcate
65. Stuffed
66. Growls
72. Lab lamps
74. Cool

PUZZLE 624

76. Canal Zone lake
77. Fakes
78. Guide
79. Over
81. Farm measures
84. Leg bone
85. Business
87. German river
88. Yemen port
89. Wilander of tennis
90. "___ a man with . . ."
95. Grade
97. Plans
99. More considerate
101. Intaglio print, for short
104. Decline
106. Purse
108. Picky person
111. Like most races
113. Beau
115. Nest
116. English composer
117. Place
118. Trim
119. Sleuth Wolfe
120. European
121. Eve's address
122. Carnival attraction
123. Pack
124. Food fish
125. "The Heat ___"
126. Seizes
127. Naughty

PUZZLE 625

ACROSS

1. Two-wheeled vehicle
5. Lighthouse
10. Omit
14. Length times width
15. Mend anew
16. Italian river
17. Juggle the books: 5 wds.
22. Flightless bird
23. Drinks like a dog
24. Musical motif
25. Annoy
26. Met in session
27. Period in history
28. "Le Coq ——"
29. Afternoon beverage
30. Flame condenser
32. Locate
33. —— Morgana
37. Wedding response: 2 wds.
38. Lower limb
39. Parted with for money
43. Excuses
45. Earth's satellite
47. Eagle's nest
48. Welcome elaborately: 4 wds.
51. Climbing vines
52. Decomposes
53. Diversify with blotches of color
54. Back end
55. Saloon
56. Gorilla
58. Fortune-teller
59. Toward the setting sun
60. Additional
62. "—— Ballou"
65. Become older
66. Deposit, as eggs
67. Not on
70. Strong beer
71. Arrived
73. Storm wind
74. Songstress Zadora
75. Carry out a plan skillfully: 4 wds.
79. Life of Riley
80. Ruth's mother-in-law
81. Unrefined minerals
82. Colors
83. Toothpaste containers
84. Walk in water

DOWN

1. Worries
2. Scent
3. Contradict formally
4. Spigot
5. With money up front
6. Towel pronoun
7. Sternward
8. Civil disturbance
9. Appropriate to the moment
10. Tree fluid
11. Asian snake
12. Harden
13. Bohemian dance
18. Power supply: abbr.
19. Black and ropy
20. Amid
21. Three feet
31. Solace
32. Shipwreck remains
33. Hindu ascetic
34. —— and kicking
35. Linden tree
36. More competent
39. Religious groups
40. Make a speech

41. French city
42. Postpone
44. "—— a Lovely Day Today"
46. Cereal grain
47. "Much —— About Nothing"
49. Deletion
50. Green gem
55. Started
57. North Star
59. Texas city
61. Potato buds
62. Cloaked
63. Mitigate
64. Twit
67. Music drama
68. Stored correspond- ence
69. Untrue
72. Jacob's twin
73. Pastime
76. Word of permission
77. Corn holder
78. Exclamation of surprise

PUZZLE 626

ACROSS
1. Soak up
7. Lock of hair
12. Discards
18. Disappointment
19. Cowboy's rope
20. Shandong province city
21. Garden flower: 2 wds.
23. Church officials
24. Present!
25. Phrase of comprehension: 2 wds.
26. Banana skin
28. King of Judah
29. Gels
30. Army insects
31. Gasp
32. Noble: Ger.
33. Actress Dawber
34. Accomplishes
35. Summon: 2 wds.
37. "—— Evalyn": 2 wds.
39. Punching tools
40. Hebrew prophet

44. "Abie's Irish ——"
45. Away from the wind
46. Los Angeles artery
47. Hindu king
49. Ron Howard role
50. Prohibits
51. Geological division
52. —— Alonzo Stagg
53. Furniture-wood trees: 2 wds.
55. Clockmaker Thomas
56. "High ——"
57. Decorative pitcher
58. Unadulterated
59. For —— sake!
60. Went by
62. Annoyance
63. TV series
64. Break in rank
65. Layer (of paint)
66. Do the impossible: 2 wds.
69. Colonizes
71. Motion-picture theater
72. Sock end
73. Rhythmic swing

76. Passion
77. Very: Fr.
78. Program of events
79. Actress Munson
80. Passing grades
81. Hellion
82. Nibbles
83. New York city
85. —— meatballs: hyph.
89. Baseballer Tom
90. Goddess of peace
91. Front: prefix
92. Thoroughfare
93. Vesicles
94. Long-eared hound

DOWN
1. Classifieds
2. Baleen whale
3. Cookery herb: 2 wds.
4. Extraordinary things
5. Anatomical network
6. Bikini part
7. Lovers' meetings
8. Stands
9. Simplicity
10. Actor Erwin
11. Chinese boats

12. Aromatic shrubs: 2 wds.
13. Battery unit
14. Unburden
15. Winning
16. Analyze grammatically
17. Agave
22. Feathered (a nest)
27. Goal
29. Soda fountain
30. Tops: 2 wds.
31. Edson Arantes do Nascimento
32. Ohio Indian
34. Short race
35. Vine flowers: 2 wds.
36. Bullfighting sounds
38. Flightless birds
39. "It's a Sin to Tell ——": 2 wds.
41. Yams: 2 wds.
42. Writer Bret
43. Hindu nurses
45. Copycat
46. Celebrity
47. Scolded
48. Soap plant
49. Had creditors
50. Actor Reynolds
53. Lover

54. Blast of wind
55. Official stamp
57. Princely Italian family
59. Warsaw resident
61. Military station
62. Rhymer
63. Bleaches

65. Golden oldie
66. Michelangelo statue
67. As a certainty: 2 wds.
68. Nourished
70. Plumbing joint
71. Cartons
73. Loamy deposit

74. Arm of the sea
75. Missouri city
77. "The Romance of Helen ——"
78. Throws
80. Manitoba Indian

81. Hive swarm
82. Texas city
84. "—— Told Every Little Star"
86. Bitterly ironic
87. Catch
88. Rubbish!

PUZZLE 626

PUZZLE 627

ACROSS
1. Poodles, e.g.
5. Rapier
10. Drink greedily
15. Siamang or gibbon
18. Inter ____
19. Check
20. Climbing plant
21. Drowse
22. Baffle
23. Desert animals
25. Normandy town
26. Child
27. Periods
28. Portend
29. Indian chief
31. Detroit athlete
33. Bartolome de Las ____
35. Submarine detector
36. Natty
38. Gutter site
39. Greek letters
42. Get rid of
43. Burrowing animal
46. Legendary
47. TV host Jay ____
48. Scot
49. Fertile locale
51. Spanish title
52. Shaver
53. Grampus
55. Statement abbr.
56. Martens
59. Rower's need
60. Like a marsh
63. Baltic language
64. Rural deities
66. Photographer's purchase
67. Religious composition
69. Surface measure
70. Madagascar mammals
73. Swiss river
74. Soldiers
80. Glutton
82. Swine
84. Balances
85. "He spoke ____ word ..."
86. Spanish painter
87. Bird of prey
88. Pronghorns
90. Holiday visitor
91. Fibrous tissue
94. Conception
95. Well-nigh
96. Certain tests
97. Designated
99. Pertaining to a pelvic bone
100. Reunion attendees
102. White or fire
103. Baseball's Lynn
104. Goal
107. Night fliers
108. Draft animals
112. New York Indian
113. Actress Merkel
114. Chemical bond
115. Amphitheater
116. Sound
117. Playing card
118. Stories
119. Dutch painter
120. Glacial ridges

DOWN
1. European flatfish
2. Butter replacement
3. Chinese animal
4. Datebook abbr.
5. Wisconsin native
6. Enticer
7. Hums
8. Vague
9. Savoy season
10. Alpaca's cousin
11. Spanish tunes
12. Bother
13. French article
14. Novelist Dos ____
15. Gorilla
16. North or South
17. Biblical kingdom
24. Medicated
25. Climbed over
27. U.S. author
30. American cuckoo
32. ____ jure
33. Nautical float
34. " . . . the shady sadness of ____"
35. Coddle
36. Farmer's home?
37. Places
38. Of a time division
39. "Lohengrin" heroine
40. Simpleton
41. Go away!
43. Pasture for a fee
44. Hawkeye
45. Comic Bert and family
50. Progression
53. Fish holder?
54. French cathedral city
57. Sandwich-shop letters
58. Politician Atwater
61. Nightmarish street
62. Aussie bird

508

64. Cowardly
65. Sprang
66. Leaping insects
67. Polynesian language
68. Big ape: French
71. Horned animal
72. Organizes
73. Genesis name
75. Swimmer Janet ____
76. Guy

77. Battery terminal
78. Fastened, in a way
79. Willow genus
81. Agile ruminant
83. Prepares for war again
86. Vicki Lawrence role
89. Green fruits
90. Fell

92. Douglas's isle
93. Prompt
95. Light brown
97. Bottom
98. Baldwin and Templeton
99. One of the Horae
100. Border on
101. Highway division

102. Later: Scot.
103. Speed
105. Singer Simone
106. Moose's cousin
109. French law
110. "____ Boot"
111. Skill
112. Region for DDE

PUZZLE 628

• AUTHOR, AUTHOR •

ACROSS
1. Visit
5. Helen's mother
9. Blind as ____
13. Trudge
17. Base or plate
18. WWII alliance
19. Starchy root
20. Read, to Jacques
21. Indigo
22. Church service
23. Trolley
24. Actor Mowbray
25. Poet/journalist
29. Some railways
30. Actress Busch
31. Behold
32. Traffic problem
35. Hi-fis
39. Wimps
43. Make leather
44. Type of camera: abbr.
45. Man: Lat.
47. Water tester
48. Diet's word
50. Crossed letters
52. Colorless
53. Mailed
54. Writer/physician
58. "The ____ of St. Mark"
59. Always, to a bard
60. Actress Miranda
61. Novelist/abolitionist
71. Assist
72. Saline drop
73. Beast's neck gear
74. Hold it!
75. Nest egg: abbr.
76. Relative
77. "____ Miserables"
78. Unrefined metal
79. British sailor
82. Erudite
86. Stage setting
88. Zodiac sign
90. Grande or Bravo
91. Baseball's Maglie
92. Writer/social critic
102. A Waugh
103. Binds
104. Markdown
105. Forearm bone
106. Venison, e.g.
107. Being, in Spain
108. Ireland, to poets
109. "____ Ringer"
110. Water and feather
111. Loch ____
112. House position
113. Talk back

DOWN
1. Irish dramatist
2. Singer Tennille
3. Indian revenue collector
4. Gipson's "Old ____"
5. Tibetan monks
6. Test
7. Type of brake
8. Undertake
9. British prime minister
10. Nude
11. Irish islands
12. Catacombs
13. Golfer Gary ____
14. Silents/talkie star Lee
15. African port
16. Inroad
26. "____ Be Seeing You"
27. Roman spirit
28. Herring color?
32. WWII battle site
33. Hammer in
34. Opposed
35. Scads
36. Shoe stretcher
37. Ellipse
38. Threshold
40. News bit
41. Corn dish
42. Congeals
44. Arteries
46. Puts back on the payroll
49. Tennis star
51. Scoff
52. Shelley or Faith
53. Blind parts
55. King of Midian
56. Billy ____ Williams
57. CIA forerunner
61. Call
62. Hillside dugout
63. Paper amount
64. Linden
65. Athlete Zaharias
66. ____ in one
67. ____ out a living
68. Sioux Indian
69. Threadbare
70. Fencing weapon
80. Votes in
81. Of course!
83. Comes up
84. Border
85. Knotted loops
86. ____ Miguel
87. Thunderheads
89. Frequently
91. Perfume
92. Door part
93. Hard ____ (captain's call)
94. American anthropologist
95. One, in Frankfort
96. Weir materials
97. Unusual
98. English essayist
99. Type of bargain
100. Spanish queen et al.
101. Physics units, for short

510

PUZZLE 629

ACROSS
1. Cicatrix
5. Flunk
9. Coarse file
13. Spats
17. Conduit
18. Rope
19. Concluded
20. Entertainer Adams
21. Component
22. Coffee makers
23. Great dog
24. Winning margin
25. Cutting replies
27. Diocese
29. Narrowed down
31. Golfer's aid
32. Esteem
34. Cut down
35. Preserved
38. Discover
39. Free from prejudice
44. Sly look
45. Limousines
46. Stringed instrument
47. Deep affection
48. "You —— My Sunshine"
49. Misplaced
50. Gasped
52. Zilch
53. Sign
55. Confused struggle
56. Bird of prey
58. First number
59. Blanched
60. Peter ——
61. Weary
64. Serves
65. Delayed
69. Commotion
70. Rapiers
72. Charter
73. Choler
74. Caldrons
76. Pismires
77. Legumes
78. English sand hill
79. By the bill of fare: 3 wds.
81. Trolley
82. Apple juice
83. Priestly vestment
84. Wiped
86. Public vehicle
87. Syndicates
91. Wee sprite
92. Spotted
96. Came to earth
97. Actress Lanchester
99. Eternally
101. Dwell
102. Allot
103. Building division
104. Peel
105. Singer Ed ——
106. Partridge's tree?
107. Matched collections
108. Utters
109. Jerk

DOWN
1. Mix
2. Attractive
3. Encourage
4. More distant
5. Woodwind
6. Broadcasts
7. Stopping place
8. Instructive examples
9. Cowboy exhibition
10. Star of "The Barefoot Contessa"
11. Mailed
12. Introductory statement
13. Renovation
14. Stench
15. Judicious
16. Pip
26. Comedian Buttons
28. Terminate
30. Hawaiian dish
32. Trumpeter Al ——
33. Devastated
35. Rebuff
36. Of flying: pref.
37. Swerve
38. Rapid
40. Memo
41. Melody
42. Wicked
43. Erase
45. Construction marker
46. Farewells: Lat.
49. Advances
50. Hurls
51. Distributed cards
54. Hallux
55. Young girls
57. Collection of sayings
59. Separated
60. Corrals
61. Bark cloth
62. Graven image
63. Jury
64. Accustomed
65. Smile with joy
66. Made a knot in
67. Marine bird
68. Forest denizen
71. Songbirds
72. Peruse
75. Disperse
77. Favors
78. Exhibit
80. Fermented drink
81. Sesame
82. 8 ounces
85. Quantities of paper
86. Poets
87. Group of tents
88. Away from the weather
89. Actress Moreno
90. Blackthorn fruit
92. Declare untrue
93. Flat bean
94. Flat
95. Writing table
98. Toper
100. By way of

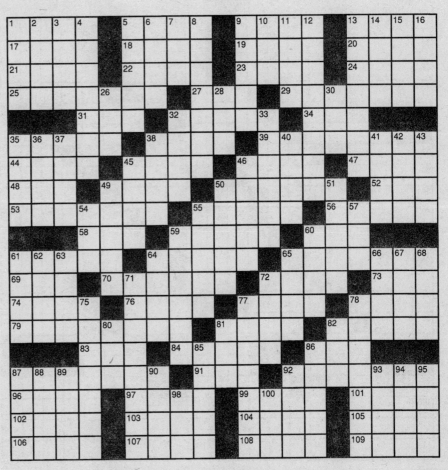

511

PUZZLE 630

• STATE CAPITALS •

ACROSS
1. Distress
5. Expert
10. Judges' wear
15. Mix
19. Othello's ensign
20. Of sheep
21. Muse of poetry
22. Pine fruit
23. Capital of the Ocean State
25. Capital of the Pelican State
27. Graffiti artist?
28. Alloted
30. Wall hanging
31. Model Carol ____
32. Skirt feature
33. Glossy fabric
36. Chars
39. Cubic meter
40. Wolverine State capital
44. River duck
45. Haggard novel
46. Inventor Thomas and kin
49. Fish eggs
50. Church recess
51. Cappuccino trait
52. Beau's offering
53. Merchandise
54. Easy as ____
55. Type of jacket
56. Author Truman ____
59. Talks wildly
60. ____ City (Utah's capital)
62. Lena ____
63. Free-for-all
64. Sturdy trees
65. Singer Mariah ____
66. Soliloquy start
67. Actress Jessica ____
69. Sheds
70. Buckeye State capital
74. Speechless actors
75. Alaskan coats
76. Sentry's command
77. Singleton
78. Baseball's Cabell
79. Now hear ____!
80. Shipshape
81. Transport
82. Poet's forever
83. Oklahoma natives
86. Actor Ron ____
87. During
88. Garden State capital
90. Let up
92. Nurture
94. Conger catcher
96. Tournament passes
97. ____ up
98. Furious
101. Uneven
103. Gathered
108. Green Mountain State capital
111. Golden State capital
114. Malefic
115. Taut
116. Tie
117. Prong
118. Part of TV
119. Tosses
120. Artful behavior
121. Mast

DOWN
1. Die spots
2. Senior citizens' org.
3. Stravinsky
4. Certain star
5. Paragons
6. Prevent
7. Wine: Fr.
8. Ref. book
9. Tailor's need
10. Blunted a weapon
11. By mouth
12. Sheets of wool
13. Ike's command
14. Scion
15. Ridicules
16. ____-de-France
17. Actress Swenson
18. Ruffs' mates
24. Hebrew month
26. Drizzles
29. Irish land
32. Petiole
34. Secluded
35. Zest
36. Dark brown
37. Atelier stand
38. Pub potion
39. Get rid of
41. Zeus's daughter
42. "Weeds" lead
43. Hairstyling aids
44. Faucets
45. Souses
47. Writer's ploy
48. Location
51. Fragment
53. Oregon city
55. Banners
56. Powdery limestone
57. Heart artery
58. One of the media
59. Contradict
61. Musical sounds
63. TV's Dodd
65. Ajaccio's locale: Fr.
66. Sycophant
67. Ocean vessel
68. Love, in Lecce
69. "____ Street"
70. Juvenile
71. Explosions
72. Disengage
73. Planter's need
74. Convene
75. Call
79. Cat's-paw
80. Letters
81. Skater Babilonia
83. Brew
84. Drills again
85. Comments
89. Stinging plant
91. Teetertotter
92. Frames again
93. "____ Bede"
95. Bridle parts
97. Denmark's ____ Islands
98. "____ a man . . ."
99. Traipse
100. Indigo plant
102. Pause
104. Solidifies
105. Prune
106. Italian peak
107. Go-getter
109. Kin of et al.
110. Actress Massari
112. "____ Lay Dying"
113. 250, to Cato

PUZZLE 631

British-style or cryptic crosswords are a great challenge for crossword fans. Each clue contains either a definition or direct reference to the answer, as well as a play on words. The numbers in parentheses indicate the number of letters in the answer word or words.

ACROSS

1. Anger in homestead leads to weapon (7)
5. Storm warning flusters Ruth and Ned (7)
9. Formulas are sometimes precise (7)
10. Reveals former mannerisms (7)
11. Leather became visible when Ed backed into Cash's boy (5)
12. Putting right male in spot makes him inactive (7)
13. Godly absorb fifty to furnish Yuletide foliage (5)
15. Ale is sprinkled in bride's path (5)
16. Coven usually conceals a goddess (5)
18. Nothing is in Alaska town to make it malodorous (7)
19. Fastened transfer backwards (5)
21. Kitchen tool upsets crier (5)
23. I heard smoked salmon curls (5)
25. Pete led wildly to drain (7)
27. Open to reveal a gap elsewhere (5)
28. Country hotels contain small territory for certain doctors (7)
29. Salary needed; please mail with gratuity included (7)
30. Spanish ship exhibits temerity with age (7)
34. Laundry worker will impress Erma in part (7)

DOWN

1. Get ahead of broken store in fall (9)
2. Fraudulent schemes used on tennis courts (7)
3. Should Red happen to change, arrest follows (9)
4. Prayer book taken from Miss Alice (6)
5. To become up-to-date use dry net (6)
6. Part of the shoe is higher (5)
7. Dad is in an odd state of contempt (7)
8. Bum steer: change the clock (5)
14. Cowboy's rope captures girl with ring (5)
16. Talented to develop evil stare (9)
17. Tear is involved in more certain submission (9)
20. Net worth of disorganized laic PTA (7)
22. Tracers unsteadily outline holes (7)
23. Deighton brings in upset spy group for instruction (6)
24. Seasoned puree has felines above (6)
25. Performing in a rondo in Greece (5)
26. East lake is very weird (5)

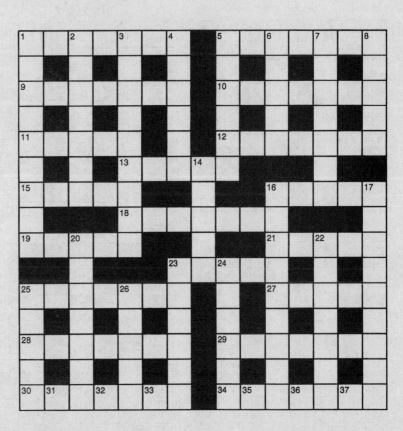

PUZZLE 1

```
SPAT  STAG  ATTA
HARE  TOKEN EWER
ONEATATIME  DOTE
PEA EBAN  TRIBES
    BALL  ITALY
REFUSE    BEREFT
ATONE SLIDE  OER
SHUT  CAD   DUPE
PAR SHAMS  LOREN
 NICKEL   LAPSED
 NOIRE    GONE
ETHANE  ERNE  TAP
LIAR THREESCORE
INNS  OILER  ANTE
SADE  SETS   BEER
```

PUZZLE 5

```
WAFT  DALE   EDE
ALAI  LINED OVID
REDSKYATMORNING
NEE ERLE   ESTEE
   DYES  ENDEAR
ARNESS  START
REAL  TORA   MID
INBLACKANDWHITE
LOS  LEER   AMAN
   AMENS  LAZILY
 ACROSS  TONY
AGAIN  PAVE  PIE
BLUEDANUBEWALTZ
BOSS  MANOR  PEER
EWE   OTTO   TARA
```

PUZZLE 9

```
LASS   LIS   BEAR
ALOU  SELMA  ELLA
PENN  POLER  LAIN
SNARLY  BLAZONED
EERIE  SULLEN
   STRAYS  AGREE
ERIE  ART  ALTERS
RUNS  MAHAL  ONAN
STREWS  ADA  MOLE
THERE  STORMY
   ELANDS  AHEAD
CHANDLER  AHERNE
LIRA  SEERS  ANIL
AVID  OZARK  RISE
MEDE  EMS    TEED
```

PUZZLE 2

```
RATS  SMEE   FANS
ETUI  WORSE  IDOL
GOLDFINGER  NATO
ANS  IVES  REGRET
LEAFLET   CANE
   ILL  MANDRELS
EARNS  FORD  PLEA
STAG  BARES  RANG
TOME  OUST  MINTS
APPRAISE   SIN
  LILT  SHATTER
ABRADE  SIAM  IVA
SOAK  RINGFINGER
TONE  STINT  RENE
ATTS  APES   ARTE
```

PUZZLE 6

```
OLAF  EGADS  CRAB
POUR  ARMEE  ROBE
SNEE  TOAST  OTOE
GREATWHITEWAY
   DAHL   LAD
BEFORE  PRESSURE
ANAME  HOARY  NEP
LARS  PALMS  PILE
ETO  ERIES  ARTIE
REENTERS  SLEETS
   OAT   EELS
ROUTESIXTYSIX
TANG  NONET  MARE
AREA  SUCRE  AMAN
PERT  ELATE  NAYS
```

PUZZLE 10

```
SPAR  SATAN  ALAN
LORE  ANODE  HOBO
ACNE  TIMEPIECES
GOODTIMES  DAISY
   ERA    PER
SIMONE  BERATED
LOIN  DEPOT  MAC
ONCEINALIFETIME
TIA  GENIC  ILED
CHINESE  CREESE
   COD    AHA
LITER  TIMEFLIES
ATIMEFORUS  OVAL
VERA  CREST  DERO
AMEN  CODES  ISLE
```

PUZZLE 3

```
GOLD  CARTA  AFAR
ARIA  ADIOS  ULNA
GARDENOFTHEGODS
ENE  LYRE   PURSE
   LION   MAORI
EVIAN  TALC   DEC
RAIDS  BRITH  AMA
AGES  PIANO  SKIS
FLU  PENCE  OPERA
TEX  RAGE  FLAYS
  COOKE   FLAN
SCALP  IOOF   GOA
CARLSBADCAVERNS
AGRA  ALEUT  VALE
TEES  GLASS  ANYA
```

PUZZLE 7

```
GONG  ESTER  BART
EVIL  GHANA  ADUE
TATA  RAGGEDYANN
LADDERS   ALIEN
ROTI   COLORS
PRIAM  FERBER
RANGER  VEES  FER
IRIS  EPEES  RUSE
MAT  TARN  ECARTE
PALATE  OGLED
STORMY  MAUD
STINT   AIRPORT
RAGGEDEDGE  LOOP
AGEE  APART  LAGO
SERE  SAREE  SNOW
```

PUZZLE 11

```
SHAM  ARRAN  PLAT
TUNA  NOOSE  AIDE
ELON  JOSHUATREE
PANGLOSS   RTES
   ROUT   SAME
STOOP  SANDARACS
CARVER  CADS  DAP
ABIE  ELOPE  MARE
MOB  OMER  DRAGON
POINCIANA  AGENT
   OUTS   VAIN
DILL    MINDOVER
COTTONWOOD  LIDO
CREE  EVANS  IDES
SEMS  TASSO  AINE
```

PUZZLE 4

```
RAPT  SPIN  BALIN
ARIA  PACE  ELUDE
JACKPINES  DAMON
ALTERED  TREMBLE
   ELAM   EVOE
ENJOYS  ASTI  RFD
LOADS  SNAIL  JAI
VICE  CAJUN  TARN
IRK  MORAL  BACON
SEA  EPIC  LACKEY
   DANE   KNIT
GRANADA  ANISEED
RUNIC  JACKKNIFE
ADDLE  ACRE  ENTR
MEYER  REED  ESSE
```

PUZZLE 8

```
STY  CHITA   MIA
LEAH  OATEN  DINS
ALWAYSTOTYRANTS
PASTA  ENE  ELTON
   TWA    ISL
WEWILLMAINTAIN
ASHE  FOLDS  SLOB
STA   LIE    IRE
HOLD  STEAD  IATE
PEACEONLYUNDER
   TAT    ESS
ALAIN  MAP  EIDER
MOUNTAINEERSARE
MING  PENNY  TRIB
ONT   ENATE  TEA
```

PUZZLE 12

```
BABY  SOFAS  SASH
OSLO  ARISE  ECHO
SHOULDERPATCHES
SEW  EDAM  IRENE
   BALD   AIRE
PARADE  ERRATIC
ALUR  PRIED  MOA
COLDSHOULDERING
TOE  HOOPS  ETTE
FREIGHT  CHASED
   NESS   CHAD
ATOLL  CHIN  BRA
BROADSHOULDERED
BANC  PEARL  VINE
APSE  YELLS  AMOS
```

514

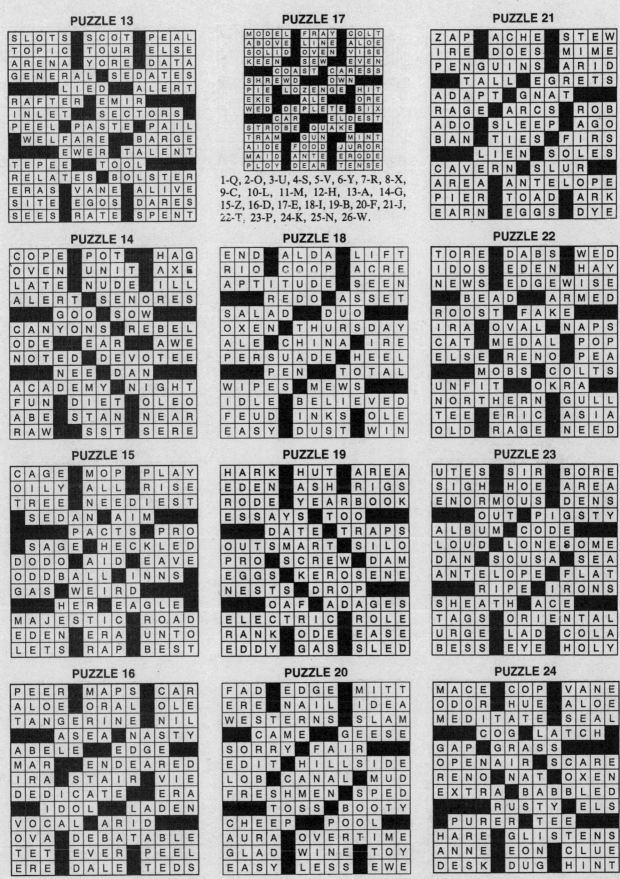

PUZZLE 13

```
S L O T S   S C O T   P E A L
T O P I C   T O U R   E L S E
A R E N A   Y O R E   D A T A
G E N E R A L   S E D A T E S
      L I E D     A L E R T
R A F T E R   E M I R
I N L E T     S E C T O R S
P E E L   P A S T E   P A I L
  W E L F A R E   B A R G E
    E W E R   T A L E N T
T E P E E     T O O L
R E L A T E S   B O L S T E R
E R A S   V A N E   A L I V E
S I T E   E G O S   D A R E S
S E E S   R A T E   S P E N T
```

PUZZLE 14

```
C O P E   P O T   H A G
O V E N   U N I T   A X E
L A T E   N U D E   I L L
A L E R T   S E N O R E S
      G O O   S O W
C A N Y O N S   R E B E L
O D E   E A R   A W E
N O T E D   D E V O T E E
      N E E   D A N
A C A D E M Y   N I G H T
F U N   D I E T   O L E O
A B E   S T A N   N E A R
R A W   S S T   S E R E
```

PUZZLE 15

```
C A G E   M O P   P L A Y
O I L Y   A L L   R I S E
T R E E   N E E D I E S T
  S E D A N   A I M
      P A C T S   P R O
  S A G E   H E C K L E D
D O D O   A I D   E A V E
O D D B A L L   I N N S
G A S   W E I R D
    H E R   E A G L E
M A J E S T I C   R O A D
E D E N   E R A   U N T O
L E T S   R A P   B E S T
```

PUZZLE 16

```
P E E R   M A P S   C A R
A L O E   O R A L   O L E
T A N G E R I N E   N I L
    A S E A   N A S T Y
A B E L E   E D G E
M A R   E N D E A R E D
I R A   S T A I R   V I E
D E D I C A T E   E R A
    I D O L   L A D E N
V O C A L   A R I D
O V A   D E B A T A B L E
T E T   E V E R   P E E L
E R E   D A L E   T E D S
```

PUZZLE 17

```
M O D E L   F R A Y   C O L T
A B O V E   L I N E   A L O E
S O L I D   O V E N   V I S E
K E E N   S E W   E V E N
    C O A S T   C A R E S S
S H R E W D   O W N
P I E   L O Z E N G E   H I T
E K E   A L E   O R E
W E D   D E P L E T E   S I X
    C A R   E L D E S T
S T R O B E   Q U A K E
T R A M   G U N   M I N T
A I D E   F O O D   J U R O R
M A I D   A N T E   E R O D E
P L O Y   D E A R   T E N S E
```

1-Q, 2-O, 3-U, 4-S, 5-V, 6-Y, 7-R, 8-X, 9-C, 10-L, 11-M, 12-H, 13-A, 14-G, 15-Z, 16-D, 17-E, 18-I, 19-B, 20-F, 21-J, 22-T, 23-P, 24-K, 25-N, 26-W.

PUZZLE 18

```
E N D   A L D A   L I F T
R I O   C O O P   A C R E
A P T I T U D E   S E E N
      R E D O   A S S E T
S A L A D   D U O
O X E N   T H U R S D A Y
A L E   C H I N A   I R E
P E R S U A D E   H E E L
      P E N   T O T A L
W I P E S   M E W S
I D L E   B E L I E V E D
F E U D   I N K S   O L E
E A S Y   D U S T   W I N
```

PUZZLE 19

```
H A R K   H U T   A R E A
E D E N   A S H   R I G S
R O D E   Y E A R B O O K
E S S A Y S   T O O
    D A T E   T R A P S
O U T S M A R T   S I L O
P R O   S C R E W   D A M
E G G S   K E R O S E N E
N E S T S   D R O P
    O A F   A D A G E S
E L E C T R I C   R O L E
R A N K   O D E   E A S E
E D D Y   G A S   S L E D
```

PUZZLE 20

```
F A D   E D G E   M I T T
E R E   N A I L   I D E A
W E S T E R N S   S L A M
    C A M E   G E E S E
S O R R Y   F A I R
E D I T   H I L L S I D E
L O B   C A N A L   M U D
F R E S H M E N   S P E D
    T O S S   B O O T Y
C H E E P   P O O L
A U R A   O V E R T I M E
G L A D   W I N E   T O Y
E A S Y   L E S S   E W E
```

PUZZLE 21

```
Z A P   A C H E   S T E W
I R E   D O E S   M I M E
P E N G U I N S   A R I D
    T A L L   E G R E T S
A D A P T   G N A T
R A G E   A R C S   R O B
A D O   S L E E P   A G O
B A N   T I E S   F I R S
    L I E N   S O L E S
C A V E R N   S L U R
A R E A   A N T E L O P E
P I E R   T O A D   A R K
E A R N   E G G S   D Y E
```

PUZZLE 22

```
T O R E   D A B S   W E D
I D O S   E D E N   H A Y
N E W S   E D G E W I S E
    B E A D   A R M E D
R O O S T   F A K E
I R A   O V A L   N A P S
C A T   M E D A L   P O P
E L S E   R E N O   P E A
    M O B S   C O L T S
U N F I T   O K R A
N O R T H E R N   G U L L
T E E   E R I C   A S I A
O L D   R A G E   N E E D
```

PUZZLE 23

```
U T E S   S I R   B O R E
S I G H   H O E   A R E A
E N O R M O U S   D E N S
    O U T   P I G S T Y
A L B U M   C O D E
L O U D   L O N E S O M E
D A N   S O U S A   S E A
A N T E L O P E   F L A T
    R I P E   I R O N S
S H E A T H   A C E
T A G S   O R I E N T A L
U R G E   L A D   C O L A
B E S S   E Y E   H O L Y
```

PUZZLE 24

```
M A C E   C O P   V A N E
O D O R   H U E   A L O E
M E D I T A T E   S E A L
      C O G   L A T C H
G A P   G R A S S
O P E N A I R   S C A R E
R E N O   N A T   O X E N
E X T R A   B A B B L E D
    R U S T Y   E L S
P U R E R   T E E
H A R E   G L I S T E N S
A N N E   E O N   C L U E
D E S K   D U G   H I N T
```

PUZZLE 25

```
SPOT  FATA  TIMES
OENO  ADAM  ARISE
RATE  SALO  MALAR
ASH  STICKSITOUT
   ESTER  ENE
PASTOR  BRAG  SAC
ASTOR  BEIT  SANA
STICKSANDSTONES
TICK  TREE  ADDLE
ARK  GENT  ERASES
   ARA  ANEST
STONEMASONS  OWE
CALEB  GORE  ANON
ALINE  RITA  NERO
RENTS  ALAD  ASKS
```

PUZZLE 29

```
EBBED  WASH  OLEG
CRONE  IDEA  NOPE
HANDMEDOWN  ERIN
ONE  EATS  DEVICE
   HASH  ABLE
PEDANT  UNAFRAID
OMENS  TRIG  YMCA
KIND  CHATS  HAIL
ELSA  LOLA  MAZEL
REENTERS  WINERY
   DEAN  LARD
DEAFEN  SORA  TKO
OLIO  SECONDHAND
LIMO  ERAS  OARED
LAST  RENE  RITES
```

PUZZLE 33

```
PARK  IMAGE  DEAR
ALEE  MERIT  ELMO
PITY  PRINCIPLES
EVA  BOLD  TEASE
RELEASE  SWAN
   INST  CHILDREN
TRADE  GLORY  EVE
OATS  PEONY  AGES
LIE  DANTE  GLINT
ENDORSES  POPS
   BITT  BLASTED
SHELF  RAIL  ELI
PILOTHOUSE  ARAN
ALAN  OLDER  METE
TONG  PEELS  IDES
```

PUZZLE 26

```
SALAS  STAR  ELSA
APART  PINE  LEND
FENCE  ITES  EGAD
EXASPERATE  CAKE
   INON  ANTLER
PLIANT  IGLOO
AIRS  ESAU  TRADE
LEISURE  SPEARED
MUSES  ECHO  TILE
   VERSO  SWEDEN
ADHERE  NATE
DEAR  MAGISTRATE
ALGA  OLES  TALON
GHAT  TARN  ELAND
EIRE  ERSE  RENES
```

PUZZLE 30

```
GABE  SWOON  RIDE
OPAL  EARTO  EVIL
YELLOWSTONEPARK
ADD  RINSE  RANTS
   PANT  JAY
HAVING  SKIT  HUE
OWING  ANIL  GUTS
BASKETBALLJONES
BRAY  REIN  OUTRE
YES  BELL  PARSON
   POE  MEND
SOARS  OCEAN  LEO
CHRISTMASCAROLS
AILS  EARTH  OVAL
BOOM  ARRAY  NEMO
```

PUZZLE 34

```
LAMB  SWAM  SALEM
ORAL  TIDY  TWICE
RIGA  ALIT  ALOHA
ELIZABETHII  NOT
   ELLS  MRS
SPARSE  MEASURES
TORSO  SONG  BOLE
AWE  SPADE  BIN
RENT  CATS  PHOTO
TRAILERS  PLATER
   PUN  FUEL
CAN  RECLAMATION
ABACK  HARP  EDGE
REVUE  ONCE  ROLE
STEED  WEED  SLED
```

PUZZLE 27

```
URAL  TALE  SABOT
SOLO  AWED  ELOPE
ELAN  RANG  CONAN
EIGHTISENOUGH
   OAT  END
STRAIN  SHAD  BAT
LOESS  MEET  ABE
EIGHTEENWHEELER
ELA  VATS  LASER
TEL  SODA  BERATE
   AUK  ARM
DINNERATEIGHT
PARIS  ANON  RARA
AROSE  GILD  ALUM
TENET  ELLA  STEP
```

PUZZLE 31

```
ARTY  HAILE  EBBS
CARE  UNTIL  NEAT
THANKSGIVINGDAY
ASP  ETES  AISLE
   DELL  LOIN
DOCILE  FILLETS
ASEA  SABLE  RIO
WILLIAMBRADFORD
SEL  GUILE  ATEE
ROSETTE  TWISTS
   OTOE  THAT
ATILT  CARL  ADD
NATIONALHOLIDAY
AXED  ONION  RARE
TIMS  RUPEE  EYES
```

PUZZLE 35

```
TILE  JOEL  AAR
ORAL  ABOUT  UNTO
MONK  LONGWINDED
END  WOES  IRISES
   LOOPS  GNAT
SCURRY  MAKEEYES
LOBES  BALL  DALE
ALB  TRAILER  RIP
TIED  OWNS  HEDDA
SCRAMBLE  MORSEL
   NIBS  TENET
ASSUME  BILE  ITS
CUMBERSOME  ACRE
TRUE  SAREE  SKIN
SET  LESS  ASPS
```

PUZZLE 28

```
SLAM  CAPP  CACAO
TORO  AGIO  OPHIR
EKER  MICK  REINS
PIANOPLAYER  LEO
   WEE  GARDEN
COPPER  CALLES
ALLAN  MINI  APSE
RIAS  SAVIN  PLEA
TOYS  ERIS  DEALT
   PENPAL  BERYLS
SCORIA  ALE
HRS  PLAYFORTIME
AESOP  ROTA  ITER
NEURO  TROT  LEON
ELMAN  YENS  LAWS
```

PUZZLE 32

```
CATO  LILAC  DRAY
OLAV  ERATO  RALE
RAKE  VIXEN  OCTA
PIERCES  COOKER
   CURED  OGLE
SOLAR  SEQUESTER
AKIMBO  PURE  ERA
LATE  LARAS  SENT
APE  EDNA  ESPRIT
DIRECTIVE  NOSEY
   ASTI  EMMET
BOTTOM  BEELINE
AMUR  EVILS  ENOS
RARA  RISES  STET
TREY  SAMMY  SOLE
```

PUZZLE 36

```
BAG  ASPER  SCAR
ACRE  SUITE  LOCO
AHOLEINTHE  EMMA
LEGENDS  SLEEPER
   CREED  SETA
SANTA  TAN  LENIN
CLASPS  REA  DINE
AIT  TAILORS  OLA
LEAR  TRI  KERNEL
ENTER  ANT  CASTE
   OPUS  GAITS
STREETS  PROCEED
ARIA  APPEARANCE
NEUT  BEARD  LIRA
GEMS  SENSE  DUN
```

PUZZLE 37

```
M A R K   A T L A S   C A V E
A N O N   L O O S E   O R A L
I T T O   E A G L E   N E S S
D I S C A R D   E D U C A T E
      K I T   J E S S E
R I P E R   L A P   H A B I T
A R I D   F I N   F E L I N E
D E N   P O L I T E R   S A D
A N T L E R   T O W   F O N D
R E S E T   B O Y   M O N E Y
      T A P E R   S I R
C A S T L E S   C I N E M A S
R I T E   S T E A L   V E I L
O D O R   T O R S O   E R M A
P E W S   S W A T S   R E S T
```

PUZZLE 41

```
S A S S   S E T   R I P S
E L L A   T A R   E R I E
W O O D   E T E   T I L E
N E E D L E   E R A S E R
      E E R   S I P
S T A R T E D   M E R G E
A I R   D O C   O A R
P E K E S   G A N D E R S
      S E A   N E A
T I L T E D   D E N T E D
A T E E   O W L   C I T E
R E N E   R A E   E D N A
T R A M   E S S   R E A R
```

PUZZLE 45

```
N E B   T A S K       G O B
A O N E   A T T I C   F A D E
S W E E T T O O T H   A L O E
T O R T I L L A   A S T E R
O R O   T E L   B R I C
      C A R   S A T C H E L
A C O R N   T H R E E A C E S
S O L E   B R E E D   N O N O
S O L A R Y E A R   A C N E S
S A M O A N S   S S E
      P A N T   P O T   T K O
S O U N D   A E R A T I O N
S E R F   B U T T E R B A L L
H A L F   Y P R E S   A R A Y
E L Y       S O R T   R A S
```

PUZZLE 38

```
A R A B S   T A R P   E S T E
C A B O T   H I E K   L E O N
C R A Z Y H O R S E   I A G O
T A T   G U N S   P A T H O S
S E E M I N G   C A M E O
      E A T   H A R I   R T E
C O H A N   O V E R U S E D
A V O N   R U L E S   B E N D
P A R T N E R S   B O S S Y
E L S   O M I T   M I A
      E L L I S   D U S T P A N
L E S I O N   G U S H   O R O
A C H E   D A R K H O R S E S
I R O N   E D I E   P A S T E
R U E S   R A P S   S T E E D
```

PUZZLE 42

```
M A S K   T O T U P   C A T S
A S T I   A V E N A   A T R I
S H U N   H E L I C O P T E R
S E N D F O R   S A B I N E S
      T R U E   B E S E T
O F F E R   N I X   R A C K S
C O L D   L I P   M O N R O E
C R Y   B A L L O O N   O L E
A G E N A S   A P T   S P A D
M O R A Y   K N T   S U D S Y
      N I C H E   M A R U
S P I N N E Y   M O O N S E T
D I R I G I B L E S   A T T A
A L E E   L E A S E   M E O W
K I S S   S R T A S   E R N S
```

PUZZLE 46

```
F O R   H E D G E       E R E
O L E O   O S I E R   A Q U A
E D E N   S P E A R   L U S T
S L E E P Y   R A L L I E S
      L E I   S T A M P S
S P L I N T E R   A N Y
H O O F   A X I S   A C R E S
A L I E   L I V I D   H I V E
G E N T S   T E T E   I D E A
      O N S   R E S T L E S S
P I L I N G   S O D
A U D I T O R   S E A R C H
S L A V   R O V E R   E R O S
A S H E   E V I C T   N O M E
N E O   S E A T S   W E T
```

PUZZLE 39

```
  I D E   J A F F A   A B I T
A N I L   A P A I L   D O D O
B O X I N G R I N G   R T E S
A N O S E   I R E   C O T E S
S E N S I B L E   J A I L
      A N A   S M A R T E R
K I S S   S A T I R E   D O G
E M U   R I G   S G T   U N A
G A G   E N R I C O   S P A T
M A D I S O N   O T T
      R A N T   G E N E R A L S
T I B I A   P E R   R A T I O
I S O N   C A N N E R Y R O W
N E W T   B R U I N   E E N S
E E L Y   S T E E D   R E S
```

PUZZLE 43

```
B E T       L A S   J A D E
A D E   P I L E   A L A N
B E N J A M I N   S E N D
E N T I R E   A D O
      L E S   T E N N I S
M A L L   R O N   O D E
O R E   T S A R S   P O E
S E A   A P E   H E L P
S A N D R A   A T E
      E A R   R E L A T E
I R O N   R E M E M B E R
T O N I   O V E N   L A M
S T E M   W E D   E R A
```

PUZZLE 47

```
O N T O P   E R S E   A P R A
L O O S E   T O P S E C R E T
P I P E S   H O U S E T O P S
A S H   T H E F E E L   V E E
E Y A S   O R T   E N O L A
      M U S T   O H A R E
T O P P E R   P A C   S T O A
O V E R T O P   T H E T O P S
M A R E   D E B   E L O P E S
      M A S A I   S U R F
F I V E S   G P O   S L A T
A S E   H E S T O N S   I G O
C A R R O T T O P   L E G U P
T A B L E T O P S   A C H E S
O C A S   U P S Y   G U T S Y
```

PUZZLE 40

```
S A S H   M A S S       G A S P
T R I O   A C T O R   A L E E
O G R E   R O U S E   R A R E
R U E   T O R N   T A N N E R
M E N T I O N   C A N E
      I N N   P A I N T E R S
S H O R T   C A R N E   V I E
P O R E   B A R E S   P I P E
A L A   S A V E D   T I L E S
R E L E N T E D   M A N
      R A T S   T I C K L E D
D A M A G E   L E S T   O N E
I R I S   R O A R S   C O D E
M I N E   S E N S E   U S E D
E A T S   R E E D   R E D S
```

PUZZLE 44

```
S H O E   O R A T E   P A D
E O N S   T O W E L   B A S E
W H A T S H A L L I S A Y H E
S O N   T E S S   C R E E D
      H A R T   C A R E E R
M O L A R S   A R L E S
I V A N   S T A T E   H U E
K I N G S O L O M O N S E N T
E D E   E R I N S   E R I E
      P R I D E   W R E S T S
A R L E N E   P R O S
A L A I N   T H I S   B S A
M I N E E Y E H A T H S E E N
A S K S   E R A S E   A N E T
S T S   W A T E R   C E D E
```

PUZZLE 48

```
D A L I   A L O H A   C A M P
U P O N   D A W E S   O B O E
P E S T   E L E M I   L O O T
E X T E M P O R A N E O U S
      R O T   O W N
P O S I T S   A C R E   G P O
A L L O T   E C R U   E R I C
S P U R O F T H E M O M E N T
T E E S   A N E W   N I E C E
A S S   A L A S   R E G R E T
      S I S   E A R
U N P R E M E D I T A T E D
O N O R   T E N O N   N A V E
D I V A   T A I N E   T R E E
S T A Y   O L D E R   S O L D
```

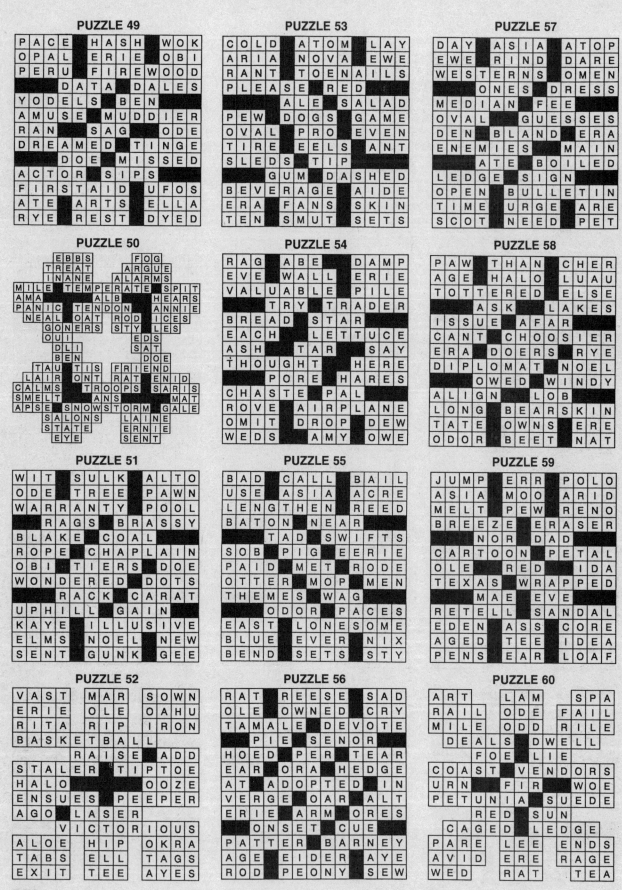

PUZZLE 49
```
PACE HASH WOK
OPAL ERIE OBI
PERU FIREWOOD
  DATA DALES
YODELS BEN
AMUSE MUDDIER
RAN SAG ODE
DREAMED TINGE
  DOE MISSED
ACTOR SIPS
FIRSTAID UFOS
ATE ARTS ELLA
RYE REST DYED
```

PUZZLE 53
```
COLD ATOM LAY
ARIA NOVA EWE
RANT TOENAILS
PLEASE RED
  ALE SALAD
PEW DOGS GAME
OVAL PRO EVEN
TIRE EELS ANT
SLEDS TIP
  GUM DASHED
BEVERAGE AIDE
ERA FANS SKIN
TEN SMUT SETS
```

PUZZLE 57
```
DAY ASIA ATOP
EWE RIND DARE
WESTERNS OMEN
  ONES DRESS
MEDIAN FEE
OVAL GUESSES
DEN BLAND ERA
ENEMIES MAIN
  ATE BOILED
LEDGE SIGN
OPEN BULLETIN
TIME URGE ARE
SCOT NEED PET
```

PUZZLE 50
```
EBBS        FOG
TREAT      ARGUE
INANE     ALARMS
MILE TEMPERATE SPIT
AMA   ALB    HEARS
PANIC TENDON ANNIE
NEAL OAT ROD ICES
GONERS  STY LES
OUI        EDS
DLI        SAT
BEN        DOE
TAU TIS FRIEND
LAIR ONT RAT ENID
CALMS TROOPS SARIS
SMELT  ANS    MAT
APSE SNOWSTORM GALE
SALONS    LAINE
STATE     ERNIE
EYE       SENT
```

PUZZLE 54
```
RAG ABE DAMP
EVE WALL ERIE
VALUABLE PILE
  TRY TRADER
BREAD STAR
EACH LETTUCE
ASH TAR SAY
THOUGHT HERE
  PORE HARES
CHASTE PAL
ROVE AIRPLANE
OMIT DROP DEW
WEDS AMY OWE
```

PUZZLE 58
```
PAW THAN CHER
AGE HALO LUAU
TOTTERED ELSE
  ASK LAKES
ISSUE AFAR
CANT CHOOSIER
ERA DOERS RYE
DIPLOMAT NOEL
  OWED WINDY
ALIGN LOB
LONG BEARSKIN
TATE OWNS ERE
ODOR BEET NAT
```

PUZZLE 51
```
WIT SULK ALTO
ODE TREE PAWN
WARRANTY POOL
  RAGS BRASSY
BLAKE COAL
ROPE CHAPLAIN
OBI TIERS DOE
WONDERED DOTS
  RACK CARAT
UPHILL GAIN
KAYE ILLUSIVE
ELMS NOEL NEW
SENT GUNK GEE
```

PUZZLE 55
```
BAD CALL BAIL
USE ASIA ACRE
LENGTHEN REED
BATON NEAR
  TAD SWIFTS
SOB PIG EERIE
PAID MET RODE
OTTER MOP MEN
THEMES WAG
  ODOR PACES
EAST LONESOME
BLUE EVER NIX
BEND SETS STY
```

PUZZLE 59
```
JUMP ERR POLO
ASIA MOO ARID
MELT PEW RENO
BREEZE ERASER
  NOR DAD
CARTOON PETAL
OLE RED IDA
TEXAS WRAPPED
  MAE EVE
RETELL SANDAL
EDEN ASS CORE
AGED TEE IDEA
PENS EAR LOAF
```

PUZZLE 52
```
VAST MAR SOWN
ERIE OLE OAHU
RITA RIP IRON
BASKETBALL
  RAISE ADD
STALER TIPTOE
HALO OOZE
ENSUES PEEPER
AGO LASER
  VICTORIOUS
ALOE HIP OKRA
TABS ELL TAGS
EXIT TEE AYES
```

PUZZLE 56
```
RAT REESE SAD
OLE OWNED CRY
TAMALE DEVOTE
  PIE SENOR
HOED PER TEAR
EAR ORA HEDGE
AT ADOPTED IN
VERGE OAR ALT
ERIE ARM ORES
  ONSET CUE
PATTER BARNEY
AGE EIDER AYE
ROD PEONY SEW
```

PUZZLE 60
```
ART LAM SPA
RAIL ODE FAIL
MILE ODD RILE
DEALS DWELL
  FOE LIE
COAST VENDORS
URN FIR WOE
PETUNIA SUEDE
  RED SUN
CAGED LEDGE
PARE LEE ENDS
AVID ERE RAGE
WED RAT TEA
```

PUZZLE 61

```
LOPE TASS
ACRE ELITE
STEN STRIVE
SAP ETO PET
 AHOY BUNT
LORAN DELTA
OPAL SODA
SET TEN TOM
TRIPOD VINE
 AORTA IOTA
 NOON ANON
```

PUZZLE 62

```
   RAW   PRY
  RIATA  LIE
 HAMMER BOOT
 CAMP    SIT
 LIP    TON
SOL   MONSTER
EWE  LAY  ELA
ENDURED   MAP
   GAG   APT
   FLY  TILE
FURY  DERIDE
ORE   ATONE
END   MAT
```

PUZZLE 63

```
 FLAW    PLAN
 IOTA RIB ROPE
NOON SOLO ODES
RASP HALT NEXT
ALE  FEN  HOT
GENERAL  ROYAL
 LILT LAD EWE
GLIMPSE ELAPSED
AIR PER OLIO
STEAL  PENDENT
 BEG JAY VIA
MOSS AFAR HAND
ANTE VOID CODE
ICON EEL  ABET
NEWT      BODY
```

PUZZLE 65

```
DUD   CAP   COW
ITEM RAPID PONE
PANE ENTER LACE
HYMNS ROTATE
  BET    POT
 CREW    WEST
FAIR      ARE
END       LAY
DOE       PACE
ERIN     MODE
  RIB    TOT
 SLOPES APART
RUIN STAMP TOOT
ARMS TAXIS ODOR
GEE   RED   SKY
```

PUZZLE 66

What the world really needs is more love and less paperwork.

1. Skeleton, 2. Tomorrow, 3. Salad, 4. Pawned, 5. Wherever, 6. Shrilly, 7. Pleased.

PUZZLE 67

```
          ARAM
          MICA
          ACED
          HERESTO
SHOP       BACON
LIVID      NONE
ALINE ADAM NITER
MODES TALE RIGID
 CARROT    AGHA
 CRYINTHENIGHT
 BRIE  OMELET
NOYES  DINE OSAGE
VALID  STET WARES
ADEN       LAMAS
MERGE      RARE
PROJECT
ARUM
GIBE
SEEN
```

PUZZLE 68

Paula's last name must be Rubin (1 and 4). Since Judy danced with Mr. Turner (2) and Paula danced with Mr. Adler (4), Angela danced with either Mr. Rubin or Mr. Tucker. Angela did not dance with Mr. Rubin (Paula's husband); she danced with Mr. Tucker (Janice's husband, 3). Mr. Turner, Angela's husband, danced with Judy (whose husband is Adler), and Janice danced with Mr. Rubin.

In summary: Angela Turner, Mr. Tucker; Janice Tucker, Mr. Rubin; Judy Adler, Mr. Turner; Paula Rubin, Mr. Adler.

PUZZLE 64

1. Work, Word, Lord, Load; 2. Fire, Dire, Dare, Dale, Sale; 3. Back, Beck, Beak, Beat, Seat; 4. Leaf, Lead, Mead, Meld, Mold.

PUZZLE 69

```
            CASTE
      DEE  ABORT
      ELLE ANTIC
SHANA  CASTANETS
COLOR ONION ROTH
ALIBI  DENT  RAMP
TECH    ALF ARIAN
 SEIDEL  BRIE MANNA
 SLAVE  PECKS SNAP
 LIENS  RATES SOME
 SLOT  NAOMI   WAS
CHI    FOILS CLEM
HINT   UNCLE AIDES
EASE    ECHO CIGAR
STOPE   LEO  KEATON
TULES   LOAD  CLUB
SEEP  SILO AUDIE OHARE
      RECESSION MENSA
      PINTA TODO ALDEN
      OTTER  SES
      TOOTS
```

PUZZLE 70

```
CAN   ITEM  FALL
OVAL  RAVE  ALOE
TIMID ICES  MOOT
 DEMONSTRATION
      BOA  ELF
ORNERY    VARY
GEAR  STERN RED
LEI  CLAIM  ODE
ELL  MOURN PAIN
  WING  SHANTY
   TAN   EAT
 TENDERHEARTED
WAND  MOOD DELAY
ELSE  ISLE RATE
DEER  TEEN  NEW
```

PUZZLE 71

FLAVORINGS: Cinnamon, Lemon, Orange, Peppermint, Sage.
ANIMALS: Chamois, Llama, Oryx, Panda, Skunk.
MUSICAL INSTRUMENTS: Cello, Lyre, Oboe, Piano, Saxophone.
VEHICLES: Car, Liner, Oxcart, Plane, Submarine.
FOOTWEAR: Clogs, Loafers, Oxfords, Pumps, Sandals.

PUZZLE 72

PUZZLE 73

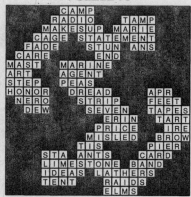

PUZZLE 74

No time like the present.

PUZZLE 75

PUZZLE 76

PUZZLE 77

Correction does much, but encouragement does more.

1. Course, 2. Bonn, 3. Enough, 4. React, 5. Medium, 6. Cored, 7. Cost, 8. Remote.

PUZZLE 78

PUZZLE 79

1. Pneumatics, 2. Jargonized, 3. Hockey fans.

PUZZLE 80

PUZZLE 81

1. Walt Disney, 2. Taking over, 3. Workplaces.

PUZZLE 82

PUZZLE 83

1. Camp, Came, Fame, Fare, Fire.
2. Wild, Wind, Bind, Bird.
3. Cork, Core, Sore, Sole.
4. Mole, More, Core, Corn, Coin, Chin, Shin, Skin.

PUZZLE 84

PUZZLE 85

1. Rite + Clan = Clarinet
2. Boast + Tine = Obstinate
3. Avon + Rete = Renovate
4. Race + Sole = Escarole

PUZZLE 86

PUZZLE 87

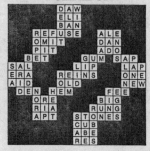

PUZZLE 88

Pumpkin, Kindred; Garden, Denizen; Shade, Adept; Scarlet, Lettuce; Parson, Sonnet; Portage, Agent; Attend, Endure; Bitten, Tenor; Carob, Robot; Concur, Curtain.

PUZZLE 89

```
DEAR  PARS  DUMB
ARLO  ELATE  INEE
BALD  RECOLLECTS
SLEEP   ERIE  LES
   VOID   YONDER
SKI  CATS  TIN
ANA  KNOTS  NAIVE
POT  KNEEL   NEW
SWEET  EAGER  VEE
   MAP  LONE  ERR
TASTED  DEAN
PAL  EARS   FETED
INTERLOPER  RITE
AGES  SPATE  IVAN
FORE   STAY  EELS
```

PUZZLE 90

```
MARINE  FIRS  BIB
OBERON  ARIA  ARI
DEMAND  NAST  LON
   ATE  HANKERING
LORE  PIT  SEA
IRK  MEDIC  NICKS
MIA  ICECAP  DANA
BOB  TOO  BAG  MAN
ELLA  SUPINE  EVE
REESE  TENET  RES
   KIT  REL  EAST
CONSTRUCT  DAB
AVE  HATE  TUMULT
PAW  EDEN  APOGEE
ELS  REST  TENSED
```

PUZZLE 91

```
AGAR  SATE  SOD
TUBE  CARL  HUR
ALEC  EMISSARY
SPLEEN  MAAM
   DREAM  NEFS
LAGER  NEEDFUL
ATE  OVERT  USA
MINERAL  HOLEY
APEX  CERAM
   RAMA  ENAMEL
PROMOTER  SOMA
IOU  VERA  UNIT
GAS  EDEN  MATE
```

PUZZLE 92

```
ANTE  PTA  SARI
NAUT  EON  STEN
CHROMATOMETER
ESQ  ERODE  ELI
   URAL  ETON
CLOUDY  SECTOR
HAIL    HIDE
INSEAM  REEVED
   ERMA  INRE
SOB  ELAND  NSA
COLORLESSNESS
AZUL  ERE  ESTE
REED  TOD  OSSA
```

PUZZLE 93

```
GARP  BORIS  CHIT
OLIO  ALONE  AUTO
LAND  TASKMASTER
FIG  CONE   MISSY
   MOUND  BEAN
STARTS  POMPOMS
OASTS  MOMMA  APB
SITS  ZORBA  ASIA
ONE  SORTS  OCTET
TREMORS  DURESS
   LIMO  PURER
TRAIL  SANS  KIM
MASTERHAND  ZERO
ELKE  OAKIE  EYED
NESS  ONICE  ESSE
```

PUZZLE 94

Difficulties are meant to rouse, not discourage.

1. Soar, 2. Families, 3. Defect, 4. Gait,
5. Detour, 6. Reunion, 7. Scout.

PUZZLE 95

```
CROWD  JOKE  DELI
LABOR  EVEN  EXAM
IVORY  WEED  LUMP
PEEK  TERN  AIDES
   MAILS  ANGER
ETHANE  EARTH
LEANT  TEXT  TAG
FEZ  EAR  LYE  JAB
NEE  LORE  AMAZE
   QUITE  STARED
SPURT  QUEST
OCEAN  BUNT  AFAR
DEAL  ARID  ADAGE
ONCE  WORE  CODED
REED  EWER  TRESS
```

1-R, 2-E, 3-J, 4-M, 5-P, 6-S, 7-F, 8-O, 9-U, 10-K, 11-W, 12-Z, 13-D, 14-Y, 15-N, 16-T, 17-G, 18-X, 19-Q, 20-H, 21-V, 22-B, 23-L, 24-A, 25-I, 26-C.

PUZZLE 96

1. Mature, Nature; 2. Staple, Stable; 3. Funnel, Tunnel; 4. Simple, Sample; 5. Squirt, Squire; 6. Number, Lumber.

PUZZLE 97

PUZZLE 98

```
INA  STAB  MISS
MOW  PENITENCE
PRECIPITATION
   ARIL  BEATS
SHARED  FOR
HOMES  FIR  SOB
ABET  LAX  COME
DON  TON  ROMAN
   MOB  REVERT
SMEAR  COPE
PARTICIPATION
INITIATES  TWO
TEES  PEST  SEW
```

PUZZLE 99

```
TOPE  PAM  PORT
ABOY  ELI  ERIE
LONESTARSTATE
KEY  CARAT  LAM
   TEAL  GET
STARTS  ERASER
RAIN    STEN
OWLETS  METALS
   SUE  EVEN
SPA  TEASE  DAM
CORPUSCHRISTI
ALTO  ARE  DUES
REED  WED  APES
```

PUZZLE 100

```
EAST  BARON  HALO
ALAS  ELITE  OVID
GILA  HONOR  RIME
LEARNING  VENDOR
END  ONE   ORE
   ODD  TRUSTING
TRAPS  BOAST  DEE
RUNT  ANT  LOAM
ALE  DELIS  WILLS
METEORIC  BIT
   AVA  FAN  CIA
SHARES  LAKELAND
CORN  EMOTE  ORAD
ALEE  ROVER  ANNE
READ  SEEDY  DEED
```

PUZZLE 101

521

PUZZLE 102

```
TENT ASIA SAW
ALEE TIDY APO
TARE OBOE COO
ANOMALY SERGE
REL ILLS PEER
STIRS ABODE
ALA DUD
LATEX RECAP
DIRE EARS ORA
UNCLE PITCHER
LEA COAT LENE
SAN HARE URAN
ELA ORTS BEST
```

PUZZLE 103

```
SETA AWAY CAM
IRON JAVA ORE
REYKJAVIK NIS
LURED PTAH
FACET FIR
EXIT AMBITION
SIT ONION VIA
SLIGHTLY LEST
ZOO HIDES
ABET DATES
NUN HAVERSACK
ERR ODOR OBOE
WRY GOWN MANY
```

PUZZLE 104
Tape

```
THEE PITS SMA SOHO
OATS ESSE ILL PRAY
WHATISREDINVISIBLE
NATANT TARE VERSOS
TIS STOW ERA
ONSET EENS BLAME
POT LEA
TRYSTS TRAP TOPPER
POE HALO ROASTS
EMPIRE EMPS ANT
MOANED ESSE PASTOR
PSI ERE
STRAP BETA SPEED
NOD USES BEL
BEETLE RAMS LEAPED
ANDHOLDSUPEVERYONE
NODE ADE TRIS ESTE
SLAM YES STES REED
```

PUZZLE 105

```
LLAMA ABACI IRK
AURAL WAGON CUE
STILE ABETS ESP
HEAL RED UPSET
EASE ALL
SWITCH CAPTURES
TAN TYRANT MEET
RIFE OUT BARE
AVES VASSAL DIM
PERSPIRE CEASES
AIM FEES
PLOYS SKI SOLO
LAW CHAIR DUPED
EVE EAGLE AMEND
DAD STAND MENDS
```

PUZZLE 106

```
S CHASTE TEACH ACHE T
P POUTER ROUTE TRUE O
R ANSWER WANES AWES N
I INSIDE DINES SEND I
N TRANCE CRATE TEAR C
G GRAPES SPARE REAP S
```

PUZZLE 107

```
SLAW SPIN BETA WANT
PITY TIME AVER AREA
AVON REPRESENTATION
NEMESIS VAIN BEANS
TOP BOSC REAR
DEBTS TAUT SORT POP
ERLE BOSS SHARE RUE
EMU ALES APERS TEST
MARKIE AGREE COSTS
REDWHITEANDBLUE
SWINE IRONY EARNED
TIES GRANT IDLY TAR
ASS TRITE EDIT MESA
YET WINE SNAG CADET
WING DOGS BAR
SEDAN SOAR SATISFY
AMUSEMENTPARKS NILE
LINT ALOE VIII ELAN
TREE RIBS EONS SOWS
```

PUZZLE 108

```
SALAD FLOSS RAGES
SQUIRE RIATA EVADED
OUTLAW ESTER FELINE
RAH BERET WATER TIN
EROS YODEL HER MOLT
RERAN DONOR DESIRES
MIB METER EON
DENOTES DUPED WOMEN
AQUARIUM SEVER RAMA
RUR ONSET LEVEL DOM
TASK GATES LIBERATE
SLEEP NAPES LEGUMES
NOT LIVER LAM
SLENDER DENIM LORDS
HOLY AIM NOVEL ROIL
ICE CRAIG RENEW TAO
NAVAHO LIMIT MORALE
STEVES ELATE ORATES
ENATE STEAD NEWER
```

PUZZLE 109

```
TOME LAPS CASK
OMEN OPAHS AGIN
LORD SERAC NATO
DOR MERRYANDREW
YEARS NIL
TOWERS CONDEMN
EMILE PAREE EEN
TIDY VIPER TRUE
ETO DIKES BURRO
SWEETER CANYON
RNA SHREW
MERRYMAKERS ILE
ARIA IMAGO AVON
ZOOT NAHUM KERN
ESSA SNEE ASEA
```

PUZZLE 110
A groundhog is a land baron.

522

PUZZLE 111

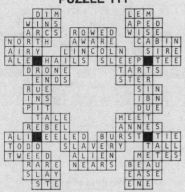

```
        DIM              LEM
WINS                     APED
ARCS    ROWED      WISE
NORTH   AWARE      CABIN
AIRY    LINCOLN    SIRE
ALE  HAILS  SLEEP  TEE
DRONE              TARTS
ENDS               STER
RUE                SIN
INS                IBN
PIT                DUE
TALE               MEET
REBEL              ANNES
ALI EELED BURST    TIE
TODD  SLAVERY      TALL
TWEED  ALIEN       METES
RARE   NEARS       BEAU
SLAY               EASE
STE                ENE
```

PUZZLE 112

```
ART              APT
NOR              EWER
OPT GLOB         LENA
PAULREVERE  MIDNIGHT
ANNOY ESTATE    LOON
LEAP   EERIE     NOT
PLAT  ETA  BLED
TAP AIL          RARE
ALA TSP          SWIFT
REPORT           ATTACK
ADIEU      TRI   SEA
IONS       EDS   KEY
CENT  AHA  SASH
SOT   EVENT      HARM
AMAH  WARNED     MARIA
COLONIES  REVOLUTION
RIDE       EVAS  ATE
SPAR       EVE
ESS        RED
```

PUZZLE 113

```
TEN  SARI  BURR
OPE  PLOT  ARIA
SEW  EMBELLISH
SEDANS     ASSES
     END   LAMA
HALT  RESEMBLE
ASH  SEEKS  RIO
SPINNERS   RAPS
     OILS  TAN
SLURP      GANDHI
PALMETTOS  NOS
ANNA  LOOT  ELL
REAL  COPE  WEE
```

PUZZLE 114

```
WASP  PAT  PANS
INTO  ARI  ONIT
STUDENTPRINCE
HER  LEYTE   EER
     DELL  ODA
CAINES     ESTHER
CLEO       AERO
CARLOS     ATLAST
     APE   TOED
SPA  ERIAN  LID
PRINCESSGRACE
EIRE  NET  ANEW
TEED  ERE  EDDY
```

PUZZLE 115

```
BLABS     PERIL
REMIT   PARADE
CASINO  LUGGED
OISE  OVAL  GAG
SSE  FLAY  RETE
ENOL   RESIDES
    RETIRES
DECLARE   LETS
INRE  ETAL  OER
PTA  WAYS  HIVE
PITIED  NAILED
ERECTS  ELDER
REDES    REEDS
```

PUZZLE 116

```
PELT      PALP
ROVER   AWARE
DAMAGE  RECORD
AIM  SALAD  FAY
USES  TAG  SITE
BELOW   MONITOR
    LOA  NOD
BALANCE   BLAST
OMEN  TAB  EVER
LOT  ARTEL  ERE
ENTIRE  LOUNGE
GENUS   LUNGE
RAMS     EDIE
```

PUZZLE 117

```
COTE  LAPSE  SERA
OVAL  ARIES  OMAR
DEPARTMENT  LIVE
ERE  ETES  IBERIA
      SPED  IMAM
MATTER   STAGNANT
ORIEL  MEETS  MAR
TERM  MADRE  LAVA
ONE  PAGES  SATED
RADIATOR  SENILE
      OLEO  SUNK
LOUDER  ETNA  HER
ANTI  ILLUSTRATE
STEN  AISNE  AVON
HOSE  LEAST  PENT
```

PUZZLE 118

MASQUERADE

PUZZLE 119

```
MARY    ABLE    DRAW
VALUE   POOL   SEINE
ARENA  CHARLEMAGNE
SAXE   THIRD  DENSER
ETA   VIED   GWEN
  NAILS  BOA  AJAR
  DUNES LEAR  UNI
JEERER  FIELD  SLED
ARRAS  PACES  BEING
MOTE  LOUIS  CANUTE
EDH    ASST   FLITS
SEEM   BET    LILAC
  ENOS  LAMS  AHA
ABUSER  SPIKE  SEEN
CONSTANTINE  WASNT
ERIES   NAPE  IBARS
RUTS    WREN   GARY
```

PUZZLE 120

```
HALE  OTHER  STOW
ELAN  LEAVE  PINE
LEND  ESTES  LEER
DEDICATE  COURSE
    NOSY  CURT
FORGET  CHEATERS
ATE  DELLA  LEVEL
UTES  ROUST  RACE
LEVIS  VEERS  DUD
TRESTLES  OATERS
    TEES  ATTA
ADHERE  ATTENDED
LIAR  WASTE  NUDE
EVIL  ALTAR  EPEE
CARY  YEARS  REND
```

PUZZLE 121

1. Stage, 2. Spare, 3. Swine, 4. Spite,
5. Smile, 6. Spode.

PUZZLE 122

```
TOPS  CAUSE  COWL
ALEE  ALLEN  AMIE
TERN  REARS  MELT
SOUTHERNACCENT
    EAST  OUR
STINTS  TENTACLE
PENCE  LANCE  LEA
EPEE  DIXIE  PEAT
EER  SOLID  BRAVE
DETRACTS  SOONER
    ANT  SCOP
SONGOFTHESOUTH
PANG  ROMAN  SNEE
RICE  EXERT  ADAR
ODER  DYNES  LORE
```

PUZZLE 123

JUDY GARLAND

PUZZLE 124

```
POMP  STOWE  JADE
ADAR  HARRY  OTIS
COMA  OXEYE  UTES
TRANQUIL  GYRATE
    CUL  ALAN
UNREADY  TAKEOFF
DAIRY  EATS  YULE
DIP  BASIS  NOR
EVEN  ORAL  OSCAR
RENEWAL  ANXIETY
    ROSY  EEN
TRIVET  THANKFUL
AERO  FUROR  SIRE
LIEU  USUAL  OLGA
ENDS  LEERY  REEF
```

PUZZLE 125

Families are forever.

PUZZLE 126

```
REWARD JIB AMY ELGIN
ELIXIR AVA KLEE FARCE
ALLEGE MARRIERS FREED
MELD ADEN ETAL LUGE
ERI AMOS CDT ERASERS
RYANS DEVISE GENE MOM
MOP GREATNIECES ALE
RABI PEWS ASTOR ERIN
ODAS EDITOR ORIGAMI
WEBERN NEW GEEGEES
SEE ASPREE TRESOR COW
PRIMERO RAS DANUBE
UNSEAMS VACATE OREL
ACTA IMAGO INES BIRD
DAH FIREBRIGADE OLE
ORB EMIL OCELOT DEGAS
PERDIEM LET BETE ANT
NEON AMIR MERE ARGO
RADAR ASSESSOR SENSOR
EVITA BOER IDO LENORE
TEXAS END PEN ARENAS
```

PUZZLE 130

```
ABATE SAGA SPAS
BAGEL ICON HUNT
BREAKFRONT ARCA
ADS LIRE ARGON
CHOU IMPEND
ISSUE SHARES
LEARNS ODIN POE
LAMB TUNES IOTA
STA PAVO HEROIC
BOMARC MARCH
ESCARP OPUS
SMACK CLUE SHE
KINK SHOPLIFTER
ALOE REAL FEARS
REED ORFE SENSE
```

PUZZLE 135

```
LURCH SHEAF SIFT
AGE ERROR NAVAL
SHEAR BORES CORES
PEST TIMER
ALARM LOOKED PRESENT
PACE ADDRESSES SOAP
ADJOIN SEAS RED
KINGS NEST
DING TEAL DEEPER
ANGEL ELBA PEEL
TESTY DENSE RARE
```

PUZZLE 131

1. hoLly, 2. spLat, 3. haLve, 4. muLch, 5. unLit, 6. deLft, 7. soLar, 8. saLve, 9. tiLed, 10. spLit.

PUZZLE 136

WOLFGANG AMADEUS MOZART

PUZZLE 127

```
ABCS BABES RIMS
SEAT ADORN ERIE
ELSE NOOSE MOLE
ATTEST REASONED
LEAP KAT
STREAMER EVERTS
CHARM TERRE HOE
ARTS TACOS POKE
NEE SALAD RIDER
SESTET PELICANS
RAT OAST
RECALLED SKULLS
ADAM EXIST ROOT
SNAP RINSE ERNE
PANS STEED DEEP
```

PUZZLE 128

A. 1. Puma, 2. Upon, 3. Mole, 4. Anew.
B. 1. This, 2. Hunt, 3. Inca, 4. Stag.

PUZZLE 132

```
TWOS MAID MER
OATH ANNA ERE
SLOOPJOHN RIA
STEREO ANTHEM
TAR LERO
BLISS MERINOS
ION FAD DUE
GUMSHOE SCARE
YEAR BAR
TYRANT ERUPTS
WOO SURFINUSA
AGO ONEI CRAM
SAM MEET HERE
```

PUZZLE 133

```
NTH WELD EAT
ARE IDEA UNDO
SUSANSARANDON
HEARD MISSY
MOB OAT
RAT WITCHESOF
ESAU TAT DUNE
SKIPPERED NEW
DES TON
AGAIN NIECE
JACKNICHOLSON
AMIE CHER PTO
RED EARS YES
```

PUZZLE 137

```
ROSES COWED PAW
ALAMO AGILE CHORE
GENUS BILLYTHEKID
EAT OLIVE EASEL
DNAS INE SHEDS
FILES TAU REAMS
ENID BRONCO PAP
STEP LEA TIN AMA
CARS RANCHES SCAR
LOA SOS TAR RAHS
UNI PISTOL MOLE
BELLI EAR PATTI
ORANT LAS SNAP
TITAN SOTTO DCI
FORTLARAMIE CAIRN
ARIES ADORN AWAIT
DOS PAGET SENDS
```

PUZZLE 138

```
STOP TAMPS ICED
LONE AWAIT RAVE
OUTS PARTY OMEN
BROTHERS INERT
ERE FOCI
SHEARS AVOCADO
HORSE RAVEN PIN
AMOK RIGOR ARTS
RED HOVER ELITE
PRESIDE BALLOT
ERST BAR
SPREE BARNACLE
ERAS ATOLL CLAD
TOGA DOWSE EAVE
SPEW DELAY SWAN
```

PUZZLE 129

```
LEAP CUTE TIRO SLAW
ALLA OBEY IDEA CUBA
BLACKBOARD BLACKWATER
ANKARA EAGLES OREL
ELATE GAUR SIMA
OMBRE ANGIE SCRABBLE
PALS STEEL BARON LUR
ENA SPEAR HELEN HALO
ROC SPORT MATTE HOCUS
ARK TROY SASSY PORK
BREAK MARTY HARSH
EERY MALTA CEPA EOS
SHANE LIRAS BARAS AVA
POUT SOLID ARROW ROT
ANT KOREA SPEED ATLI
REYNOLDS FALLS ARSON
APES SINO START
ESNE SALOME ANTERO
BLACKHILLS BLACKSMITH
ALLY ARES ARIL IDES
DEES SADA MATE SEAT
```

PUZZLE 134

```
RATE CLOSE APER
LEVER HAVEN BORES
CAPONE ENACT LOAVES
UPON CREE ORDER EVE
RES STIR SNEER TREE
ELECTED SUDAN BOERS
LAD CARAT DER
SPEAR BAKER REROUTE
LEND CORE YOUNGSTER
ANT BURG PITS TAR
SCENARIOS PENS PESO
HERETIC PEONS RARER
WEE RIDES MAN
PARED MERIT FANTASY
OWER REFIT MINT THE
LAW PILOT BARA WHOA
ORATES RURAL GREETS
DRONE MAINE EARNS
DOTS SLOGS SPES
```

PUZZLE 139

Canary, Cuckoo, Falcon, Grouse, Magpie, Oriole, Parrot, Pigeon, Toucan, Turkey.

PUZZLE 140

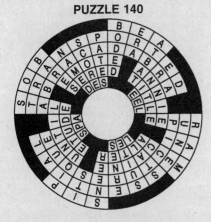

PUZZLE 141

```
OCEAN SLOB  PAIR
PIECE HIDE  RISE
TARTS ENDS  IDLE
SOY   THEE  INDEED
      SLAT  DUE
MALLET DEEM  AND
ARIAS  SEA   BELOW
CELT   TAR   LIVE
ANTED  ALL   RIVAL
WAS    OARS  DETEST
       ELF   ROLE
CLOVER BETA  SET
RAVE   ICON  TRADE
EVER   COLD  EATEN
WARY   ADDS  SPEND
```

PUZZLE 142

1. The bigger they come the harder they fall.
2. Half a loaf is better than no time off at all.

PUZZLE 143

```
ASK        SLIP
SEAT       TEALS
ANTI       RENAME
   DETOUR  NIX
      HIM  DELE
CAMEL   MOSES
ALIS    DAN
STS     MARKET
SETTER  ERAS
REESE   YORE
READ    SAW
```

PUZZLE 144

```
ANTE   BOW  DIGS
VAIN   ADE  IDEA
EVER   RED  FLAG
RESORT   DEFERS
LIE    ERE
TAILOR   DARTED
OWN         AGE
TENDER   BORROW
ROE      APE
BELONG   STARED
AVOW   ELK  CAPE
RIGS   NEE  TREE
SLOE   TAT  SEED
```

PUZZLE 145

```
SEA      HEP
POLL     FAVOR
OUST     AGILE
DREAMS   LIVE
     RICH   CUR
DEB    LIE  YEN
OLE    KNIT
MILE     ARREST
  TOAST   ACHE
  ENSUE   SHUN
   GEM    HOT
```

PUZZLE 146

```
ASSET  IRE  GAB
SALVO  NEE  UTE
PLAID  CALMEST
  CLAMOR   USES
OAK   YAM   ASSAY
AGES  JESSE
FOREGO   CHUMPS
  CARGO    MARE
CAROL  AUK  NOW
AVON     ERRAND
LOWDOWN  ROARS
LIE   WEE  ESTOP
ADD   ERR  NEEDY
```

PUZZLE 147

```
OLD   ABUTS  TSAR
WORK  RESET  RICO
EDEN  BLEND  ODES
SIDEBOARD    APERS
    EERY     ELIS
LISLE    SIDECAR
ARIES  SWAG  DIN
TODD   STAGE EDDA
ENE    TARO  SALEP
   SIDEARM  AGERS
   SWAB     IDLE
LASER    SIDETRACK
ELUL   PATEN  LVII
NOEL   IDEAS  YANK
SESS   PERLE  LEI
```

PUZZLE 148

```
G  RUGGED  URGED  RUDE  G
A  PARADE  DRAPE  APED  R
R  ARREST  STARE  REST  A
N  ISLAND  DIALS  LADS  I
E  DANGER  GRAND  DRAG  N
R  SCRAPE  SPACE  CAPE  S
```

PUZZLE 149

```
BARS   STES  NEPAL
ABEE   TRET  ORATE
LEAR   AIRE  ANDTO
ILLFOLLOWTHESUN
        MEL   ASS
PASHA   SCAR  TRAP
ASPENS  ANTS  ALE
SKYWITHDIAMONDS
SER   SEAR  REHEAT
EDIT  LYES  LOESS
       OIL   PAT
GOODDAYSUNSHINE
EXUDE  SAND  AREA
TESLA  ELKE  ROOT
SNEES  RAYS  INNS
```

PUZZLE 150

IN THE BATHROOM: 1. Tub, 2. Soap, 3. Cloth, 4. Mat, 5. Brush, 6. Towel, 7. Water.

PUZZLE 151

```
FLED   FLOP   FAN
LOVE   PLANE  SAVE
ODES   LINEN  AREA
OGRE   ARA    ALERT
DETRACT   CANE
    VIE  ROPY  BAN
MOWED  GIVE  ACE
AGE    EARNEST IRE
ILL    LIST   ACTED
LED    DUPE   SIR
   FUME   RELAPSE
CHORE   WIN   CRAM
HAVE   YARDS  KITE
ALEE   ADAGE  LEER
TON    MOPE   EDDY
```

PUZZLE 152

1. Ease/Because, 2. Sear/Sneaker, 3. Pile/Reptile, 4. Lion/Clarion, 5. Bush/Bulrush, 6. Brad/Bravado, 7. Sour/Sojourn, 8. Rang/Wrangle, 9. Vary/Variety, 10. Need/Annexed.

PUZZLE 153

```
COLD   RARE   ASH
ALOUD  AVOW   SHOO
LINER  PILE   HERO
FOG    ELIDE  BOARD
   SAID      TARDY
  PLUMP   BLAST
DOOR   SLATE  DIG
ALOFT  PUN    SHARE
MET    AWARD  ATOM
   SPORT    RAVEN
   LINEN    HUGE
MANOR  SHINE  EVE
ONER   FOUR   NAVAL
ACRE   ISLE   TRESS
NET    BOLD   KNEE
```

PUZZLE 154

OUT: 1. Bush, 3. Turtle, 5. Vary, 7. Alert, 9. Saps, 11. Sorcerer, 13. Fare.
IN: 14. Era, 13. Frere, 12. Cross, 10. Past, 8. Relay, 6. Ravel, 4. Truth, 2. Sub.

PUZZLE 155

```
CALLS  MEW   BEAST
AXIAL  AGE   ERROR
SLOPE  SOL   SNIDE
HENPECK     TUESDAY
    EKE    PERT
FAST   LEARN  AQUA
EVE    STAR   FLUNG
NORSE  RAY    ELATE
CIVET  GALE   KIN
EDEN   AROMA  PELT
   SPIN     TAR
HATCHET    JEWELER
ALOHA  UTE   AWARE
FORUM  AWE   RAMIE
TEEMS  LOP   DRANK
```

PUZZLE 156

1. Underpay, 2. Baseless, 3. Flashing, 4. Jamboree.

PUZZLE 157

```
LAPS  SLATS   SLED
OBOE  PIVOT   LODE
FLOE  ENEMY   URGE
TERRACE    ORDER
      MINERALS
SESAME  LAND  FIG
HALLO  LEST   SIDE
ERAS  ROMPS   TEEN
ALTO  ICES   LUNAR
RYE   SPAN  WADDLE
      SHELTERS
ABATE     RESULTS
COLA  GALES   REAP
ROAR  ELECT   NAME
ERST  MEETS   SKEW
```

PUZZLE 158

T	TARGET	GRATE	TEAR	G
W	WANGLE	ANGEL	GLEN	A
O	COARSE	SCARE	CASE	R
C	ASPECT	PASTE	PEST	A
A	MIRAGE	GRIME	EMIR	G
R	SEARCH	CHASE	CASH	E

PUZZLE 159

```
FO RTY    NON E S    PU RES T
R EA R     SEN AT OR   BL U E
MER CH AN DI SE   EST ABL ISH ME NT
      NIC E            O ER
RA DIC AL    BO RE D OM     O VEN
IN K          E D ICT      PER T
BOW ER     VE R S ION     ME AS URE
       BA RD       FI ND
RES TAU R ANT S    EXP END  I TU RE
TI GH TER    C HO OSE    CAN N ED
VE T S       AB USE D     T IC S
```

PUZZLE 160

1. Poke, 2. Heap, 3. Oily, 4. Trek, 5. Omit, 6. Gods, 7. Roof, 8. Also, 9. Pact, 10. Hood, 11. Espy, 12. Reel.
OUTER RING: Photographer
THIRD RING: Kaleidoscope

PUZZLE 161

```
ODD  COLD    NOW
WOE  ALEE   NOVA
ETC  REEF   ONER
REESE    LONERS
    NOR  GAMES
ANTS  DATA   STY
PER  METER   EWE
TEA  UTES   ENOS
    LOSES  SAT
SLIDER     TRIAL
LAZE  ROLE   ARE
ICES  ERIE   LEA
TED   DEER   SAP
```

PUZZLE 162

```
ART  BEAD   POLL
SEA  RELY   AREA
EAR  ELSE   LEAD
AROMA  ORAL
     ATE  SLIDER
FARTHER   ADORE
AVA   NET    LIE
SETTO  SIGHTED
TRAILS  PRE
     EDEN  ARENA
ARID  DINT   VOW
SEMI  ALEE   ENE
SPAN  NEED   NOD
```

PUZZLE 163

```
SKIS  MACE   BORA
COST  ORAL  DELON
ARLO  BALI  UNLIT
LEAN  CLYDESDALE
PAMELA  PELT
     HOPES  MYRTLE
BASEL  POME  EWER
EMANATE  EROSION
DING  HEAT  TENSE
ENDEAR  MESTA
     LEDA  NORMAN
FUZZYWUZZY  CORE
ISAAC  FOOD  HOOP
SENNE  ANNE  ERMA
TREY  YSER  SEAL
```

PUZZLE 164

TV SHOW HOSTS: Moore, Adams, Rayburn, Carson, Hartman.
TOOLS: Monkey wrench, Awl, Rammer, Crowbar, Header.
ANIMALS: Muskrat, Addax, Raccoon, Cougar, Hamster.
SENATORS: Mansfield, Allen, Roth, Case, Hatfield.
RIVERS: Mississippi, Allegheny, Red, Columbia, Hudson.

PUZZLE 165

```
IMPS  PACT   PTA
LEAP  ARLO   OIL
SALA  DEADLINE
ALEC  DADDY
     EGO  YOLKS
RAT  ACHE   NEAT
ELO  SKIMP   ALA
EDAM  STIR   KEY
FADED   SOS
     MIMES  CAKE
SAYONARA   ORAL
ICE  EMIR   RITA
PEN  DENY   EDEN
```

PUZZLE 166

```
COPE  SCAN   AGE
APEX  CEDE   BEN
SERE  ENDORSED
ENTRANT    NOT
    TREES   TROT
ARCED  RAT   ALE
SELDOM  DANCER
ENE   RIP  BATON
ADAM  DONOR
    RAM  REORDER
INITIATE   ARIA
CON  CLAD   TARP
EGG  ALLY   EWES
```

PUZZLE 167

```
CLAP  BLASS   POLE
HAIR  RANEE   OMIT
ACRE  ASTIR   PARA
RESPECT    NATURAL
     AWE  REPEL
UMBRELLA  ENABLE
TORE  EON    TREED
TIE  STOGIES  GAG
ERASE   ERA   POSE
REDCAP  RESPITES
     ATOMS  TAR
RECLOSE  PENANCE
ARID  SAPOR   TARA
MITE  ENROL  EVER
SEED  STORY   SEWS
```

PUZZLE 168

1. Fruit bowl, 2. Hairstyle

PUZZLE 169

```
AWE  PASS    RENT
LAX  ALOHA  RUMOR
TIP  RADAR  ASIDE
EVER  SAFE  VERSE
RELIC  STALE
    POD   ALLEGE
ORT  DEFEAT  IDEA
DOER  SUAVE  DENS
OLEO  INTEND  NEE
RENDER    TIE
     LEASE  MALES
CHILI  LENS  RAMP
LACED  MANIA  YEA
ATONE  STUNS  ERR
DENT   SIKH   RYE
```

PUZZLE 170

1. Ankle, 2. Blink, 3. Noble, 4. Blend, 5. Skill, 6. Alike, 7. Solid, 8. Linen, 9. Bless, 10. Sable.

PUZZLE 171

```
SPARS  PASTA
HABIT  ACTOR
ARENA  SHAPE
    GRATER
RECORD    TEA
IWO  YES   LAD
GEM   PETERS
    PESTER
CRATE   SORRY
BARON   AVOID
SPEND   WEEDS
```

PUZZLE 172

```
WEB  CHEF   METE
OAR  IOWA   ICED
WRIGGLED   DRAG
    GLAD  PAUSE
USHER   ALI
TOTE  PANORAMA
ALE  TAPED   VAN
HONEYDEW  LINT
    UPS   LEASE
SPIRE   FIST
ALTO  MEALTIME
PEEP  ARIA   OAK
SAME  TALC   NEE
```

PUZZLE 173

```
BEAN  RIVAL   DARE
OSLO  ONICE  ELIS
USER  WASHINGTON
TEETH  NAE  ORATE
     HONES  DIE
SLEEPER  ARRESTS
TURRET  TREE   TOT
INAN  THETA  BONA
LAS  SLID  MEANER
TREATED  TEASERS
     SAD  PURSE
AMATI  ERR  EBERT
DETENTIONS  AVER
AMOR  ANVIL  LODE
SOPS  WEEPY  LEST
```

PUZZLE 174

Though money does not go as far as it did, it certainly goes much faster.

PUZZLE 175

```
B O S C   E S S E N   W A A C
L A I R   A L I V E   E N N A
O T T O   R A N E E   E G O S
T H E M U L B E R R Y B U S H
      W A Y S       O I S E
S T E E R       G A M U T
W A L L   S A I L O R   S P A
I M A L I T T L E T E A P O T
M E N   R I L L E S   L I N E
      T A R E S   F A T E S
      L O O T   U S E D
F A R M E R I N T H E D E L L
A I D A   E N A T E   I D E A
S T E T   A R M E D   N E S T
T Y R O   L E E R S   S N E E
```

PUZZLE 176

1. Other, 2. Reason, 3. Glance, 4. Builder, 5. Hypnotism.

PUZZLE 177

```
L A M   S T I R       C P A
I D A   P U R E   S H A M
S A D D E N E D   T A R O
T R A I N   D E A R E R
      M E T   P E A R L
S T E M   D I N S   E A R
P O D   M O N E T   S H E
A Y E   A G E D   A D A M
      F A N G S   E L A
T R A L E E   C O R E A
H A R E   R E C O U N T S
I N G E   E V I L   A T E
S T E   L A D E   Y E A
```

PUZZLE 178

```
A D S   L O T S   T H E N
B E E   A L A I   R A G E
B A W L B A L L   U R G E
E R N I E   C L O S E
      S L Y   E T H E R
L I F T   E W E R   A S A
A D E S   A I R   S I N K
S E E   E R G S   C R E E
T A T E R   T A R
      F A R E S   D U N C E
D E E R   B A R E B E A R
A L A N   B L I P   A N I
B A T S   S T A T   T E E
```

PUZZLE 179

```
G O L F   T A M P   A B B A
L I A R   R I S E R   R O A D
A L T I T U D I N O U S A N D
D Y E   A S E A   S N O R E S
      F R E D   S P I N
S P R I G S   S T E T   O L E
A L O N E   A M O R   U R A L
L A T I T U D I N O U S A N D
E N O S   N O T E   B I N G E
S E R   W I R E   R A N G E R
      D I V E   S I N G
A C C U S E   S M O G   H O E
P U L C H R I T U D I N O U S
E R I K   S A U T E   E R R S
D E P S   E N D S   E A S E
```

PUZZLE 180

1. Senate, 2. Deputy, 3. Decree, 4. Leader, 5. Govern, 6. Record, 7. Recess, 8. Report, 9. Treaty, 10. Regime.

PUZZLE 181

```
WE SKI T    PA V ED    SU CH
A PP ROV AL    T AN GY    PER IL
VE ER E D    CH ILL    REF IN E
      ER UPT    A ST U TE
FL EX    OW LET    A GEN D A
O PEN    GE N T LE MEN    EN D
UR S IN E    ER ASE    T ORN
   I N SE T    D OPE
LO V ING    ANG LE    RA PI DS
G EL    SH EL VE    TOR N AD O
IC Y    ARD OR    T O UR
```

PUZZLE 182

NECKWEAR: Scarf, Muffler, Ascot, Ruff, Tie.

SEATS: Stool, Morris chair, Armchair, Rocker, Throne.

TIMEPIECES: Sundial, Metronome, Alarm clock, Repeater, Timer.

CONDIMENTS: Salsa, Mustard, Aioli, Relish, Tabasco.

COUNTRIES: Spain, Mexico, Australia, Russia, Thailand.

PUZZLE 183

```
R E A P   P O D   S L A W
A L T A   I R E   L O V E
N A I L   R A P   O D E R
I M P A L A   E M P I R E
      C O T   N I P
D E L E T E   D A Y T O N
A V E       E R A
Y E S S I R   S I D N E Y
      I R A   A T E
F L A S K S   D E C I D E
R A N T   H A D   A R E S
E R N E   E W E   D O N T
T I E R   R A N   E N T E
```

PUZZLE 184

```
G A S   S T A Y   C L E F
A P T   H A L E   H O L E
G E E   I L L A T E A S E
      P A N E   W A D E
G L O R Y   C L A P
A U N T   S H I N   G I N
S K I   S T U N G   O D E
P E T   H A R E   S T O W
      F E R N   F O O L S
L O L L   L I N T
M A K E F U N O F   O D D
A C R E   S O R T   W O O
N E A T   E D D Y   N E T
```

PUZZLE 185

```
E L L   S P A S   E L O P E
T R A Y   P I T H   R O V E S
U R G E   A L O E   O V E R T
B E E   D E P E N D E N T
D R I V E   N E E
      N E S T S   A D D E D
P R O S E   E W E R   A D A M
P A R E   H E E L S   R I L E
S T A R   O N E S   U N T I L
A L T E R   T E A S E
      R A W   R A D A R
R E F A S H I O N   N O D
C O R E S   E D I E   T O T E
A L I N E   E E L S   I D O L
D E E D S   L A S S   P E R
```

PUZZLE 186

OUT: 1. Rapt, 3. Carts, 4. Baleen, 6. Kerosene, 8. Gannet, 9. Nap, 11. Mar.
IN: 12. Ramp, 10. Antenna, 8. Genes, 7. Ore, 6. Kneel, 5. Abstract, 2. Par.

PUZZLE 187

```
C R A M   G A M E R   J A V A
R E P O   A G A P E   A W E D
O D I N   R E G I S   W A N D
C O N T R A D I C T S   S U E
      H O G   R U S H E R
T A T   G E L   S O R T
E L O P E   A L T O   O T I S
C O M E T O T E R M S W I T H
H U E D   P I T A   T E N S E
      A M E N   W A R   T A D
F A L L I N   T I S
O D E   D I S P U T A T I O N
N E A R   N O I S E   I N G A
D A D E   G U L E S   C O R M
A L S O   S L E E T   K N E E
```

PUZZLE 188

1. Delicate, 2. Reliable, 3. Domicile, 4. Recanted, 5. Regiment, 6. Magician, 7. Shadowed, 8. Cashmere, 9. Remarked.

PUZZLE 189

```
KARL ROLE MIG
ELIA EPOS ORE
RANT VENT DAM
NIGHTINGALE
    EASES ERGO
SIR LED TEALS
ERODES PORTAL
ROBES PAN EDO
ANIL PARIS
NIGHTSCHOOL
ADS ROTO OGRE
COO ANON PLAT
TEN YENS SENT
```

PUZZLE 190

```
CAB ERAS CAD
ALA VAST AIRY
RUM APER BRIE
EMBED ARECAS
OWED TUTU
ALOE IRAN MAT
FEZ OSAGE VIE
TIL OSTE SELL
ERNE MEAN
TAMTAM NOTES
OGEE BRAT IRA
PENS LACE OIL
SET EWER NET
```

PUZZLE 191

```
PAGER ALEC MALE
ALINE LARA AMAS
CANDYISDANDYBUT
ESAU SOY ASIDE
RAM ASI
LEVER OGDENNASH
EVE CARROT AUTO
AILE DIANA TROT
STAN METIER AWE
HARDLINES CREEL
ITT SAO
CHARM IST SAGA
LIQUORISQUICKER
ARUM ORLY NOISE
NEAP WEED CENTS
```

PUZZLE 192

1.
```
1 2 4 6
7 3 1 5
9 2 4 8 1
3 4 1 2 7
6 6 2 1 2
```
27

2.
```
7 1 4 6 3
9 2 1 5 8
4 6 1 7
5 2 4 9 3
5 4 8 1 1
```
49

PUZZLE 193

```
DEBIT MAPS PEPE
ARETE ARAT IVAN
MISSMARPLE REST
ENS PRISM CARTE
BETA MATTER
EDGARS UTILE
TALKS TSAR SUFI
ALEE TAHOE GROT
LEER ETES BOGUS
STEER ELLERY
DANTON FEUD
EVORA SNARE ALA
LIRE THEGOLDBUG
LOGE RANI ARENA
ANET AMEN WYLER
```

PUZZLE 194

There was an old soldier of Bister
Went walking one day with his sister,
    When a cow at one poke
    Tossed her into an oak
Before the old gentleman missed her.

PUZZLE 195

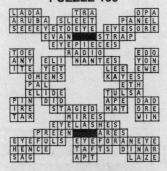

PUZZLE 196

```
HOPI BACKS ALOE
ARAN ABONE BELA
HART NOWORNEVER
ALLERGY CAUTION
IRES SKIRT
STAIR KEW LORAN
COMMUNIQUE REDO
AXE NATURAL MAT
LINT GHOSTIMAGE
ANTED AIT BARED
ARENA TREK
EMERALD SHOWAND
KISSMEKATE EBER
ENTO MITER SLOE
DEAN INANE TEND
```

PUZZLE 197

```
  LOP
ELIDE
RIVET
APE
```

PUZZLE 198

PUZZLE 199

1. Storage, 2. Heroism, 3. Juniper, 4. Aviator, 5. Qualify.

PUZZLE 200

PUZZLE 201

```
BATT AHAS LAIC LASH
OLEO VOLT UNTO ARLO
STAG ELLINGTON SMOG
HAGGARD NYES TASSES
ALMS AGES RELIT
BARES STET DESSERTS
ENDS POOR PINTO ORE
ENE CLAM WANDS KNEE
PANTHER SORES WAGER
AAA SHUTS TAN
MAJOR ENOLS BANTAMS
ARES CROWD SERE NIT
TIL BARON ROSE PISA
HALTERED PEST BETTY
YIELD ALTO RONA
EGRESS ALOU SEASONS
DOOR BUDDYRICH IDOL
ABLE ASEA NCAA VANE
MILD DENS SERB EYED
```

PUZZLE 202

```
SHASTA STAIR BEST
PEPPER TARDE EARWIG
SOWHATABOUTIT TRAINER
TROIS BOK YOUWANTMETO
URNS PIPER TRAPS WASP
KAT GRASSED NNE DIRTY
ANEURIN UNITED FATSO
ARAM OPENED SIGH
LATENESS WEE GALAHAD
ORA TRUMPED JAM NITER
LILT ANOLD DIMAG MLLE
ALOHA SNY SIBERIA AID
STAINED BEN SARGASSO
TROT TAMEST DIST
DAWES AWHITE SELKIRK
REBID FLO STATURE TEA
EVEL GEESE EMIRS TSAR
DOLLAREXTRA INF PABLO
STABBED ONMILKALLWEEK
ERECTS RIODE CEASES
DADA YESES EXTENT
```

PUZZLE 203

```
BAH HATS BEA PATS
ANET OMIT MAIL ALEE
NORA RIFE ARNO TORE
DANTES FRANKENSTEIN
ASTER ERN GEE
RAN TAIL KEPT ARTES
END ANDES ROOD ROT
ATOM DEVIL TART ENE
LEDA BRIDES DEW ASP
ECRU SEVER SOUS
GAS EGG SERINS SUMS
ADO EGOS RULED ERIN
PIT YEAS MERES ETE
STORE SPIT DOSE ITE
OLD LES SITES
DOUBLEAGENTS GALLEY
ERLE GRAN ALAN LARA
ALAR ALIT NOTE ANIL
LENT SON DEER DEE
```

PUZZLE 204

```
NETS SWAP DRUG ACRE
ERAT HOMER ARENA COOS
WIRETOWIRE RIDINGCROP
SEAROVER VAMPS GREEDY
NEED SILAS SOS
UPPED PAVED STASHES
NAHS STEVECAUTHEN AXE
SPOT CREE BEER ONCE
EAT HORSESHOE ORDER
TWOSTEPS ANOA AVAILS
FLAME STOUT FRANC
TRIODE HEWS TALLTALE
HUNTS HORSERACE POD
ELIS SHEA AMEN SPIN
DES STARTINGGATE HERA
ASHAMED RARER MORES
LEE ROPED APER
REFILL RANEE OVERTURE
STABLEMATE TIMEKEEPER
TERI ROTOR SNARE STAG
USES SEEN ARTS TODO
```

528

PUZZLE 205

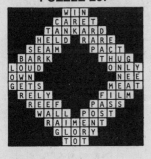

```
A R C       W A S P
R O O M   C E R E A L
M A M A   U N I Q U E
  D E S E R T   U S E
    C A B   B E E R
B O O T   B A L D
P A R T     E A R
E R N   H A R B O R
E R A S E R   E D E N
R E T U R N   R O N A
  L E N D       R O B
```

PUZZLE 206

```
  T U B
S O L A R         P I N
E X T R A       O D O R
A I R   N O W   D I V A
C A R   M A D     O A T
    O B E D I E N T
      P A L   L E E
    G E N E R A L S
F A R     T O T   T A D
E M I T     Y E N   F E N
W I P E       A L I B I
  D E N       P E R I L
                G E T
```

PUZZLE 207

```
        W I N
      C A R E T
    T A N K A R D
    H E L D   R A R E
  S E A M     P A C T
B A R K         T H U G
L O U D         O N L Y
O W N             N E E
G E T S         M E A T
R E L Y         F I L M
  R E E F       P A S S
  W A L L   P O S T
    R A I M E N T
      G L O R Y
        T O T
```

PUZZLE 208

1. Patronized, 2. Thermos jug, 3. Any old time.

PUZZLE 209

```
    H U B     O F F
  M O R A L   A L I
L A U G H A T   K I S S
E L S E   C A P   T H A T
G E E   K N O B   S L Y
        K I T   T I P
  N A P   L E T A L O N E
C E L L   M A R   S I R E
G I V E A W A Y   K E Y
A T E   N A G
S I R     R I N D   A R M
H E M P   C A R   O B O E
  S I L L   B I G S H O T
  N A Y     P I L O T
  D Y E       N O R
```

PUZZLE 210

1. Well, Dell, Doll, Dole, Done.
2. Fore, Fork, Cork, Cock, Lock.
3. Good, Wood, Word, Worn, Torn, Turn.
4. Last, Cast, Cart, Wart, Ward, Word.

PUZZLE 211

```
P A L M   F E N     W E B
  A R I A   L O U D   H A Y
G A S K E T   A N T I D O T E
L I T   N E S T   M U D
A D E     S I T   D U T Y
D E L A Y   M E N   N E E
    D E S I R E S   I N N
    H O T E L   C O M E T
Y O U   W A L K W A Y
A I M     R O T   P E D A L
P L A N   T I P   E K E
  N I B   T E A L   F I N
F L E X I B L E   P O T E N T
E E L   D O O R   E V E N
D A Y   B O Y   R E A D
```

PUZZLE 212

1. Clustering, 2. Silk thread, 3. Motherland.

PUZZLE 213

```
W E B
A C E S
S H A P E           S P A
  O C E A N       S H A D
  H A R E M     T E A S E
  K N E A D     E A R S
    D I E   D E S K
    A L L U D E S
  G A L E   C A N
  C A M P   E N T E R
M O V E S   E A T E N
O P E N     L O G E S
M E L       N A V A L
            L E N A
            R E D
```

PUZZLE 214

Silence and modesty are valuable qualities in conversation.

1. Equality, 2. Sconces, 3. Nation, 4. Adverb, 5. Various, 6. Elemental, 7. Sailed in.

PUZZLE 215

```
S T U B     B R A G
N O V A   P O I S E D
A D E N   G A N G S T E R
G O A T   A R I D   S L O W
    E L T O N     A L E
    R A T S       Y E T
    W I S P
    C E L L O
      Y A L E
A R C       G I V E
N I L     C O V E N
A L A S   S L O E   D A N A
E M I S S I O N   U P O N
  P L I A N T   R E N O
  O P T S       E D E N
```

PUZZLE 216

1. Sympathize, 2. Defrosting, 3. Light cream.

PUZZLE 217

```
    F U R       C O P
    H E R O     A M O R
    P O R G Y   S P A R E
    D U N N E   H I N T S
E R N E S       S O T
R A G S       P L E A T
A P E     G E E   L U G
E N D     R A P     B O Y
T A G   A C T       S E E
  M A R C H       S L A M
    R U E       S T I R S
I R O N S       S H U N S
C A D E T       A L O N G
E V E R       R I O T
E S S         A P T
```

PUZZLE 218

No man has a right to do as he pleases unless he pleases to do right.

1. Sharpeners, 2. Highest, 3. Student, 4. Lemonade, 5. Spools, 6. Aloha, 7. Stogies, 8. Aha.

PUZZLE 219

```
          B E E
          S O A R
L E S S   P L A C I D
O R A L   H E A R H E A R
G A L E   E A T     M I D
    T E A R     C A F E
    T I M I D   O G L E
C A R T   R I D E R   W E E P
O L E O   T O T A L
S I G N     E P I C
T A R     S O S   G L A D
S E E A B O U T   H U L A
    T A L E N T   T E E M
    S T A G
    T O T
```

PUZZLE 220

1. Half crowns, 2. Manuscript, 3. Subheading.

PUZZLE 221

```
            S A G
    M O B   R I S E
    A P E   O N S E T
    R E N T   B E G   A P T
F I N   O W E     P E A
O N E   L O T     P I T
R E D   D O T     L O G
          L E S     O D E
P A R     R O D     R O T
A T E       D I P
L O S       N E T   D E N
M U D       N E O   A V A
L O W       E L L   R A P
T E A     H E R   L A N D
    C A M E L     L E E
    W A L K       A D D
    E N D
```

PUZZLE 222

1. Lose, Lone, Line, Fine, Find.
2. Read, Bead, Beat, Boat, Boot, Book.
3. Work, Word, Wood, Good, Goad, Goal.
4. Tree, Free, Fret, Feet, Beet, Beat, Bead, Lead, Leaf.

PUZZLE 223

```
CALL
OLIO        WATT
WALDO       ELIA
ARSON   ALGERIA
LST     UCA   DONE
LEAP   FROE  YUCCA
  RECLAIM     ERS
  TRANCE    ISUP
  RAYS      MITT
AGOG     CHOLER
NIL      LINEMAN
DREAM  FELT   LUCK
 DUDE  RAT     GAL
 MOTIONS    ARGUE
 ERNS       GEESE
 RATE       ANTE
            ROSS
```

PUZZLE 227

```
            PIE
  WIT     EARL
  ONE     TRAMP
  OLEO  SAT    ASP
ELA   RAT     LEO
YEN   ERE     ALE
END   SEE     APT
      ADE     NEE
HAD   SAD     DEN
AVE   RED
MOB       BAG  PAT
WAS       UTE  EGO
SOY       TAM  TRY
EWE   ELS  SURE
    SLIDE     FEE
    ACID      OLD
    WET
```

PUZZLE 228

1. Apace, Space, Spare, Share, Shore, Short.
2. Creel, Creek, Cheek, Check, Chock, Shock.
3. Cling, Clink, Click, Slick, Slack, Shack.
4. Least, Lease, Cease, Chase, Chose, Chore.

PUZZLE 229

```
BESOM
RIETI      HERA
UNTIL      PANAMA
TEASES  ELATER
        MILESTONE
ALAR   ENDS
DROP
TRUK
REPEAL      BAMA
AMERCE  TOLLAGES
MISSISASGOODASAMILE
   DEPARTED  SLIVER
   ORES      EASING
            SETS
           AMID
   ASEA  ELAN
   MISSAYING
   METTLE   SLICER
   OPERAS   INURE
   IRON     NORIA
            KNEED
```

PUZZLE 224

6	7	4	5
3	3	3	6
5	2	8	7
1	5	4	8

PUZZLE 225

```
   GET
   PAVE  TOW
   SEVER  AVE    ARM
   FLEE  MOVED  LEA
PIER  SIREN   SAND
ARE   LATER  ACME
REPTILE  NARROW
   AVA    BOA
TUXEDO  POMPOUS
ONES  RHODA  IRE
SKID  CAUSE  OLGA
PET  WANTS  EPEE
ANY   EGG  ENDED
   TEE   SEEN
       SEN
```

PUZZLE 226

Worry is interest paid on trouble before it is due.

1. Dares, 2. Lei, 3. Trousers, 4. Wife, 5. Rein, 6. Point, 7. Tire, 8. Boy, 9. Doubt.

PUZZLE 230

```
               CUB
     LAP       USA
     ARE       RED
  SHRIMP    SAFE
  HOUR      LIE
  ONE       ALL
  BEE     PAT  TOP
BRA    HOP      WIG
OAR   TRITE    NEE
BIG   EAT      ERE
NEW  BEG      FUR
  ICE        SIP
  DON       SOLO
  TENT    HAPPEN
SHE        IDA
AIR        DOT
GEM
```

PUZZLE 231

1. Shoe, Shot, Soot, Boot.
2. Past, Pest, Peat, Pear, Year.
3. Cock, Cook, Cool, Coil, Toil, Tail.
4. Tree, Free, Fret, Feet, Fees, Foes, Toes, Tops.

PUZZLE 232

```
LISP        LAVA
AREA        USED
PEACH       REED
 STEAM  YEAR
   LOGO      PROW
   LAYS  LANE
  CAROL  JOKED
   SCORN  ORATE
ALLAY  EAGER
SEAR    TRAP
HOPE     ONLY
     FLAW YANKS
  TIER    MONEY
  ALEC     TORE
  MESH     EWES
```

PUZZLE 233

Light is the task where many share the toil.

1. Whirl, 2. Sight, 3. Relate, 4. Sheik, 5. Moth-eaten, 6. Hasty.

PUZZLE 234

```
      NODE    HELP
  MAILED      OLIO
CHALLENGE  MEETS
LISP     YORE  VET
ADO   GAS  NOT  ARE
PEN   RIP  SEE  TAR
   SLALOM    GEL
    OBSTINATE
VAT      DONATE
RAP  DAB  PEP  NAP
ANT  ERR  EWE  RUE
SIN  STEW     TIRE
CLERK  WHIMSICAL
ALSO     AVOUCH
LAST     TYPE
```

PUZZLE 235

1. Harvesting, 2. Speculator, 3. Run like mad.

PUZZLE 236

```
ROSE
ANTS
FEET     SEEP   RACED
TREE  THERE    ADORE
   RETAILER    MOORE
   MERV         LED
   NEED        SPED
   HEED
   RIO  TENT
  AMENDMENT
  OWED  DEN
  DUET   NEST
  POTS   MEAT
PAL     REPEATED
AILED    EVENT  ARES
SNARE    VENT   SOLE
STRAW          EVIL
               DEAL
```

PUZZLE 237

1. Meat, Melt, Malt, Mall, Ball.
2. Dill, Dial, Deal, Dead, Deed, Weed.
3. Shoe, Shot, Soot, Boot, Boon, Born, Horn.
4. True, Tree, Trey, Tray, Tram, Gram, Grim, Grit.

530

PUZZLE 238

```
A L P   E L D   G R A D S   M E S T A
B O A   P O E   L I M I T   O M E R S
C A R T O O N   I M P R E S S U R E S
    R E S P O N D S   E R O S   E N E
L O I N   T O E   I C E D   T N T S
A W E S   H E M   D O T S   P O D
I N D I T E D   L E N S   S E M I T E
    O E R   G A M S   S E R A P E S
C R A N E   A L M A   B E E T   I R K
H A L S   C R A B G R A S S   E T R E
A N T   C O E D   O I L S   P A Y E R
T E E T E R S   E G A D   L E S
S E R E N E   F O U L   S E A T T L E
    N A T   S I N E   P T A   W A I L
A L A S   C H A S   E R A   I T E M
N U T   E A R N   E M E R G E N T
G R I D D L E C A K E   R U D D E R S
L I V I D   W E S E R   E D E   R I O
E D E M A   S E E D Y   D E N   S A N
```

PUZZLE 239

```
  S E N D S   L A B O R   A B A S H
S T R A I T   I N A N E   C A C H E S
C O M P A R E N O T E S   R F T O R T
A L I   L I V E N S   O V E R   W A R
D E N S   D A N   U R I S   C O L A
S N E E R E D   A O R T A   H A N D Y
    D U N E   L U G S   R O S E
T E N A N T   S I T E   C A N A S T A
E L A T E   S A G O   H O P E   F E D
S I R E   S K I N F L I N T   C A R D
T O R   A N I L   H A R E   N A C R E
S T O P G A P   W A K E   C A R E E R
    W E E P   C A N E   D O M O
T A M E D   R A N D S   I R E L A N D
R U I N   M E R E   A G O   S T A R
E R N   S I V A   S A L I N A   E N E
N O D D E D   F E E L O N E S O A T S
D R E A M S   E R A S E   T E N S E S
  A D M I T   S I L O S   S A T E S
```

PUZZLE 240

```
P R I M   Z I N G   S T O W   R A F T
R I C E   O R A L   H O M E   E G I S
O P E N   R O T I   A M I D   B A R K
W E S T E R N O M E L E T   T E R N S
    O S O   M O T   L A C
A L E R T   A M E N   P R A N C E R S
L A Y S   L I A R   R U I N   A M A H
E T E   P O R T   A O R T A   W I P E
S H O W E R   S A D D L E   T E S T A
    P E R E S   G I E   S W I S S
C R E S T   P I N T O S   A C T I O N
H I N T   A I R E S   C O R K   O B I
I T E M   S K I S   E A R N   S N O B
C A R I B E E S   A N T E   R U S E S
    N E A   E N D   S A M
C H A S E   W E S T O F T H E M O O N
L I L T   L A S S   R A R E   E L M O
E D G E   E L S A   S L I D   R E E D
F E A R   O K A Y   E L M S   Y O R E
```

PUZZLE 241

```
B A N K     A R O W   C H A P
E B O N   O C A L A   L A N A
G E T O F F T H E G R O U N D
S T A T U T E S   E A G L E S
        R E D   U R I S
A S T E R N   S K I N   E L S
T E R S E   S T A N   P L E A
S T A N D O N E S G R O U N D
E A V E   P I P E   I N D I A
A L E   F E D S   O D D E S T
      E R N E   P R E
A P P L E S   S A L A R I E S
F R O M T H E G R O U N D U P
R O L E   O A T E N   A E R O
O D E R   P U S S   S O O T
```

PUZZLE 242

```
S L E D   P R O O F   S C O T
T U N A   L E M U R   T A P A
A N D Y E A R E R I S E N U P
G A S   S C A N   A M A S S
      S E E N   T I P
H A S P   E O S   T E E
O R C A S   A D A M A L S O
G R A C E U N T O Y O U A N D
S O R E N S E N   A N T E D
  W E D   E T O   T E S S
      M R S   A C T S
S T O V E   L I A R   L A G
H A V I N G D A M N A T I O N
A M E N   I N S E T   A N N A
M E R E   S A T E S   M E E T
```

PUZZLE 243

```
T I L E   G A B   G A S   C A P T
O D E S   A L E   O T T   A R A R
N E A T   G A I   O H O   V I S E
E A V E S   S O P   L A R I A T S
S L E E P S   W I D E   E A S E S
    M O O T   E I T H E R
P A W   T O O T   V E A L   W A S
A G E S   N O O S E   T E N A N T
I R A T E   L O O S E   D O D G E
N E V A D A   T O T A L   B E L A
T E E   D I S H   S T A Y   S O L
    S I D L E D   S W A M
M A R I E   O D O R   S L E I G H
A M A S S E S   T O P   E R N I E
L I N T   T H Y   U R N   T A L L
E D G E   N E E   T I E   O N T O
S E E R   A D S   E G O   N E S T
```

PUZZLE 244

```
B A C H   M O P   S A G E
E C H O   E R A   E N I D
A R I D   L A S T W O R D
N E T   D E N   H E A D Y
    C L U E   F U R
A S H E N   R I G   C O G
R E A D   H U B   H A V E
M E T   H U E   M U R A L
    G I G   F A M E
S C A R F   E R R   F A R
N O S E I N T O   A R G O
I N E E   I N N   S E R A
P E A T   B A D   S E A M
```

PUZZLE 245

```
C A T   H A R D   R A N K
A L I   E P E E   E L A N
S I D E S T E P   J A N E
S T Y L I   F O R E S A W
    S T U   T I C
R E L E A S E   S T E E P
I R A   T A R S I   M O O
B A M B I   R E B O U N D
    L O G   T I M
T I T A N I C   L E A S E
A D A M   B E G I N N E R
S E R E   E D I T   N A G
S A S S   D E N Y   O N O
```

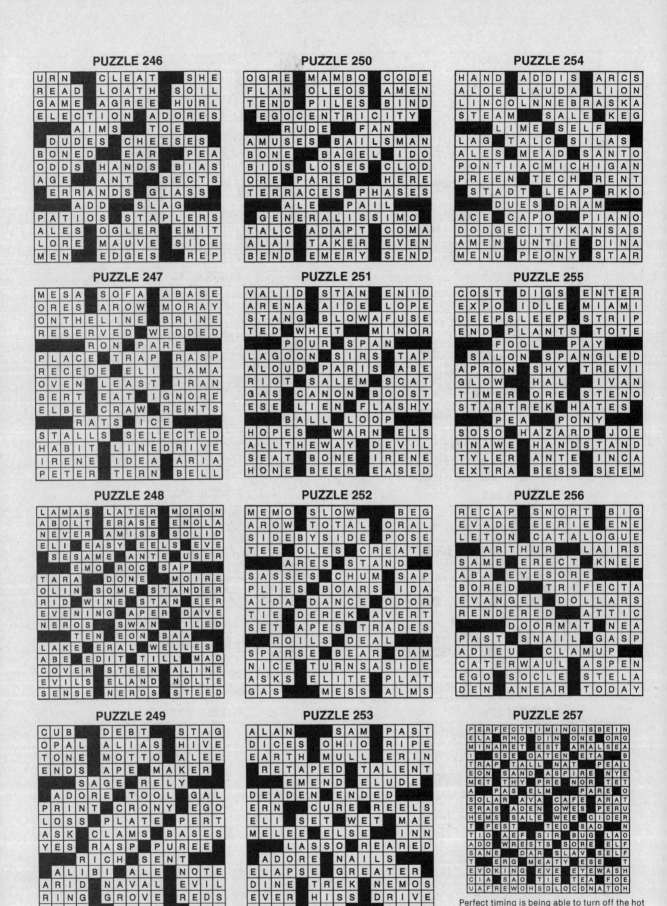

PUZZLE 246

U	R	N			C	L	E	A	T				S	H	E
R	E	A	D		L	O	A	T	H			S	O	I	L
G	A	M	E		A	G	R	E	E			H	U	R	L
E	L	E	C	T	I	O	N		A	D	O	R	E	S	
			A	I	M	S				T	O	E			
	D	U	D	E	S		C	H	E	E	S	E	S		
B	O	N	E	D			E	A	R				P	E	A
O	D	D	S		H	A	N	D	S		B	I	A	S	
A	G	E		A	N	T				S	E	C	T	S	
	E	R	R	A	N	D	S		G	L	A	S	S		
			A	D	D			S	L	A	G				
P	A	T	I	O	S		S	T	A	P	L	E	R	S	
A	L	E	S		O	G	L	E	R		E	M	I	T	
L	O	R	E		M	A	U	V	E		S	I	D	E	
M	E	N			E	D	G	E	S			R	E	P	

PUZZLE 250

O	G	R	E		M	A	M	B	O		C	O	D	E
F	L	A	N		O	L	E	O	S		A	M	E	N
T	E	N	D		P	I	L	E	S		B	I	N	D
	E	G	O	C	E	N	T	R	I	C	I	T	Y	
			R	U	D	E			F	A	N			
A	M	U	S	E	S		B	A	I	L	S	M	A	N
B	O	N	E			B	A	G	E	L		I	D	O
B	I	D	S		L	O	S	E	S		C	L	O	D
O	R	E		P	A	R	E	D		H	E	R	E	
T	E	R	R	A	C	E	S		P	H	A	S	E	S
			A	L	E			P	A	I	L			
	G	E	N	E	R	A	L	I	S	S	I	M	O	
T	A	L	C		A	D	A	P	T		C	O	M	A
A	L	A	I		T	A	K	E	R		E	V	E	N
B	E	N	D		E	M	E	R	Y		S	E	N	D

PUZZLE 254

H	A	N	D		A	D	D	I	S		A	R	C	S
A	L	O	E		L	A	U	D	A		L	I	O	N
L	I	N	C	O	L	N	N	E	B	R	A	S	K	A
S	T	E	A	M			S	A	L	E		K	E	G
			L	I	M	E			S	E	L	F		
L	A	G		T	A	L	C			S	I	L	A	S
A	L	E	S		M	E	A	D			S	A	N	T	O
P	O	N	T	I	A	C	M	I	C	H	I	G	A	N
P	R	E	E	N			T	E	C	H		R	E	N	T
	S	T	A	D	T		L	E	A	P		R	K	O	
			D	U	E	S			D	R	A	M			
A	C	E		C	A	P	O			P	I	A	N	O
D	O	D	G	E	C	I	T	Y	K	A	N	S	A	S
A	M	E	N		U	N	T	I	E		D	I	N	A
M	E	N	U		P	E	O	N	Y		S	T	A	R

PUZZLE 247

M	E	S	A		S	O	F	A		A	B	A	S	E
O	R	E	S		A	R	O	W		M	O	R	A	Y
O	N	T	H	E	L	I	N	E		B	R	I	N	E
R	E	S	E	R	V	E	D		W	E	D	D	E	D
			R	O	N		P	A	R	E				
P	L	A	C	E		T	R	A	P		R	A	S	P
R	E	C	E	D	E		E	L	I		L	A	M	A
O	V	E	N		L	E	A	S	T		I	R	A	N
B	E	R	T		E	A	T		I	G	N	O	R	E
E	L	B	E		C	R	A	W		R	E	N	T	S
			R	A	T	S		I	C	E				
S	T	A	L	L	S		S	E	L	E	C	T	E	D
H	A	B	I	T		L	I	N	E	D	R	I	V	E
I	R	E	N	E		I	D	E	A		A	R	I	A
P	E	T	E	R		T	E	R	N		B	E	L	L

PUZZLE 251

V	A	L	I	D		S	T	A	N		E	N	I	D
A	R	E	N	A		A	I	D	E		L	O	P	E
S	T	A	N	G		B	L	O	W	A	F	U	S	E
T	E	D		W	H	E	T			M	I	N	O	R
			P	O	U	R		S	P	A	N			
L	A	G	O	O	N		S	I	R	S		T	A	P
A	L	O	U	D		P	A	R	I	S		A	B	E
R	I	O	T		S	A	L	E	M		S	C	A	T
G	A	S		C	A	N	O	N		B	O	O	S	T
E	S	E		L	I	E	N		F	L	A	S	H	Y
			B	A	L	L		L	O	O	P			
H	O	P	E	S			W	A	R	N		E	L	S
A	L	L	T	H	E	W	A	Y		D	E	V	I	L
S	E	A	T		B	O	N	E		I	R	E	N	E
H	O	N	E		B	E	E	R		E	A	S	E	D

PUZZLE 255

C	O	S	T		D	I	G	S		E	N	T	E	R
E	X	P	O		I	D	L	E		M	I	A	M	I
D	E	E	P	S	L	E	E	P		S	T	R	I	P
E	N	D		P	L	A	N	T	S		T	O	T	E
			F	O	O	L			P	A	Y			
S	A	L	O	N		S	P	A	N	G	L	E	D	
A	P	R	O	N		S	H	Y		T	R	E	V	I
G	L	O	W		H	A	L			I	V	A	N	
T	I	M	E	R		O	R	E		S	T	E	N	O
S	T	A	R	T	R	E	K		H	A	T	E	S	
			P	E	A			P	O	N	Y			
S	O	S	O		H	A	Z	A	R	D		J	O	E
I	N	A	W	E		H	A	N	D	S	T	A	N	D
T	Y	L	E	R		A	N	T	E		I	N	C	A
E	X	T	R	A		B	E	S	S		S	E	E	M

PUZZLE 248

L	A	M	A	S		L	A	T	E	R		M	O	R	O	N
A	B	O	L	T		E	R	A	S	E		E	N	O	L	A
N	E	V	E	R		A	M	I	S	S		S	O	L	I	D
E	L	I		E	A	S	Y		E	E	L	S		E	V	E
	S	E	S	A	M	E		A	N	T	E		U	S	E	R
			E	M	O		R	O	C		S	A	P			
T	A	R	A		D	O	N	E			M	O	I	R	E	
O	L	I	N		S	O	M	E		S	T	A	N	D	E	R
R	I	D		W	I	N	E		S	T	A	N		E	E	R
E	V	E	N	I	N	G		A	P	E	R		D	A	V	E
N	E	R	O	S			S	W	A	N			I	L	E	D
			T	E	N		E	O	N		B	A	A			
L	A	K	E		E	R	A	L		W	E	L	L	E	S	
A	B	E		E	D	I	T		T	I	L	L		M	A	D
C	O	V	E	R		S	T	E	E	N		A	L	I	N	E
E	V	I	L	S		E	L	A	N	D		N	O	L	T	E
S	E	N	S	E		N	E	R	D	S		S	T	E	E	D

PUZZLE 252

M	E	M	O		S	L	O	W			B	E	G
A	R	O	W		T	O	T	A	L		O	R	A	L
S	I	D	E	B	Y	S	I	D	E		P	O	S	E
T	E	E		O	L	E	S		C	R	E	A	T	E
			A	R	E	S		S	T	A	N	D		
S	A	S	S	E	S		C	H	U	M		S	A	P
P	L	I	E	S		B	O	A	R	S		I	D	A
A	L	D	A		D	A	N	C	E		O	D	O	R
T	I	E		D	E	R	E	K		A	V	E	R	T
S	E	T		A	P	E	S		T	R	A	D	E	S
			R	O	I	L	S		D	E	A	L		
S	P	A	R	S	E		B	E	A	R		D	A	M
N	I	C	E		T	U	R	N	S	A	S	I	D	E
A	S	K	S		E	L	I	T	E		P	L	A	T
G	A	S			M	E	S	S		A	L	M	S	

PUZZLE 256

R	E	C	A	P		S	N	O	R	T		B	I	G
E	V	A	D	E		E	E	R	I	E		E	N	E
L	E	T	O	N		C	A	T	A	L	O	G	U	E
			A	R	T	H	U	R		L	A	I	R	S
S	A	M	E		E	R	E	C	T		K	N	E	E
A	B	A		E	Y	E	S	O	R	E				
B	O	R	E	D				T	R	I	F	E	C	T	A
E	V	A	N	G	E	L		D	O	L	L	A	R	S
R	E	N	D	E	R	E	D			A	T	T	I	C
			D	O	O	R	M	A	T		N	E	A	
P	A	S	T		S	N	A	I	L		G	A	S	P
A	D	I	E	U		C	L	A	M	U	P			
C	A	T	E	R	W	A	U	L		A	S	P	E	N
E	G	O		S	O	C	L	E		S	T	E	L	A
D	E	N		A	N	E	A	R		T	O	D	A	Y

PUZZLE 249

C	U	B		D	E	B	T			S	T	A	G
O	P	A	L		A	L	I	A	S		H	I	V	E
T	O	N	E		M	O	T	T	O		A	L	E	E
E	N	D	S		A	P	E		M	A	K	E	R	
			S	A	G	E		R	E	L	Y			
	A	D	O	R	E		T	O	O	L		G	A	L
P	R	I	N	T		C	R	O	N	Y		E	G	O
L	O	S	S		P	L	A	T	E		P	E	R	T
A	S	K		C	L	A	M	S		B	A	S	E	S
Y	E	S		R	A	S	P		P	U	R	E	E	
			R	I	C	H		S	E	N	T			
	A	L	I	B	I		A	L	E		N	O	T	E
A	R	I	D		N	A	V	A	L		E	V	I	L
R	I	N	G		G	R	O	V	E		R	E	D	S
C	A	K	E			E	W	E	R			N	E	E

PUZZLE 253

A	L	A	N			S	A	M			P	A	S	T
D	I	C	E	S		O	H	I	O		R	I	P	E
E	A	R	T	H		M	U	L	L		E	R	I	N
	R	E	T	A	P	E	D		T	A	L	E	N	T
			E	M	E	N	D		E	L	U	D	E	
D	E	A	D	E	N		E	N	D	E	D			
E	R	N			C	U	R	E		R	E	E	L	S
E	L	I		S	E	T		W	E	T		M	A	E
M	E	L	E	E		E	L	S	E			I	N	N
			L	A	S	S	O		R	E	A	R	E	D
	A	D	O	R	E		N	A	I	L	S			
E	L	A	P	S	E		G	R	E	A	T	E	R	
D	I	N	E		T	R	E	K		N	E	M	O	S
E	V	E	R		H	I	S	S		D	R	I	V	E
N	E	S	S		E	D	T			S	T	E	W	

PUZZLE 257

P	E	R	F	E	C	T	T	I	M	I	N	G	I	S	B	E	I	N
E	L	A		R	H	O		D	I	N		O	N	E		O	R	G
M	I	N	A	R	E	T		E	S	T		A	R	A	L	S	E	A
I		S	S	E		O	A	T	E	N		E	T	A			B	
T	R	A	P		T	A	L	L		N	A	T		P	E	A	L	
E	O	N		S	A	N	D		A	S	P	I	R	E		N	Y	E
M	E	T		T	H	Y		P	R	E		N	O	R		T	E	T
A			P	A	S		E	L	M		P	A	R	E			O	
S	O	L	A	R		A	V	A		C	A	F	E		A	R	A	T
E	R	A	S		A	D	E	N		O	W	E	S		P	E	R	U
H	E	M	S		S	A	L	E		W	E	E		C	I	D	E	R
T		P	E	S	T			T	E	D		S	A	D			N	
T	I	O		A	E	F		S	I	R		B	U	G		L	A	O
A	D	O		W	R	E	S	T	S		S	O	R	E		E	L	F
S	A	N	E		D	A	R		S	L	A	V		S	E	L	F	
T		E	R	G		M	E	A	T	Y		E	S	E			T	
E	V	O	K	I	N	G		E	V	E		E	Y	E	W	A	S	H
C	I	A		S	A	O		T	I	E		T	E	A		F	O	E
U	A	F	R	E	W	O	H	S	D	L	O	C	D	N	A	T	O	H

Perfect timing is being able to turn off the hot and cold shower faucets at the same time.

532

PUZZLE 258

```
DIRT PLOT THIS INTO
ODOR LINE RANT NEON
ELSE APER ERNE DANE
SEASONS MEND WAITER
    TIE WIND LANA
STILL BITE PARTNERS
LODE DOTE PRIDE TOE
IDO TEA SPEARS LOST
TOLERATE LENS BONES
   LIL DRANK PEA
SCALP SWAN STRENGTH
TORS SHACKS ION LEE
APE MERRY TEND SEER
REASONED TART DEEMS
   TOAD PONE HEN
RECENT MIND SANDALS
ACHE OPEN ARTS ERIE
SHOD RATE RIOT RISE
POPS SLED DOPE SAPS
```

PUZZLE 262

```
OLLA  ALAS  LETT
RIANT TILE  ALAR
CONTRITION  MALE
AND INE ESSENCE
    CONN  EON
PRO ITS SATED
TRAM NICE PALED
ROMP GOONS TATI
ABOUT NOLA ITEM
ENNIS PAL OER
    CRT  ROON
CANTEEN GOT AIM
AMOI REPENTANCE
NATO EWER OTTER
STEN OTIS EIRE
```

PUZZLE 266

```
EDAM   PASS  OTOE
DORA MARTA  URAL
SWONDERFUL  TERM
ENS OLES UNLESS
LYE BON STOA
  AINTSHESWEET
ALICE  EERY APE
LOGE READS EVER
MOO SECT PREEN
 APRILSHOWERS
 SOHO ADO ASK
REDSEA MLIX RAE
ABOU PRETTYBABY
FREE EASES ABLE
TOSS SPAR DYED
```

PUZZLE 259

```
MARC MUFTI  TMEN
AREA ARIES HALE
SPAT CATERWAULS
CARTOONS  ALIAS
   ANNI ABRI
TACIT CATAMARAN
ANALOG GIGS HIE
BINS ARETE COME
ATA STAN LEADED
CALICOCAT STARS
   TARE ROTC
INCAN  SEAHAWKS
BELLTHECAT LANE
AMOI AGATE LIEN
ROTA TONYS SLED
```

PUZZLE 263

```
REAM ALSO SOHO WALK
AINU PSALM PROMS IRON
IDEM RAMIE ACTUP LESE
SEABEE EGGER STE LATE
ERRORS HANKYPANKY
JETSET CLIO DENSE
ECRU OIL SLEPT VIEWS
ROOMS PURPOSE SHELVES
ARABIC LOIS SPELLERS
SENORES ADES OAR YRS
  ENCORE PATROL
ASH TOP RAID SNIFFAT
SCOOTERS TRAP SKULLS
ARRIERE CREAMOF EDEMA
TEETH SHELL SRO DEAR
DRYER KEPI HEYDAY
TEENYWEENY ENDALL
HOBO NAH ARIEL STUDIO
ALAI EVICT ETUIS DODO
LINT SEGUE CANNA DROP
LOGY SHED ELAN YENS
```

PUZZLE 267

```
REAR  SLAM  MAJOR
AGRA TODO  AWAKE
JACKFROST  TACIT
ADHERES  STRIKES
   OWED ROTH
CAJUNS ERIN AGA
ORANT CLOTS MLS
RICA ROUTE AMOS
ASK BORGE STEVE
LEA RUNE SCARES
  NEON DATA
GRANADA SARDINE
LOPED JACKPINES
ISERE ALOE STEP
MASON RATS CODY
```

PUZZLE 260

```
  CLIM BGIST
A RO MAR  OE
RA GLA D OUR
 BU OY ARM
CL ING EIDER
HESS IBE  RIA
  H   ADE S
ER ANE AREST
ST ER N NUT
 PI  LG  EE
BEGIN OMEN S
ASHCOOP LE  T
DOTS BEA  DS
```

PUZZLE 264

```
ADHOC CARMEL  COMET
DRAPE ARCADIA ATONE
LAPEL MRANDMRSNORTH
IMP ASEA DOODLE SEE
BAYS LONER NEE SERE
 HOLY TRAM NEAT
SORE SKAT PLAGUE
TOTALS TEXAS STAND
SOL NOTE TIMES ESTA
NOIL PARCHMENT DORM
ALGA ERNIE DOLT LIS
PIANO SELMA ROOKIE
SENORA SIAM WIND
 SERB AGOG ANTE
LACE ERS IRREG SAKE
AIL STATIC AXED LES
PRINCEVALIANT RELET
SENNA ORLANDO IRENE
EDGED KENNEL PAYER
```

PUZZLE 268

```
TITI  SHAY  FATAL
ANON TOGS  AMORE
GIRT INTERLAKEN
STEEPLE RAT END
   RYES REINAS
WHIRLS STERN
ROGUE DIRE TARN
ALOP SIDES ELIA
PERT COLE CRIMP
 ERASE WASTES
STARER RANT
WAN GUM AGAINST
INTERMEZZO COTE
STAGE LOON ETON
HELOT TORS SEAT
```

PUZZLE 261

```
LEAF  CARR  COHAN
ELLA ABEE  ORATE
HAIRBRUSH  REINS
ATE OUTTALK ROT
RENEWS  BEEPS
 NEONS GRETNA
BAHTS EIRE RYES
ALAE LANES CLII
HEIR APED PEELS
SCRAPS WOMAN
 SLOES ENTIRE
ASP PRECISE NAE
STRIP CROSSHAIR
SLAVE TOTE ANTI
TOYED SPAS METE
```

PUZZLE 265

```
CARR  PAGET  SALS
ALOE ADELE  IRAE
BOBBYDARIN  NOVA
SPREE   DOC SET
 ELATE ERASERS
ALI ROME SIL
DAN SMILE NOMAN
ARES STILL WAGE
MARCH SALAD RES
 OIL SISI  YES
SETTLER SHANA
AVA ONE  NESTS
NELS DEANMARTIN
TRIO ESTER VOTE
ETAL REEDS ERIE
```

PUZZLE 269

```
AMBLE  BALI  VAST
SOLID OMEN  ULTO
ELUDE RAND  LION
ADE NIGHTINGALE
 BAITS  CEASED
PRINCE  ALTAR
HORN RAREST CRO
INDIA ILE HAHAS
LAS MODEST VINO
 TAPES ERECTS
ANSATE  FRISK
MOCKINGBIRD ASP
ETRE ERIN EYDIE
NEAR RITE REEDS
TSPS SPED SWEET
```

PUZZLE 270

L	E	S	S		P	A	R		C	R	I	B
A	L	E	C		A	L	E		A	O	N	E
U	S	E	R		N	I	L		N	O	S	E
D	E	N	I	E	D		A	T	O	M		
			B	L	A	S	P	H	E	M	E	D
B	R	I	E	F		T	S	E		A	R	I
E	E	L	S		W	O	E		S	T	I	R
A	I	L		S	I	R		S	H	E	E	T
U	N	I	F	O	R	M	I	T	Y			
		N	I	N	E		D	U	S	T	E	D
G	O	O	N		T	E	E		T	A	K	E
E	R	I	C		A	V	A		E	P	E	E
M	E	S	H		P	A	L		R	E	D	D

PUZZLE 274

C	O	P	E			B	A	A		D	E	N
A	G	E	D		D	O	G	S		A	P	E
D	R	A	G		E	G	O	S		Y	E	A
	E	R	E	C	T	S		E	M	B	E	R
			S	E	A		T	A	R			
R	A	G		D	I	A	L		R	E	E	L
O	R	E		E	L	D	E	R		A	W	E
T	E	N	D		S	O	D	A		K	E	G
		E	O	N			G	I	G			
S	P	R	E	E		C	E	L	L	A	R	
T	E	A		W	E	A	R		I	R	O	N
A	R	T		E	R	R	S		N	I	C	E
R	U	E		R	E	D			T	A	K	E

PUZZLE 278

N	I	G	H	T		S	P	R	A	Y
D	I	N	N	E	R		C	L	O	S	E	D
R	E	S	U	M	E		R	A	T	T	L	E
A	C	T		P	A	G	A	N		E	L	I
M	E	E	T		T	A	M		F	R	E	T
A	S	P	I	R	E	D		C	A	N	D	Y
			B	E	D		E	A	R			
R	U	L	E	D		D	E	T	E	C	T	S
O	M	I	T		S	I	R		S	A	R	A
U	P	S		R	A	P	I	D		B	A	R
N	I	T	W	I	T		E	A	S	I	N	G
D	R	E	A	M	Y		S	T	A	N	C	E
	E	D	G	E	R		T	E	N	S	E	

PUZZLE 271

S	O	F	T		M	E	T		S	H	O	P
I	D	L	E		O	R	E		L	I	M	E
L	O	O	N		W	A	N		A	D	I	T
T	R	E	S	S		S	O	N	N	E	T	S
			E	N	T	E	R	E	D			
L	O	S		E	A	R		S	E	W	E	R
O	U	T	L	A	W		S	T	R	I	V	E
B	R	E	A	K		S	A	L		T	E	D
		D	E	M	O	T	E	D				
C	A	L	D	R	O	N		D	R	A	P	E
E	R	I	E		R	A	H		A	R	I	D
N	E	A	R		A	T	E		M	U	L	E
T	A	R	S		Y	A	M		A	M	E	N

PUZZLE 275

E	A	T	E	N		T	O	T		A	D	E
S	C	A	L	E		E	R	R		D	I	M
S	T	R	A	P		A	B	A	L	O	N	E
			T	A	B		S	N	O	R	E	R
D	E	V	E	L	O	P		S	A	N	D	Y
O	W	E	D		R	A	B	I	D			
G	E	T		I	N	G	O	T		G	A	Y
		C	L	E	A	N		C	E	D	E	
M	U	R	A	L		N	E	A	R	E	S	T
E	N	A	M	E	L		D	U	E			
A	L	L	E	G	E	S		D	A	R	E	D
N	I	L		A	V	E		I	T	A	L	Y
S	T	Y		L	Y	E		T	E	N	S	E

PUZZLE 279

P	I	T	S		L	I	D		S	I	L	L
E	R	I	E		A	C	E		T	R	U	E
P	A	N	C	A	K	E	S		R	I	T	A
			E	W	E		E	R	A	S	E	D
P	R	I	D	E		D	R	E	W			
R	A	T	E		N	O	T	E		P	E	T
I	V	E		N	O	V	E	L		A	L	E
G	E	M		O	V	E	R		R	I	L	L
			O	N	E	S		P	E	D	A	L
T	O	M	T	O	M		S	A	P			
E	M	I	T		B	A	L	L	O	O	N	S
N	I	N	E		E	Y	E			S	L	I	P
S	T	I	R		R	E	D		E	E	L	Y

PUZZLE 272

C	O	T		S	T	O	P		B	R	A	N
A	P	E		W	A	D	E		L	O	G	O
V	A	N		O	N	E	S		O	D	O	R
E	L	D	E	R		S	T	E	W			
			A	D	S		O	N	I	O	N	
A	G	E	S		T	E	E	N		D	I	E
C	O	A	T		O	R	B		G	E	L	S
E	R	R		S	W	A	B		L	A	S	T
S	E	N	S	E			S	E	E			
			C	A	S	E		D	E	C	A	Y
C	O	M	A		C	R	A	G		A	R	E
O	R	A	L		A	I	D	E		P	E	A
W	E	R	E		T	E	E	S		E	A	R

PUZZLE 276

A	B	E	D			D	A	D			R	U	D	E
R	A	R	E		F	I	N	E			O	N	E	S
C	H	A	N	G	E	H	A	N	D	S		A	D	D	L	E
		A	M	I	D				M	O	R	S	E	
H	A	N	D	G	U	N		E	T	S		A	D	E		R	N	S
O	V	E	R		D	E	C	K	H	A	N	D		A	H	O	Y
P	E	T	S			B	U	O	Y	S			A	L	A	R	M
			C	O	B			H	A	N	D	I	N	
P	A	H		C	A	N		R	E	D		D	A	Y
A	G	A		L	P	S		O	P	E		E	T	A
T	E	N		O	R	E		M	A	D		D	E	M
		D	I	G	I	T	S			G	A	L	
M	E	M	O	S		A	I	S	L	E		N	O	R	M
O	V	E	N		H	A	N	D	S	O	M	E		O	D	O	R
P	A	D		C	O	P		A	W	N		M	I	T	T	E	N	S
			O	R	A	T	E			A	I	D	A	
S	O	W	E	D		H	A	N	D	T	O	M	O	U	T	H
H	A	N	S		A	L	A	S			A	R	I	A
E	R	S	T			L	E	G			T	I	N	T

PUZZLE 277

O	F	F		O	W	E	D		C	O	D	E
I	R	A		T	O	R	E		O	P	A	L
L	O	N	G	H	O	R	N		P	E	R	K
		N	E	E		D	I	R	K	S		
	A	W	A	R	D		G	O	N	E		
K	N	I	T		L	E	N	G	T	H	Y	
I	N	N		P	O	E	M	S		T	E	A
T	A	D	P	O	L	E		M	A	R	K	
	F	O	N	D		G	E	E	S	E		
T	R	A	C	E			A	D	S			
H	U	L	K		T	A	L	I	S	M	A	N
I	D	L	E		A	L	E	C		E	G	O
N	E	S	T		P	A	S	T		L	E	D

PUZZLE 273

G	A	L	E		S	A	D		D	A	M	P
A	D	A	M		P	I	E		E	R	I	E
S	A	P	P	H	I	R	E		L	E	N	T
			I	A	N		P	L	E	A	D	S
S	T	A	R	T		B	E	A	T			
C	I	T	E		C	O	N	S	E	R	V	E
A	D	O		T	O	N	E	S		O	A	K
R	E	P	E	A	L	E	D		V	A	S	E
			A	I	L	S		P	A	N	T	S
T	A	N	G	L	E		B	E	N			
O	R	A	L		C	A	R	R	I	A	G	E
L	I	V	E		T	W	O		S	C	A	N
D	A	Y	S		S	E	W		H	E	R	D

PUZZLE 280

M	I	L	L		A	T	O	P		A	P	E
I	D	E	A		T	R	I	O		R	E	D
L	O	A	M		H	A	L	L		G	A	G
E	L	D	E	R	L	Y		A	M	U	S	E
			D	U	E		R	A	M			
M	A	N		I	T	E	M		D	E	F	Y
A	G	E		N	E	V	E	R		N	E	E
T	O	A	D		S	E	R	E		T	E	N
			R	O	T		R	A	W			
T	I	N	G	E		S	I	L	I	C	O	N
W	O	E		N	I	C	E		D	A	M	E
I	T	S		E	R	A	S		E	P	E	E
G	A	S		T	E	N	T		R	E	N	D

PUZZLE 281

P	A	L		A	C	T		R	A	Y
E	X	I	T		F	O	O	D		O	W	E
E	L	S	E		T	O	N	E		L	E	T
L	E	A	N			E	E	L	S			
		D	A	Y		T	R	Y				
J	A	W		B	E	A	R		E	A	S	T
E	G	O		E	A	S	E	D		R	U	E
T	O	W	N		S	P	A	R		M	E	N
		O	U	T		D	Y	E				
D	U	D	S					L	A	K	E	
S	O	T		E	M	I	T		K	I	N	D
P	E	A		D	I	V	E		S	M	O	G
A	S	H		L	Y	E			S	T	Y	

PUZZLE 282

```
BEATS FLEA  RAJ
AUDIO LAWN  FILE
GRENADINES  IDEA
SON PINK WORSEN
    PENT MERE
REBORE HEROICAL
ORALS DOLE  SORE
BOGY AIRED  LOOP
EDEN CEDE  LAPSE
DELEGATE  DENSER
    SUDS GOOD
SHIITE AUNT  OLE
COCA MADAGASCAR
OPEN IRAN  RATIO
TED AMMO  DOORS
```

PUZZLE 286

```
SAD LIME  TROT
ELI ADOS  RAVE
WILLIAMS  ACES
   EAR ACCENT
ALMS  DOYLE
GUM DEW  EDITS
ERA INNER  MAE
DESKS ELK  PIE
   ACIDS BULK
BURROS  WAD
ASIA  LABORERS
BENT EVER  NIP
EDGE TEEN  TOY
```

PUZZLE 290

```
WERE ALTO YOWL ELSE
AMEN LOAN AREA MOPE
DINOSAURS NEED OVAL
STOUT PEAK PESTERS
   GABS TIED NAIL
ENTHRALL DEEM TOILS
MOO GOAL SLAM NEAT
URNS STYLE IRIS SKI
SMEAR EARP SCEPTER
  PETERMARSHALL
PASSION ASIA FADED
UFO NASH EDICT NERO
LAMP DUEL ELLA SIN
PREEN EWER SOLSTICE
  TRIM SAUL DEAR
DRIFTED TEAR RABBI
ROME LASH PETTICOAT
ALEC TRUE SEAR TAKE
WEST SEER EDGY STEM
```

PUZZLE 283

```
BEET SCUM ALMA SPUD
RILE NANA CAIN LARA
AREA ORIG CONN EGAD
TEMPERATURE GORILLA
  OAK SAND YOGI
MATTERS PTAH CHASE
DIP SLACK SNAP SCOT
EDEN SHAHS EWER COT
FIDEL SMACK KACHINA
  COL SKEET SPA
BACKLOG INERT TUBED
LEA AAHS ELIOT LACE
TRUE DAHL SADAT RUB
SOLAR TEES LOCALES
  DRAB SORA OLE
GARNERS PACKANIMALS
ALOE OHIO TAXI OBIE
FANS TOLL EMIT NEER
FIST HELD DALE SLUE
```

PUZZLE 287

```
WOOD SET  ASHE
INTO WEE  CHEF
NEON ELEPHANT
GREASE  LET
   LOT MASTER
CANDY WAY  EDA
ORO PAN  RIC
GER AIR  PASTE
LATENT  DES
   HAT EASTER
AMERICAN  ERIE
CORN ADS  TERN
TONS TOE  SEED
```

PUZZLE 291

```
GIBE MAPS SWAP WASH
ORYX AMAH ERNE ISLE
BARCAROLE PETROLEUM
INDUCTS BRAN FRIARS
   STY HAUL HUGE
WALES WINE FUMAROLE
HIED KING SIREN DAD
IDA PAST SCOLD SEMI
REPTILE SPARS ONSET
   ICE SWORD RHO
FLANK CHIRP PIEBALD
LOLA GOOSE FUND TOE
USE PLANS MUCK DEAF
ESCAROLE WIRE PENNY
  MOWS EONS HIP
AROUSE GLEE OUTAGES
CASSEROLE RIGMAROLE
RILE ERIC ARLO TAKE
ENOS DEBT LEER SLED
```

PUZZLE 284

```
ABEE ORAL PABA BALMS
COMB MOVE MEDAL ELIOT
HUMBLEPIE ORATE FILLE
ETA OLES TOUGHCOOKIES
  TRES MORSE ARE
REGRET PAREE RATE TIS
ALIEN MALT SEERS PASO
NINE SALT LET NAKED
TAG CREAMPUFFS OPERA
SSE LOTS OASIS GRATE
  ROOTS EVIAN CRASH
ABBOT SLING COED ELS
SCRIP CHEESECAKE CAT
POETS RAN OMIT DATA
ERAS CARAT CLUE LAKER
END TAME ETHOS LONERS
  ARM SMEAR PARE
CANDYSTRIPER LAWN OLD
AREAS EATEN EASYASPIE
SLANT EVERY ANTE TARA
TOROS NESS REAR ALAN
```

PUZZLE 288

```
UTAH LAMB CHUM WALK
SALE OVER OOLA ERIE
ERMA DESI BONG ALEE
SPARSE HEARTANDSOUL
  TOSS FRA ORE
ARSON PELF DELILAH
WOLF VERY TULIP ROB
ELAPSING MAMBA TAB
DEBATED COMMA OPERA
  LAW BOGEY SHU
ENEMY ALOUD LEERIER
RAM SCULL WORDPLAY
ARI BORES DAUB LIRE
CREOLES TICS PEALS
  ABE MEG EACH
CROSSMYHEART STEADY
REST NOEL EONS ALAS
IDLE LYRE SIRE RIDE
BOOR YORE SLAT TIER
```

PUZZLE 292

```
BREW ERODE  DADA
AUTO NITER  EGER
ISTO SAILS  FAME
LEAD UNCLEREMUS
   STET INART
ROAMED PLEAD
ALCAN VIOL  HOE
JOHNNYAPPLESEED
ARE USES  PURSE
  BOLTS TENDER
ALGER  BEES
PAULBUNYAN HORA
ANIL ROARS  IRES
RASE SURGE  NEAT
TIES ANDES  ELLA
```

PUZZLE 289

```
HER ALAI ADLIB KALE
ATE CORN DRACO OBEY
MAVERICK DENEB DEAR
  OPEN LIEGE WRITHE
GALES LIARS WHOA
LIVE FANGS BRICKBAT
ADE FARGO BLOTS OHO
DERRICKS PRATE NOEL
  ARES TRACE CANAL
ASSIST TRICK MOPEDS
STINT PIECE LONE
PANS SLEEK RICKSHAW
IRA SPARS PUNKS EDO
CRICKETS WEEKS DAZE
  LICE CHEFS SIDES
GEMINI HAIKU AWOL
EDAM ABOUT LIMERICK
TINA LAPSE LOOP NAE
STYX SHEEN YURT EPA
```

PUZZLE 293

```
AVEC SHEET  LADY
LIMA HARSH  ALOE
EDIT RISER  SIVA
CATAPULT EASTER
   LEGS HALE
GAPES CATARACT
REGAL MOLE  NOR
ONES DEMON  CEDE
TON ETES  HONES
CATAWBAS COOTS
  GOAL BALL
GREENS COPYCATS
LORN INANE  ASEA
AMID NEVER  TILT
DANA GEARS  SALE
```

PUZZLE 294

```
ARC      GAS
SOLD  MAINE
HOAR  ARRIVE
 TWISTS  PEN
   VIE  SEND
 STEP  PART
JAWS  JAM
AGE  HELPED
BANTER  LARK
 STEAK  ERIE
   YAP    SPY
```

PUZZLE 295

```
AGES  BASE  APT
TAXI  ALAN  NOR
ASTRONAUT  TOE
  EEL  STERILE
CURSES  ERE
ALI  OLD  SIDES
SNOB  YET  NERO
HARES  WIT  LIL
  AHA  PALACE
RUNDOWN  LOW
ORE  RAINCOATS
AGO  TILE  TRIO
DEN  STEW  SEND
```

PUZZLE 296

```
RIATAS  DEBTS
UNROLL  ELAINE
THEEVERGLADES
TAN  APERS  IAN
ELAM  TVA  BEDE
DESIS  EDGARS
   DECREES
STATUS  RITAS
TEAS  TIS  NOTE
ASP  AROMA  REL
CAPECANAVERAL
OMELET  REVISE
ERASE  TRADER
```

PUZZLE 297

```
APE  EDIT  FRAY
TAX  LORE  LONE
EWE  AMEN  IOTA
  RATE  DANDER
UNCLE  BELT
NAIL  RENO  AWE
ITS  FENCE  MEN
TOE  LADY  FOLD
  GALS  FEUDS
ACCEPT  LIEN
BEAN  OBOE  TOT
EDGE  REAL  ERA
TEES  SEND  DEN
```

PUZZLE 298

```
PEAT  SLAG  SERT  MANE
ELLA  LIRA  ARAN  AMOK
AMEN  EMMY  GEST  RODE
ROCKAWAYBEACH  ABYSS
  TIS  LENT  MIL
BROOM  CHAN  CATERER
LUMP  SLED  PEAL  HONE
ASE  STONEHENGE  AMOS
BERATED  ARNE  BLAST
  TOP  HAMES  PAL
SAMBA  BELA  BASSOON
NEAL  MARBLEARCH  RUE
ARIA  OARS  XMAS  PASS
PONCHOS  SPAT  WILTS
  KON  BRAE  EVA
APORT  BOULDERCANYON
DADO  FIRN  IDOL  IONE
ERIC  ANNE  TATA  SKUA
SINK  AGES  EMIT  TEST
```

PUZZLE 299

```
MARPLE  IRENE  HST
ACADIA  CATON  ETES
MURDERWITHMIRRORS
ATE  SLICES  GOCART
SERA  YELL  IMPUTES
  RUBLE  KRAAL
CAROTID  ROKS  EVES
REAMER  PALE  ABC
ARIA  DOODADS  AROA
MID  ALAS  TUMULT
PEST  STER  NEMESIS
  OPTED  RIPEN
SARTRES  GETS  SALT
ORATOR  TRIODE  NOR
ORDEALBYINNOCENCE
NOIR  EARLE  WREAKS
WIS  TAELS  NURSES
```

PUZZLE 300

```
CADGES  RAGS  STRAND
EMERGE  BUILT  PRANCE
ROBERTTAYLOR  LANDAU
UTE  ALL  AURIC  SAX
FEGATELLOATTACK
LAGS  LEAPS  STE  SAGA
ORE  MODEST  ASPIRED
ELDER  FEZ  OTB  EDGED
  GAP  GOALIE  OSE
KINGSGAMBITDECLINED
IRA  PATTEN  HEN
CADRE  TNT  NSC  RAGES
KNEADER  AMATOL  LEO
SIRE  MAC  OZONE  FALL
SICILIANDEFENSE
HOS  INTRO  RIO  UNC
ENTIRE  QUEENSINDIAN
ACUMEN  USING  AGENDA
PEDANT  EYRE  MORGAN
```

PUZZLE 301

```
WHEAT  SHA  BET  BACH
AERIE  CUR  ARE  APRON
SANDSTORM  SANDSTONE
PRI  SANDY  ESTES  WED
STEW  TEL  EEL  ENDS
  ABASES  ERRING
HARTE  STARS  BAILS
AMEERS  ONE  MADDER
GEORGESAND  PTA  SEGO
  LACE  PEAR
ALEC  LOT  SANDCASTLE
DALLAS  GAT  STORES
SOFAS  SATES  TAINT
  SHOCKS  REWRAP
LETS  ARI  REE  SPAT
IMA  ARENA  TRANS  ANI
AMPERSAND  SANDPIPER
REESE  TEE  ATE  IRENE
TRES  ERS  RED  TARTS
```

PUZZLE 302

```
  SPAR  TOTS
  SPARE  ARENA
  AIRED  TENOR
FEE  SAT  TRI
ELSE  LEASED
  STIRS
CAREEN  PALS
ADE  NEW  LEE
RATED  OLIVE
SPIRE  RIVER
TEAR  DEER
```

PUZZLE 303

```
TAM  RAPS  SPOT
ALE  OHIO  TAPE
BASEBALL  AREA
  SOB  LISTENS
PLANES  DUE
LOG  RIN  ESSAY
ONE  TOP  INA
TESTS  RIB  LOP
  OAR  PREENS
POSTMAN  ERN
ARIA  DEPARTED
CALL  ARID  LYE
ELKS  ROTS  YEN
```

PUZZLE 304

```
SWIM  BALSA  PAST
PANE  ALIEN  ERNE
AFAR  PLANTATION
CEDE  TORT  STABS
ERE  NIT  SPY
  QUIZ  JET  RAT
SOURCE  ANY  HENS
ADAGE  DUD  PASTA
ROTE  GIN  PAUPER
IRE  OPT  RILE
  WEB  DAD  CAP
BATHE  FRAY  STIR
EXHILARATE  TIDE
ALES  SEVER  EVES
MEEK  HEEDS  MESS
```

1-F, 2-G, 3-T, 4-K, 5-W, 6-S, 7-O, 8-A, 9-D, 10-Y, 11-H, 12-N, 13-Q, 14-M, 15-X, 16-C, 17-J, 18-P, 19-Z, 20-V, 21-R, 22-E, 23-U, 24-B, 25-L, 26-I.

PUZZLE 305

```
M  WARMER  RAWER  RARE  W
A  DETAIN  TINED  TEND  I
R  NERVES  SEVEN  EVES  N
C  SCARED  DEARS  ERAS  D
H  SHARED  READS  DARE  S
```

PUZZLE 306

```
OATS  SCAN  STRAP
DRAW  TALE  PROVE
DINE  ONTO  YODEL
SAGA  COON  WEST
  TYKE  FEE
PASSE  SCARLET
ACT  TAPIOCA  VAT
IRE  GENIE  APE
LEE  RESULTS  DEN
SPRINTS  AVERT
  OPT  DATA
LIST  ATOM  STEP
ANNAL  TUNA  SODA
STATE  ONUS  AMID
HOPED  PETS  LETS
```

PUZZLE 307

PUZZLE 308

```
LOTTO CERO  BROW  AVER
OMAHA ABED  POONA NAVE
TARES ROME  ASSET ILET
ONOR  HALE  ARSINE MIRE
FITASAFIDDLEANDREADY
    PAVE  YOUR   INLAWS
REVIVE FIRM CLUNG THE
ABASE LANK  DOING PIED
MOST  BANG  DOLLOP LORE
ANT  PRIG  RALLY LEANER
    VAIN MERLS CART
BASING TESTS RACE  SPA
OPUS  HEALTH SURE SPIN
APSE  TALES SINE PAULO
RAT  AERIE LUNT MENDED
DRESSY    SORE  SERI
INTHEPINKOFCONDITIION
STAR DADOES URIS ARNE
AINU ARETE TRAP AROSE
NOCT NEARS RENE LIINED
ONES DELE  ASTR LASTS
```

PUZZLE 309

```
MOTS  SAFE  CODA  SCAN
ALOE  WRAP  AWAY  COTE
RIDE  ANNI  RENE  ROLE
COOKONESGOOSE  PIKER
   ELK  RAM  GOBI
SUCRE BOAR  CANTEENS
PROS  FOAM  ALIAS  COW
OSO   ROOK  STARR ARTA
TAKEON SALOME BLUET
UNITE MON  SERUM
TAPIS REAPED TIMBER
ROAD  CRAZE ARAM  LIE
INN   CLOVE PLAT  MERE
PEEPHOLE REIN EASEL
XRAY  SOL  ANS
ASCOT COOKINGSCHOOL
GLUM  CRIB  COOT  ISBA
HASP  HOSE  APER  ESAU
ABET  EWER  NERO  SAND
```

PUZZLE 310

```
HOPS  PACT  CRAB  BRIM
ALEC  OMAR  HIVE  IONE
NINO  TYRO  ICER  SORA
DONNA PUMPERNICKEL
   YEMEN  TOM  EMU
BAD  ECON  OUR  PIQUE
ERR  SCOUT NEAP  TUNE
ALES  ENDO  KOREA AIL
NOAH  NEEDY CAVORTS
   DEFT  SOARS  RENT
AFFAIRS METAL CELT
CLU  TIARA DAUB  ERIE
HELP  CLAN  STRUT MEN
EASEL ETA  EACH  ANT
   PAL  IRE  SKIMS
STOPSONADIME  NOTED
COPE  COMO  EVEN  VETO
AGER  ANET  NERO  IRON
MANY  LONE  DRAB  ESNE
```

PUZZLE 311

```
 GANEF PILLAR EROS
CAREER ANYONE GOTHS
JAMIELEECURTIS RATITE
ORB DESPISE MIMED RAT
KOLA RHONE SADAT ALPH
ELENA EDO MITER ADELE
DEDICATE CIITED GRAYER
   MUGS SOCKS ALIMB
ABATE OMAHA DRESSAGE
AGATE GRETA CARNE SEE
MIRO LESLIECARON OSAR
ALB MINOT LOIRE AVERY
SEARAVEN SKINS PREYS
   RIVET SPINE CARR
ONAGER BARDS CATALPAS
ROBIN WALED DAL HARSH
GRAD PASTE DINES POPE
AIR MODEM EUGENES MII
NARROW MILDREDDUNNOCK
SIEVE ANODES ALEUTS
 EYER NEWART REESE
```

PUZZLE 312

```
CHAISE  COMPOSE  TWISTS
LID  ABREAST  ORNATE
CASE DENT  HUNDRED
ETERNAL  POLKA
   VEIN  FAKE  DRAWS
REAP ESCORT  SOOTHE
PAINT LIMITED  EARN
ASCEND GARAGE  FILE
TENDON  CLUE  N AB
   SEDAN  PREACH
REVENUE SOON  TEASE
STIRS FOUNDER  HELM
SCENE RESTORED  WET
```

PUZZLE 313

```
DORM  DART  SCAM  COST
ALOE  ITER  TRIO  ATTU
BATS  VENI  ROMP  PHIL
FISHANDCHIPS  STERE
IAN  KIP  BEAR
CAFES FAYE  TERRIFIC
HEIR  BUS  KITE  NINO
IRS  FISHMONGER  SRO
COHORTS OMARS ATHEL
OTOE  STAVE  FLAT
FLUTE MAINE PROMOTE
LOT  CATFISHROW  FIR
ENOS  ODES  RAG  ARES
DEFENDED BUSY  TRYST
WARY  GIN  SUM
SCALA GOLDFISHBOWL
TATA  TOLE  OTTO  RAIL
OVEN  SAGA  LEER  EDNA
PERE  PLAN  DAWN  DIDO
```

PUZZLE 314

```
LOUD      SOPS
EASE      IDEA
TREESURGERY
   RERUN
LOS  EAR       PAM
EMU  POPLARS   ICE
NAG PODS LOAD  NEE
DRAB RED EGO  WEST
REBUT  AGAIN
MAIN       WINE
ASTER      FORCE
RAPT RUB  TOO EDEN
OIL  SEAS SEND LAO
ADE  STUMPED   ESS
DES       DEL  STY
    MANIA
COCONUTPALM
ORAL      ERIE
TEND      SEEN
```

PUZZLE 315

```
REEF  TRAPU LACES CHAR
ELLA  ROSIN EVORA RAMA
STIR  ASTER SORAS ARES
TOOMANYIRONSINTHEFIRE
ANTONS  LEEDS  AIT
UNI POLERS  AYR  CAT
TEETOTALLER TWEEZERS
OMA  LAID  STEAD ODEA
RET SETTO SORRY DREAR
ASO  ADO  EATEN  AIR
HANDLINGWITHKIDGLOVES
OAT RADIO  HAL  YET
SPEND SAREE GLORY IRE
LOAN  RISER TOIL  NIE
INVADERS THREEBAGGER
DEE EDE BIRRED  AWE
   ANE  SERIE ROLLIE
STARTEDTHEBALLROLLING
ORNE MORON DAYIN INCA
RIOT EDILE EMOTE NEON
TONE ROADS RANAT GAGS
```

PUZZLE 316

```
SCORE SWAMP PER
TUBER TEPEE AXE
ALOHA ARENA NIL
GLEE  RED  NATTY
      ALMS OUT
PATTER CONTORTS
USE ESCAPE LOOP
LIES  AVE  LUTE
SATE AGENDA TEN
ENHANCES ATTEST
   TOE  OBEY
CHASM RIB  REEL
LAB AROSE HARDY
ARE DIALS ANGER
NET SPREE STONE
```

PUZZLE 317
MISFORTUNE

PUZZLE 318

```
BRIG TEAL VAN
LOLL URDU EGO
OSLO BULLFROG
TYSON  PAULA
  MUFTI  ACME
SHH LAS SIRUP
POORLY SALUTE
ANNES HOG ZEE
TEEM  GAYER
   SILLS RADAR
WITTIEST  RATE
ALL MALE EDEN
SKY AMEN RANT
```

PUZZLE 319

APPLIANCES: Air conditioner, Refrigerator, Oven, Stove, Electric fan.
SEATS: Armchair, Rocker, Ottoman, Stool, Easy chair.
MYTHOLOGY: Achilles, Romulus, Orion, Satyrs, Eros.
MATH TERMS: Addition, Radius, Ordinate, Square root, Ellipse.
BOATS: Ark, Rowboat, Outboard, Scull, Excursion.

PUZZLE 320

1-Q, 2-V, 3-T, 4-S, 5-X, 6-I, 7-B, 8-O, 9-W, 10-Z, 11-R, 12-F, 13-J, 14-H, 15-D, 16-Y, 17-M, 18-E, 19-A, 20-U, 21-L, 22-N, 23-P, 24-G, 25-C, 26-K.

PUZZLE 321

```
JEWEL F HEEDS
UR EAR A X N
RHYME A WITHE
OL KAYAK R A
RAYS E TACK
 D E ODE H H
QUIVER WRITER
 L EVE N S
STUN A GASP
 C N TULIP L A
RITZY L URBAN
U I P ELF U T
BULGE Y FUMES
```

1-Y, 2-M, 3-X, 4-S, 5-D, 6-G, 7-N, 8-T, 9-Q, 10-U, 11-E, 12-O, 13-Z, 14-R, 15-W, 16-J, 17-F, 18-A, 19-L, 20-P, 21-I, 22-B, 23-H, 24-V, 25-K, 26-C.

PUZZLE 322

```
PLAN NESTS COAL
AERO ETHER AURA
PAINTTHETOWNRED
ASSORTED  HESSE
LEE ILL SHY
  BEE BOO ODOR
FACES SOAPOPERA
AWHITECHRISTMAS
TRAGEDIES SEINE
SYNE GOA CID
   PEN ARC AID
HOSTS  IDOLATRY
ONCEINABLUEMOON
ETAT ARIES ANNE
ROBE PADRE HESS
```

PUZZLE 323

```
1. PEAR   2. SPOT   3. RICE
   EDGE      PURE      IDOL
   AGES      ORBS      COAL
   REST      TEST      ELLS
```

PUZZLE 324

```
LAGS ESS BAIL
IDLE RAH EDNA
MAIN AGE REND
AMBASSADOR
   TIE DAYTON
HERON BET IRE
AVER JAR ONES
MOB TAG TRYST
SEASON SEA
  TOUCHANDGO
SODA ARA GOAD
ODOR RED ENID
SENT YES SETS
```

PUZZLE 325

ACROSS: 1. Laurel, 2. Spruce, 3. Banyan, 4. Walnut, 5. Willow.

DOWN: 1. Alder, 2. Birch, 3. Aspen, 4. Beech, 5. Cedar, 6. Maple.

SAYING: Children and fools have merry lives.

PUZZLE 326

```
MOSS CARAT BASE
ERLE AMINO AVON
SEATTLEMARINERS
ASP ALES  CARE
  AGAR OMEN
BALL  ARE  ALP
ERASES BANG ERE
TORONTOBLUEJAYS
ASK DARE SEASON
 ESP RAY  MERE
  LIEN ARAB
 STAR SPAR UTE
CHICAGOWHITESOX
HARE AVAIL VEGA
IDES BANDS EDAM
```

PUZZLE 327

1. Utter, 2. Stare, 3. Shark, 4. Penny, 5. Boxer, 6. Clash, 7. Braze, 8. Weird, 9. Scoop, 10. Fluid.

PUZZLE 328

```
FIRS DIET TSP
EDIT ACRE RUE
ELSE YEARLING
LEERED SNAP
  EARL SILKS
HONOREES RENO
ALE NAMED TEN
LEAP MOLASSES
TOTEM NEST
  NEAR CHARMS
OVERCAST MOAT
WAS AGUE PILE
ENS WEED SLEW
```

PUZZLE 329

```
ASP MACAW LED
RAE ALIBI AXE
FORBIDDEN YUL
 TINA DWELL
ELUDE ALBERTA
RARE OCEAN
SOB STUNG GOT
 ANITA LOBE
CHINESE DAVID
HARTE PIKE
IRA RECOVERED
MEN EVOKE NAY
PSI DATED SUE
```

538

PUZZLE 330

```
MOVES ARIA STIR
ADORE RENT TOGA
MOTEL MAKEFUNOF
ARE FOOL INERT
LIAR PEST
REPAST FLAT TAD
IRISH GRASS USE
VOLT CRANE FLIT
ADE BLAME GLIDE
LED RACE PROPER
TOME CROW
ASSET SHOW CAR
MAKEHASTE NOOSE
OMIT PEAS UNITE
SETH TENT PENAL
```

PUZZLE 335

```
SEERAIMSTHAWAHA
ARMISTICEAMIGOS
CROOKEDRAVENEST
ROTTERDAMENTREE
ARESRAYMONDAGAR
MARSHCABLEGRAMS
ELATECULTDRIVEN
NOVAROGERDINERO
THIMBLEDAISTOGS
CAVILARISETEPEE
ALANADDLEDARENA
RELAYEREMITERIG
RAGEELARENOSAVE
OVERRAKEDANTTEN
TEENSPETERESENT
```

PUZZLE 339

```
JABS STAN EWE
ACRE HERO LOG
YEAR EXISTING
STIR EYE
OOZES DOOM
SHOUTED MAE
TAPS EGO PART
ALE ENDORSE
GONE AREAL
SAG BEAR
QUESTION CLAM
USA OLIO ASIA
OER PELT TOLD
```

PUZZLE 331

1. At birth an elephant weighs from one hundred and sixty to two hundred pounds.
2. You share your birthday with at least nine million others.

PUZZLE 332

```
ONES FOR SHED
POLO AWE HERE
TRIFLING RAIN
TAR UNITES
SAFES SLIM
TURN SCALPERS
ERA SPATE VAT
MANICURE SERE
DATE SCREW
DESERT CUR
ARIA EVENINGS
TILL RID BEAT
ANTS SEE EELY
```

PUZZLE 336

```
REAP ANT
ONCE DAUBS
BEET AGREE
IMP FLAW
ROTATE ONE
BERET DANCE
ADD EMERGE
DUET END
CAROL EVIL
ELOPE NINE
TEE TAKE
```

PUZZLE 340

```
CRIB SWAP HIM
HONE CAGE ODE
ABUT ADORABLE
PEN ALE POET
DALE JET
CHASM PUN LOG
AUTHORITATIVE
BEE SAG METAL
STY CONE
DELI WAR RAP
RAINCOAT HALO
AVE URGE ITEM
YEN BEER DEEP
```

PUZZLE 333

```
CUPS GRAB SPA
OPAL RUDE TON
WORE EGAD APT
SNEEZE MILL
TENT MOLAR
HAT REAP TIRE
AIR ORGAN NEE
IDEA YULE GAD
REMIT SEAT
BLOB TRAMPS
ELL WANT SORE
BEE ERIE KNOW
BAD RAPS SAPS
```

PUZZLE 337

```
GOLD HAM LIAR
AREA ACE ALTO
LACY TRAMPLED
ANT SCENES
UTAH DEEPEN
CORED JET ODE
AMEN PAR LOGS
PER AIM BERET
ENSIGN PATH
NECTAR OAR
LAUNDERS CURE
ELSE RUT ASIA
DEER SEE TEAM
```

PUZZLE 341

```
WRAP JAM
NAIVE LIBERAL
INFER AGITATE
LET MIX DATED
TIC EEL
FORETELL AFT
ARIA BOA IDEA
RED OPPONENT
LOX SUN
MOTOR BET PAW
EDUCATE INANE
NEGATED NOTED
LEE GREW
```

PUZZLE 334

```
TALON J MAGIC
O IDECIMALA O
TF ETAGERE GS
HOD LP MI SUM
EWEE SOB RERE
REPAST ERRANT
EOS AIR OM I
AR ANTSR SC
ET RPCLE TE
MMO AHA VRL
PREFER TWEEZE
TUNI VIE SIP
RET LE RE SPA
EL FANTAIL UT
S LUSUALLYR H
SHANK X LEFTY
```

PUZZLE 338

```
BEG POUR ADDS
AYE EASE ROUE
TEMPERED MOST
OVER PARTS
AGREED ROD
CLAM PYRAMID
TOT SHEET ODE
SWEATER SALE
CAN PANTED
BERRY POLO
OLEO LASTWORD
LASS ELSE WOE
ANTS DEER NEW
```

PUZZLE 342

```
ANTELOPE CHECKS
C I A I E O I
CATATONIC LINEN
O H C K O I T I
SEETHE INJURIES
T I A T M N T
MANICURE HERE
T O G C A B N R
ETNA VISCOUNT
R A I D T C
RESIGNED SKEWER
A T N N P S E O
CREDO TOOTHPICK
E R R S O G E
STYLED THATCHER
```

PUZZLE 343

```
ROOT  HOPS  RIVER
EACH  ERAL  ERASE
ATTU  RARA  PASTA
THELIONINWINTER
ASTERN  STAN
       ASH  DEBATE
ECLAT  ABIE  RAID
MOUSETHATROARED
INIT  RAYE  SEEDY
RESALE  MAA
     ENOS  SKATED
CATANDTHECANARY
LURID  HAVE  ESNE
ERODE  EDEN  STIR
OATER  REND  TEES
```

PUZZLE 344

1. Turtle (E, O); 2. Gratis (H, T); 3. Expel (A, M); 4. Clear (Q, U); 5. Plait (C, Y); 6. Poetry (P, R); 7. Orate (G, S); 8. Sewer (I, V); 9. Least (W, Z); 10. Trite (K, N); 11. Stead (B, L); 12. Stole (D, J); 13. Yield (F, X).

PUZZLE 345

```
DAMP  SAM  FEUD
ORAL  ADA  EASE
DATA  USE  WRAY
OBEYED  SEEM
     PAINTBRUSH
SORER  ORB  FEE
AMEN  RIO  AFAR
GAL  SOS  GUSTO
ARITHMETIC
     AREA  ENTREE
BABE  NOR  IOWA
IDLE  CAR  ODES
TOES  ETA  NEST
```

PUZZLE 346

```
RITA  OBI  SLAB
AVID  PAN  POLO
MENU  INNUENDO
     PLANE  SNEAK
SILAGE  BET
ERATO  CAR  AIR
RATE  LOT  ONCE
ENE  DEN  MUTES
     POT  LATEST
SPURN  PANDA
ARRESTED  ATTU
POSE  EEL  TEAR
SPAN  ARE  ERIN
```

PUZZLE 347

```
SOME  SCREW  REDS
EVER  QUAKE  EXIT
LASS  URGES  LAVA
FLATTER  STEAMER
     RAY  WAX
SHRIEK  AJAR  PRO
PEACE  ONER  FLAW
LAZE  TUNED  RAIN
AVER  ATOP  TENSE
YES  BUSY  JUTTED
     WAN  PEN
SQUIRTS  REALIZE
OUST  ICHOR  ODOR
DIET  NAIVE  GONG
SPRY  GREED  OLEO
```

1-D, 2-P, 3-K, 4-C, 5-N, 6-Q, 7-I, 8-V, 9-X, 10-W, 11-O, 12-J, 13-R, 14-F, 15-G, 16-Z, 17-E, 18-L, 19-M, 20-Y, 21-S, 22-B, 23-A, 24-U, 25-T, 26-H.

PUZZLE 348

D	DARING	GRAIN	RANG	I
E	CREASE	SCARE	RACE	S
S	SALTED	DEALT	DATE	L
E	REPEAT	PRATE	PERT	A
R	DRONES	NODES	DOES	N
T	DESPOT	SPODE	POSE	D

PUZZLE 349

```
GAME  GAITS  EKES
ELAN  ANNIE  AUNT
TACT  RACECOURSE
SEARED  ARAB  SUE
   DARED  SNEAKER
WEAPONED  TYS
ARM  SIEVE  SHISH
DRIP  ADITS  YMCA
ISAAC  SNAIL  PAD
  CAB  APTITUDE
EMPEROR  EARED
PEA  EDIT  RANEES
STRADIVARI  SNIP
ORES  CENIS  ECRU
MODS  ERGOT  SEED
```

PUZZLE 350

1. 48, 2. 48, 3. 36.

PUZZLE 351

```
TART  LAVA  WEB
ALES  ARAB  OLE
UTAH  BILLFOLD
TOPIC  DUEL
   RAT  ERODED
JOSTLED  WERE
EKE  LEASE  LIE
TRAP  BUMPIER
SALARY  BUY
   DOOR  STEAL
CRUSADER  HARE
OAR  MENU  OVEN
OWN  SLOT  NEAT
```

PUZZLE 352

```
 BASTE  OCCUR
ROTTEN  LOANED
INTENT  INDIGO
SNIP  RAVE  SET
EEL  GENE  ZONE
STARRED  TINTS
   YES  DAN
SHREW  PARCHES
CUES  AIMS  ALA
ORB  DIPS  ENDS
LLAMAS  EVADES
DETAIL  LIVERY
DENSE  SEEDS
```

PUZZLE 353

```
HAS  CREAM  COY
ART  HALVE  HUE
MAIM  INLET  VISA
  BRAWL  REJECT
   NEIGH  SUN
TROT  LID  IDOL
MOOR  ZODIAC  RAP
ODD  COB  EWE  ATE
ODE  HOARSE  STEW
  YOGA  LIE  FLEX
   OFF  GLARE
  SQUEAK  VODKA
TAUT  LEASE  SING
ERA  LEVER  LEE
AID  SLEET  OWE
```

1-C, 2-V, 3-F, 4-M, 5-X, 6-O, 7-U, 8-N, 9-R, 10-K, 11-L, 12-T, 13-E, 14-G, 15-D, 16-B, 17-J, 18-Y, 19-Q, 20-H, 21-I, 22-A, 23-P, 24-S, 25-Z, 26-W.

PUZZLE 354

Etiquette is the art of yawning without opening your mouth.

1. Quip, 2. Twenty-one, 3. Inge, 4. Youth, 5. Hawthorne, 6. Mitigate, 7. Fortuitous.

PUZZLE 355

```
TAFT  HAM  AAR
AREA  ERAT  SPA
BEAR  AFEATHER
  TROTS  THERE
USHERS  REO
SWEDE  SORROW
EAR  EON  NAT
  PSHAWS  TREVI
   ERE  REESES
FERMI  SATAN
INHISCAP  TELL
LOO  ELHI  ASIA
ESS  ELD  STEM
```

PUZZLE 356

```
 SPAT  CHOW
PLANET  ROBE
LARDER  ANON
ALA  INDEED
NOD  OIL
  MEEK  BEST
   LID  PEN
INMATE  ONE
SOAP  AGENDA
LESS  FORGET
ELSE  BEER
```

540

PUZZLE 357

```
REAR WASH SLAP SCAT
IDLE RITA HOPE LANE
MESS EDIT AWED IRON
SNOUTS REST DAMPENS
   LOTS SOTS LAP
PRATTLES DEER TENSE
RID SEDAN REAM DEAR
OPAL SEPAL SNIP ELI
DEMON ROVED GLADDEN
   NUT RAGED DIE
DANGLES LAPEL DEBTS
ABE LEER LOVED PART
SLOT SEEP TIMES LEA
HENRY DARN LOCALITY
   EEL PEER NOTE
TREATED STAG REDDER
AULD AIMS DATA GALE
ISLE SLOE ALIT ERIE
LEAR ELMS RACE READ
```

PUZZLE 362

```
SPAR SLED PRO
LOGIC HERO BLOW
ELUDE EARN RUSE
WOE NEED TAMED
  STEP PLUG
PASTEL LOBSTER
ABLER STAB ONE
POEM ALONE GATE
EVE LINE POSED
RETREAD SENTRY
  ELSE DUPE
STALL RAMP WIG
ARIA OPAL ERODE
WARY FELL RIVER
SPY TREY BEAM
```

PUZZLE 363

1. Float, Gloat, Groat, Great, Greet, Green.
2. Paper, Pacer, Paces, Races, Racks, Rocks.
3. Perch, Peach, Peace, Place, Plate, Slate.
4. Share, Shale, Shall, Shell, Swell, Dwell.

PUZZLE 368

```
MOLT CLAW AGED RILE
APER RICH LORE EDEN
RAGE ANTE LARD MEND
ELEMENT TROT ILIAD
  NONE THAW ACES
PADRE CHEW TRANSMIT
ERAS HAIR BOOTS IRE
AIR SINS TEASE GRID
LAYETTE GRADE BLESS
  LAS SEATS SEA
RADAR STAYS CHEDDAR
ERIN TIERS SOAR AXE
AMP DALES WORM ERLE
MYSTICAL SEAN FREED
  HATS HEAP CLAD
STALL BOWS MOUSERS
TEAM ECRU EDIT EVIL
WAKE SPAS LUTE RITA
ORES SAGE SETS SLEW
```

PUZZLE 358

```
SAME SAT PEWS
AWARE WOO CANAL
BORAX ART ARENA
EKE TOTTERS MEN
RESTED AMETHYST
  ANON SALE
TEARDROP PEWTER
IMP DUE EGO
CUTOFF BREAKAGE
  PILE RAVE
CANTEENS SENTRY
ARE LACQUER HUE
ROVED OUR SHELL
OMENS RAG EASEL
LARD EWE MESS
```

PUZZLE 359

```
T  SALTED  DEALS  LADS  E
H  HANDLE  ALDEN  LEAN  D
O  ORIENT  INTER  TERN  I
M  STREAM  ASTER  TEAR  S
A  SALOME  MOLES  ELMS  O
S  STONES  NOTES  TOES  N
```

PUZZLE 364

```
ALEC PECOS TELL
MOTH ADORE RAYE
MOTO RIDER UPON
OPERETTA EGMONT
  AMOS SNIPES
VIOLIN DIANE
INLET BANDSTAND
ETA SEDGE REO
SONGBIRDS ALICE
  RANGY BREAKS
ARENAS TATA
PRIEST BASSDRUM
HILT ROAST EYRE
ISLE ANISE ROSE
LEER SOLOS STAT
```

PUZZLE 365

HOSPITABLE

PUZZLE 360

```
PRAY AGHA BEEF
LOGE LAIN ERROR
AGRA LINT AESOP
TEE SITTERS ELM
ORESTES ETC
  CAD ERASURES
ALLAN GLUM ROLE
WOOL CLASS TILE
ORAL LATE SALAS
LEMONADE SKI
  PAR SPINNER
ALE BASTION ELA
CAMEO LARK SWIG
TIMER ELEE PETE
CARS DENS ARES
```

PUZZLE 369

```
SERENDIPITY   A
I G VELA T     R
SURGEON UGLIEST
S E R T M L L  I
UNTIE UMBRELLAS
S E R S S T T
DEVOTEES STRAYS
A       S B   L
SCRIBE SLUMBERS
E I L S U A
CLAMOROUS CIGAR
E B O N H A R E
DILEMMA INDOORS
E E E T N A A T
D ARRANGEMENT
```

PUZZLE 370

```
TURF LASS BART
AGUE EROS BELIE
BLIZZARDS ACADS
SYN ANOA GRADES
  SNOWSTORM
HASTEN EMEERS
ELLES SLED EWE
MOAT SLIER TSAR
SET CHAT ROOMS
SEARED PUNDIT
  COLDSNAPS
SCHOOL NOSE RAG
ALARK WINTERIZE
DARNS IDEE AVON
APES NESS NAVE
```

PUZZLE 361

Jewel, Ivory, Caper, Mouse, Aisle,
Lasso, Knead, Dwarf, Growl, Royal.

PUZZLE 366

```
WAN ARTS SPA
MIRED PEAL STAG
SMITE EDNA POLE
SPATTER TAILED
  LEASE ERNES
STEERS ROSIE
AIR EARN STASH
LEI ADD CUE LEA
TREED EVER SAL
  LORNA ASSORT
CADRE TALON
PARENT ISLANDS
ORES IRAS AREAS
SENT ROLL REMIT
ERA EDIE SOS
```

PUZZLE 367

1. Usage, 2. Nymph, 3. Zebra, 4. Burst,
5. Idiom.
GUEST STAR: Zubin Mehta

PUZZLE 371

1. Hail, Snow, Sleet, Rain; 2. Hula,
Jig, Tango, Reel; 3. Lute, Fiddle,
Cello, Harp; 4. Dewy, Wet, Moist,
Damp; 5. Filly, Pony, Mare, Steed; 6.
Perch, Cod, Sole, Hake.

PUZZLE 372

```
  GRADES   B ART   CRAB
FLIPPER  LON I   RYDER
UNSEAT  DESCRIPTION
   IRAN  ANTI
CORRESPONDENT C CAMELOT
RAIDERS  OMICRON  RISE
LEONS    EDUCATED
  PEKIN   ONS
DEPTHCHARGE  UINTAS
AREAS   DON  TABORET
TREE    MATE  LEVELS
```

PUZZLE 373

Dog, Dot, Doe, Did, Dig, Dim, Day,
Dab, Dam.

PUZZLE 374

```
ROAM  AFT   DECK
IDLE  SIR   OXEN
FOOT THROB  TILE
FREEBIE  TRESTLE
   INN  HIM
   JOB    QUIZ
FLAB BAYOU   MEAN
AIDE AGAPE   ABLE
TEES COMET   GREW
   DESK    YEA
   PIT  COO
SOPRANO  RINGLET
TREE GAVEL   RAVE
EASE  SOD    AKIN
PLOD  TWO    MELD
```

1-P, 2-J, 3-G, 4-U, 5-M, 6-D, 7-L, 8-V, 9-Q, 10-I, 11-R, 12-A, 13-N, 14-B, 15-T, 16-E, 17-Y, 18-S, 19-H, 20-K, 21-C, 22-W, 23-F, 24-O, 25-Z, 26-X.

PUZZLE 375

1. Talent; 2. Howler; 3. Eli, Eli; 4. Embark; 5. Mosque; 6. Pisces; 7. Intomb; 8. Retina; 9. Exotic; 10. Struck.
FILM: The Empire Strikes Back
RELATED FILM: Star Wars

PUZZLE 376

```
CAST      PRAY
ALOHA    IRATE
PINES    DIMES
    SHEEN
PAGE   LATHER
ERA  HIS   ALA
PELLET    EMIT
    ARENA
STAND    ARROW
HANDS    GLIDE
ENDS      SPED
```

PUZZLE 377

```
LOFT  TART   ASP
EMIR  AVER   FOE
SIRE  MENU   ALP
STEEP  RECORD
    ANSWER
NOMINEE   DAFT
ORANGE  STEREO
WEPT   TORRENT
    ESTATE
STRAIT   KNIFE
BAR  LATE   ODOR
EGO  AREA   DEAN
TAT  DART   SAME
```

PUZZLE 378

```
RASP  SPRY   FIAT
EPEE  CLUE   LIMBO
BANG  REEL   INPUT
URN  SEA  PAD  ATE
STACCATO   MOOR
    ARM  RAP  ITCH
AMATI  WELL  LIRE
BAD  PLAGUES  AIR
LIVE ADAM   MELBA
EDEN  PEN   HIT
    NESS  OVERALLS
MET  EEL  IRK  OAK
EXUDE  ELSE  ACRE
SIREN  TATS  SAGE
STEW   SWAY  PLOT
```

Children are obedient whenever it's expedient.

PUZZLE 379
BROTHERHOOD

PUZZLE 380

```
STAG    TRAM
TIBET   ROBOT
AGILE   AWARE
RED  ASP   TON
REACH   LENT
   SHAVE
LANK  POISE
APO  NET  TAP
TRITE   ERASE
HOSES   DARES
NEAT    PELT
```

PUZZLE 381

```
FAR  ATOP   BEAM
ORE  DOLL   URGE
EMPLOYEE   RIOT
   OARS  ALLEGE
BARGE  ASIA
RUTS  TRUMPETS
ATE  SHORE   NAP
TORTOISE   ETNA
   RARE  LARKS
DESERT   FACE
EDEN  ELEPHANT
AGED  EELS   TEA
LENS  NILE   YEN
```

PUZZLE 382

```
CHAMP    MAGIC
RETAIN  CANADA
ORANGE  LITTER
SOB  SATIN  HAD
SEAT  TAP  EELS
  SLIVER  JARS
   BAR  GUS
  SUET  SAGEST
CANT  MIL  LARD
ALE  GIRLS  HOE
RAVENS  OTTAWA
OMEGAS  PEERER
MINOR    WEALS
```

PUZZLE 383

```
SAND  PLEA   SPY
OVER  ROAD   TIE
MERE  INTERACT
ERODING   PER
   GOT  STARES
WOMEN  RESPIRE
AGO   PEW   ELL
TROOPED   MOREL
TENDON   FUR
   BET  SUMATRA
ONESTEPS  TRIP
LEA  ERIE   EASE
DEM  DANE   SPED
```

PUZZLE 384

```
RA TE S    IND ITE    CO LU M BUS
THE RM OME  T  ER  R    UN RE AD Y
R   ING    ALE  C    SPA  T   LY ING
           S IS TI N E
HA  P  PEN   I  RAN   RED LI GH T
R   O  AN   VE ST    T   L  OS E
P   RE CE DE  SHI RE    AC T  ED
            S LO P PI ER
RE  S      P UT    DAT A    MAR S
T   H  UND ER    PRA I SE WOR TH Y
INT IM ID ATE    Y  ON    K  A  NE
```

PUZZLE 385

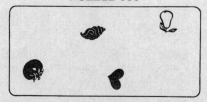

PUZZLE 386

```
BACH  SALE   PRIM
EQUAL ARIA   LORE
NURSE FINS   ASIA
TASTE EDGE   NEST
   ERR  ELAN
TURN OVER   GERM
ONE  PIN  SODIUM
SIP FEARING  FRO
STEALS ORE   LAS
  ELSE GLEE PELT
   HEAR  ROE
AREA  LEAF  PALER
SIAM  TAME  ALIKE
ACRE  ASEA  LEVEE
PEND  RENT  DESK
```

PUZZLE 387

1. Decanter, 2. Treaties, 3. Heaven, 4. Sherbet, 5. Scallops, 6. Respondent, 7. Touchier, 8. Spillage, 9. Pirates, 10. Delayed.

PUZZLE 388

```
CALF  BARD  ADOBE
RAIL  ETUI  NOMAN
ARNO  ROSS  ONERS
BETWEENTHEDARK
   ENTE  PET
  BIRD  SAGO  ESTE
CAMEO  RICA  CID
THETWILIGHTZONE
NAT SRAS  OILER
SIAM ITER  NODS
   ESS  ELAN
ANDTHEDAYLIGHT
GRADE WADI   SLUR
AGILE EDEN   TOLE
DOLED SARG   SWAT
```

PUZZLE 389

M	SCREAM	SCARE	RACE	S
A	ENTAIL	INLET	NILE	T
R	ORNATE	ATONE	NOTE	A
B	TRIBAL	TRAIL	LIAR	T
L	CLAUSE	SAUCE	ACES	U
E	CREATE	TRACE	CART	E

PUZZLE 390

```
LAD   SPAT   WANT
ODOR  EASE   RACER
OOZE  ELSE   ARRAY
PREPARE  TAMPER
   EDEN  HIM
   LYING  LEERED
JAB   READ  DRIVE
ARAB  EXTRA  ALEE
MINED  TEAR   END
SADDER  SWEAR
   POP   RASP
ASTUTE  RECITES
AWAIT  DEAR   SORE
PENNY  ARTS   EVIL
EDGE   LEST   ELF
```

PUZZLE 391

1. Saint Bernard, 2. Cocker spaniel, 3. Afghan hound, 4. French poodle, 5. Irish setter, 6. Alaskan malamute.

PUZZLE 392

```
ASS  SSW  RAP
OTT  TOA  ALI
REO  APRICOT
TRACY   IDEES
ANTI   LEERS
     TIARA
   FORMS  LONE
SAMOA  ASTER
ORANGES   TEA
ACH  ESP  EDS
PEA  SSS  RYE
```

PUZZLE 393

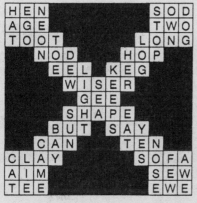

PUZZLE 394

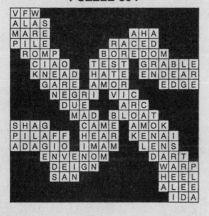

PUZZLE 395

1. Phantom, Hamper, Charm, Math;
2. Central, Letter, Title, Tile; 3. Conceit,
Beyond, Tenor, Neon; 4. Gesture,
Bought, Tough, Gust.

PUZZLE 396

```
          RAPT
   LIP   ODOR
  JOKE  DEPOT
 RAVEN   COOK
MAZE    COPPER
DAZZLE  CUR  INA
IDO  YAM THEN COT
PER  COCOA
     HOLDOFF
       EASEL  EFT
ANT  STAY  WAN  SEA
SOU  HEN   TOSSUP
HANGON     GOAD
HERO       STORY
 SATAN     HOOT
 SALE      END
 STEW
```

PUZZLE 397

1. Back, Beck, Beak, Beat, Seat.
2. Junk, Bunk, Bank, Bark, Bard, Yard.
3. Head, Lead, Lend, Land, Lane, Line.
4. Life, Lift, Loft, Loot, Boot, Boat.

PUZZLE 398

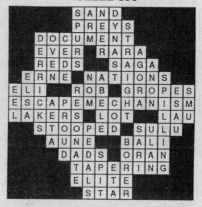

PUZZLE 399

1. Presumably, 2. Backfields, 3. Patronymic.

PUZZLE 400

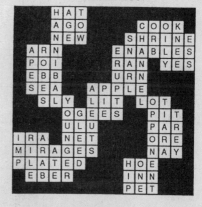

PUZZLE 401

WALLFLOWER

PUZZLE 402

```
      PACE
      EROS ODER
      ALIT URGE
JACKOLANTERN        AMAH
OVA   TARGET        LASE
KEEP    EYE SAT     ARIA
ESNE        SLAM    TAT
        TAR     LOCI
      PELE      CRANE
      ERIC      ARGO
      ASKEW     LOAN
      PESO      ELL
ICE  SLOB           EAST
BAND FRA  HAS       SLAY
INCA    ASSAIL      ASP
DEEM    CHARLEYHORSE
        LEND ZOEA
        EDGY ARES
             KELT
```

PUZZLE 403

Addend, Addled, Assets, Attest, Beetle, Egging, Eggnog, Essays, Feeble, Issues, Needle, Seethe, Weenie.

PUZZLE 404

```
NAG     GAS     BAT
OMAR    RIP     ERA
DELE    ADO     AIR
SAINTBERNARD
SNOW        TOP
  SRO       RIO
      SEAMAN
    GREATDANE
    SUNDAE
    ADD     APT
    EEL     GAIT
  BORDERCOLLIE
HOP   MOO     TRIP
IRA   OLD     SERE
TEL   NEE     DEN
```

PUZZLE 405

1. Goose, 2. Doors, 3. Lost polar bear, 4. Tarzan, 5. Hare spray.

PUZZLE 406

```
    PAST          ERIE
    OVER          ADORE
    TOME          LEVEL
    NIECE   PINE
      OTOE
SPA   ACRE        BAR
  TOGETHER        DOLE
TUREEN          ERASED
ITEM    ABANDONS
PEW     MORE      BAY
        EWES
    REAL    ATTIC
HEARD       ARES
AMISS       LODE
MULE        KNEW
```

PUZZLE 407

Humility, that low, sweet root from which all heavenly virtues shoot. (Thomas Moore)

1. Rich, 2. Motto, 3. Youth, 4. Hollow, 5. Shelter, 6. Whitewash, 7. Eventually, 8. Favoritism.

PUZZLE 408

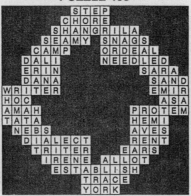

```
        STEP
        CHORE
        SHANGRILA
        SEAMY SNAGS
    CAMP      ORDEAL
    DALI      NEEDLED
    ERIN          SARA
    DANA          SAND
WRITER            EMIR
HOC               ASA
AMAH          PROTEM
TATA          HEMI
NEBS          AVES
DIALECT       RENT
TRITER        EARS
    IRENE ALLOT
    ESTABLISH
        TRACE
        YORK
```

PUZZLE 409

JOURNALISM

PUZZLE 410

```
ARC                   BIG
PAL                   USE
ACID                  BILL
RENEE                 FILE
TRIALS          FOLD
  SCREAM        AUK
      VIA   BALEFUL
      HUT LOX
      MATISSE
    KIN NUT
  WELD  GIRDED
  HEED  TORRID
HEAP      MARLO
OAR       MALT
PLY       NET
          DRY
```

PUZZLE 411

1. Cool, Wool, Wood, Word, Ward, Warm.
2. Dull, Full, Fell, Feel, Keel, Keen.
3. Head, Held, Hell, Tell, Tall, Tail.
4. Stay, Slay, Slat, Slit, Suit, Quit.

PUZZLE 412

```
AMAH
GINA
AMIND
SITDOWNS            GLOP
 AMORAL             LANE
  ADIME             ANTE
STILTED             DIOR
HIDES               THEP
ITE    TROP         PHAR
PONS ARABIC  OLIN
SITSONONESHANDS
TOED LENITY  SIVA
DURA    SOSO TIL
DRAT         OSTEO
ARAT         MORTISE
GIGI         ASLAN
OLEO         THONGS
GLEN         HANDBAGS
                SUMAC
                LOLA
                LAST
```

PUZZLE 413

```
AWE             SAT
FOX             TIE
TOADS           SHADE
  CRAM       SOOT
  TILE       PALE
  PEER HARD
      TUTOR
      LOT
      REPEL
      PAIR LOSS
  CLIP      ACTS
  HARE      MOAT
SHINY           WREST
OIL             AHA
WED             MEW
```

PUZZLE 414

1. Shrinkable, 2. Exhausting, 3. Mistakenly

PUZZLE 415

```
              ARM
COST          BEAT
ALTO          EMIR
DIET    SLY   ODE
EVE    STOAS  VEE
TERN   TRAMP  TEN
    ACRID OAR
    SOAP MICE
    TOY RULES
CRY  ERASE    SPED
ALE  DATED    OVA
LOT   YES     PIER
AVID          ESNE
SERA          NETS
RED
```

PUZZLE 416

We do not know one millionth of one percent about anything. (Thomas Alva Edison)

1. Delightful, 2. Nomination, 3. Know-how, 4. Pontoon, 5. Cone, 6. Nee, 7. Battery.

PUZZLE 417

```
        BAR
       TABOO
      ERRATUM
    MEEK   ASIS
    TALK     TEND
  WILY         NAIL
GAPE            PRIM
ART              TEA
SPOT            PINT
  SERE         FEES
  DIVA       BURR
    PECK   WEST
    NINNIES
     DEEDS
      EWE
```

PUZZLE 418

1. Plastering, 2. New product, 3. Fights back.

PUZZLE 419

```
ERECT TABLE
SNARE OBOES
PARER REWET
   ASSET
INSTEP   OPA
VETERANSDAY
YES   DELETE
   CREPE
SPARE HEWER
TAHOE EVERY
DRAWL WEDGE
```

PUZZLE 420

```
CAD ATLAS SPA
ODE CHOSE YES
TOMAHAWKS RAT
  AMEN SAUCE
WINES SHIPPER
ADD3  CIIOOT
GAS SPOON AXE
  AWARD SILK
VIBRATE SERVE
EDICT  SLAB
RIB TEMPERATE
SOL ERRED SAW
ETE DISCS ERE
```

PUZZLE 421

```
        DEW
MAT     IRIS
CAVE   WEALTH
DOZEN TOT DRIP
LAME DRUM  IRE
ONE ABE BAKER
SCANT PAN APE
TENOR    REIGN
DEE SHY EXTRA
ANGLE HUE  RAM
DOE  ALTO PIPE
DATA IRK PEACE
HIJACK   ARCH
TALE      LET
RED
```

PUZZLE 422

School is a building that has four walls—with tomorrow inside.

1. Understood, 2. Christmas, 3. Fail, 4. Willow, 5. Toothbrush, 6. Losing, 7. Hawaii.

PUZZLE 423

```
 PAW
 PIPE
BELLE   YEA
MACAO  BEAR
ATARMSLENGTH
PEN BIAS LYON
  PRIDE BABY
GAS EDIT OBOE
IMP DEN  OATH
BYANOSE BRIER
ELSE     LEES
 MAGIC EARMARK
 RENO  AGE DIE
 SCAB PREP YEW
 TACO ALLOT
 TALC EROS TEA
 TAKESTOHEART
   MEWS  AMUSE
   PRE  ADEPT
        GENE
        ODD
```

PUZZLE 424

```
     SAFE   GAY
     AREA   RYE
     ROAR  BEET
    POST  BOW
    PINE PIN
    DING BENEATH
STREET BAT   COO
IRONS  OUR TWIRL
PAD   LID TRADED
SPECIAL  TOUR
     END BALE
     ELK COLD
OVAL  FARE
AIR   OPEN
RAN   REST
```

PUZZLE 425

1. Hypnotized, 2. Introduces, 3. Hospitable.

PUZZLE 426

```
          CHAP
    TAT  HARE
HUE ZERO ERNE
ALSO EXTENSION
MUSKRAT  SET
  ARAL   ESTES
MAYAN     EAU
BARS     GASP
ELM   ERASE
DESKS AMEN
  IAN ECUADOR
FORTWORTH RENO
ALIT DONE  RED
RICE SEA
MOAN
```

PUZZLE 427

Dollars and sense do not necessarily go together.

1. Honesty, 2. Creation, 3. Staggers, 4. Ended, 5. Rolled, 6. Saloons.

PUZZLE 428

```
       DIM
 SHE  MORON
TEACH SOFABED
FRESHOUTOF SWIM
CLAM OWNER  EVE
AID   LAW  GNAT
TREK      SIGN
TIED      ALL
NEAT     GLAD
PRO      SNIP
STEM    DALE
GOAD RAW  GAL
EBB VISIT TRIM
MESS PASSTHEHAT
ROUTINE HAREM
 NIECE   WAN
  TEA
```

PUZZLE 429

1. Pole, pose, post, past, mast.
2. Work, cork, cook, cool, coil, toil.
3. Ring, rind, bind, bend, bent, belt, bell.
4. Drop, crop, coop, cool, pool, poll, pall, fall.

PUZZLE 430

```
       HAJJ
       OMOO
       PATHS
       STANTON
        SERE
  DAIS  WENT
  BARRE POLES
  CELLARS SIRS
JOHNNYONTHESPOT
ELIOT   ASWAN  SLOE
LISTS   ARTAR WOULD
LOSE   SCOOT  ELLEN
  JOHNPHILIPSOUSA
  SONE STOGIES
BATHS  ABONE
ELAN   LORE
LETS
ACUTELY
 SORES
 WISE
 NEER
```

PUZZLE 431

```
  CLAP
AIDE    PAT    SEE
PEEL   RULE    PAN
  TAKEPLACE  USE
     GIN    APART
   WENT     FIN
  TIE      SECT
PACT   MATE    STY
LACE   ANEW   HOE
PORT   IDA   TOWS
ELI    ONER  FERN
GAS    LESS  CORE
  MIND      ARM
  ADO    PEAR
 DEPOT   EEL
POD  LETHERRIP
AVE  RUST  EASE
YEN  YET   ARIA
           LENT
```

PUZZLE 432

(Less common words in capital letters)

Accent, Accomplish, Accost, Ace, Ache, Acme, Aim, Ale, Alien, Alit, Amen, Ample, Ant, Ape, Apish, APSE, Apt, Ash, Ashen, Cent, Client, CLIME, Coin, Colt, Come, Comet, Comment, Con, Cop, Cope, COPSE, Cost, Hen, Lent, Let, Lie, Lime, Lint, List, Lit, Men, Met, Mime, Mint, Mist, Omen, Omit, Open, Opt, Pen, Pent, Pie, Pin, Pint, Pit, Sent, Set, She.

PUZZLE 433

```
  HAD
 OREM
CABOT       SPA
PARIS      GOOD
REGAL     CLANS
 LEWIS   BOARD
ROW   REMUS WARDS
AMOK  DEPOSITS
NEVIS   PRESSED
GREET DEPLETE TRUNK
VANILLA    SATIN
  TORMENTS GALE
 TRUST ATOMS HEW
SHARE   STEAK
APACE   SAVED
MANY    ROYAL
ARK     RUMOR
        POLE
        NAP
```

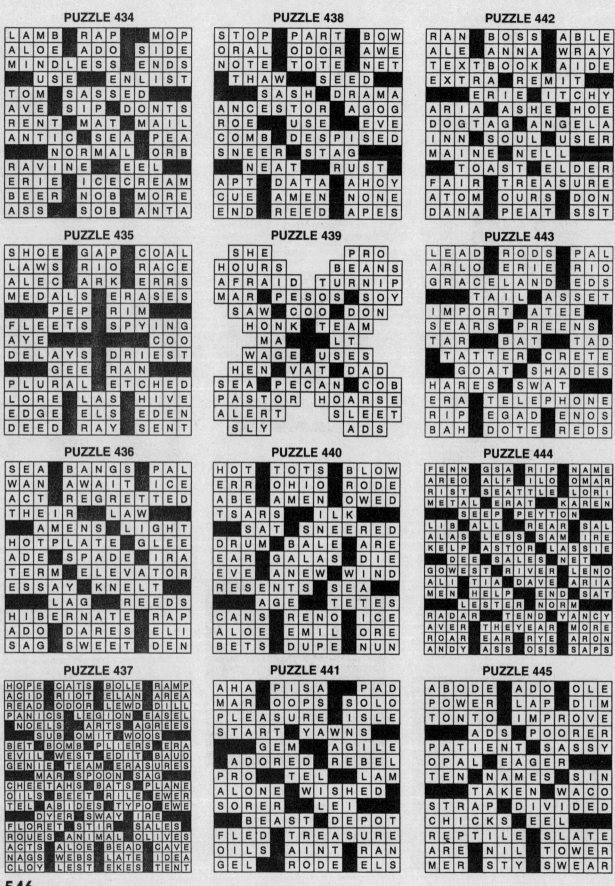

PUZZLE 434

```
L A M B   R A P       M O P
A L O E   A D O   S I D E
M I N D L E S S   E N D S
      U S E   E N L I S T
T O M   S A S S E D
A V E   S I P   D O N T S
R E N T   M A T   M A I L
A N T I C   S E A   P E A
    N O R M A L   O R B
R A V I N E   E E L
E R I E   I C E C R E A M
B E E R   N O B   M O R E
A S S   S O B   A N T A
```

PUZZLE 438

```
S T O P   P A R T   B O W
O R A L   O D O R   A W E
N O T E   T O T E   N E T
  T H A W   S E E D
  S A S H   D R A M A
A N C E S T O R   A G O G
R O E   U S E   E V E
C O M B   D E S P I S E D
S N E E R   S T A G
  N E A T   R U S T
A P T   D A T A   A H O Y
C U E   A M E N   N O N E
E N D   R E E D   A P E S
```

PUZZLE 442

```
R A N   B O S S   A B L E
A L E   A N N A   W R A Y
T E X T B O O K   A I D E
E X T R A   R E M I T
    E R I E   I T C H Y
A R I A   A S H E   H O E
D O G T A G   A N G E L A
I N N   S O U L   U S E R
M A I N E   N E L L
  T O A S T   E L D E R
F A I R   T R E A S U R E
A T O M   O U R S   D O N
D A N A   P E A T   S S T
```

PUZZLE 435

```
S H O E   G A P   C O A L
L A W S   R I O   R A C E
A L E C   A R K   E R R S
M E D A L S   E R A S E S
    P E P   R I M
F L E E T S   S P Y I N G
A Y E           C O O
D E L A Y S   D R I E S T
    G E E   R A N
P L U R A L   E T C H E D
L O R E   L A S   H I V E
E D G E   E L S   E D E N
D E E D   R A Y   S E N T
```

PUZZLE 439

```
  S H E           P R O
H O U R S       B E A N S
A F R A I D   T U R N I P
M A R   P E S O S   S O Y
  S A W   C O O   D O N
  H O N K   T E A M
    M A       L T
  W A G E   U S E S
  H E N   V A T   D A D
S E A   P E C A N   C O B
P A S T O R   H O A R S E
A L E R T     S L E E T
S L Y         A D S
```

PUZZLE 443

```
L E A D   R O D S   P A L
A R L O   E R I E   R I O
G R A C E L A N D   E D S
    T A I L   A S S E T
I M P O R T   A T E E
S E A R S   P R E E N S
T A R   B A T   T A D
  T A T T E R   C R E T E
  G O A T   S H A D E S
H A R E S   S W A T
E R A   T E L E P H O N E
R I P   E G A D   E N O S
B A H   D O T E   R E D S
```

PUZZLE 436

```
S E A   B A N G S   P A L
W A N   A W A I T   I C E
A C T   R E G R E T T E D
T H E I R     L A W
    A M E N S   L I G H T
H O T P L A T E   G L E E
A D E   S P A D E   I R A
T E R M   E L E V A T O R
E S S A Y   K N E L T
    L A G     R E E D S
H I B E R N A T E   R A P
A D O   D A R E S   E L I
S A G   S W E E T   D E N
```

PUZZLE 440

```
H O T   T O T S   B L O W
E R R   O H I O   R O D E
A B E   A M E N   O W E D
T S A R S     I L K
  S A T   S N E E R E D
D R U M   B A L E   A R E
E A R   G A L A S   D I E
E V E   A N E W   W I N D
R E S E N T S     S E A
    A G E     T E T E S
C A N S   R E N O   I C E
A L O E   E M I L   O R E
B E T S   D U P E   N U N
```

PUZZLE 444

```
F E N N   G S A   R I P   N A M E
A R E O   A L F   I L O   O M A R
R I S T   S E A T T L E   L O R I
M E T A L   E R A T   K A R E N
    S E E P   P E Y T O N
L I B   A L L   R E A R   S A L
A L A S   L E S S   S A M   I R E
K E L P   A S T O R   L A S S I E
    D E E   S A L E S   N E T
G O W E S T   R I V E R   L E N O
A L I   T I A   D A V E   A R I A
M E N   H E L P   E N D   S A T
    L E S T E R   N O R M
R A D A R   T E N D   Y A N C Y
A V E R   T H E Y E A R   M O R E
R O A R   E A R   R Y E   A R O N
A N D Y   A S S   O S S   S A P S
```

PUZZLE 437

```
H O P E   C A T S   B O L E   R A M P
A C I D   R I O T   E L A N   A R E A
R E A D   O D O R   L E W D   D I L L
P A N I C S   L E G I O N   E A S E L
N O E L S   A R T S   A G R E E S
  S U B   O M I T   W O O S
B E T   B O M B   P L I E R S   E R A
E V I L   W E S T   E D I T   B A U D
G E N I E   T E A M   E R A S U R E S
  M A R   S P O O N   S A G
C H E E T A H S   B A T S   P L A N E
O I L S   B E E T   R I L E   E W E R
T E L   A B I D E S   T Y P O   E W E
  D Y E R   S W A Y   I R E
F L O R E T   S T I R   S A L E S
R O U E S   A N I M A L   O L I V E S
A C T S   A L O E   B E A D   C A V E
N A G S   W E B S   L A T E   I D E A
C L O Y   L E S T   E K E S   T E N T
```

PUZZLE 441

```
A H A   P I S A       P A D
M A R   O O P S   S O L O
P L E A S U R E   I S L E
S T A R T   Y A W N S
    G E M   A G I L E
  A D O R E D   R E B E L
P R O   T E L   L A M
A L O N E   W I S H E D
S O R E R   L E I
  B E A S T   D E P O T
F L E D   T R E A S U R E
O I L S   A I N T   R A N
G E L   R O D E   E L S
```

PUZZLE 445

```
A B O D E   A D O   O L E
P O W E R   L A P   D I M
T O N T O   I M P R O V E
    A D S   P O O R E R
P A T I E N T   S A S S Y
O P A L   E A G E R
T E N   N A M E S   S I N
    T A K E N   W A C O
S T R A P   D I V I D E D
C H I C K S   E E L
R E P T I L E   S L A T E
A R E   N I L   T O W E R
M E R   S T Y   S W E A R
```

PUZZLE 446

```
PAPA  AWARE  SPCA
OWES  RAVED  WEAN
PERPENDICULARLY
   MILO   ICONS
CRACK CAPET  ODS
HENS  BATED ENOW
AVE  PUSH  PLATA
TENNESSEEVALLEY
EATEN   ISIT  PSI
ALMA GASPE  ARON
USA BALMY  ALONG
   GEESE   KILN
CONTEMPORANEOUS
OPEC  APART  NUDE
BATH  NORSE  SNOW
```

PUZZLE 450

```
OWED   HIS   SPUR
DALE   ADO   PERU
DRIVEWAY    RAGE
    IRK  BOOKED
AISLE  BEAU
LOTS  FLATTERY
EWE  PLANS   DOE
CAPTAINS   MEOW
    RICK  HINTS
REMARK    RAM
ARID   EMOTIONS
FIRE   RAP   CLUE
TEES   SEE   SENT
```

PUZZLE 447

```
ASHES  AFAR  ANEW
PEALE  DICE  CORA
ATTIC  INTO  ORES
THEATREDISTRICT
    IOU   ENATE
DESPOT   STOA
ASPEN  ETRUSCANS
MAUL  AVOIR  ARIA
SURETHING  PAINT
   YALE  SUNDAE
ADDER    TIN
PERSONANONGRATA
PLOT  AVID  EULER
LANE  SEND  NEVER
EYES  TREY  TRAMS
```

PUZZLE 451

```
GRATE  TRAP  RIPS
NOVEL  RODE  ORAL
ALINE  ICON  SANE
WED  MOCK  DAINTY
   PEAK  MANE
LATENT  SENTRIES
EGRET  ENATE  RAH
VIAL  FRETS  HAVE
ELM  GENES  RATED
REPORTER  CARESS
   PITS  SADE
MARINE  GOBI  ERE
ELAN  ROAD  ALTAR
SORE  ELMO  NEONS
HEED  DEEM  TINGE
```

PUZZLE 448

```
FACEUP  AWNS  ZOO
ORANGE  VRAI  UVA
GOTTHEPOINT  LES
USER  POINTCOUNT
PECAN  EDGEOF
   HIED    SMILED
COUNTDOWN   TALE
ADM  HEDONIC  NEE
REED  DOWNUNDER
RANOFF   ABES
   SIESTA  ASCOT
UNDERSCORE  TAPE
TOE  SCOREKEEPER
ADE  TUTU  EDGERS
HEP  SETS  DEGREE
```

PUZZLE 449

```
APAR  GILA  COMTE
LOSE  EBON  OMAHA
IMPELLING  NIGER
SPINE  SELECTION
TEETHE  REMIT
   EARS   USEFUL
REARRANGE  EDILE
ALL  TIARA  VAN
PIECE  TRANSIENT
TACOMA   STEM
   RAILS  ANITRA
MOMENTOUS  STEIN
ADELA  VENGEANCE
DEALT  EDIE  TOES
ERNIE  DEPT  ERST
```

PUZZLE 453

```
HOT   MOB   SPLIT
ALABAMA    ALAMO
REBATES    CARAT
MOLT   LIP   NAG
SSE   MESAS   MIG
   SAT  RAPINE
SOLOS    GREET
AVALON   DAY
WET  NEARS   DON
   REB  WOE  TRUE
BARON   RADIATE
AWARE   TRIPPED
RELET   AYE   ERS
```

PUZZLE 452

```
HORA  DAMES  ABBE
EROS  AWARE  TAIL
SASS  MORSE  ARTS
ALE  TOLL  ALBEE
   MEIN  ERASER
TOATEE  NASA  ASI
ERRED  HERON  STS
PAYS  SEDER  ETAL
ETC  MAMIE  SARGE
EEL  AGEE  STREET
   ORIENT  COSI
SHOED   RHEA  SID
LENA  ONION  MADE
ABED  CACHE  INEE
BEYS  ATHOS  ADAM
```

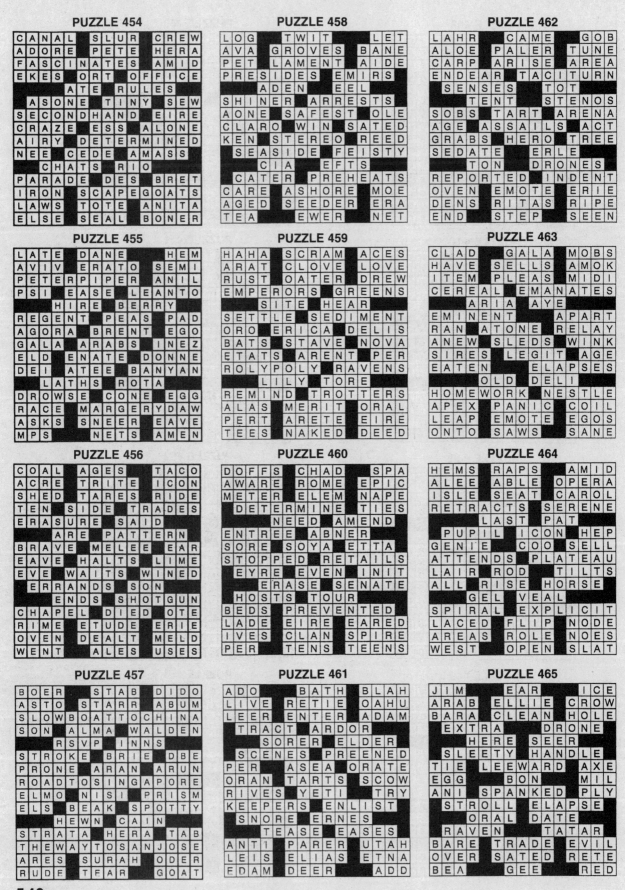

PUZZLE 454

```
CANAL   SLUR   CREW
ADORE   PETE   HERA
FASCINATES     AMID
EKES  ORT   OFFICE
      ATE  RULES
  ASONE  TINY   SEW
SECONDHAND     EIRE
CRAZE  ESS   ALONE
AIRY   DETERMINED
NEE  CEDE   AMASS
   CHATS  RIO
PARADE   DES   BRET
IRON   SCAPEGOATS
LAWS   TOTE   ANITA
ELSE   SEAL   BONER
```

PUZZLE 455

```
LATE   DANE    HEM
AVIV   ERATO   SEMI
PETERPIPER      ANIL
PSI  EASE   LEANTO
    HIRE   BERRY
REGENT   PEAS   PAD
AGORA   BRENT   EGO
GALA   ARABS   INEZ
ELD   ENATE   DONNE
DEI   ATEE   BANYAN
    LATHS   ROTA
DROWSE   CONE   EGG
RACE   MARGERYDAW
ASKS   SNEER   EAVE
MPS    NETS   AMEN
```

PUZZLE 456

```
COAL   AGES    TACO
ACRE   TRITE   ICON
SHED   TARES   RIDE
TEN  SIDE   TRADES
ERASURE   SAID
    ARE   PATTERN
BRAVE   MELEE   EAR
EAVE   HALTS   LIME
EVE   WAITS   WINED
  ERRANDS   SON
    ENDS   SHOTGUN
CHAPEL   DIED   OTE
RIME   ETUDE   ERIE
OVEN   DEALT   MELD
WENT    ALES   USES
```

PUZZLE 457

```
BOER     STAB   DIDO
ASTO   STARR   ABUM
SLOWBOATTOCHINA
SON   ALMA   WALDEN
    RSVP   INNS
STROKE   BRIE   DBE
PRONE   ARAN   ARUN
ROADTOSINGAPORE
ELMO   NISI   PRISM
ELS   BEAK   SPOTTY
    HEWN   CAIN
STRATA   HERA   TAB
THEWAYTOSANJOSE
ARES   SURAH   ODER
RUDE   TEAR   GOAT
```

PUZZLE 458

```
LOG    TWIT     LET
AVA   GROVES   BANE
PET   LAMENT   AIDE
PRESIDES   EMIRS
    ADEN   EEL
SHINER   ARRESTS
AONE   SAFEST   OLE
CLARO   WIN   SATED
KEN   STEREO   REED
  SEASIDE   FEISTY
    CIA   EFTS
  CATER   PREHEATS
CARE   ASHORE   MOE
AGED   SEEDER   ERA
TEA    EWER    NET
```

PUZZLE 459

```
HAHA   SCRAM   ACES
ARAT   CLOVE   LOVE
RUST   OATER   DREW
EMPERORS   GREENS
    SITE   HEAR
SETTLE   SEDIMENT
ORO   ERICA   DELIS
BATS   STAVE   NOVA
ETATS   ARENT   PER
ROLYPOLY   RAVENS
    LILY   TORE
REMIND   TROTTERS
ALAS   MERIT   ORAL
PERT   ARETE   EIRE
TEES   NAKED   DEED
```

PUZZLE 460

```
DOFFS   CHAD    SPA
AWARE   ROME   EPIC
METER   ELEM   NAPE
DETERMINE   TIES
    NEED   AMEND
ENTREE   ABNER
SORE   SOYA   ETTA
STOPPED   RETAILS
EYRE   EVEN   INIT
  ERASE   SENATE
  HOSTS   TOUR
BEDS   PREVENTED
LADE   EIRE   EARED
IVES   CLAN   SPIRE
PER   TENS   TEENS
```

PUZZLE 461

```
ADO     BATH    BLAH
LIVE   RETIE   OAHU
LEER   ENTER   ADAM
  TRACT   ARDOR
  SORER   ELDER
SCENES   PREENED
PER   ASEA   ORATE
ORAN   TARTS   SCOW
RIVES   YETI   TRY
KEEPERS   ENLIST
  SNORE   ERNES
  TEASE   EASES
ANTI   PARER   UTAH
LEIS   ELIAS   ETNA
EDAM   DEER    ADD
```

PUZZLE 462

```
LAHR    CAME     GOB
ALOE   PALER   TUNE
CARP   ARISE   AREA
ENDEAR   TACITURN
SENSES   TOT
    TENT   STENOS
SOBS   TART   ARENA
AGE   ASSAILS   ACT
GRABS   HERO   TREE
SEDATE   ERLE
    TON   DRONES
REPORTED   INDENT
OVEN   EMOTE   ERIE
DENS   RITAS   RIPE
END    STEP   SEEN
```

PUZZLE 463

```
CLAD    GALA   MOBS
HAVE   SELLS   AMOK
ITEM   PLEAS   MIDI
CEREAL   EMANATES
    ARIA   AYE
EMINENT     APART
RAN   ATONE   RELAY
ANEW   SLEDS   WINK
SIRES   LEGIT   AGE
EATEN   ELAPSES
    OLD   DELI
HOMEWORK   NESTLE
APEX   PANIC   COIL
LEAP   EMOTE   EGOS
ONTO   SAWS   SANE
```

PUZZLE 464

```
HEMS   RAPS    AMID
ALEE   ABLE   OPERA
ISLE   SEAT   CAROL
RETRACTS   SERENE
    LAST   PAT
PUPIL   ICON   HEP
GENIE   COO   SELL
ATTENDS   PLATEAU
LAIR   ROD   TILTS
ALL   RISE   HORSE
    GEL   VEAL
SPIRAL   EXPLICIT
LACED   FLIP   NODE
AREAS   ROLE   NOES
WEST    OPEN   SLAT
```

PUZZLE 465

```
JIM     EAR     ICE
ARAB   ELLIE   CROW
BARA   CLEAN   HOLE
EXTRA     DRONE
    HERE   SEER
SLEETY     HANDLE
TIE   LEEWARD   AXE
EGG    BON    MIL
ANI   SPANKED   PLY
STROLL   ELAPSE
    ORAL   DATE
RAVEN     TATAR
BARE   TRADE   EVIL
OVER   SATED   RETE
BEA    GEE     RED
```

PUZZLE 466

```
MASH MILO  CHAT
AREA IRONS ROLE
DENT RAVEL ERIN
AND RATE EVENTS
MASSAGE  SNIP
   EVE MODESTLY
STALE LOBES  ROE
TOLL SEVER LANA
OUT STEER PAPER
PROSPERS LID
   HAMS CANDLES
REFORM DATE ELL
OLEO ENURE FADE
DIET DINES ISEE
EATS  PEST  BERT
```

PUZZLE 467

```
DOME AGATE MARS
EVES PALOS AMAH
BEETHOVENSPIANO
TNT OGEE  UNTIE
  OREL NOBS
BUTANE CARL AVA
ARAT ALIBI MER
BACHSCLAVICHORD
ELK CHASE  INDO
SSS RAMP HANGER
   AERO BALD
STALE  FALA ADO
PAGANINISVIOLIN
APER TANTE ROVE
TERM SPEED TEES
```

PUZZLE 468

```
SIPS GASP CHALK
AREA ALOE HUMAN
FANTASTIC ABIDE
ENTER  LAGS DEE
  ERSE NEST
TOPNOTCH TIRADE
ALA WALES SOLAR
PINS YARNS TITO
EVENT TOOTS BUS
RESORT NOONTIME
  WOOD PAIR
WOO LEAP  PINCH
ANVIL TURNSTILE
SCENE ERIE OLES
PENNY SEAT NEWS
```

PUZZLE 469

```
 PAW SHAD GROOM
BALE POUR AERIE
ORAD INTO STALL
BRIDALGOWN  TED
  ILL SOMBER
 VENEER EVER
TANG DUB STITCH
ALICE GAP EDILE
CEDARS NUB EDAM
 KNEW NURSED
 OBESER  BUM
AMO RINGBEARER
LARGE TOIL IAGO
SHEET HOLE DRAB
OASTS ENDS  SEN
```

PUZZLE 470

```
ADAM SMOTE ETTA
BELA PEARY SWAN
EBAN ISSUE TORN
STRAIGHTS SHONE
  GOO THIEF
PARENTAL ERRATA
ADORE MACLE KAN
RAYS BINAL CIST
ELA HONER MONTE
SELLER STRANDED
 FARGO  ETC
SALSA FULLHOUSE
OPUS ATRIA RTES
DESI TENET DART
ASHE ENSUE SHEA
```

PUZZLE 471

```
RASE RAPT SELLS
ARAL ELLA ODEON
GELS TAAL LITRE
ENE ANIL ATONE
DAMASKSTITCH
 LYE ERE  ORB
SOON ARE STOA
HALFCROSSSTITCH
ANET AUK ENOS
SEA BIT ANA
 SINGLESTITCH
ADOPT ALBS ALA
DAVIT TALE ASOR
EDILE EMIT ESNE
SEDER SASS SEEM
```

PUZZLE 472

```
FLAY MASS ROLL
RARA HELLO EVOE
APER ANEAR NEST
SPADES EYESORES
 ACTS HOI
 TARHEEL EUROPE
PROMO NEPAL NON
OARS EDGED FEUD
EDT BASIS ROANS
TEASER TOEHOLD
 PAL STET
CHEEKIER HANKER
HALL EMILY ONLY
OVAL SISAL TELE
PENS TREY EWES
```

PUZZLE 473

```
SWIM CLAW COLUM
ARNO LARA AROSE
DESTROYER RAVEN
ENTHUSE PORTERS
 PER RIO
CREME SINCEREST
LEVEE BEAR APR
OLEG MOSES BRIE
VAN CUBE POETS
EXTORTING ANDES
 CUE ITS
LEFTIST BETWEEN
IDEAS SUBMARINE
KNAVE ATOP IRIS
EATER RENT TEDS
```

PUZZLE 474

```
CLAP MEETS ARIL
HARE ATRIA PARE
ITER RHINO PROS
CHAMPION TALENT
 EONS SIRE
CABANA SWANSONG
AMITY DIEGO VOL
RIDE RONDO CAVA
AGE ROUGE GATES
TORTOISE HOTELS
 IPSE RUNS
FORGET KANGAROO
ALEE ELECT WIRE
REAR RANEE ALAI
MODS SWORD YELL
```

PUZZLE 475

```
POPS TSAR CHAT
AGEE SAUTE PIER
SLAT OWNED OGRE
SECTOR SNAP HOE
 HOARSE CREW
APT TOOT TORAHS
BAR SWABS PAYEE
ASEA SPOTS STAN
SHELL SURER ORA
EASTER LUNA HST
 TONE EMERGE
OAR SLAV CARAFE
PLEA AMANA EVIL
AGED TIRES EELS
LATE EDDY KNEE
```

PUZZLE 476

```
MAID HOSS  TAM
ARTY ACORN THEE
REIN MEDIA EARS
CAS ALAS PORTIA
 ADMEN BLANK
 AWAIT LEES NAB
CHILD FIRST OLE
ROSE LOT TWOS
ALE SPANS HASNT
BEF IRKS CACHE
 ALGAE PATTI
ANTONY GRES SAD
LEHR ETUIS PORE
SMEE DRAMA TWIN
OAR  EMIR ANDY
```

PUZZLE 477

```
BITS CHAPS GEMS
ACRE LANAI ALOE
BOOR ALARM LION
ENTRUST DULLARD
 ASPS LOO
STATES TRAINERS
CONES FEATS PAT
APED PIXIE SERE
LEA NOLAN STEEP
PERFORMS HORSES
 ART HULA
GRAMMAR IRONTON
LEVI BEARD GAME
IDOL LABEL ERIN
BONY ERASE RATE
```

549

PUZZLE 478

```
ROMA  RARAE  SIZE
EDIT  ERODE  TOOT
NONO  AMAZE  ETNA
DRIZZLED   LEAKS
    OLD   MEAL
BARONY   PIZZERIA
OZONE  PADRE  ENL
RUST  MARIA  ZANE
ERE  POSES  RATER
DESOLATE  DEPART
    CANE  PAN
ZESTY   ZEROHOUR
ELIA  SPORT  ANTA
ALAN  AROSE  ZEES
LAME  GOMER  ESSE
```

PUZZLE 482

```
MASS  SPEAK  DEED
ASTI  AURAE  ADDA
THEREDLILY   IDOL
TEA  EDEN  SESAME
ENDURED    STAY
    LIN  STORMING
HASTE  CLAN  INEE
AMOR  SLAVE  LIEN
LIRA  CAKE  BLADE
TRAVERSE    TEE
    IRIS  CHERISH
INFORM  SOAR  RHO
TOIL  PANSYYOKUM
ELLE  EMOTE  TETE
MALT  DEBAR  ODER
```

PUZZLE 486

```
SAFE  POGO   COST
ISIS  AVERS  ANOA
THREERINGCIRCUS
SEE  LANE  ENTERS
    MADE  ANNS
STATE  BITS  BOA
SPINE  RODS  DRIP
CAGED  ONE  SEALS
ACES  SPED  LEVEE
TER  PEER  RIDER
    JEER  SUES
SHOOTS  LOSS  LAD
WALKSATIGHTROPE
ALEE  WEDGE  EVEN
BOOR   TOYS  BEST
```

PUZZLE 479

```
SHAW  ADELE   RUT
POSH  BEDIM  OPEN
OUTONALIMB  STLO
TRA  ATEE  RATHER
    FRED  SABRE
EDDIED  DECLARED
LOONS  RANEE  IRE
SOWN  HEROD  EVEN
ANN  RULER  ELECT
SEASONED  FLIRTS
   NUDGE  CABS
CADGER  CLIO  ART
STOA  INHOTWATER
TOUR  LEACH  LONE
MTS  YANKS  EPEE
```

PUZZLE 483

```
LANE  TITO  BINGE
IGOR  IDES  IDEES
LOVE  SEAS  KARAT
ARE  ASA  AMI  ORA
CALIGULA    ANI
    CEE  PERICLES
FARES  PEA  HILO
ILE  ALERT   EST
LAIT  GOA  TIDES
MINOTAUR    SAM
    ORT  SOCRATES
STA  AEF  BAN  ORE
HIRED  REEL  ETNA
ORATE  ERSE  RAIL
EELER  TIES  ALES
```

PUZZLE 487

```
GAME  ESTES  SILO
ADAM  APORT  CROP
LIMB  SINGE  RANI
STALLING  AVENGE
    AYES  SMEW
GLAZER  BLESSING
LOSE  HEART  REL
OUTS  SORTS  PAVE
SIE  HERES  UTES
SERGEANT  LINERS
   RARE  GATS
TOLEDO  SENATORS
ALOE  VOTED  EVIL
CLAN  ERASE  RATE
KANE  RAGED  SLAW
```

PUZZLE 480

```
SPRAY   WED  STAY
PEARS  DEER  PACE
ARNIE  ELLA  ARTS
SUGARANDSPICE
    SOS  ERE
RAT  BIT  ABAS
ANI  ADEN  ARES
PEACHESANDCREAM
TARO  HERA  ATE
RAMS  VOW  SOW
   MOA  SAO
SALTANDPEPPER
SPAN  ASEA  LEASE
SAND  LIEN  SEINE
TRES  EAR  ERRED
```

PUZZLE 484

```
MOLAR  ASSET  BBC
AWARE  READE  LAY
HEMEN  GAMESTERS
   PATROL  TWEET
AMOS  OSIER  ODDS
NEO  MAYORAL
TANNA  NAVIGATE
IDEAMEN  SENORAS
CEREBRAL   EATIT
   ASSENTS  INE
ACID  EAGER  AFTS
ARNEE   GEISHA
RESERVOIR  LOCKS
ODE  ROUND  ALTAR
NOT  SARGO  PESTS
```

PUZZLE 488

```
SLID  REGIS  CHAT
CARE  EMOTE  ROPE
ATOP  FEAST  ELSE
TENEMENT  TRADES
   NERD  BEET
PONDER  PERSUADE
ORE  TENOR  TREES
SIRS  DARED  ERNS
SEVEN  METRO  ITE
ELEVATED  ARNESS
   EVES  MITE
SORREL  PUNSTERS
ALAI  LOOSE  TRIO
MEIN  ELMER  LILT
SONG  REEDS  EELS
```

PUZZLE 481

```
FAST  OBESE  OHIO
ANNE  BABEL  RAND
COUNTERBALANCED
TAB  ORES  CAKES
   PROD  BLAT
SCREEN  PROJECT
TAIL  TRURO  ORB
UNDERTHECOUNTER
BAG  ERASE  ETNA
LESSENS  TREATY
   LEEK  FOOD
ATMAN  ARTS  PRO
COUNTERMEASURES
HINT  LIBEL  RODS
ELIS  MOODS  NASA
```

PUZZLE 485

```
CAMEL  LAWS  FLAM
ATONE  IRAE  RENO
LEWIS  TERN  OVEN
LENDSAHAND  NEAT
   ENOW  EATERY
SEABEE   ARROW
CREE  MAYO  NAMED
AIRFLOW  THERETO
BAYOU  ESAU  DEAR
   RAISE  MOSTLY
ADIEUS   ATON
ROSH  AFTERWARDS
ITSA  BAIT  AVERT
STUN  ERNE  REDYE
EYED  LEGS  DROSS
```

PUZZLE 489

```
SWAT  ARCH  SPRAT
EASE  BOLE  ORONO
TIER  OSAR  NATTY
FAMOUSPOTATOES
    UTE   ARE
FLAGS  SOAR  SAME
REMOTE  ARIA  LIL
YOUVEGOTAFRIEND
ENS  DOTE  FRANCE
REES  IONA  EMEER
   PAS  RES
VOLUNTEERSTATE
IRANI  ADIT  BALE
SACKS  RIVE  URAL
ANEYE  NEER  TONY
```

PUZZLE 490

```
C L O P   P L A N E   S P I N
R U D E   E A R E D   T A R A
A L A R   E R N S T   E P O S
G U Y F A W K E S   E V E N T
      O L E S     O V E R
   A G R E E   C A L E N D A R
B R U M E   S U G A R   O R E
R O Y S   L O R E N   S L I D
I S M   R U L E S   A T L A S
M E A S U R E D   C L A S S
   D U N K     S H A N
F A I R E   S A T I N D O L L
E L S E   M A D A M   P R O A
S O O T   A G A T E   A L O T
T U N E   D A M E S   T Y K E
```

PUZZLE 491

Fairyland, Fallout, Federal, Fiend, Finale, Firearm, Flagon, Flashlight, Flotsam, Forbear, Forelock, Forever, Fragrant, Frankincense, Frigate.

PUZZLE 492

```
O P T E D   S A S S   B L A B
D I O D E   A L O E   A I D A
D E G A S   T A R N   T E E N
R A M I F I C A T I O N S
      R I N K     I O N
V E S P E R   I N U R E S
A R T I S   T U B E   O X E N
S L O G   B A S I L   U T W A
T E A M   R T E S   E G R E T
   S T E L A E   S M E A R S
      N A G   G R A B
C A T E G O R I C A L L Y
C O L A   A P O D   R O U S T
A L A R   R I V E   K O R E A
D E N Y   T E E S   S T E R N
```

PUZZLE 493

INSECTS: Ladybug, Earwig, Aphid, Silverfish, Termite.
SUPERNATURAL: Leprechaun, Elf, Angel, Specter, Troll.
ROYAL TITLES: Lord, Emperor, Archduke, Sultan, Tsar.
BODY PARTS: Leg, Ear, Arm, Scalp, Throat.
FIELDS OF STUDY: Law, Economics, Accounting, Sociology, Theology.

PUZZLE 494

```
P A C T   N A Y S   B E T   S O M E
A L A I   O B O E   E R E   T I R E D
C O R E   M O U N T A I N   E R A S E
E E N   H A Y   N A M E   A R E N A
   A R I D   N E T S   S T I N G
A R T I E   S E T   H A L   S E A M
M A I D   E M O T E   A G A   A M I
A G O   S T A N   M A L E S   O D E S
S E N A T O R   G U L L   O V E N S
      C E N T E R   A S H O R E
T U L I P   M A T S   O P E R A T E
A P E D   C O I N S   A N T S   F A R
B O X   A C T   E R N E S   E T T A
S N I P   G A S   E N D   S T E E L
   N A P E S   T A L E   S P A R
E G G E D   S A R I   S T Y   W A D
A S T E R   S T R A G G L E   M A R E
S T O R M   A I D   H E A R   A R N E
H E N S   D R Y   T E T E   O D O R
```

PUZZLE 495

```
D E A L S       W A S T E
P E N C I L   C A R T E D
A C C E D E   U N I O N S
L E O   S E C T   D O S E
L I R A   T O L E   G E L
S T E L E   N E E D E D
      B R I T T L E
R E S I D E   S E R F S
B A L   S I N G   P E L E
E T A S   O T I S   P A W
A T T E S T   B E C O M E
S L E E P S   E R A S E D
T E D D Y       S A T E S
```

PUZZLE 496

```
D E K A L B   R A T E D
E V A D E R   E R O D E S
F I N D F A U L T W I T H
E N S   T Y P E S   T E A
A C A D   S P A   F O R M
T E N E T   E S T E R S
      N E A R E S T
A N S E L M   P E S T S
S P E E   L O S   S T A N
A R A   L O S E R   A L E
B O R R O W T R O U B L E
E N L A C E   B U T L E R
S Y N O D   S T E E R S
```

PUZZLE 497

```
            O F F
A R T     T R E A T       F E D
H A H   C R A N B E R R I E S   A Y E
A G A   A U N T       I N T O   M E N
   N A T T Y   H U E   C A P R I
A N K L E   F U N N Y   S A L A D
G A S T R   P A R A D E S   T Y R O
O R G   E E N     T A B   G I N
   D I N I N G   M A S H E D
      V O L T   T A C T
   G I B L E T   P O T A T O
C O N   R O B   D A N   O L E
U R G E   T U R K E Y S   E G G E D
D E F E R   M A I N E   G U E S T
   E L A T E   E T E   S L A N T
E R A   S A L S   A K I N   H E N
L O S   P U M P K I N P I E S   E V E
L E T     A E R I E       R A W
            N A P
```

PUZZLE 498

```
W A R M     B L E A T
O L E O   P R O N T O
N E S T   L A R D E R
      P I R A T E
P R O F I T     B E G
E O N   B I T   A V E
A D D     T A S S E L
      C H U R C H
F A I L E D   A F A R
I G N O R E   R U D E
T E N T S     S L E D
```

PUZZLE 499

```
R O B   T H A N   G A P S
A I R   W O R E   O P A L
C L A R I N E T   R E L Y
E S T A T E   W A G
      I C Y   O C E A N S
F L E S H   A R T   T O E
L A C E   A R K   S O M E
A S H   H U M   W O M E N
P H O N E S   C O N
      A N T   H O A R S E
C O B S   R A I L R O A D
A R E A   I S L E   A L E
R E E L   A K I N   D E N
```

PUZZLE 500

```
O X I D I Z E   P L A N N E R
S   N D X O X   U   A
C A D G E   A Z U R E   M A N
I   R   A   C   R   E   K
L E A F L E T   S Q U I R E S
W     N         A
A W N   B Y W A Y   F I L E S
T     R   A   O   I     U
E V A D E   S Q U A T   F O R
M     W         I     P
C H O O S E S   C A R E F U L
R   N   A   A   T   U
E G G   P A C E R   J E E R S
E S I K   O   A E E
K I T T E N S   B E H I N D S
```

1-B, 2-S, 3-W, 4-V, 5-J, 6-C, 7-T, 8-A, 9-X, 10-H, 11-F, 12-U, 13-O, 14-Y, 15-D, 16-L, 17-N, 18-Q, 19-G, 20-M, 21-I, 22-R, 23-K, 24-E, 25-Z, 26-P.

PUZZLE 501

Show me a man who is a good loser and I'll show you a man who is playing golf with his boss.

PUZZLE 502

```
R O S T E R S   P A B L O   C A T T
M A N A G E M E N T   T E R N   P R E E N S
I N E R T   D E S P E R A T I O N
A S S   Y A R D S T I C K
S A R A H   R A G E S   E N I G M A T I C
E S C U T C H E O N   S T I N G A R E E
S E N S E   T R A P   S L O P
P E N I N S U L A R   T A C K
P R O F O U N D E S T   T E H E R A N
F I R S   L I N G O   T O C S I N
T E S T E R   G O D S   R I C H N E S S
```

PUZZLE 503

(Less common words in *italics*)
Abed, Abode, Adobe, Adore, *Aery*, *Ardeb*, Bade, Bake, Bakery, Bard, Bare, Bark, Bayed, Bead, Beak, Bear, Beard, Boar, Board, Bode, Body, *Bora*, Bore, *Boyar*, Brad, Brake, Bray, Bread, Break, Bred, Broad, Broke, Dare, Dark, Dear, Debar, Debark, Derby, Doer, Dory, Drab, Drake, Dray, Dyer, Kayo, Oared, Obey, Okay, Okra, *Orbed*, *Oread*, Rake, Rayed, Read, Ready, Road, Robe, Rode, Yard, *Yare*, Year, Yoke, Yore.

PUZZLE 504

There are very few people who don't become more interesting when they stop talking.

PUZZLE 505

PUZZLE 506

```
M  EMBARK  BREAK  RAKE  B
A  EASTER  STEER  TEES  R
R  RAVINE  NAIVE  VEIN  A
L  LANCER  CRANE  RACE  N
O  RODENT  TREND  RENT  D
N  APRONS  SAPOR  SPAR  O
```

PUZZLE 507

```
BALD WASH ASSAM
ASEA ECHO SHARI
SHORTSTOP SOLAR
SESTET PETERED
    STOPSHORT
EFT ENE ATWILL
FLOSS NERD ARIA
LODE PALES VETS
ARAL ALMA TENET
TAYLOR CHA ERS
   SHORTHORN
MAHALIA TOILER
SAVOR SHORTCAKE
AGORA KOLO HIES
MINTS SEED ERST
```

PUZZLE 508

1. Ace, Deuce, Trey; 2. Beaver, Whale, Seal; 3. Ship, Boat, Liner; 4. Moe, Curly, Larry; 5. Stone, Rock, Boulder.

PUZZLE 509

PUZZLE 510

If a one hundred seventy pound man used up as much energy as the tiny hummingbird, he would have to eat three hundred forty pounds of potatoes or two hundred eighty-five pounds of hamburger daily just to maintain his weight.

PUZZLE 511

PUZZLE 512

A wise man makes more opportunities than he finds.

1. Hawaii, 2. Tenant, 3. Memories, 4. Friend, 5. Spunk, 6. Peas, 7. Smooth.

PUZZLE 513

PUZZLE 514

Pagan, Pearl, Pluck, Probe, Putty.

PUZZLE 515

```
MUS CLE P SAL M LEA PS
TAR OT A ESOP STE W
DRES SER S S ING STAN
     VIC TOR S OTTERS
M ARRIES A B SENT
ARGON B L ANK ACTIVE
   S EALION B LESSES
S W INGS S L ANG
L ASH SAYS O AN SWERING
A PERS F RED AR GUES
S STS TAPING SOTS
```

PUZZLE 516

20

PUZZLE 517

PUZZLE 518

IN: 1. Spare, 3. Tales, 5. Leered, 7. Artless, 9. Ever, 11. Islam, 12. Ron. OUT: 14. Normal, 12, Sire, 8. Trade, 6. Reels, 4. Elate, 2. Raps.

PUZZLE 519

```
EGG FEDS SHIED
SARI ORAL EARLY
IRAN DIRE AROSE
RED DETERMINE
DENSE TOE
EERIE ORDER
SPATE CASK EVES
PART LOSES PEST
ALEE ONER AORTA
LADEN DEALS
NEW SIEGE
RESTRAINS EMU
MATTE KNEE ALES
ATTAR EDIT VINE
PEERS DONS ADD
```

PUZZLE 520

```
V  GRAVEL  LARGE  REAL  G
I  SUITOR  TOURS  ROTS  U
O  RATION  TRAIN  RANT  I
L  LASTED  STEAD  ADES  T
I  ALBEIT  BLEAT  BELT  A
N  RINSED  DRIES  SIDE  R
```

PUZZLE 521

```
AHA DAB TRA
PAL ARE WAD
ETA REASONS
   BANANA
STARS SNAIL
SOME DROP
WEANS VEINS
   ALTERS
LASSOES ILL
ICE PAT NEE
PETERS GOT
```

PUZZLE 522

```
SCAR STAN
RELIES FLARED
ICEMAN EARNER
TEA DOPEY ODE
EDNA OIL BLEW
ESCAPE LADD
TIS ROT
AGED RIGHTS
BIRD DUD ERAS
ARE DANDY AGO
BIASED LEADER
ENSUES ELDEST
GEMS PERT
```

PUZZLE 523

```
IMAM FANS  SAIC  SHEM
TUTU EPIC NARCO  HARI
ENOS NOTA OLEAN CARNE
MINTANDANISEANDCUMMIN
 AGES  DIMS  ILLUSE
MITRAL BALES EMITS
ACIDS  SEDER WEEPS LFS
CONS SALAD MORNS WERE
ENE BETTY TAROT HARAN
 SADIE  SALT  AARONS
SPICEANDALLTHINGSNICE
MODERN  SALS  GOATS
IRONS BITTY CLOVE RED
TELE GATES BOONE PETE
ESS COYER FAROE DEMON
 BURLS KILNS JAPING
SPARSE VILS  GASP
THEGREATESTAMONGHERBS
RANGY VERSE ALOG RARA
ANTE ELDER TIME ELAN
PEAR  SLED ONER DESK
```

PUZZLE 527

```
BITT CALL OVOLO TAMIS
ACHY AREA RIVER ORANT
TEEN CRAM CRIMSONTIDE
ABSENT SASH DOWNY LIE
VEE OUST PEP NIT HEAP
IRANIST MASON MODERNS
AGARS EPISTLER PES
 RAIDERS REVET MIRED
AGO NILESTAR MARITIME
LOUNGE CEIL SALE ADIT
TONE SHUTE SPICA TELE
ODDS EARS CORN CLERIC
NAUTILUS VALIDATE SAT
ASSET LOMAN TENSPOT
 GEM ROTIFERA APORT
STIGMAS PESOS MANATEE
KANS RAW SMU PERT HAS
EMS TIRES IRMA ROBERT
WATEREDDOWN ASHE ASIA
ELEVE IGLOO THIS RENT
REPAY SEDER HAST SAGE
```

PUZZLE 524

```
TALC SPAR BELL PODS
ELIA MESA ISEE EDIE
DEAL EASYASPIE ROMA
CRAVAT MOO BURST
MAR BONN CAR
ALLIN DANE HOPALONG
FEAT WAND SOME EVIL
ANDY ARK ANNEX VALE
RAY GIN SLEET HELEN
HAL DELAY PAL
BIDES LIVED GUY BED
EDAM LINEN BUS PAVE
ELLA EVEN SASH AREA
REINDEER GIST DWARF
FRR HAGS BAN
TWAIN ANN KANSAS
HALO EASYGOING HULA
IVAN BLUE FREE OTIS
NESS BEES FEEL POMP
```

PUZZLE 528

```
SEAM PEARS SWAB
TARE JULEP HAIF
USED SLIER ELOR
BEADS CANES LET
LEG SLAPDASH
REPEALS IDEA
APE TOTES DRIFT
MESH WROTE EDIE
PETAL INERT ONE
RISK DANGLES
REPEATED FIR
EVE RASED PASSE
ARNO NOVEL YALL
PANE DUOLA EVIL
SCAR STREW REPS
```

PUZZLE 525

```
LOAD TRUMP RABAT ARAM
ERLE HEALS ERODE MAXI
FLUSHESWITHPRIDE PILE
TYMPANI ISEE LEST SEN
IRONS LAT RUEDE
CRETAN TRIPLED PAUSED
LUNES TRANS PRE RECTO
ALL STRAND VEALS SAUR
NEAR HAIG PEEWEES IDI
GRIPPE GEARS INRE NEA
MARCH BIT NAVAL
FRO ROUT BEING IMARET
IES CATERED ABEL SOAR
RICO DIDOS SCONES URI
SCABS EGO FARAD ADELA
THRONE EMPOWER PHENYL
WEIRS SAY DORIS
MAI PEPE RETE REBORES
ABLE CUSTERSLASTSTAND
MEDE TRAIN ALLOT ORCA
EDEN STUNT RAINY SEEK
```

PUZZLE 529

```
DAHS CARED SOLO TOTO
AMAH ABELE IDEAS IVAN
TIMETRIALS TICKERTAPE
ASSERTER THANT DALLAS
ROE RARER UNITE
BATED BARON TRIMESTER
ERAS GUNNY SEEDER WEE
LETTINGGO DEL INSPIRE
OTT TALE AIRLIFT ENID
WELFARE SLAVERY RAKES
EELS SHAPERS DILL
APTLY REAMERS GOSSETT
TEAL DEALERS CONK TAW
ECLAIRS LIS MOONSTONE
SHE NATION HENNA RETE
TESTAMENT GOADS BIDED
APART MAINE TAM
SECRET AMASS MARBELLA
TRIPTICKET TONGUETIED
ONTO CHEAT EVERS EDDA
PEEN ESTE DADAS ROAM
```

PUZZLE 526

```
SODS BESS STAR JEEP
IDEA ARTE CUBE ULNA
MOLL SLAV ANEW LEER
PRIVATESECRETARIES
ERE ROE TREE
CLERK OVEN SENATORS
HITS ARE MUD TAI
EMU AVER JAM YOUTHS
FID SOLDIER PUFF
TENNISINSTRUCTORS
CEDE ESSENCE ONE
RUMORS ORE STAN DEL
AAA KAT IES MEAL
PRODUCER WEND COOKS
IGOT CHE BIT
HIGHSCHOOLTEACHERS
RUNG THAT ERRS EVOE
OGRE AUNT RUSE RISE
DEER LPGA SEER SLED
```

PUZZLE 530

```
JACK ASSET ATHOS ROW
ARAN READE TRAMP EVIL
BELA MATED HANNA SODA
SAMP AMUR BEGS NAILED
WADER ANI IGNORE
QUEENANNESLACE SIS
UNWED VOL COHO ADS
ICED HOPED RAHAB PTAH
ELL PORES SONORA IONA
TEL ALAR SEAT YIPPED
WILLIAMPRIMROSE
DEARLY LEOS AUNT ASS
ULNA GAMELY DINES LOT
SLOP ORIEL GENET GALA
TAN FLIC BUS CAMEL
POI ABIESIRISHROSE
ACHING UMA ARMED
BREATH CRAM MMVI ETTA
BARN TWANG PERIL NEAT
ENDO LEVEE ILONA INTO
ESS YEARS CODEX ADAM
```

PUZZLE 531

```
MERE  FAD  GAS
NOVEL  ADO  RUE
IDEAL  LANTERN
BEND  ALP  READ
   YAK  TWIT
HAD  GIG  AMISS
EVE  INEPT  NET
METAL  TIE  GAY
   OPEN  PRO
VANE  ADE  BRAD
EVASIVE  PEACE
TOT  MEN  ASKEW
OWE  PLY  NEED
```

PUZZLE 532

```
VATS  PASS  ROD
EVIL  RIPE  ODE
SETA  EMERALDS
TROLLS  DULL
   OISE  MACAW
CRAMMING  RARA
LOS  ANDES  LEG
ITSA  GORILLAS
PAULS  WADE
   AMAH  NESTLE
RIGATONI  SOUR
ACE  ABOU  ETNA
YES  NORM  NETS
```

PUZZLE 533

```
SLAP  ATE  STOP
HOLE  RAN  PAVE
EVER  ERR  OMEN
DESIGN  OTTERS
   SEA  LET
LIGHTS  LAYOFF
ARE       WOE
DELETE  CHANGE
   AIL  OUR
RAGGED  FEASTS
AWOL  ELF  BOAT
CANE  SEE  IDLE
EYES  TEE  CALM
```

PUZZLE 534

```
ACT    LAIR
MARS  ALTER
ASIA  PASTOR
HORSES  USA
   GAL  TREK
EDSEL  DENSE
PEPS  LON
EER  WONDER
EDITOR  EROS
STARE  RIVA
   EDEN  EEN
```

PUZZLE 535

```
ORE  HALF  PALS
FOR  OREL  ATOP
FINANCIALPAGE
   RES  TEEPEE
ASHES  STAR
BOAT  SHOP  RIO
BLUECHIPSTOCK
EEL  ARES  IDOL
   MRED  ARENA
RESOLD  AGE
EXTRADIVIDEND
APES  ERAL  LEA
DOTE  DELE  KEY
```

PUZZLE 536

If you want to kill time, try working it to death.

1. Grotto, 2. Dotty, 3. Militia, 4. Wink, 5. Woeful, 6. Hay, 7. Trinket.

PUZZLE 537

```
OILS  SACS  SAP
PROA  TROT  ALA
SEAM  ACTA  LEG
   BOTH  BRACE
SAFARI  ALE
PIE  CONSENSUS
ADAR  NAP  TERA
RERIVETED  RAM
   BAD  RAMBLE
GLASS  OSSA
ROB  SATI  KEPI
AGE  ALTO  EVER
YET  LION  RANK
```

PUZZLE 538

```
   HOG       BAG
QUART  TEXAS
AUNTIE  REELER
DIG  MAJOR  LIE
STEW  SAY  BOND
ERASER  ZONE
   TED  TAX
FACT  PAPERS
RUSH  SUB  SAIL
AMT  BIBLE  IRE
FEUDAL  EVADED
STINK  SEVEN
   END       NED
```

1-E, 2-L, 3-X, 4-Q, 5-W, 6-F, 7-P, 8-K, 9-A, 10-G, 11-O, 12-V, 13-B, 14-U, 15-Y, 16-T, 17-H, 18-N, 19-Z, 20-S, 21-J, 22-C, 23-R, 24-M, 25-D, 26-I.

PUZZLE 539

PUZZLE 540

A = 9, B = 3, C = 7, D = 4, E = 6, F = 5.

PUZZLE 541

```
SODA  ERASE  HAM
LOAM  MALTA  ISA
EZRA  SITAR  THIN
DENSE  NON  HOAX
   SLIM  GAME
ART  SWAB  REMUS
REEL  OKEFENOKEE
AARON  ELL  USAGE
BRIDEGROOM  TSAR
MAGOO  WRAP  ELY
   INTO  IRAQ
JOHN  PAD  YUCCA
ARUG  MEDIA  AHAB
PAN  AREAL  SILL
ELK  HANNA  ISME
```

PUZZLE 542

1. Deck, Heck, Hack, Hank, Hand.
2. Port, Pore, Sore, Sire, Side.
3. Wind, Wand, Sand, Said, Raid, Rain.
4. Sail, Bail, Boil, Boll, Bolt, Boat.

PUZZLE 543

```
FADE  CAJUN  ZEST
IGOR  ELATE  AXLE
LENO  LIVID  NEON
ERAS  ETAL  CODES
   ERR  ETA
STA  AYES  APPEAR
THROW  TALK  ANNE
ARAM  DOGIE  AVIS
GOBI  ONES  AROSE
SESTET  SAWS  YET
   LES  AHA
SWANK  QUOD  MODE
TARA  CURVE  ITER
IDEM  EAGER  SHAG
RISE  EWERS  SONS
```

1-S, 2-Z, 3-C, 4-P, 5-Y, 6-D, 7-H, 8-W, 9-E, 10-A, 11-M, 12-R, 13-G, 14-L, 15-Q, 16-K, 17-N, 18-J, 19-U, 20-T, 21-I, 22-B, 23-F, 24-X, 25-O, 26-V.

PUZZLE 544

1. Wagon, 2. Service, 3. Box, 4. Quick, 5. Powder, 6. Little, 7. Milk.

PUZZLE 545

```
CAM  SAUL   EST
OARED TIKE BATE
SPITE AMEN EVAS
SPATTER  TOWELS
  LEASE EVADE
CAPERS  LINER
AVA   EMIT NEWER
PER ADO ELS IRE
TRESS TOME  LIE
  ENDED MENDED
  DARER DRONE
SEVERE  INTENSE
OMEN AMID EDITS
FORE MACE RENES
ANT  SEER  DEW
```

PUZZLE 546

1. Bouquet, Flowers; 2. Conduct, Manners; 3. Animals, Zoology; 4. Weather, Almanac; 5. Compose, Anthems; 6. Weapons, Arsenal; 7. Portico, Veranda.

PUZZLE 547

```
GAB   QUIT  WISH
TAXES UNDO  EDIE
ALIEN IDEA  NILE
PASTE TESS  DOLL
   APER  TESTY
   FLAKE  ASK
MEAN GRIP EJECT
RENTS ANS SARAH
STEEL INEZ VANE
    AID ABASE
    PLAYS MOPE
SLED LEAD ALTAR
HEAD ARID CEASE
EAVE NINE HALED
STER DEER  PEA
```

1-E, 2-G, 3-I, 4-A, 5-L, 6-N, 7-R, 8-T, 9-W, 10-P, 11-X, 12-Y, 13-C, 14-F, 15-H, 16-J, 17-B, 18-K, 19-M, 20-Q, 21-S, 22-U, 23-V, 24-Z, 25-O, 26-D.

PUZZLE 548

1. Apace, Space, Spare, Share, Shark, Shirk.
2. While, Whine, Shine, Shone, Stone, Stony.
3. Maker, Baker, Baler, Bales, Balls, Bills.
4. Scarf, Scare, Score, Store, Stone, Atone.

PUZZLE 549

```
SOBS  GAEL  RANI  MAMA
PLAT  ELSA  ATOM  ELAL
ALBATROSS   CORMORANT
DAYTIME STEP  EUGENE
   ERS  BOAR  ARTE
CABLE DOER  ASSESSED
ORLY  WOODPECKER  ARE
LEA WANT  SHED  INGE
TACTILE ANTED  ARDOR
KANT  PRIED  SWAP
RABID BEEPS BEANIES
EVIL CORN  MARY  PRO
PER KOOKABURRA  DEMO
ORDINARY ASEA  CARAT
   CATS  STUD  MAI
ASPECT STER  PERSIAN
CHICKADEE  PARTRIDGE
TUNA  IDEA  ERIE  ELEE
SNAP  LEND  DIMS  SEED
```

PUZZLE 550

```
HACK  BURG  ABBA  OATEN
COBRA ONER  MILL  ALATE
APEAR OSSA  IDOL  KILOS
MILWAUKEETONEWORLEANS
   STRIATED  STOA
CHI GET DRU  SNAPS
LATCHES BIBAND ADLOC
IDAHO PARADISE TILER
FTLAUDERDALETOSPOKANE
FOOTSORE ELKE PUBERTY
   TNOTE SPIRO
SELLOUT SCAR HESSITES
ATLANTICCITYTODETROIT
CHANT COATLESS OMUDA
INION GREASE MANAGER
CONDO  PRN PAL  HRS
   UVEA  TEARSOFF
PORTLANDTOALBUQUERQUE
ADIEU TEAL MENU ROUSE
ROGET RAND ALEE AMIEL
TRASH ELSE NEDS LETS
```

PUZZLE 551

```
TUBE  ELLA  HOT
ASEA  LEAD  ALA
PFRT  FAULKNER
ERNES    DIE
   SNAKE BAHIA
HAT FEAR  ELL
ERE ELMER MLI
LEI  PETE IST
PANDA  SEVEN
   ACT  SAGAS
GERSHWIN SWAY
ARI  EIRE EARN
MAO  STET DYES
```

PUZZLE 552

```
CODE  JET  ACTS
AWED  AYE  TOIL
BEWILDER  TONE
   TOE REEKED
   BLOW RIMS
TEAR HABITUAL
OAT GUILT  SLY
ONEHORSE  METE
   ANTE  HERO
TRAVEL  PAT
ROPE IMITATOR
AMEN NAP  LODE
MESS GEE  SPED
```

PUZZLE 553

```
BOWL  TEDS  PAN
OBOE  ERIA  RIE
TINT  ENVIRONS
   HOT ANIMUS
LEVERET  TAP
ILO ARAR  STOW
PAL LEMUR  ITO
SMUT DATA  NOR
   NOD RAVAGED
FUTURE   BED
ATARAXIA MYNA
CAR KING  IOUS
THY ETNA  TUNS
```

PUZZLE 554

```
SANTA    SAMOA
KNEADS  SHIELD
INSTEP  CALLED
PUT SALAD  LIE
SALT RUR  BOND
LEAP  MACAWS
   BOMBBAY
KELPIE  MESS
DOSE TRI  DEER
ART HESTS  CRI
READER  ELATED
EATERS  REDONE
SNEER    WARES
```

PUZZLE 555

```
IMPART  BASIE  STRAINER
ROLES  RENT  CANNON
VESPER  GONG  SINE
   SONIC  ARDENT
WHOLESALE WANES  SHIN
OPS LAND HOLDER ATEN
SON  DIME  TEMPEST
   INHERIT  ROUT
CRUDER YOURS HEDGEHOG
SIENNA PAINTER ORA
TESTY  QUEEN  GIAN
```

PUZZLE 556

A. Geese, Peeve, Added, Asses, Error; B. Epees, Daddy, Mommy, Emeer, Lolls, Lulls, Sassy, Sissy, Nanny, Ninny, Bobby, Mummy, Puppy, Poppy, Peppy; C. Belle, Femme, Freer, Lotto, Motto; D. Eleven, Evened, Eyelet; E. Bazaar, Salaam, Redeem, Reseed, Veneer.

PUZZLE 557

```
ACID  LOVER  CATS
VASE  ANODE  OLEO
EVIL  DENIM  NEAT
RESENDS  TINTERS
   TIS  VOTER
CAMEL  CAR  VOLES
AVID  OAR  MELODY
SON PADDLER  SUN
TICKET  EAT  DECO
EDENS ENS  PARED
   ETONS  FUR
SCISSOR  MENTORS
HATS  ZAMIA  IRIS
OGEE  EGEST  NEST
PERT  DENTS  GOES
```

PUZZLE 558

```
FARE  ROOF  CHIC  SHED
AMEN  ANTI  LOCO  PURE
CONDUCTOR  EMEU  URGE
EST NEO EIRE  PARLOR
   SIR AMOK  ALMS
STRUT PLAN FREE  IRE
THAN SEAN LAIRS ROW
ERI  APES TONES TOME
PULLMAN FROGS DINER
   RAIN CLAMS BATH
CLOSE DRAMS CABOOSE
HEAT MEETS LAGS  ROT
AND DOPES TABS  ESTE
PAS ENOS  SASS PRESS
   SLOT TENS  FUN
PORTER SEEK NUT  HST
AREA ABLE CROSSTIES
WANT IRAN AIDE  OKRA
SLOE LAMS ROSE  PEER
```

PUZZLE 559

```
DUFF  DAME   COS
OPIE  AMORE LATE
COLE  MEDAL OMIT
NELSON  SLAVES
   IAN  EASE
MANY  ARR  TROG
SING FRO  COSTAS
ALI MATADOR HIE
LETTER DON  TELE
SARA  SSE  DORS
   AROW  GET
MADAME  MEETME
ROPE EDDIE EARL
OVER NEALS RIME
BED  SNEE  SLAW
```

PUZZLE 560

TARE TRAIT COMA
STUN WILDE AMES
ETHANALLEN BEET
URBANE ATLANTA
LEG OTHER
VASE EVE VENUS
ADE SORE PETITE
PAD QUARTER OTT
INARUT LOTS BET
DONEE AIM HERO
MAMIE AGE
PAROLED STAROF
AVIV RESTORABLE
LOVE IDIOM LOUS
OWED TEXAS DEEP

PUZZLE 561

Adit, Afar, Agar, Ajar, Aloe, Arid, Bead, Beam, Bear, Best, Bola, Bolo, Bowl, Dada, Dart, Dead, Deaf, Deal, Dear, Dirt, Drag, Dram, Edit, Fade, Flag, Floe, Flow, Gala, Grad, Gram, Grid, Grit, Idea, Jade, Jest, Jowl, Lama, Lard, Lobe, Lobo, Made, Mama, Mart, Oboe, Peal, Pear, Pest, Raga, Ride, Rite, Seal, Seam, Sear, Sped, Step, Stet, Stir, Teal, Team, Tear, Test, Tide, Tram, Wolf.

PUZZLE 562

VAMPS PAT AMT
AGORA EGO FIR
TENOR COMBINE
SWIFT BURIN
WITS RIA REED
EWE TANKER
BARSAC IRONER
QUALMS UTE
MENU SIB SCAD
ARIAS FOREL
CANDENT OREAD
ETO LEE UVATE
SON FED XERES

PUZZLE 563

BIRD IRES BAD
ODOR NERO IDA
ALOE IPIL GEM
REDACT NIPA
DAIS DEMIT
CONSTANT RICH
ODA OTOES SEE
SETA ERRANTRY
TRIBE ERIE
VILE IDEALS
ELI BAKE DRIP
ROT OVER LEDA
RAY WENS EAST

PUZZLE 564

ALIT CANT MARIE
SIDA AREA ELAND
CLOCKWORKORANGE
OLLIE NOEL DEN
TESTED NEED
LAVA GAELIC
AGES VENT CLONE
FORTYEIGHTHOURS
ANGIE LEAR STES
RESETS LIAR
SILO POMMEL
AHA ECHO LIANA
SECONDHONEYMOON
TAHOE EMUS ERLE
ADEPT REST DIAS

PUZZLE 565

A. 1. Aloft, 2. Flock, 3. Cargo, 4. Gnome, 5. March, 6. Cable, 7. Least, 8. Spear.
B. 1. Loft, 2. Lock, 3. Argo, 4. Nome, 5. Arch, 6. Able, 7. East, 8. Pear.

PUZZLE 566

STUB ADAM STEM FOLK
CURE DELA TERI OVEN
ANNE DELL RAID RANI
MASTERPIECE CAMELOT
DELE RAG SUP
EMBASSY LAMAS GATES
DIODES CATERED WORE
ANNUL WATER ROY NIN
MEAL FINER SALARIED
TELLER TOPEKA
BRUSSELS TIRES CHOP
RAN SEA MOLES WHINE
AVID TRAILER THENCE
DETER DINER BUILDER
DEB MUD TURF
ARDUOUS TOURDEFORCE
LAIC ROTE SAGE BORE
ACME SAWS EDEN ODOR
SEED TROT SETS ESPY

PUZZLE 567

RAGE SCOWL ABET
OVAL WHERE WAVE
METE EERIE AREA
PREVIEW TRAINS
ACT BESET
SKATE BAR REAPS
WAGE WAR FIDDLE
ARI CHARLIE DUE
PALTRY EAR SEND
STERE PLY BARKS
ESSES RED
HEATER HINDERS
PORT AMAIN EDIE
OPIE TILLS NILE
DEED STALE STEP

PUZZLE 568

CABINETMAKER

PUZZLE 569

SPLAT FARE CRINGE
CRANER ARABIC RIGORS
RETILE ROMANO AGOROT
BETHLEHEMSANDHAWS FUR
RARE PELEE IONS TOPE
AMA HAIR VARY CILIA
TEC HORAS MINT JUNKET
DEMANDS NEE LURED
EWE METRE ILL ALA
PECAN BOAR XRAY MNOP
IRON NEWPORTER ACRE
KILT MOTE NEOS COEDS
ECU BAS DROLL EAR
MERRY AMY COLLIER
LABIAL SEVE LAPEL NEA
ENURE WERE OREM END
VISE FARO SCONE DRIED
EMS BIRMINGHAMANDEGGS
RATTAN OCELOT ITALIA
ETOILE NATURE RANTED
TEPEES SEND LEASE

PUZZLE 570

THAW SAGA BRAGS
RUSH CROP RESET
ALEE RETE APPLY
PLAYPEN DOVE
LEA BEACH
SPAIN PIE THIN
SCARE LACY ONE
TARTS AGO SLIDE
ERA EVEN PACED
MADE CAR BOWER
BENCH ERR
TOOL RETORTS
DENIM AVOW MIRE
AWARE SIDE IDEA
METES HEED TEEM

PUZZLE 571

1. To err is human, to forgive divine.
2. Fiddler on the Roof.

PUZZLE 572

PUZZLE 573

TAM SOFA SHOW
ATOP EVICT TALE
CORE SANTA RIDE
OMEN ALE FEAR
CAM FRY
RECIPE PEASANT
ORALS FEET FOE
MOP ETERNAL TON
ADE REED OBESE
NERVOUS GARRET
ARM ADO
PREP AWL KEYS
DELI EASEL EXIT
AGUE TRIBE NAPE
MOSS EASY MEW

PUZZLE 574

1. Rim in grime, 2. Ode in yodel, 3. Tee in steer, 4. Owl in bowls, 5. Rap in craps, 6. Ire in siren.

PUZZLE 575

MAST SAMP STEED
SOBER OLEO EASTER
ELATE LINT CREASE
NAT ADIT TOTE PIN
DRESSED BEDS PERT
TOW PORE RASES
ASPEN DAD UAR
BEET ROSEOFSHARON
ETE LIFT PIES ONE
THREEOFAKIND RACE
ANT AND BORED
SWARD HALE ALL
OARS SINE CHALICE
DID ENDS BOAS ROW
AVERSE WOOD THANE
SENATE ERLE EATER
STEER REDS DYES

PUZZLE 576

```
C O H O   S O D A S   A B E   L O S T
A M O R   I R I S H   P O X   A N O A
R O L L I N G S T O N E G A T H E R S
T O Y E R S   R U E S   M O R S E S
    S S S   A R I L S   F I R S T
R A T S   G R I N D S T O N E   O N A
E L O   M A L I G N   I R E   O N U S
D I N   A L E S   T A M E R   P E T S
O V E R R A N   S T L O   S A T
  E D E N   E A C H O N E   R I S K
    M E G   D A R E   S A N C T U M
B A B A   A L A M O   I S N O   O D A
A D E N   L O N   W I D E N S   N O R
G A S   B L O O D S T O N E   B E S T
  T R U S T   A T A L E   M A H
A C O U R T   O D O R   L A R E D O
L E F T N O S T O N E U N T U R N E D
A B I T   N A T   E S T E R   O G L E
D U T Y   E G O   S T E W S   W E I R
```

PUZZLE 577

```
P E N   D E G A S   L O S E R   D O N
L I E   O V A T E   A W A R E   E M U
A R C   N E W E R   P E T A L   T A N
N E T W O R K   M A S S   S A B E R
  A I R Y   D O N E   M E T E R
T E R N S   P O N Y   R E D E E M E D
A M I D   P A S S   T I E   I R A
F I N   B A L E   T R O T   K N O T
T R E L L I S   F R E T S   G E E S E
  O U R   B L I S S   F R Y
C A S T E   S L A P S   P L A S T I C
A B E S   L A S S   S L A M   E R A
R E P   A S K   F L O W   S N I P
S T A G N A N T   F O O D   C H E S S
  R O O S T   P O R T   B O O M
G A T O S   B O R E   C R A T E R S
R U T   D A L E S   S H O U T   N E T
I R E   L I E N S   T O R T E   T E A
M U D   E L A T E   S T E E D   S L Y
```

PUZZLE 578

```
W H I M   T R A M   F L A P   C R O W
A I D A   R I V E   L A I R   H E R E
I D E N T I C A L   A C M E   E A R L
L E A S E   H I L L S   S E V E R A L
    E B B   L O O K S   N I T
A S P   E L F   W A S T E   M A T E R
M E R   T A L K E D   R A M   H A V E
B E E S   N E E D   E E R I E   K E N
I N C A   D E E   A W E   D E S E R T
  I R A   S P I N E T S   L E A
B E S I D E   S L Y   C A B   A F R O
A L E   S P E A K   C A P E   S T A R
L I L Y   I N K   C E R I S E   E V E
L A Y E R   D E T E R   D E N   R E S
    A I T   S I D E S   T U B
E M E R G E S   L E M O N   R A N E E
W A R N   N U L L   O D O M E T E R S
E L S E   T R E E   N A T O   O R A N
R E E D   S E E R   Y S E R   N O S E
```

PUZZLE 579

```
S H A D Y   T R A S H   C R A S H
C A N O E   R A R E E   A U D I O
O M I T S   A F T E R   R E A D S
P A L   T A C T   D O E R   G E T
E L E M E N T   D I N G I N E S S
  O R T   F I E   G E E
F A R A D   P A N S Y   R A J A H
I M I T A T O R   T O M   R A C A
R A G   Y A K   K I P   P U T
S T O P   N E W   R E L E G A T E
T I R O L   R A T A L   C A N E D
  R O C   T A P   C U R
S C H E D U L E D   T A L B O T S
W O O   G E A R   L I R A   R I N
E L U D E   S L O O P   T A B L E
P O S E R   T O F F S   E L I D E
T R E Y S   S O F T Y   D E T E R
```

PUZZLE 580

```
E M S   F A L A   P U P A S   S I L O
B I T   A R A B   A T A L E   O D O R
B L A C K E Y E D S U S A N   R O S E
  R U E S   R E T R O   H A R L E M
S W O R D   A D M E N   N O M E
T A F T   F R E U D   M A R Y L A N D
A C T   S L I E R   M O R A L   B O O
B O H E M I A N   P A R I S   F R O G
  E R I N S   T R I E S   C E A S E
P E N U L T   F O I L S   B A T H E S
S L O P E   Y O K E S   B E R E A
H A R T   G A L E S   G R A N D M A S
A T T   E R W I N   C L A R E   L I E
W E H A V E N O   T R E S S   P I R N
  L E E S   R U I N S   T E N T S
A S T E R N   O A R E D   M A R C
T H O U   W E S T B R A N C H I O W A
T O R T   A T S E A   L O C O   L A C
U T E S   Y E A R N   E R I E   N R A
```

PUZZLE 581

```
F A D S   M E S A   C A D S   R I T A
A B E T   O V E R   A L A N   E D E N
I B A R   S A N M A R I N O   V E N T
R E L A T E   D U L I   K U H E A N S
    N E L L   R E E F   P A R
M O N D A L E   S L A P   W E L L S
I N A   M E A D E   S U E Z   S O O T
C U S S   P O L L   N E E D   V I A
A S H E N   T O M E S   L A R C E N Y
  V E E R   R E M I T   L O O S
S T I N T E D   R U M O R   P A T S Y
L I L   S A R K   R O T O   L O L A
E E L S   L A I C   N E A R S   R U R
W R E A K   B L O B   D E C O Y E D
  L E T   O M E R   S P A R
P E T U N I A   P E A T   E R A S E S
A L I T   D E C E P T I O N   T O T O
L I N E   A R A T   E T A T   O D O R
L A G S   L O N E   D O T S   R A N T
```

PUZZLE 582

```
S P A T   B I L L   A P S E   S T E P
E A S E   A R I A   B O O R   C O R E
E T T A   G O L D E N E Y E   R O L E
S H A R P E N   D I E T   D E T E R
  G A L   E R R   A S I A
C O R A L   H A R E   D I A M O N D
I R I S   B O S S   S P E L L   D O E
T A N   A L P   H A R P O   H O S E
E L D E R L Y   C A R A T   H A R E M
  T I E   A R R A Y   T A R
S T R O P   B L U S H   S U M M A R Y
I R A N   B R A S H   P U N   R O E
T A G   S A I N T   C A R E   P E A L
E M E R A L D   L A T E   P E A R L
  A I D E   P U B   T E L
B R A N D   B A R A   C A P I T A L
I O N S   S I L V E R F O X   C O L A
T O T O   I D E A   E R I E   A G E S
S T E M   P A W N   T O L D   N A S H
```

PUZZLE 583

```
S P A R E   F O S S E   S O L O S
S C O R E S   A S H E S   O L I V E R
W A L K I N G S T I C K   R E V E R E
E R I   N E A T E R   I D E A   R E D
A C T S   S T E   A M E S   M O N A
T E E N S   E D I T I O N   L I N E N
  E I N S   R I D S   S A N E
S P H E R E   P O N E   I N V E S T S
H E A R   S T I N T   T R U E   H E A
E A R S   T I P S   S W A G   L E A F
E L D   A L E E   G O I N G   E A S E
R E T I R E D   B O U T   L O A D E R
  O R T S   R O S S   D E A N
A C H E S   R E S H A P E   R E F E R
B R A D   B I D S   A N T   D E L E
Y E N   E L A H   S O D I U M   N A N
S E D A T E   O N E A R M B A N D I T
S P L I T S   T E N S E   A L I E N S
  S E R E S   S E T T S   S T E R E
```

PUZZLE 584

```
APSE    PLAN
TRIPS   RIGID
PICNIC  IRONED
BACH NAIVE  EVEN
INK   PEA   INE
DELS RESTS  ELSE
ELECTED  ELAPSED
AWE        ADO
CHARADE  ENACTED
LOSE SPENT  HERO
USS   INT   MEN
BEEN STEEL  SPCA
STEREO  REVOLT
STEAM   EVADE
SOLE    DINS
```

PUZZLE 585

```
TELL  MOTT  OSLO
ELEE  OAHU  CHARS
ASIF  STAR  SONIC
LEFTBEHIND  ROSE
YUL    LIT   SON
CUDGEL  REDOLENT
ANYONE   AFORE
DIEM   FIT   FARO
ERROL   BATTER
FRAZIERS  UNWISE
REB  BEL   SKI
ABAS  LEFTHANDED
MACON FREE  GOAD
ETUDE TOLL  EZRA
ESAU  YMAS  RELY
```

PUZZLE 586

```
CRISP VETCH  TSK
RETAR OCALA  HAL
ANCHORWOMAN  EYE
BEHAVE  LARGESSE
REDS   LEMOKO
HAHA  FILE   ALI
ELI   ODE  SNIPPY
MATS REATA  CPAS
PITTED  ROY   ERE
HUN  ANEW  BRER
CENTER   SHUL
OLDTIMES  EPOPEE
SUE  COTTONSWABS
SEC ETHER  EEROS
ASK  DEARS  TRINE
```

PUZZLE 587

```
TUB  END    ROSE
ORE  LOOT   EVIL
ENGRAVER   LENS
IOTA   ORANGE
ANTE   SUIT
DINE  PEPPERED
ODE  DOVES   AGE
TERMITES   LION
OMEN   PANS
GARDEN   HAND
OBOE  CHILDREN
BLUR  YORE   OWE
SEEN    WED   PET
```

PUZZLE 588

```
ISLE  DUMAS  ATIP
OHIO  AROMA  RARE
LANSINGMICHIGAN
EWE  DIES   ESSEN
MESS   HALE
PARISH  CARP  HMS
ONES   SETAE  AIL
LINCOLNNEBRASKA
ESE  ROOTS   STEN
SEW  OARS  LATEST
HIDE   SALA
STRAD  NEWS   LEO
CHEYENNEWYOMING
ARNE  AIMEE  IDOL
RUTS  STARR  ROSE
```

PUZZLE 589

```
LOFT  ABAS  RENEW
ADAR  PERT  EVADE
RITE  OLLA  GAVEL
KNEES  TERRA  END
SEA   STILL
SHE  VIE  LEASES
COMMERCIAL  TIRE
AMBER  TOR  SEDAN
REED  SONGSTRESS
ERRANT  OLE   SEE
LOOSE   YES
ALA  DANTE  PAGAN
VALID AURA  TORE
OVATE IDOL  IRIS
WANED LEST  NEAT
```

PUZZLE 590

```
ROW   SPUD  MAZES
OCHO  PORE  ASIDE
ATOP  ASIR  RANGE
MELEE TAMER  CYD
STEREOPHONIC
WALDO   GEORGE
BAH  SONIC  SLEET
ELEA  RENAL  AFAR
STAMP DATUM  IRE
TATARS   ANION
TOASTMASTERS
IWO  FOLIO  STRAW
BAMBI  ABUT  EINE
IDEAL  CINE  REEL
DENSE  KATE   SEL
```

PUZZLE 591

```
LOOP  SQUAD  AJAR
IDLE  PURSE  PELE
NEER  RINSE  RAIL
GROUPIES   HONEY
ANT    COIN
SARONG  GANGSTER
CLING  TOUCH  AXE
RAVE  CHOSE  SPIN
ATE  SUEDE  CHEST
PERFORMS  HEARTS
LATE   HAL
BORER   BELLWOOD
APEX  KARAT  HOUR
RITE  OLIVE  EZRA
NEED  STEER  TEST
```

PUZZLE 592

```
CHORD DAMP  NOME
ROVER ELIA  ICED
AMANA PUNT  BANG
BOLTFROMTHEBLUE
ETAS   GLASS
SCAR   PEERAGE
WORST   LOVESEAT
ALA ATELIER  SRO
PALLIATE  SANER
APPENDS  DEAN
TASTE   IOTA
ONCEINABLUEMOON
IGOR  ORAL  RANGE
LIRA  DIRE  SNELL
SEEL  SAAR  EDSEL
```

PUZZLE 593

```
MARC  CARET  THAW
ADAH  OSAKA  IONA
HAVINGTHEJUMPON
RENEGES   SEINE
AVER   BRED
ABASED  DRED  APE
LOPE  SAINT  RUN
TOHAVEANDTOHOLD
ANI  EDUCE  EASE
RED  RICE  SNARED
ANTE   PAID
STENO   CESSION
HAVINGNOTHINGON
IRIS  AERIE  GLUE
POLE  DENTS  SENT
```

PUZZLE 594

```
NEPAL MOTOR  SEC
ARENA CLARE  WPA
BRIDGECLUBS  EON
GLOAT   THEDA
SNEAKY  HOSTEL
PIERRE  DEARTH
ILIAD ARISE  EMU
LOLL GLINT  LAOS
LSD  PEALE  HARTE
ISRAEL  TOTTER
SLATER   FINEST
TOMES  EDILE
ORO SAMUELSPADE
WEN ELMAN  TRUED
END ROALD  YOKES
```

PUZZLE 595

```
FLAIR  BLAB  RUST
LAPSE  RILE  ANTI
EVENTUALLY  IDOL
WEST  MILES  SEAT
ABNER   BERTH
BESTIRS  GRASS
ARCADE TEEN  TAT
SLAM LEANS  LAME
HEM SLAG  TRITON
PLEAS  LOITERS
SHEET   THIRD
HORA  SWINE  GAPE
AMIS LANDSCAPES
RENE  URGE  ASSES
ERGS  EDEN  THERE
```

558

PUZZLE 596

```
SACK THINE ALMA
AREA RERAN LEAP
WILLIEMAYS LORE
SALESMAN LEANER
   LON LAWNS
SALTER ROVE PST
TREAT PAPER ICE
ABET WAGES GNAT
GOT HIRED ANKLE
ERR ARID AMUSES
  ERIES UTE
COVERT ASTERISK
AMIN ARTHURASHE
MANE PATEN SEEP
PROW SPARE HEAT
```

PUZZLE 597

```
LAPP BAM SPED
ALEE AHAB AORTA
BIRR NERO CLOUD
SAUCEJACKANDPIE
   ASOR DEE
HILT TEAM RARA
RODEO ABEE DEW
OILSPLITANDPEEL
USE SANE WALKS
ETRE NANA ARES
   SPA LIRA
JUICEICEANDBOWL
ORSON ORSK LURE
AGERS ELKE ERIN
BEET EAR SSTS
```

PUZZLE 598

```
POMP SILT MERV
ALEE ANWAR ALOE
CLARABOWWINDOWS
TAT VOWS CORNET
   BEDS BYTE
RELINE LUCE SIB
ALONG MALL SANE
JUDGEROYBEANBAG
ADES EVES LEONI
HEN EVER STATEN
   SAID SHAD
MATURE STAR LEA
ETHELWATERSDOWN
GOAD ELOPE ACED
ANNE DIPS NOSY
```

PUZZLE 599

```
ALFA ABASE ACRE
GOAL BENIN THEN
ONCE HANDTOHAND
GEE MONA IRENE
   TSARS STAN
MOONS SUITABLE
NIFTY PAREE AID
ALAS SITES ACME
PAC SHEER LIKEN
SNEAKERS DONTS
   MELS SETTO
STEEL STAS BOB
REELTOREEL MADE
OMNI UNCLE ACID
TINA TATER EKES
```

PUZZLE 600

```
MATS UCLA CHA
ELAN THING SHOW
WARADMIRAL LAME
SIT IOTA ELATED
   MASS PEEVE
ESCORT SOFT AAR
STORY MODUS URI
NOUN PUPIL AGED
ERN SASHA ALATE
SET TRIS PLAYER
  FOLIC ELIS
GALLON ALEE AGA
OREL GALLANTFOX
OLEA SHEET VANE
DOT ANNS ARES
```

PUZZLE 601

```
BARE PART SOP
EMIL ALOE EGO
LIMA SIDEWALK
  TEST MELEE
SPHERE FEN
ERODE FADDIST
ROO YON LOU
EMPOWER BALIN
  GAS HASSLE
STORY LONI
COMELIER DUDS
ALE ADES ETUI
TEN YOKE SAND
```

Repartee is what you wish you'd said.

PUZZLE 602

```
BOSS TARO SLAP STAB
AREA ROAN PALE TOLE
SALT UNDECIDED ERIE
ELLIPSE SLED EVENTS
   SAT READ TSAR
GAFFS BALM ARTISTIC
ALLY TIFF CLEAN ARE
USE PUNT CREEL TROD
LODGING PEERS CRANE
GALA BLAST MAIN
BELIE GRASS BIGOTED
LAIN PRATE SALE UTE
USN TEASE CONE SLOE
REGRINDS RAID PLANS
   ALEE PAIL FEE
PARCEL SETS CORNCOB
AMOK OPPRESSOR DOME
TALE PEAK OUST EDIT
SHED EATS NETS RETS
```

PUZZLE 603

```
RATES LISP PLOP SCABS
ORALE ASHE RODE CARAT
URBBEGCLEASIGERMANRABI
GALA REED AMAS OPENER
ESE FAST ELON SLED
   HIS SNAG ALA RAM
LAGOAPRSPODEMPARDMARO
INERT ETAS NAST RONDO
ATLI AGER TIRE DENIES
RITZ RAE LOTS ARGONNE
  OUTRPRONOHOMESP
CRANKED ONER TOA OSLO
RENTAL LAGS DOUR LEES
IDEAS BESS BEEN MIENS
MATLENLATHERESTACERTA
ENS OAK OVID TIS
CRJB PRIM KNOX ALI
ALLIES GAEL SOON GNAR
MAIDSEVRUMSHEPRECANTE
ONSET EASE AMES ALIEN
REARS EDEN DIKE DEERE
```

PUZZLE 604

```
HARE BOOK LAST
EVEN CRANE OBEY
RIDE LOSER GULP
ODOR EAT NESTLE
   GLAD SEW
CRAYON PLEDGE
LIT TEASE ROLLS
AGOG DREAD NAVE
MINUS MAKES DEN
DEMOTE FOREST
  LAD CEDE
SLOWER SON POSH
HAVE GENES ALTO
OMEN ERODE SEEP
PERT TABS TOWS
```

PUZZLE 605

```
PARES OFF COTS
ABIDE ZOOM UPON
TEPEE AREA REDO
SLENDEREST DRAB
   ELKS ESSAYS
TOLEDO TASK
ADAM PAST IOTA
NOVICES ORDAINS
RATE PIPE RENO
   DUST LESSEN
FASTEN EVIL
LICE IMMACULATE
ADOS TAIL DINER
MELT SIZE EATER
EDDY NET DRESS
```

PUZZLE 606

```
CAGE SPUR SLIM DREG
OMER CORE TONE EATA
METE RUNAROUND SNAP
ANN CAT SILT IDEALS
   EDAM MOVE STIR
MAXIM GENE BEANTOWN
ANTE RAN RELATE LOO
SET POPUP DATE CLOT
TWOTIME AMISS TRADE
ONE CRATE FRA
SPITE CLARO ALIBABA
NETS BRAD RODEO BOP
ORE CLOSES MAW MOWS
BUMSRUSH TRAM PAUSE
   LEES LEER BENT
RENOWN LAPS SEW FOE
AROW OVERSIGHT ZARF
SINE SING SOOT ACCT
PEER EASE TOPE PEAS
```

PUZZLE 607

```
BATS BRAT ALOE FOLD
EXIT RECEIVERS ELIA
ELLA ENERVATES NEAR
RETREAT MISS ENCORE
   RED DIET KNEE
SHEEN RATS ENCIRCLE
MIND PETE SPIEL EON
EGG SAME TWIGS CLOD
WHISTLE BEECH SEEPS
NEE MEANEST ORB
STEAM BESET HONORED
TRET RELIT FOES AGO
OUR HARES DOOR STAG
PESTERED MEAD DEEDS
   ARID CALM TIN
PARROT MADE MENACES
ATIP ITERATION TAKE
COCO EASEMENTS OPEN
AMEN SWAT SKEE REST
```

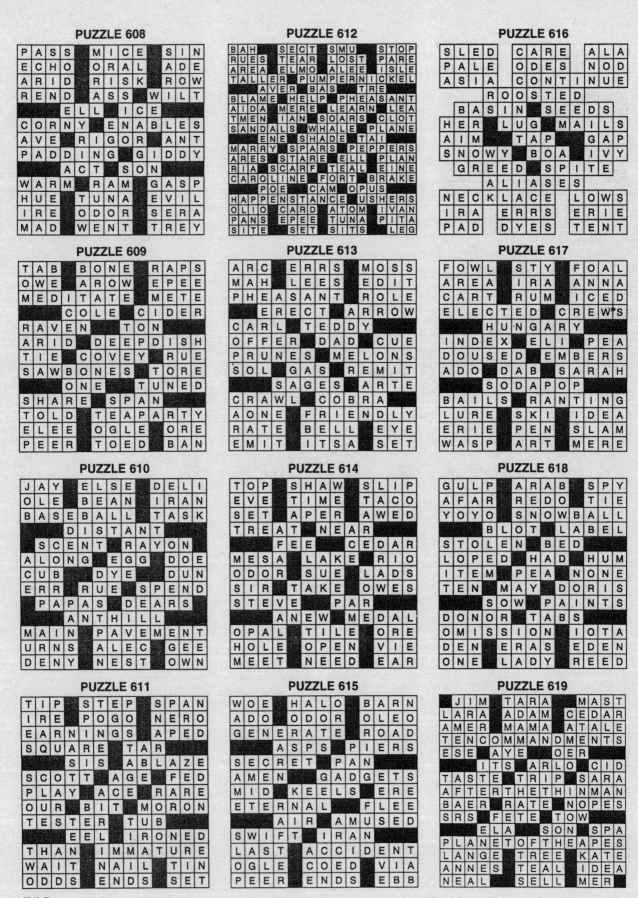

PUZZLE 608

```
PASS MICE SIN
ECHO ORAL ADE
ARID RISK ROW
REND ASS WILT
     ELL ICE
CORNY ENABLES
AVE RIGOR ANT
PADDING GIDDY
    ACT SON
WARM RAM GASP
HUE TUNA EVIL
IRE ODOR SERA
MAD WENT TREY
```

PUZZLE 612

```
BAH SECT SMU STOP
RUES TEAR LOST PARE
AREA ELMO ALEE ISLE
TALLER PUMPERNICKEL
AVER BAS TRE
BLAME HELP PHEASANT
AIDA MERE LEARN LEA
TMEN IAN SOARS CLOT
SANDALS WHALE PLANE
ENE SHADE TAI
MARRY SPARS PEPPERS
ARES STARE ELL PLAN
RIA SCARF TEAL EINE
CAROLINE FORT BRAKE
POE CAM OPUS
HAPPENSTANCE USHERS
OLIO CARD ATOM IVAN
PANS EPEE TUNA PITA
SITE SET SITS LEG
```

PUZZLE 616

```
SLED CARE ALA
PALE ODES NOD
ASIA CONTINUE
   ROOSTED
BASIN SEEDS
HER LUG MAILS
AIM TAP GAP
SNOWY BOA IVY
GREED SPITE
  ALIASES
NECKLACE LOWS
IRA ERRS ERIE
PAD DYES TENT
```

PUZZLE 609

```
TAB BONE RAPS
OWE AROW EPEE
MEDITATE METE
   COLE CIDER
RAVEN TON
ARID DEEPDISH
TIE COVEY RUE
SAWBONES TORE
  ONE TUNED
SHARE SPAN
TOLD TEAPARTY
ELEE OGLE ORE
PEER TOED BAN
```

PUZZLE 613

```
ARC ERRS MOSS
MAH LEES EDIT
PHEASANT ROLE
  ERECT ARROW
CARL TEDDY
OFFER DAD CUE
PRUNES MELONS
SOL GAS REMIT
  SAGES ARTE
CRAWL COBRA
AONE FRIENDLY
RATE BELL EYE
EMIT ITSA SET
```

PUZZLE 617

```
FOWL STY FOAL
AREA IRA ANNA
CART RUM ICED
ELECTED CREW*S
   HUNGARY
INDEX ELI PEA
DOUSED EMBERS
ADO DAB SARAH
  SODAPOP
BAILS RANTING
LURE SKI IDEA
ERIE PEN SLAM
WASP ART MERE
```

PUZZLE 610

```
JAY ELSE DELI
OLE BEAN IRAN
BASEBALL TASK
  DISTANT
SCENT RAYON
ALONG EGG DOE
CUB DYE DUN
ERR RUE SPEND
PAPAS DEARS
  ANTHILL
MAIN PAVEMENT
URNS ALEC GEE
DENY NEST OWN
```

PUZZLE 614

```
TOP SHAW SLIP
EVE TIME TACO
SET APER AWED
TREAT NEAR
   FEE CEDAR
MESA LAKE RIO
ODOR SUE LADS
SIR TAKE OWES
STEVE PAR
  ANEW MEDAL
OPAL TILE ORE
HOLE OPEN VIE
MEET NEED EAR
```

PUZZLE 618

```
GULP ARAB SPY
AFAR REDO TIE
YOYO SNOWBALL
   BLOT LABEL
STOLEN BED
LOPED HAD HUM
ITEM PEA NONE
TEN MAY DORIS
  SOW PAINTS
DONOR TABS
OMISSION IOTA
DEN ERAS EDEN
ONE LADY REED
```

PUZZLE 611

```
TIP STEP SPAN
IRE POGO NERO
EARNINGS APED
SQUARE TAR
   SIS ABLAZE
SCOTT AGE FED
PLAY ACE RARE
OUR BIT MORON
TESTER TUB
  EEL IRONED
THAN IMMATURE
WAIT NAIL TIN
ODDS ENDS SET
```

PUZZLE 615

```
WOE HALO BARN
ADO ODOR OLEO
GENERATE ROAD
  ASPS PIERS
SECRET PAN
AMEN GADGETS
MID KEELS ERE
ETERNAL FLEE
  AIR AMUSED
SWIFT IRAN
LAST ACCIDENT
OGLE COED VIA
PEER ENDS EBB
```

PUZZLE 619

```
JIM TARA MAST
LARA ADAM CEDAR
AMER MAMA ATALE
TENCOMMANDMENTS
ESE AYE OER
  ITS ARLO CID
TASTE TRIP SARA
AFTERTHETHINMAN
BAER RATE NOPES
SRS FETE TOW
  ELA SON SPA
PLANETOFTHEAPES
LANGE TREE KATE
ANNES TEAL IDEA
NEAL SELL MER
```

PUZZLE 620

```
BOSC  SANG  CRAB  DOTE
OLEO  EPEE  RACE  IVAN
HILL  REENTERED  VERO
ROLLERS  ERSE  WARES
      INA  STAT  BRAN
BIDED  EPIC  MOAN  BAA
ADIRONDACKMOUNTAINS
NEB  RIDS  AUNT  GLAS
DARESAY  RIND  CAINE
   OLES  TRENT  SHIN
LAMBS  LEAS  CHANGES
APIO  BARN  LOOP  URI
REDWOODNATIONALPARK
AXE  VOLS  ENID  ALLAH
    LUTE  TMEN  LII
SALEM  DOPP  SENATOR
AREA  PROMOTION  BONE
KIEV  RAGE  LIAO  LOUD
EASE  EYES  YIPS  ELSE
```

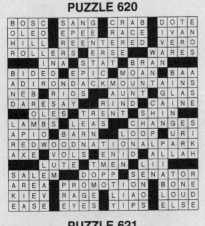

PUZZLE 621

```
ABE    GAMES    TOO
ROE    ALIVE    ELL
CALLASPADEAJNADE
       OPTS   TEE
ASEA  ERA  TACT
PIE  START  HAT
RODS  PLAYERS  ERR
IKE  PAY  ITSA  URN
IVE  SIS  ATT  MAE
DAR  YES  SEE  PIT
ELF  SCI  HID  ESS
ASA  TENS  HEN  ODE
CEE  GAMBLED  STUD
ELM  TREYS  TIP
ISLE  STE  IDAS
      EMS  TREK
CARDUPONESSLEEVE
OWE   ARENA   BIN
BED   SEWER   BAD
```

PUZZLE 622

```
OPT  LURE  ASHE  TWO
FOE  ARID  REAL  EAR
FIELDGOAL  SCRIMMAGE
ODES  ANN  ELSE
OPQR  STOOP  ACT
LOUD  SUPERBOWL  THAN
ALAS  ARA  SOU  SEMI
FAR  FLIT  TOGA  EEL
TILE          GAR
ERAS          BALL
RAM           RILE
JAB  EPEE  SPIN  APT
ARAB  EVA  IAN  IDLE
INCA  RECTANGLE  LEER
OKS  HAVEN  IRAN
TRAP  REX  PISA
RECEIVERS  TOUCHDOWN
AGO  CORE  AREA  URN
WOW  ANTS  REDD  RYE
```

PUZZLE 623

```
ERA  KEATS  RAMIE  ANAT
LOGS  OASES  ECOLE  VEGA
ITHINKTHATISHALLNEVER
CAMEO  LIEN  ISERE
IAM  PROD  MEN
SEEAPOEMLOVELYASATREE
TERNS  LOUPE  AUKS  IONA
URN  CHIME  ITE  TAOS
BIER  RILE  ADAS  MORSE
SESAME  AMINUTE
THEMURMURINGPINES
RESEATS  GUSHED
HASTE  URSA  MUSE  ERLE
ERIA  ROC  CATER  ILE
ACTS  BELL  TATAR  SOLID
THESCARLETOFTHEMAPLES
ADS  EYES  YIP
ESTES  ALTO  STOOL
THECHERRYHUNGWITHSNOW
NOAH  LOIRE  IRANI  ELBA
AERO  MILER  PANIC  YET
```

PUZZLE 624

```
LANDS  PERI  PESO  ETAPE
APART  OVEN  ATEN  TALIA
CEDAR  LIED  RUED  ERECT
EXAMIPOLLIELIMIPROFA
AVA  AGO  TIN
AGA  ELMER  GUST  TABBED
COLT  SARAN  SARA  LORRE
TOGAS  ILIAD  TUBA  RIGA
FASCIDESTIRESIGSUBOR
SETON  EAVE  SEEN  ETS
ERSE  STEPS  SNAG
SPA  ETTA  ORLE  DRAFT
HIBERINCARTERMIALTER
ALOD  LARD  STEAM  SUMAC
MOVED  SEEP  ENTER  NUDE
STERES  SNOB  ESTOP  REE
SAT  LAS  TEA
ASSIGINDIGPERSODESIG
BRING  MEAT  ADIT  AROSE
ANTIN  ERNE  REDO  NILOT
DEEPS  DOER  KNEW  TEENS
```

PUZZLE 625

```
CART  PHARE  SKIP
AREA  REFIX  ARNO
ROBPETERTOPAYPAUL
EMU  LAPS  TEMA  IRK
SAT  ERA  DOR  TEA
CRIC  FIND
FATA  IDO  LEG  SOLD
ALIBIS  MOON  AERIE
KILLTHEFATTEDCALF
IVIES  ROTS  MOTTLE
REAR  BAR  APE  SEER
WEST  MORE
CAT  AGE  LAY  OFF
ALE  CAME  GALE  PIA
PLAYONESCARDSWELL
EASE  NAOMI  ORES
DYES  TUBES  WADE
```

PUZZLE 626

```
ABSORB  TRESS  SCRAPS
DOWNER  RIATA  WEIHAI
SWEETALYSSUM  ELDERS
HERE  ISEE  PEEL  ASA
SETS  ANTS  PANT  EDEL
PAM  DOES  SENDFOR
ADAMAND  AWLS  ELISHA
ROSE  ALEE  FREEWAY
RAJAH  OPIE  BANS  ERA
AMOS  SWEETGUMS  SETH
TOR  EWER  PURE  PETES
ELAPSED  PEST  SOAP
DEMOTE  COAT  PULLOFF
SETTLES  CINE  TOE
LILT  HEAT  TRES  CARD
ONA  CEES  BRAT  EATS
ELMIRA  SWEETANDSOUR
SEAVER  IRENE  ANTERO
STREET  CYSTS  BASSET
```

PUZZLE 627

```
DOGS  BLADE  LAPUP  APE
ALIA  AUDIT  LIANA  NOD
BEAT  DROMEDARIES  STLO
SON  AGES  OMEN  SACHEM
TIGER  CASAS  SONAR
DAPPER  EAVE  EPSILONS
ERASE  ARMADILLO  EPIC
LENO  GAEL  OASIS  DONA
LAD  KILLERWHALE  INT
SABLES  OAR  REEDY
LETT  FAUNS  FILM
MOTET  ARE  LEMURS
AAR  LEGIONARIES  HOG
BOAR  EVENS  NOTA  MIRO
ERNE  ANTELOPES  SANTA
LIGAMENT  IDEA  ALMOST
ORALS  NAMED  ILIAC
ALUMNI  SALE  FRED  END
BATS  CLYDESDALES  ERIE
UNA  IONIC  ARENA  TONE
TEN  TIERS  STEEN  OSAR
```

PUZZLE 628

S	T	A	Y		L	E	D	A		A	B	A	T		P	L	O	D
H	O	M	E		A	X	I	S		T	A	R	O		L	I	R	E
A	N	I	L		M	A	S	S		T	R	A	M		A	L	A	N
W	I	L	L	I	A	M	C	U	L	L	E	N	B	R	Y	A	N	T
			E	L	S			M	A	E				S	E	E		
S	N	A	R	L		S	T	E	R	E	O	S		D	R	I	P	S
T	A	N		S	L	R			V	I	R			T	O	E		
L	I	T	E		T	E	E	S		P	A	L	E		S	E	N	T
O	L	I	V	E	R	W	E	N	D	E	L	L	H	O	L	M	E	S
	E	V	E		E	E	R			I	S	A						
H	A	R	R	I	E	T	B	E	E	C	H	E	R	S	T	O	W	E
A	B	E	T		T	E	A	R		Y	O	K	E		S	T	O	P
I	R	A		S	I	B			L	E	S			O	R	E		
L	I	M	E	Y		L	E	A	R	N	E	D		S	C	E	N	E
	L	E	O		R	I	O			S	A	L						
J	A	M	E	S	F	E	N	I	M	O	R	E	C	O	O	P	E	R
A	L	E	C		T	I	E	S		S	A	L	E		U	L	N	A
M	E	A	T		E	N	T	E		E	R	I	N		D	E	A	D
B	E	D	S		N	E	S	S		S	E	A	T		S	A	S	S

PUZZLE 629

S	C	A	R		F	A	I	L		R	A	S	P		R	O	W	S
T	U	B	E		L	I	N	E		O	V	E	R		E	D	I	E
I	T	E	M		U	R	N	S		D	A	N	E		N	O	S	E
R	E	T	O	R	T	S		S	E	E		T	A	P	E	R	E	D
				T	E	E		H	O	N	O	R		M	O	W		
S	A	V	E	D		F	I	N	D		U	N	B	I	A	S	E	D
L	E	E	R		C	A	R	S		V	I	O	L		L	O	V	E
A	R	E		L	O	S	T		P	A	N	T	E	D		N	I	L
P	O	R	T	E	N	T		M	E	L	E	E		E	A	G	L	E
			O	N	E		P	A	L	E	D		P	A	N			
T	I	R	E	D		W	A	I	T	S		B	E	L	A	T	E	D
A	D	O		S	W	O	R	D	S		R	E	N	T		I	R	E
P	O	T	S		A	N	T	S		P	E	A	S		D	E	N	E
A	L	A	C	A	R	T	E		T	R	A	M		C	I	D	E	R
			A	L	B		D	R	I	E	D		B	U	S			
C	A	R	T	E	L	S		E	L	F		D	A	P	P	L	E	D
A	L	I	T		E	L	S	A		E	V	E	R		L	I	V	E
M	E	T	E		R	O	O	M		R	I	N	D		A	M	E	S
P	E	A	R		S	E	T	S		S	A	Y	S		Y	A	N	K

PUZZLE 630

P	A	I	N		M	A	V	E	N		R	O	B	E	S		S	T	I	R
I	A	G	O		O	V	I	N	E		E	R	A	T	O		C	O	N	E
P	R	O	V	I	D	E	N	C	E		B	A	T	O	N	R	O	U	G	E
S	P	R	A	Y	E	R		D	E	A	L	T			A	R	R	A	S	
			A	L	T		S	L	I	T		S	A	T	I	N				
S	E	A	R	S		S	T	E	R	E		L	A	N	S	I	N	G		
T	E	A	L		S	H	E		E	D	I	S	O	N	S		R	O	E	
A	P	S	E		F	O	A	M		R	I	N	G			S	E	L	L	
P	I	E		F	L	A	K		C	A	P	O	T	E		R	A	N	T	S
S	A	L	T	L	A	K	E		H	O	R	N	E		M	E	L	E	E	
			O	A	K	S		C	A	R	E	Y		T	O	B	E			
L	A	N	G	E		M	O	L	T	S		C	O	L	U	M	B	U	S	
M	I	M	E	S		P	A	R	K	A	S		H	A	L	T		O	N	E
E	N	O	S		T	H	I	S		T	I	D	Y		T	O	T	E		
E	E	R		S	O	O	N	E	R	S		E	L	Y		A	M	I	D	
T	R	E	N	T	O	N		E	A	S	E	D		R	A	I	S	E		
			E	E	L	E	R		B	Y	E	S		F	E	D				
I	R	A	T	E		E	R	O	S	E		A	M	A	S	S	E	D		
M	O	N	T	P	E	L	I	E	R		S	A	C	R	A	M	E	N	T	O
E	V	I	L		T	E	N	S	E		A	S	C	O	T		T	I	N	E
T	E	L	E		C	A	S	T	S		W	I	L	E	S		S	P	A	R

PUZZLE 631

| | | | | | | | | | | | | |
|F|I|R|E|A|R|M| |T|H|U|N|D|E|R|
|O| |A| |P| |I| |R| |P| |I|E|
|R|E|C|I|P|E|S| |E|X|P|O|S|E|S|
|E| |K| |R| |S| |N| |E| |D|E|
S	U	E	D	E		A		D	O	R	M	A	N	T
T		T		H	O	L	L	Y		I			
A	I	S	L	E		A		V	E	N	U	S	
L		N	O	I	S	O	M	E			U		
L	A	C	E	D		S		R	I	C	E	R	
A			L	O	C	K	S		R		R		
D	E	P	L	E	T	E		A	G	A	P	E	
O		I		E	S		T	T		N		
I	N	T	E	R	N	S		S	T	I	P	E	N	D
N		A		I	O	U		L		R	E		
G	A	L	L	E	O	N		P	R	E	S	S	E	R